CW00735701

EMANUEL SWEDENBORG was born in Stockholm in 1688, the third child of Jesper
Swedberg, a Lutheran bishop, and Sara Behm, who came from a wealthy mine-owning
family. After graduating from Uppsala University in 1709, he travelled across Europe for
a number of years, seeking knowledge, learning crafts and publishing three volumes
of poetry. In England he studied briefly with Edmond Halley and John Flamsteed, and
was much influenced by the work of Isaac Newton. On his return to Sweden, he set up
and edited the nation's first scientific journal *Daedalus Hyperboreus* whilst working
alongside the great inventor, Christopher Polhem, with the pair assisting Charles XII's
military campaigns with innovative engineering projects. Swedenborg was appointed to
the Royal Board of Mines in 1716. He continued to write on scientific subjects, such as
mathematics, geology and cosmology, conceiving the nebular hypothesis for the origin
of the solar system in *The Principia* (1734). Swedenborg's interest in the soul led to a
study of anatomy resulting in the publication of *The Economy of the Animal Kingdom*
(1740-1) and *The Animal Kingdom* (1744-5) which, along with numerous unpublished
manuscripts, showed his deductions, particularly those on the workings of the brain, to
be years ahead of his time. In 1743 he underwent a spiritual crisis, accompanied by vivid
dreams and visions. He later wrote that at that time the spiritual world was opened to him,
that he could visit the afterlife, and converse with angels and devils. In 1747 he began to
write *Arcana Caelestia* (1749-56), a lengthy exegesis of the Books of Genesis and Exodus
followed in 1758 with his most famous and enduring work, *Heaven and Hell*. In this
and other books, Swedenborg outlined his notion of correspondences: that everything in
the physical universe corresponds to a spiritual value. Swedenborg's theory has had great
resonance in the succeeding centuries, influencing the Symbolist movement and literary
and artistic figures such as William Blake, Honoré de Balzac, Helen Keller, W B Yeats,
C G Jung, and Jorge Luis Borges. Swedenborg published his mystical works anonymously
whilst continuing to serve as a valued member of the Swedish House of Nobles, where
he contributed papers on industry and financial reform. He died in 1772 in London.

PHILOSOPHY, LITERATURE, MYSTICISM is the first in a series of anthologies exploring
Swedenborg's place within the history of ideas. Drawing on new research by international
academics and scholars, the aim of the series is to gather together leading research on themes
related to Swedenborg and his subsequent influence. Future volumes are to include essays on
key Swedenborgian concepts and terms, plus studies on Swedenborg in relation to Aristotle,
Locke, Malebranche, Luther, Descartes, Newton, Leibniz, Wolff and others.

philosophy literature mysticism

an anthology of essays
on the thought and influence
of Emanuel Swedenborg

philosophy
literature
mysticism

an anthology of essays
on the thought and influence
of Emanuel Swedenborg

Edited by Stephen McNeilly

The Swedenborg Society
20-21 Bloomsbury Way
London WC1A 2TH

2013

'Swedenborg and Dostoevsky' from *Beginning With My Streets: Essays And Recollections* by Czeslaw Milosz, translated by Madeline G Levine. Translation copyright © 1992 by Farrar, Straus & Giroux, Inc. Reprinted by permission of Farrar, Straus and Giroux, LLC.
Excerpts from *The Land Of Ulro* by Czeslaw Milosz, translated by Louis Iribarne. Translation copyright © 1984 by Farrar, Straus & Giroux, Inc. Reprinted by permission of Farrar, Straus and Giroux, LLC and Carcanet.

Typeset at Swedenborg House.
Printed at T J International, Padstow
Book design and artwork © Stephen McNeilly

Published by:
The Swedenborg Society
Swedenborg House
20-21 Bloomsbury Way
London
WC1A 2TH

ISBN 978-0-85448-161-3
British Library Cataloguing-in-Publication Data.
A catalogue record for this book is available from the British Library.

Contents

Preface

This volume was first proposed as far back as 2008 as part of a broader programme of publications to be made ready for the Swedenborg Society's bicentenary celebrations in 2010. The idea for an anthology was to gather a select group of articles previously printed within the pages of the *Journal of the Swedenborg Society*. Since then numerous new essays have been commissioned and others have emerged independently, and these additions have created a wider sense of the aims of the book as a whole. In total twenty essays have been selected, with six of those published here for the first time. Parts one and two explore Swedenborg's impact on the realms of philosophy and literature and are presented in a broad chronological sequence (with many themes overlapping and interlinked). The essays in the final part are more varied and point to topics to be developed in subsequent volumes. All of the essays are comparative in emphasis.

By definition an anthology cannot hope to be comprehensive, especially when dealing with material of this scope and variety. Many more articles could have been included and on a great many themes and connections. There is currently very little published on Swedenborg's influence on the visual arts and music, and even less on the important question of his role in nineteenth-century social and religious emancipation. Much more could also have been included on his political and scientific thought. With this in mind it is hoped that the present collection of essays will help to fill the gap between the cursory introduction to Swedenborg required on most courses of eighteenth-century thought, and the detailed study pursued by academics for academics. It is also hoped that the project will serve as a catalyst for new research, and a better understanding of Swedenborg's life and thought within the history of ideas.

For their help in preparing this book a warm thanks is extended to Nora Foster, Olivia Stewart and Alex Murray for their comments and observations; to Inge Jonsson for reading the material and for preparing his 'Foreword', and Edward Lines for his translation of Saori Osuga's 'Balzac and Swedenborg'. Special mention most also go to James Wilson and Holly Catling for their hard work and assistance. All have made excellent contributions to this book.

More formal acknowledgements must also go to Dr Chris Gair and *Symbiosis* (vol. 8.1, 2001) for permission to reprint Dr Hazel Hutchison's 'Ideal homes: James, Rossetti and Swedenborg's House of Life'; to Jim Lawrence and *Studia Swedenborgiana* for Dr Eugene Taylor's 'Peirce and Swedenborg' (June 1986, vol. 6 no. 1), and 'Jung and his intellectual context: the Swedenborgian connection' (June 1991, vol. 7, no. 2). Acknowledgements are also extended to Farrer, Strauss & Giroux Inc and Carcanet for permission to reprint Czeslaw Milosz's 'Blake and Swedenborg' and 'Swedenborg the Mystic' first published in English in *The Land of Ulro* (tr. Louis Iribarne, 1984); and again to Farrer, Strauss & Giroux Inc for permission to reprint 'Dostoevsky and Swedenborg', first published in English in *Beginning with My Streets* (tr. Madelein G Levine, 1992).

Contributions from the *Journal of the Swedenborg Society* include 'Swedenborg and Kant on spiritual intuition' by Michelle Gilmore-Grier (vol. II, 2003); 'Swedenborg's positive influence on the development of Kant's mature moral philosophy' and 'Schopenhauer as reader of Swedenborg' by Gregory R Johnson (vol. II, 2003); "Swedenborg's Meaning is the truth': Coleridge, Tulk, and Swedenborg' by H J Jackson (vol. III, 2004); 'Swedenborgian simile in Emersonian edification' and 'A hermeneutic key to the title *Leaves of Grass*' by Anders Hallengren (vol. III, 2004); and 'The spiritual detective: how Baudelaire invented symbolism, by way of Swedenborg, E T A Hoffmann and Edgar Allan Poe' by Gary Lachman (vol. IV, 2005); 'Jacob Boehme, Emanuel Swedenborg and their readers' by Ariel Hessayon (vol. V, 2007). A full list of the contents of previous volumes of the Society's volumes are given in a bibliography at the end of the volume.

A final expression of gratitude must also go to those contributors whose essays are published here for the first time. These include Devin P Zuber for his essay 'Spiritualized science and the celestial artist: Nathaniel Hawthorne and Swedenborgian aesthetics'; Anna Maddison for her essay '"Through Death to Love': Swedenborgian imagery in the painting and poetry of Dante Gabriel Rossetti'; Richard Lines for his 'Handel, Hogarth and Swedenborg: manners and morals in eighteenth-century London'; Saori Osuga whose 'Balzac and Swedenborg' was drawn from her doctoral thesis; Keri Davies whose article "The Swedishman at Brother Brockmer's': Moravians and Swedenborgians in eighteenth-century London' was first given as a paper at the *Blake in Contexts* conference held at the Swedenborg Society in 2008; and Gary Lachman whose article 'Swedenborg, existentialism and the active life' was first given as a lecture at the Swedenborg Society in 2007.

Stephen McNeilly
London 2013

Further reading

Standard editions of Swedenborg's works in English are published by the Swedenborg Society, London. Noteworthy new translations include *The Interaction of Soul and Body* (tr. John Elliott, 2012), *Heaven and Hell* (tr. Ken Ryder, 2010), *Arcana Caelestia* (tr. John Elliott, 1983-99), *Conjugial Love* (tr. John Chadwick, 1996), *The Last Judgment* (tr. John Chadwick, 1992), *The Worlds in Space* (tr. John Chadwick, 1997), *The New Jerusalem* (tr. John Chadwick, 1992) and *The True Christian Religion* (tr. John Chadwick, 1988). The Society also keeps in print Latin editions of Swedenborg's published theological works.

English translations of his early scientific and philosophic titles are available from the Swedenborg Scientific Association, in Pennsylvania, USA, and important editions of Swedenborg's poetry include a trio of dual language volumes edited and translated by Hans Helander and published by Almqvist & Wiksell International, Sweden. A new edition of Swedenborg's published theological works is also available from the Swedenborg Foundation under the title *A New Century Edition of the Works of Emanuel Swedenborg* (ed. Jonathan S Rose).

The most up-to-date biographies of Swedenborg are Lars Bergquist's critically acclaimed *Swedenborg's Secret* (Swedenborg Society, 2006), Gary Lachman's *Discovering Swedenborg* (Swedenborg Society, 2010, reprinted by Tarcher/Penguin 2012), Carl Robsahm's *Memoirs of Swedenborg* (Swedenborg Society, 2011), Ernst

Benz's *Emanuel Swedenborg: Visionary Savant in the Age of Reason* (Swedenborg Foundation, 2002) and Martin Lamm's *Emanuel Swedenborg: the development of his Thought* (Swedenborg Foundation, 2000).

Other important works and study guides include Norman Ryder's *A Descriptive Bibliography of the Works of Emanuel Swedenborg (1688-1772)* (Swedenborg Society, 2010-); Dr John Chadwick and Dr Jonathan S Rose's *A Lexicon to the Latin Text of the Theological Writings of Emanuel Swedenborg (1688-1772)* (Swedenborg Society, 2008); Anders Hallengren's *Gallery of Mirrors* (Swedenborg Foundation, 1998); Inge Jonsson's *Visionary Scientist: the Effects of Science and Philosophy on Swedenborg's Cosmology* (Swedenborg Foundation, 1999); Immanuel Kant's *Dreams of A Spirit Seer and Other Writings* edited by Gregory R Johnson (Swedenborg Foundation, 2002) and Henry Corbin's *Swedenborg and Esoteric Islam* (Swedenborg Foundation, 1995). For readers interested in a more comprehensive list of comparative literature, a bibliography of secondary sources has also been included at the end.

Notes on contributors

Keri Davies is a Visiting Fellow in the School of Arts and Humanities at Nottingham Trent University and Vice-President of the Blake Society. He has written on William Blake's parents (particularly his mother's links to the Moravian Church), and on the social and intellectual milieu of early Blake collectors, and other friends and acquaintances of the painter-poet.

Michelle Gilmore-Grier is a Professor of Philosophy at the University of San Diego, California. Her areas of research include Kant, Hegel, Nietzche, the History of Modern Philosophy, and Post-Kantian Continental Philosophy. She has published numerous articles on Kant's theoretical philosophy and is the author of *Kant's Doctrine of Transcendental Illusion* (Cambridge University Press, 2001) and *What Can I Know?* (Routledge, 2012).

Anders Hallengren is an Associate Professor and Fellow of Stockholm University, a Fellow of the Linnean Society of London and President of the Swedenborg Society (2011-13). He was the managing editor of *Parnass*, journal of the Literary Societies of Sweden, and a member of the editorial board of the Nobel Foundation. A prolific composer, essayist and poet, Hallengren was awarded a prize by the Swedish Academy in 2008. His publications in English include *Deciphering Reality* (University of Minnesota, 1992), *The Code of Concorde* (Almqvist &

Wiksell International, 1994), *What is National Literature?* (Current History, 1996), *Gallery of Mirrors* (Swedenborg Foundation, 1998), *Nobel Laureates in Search of Identity and Integrity* (WSPC, 2004), and *The Grand Theme and other Essays* (Swedenborg Society, 2013).

Ariel Hessayon is Lecturer in History at Goldsmiths, University of London. He is the author of *'Gold Tried in the Fire'. The Prophet TheaurauJohn Tany and the English Revolution* (Ashgate, 2007) and editor (with Nicholas Keene) of *Scripture and Scholarship in Early Modern England* (Ashgate, 2006). He has written for a number of academic journals including the *Journal for the Study of Radicalism* (vol. 2, no. 2, 2009, and vol. 3, no. 3, 2010) and the *Journal of Ecclesiastical History* (vol. 62, no. 1, 2011) and has contributed papers for edited volumes including *The Oxford Handbook of Literature and the English Revolution* (OUP, forthcoming) and *The Experience of Revolution in Stuart Britain and Ireland* (Cambridge University Press, 2011).

Hazel Hutchison lectures at the University of Aberdeen where she teaches and researches literature of the nineteenth and twentieth centuries. Her publications include *Seeing and Believing: Henry James and the Spiritual World* (Palgrave, 2006) and articles on James, Rupert Brooke and Gerard Manley Hopkins. She has edited a reprint of Mary Borden's First World War memoir *The Forbidden Zone* (Hesperus, 2008) and is currently writing a monograph about American writers of the First World War. She has edited a collection of poems about the city of Aberdeen, *Silver* (Polygon, 2009) and has also written books about essay-writing skills.

H J Jackson, a Professor of English at the University of Toronto, is the editor or co-editor of six volumes in the standard edition of Samuel Taylor Coleridge's *Collected Works*. She is also the editor of several trade editions of Coleridge including *The Major Works* (Oxford World's Classics, 2000). She is the author of *Marginalia: Readers Writing in Books* (Yale, 2001), *A Book I Value* (Yale, 2003) and *Romantic Readers: The Evidence of Marginalia* (Yale, 2005).

Gregory R Johnson holds a Ph.D. in philosophy from the Catholic University of America in Washington, DC. His doctoral dissertation, 'A Commentary on Kant's *Dreams of a Spirit-Seer*', argues that Kant adopted central tenets of his mature critical philosophy from Swedenborg. He has published widely on the Kant-Swedenborg relationship and is the translator of Immanuel Kant, *Dreams of a Spirit-Seer and Other Writings on Swedenborg* (Swedenborg Foundation, 2002). He has written editorial introductions to Swedenborg's *Divine Love and Wisdom* (Swedenborg Foundation, 2003) and *Divine Providence* (Swedenborg Foundation, 2003).

Inge Jonsson was Professor of Comparative Literature at Stockholm University, and has published widely in Swedish on the history of literature and poetics including four books on Swedenborg. He was awarded the Kellgren prize in 1995, the Swedish Academy Royal Prize in 2005 and was president of the Royal Academy of Letters, History, and Antiquities in Stockholm between 1999 to 2001. His books on Swedenborg in English include *Visionary Scientist: The Effects of Science and Philosophy on Swedenborg's Cosmology* (Swedenborg Foundation, 1999) and *A Drama of Creation: Sources and Influences in Swedenborg's Worship and Love of God* (Swedenborg Foundation, 2004). He has recently written a history of the Royal Academy of Letters, History, and Antiquities.

Gary Lachman is the author of *Discovering Swedenborg* (Swedenborg Society, 2006), and has written numerous books on the history and influence of esoteric ideas on Western culture including *The Dedalus Book of the Occult: A Dark Muse* (Dedalus, 2003), *In Search of P. D. Ouspensky: The Genius in the Shadow of Gurdjieff* (Quest, 2004), *The Dedalus Occult Reader: The Garden of Hermetic Dreams* (Dedalus, 2005), *Rudolf Steiner. An Introduction to His Life and Work* (Floris Books, 2007), *Jung the Mystic: The Esoteric Dimensions of Carl Jung's Life and Teachings* (Tarcher, 2010), and *The Quest for Hermes Trismegistus: From Ancient Egypt to the Modern World* (Floris Books, 2011).

Richard Lines has written extensively on Swedenborg's influence on literature, including 'Swedenborgian Ideas in the Poetry of Elizabeth Barrett Browning and Robert Browning', in *In Search of the Absolute* (Swedenborg Society, 2004), and 'Eros and the Unknown Victorian: Coventry Patmore and Swedenborg', in *Between Method and Madness* (Swedenborg Society, 2005). He contributed an entry on J J G Wilkinson for *The Dictionary of Nineteenth-Century British Philosophers* (Thoemmes Press, 2002). He is also the author of *A History of the Swedenborg Society 1810-2010* (South Vale Press, 2011).

Anna Maddison is a freelance Art Historian who also lectures in English Literature, having received an MA in Victorian Literature (2002). Her specialism is the Pre-Raphaelites and she is currently writing a Ph.D. thesis on Dante Gabriel Rossetti. She teaches regularly at Liverpool and Bradford Universities, and is a visiting lecturer at LJMU. She has had a long association with the Atkinson Art Gallery, Southport; lecturing there since 2003. In 2009 she co-curated their *Identity and Place* exhibition, and has recently had original research published on an Atkinson-owned pastel painting by Ford Madox Brown (*PRS Review*, Spring 2011).

Stephen McNeilly is the editor of the *Journal of the Swedenborg Society* and series editor for the *Swedenborg Archive* imprint. His edited volumes include *On the Translator and the Latin Text* (2001), *On the True Philosopher and the True Philosophy* (2002), *In Search of the Absolute* (2004), *Between Method and Madness* (2005), *The arms of Morpheus* (2007), *Blake's London: The Topgraphic Sublime* by Iain Sinclair (2011) and *Several Clouds Colliding* by Iain Sinclair and Brian Catling (Swedenborg Archive/Book Works, 2012). He Lectures occasionally on art and critical theory at the University of Creative Arts, Canterbury, and has published a number of studies on philosophy and art for Dedecus Press.

Czeslaw Milosz was awarded the Nobel Prize in Literature in 1980, and was Professor of Slavic Languages and Literatures at the University of California, Berkeley from 1961. Among his many publications are *A Poetical Treatise* (1957), *The History of Polish Literature* (1969), *The Land of Ulro* (1977), *Chronicles* (1987), *Facing the River* (1994), *In Search of a Homeland* (1992), *Modern Legends* (1996), *On Time Travel* (2004), and *Selected Poems: 1931-2004* (2006). Milosz died in 2004, at his home in Kraków, aged 93.

Saori Osuga completed her doctorate in French Literature at University Paris IV-Sorbonne in 2010, on the theme of 'Seraphita and the Bible—Scriptural Sources of Balzac's Mysticism'. Between 2007-8 she was awarded the Ambassadorial Scholarship of Rotary International and a French Government Scholarship. She was a research Fellow of the Japan Society for the Promotion of Science and is currently a part-time Lecturer at Caritas Junior College, Yokohama. Her publications include *'Séraphîta' and the Bible: Scriptural Sources of Balzac's Mysticism* (Honoré Champion Press, 2011) and a Japanese translation of *Séraphîta*, co-translated with Naohiro Kato (Suiseisha Press, 2011).

Eugene Taylor was Professor of The History and Philosophy of Psychology at Saybrook University, Lecturer on Psychiatry at Harvard Medical School and Founder/Director of the Cambridge Institute of Psychology and Comparative Religions. His publications include *Shadow Culture: Psychology and Spirituality in America* (Counterpoint, 2000), *The Mystery of Personality: A history of Psychodynamic theories* (Springer, 2009), *William James on Exceptional Mental States* (Scribner, 1983), *William James on Consciousness beyond the Margin* (Princeton, 2011), and with Robert Wozniak (eds.), *Pure Experience: The response to William James* (St Augustine's Press, 1996). He was also the curator of Gordon Allport's papers and an internationally renowned scholar on a number of subjects.

Devin P Zuber is assistant professor for American Studies, Literature and Swedenborgian Studies at the Pacific School of Religion and Graduate Theological Union, Berkeley. Before moving to California, Dr Zuber was the 2010 Eccles fellow in American Studies at the British Library, and held teaching positions at the universities of Osnabrueck and Munich in Germany. His work has appeared in

American Quarterly, *Religion and the Arts*, and *Variations*, and he is presently completing several books including a study of Swedenborg and American environmental aesthetics, a selected edition of the letters of J J G Garth Wilkinson and a smaller volume on the performance artist Marina Abramovic.

Selected works of Swedenborg

Published by Swedenborg

1709   Selected Sentences (*Selectae Sententiae*).

1714   Heliconian Sports (*Ludus Heliconius*).

1715   Northern Muse (*Camena Borea*).

1716-18 Northern Inventor (*Daedalus Hyperboreus*).

1721   A New Method of Finding Longitude (*Methodus Nova inveniendi Longitudines Locorum terra marique ope Lunae*).

        Principles of Chemistry (*Prodromus Principiorum Rerum naturalium Sive novorum Tentaminum Chymiam et Physicam*).

1722   Miscellaneous Observations (*Miscellanea Observata*).

1734   The Infinite and the Final Cause of Creation (*Prodromus philosophiae ratiocinantis de Infinito, et Causa finali creationis*).

        The Principia (*Principia Rerum Naturalium*).

1740-1   The Economy of the Animal Kingdom (*Oeconomia Regni Animalis*).

1744-5   The Animal Kingdom (*Regnum Animale*)*.*

1745   The Worship and Love of God (*De Cultu et amore Dei*).

1749-56 Arcana Caelestia (*Arcana Coelestia*).

1758   The Worlds in Space (*De Telluribus in Mundo nostro solari*).

        Heaven and Hell (*De Coelo et ejus mirabilibus, et de Inferno*).

        The Last Judgment (*De Ultimo Judicio*).

The New Jerusalem and its Heavenly Doctrine (*De Nova Hierosolyma et ejus Doctrina Coelesti*).

The White Horse (*De Equo Albo*).

1763   The Doctrine of the Lord (*Doctrina Novae Hierosolymae de Domino*).

The Doctrine of the Sacred Scripture (*Doctrina Novae Hierosolymae de Scriptura Sacra*).

The Doctrine of Life (*Doctrina Vitae pro Nova Hierosolyma ex praeceptis Decalogi*).

The Doctrine of Faith (*Doctrina Novae Hierosolymae de Fide*).

Continuation of The Last Judgment (*Continuatio de Ultimo Judicio*).

Divine Love and Wisdom (*De Divino Amore et de Divina Sapientia*).

1764   Divine Providence (*De Divina Providentia*).

1766   The Apocalypse Revealed (*Apocalypsis Revelata*).

1768   Conjugial Love (*De Amore Conjugiali*).

1769   A Brief Exposition (*Summaria Expositio Doctrinae Novae Ecclesiae*).

Interaction of the Soul and Body (*De Commercio Animae et Corporis*).

1771   The True Christian Religion (*Vera Christiana Religio*).

Published posthumously

1719   On Tremulation (*Anatomi af wår aldrafinaste Natur, wisande att wårt rörande och lefwande wäsende*).

1734   On the Mechanism of the Soul and Body (*De Mechanismo Animae et Corporis*).

1738-40 The Cerebrum (*Transactiones de cerebro*).

1740-4 The Brain (various untitled MSS).

1741   A Philosopher's Notebook (*Varia Philosophica et Theologica*).

Correspondences and Representations (*De Correspondentia et Representatione*).

1742   Rational Psychology (*Psychologia Rationalis*).

Ontology (*Ontologia*).

A Hieroglyphic Key (*Clavis Hieroglyphica*).

1743   The Generative Organs (*Anatomia Corporis*).

1743-4   The Journal of Dreams (*Swedenborgs Drömmar*).

1745-7   The Word Explained (*Explicatio in Verbum Historicum Veteris Testamenti*).

1746-8   Biblical Index (*Index Biblicus*).

1747-65   The Spiritual Diary (*Diarium Spirituale*).

1757-9   The Apocalypse Explained (*Apocalypsis Explicata*).

1759   The Athanasian Creed (*De Athanasii Symbolo*).

           The Last Judgment Posthumous (*De Ultimo Judicio Posth*).

1761   The Prophets and Psalms (*Summaria Expositio Sensu Interni Librorum Propheticorum ac Psalmorum*).

1762   On the Sacred Scripture or Word of the Lord, from experience (*De Scriptura Sacra seu Verbo Domini*).

           Precepts of the Decalogue (*De Praeceptis Decalogi*).

           The Divine Love (*De Divino Amore*).

1763   The Divine Wisdom (*De Divina Sapientia*).

1766   Conversations with Angels (*Colloquia cum Angelis*).

           Charity (*De Charitate*).

           Five Memorable Relations (*Quinque Memorabilia*).

           Marriage (*De Conjugio*).

1769   Canons of the New Church (*Canones Novae Ecclesiae*).

           Scripture Confirmations (*Dicta probantia*).

           Index to *Formula Concordiae* (*Index ad Formulam Concordiae*).

1770   Ecclesiastical History of the New Church (*Historia Ecclesiatica Novae Ecclesiae*).

1771   Nine Questions (*Quaestiones Novem de Trinitate*).

           Reply to Ernesti (*Responsum ad Ernesti*).

           The Coronis (*Coronis seu Appendix*).

           The Consummation of the Age and Invitation to the New Church (*De Consummatione Saeculi, de Adventu Secundo Domini*).

Foreword

Inge Jonsson

I n *Muttersohn* (*Son of a Mother*), a novel that was first published in July 2011, the great German writer Martin Walser tells the story of a group of people connected to a psychiatric clinic, housed in a building that was once a monastery in Southern Germany. Percy, the main character, is a paramedic, and has been allowed to offer patients a different type of therapy based on learning texts by heart. As might be expected, many of the doctors (for whom chemotherapeutical methods are the one and only remedy) despise his 'sleeping bag therapy'. But for some the new therapy appears to work. Among the authors selected by Percy, Emanuel Swedenborg holds first place in a list that also includes St Augustine, Heinrich Suso and Jacob Boehme. On one or two occasions the reader encounters Percy reading from a number of distinctive passages from Swedenborg's *Journal of Dreams* (which might, with more accuracy, be described as jottings made in The Hague between 6th and 19th of April, 1744) and in doing so he refers to Swedenborg most respectfully, as 'my prompter' ('Mein Souffleur'), 'the great man of the North' ('der grosse Grosse aus dem Norden') and even 'the Holy Spirit of the North' ('der heilige Geist aus dem Norden').

The texts Percy has chosen to recite contain dreams of heavenly blessedness but they also bear witness to how difficult Swedenborg found it for a 'philosopher' to let his intellect be a part of the game, that is, to accept Christianity unconditionally.

Swedenborg is appealing to Christ directly, to make him worthy of his search for inmost truth, although his spiritual pride makes him a greater sinner than others. For Percy the most important passages are Swedenborg's description of a vision on the night between April 9 and 10, 1744, where Swedenborg is awake and sees how everything in the universe is put together and flows into the centre of the infinite, where love has its abode. Percy himself represents love in a world where hatred is perpetually threatening to triumph, and (as a disciple of Christ, if ever there was one) he is familiar with the struggle for self-knowledge which is reflected in Swedenborg's *Journal of Dreams*. On the final pages Percy is murdered by a representative of hatred, appropriately serving as leader of a gang of motorcyclists. Nevertheless, hatred is not victorious this time: the killer breaks his neck when the driver loses control of his big BMW bike.

Martin Walser has referred to Swedenborg in previous novels, for example his *Ein fliehendes Pferd* (*Runaway horse*) published in 1978, but in *Muttersohn* he gives the Swede a more important role as spiritual guide. Nevertheless Walser must not be mistaken as a regular disciple of Swedenborg. The spiritual milieu in *Muttersohn* is strongly informed by Roman Catholicism and there is no immediate influence of Swedenborg's theology. On the contrary, it is characteristic that Walser has turned exclusively to the *Journal of Dreams* in his quest for a collage of reading material. In this text Swedenborg comes forth as a searching and suffering human being, almost as a contemporary. What fascinates Walser is how Swedenborg, under a decisive crisis, wrestled with questions that people still pose for themselves today in the mass media era. Indeed he is not particularly interested in the answers proposed by Swedenborg himself, in works such as *Heaven and Hell* or *The True Christian Religion*, which many readers might find difficult today.

In this respect, Martin Walser is representative of many writers of the last 150 years who have shown an interest in Swedenborg. However, since the majority of the studies within the following pages are devoted to writers older than that, they are unable to confirm this statement and for one simple reason: Swedenborg's notes and dreams from his fifth journey abroad were first published in 1859 in Swedish, and they only became available in English translation by James John Garth Wilkinson in the following year. We do not know how the little note book ended up in senior master Scheringson's property in the town of Västerås. In any case it was not part of the collection of about 20,000 pages of manuscripts which Swedenborg's relatives left into the custody of the Royal Swedish Academy of Sciences in 1772.

Neither as to form nor content do these notes represent Swedenborg's work as a whole, and they were clearly not meant for publication. The mere fact that they were written in Swedish make them stand out from almost all his other texts, and their frank reports of sexual experiences, which seriously upset Victorian readers, have no parallels in his literary heritage. But these very sections may, in fact, have increased the interest of a post-Freudian public, and it is hard to believe that they would shock anyone today. On the contrary, they strengthen the impression of a sincere self-examination and a desire for understanding the role of man in the Creation, which a reading of the artless Swedish evokes. Although he must have read them in translation, Swedenborg's dream notes clearly made that impression on Percy—or Anton Percy Schlugen to give his full name—in Martin Walser's extremely readable novel.

*

Czeslaw Milosz, the Polish-American 1980 Nobel laureate, was another prominent modern writer to have been inspired by Emanuel Swedenborg, and for very good reasons he has been included in this collection of studies. In a famous essay Milosz called the remarkable Swede 'a true son of the Enlightenment', a nomination which, in my view, conveys a good deal of truth but certainly not all of it. According to Immanuel Kant's well-known definition, the Enlightenment meant that man had come of age, and no doubt an enormous amount of intellectual energy was released in the eighteenth century. Still one must not overestimate the modernity of the epoch. The philosophical framework remained rather narrow, many new ideas and incentives appeared in forms which are difficult for us to understand, and there were countercurrents and adversaries: in the middle of the century Rousseau initiated a rebellion of feeling against the dominance of reason.

In fact Swedenborg is a paradigmatic example of how difficult, or rather impossible, it is to label great historical characters unequivocally. He came from a family at the highest level of ecclesiastical hierarchy in Sweden, and at the time of his birth, Sweden was also one of Europe's great powers. He was educated at the University of Uppsala, a small college of higher education, still essentially based on the Reformation combination of Lutheran theology and classical humanism, but not unaffected by the criticism of traditional learning triggered by the progress of seventeenth-century science and philosophy. It was René Descartes (1596-1650) who gave a fatal blow to the ontological structure of Scholasticism by applying a rationalistic method to systematically question all established conceptions and thereby come down to an unyielding basis of human knowledge, from which a stable new house of learning could be erected.

As a student Swedenborg drew inspiration from Descartes, but his real mentor was the autodidactic inventor Christopher Polhem. When he returned to Sweden from his first stay abroad, he implemented a long-standing plan to publish Polhem's most momentous inventions. The outcome was six issues of the first scientific journal entitled *Daedalus hyperboreus* after the ingenious inventor of classical mythology. It was published in Swedish and financed by Swedenborg himself (or Swedberg as he was called before he was raised to the nobility in 1719). King Charles XII read some articles in his headquarters in Lund and gave him *stante pede* a post in the Board of Mines (primarily to assist Polhem in a number of grandiose technical projects). This position did not prevent the newly appointed assessor from publishing a series of *scripta minora* on cosmological and geological problems, as well as the first Swedish textbook on algebra. Some of these publications presented ideas which he developed in future works, whilst others stood as valuable solo contributions to science, e.g., the small paper on land elevation in Sweden (or as he assumed, the abatement of water).

During a second journey abroad, at the beginning of the 1720s, he published further studies in the field of natural philosophy but this time (as with all his future works) in Latin. But then a decade passed in which he worked in the Board of Mines and gathered material for his three volume *magnum opus* on inorganic nature entitled *Opera philosophica et mineralia,* which he published in Dresden in 1734. A diary kept by him on this third journey abroad shows that by reading up-to-date literature and by visiting mines and smelting plants he spent much time increasing his skills as a mineralogist and mining technician. In the mineralogical parts of the work there is extensive documentation on the production of iron and copper based upon personal experience and current literature. These works were soon reported in learned journals and gave him a European reputation as an authority in the field.

From a literary point of view, however, the first volume is the most interesting. Here Swedenborg has developed a number of ideas from the 1710s into a unified grand theory on the birth of the universe from the mathematical point and its growth up to the appearance of our solar system and the earth. It is a vision, inspired by Descartes, of a divine creation *per media*, which started when the Almighty inserted a *conatus*, an effort, to motion in the mathematical point that marked the border between nature and infinity. With his classical education Swedenborg found an excellent symbol of this point in Janus, the Roman god of the gate who was depicted with two faces in opposite directions. The impulses of Descartes and other seventeenth-century physicists are still manifest, together with effects of his biblical and classical erudition, but you will also meet ideas heralding new approaches.

These ideas appear with particular clarity in two essays, which Swedenborg also published in 1734, in a little book usually called *De Infinito*, or *On the Infinite*. In one of them he addressed the problem of the interaction of soul and body. This was a complicated subject which the radical Cartesian distinction between thinking and matter, *res cogitans* and *res extensa*, had brought into focus. Swedenborg had tested a solution already in an article in *Daedalus hyperboreus*, but not until he regarded himself to have laid a solid philosophical foundation did he believe it possible to make any progress. The programme he announces for his coming research aims at no less than to prove the immortality of the soul *ipsis sensibus*, for the senses themselves, i.e., empirically.

During his fourth *iter ad exteros* 1736-40 he worked intensely with this extremely ambitious project. His focus was on the human body which, in the titles of the works already published, was presented as the kingdom of the soul, or *regnum animale*. In some of his earlier papers he had also taken an interest in the anatomy and physiology of the brain——convinced of course that it must be the seat of the soul——and these studies were now resumed with astounding energy. Modern researchers, who have acquainted themselves with Swedenborg's studies of the human brain, have expressed their admiration of his perspicacious observations, which in many cases were far ahead of his time. However, since most of them were not published until more than a century later, they could not make an impact on mainstream brain research. In addition to this Swedenborg had soon to learn the lesson of so many of his scientific colleagues, namely that the problem turned out to be much more complicated than expected. As a consequence he was not only forced to handle a growing amount of empirical data but also to look for new theories to explain it.

On quite a few occasions Swedenborg writes of the need for a thinker who could combine the intellectual acuity of the ancient philosophers with the enormous empirical data of modern science, and this, no doubt, is an ideal self-portrait. In the period that concluded Swedenborg's career as a scientist, a little less than one decade, he was desperately trying to fulfil his superhuman research programme. Among the excerpts from the years before his religious crisis between 1743-5, Plato, Aristotle and St Augustine appear together with a number of modern rationalists, (with the great Leibniz as the elite among those) from whom he expected to be assisted in his interpretation of what the microscopists had observed in human blood and brain tissue. His extensive reading led him to a tripartition of the human psyche in *anima*, the soul in the full meaning of the word, which contains all the ruling principles of mental life but is unable to communicate directly with the levels beneath, *mens rationalis,* the intellect, consciousness, and thereby the seat of the language, and *animus*, where the reports of the senses are received and transformed.

This means that everyday language cannot reach beyond the intellect and, insofar as a new language cannot be found, that what happens in *anima* will remain inaccessible to scientific analysis, which in turn had made the seventeenth-century physics possible. Swedenborg was obviously inspired by the dream of a concept calculus, a *mathesis universalium,* which a few scholars embraced at the time of the modern scientific breakthrough. However, he had to abstain from trying to construct such an artificial language, although he believed it to be feasible, because it would take too much time. Instead he was looking for a substitute, and the outcome was his doctrine of correspondences and representations, in practice an exchange of linguistic terms based on his conviction that nature is a symbol of the spiritual world.

Swedenborg returned to Stockholm in November 1740 after having published two bulky research studies entitled *Oeconomia regni animalis* in Amsterdam. He went back to work in the Board of Mines and the Parliament, which was in session, and before long he was elected to the recently founded Academy of Sciences as member number 60. However, his research programme was far from concluded, and in July 1743 he left Stockholm on his fifth journey abroad. He was able to have two parts of a new series of research reports and a fragmentary *hexaemeron* in Latin prose printed before the religious crisis—mirrored in the *Journal of Dreams*—radically changed his career. When he came back to Stockholm in the summer of 1745, he had actually abandoned his impracticable research project, even if he believed it to have been precisely the other way round. What he had experienced during his crisis proved to him that the human soul was immortal. Now he had to obey a command that Christ had given him in a vision in London: to present an interpretation of the Holy Scriptures, which would make his fellow men equally convinced.

He began a systematic study of the Bible with incomparable energy, and without letting it interfere with his duties as a public servant. However, when he was proposed for promotion to councillor, the highest office of the Board of Mines, he abstained and asked to resign in 1747. During the quarter of a century which was left to him on earth he wrote and printed thousands of pages of exegetic texts in Latin, most of them anonymously in London and Amsterdam. The ecclesiastical censorship in Sweden banned both publication and import of heretical books, and all theological writings by Emanuel Swedenborg were included in this poison-labelled category. However, this decision did not prevent his anonymity being broken at the beginning of the 1760s when Swedenborg himself put his name on the front page of *Delitiae sapientiae de amore coniugiali* in 1768, and nor did it prevent copies being incorporated in the Royal Library in Stockholm.

Already in his first published work of the theological period, the huge eight volumes of *Arcana Coelestia* (1749-56), Swedenborg appeared in the two roles for which he has become both famous and ridiculed: as exegete and visionary. The evaluation of these two varied from the beginning. Some readers accepted his hermeneutic practice and rationalistic theology but rejected his *memorabilia* (or scenes from the spiritual world) as deplorable products of a deranged mind. Others found his interpretation of the Bible and his theology false and requested him to communicate only *visa et audita* what he had seen and heard in the world of spirits. The problem, however, is that such a separation cannot be made without destroying the coherent whole. In a similar way, Swedenborg's spiritual experiences and his theology are closely connected with his work as a scientist. As many commentators have emphasized, his vision of the beyond has its roots in an extensive reading of anatomical reports of contemporary microscopists and in his own theorizing on the structure of inorganic nature. It is the peculiar combination of compiling enormous amounts of empirical knowledge and transgressing established science, even at the price of being regarded as a maniac, that makes Emanuel Swedenborg such a fascinating figure: a true son of the Enlightenment but also a herald of ages to come.

I would like to end by paying tribute to his long-standing publishers, among which the Swedenborg Society is the oldest and most respected. Without their assiduous efforts to publish and translate his writings, as well as taking good care of many of his manuscripts, he would most probably not have acquired the position in the literary hall of fame that he holds today. It is certainly a controversial one, and it came probably as a surprise to most of his compatriots in 2006, when Unesco decided to include the collection of Swedenborg's manuscripts at the Royal Swedish Academy of Sciences in its Memories of the World programme. However, Martin Walser and the valuable studies in the present book prove that Unesco had very good reasons for its decision.

I. PHILOSOPHY

Swedenborg and Kant on spiritual intuition

Michelle Gilmore-Grier

I n 1765, Kant published a mysterious work entitled, *Dreams of a Spirit-Seer, as Elucidated Through Dreams of a Metaphysician*.[1] It is well known that the work was motivated by Kant's readings of Swedenborg's *Arcana Caelestia*. Yet, the *Dreams* has long perplexed Kant scholars, who are often stymied by its ironic tone. Because of this, the book has inspired a great deal of speculation, particularly as regards Kant's motives. Was it Kant's intention in the *Dreams* to offer a scathing attack on metaphysics by suggesting that it, like Swedenborg's spiritual experiences, was the product of a delusion? Or was Kant using his 'review' of the *Arcana Caelestia* as a foil in order to ground a deeply Swedenborgian metaphysics all of his own? Many Kant scholars have assumed the first interpretation, although it is certainly clear that some have tried to find in Kant's *Dreams* a veiled endorsement of Swedenborgianism.[2] Interestingly, both of these interpretations find support in Kant's own work, and for good reason. For it seems to me that Kant's position vis-à-vis Swedenborg is neither that of an entirely dismissive critic, nor that of a closet enthusiast. Rather, Kant is conflicted in his response to Swedenborg, and despite his general sympathy for a number of deep-rooted Swedenborgian claims, he remains sceptical on both epistemological and metaphysical, and indeed on moral, grounds for those claims. As Kant himself says in speaking of this perplexing work:

It was in fact difficult for me to devise the right style with which to clothe my thoughts, so as not to expose myself to derision. It seemed to me wisest to forestall other people's mockery by first of all mocking myself; and this procedure was actually quite honest, since my mind is really in a state of conflict on this matter. As regards the spirit reports, I cannot help but be charmed by stories of this kind, and I cannot rid myself of the suspicion that there is some truth to their validity, regardless of the absurdities in these stories and the fancies and unintelligible notions that infect their rational foundations and undermine their value.[3]

I think that it is reasonable to take Kant at his word here, and to accept that he was indeed conflicted in his response to Swedenborg, rather than to try to show either that his support for Swedenborg is entirely dissembled or that he was a closet Swedenborgian who only pretended to have complaints about the latter's methods and testimonies. Even so, the above confession leads one both to inquire into the nature of Kant's agreements and sympathies and to identify precisely the nature of his rejection of Swedenborg's stories. The questions I should like to ask, then, are these: in what way is there 'truth in the validity' of Swedenborg's 'spirit reports'? And exactly what are the 'unintelligible notions and fancies' that undermine their value and 'infect their rational foundations'? Answers to these questions might prove to be illuminating with respect to the relation between Swedenborg and Kant, and may allow us to determine whether Swedenborg's writings provided the basis for any developments in Kant's philosophy. In order to make sense of this issue, we must examine Kant's views about Swedenborg more carefully.

|

As above, the *Dreams of a Spirit-Seer* is a notoriously difficult text to reconcile. Its tone is unusually and, for Kant, uncharacteristically light—almost playfully sarcastic, particularly given the very serious topic with which it is concerned (the doctrine of spiritual being). The tone is just odd enough that straight away Moses Mendelssohn was led to state that 'The jocular profundity with which this little book is written leaves the reader for a time in doubt whether Herr Kant intended to make metaphysics ridiculous or spirit-seeing credible'.[4] In a peculiar preamble, Kant himself seems to exhort his readers not to take the work seriously, indicating again the speculative, undecided and possibly experimental tendencies present in the work, and of which Kant himself was surely aware. Still, Kant seems to be calling into question the legitimacy of metaphysical theories about the nature of spiritual being and its relation to body by juxtaposing them against Swedenborg's own claims as stated in the *Arcana Caelestia*. At issue here is the philosophical conception of spiritual being as *immaterial substance* (*self-subsistent being*), a conception that Kant claims leads us into a 'knot'. On the one hand, by virtue of being immaterial, such a being would have to lack the properties of extension, spatial location, and so on. On the other hand, spiritual being is held to be (in some sense) a part of the universe, and to bear some relation to the world of body. In the latter case, it seems spiritual being must be somehow *present*, for how else could a spiritual being bear any relation to body, or exert any influence in the material world? The problems with this last view are commonly, and with no small amount of distress, discussed by academic philosophers and fall under the rubric of the 'Mind Body Problem'. That he was deeply interested in this problem when writing the *Dreams* is confirmed by Kant himself. In a *post facto* explanation of his work to Mendelssohn, Kant states that, 'In my opinion, everything depends on our seeking out data for the problem, *how is the soul present in the world, both in material and in non-material things*'.[5] Indeed, the problem that dominates the *Dreams* is how spiritual being could interact with or bear any relation to body. As such, it has been argued that Kant is concerned with the problems surrounding theories of real influx and potential mind-body interaction that were prominently discussed during the time.[6]

3

This problem becomes pronounced as Kant moves from the initial and purely philosophical conception of spiritual being above, to chapter two of the *Dreams*. What Kant offers in this chapter is essentially a Platonic or 'two worlds' metaphysical view, i.e., a view according to which 'reality' is divided into two spheres, or worlds: the physical (material) world of our sensuous experience, and the intelligible, or spiritual, world. On the view proposed, a spirit world exists in addition to and alongside of the material world. But because the material world admits of physico-mathematical (mechanical) explanations only on the basis of the material manifestations of solidity, expansion and form, the spirit world (which has none of these) cannot be explained by appeal to mechanical accounts. Instead, Kant more or less jokingly hypothesizes that the spiritual world would have to be governed by a unique set of 'pneumatic laws'.[7] Such laws would have to account for the relation between immaterial beings. More interestingly, Kant suggests that the spiritual world be viewed as the underlying principle of the life that is manifested in the material world. As such, the spiritual world acts as the explanatory ground of the material world. The philosophical outlines of this position, as we later come to see, are characteristic of both the philosophical idealists and Swedenborg, all of whom seek ultimate explanations for phenomena in an intelligible realm. Indeed, it is because of the obvious and explicitly stated similarities between them, that many have come to view Kant's *Dreams* as involving an attempt to discredit metaphysics by suggesting that it is just as 'fanatical' as Swedenborg's spiritual 'fantasies'.[8] Many take this position because it does seem clear that at least part of what Kant is doing is suggesting an analogy between the 'dreams' of the metaphysician, and the 'dreams' of the spirit-seer. And Kant often speaks in ways that seem explicitly hostile to Swedenborg's visions, visions said by Kant to contain 'not a single drop of reason',[9] and to have arisen from a 'fanatical intuition'.[10]

Nevertheless, we must be careful not to misconstrue the reasons why Kant objects to the metaphysical claims of both Swedenborg and the rationalists. Here the above-cited response to Mendelssohn is instructive. Kant repeatedly states in his letter that it is not metaphysics itself, taken 'objectively', that bothers him. Indeed, he emphatically pronounces his high regard for metaphysics. Rather, Kant objects to *the method deployed* by metaphysicians in their efforts to explain things such as spiritual being, or the cause-effect relation. It seems reasonable to suggest that in a similar way, Kant is not necessarily objecting to many of the tenets of Swedenborg's system in their own right. Rather, he is objecting to the ostensible *methods* deployed by Swedenborg to arrive at these. Whereas the metaphysician presumes to arrive at her theses *a priori*, through concepts and principles of an unaided and isolated reason, Swedenborg bases his findings on the interpretation of his own direct spiritual experience. The question for us, then, is why Kant finds each of these methods (and thus the 'dreams of the metaphysician' and the 'dreams of a spirit-seer') to be inadequate to support the two-world view and the theories of influx they support.

The problem with the rationalist metaphysicians

It might be instructive to consider the problems with traditional, rationalist metaphysics before discussing Kant's complaints about Swedenborg. As above, one problem is clearly that the metaphysician takes the soul to have some kind of 'place' in the world by virtue of which it acts or exerts forces or influences on the body. There are really, it seems, two distinct issues here. The first is a metaphysical problem stemming from the supposed notion of spiritual being as immaterial (a soul with reason), for the metaphysician assigns to an ostensibly immaterial being some kind of real relation to body. To view the soul in this way, however, is to take it to be somehow analogous with body by having some presence or place in the universe. But, as above, the fact that spiritual being is immaterial (simple, non-extended, etc.), poses serious metaphysical problems for the theory. In this regard, Alison Laywine has convincingly argued that Kant's readings of Swedenborg highlighted a number of distinct problems in metaphysics. More specifically, she suggests that Swedenborg's visions illuminated for Kant the dangers stemming from the metaphysicians' tendency to subject immaterial substances to the spatio-temporal

[handwritten margin note: Note problem with metaphysics but with the method deployed]

5

conditions under which bodies are given to the senses.[11] The second problem is, it would seem, epistemological or methodological and relates to the fact that the metaphysician's only way of deducing this consequence is by the use of pure reason, or from concepts alone. Here, Kant's criticism is that the metaphysician presumes to deduce the nature and existence of simple, immaterial beings *a priori*. Such a method is problematic, for Kant, precisely because it involves an attempt to derive conclusions about reality from concepts alone. Already, before the *Dreams*, Kant had developed a criticism of the metaphysicians' presumptions on this score. In both the *Beweisgrund* and the *Deutlichkeit*, Kant had laid the foundations for a criticism of any attempt to use the deductive method in metaphysics.[12] The problem, from Kant's standpoint, is that metaphysics is supposed to be providing knowledge about really existing things (e.g. spiritual beings). Kant's considered view, however, is that formal concepts and principles by themselves cannot deductively yield such knowledge. Indeed, Kant was increasingly of the mind that the deductive method, while appropriate for mathematics, was erroneously deployed by the Cartesians, in their efforts to acquire deductive knowledge of 'reality'.

The force of these criticisms of metaphysical philosophers, as well as the affinity with the presumed errors of Swedenborg, becomes highlighted in chapter three of the *Dreams*. There, Kant mysteriously shifts from the Leibnizian or 'Platonic' perspective of the proponent of any two-worlds view to the more 'Epicurean' perspective according to which reality is co-extensive with what is given in sensation. The latter represents, of course, a more ordinary or 'common sense' standpoint. From this standpoint, however, the notion of spiritual being appears completely unsubstantiated. Given that there is no empirical (intersubjectively accessible) data supporting the theories of spiritual being and spiritual influx, Kant suggests that such theories might be readily dismissed as the solipsistic ego-worlds, or 'dream worlds', of the sleeping. Indeed, in this chapter Kant suggests that, lacking any confirmation by commonly shared sensation or experience, the theories of spiritual being lack credibility altogether. In the *Dreams*, Kant notes that these imaginary philosophical worlds are often constructed through the enthusiastic deductions of the rationalist metaphysicians. It may be that reflecting on Swedenborg's accounts led Kant to the following question: what exactly is the difference between those who think they can access spiritual being by *reason* and those who think they immediately 'perceive' or intuit such being? In either case, the alleged spiritual sphere takes on the characteristic of an 'imaginary world' precisely because it lacks any confirmation through our shared world of experience. Speaking later on of the metaphysicians' deductive method, Kant states without equivocation his concern with the flights of the reason-dreamer: 'This approach involves a new difficulty: one starts I know not whence, and arrives I know not where; the advance of the arguments refuses to correspond with experience'.[13] One problem with the metaphysicians, then, is that in their efforts to 'prove' their theories by appealing to reason alone, they run the risk of having their arguments proceed *in abstracto*, without ever meeting up with experience or factual description.[14] As Kant's critical philosophy began to develop, however, he began to consider the possibility that reason, taken by itself, was 'empty', that it failed to deliver any experiential 'data' that could confirm the substantive metaphysical conclusions it propounded. This concern is articulated throughout the *Dreams*. But Kant goes further. Drawing on earlier developments in his thinking, he suggests that the concept of spiritual being is not only not confirmed by any experiential data, but indeed, that by itself, it provides us with a merely negative conception. To the extent that such a conception has no corresponding data in sensation, we cannot even claim to have any positive definition of what it is we are talking about.

> The principle of this life, in other words, the spirit-nature which we do not know but only suppose, can never be positively thought, for in the entire range of our sensations, there are no data for such a positive thought. One has to make do with negations if one is to think something which differs so much from anything of a sensible character. But even the possibility of such

negations is based neither on experience, nor on inferences, but on a fiction, in which reason, stripped of all assistance […] seeks its refuge.[15]

II

It would be precipitous to conclude from the above concerns that Kant is completely opposed to a Swedenborgian style (two-worlds) system. Indeed, many Kant scholars have noted the similarities between Swedenborg's spiritual system and a number of deep Kantian tenets.[16] More specifically, Kant seems to agree with Swedenborg that there is a distinction between the intelligible (or spiritual) and the sensible worlds, and that such a distinction is implicit in the distinction between 'spiritual' and 'material' beings. Here it is important to note that there are deep theoretical reasons that compel Kant's acceptance of the distinction between these two realms. Kant's views on this score coincide with his developing conception of reason as a theoretical faculty. Throughout the *Dreams*, Kant repeatedly indicates that we are rightly compelled by reason to seek ultimate explanations for phenomena in an intelligible (noumenal, spiritual) world. Reason requires that we leap over into such intelligible explanations precisely because the sensible data provided us in experience are insufficient to complete our inquiries. Thus he notes repeatedly, and ironically, that a strictly empiricist view, while perhaps able to explain various experienced (sensuous) phenomena in accordance with mechanical laws, can nevertheless not go beyond such phenomena in order to offer any reason *why* they operate in the ways they do. Although we may, Kant tells us, know from experience that matter operates in accordance with the force of repulsion, we do not know *why* this is so. The answer to our 'why questions' is precisely what reason, in its theoretical use, demands. Kant thus concedes that experience is utterly incapable of yielding sufficient information. Indeed, he recognizes that experience itself provides us with grounds for speculating about 'hidden reasons' and underlying principles. As Kant himself notes in another example, the fact that we experience in ourselves abilities that are different in kind from capacities of matter, such as

8

our abilities to think, and to choose, gives us *good reason* to conceive of ourselves as incorporeal and constant beings. The insufficiency of experience, the fact that we are aware that there is 'something left over and unaccounted for', something presupposed by our common-sense 'waking' experiences, is precisely what motivates our reason in seeking ultimate explanations in the intelligible world. Indeed, it is reasonable to assume that this is, at least in part, what Kant meant in his letter to Mendelssohn, when he stated that Swedenborg's 'spirit reports' appear to announce some 'truth', and that they have 'rational foundations'. Or so I contend. For one thing seems certain: despite the views of some commentators, Kant does not argue on behalf of a robust empiricism during this period of his career. Indeed, he does not want to distance himself entirely from the need and demand of reason to seek ultimate (and ultimately intelligible) explanations for the phenomena presented to us in experience.[17]

Since the systems of both the metaphysicians and Swedenborg can be understood to express this deep rational need, Kant is sympathetic. Indeed, Kant agrees that there are reasons which compel us to think the intelligible world 'as a whole' in its own right. As above, he admits that appeals to the intelligible world (and thus spiritual being) stem from the need to 'ground' our material (mechanical) explanations of sensuous phenomena in some intelligible and underlying non-physical source, ground, etc. What we find in the *Dreams*, however, is the view that although reason is legitimate in its demand for ultimate explanations, and although we are in a sense justified in pointing out that there must be something *beyond* experience that ultimately accounts for things, we also must recognize that because sensible experience alone provides the data requisite for (our) theoretical knowledge of reality, reason is incapable of supplying by itself alone such knowledge.

This is indeed the theoretical conclusion drawn from Part I of the *Dreams*. On this score, Kant suggests that the function of reason needs to be reinterpreted. Rather than being the source of *a priori* knowledge about transcendent reality, he suggests, metaphysics is to be viewed as the 'science of the limits of human reason'.[18] Its task is to take the questions highlighted by reason about the hidden nature of things and determine whether such an inquiry even falls within the limits of possible human knowledge.[19] Metaphysics, as a rational inquiry into the nature of things, is thus only in a position to mark out the boundaries of our knowledge. The ultimate suggestion here is that metaphysics (reason) is useful in revealing the boundaries beyond which speculation cannot legitimately go. Specifically, it cannot legitimately pass beyond the domain of experience and, when it does, its claims amount to empty speculation, or fiction.[20] Once again, the need to determine the limits of human reason/knowledge issues from the fact that we are constrained to conceive of and recognize beings that transcend our experience in order to complete our inquiries. The result, however, is a purely negative metaphysics, one that does not presume to offer knowledge of the nature of spiritual being, but which remains content with exposing the limitations imposed by our sensuous experience. The negative doctrine of spiritual being brings our inquiries to completion, not by extending our material knowledge, but rather by demonstrating that we have reached the limits of our perhaps all-too-human knowledge.

The problem with Swedenborg

Many commentators go to great lengths to emphasize the ways in which Kant might want to liken Swedenborg to the metaphysicians.[21] Nevertheless, if we are to sort through his multi-layered response to Swedenborg, we must be careful to note the way in which Kant *distinguishes* Swedenborg's 'dreams' from the 'reason-dreams' of the metaphysician. Here one thing seems abundantly clear: Kant cannot legitimately criticize Swedenborg for falling victim to the pretensions of reason. In fact, Swedenborg is quite clear in the *Arcana Caelestia* that he takes the systems and arguments of metaphysics to be empty, and inadequate (almost laughably so) for the purposes of illuminating ultimate truths.[22] As we have seen, Kant ultimately seems to agree with Swedenborg on this point, for he argues that metaphysics is only in a position to highlight the boundaries and limits of our human knowledge. Thus, despite Kant's concession that there are 'rational foundations' for Swedenborg's claims (as above), he does not think that Swedenborg errs in exactly the same ways that the metaphysicians do. *If* Swedenborg's claim were simply that he had good reasons to argue for a spiritual world, *if* he claimed to have knowledge of spiritual being simply through the empty deductions of reason, then of course Kant's response to him would be just as it had been to the metaphysicians. But this is, interestingly, *not* Swedenborg's position, and Kant knows it. Swedenborg is not engaging in a purely speculative metaphysics. Rather, his account is essentially a *testimony*, and he claims to access the spiritual world through what we might want to call 'a spiritual faculty', and to have an immediate intuitive experience of such a world.

[handwritten margin note: But, Swedenborg is not a metaphysician.]

> In order that I might know that we live after death it has been given me to speak and be in company with many who were known to me on earth; and this not merely for a day or a week, but for months and almost a year, speaking and associating with them, just as in this world. [23]

Kant himself goes to great lengths to distinguish between the case of the reason-dreaming metaphysician and the visionary experiences of Swedenborg. Relevant here is the fact that Swedenborg often seems to testify to having what amounts to something analogous to a sensuous experience of spirits (he 'sees' angels with a spiritual analogue to vision, for example). Indeed, Swedenborg suggests to us that the spirits themselves have sensations; they are said to hear, see, touch, and smell: 'Spirits not only possess the faculty of sight, but they live in such great light that our noonday light can scarcely be compared to it. They enjoy the power of hearing also, [...] They also possess the power of speaking, and the sense of smell'.[24]

That Kant wants to distinguish between the pretences of the rationalist metaphysicians (the reason-dreamers) and the experiences of a Swedenborgian style visionary is abundantly clear in the *Dreams*. For even despite the general similarities noted above (they both presume some access to a transcendent spiritual world, and there are good rational grounds for being motivated in this regard), Kant notes that the dreams of reason are distinctly different from the dreams of the visionary. Kant likens the latter to a kind of 'sensation dreaming'. Unlike the metaphysicians, who arrive at their conclusions from pretensions of reason (precipitous judgments), the spirit-seer actually experiences spirits in what amounts to something analogous to sensation. Because of this, the spirit-seer is unable to banish his visions simply by reasoning them away, for 'true or illusory, the impression of the senses itself precedes all judgment of the understanding and possesses an immediate certainty'. [25]

These considerations illuminate, perhaps, the way in which ruminating on Swedenborg's visions provided the basis for the development of some important Kantian doctrines. It may also highlight the precise nature of Kant's disagreement with Swedenborg. The main puzzle presented by Swedenborg has to do with the latter's claim to have immediate or direct (intuitive) experience of the spiritual world. This is especially puzzling in so far as Swedenborg's 'visionary' experiences include visual, auditory, tactile (i.e., sensible) experiences. Kant's *Lectures on Metaphysics* suggest little concern with the most general possibility that we may be capable of having both a sensible and a 'spiritual' intuition. Indeed, as we shall see Kant refers to Swedenborg's claim that we are members in both an intelligible and sensible world as 'sublime'. Nevertheless, Kant does seem to find certain problems with Swedenborg's claim to have both of these *at once*. Even more specifically, it seems to me that most of Kant's derision is reserved for the suggestion that Swedenborg is essentially having sensible representations of immaterial beings.[26] For how could an immaterial being be intuited sensibly? Kant's view seems to be something like this: either you've got a spiritual intuition, or you've got a sensible one. You cannot have the two simultaneously. In conjunction with this, Kant's first complaint relates to Swedenborg's claim to access this spiritual world while *still in the body*. Consider the following:

But one question still remains: whether the soul, which already sees itself

12

spiritually in the other world, will and can appear in the visible world through visible effects? This is not possible, for matter can be intuited only sensibly and fall only in the outer senses, but not a spirit. Or could I not to some extent already intuit here the community of departed souls with my soul, which is not yet departed, but which stands in their community as a spirit? e.g. as Swedenborg contends? This is contradictory, for then spiritual intuition would have to begin already in this world.[27]

Despite Kant's endorsement of many 'Swedenborgian' themes, his central disagreement with Swedenborg has to do, it seems, with our 'mode of access' to the 'spiritual world'. On this, Kant's charge is that Swedenborg claims to access the spirit world directly while still in the sensible world. In this, from a Kantian standpoint, Swedenborg has assumed to possess some kind of spiritual or mystical intuition that Kant claims we simply do not have, at least so long as we are beings governed by a sensible intuition. This view stems from Kant's epistemology, developing at the time of the *Dreams*, and fully developed in the later *Inaugural Dissertation* (1770). Kant's position is that objects are given to the human mind in accordance with a faculty of receptivity, or 'intuition'. According to Kant, our only mode of intuition is 'sensible', and it is governed by the pure 'forms of sensibility', space and time. Clearly, a spiritual being, which is immaterial, is not spatial in the sense that allows it to be intuited.

It is in connection with this problem that Kant tentatively develops a theory of metaphysical delusion in the *Dreams*. Kant suggests that the subjection of immaterial being to sensible conditions that characterizes both the metaphysician and Swedenborg might spring from and share in a deception indicative of the illusory experiences characteristic of dream states. This last suggestion clearly reflects Kant's growing concern to trace the conclusions of metaphysics back to their source in the human mind. One similarity between the metaphysician, the visionary and the 'dreamer' stems from the fact that in all cases, an individual believes herself to access an 'objective' world, a world of really existing and mind-independent things, despite the fact that such beings are not inter-subjectively accessible from the common, ordinary (sense-based) experiences of everyone else. The experiences of the visionary, in particular, share with dreaming states the quality of seeming to 'see' and 'hear' (etc.) objective phenomena, despite the fact that there are no inter-subjectively accessible objects that would allow us to confirm the experience. Kant indicates that from a common-sense standpoint, one could argue that the pretence to have access to the spiritual realm might be just as deluded as experiences grounded in 'diseases of the brain'.[28]

I should like to suggest that Swedenborg's accounts provided Kant with a striking example of the capacity and tendency of the human mind to transpose ideas and subjective experiences into objects that have mind-independent status. Later in his career Kant comes to argue that metaphysics stems from certain illusions of the mind.[29] This claim links up to the aforementioned notion that reason demands ultimate explanations, the data for which can never be met with in any sensuous experience. The result is that we are compelled to postulate intelligible grounds (e.g. spiritual beings) to account for what is given in our experiences. Kant becomes increasingly preoccupied with the way in which the human mind is led to 'hypostatize' these ideas, to ineluctably take them to be objective beings (objects) that provide the basis for our explanations. Indeed, it is interesting to note that the full-blown theory of metaphysical illusion so dominant in Kant's critical work (i.e., the *Critique of Pure Reason*) is tentatively laid out in the *Dreams* for the first time. There, Kant is deeply concerned to ask how it is that we come to take subjective phenomena (ideas of reason, subjectively experienced visions, etc.) and take them to be things that have real (mind-independent) existence:

Hence, the question I wish to have answered is this: How does the soul transpose such an image, which it ought, after all, to present as contained within itself, into a quite different relation, locating it, namely, in a place external to itself among objects which present themselves to the sensation which the soul has. [30]

Note that this phenomenon of 'transposing' subjective experiences 'as objects' [31] is not dismissed by Kant as ridiculous. Nor is such a tendency simply characteristic of 'fanatics' and charlatans. What seems to interest Kant is the utterly commonplace feature of this, for each of us does this all the time whenever we dream. The similarity of visionary and dream states, in which we find ourselves 'talking' and as it were 'sensing' objects and others who are not, presumably, actually present in any mind-independent fashion, provided Kant with the materials for these reflections. It seems to me, indeed, that Swedenborg's testimonies offered Kant with the material for a deep rumination on the overwhelming tendencies of metaphysicians to engage in their own abstract form of spirit-seeing. These considerations might allow us to refine our views about the nature of Kant's ambiguous response to Swedenborg.

It seems at times that Kant's point is that any theory of real relation that applies to both material and immaterial beings is doomed because it involves what Kant later commonly refers to as a 'subreption'. A subreption, for Kant, indicates a fallacy according to which we surreptitiously substitute concepts and terms of one kind for those of another. For Kant, the term is usually reserved for cases where we conflate concepts and principles of sensuous experience with those of pure reason. In the case at hand, Kant is concerned with a subreption according to which the immaterial beings or souls are construed by analogy with material, physical beings. [32] At issue here is the metaphysician's strained efforts to account for real interaction by surreptiously viewing spiritual being as analogous to physical being, in order to make sense of the alleged capacity to exert spiritual influences on body. More importantly, we find the general suggestion that metaphysicians (and particularly the metaphysical theories about the soul) erroneously presume to have access to spiritual being in a way that is analogous to the way we can access material objects. The metaphysician, in short, must presume to have some sort of direct *intellectual* (*rational*) access to the spiritual world in the same way that Swedenborg claims to access such a realm through a *mystical* intuition. This is precisely Kant's complaint. Indeed, the claim in the *Dreams* that there are no data corresponding to reason's pure concepts foreshadows the famous Kantian doctrine that our (human) reason is not intuitive. To state the later formulated and well-worn Kantian dictum: 'Concepts without intuitions are empty; intuitions without concepts are blind'. Or, in other words, according to Kant, we (unlike, say, God) do not have intellectual intuition. Since intuition is the capacity to be affected by and 'given' objects, Kant's real suggestion (albeit nascent in the *Dreams*) is that human intuition is in all cases sensible. The result is that, from a Kantian standpoint, the theories about spiritual being lack the epistemological support required to ground them. It is thus not surprising to find that in the main work published after the *Dreams*, Kant develops his doctrine of metaphysical error. By the later *Inaugural Dissertation* (1770), Kant had come to a full characterization of the illusions of the intellect, and a theory of 'subreption'.

III

The story does not stop here, however. Note that the thrust of the critical remarks offered by Kant relate to our *theoretical* efforts to acquire knowledge of the transcendent world. That is, Kant is clearly interested in drawing a boundary beyond which speculation and knowledge cannot go. It was in this connection, it seems, that he suggested that the 'dreams' (whether they be those of the metaphysician or the visionary) cannot serve as justified theoretical accounts. But Kant leaves opaque his actual position here. In chapter two, he suggests that the proliferation of ghost stories could equally well be explained by the fact that we *are*, each of us, truly in relation to the spiritual world.[33] In this, Kant seems to recognize that his own theoretical conclusions pertaining to metaphysics, i.e., the claims about limiting reason in its speculative or theoretical aims, leave open a number of issues relating to the moral theory. It may indeed be that Swedenborg's writings also highlight the distinction between reason in its theoretical and its moral (practical) uses, for even despite the above, Kant does not seem to want to reject a number of Swedenborgian claims. That we are each of us always already participants in the intelligible world, that each 'person' is, by virtue of a moral subjectivity (a soul) always already in communion with all other moral subjects, and that it is correct to view ourselves as subjects who participate in such a community, these are things which Kant surely seems to find attractive. Similarly, Kant does not dismiss the suggestion that heaven and hell are not 'places' to which we somehow find ourselves transported after death, but are rather the spiritual conditions reflected in the nature of our soul, or reflecting the degree of our moral development. It may, then, be that ruminating on Swedenborg's views, which place a primacy in moral, spiritual intuition (rather than simply on 'knowledge' from reason alone) led Kant to recognize that practical (moral) reason makes its claims upon us despite our theoretical limitations. And indeed, that it must do so. Here, it is interesting to note that throughout the *Dreams* Kant indicates that all the speculative tendencies of the metaphysician might actually find their real source in, and ultimately be guided by, practical (moral) interests. Moreover, the practical conclusion of the *Dreams* suggests that the speculative fairy-spinnings of the metaphysician are ultimately 'superfluous and unnecessary' for moral purposes. This in turn suggests that Kant might find some 'truth in the validity' of Swedenborg's accounts without countenancing use of Swedenborg's visions as evidence for any metaphysical knowledge.

Kant's agreement with many of the Swedenborgian theses is confirmed in the *Lectures on Metaphysics*, and it is here that Kant's emphasis on moral considerations in praising Swedenborg become most pronounced. Throughout these *Lectures* one finds Kant simultaneously praising and criticizing Swedenborg. Kant's agreements stem from his concession that there is a real (i.e., metaphysical) distinction between the bodily or sensuous world on the one hand, and the spiritual world on the other. Kant also agrees with Swedenborg that our bodily existence is governed by sensible intuition, which clouds and conceals our participation in the spiritual world. Consider the following:

We have a cognition of the bodily world through sensible intuition insofar as it appears to us […] but when the soul separates itself from the body, then it will not have the same sensible intuition of this world; it will not intuit the world as it appears, but rather as it is. Accordingly the separation of the soul from the body consists in the alteration of sensible intuition into spiritual intuition; and that is the other world.

[…] the thought of Swedenborg is in this quite sublime. He says the spiritual world constitutes a special real universe; this is the intelligible world [*mundis intelligibilis*], which must be distinguished from this sensible world [*mundo sensibili*]. He says all spiritual natures stand in connection with one another, only the community and connection of the spirits is not bound to the condition of the bodies […] Now as spirits our souls stand in this connection and community with one another, and indeed already here in this world, only we do not see ourselves in this community because we still have a sensible intuition; but although we do not see ourselves in it, we still stand within it. Now when the hindrance of sensible intuition is once removed, then we see ourselves in this spiritual community, and this is the other world; now these are not other things, but rather the same ones, but which we intuit differently. [34]

As we have seen, Kant cannot and does not want to go so far as to concede that Swedenborg's testimonies provide the basis for any theoretical knowledge of the spiritual realm, life after death, and so on. Thus, he refrains from accepting Swedenborg's testimonies for the reasons cited above, i.e., the subreptive conflation of the conditions of sensation and reason. However, Kant often seems to find in Swedenborg thoughts that are 'sublime' as expressions of a moral subjectivity. Given this, we might wonder why Kant would want to shy away from Swedenborg's testimonies. Does Kant have good reason to deny the reliance on mystical or immediate experience of a spiritual world, especially as expressions of an attuned moral (spiritual) subjectivity? And if so, what exactly are his reasons? Kant is quite explicit about admitting that Swedenborg's experiences, like the dreams of the metaphysician, can neither be confirmed nor disproved. Once again, however, Kant seems to think in the *Dreams* that in the face of our inability to confirm or deny, we must grant the rights to experience:

> If, however, certain alleged experiences cannot be brought under any law of sensation, which is unanimously accepted by the majority of people, and if, therefore, these alleged experiences establish no more than an irregularity in the testimony of the senses (as is, in fact, the case with the ghost stories which circulate), it is advisable to break off the enquiry without further ado, and that for the following reason. The lack of agreement and uniformity in this case deprives our historical knowledge of all power to prove anything, and renders it incapable of serving as a foundation to any law of experience, concerning which the understanding could judge. [35]

In the face of these considerations, it appears that Kant's only recourse is to suggest that Swedenborg's alleged experiences do not constitute sufficient *evidence* or grounds for the spiritual system he promotes. While Kant is not (admittedly) in a position to disprove Swedenborg's claims, he nevertheless feels that a reliance on such subjective and unique experiences might undermine reliance on more secure methods, not only in the theoretical philosophy, but in issues of morality. Indeed, Kant's deeper fear seems to be that a full-scale embrace of Swedenborg's accounts opens the floodgates to a mystical fanaticism or enthusiasm which Kant finds particularly worrisome. It is worrisome in some sense because it might possibly undermine the ethical position it seeks to express. One danger is that it might engender the conflation of ground and consequence. More specifically, Kant's claim is that we should not act morally in order to increase our chances of a blissful afterlife, but should, rather, cultivate a moral disposition which in turn leads to a noble hope for the future.[36] Thus, our need to 'prove' the existence of an afterlife, a spiritual realm, either by metaphysics or by reliance on Swedenborg's assurances, displaces the real ground of morality: 'What, is it only good to be virtuous because there is another world? Or is it not rather the case that actions will one day be rewarded because they are good and virtuous in themselves? Does not the heart of man contain within itself immediate moral prescriptions? Is it really necessary, in order to induce man to act in accordance with his destiny here on earth, to set machinery moving in another world?'.[37] What Kant fears is the encroaching 'enthusiasm' of mysticism or the fanaticism that he is concerned it may engender. Kant thus concludes:

 kant: against mystical experience

> Nor has human reason been endowed with the wings which would enable it to fly so high as to cleave the clouds which veil from our eyes the mysteries of the other world. And to those who are eager for knowledge of such things and who attempt to inform themselves with such importunity about mysteries of this kind, one can give this simple advice: that it would probably be best if they had the good grace to wait with patience until they arrived there. [38]

NOTES

1 Immanuel Kant, *Träume eines Geistersehers, erläutert durch Träume der Metaphysik* (1766). Passages from the *Dreams* are taken from *The Cambridge Edition of the Works of Immanuel Kant: Theoretical Philosophy 1755-1770* (Cambridge: CUP, 1992), pp. 301-59.

2 I do not mean to suggest that these two broadly opposed positions exhaust the ways in which scholars have attempted to account for Kant's response to Swedenborg. In fact, even within these two camps, scholars differ on exactly how they interpret Kant's position. For a good summary of some of these, see Alison Laywine, *Kant's Early Metaphysics and the Origins of the Critical Philosophy, North American Kant Society Studies in Philosophy,* vol. 3 (Atascadero: Ridgeview Publishing Company, 1993).

3   Correspondence to Moses Mendelssohn, 8 April 1766, in *The Cambridge Edition of the Works of Immanuel Kant: Correspondence* (Cambridge: CUP, 1999).

4   Moses Mendelssohn, *Gesammelte Schriften*, second series, vol. 4, ed. G B Mendelssohn (Leipzig: F A Brockhaus, 1844), p. 529.

5   Kant, *Correspondence*, p. 91.

6   Laywine, see especially pp. 55-100.

7   Kant suggests in his letter to Mendelssohn (1766) that his analogy between a real moral influx by spiritual beings and the force of universal gravitation is 'not intended seriously; it is only an example of how far one can go in philosophical fabrications'. See *The Cambridge Edition of the Works of Immanuel Kant: Correspondence*, p. 92.

8   See for example, Kuno Fisher, *Geschichte der neuern Philosophie*, vol. 4 (Heidelberg: Carl Winters Universitätsbuchhandlung, 1898). For a detailed discussion of this kind of reading, see Laywine, pp. 19-21.

9   Kant, *Dreams*, p. 346.

10 Ibid., p. 347. For a more detailed discussion, see my *Kant's Doctrine of Transcendental Illusion* (Cambridge: CUP, 2001).

11 Laywine, especially chapters 4 and 5. Laywine's position is essentially that Kant's readings of Swedenborg highlighted the way in which his (Kant's) early metaphysics, and particularly his theory of real influx, committed him to the possibility of a Swedenborgian account. Kant, seeing this similarity between his own and Swedenborg's views is said by Laywine to have been deeply disturbed. I agree with much of what Laywine contends, but feel that Kant's response was considerably more complex and ambiguous than she suggests.

12 See *Der einzig mögliche Beweisgrund zu einer Demonstration des Daseins Gottes* (1763) and *Untersuchung über die Deutlichkeit der Grundsätze der natürlichen Theologie und der Moral* (1764).

13 Kant, *Dreams*, p. 344.

14 Ibid., p. 345.

15 Ibid., p. 339.

16 As an example, see Hans Vaihinger, *Kommentar zu Kants Kritik der reinen Vernunft*, second edition, vol. II (Stuttgart: Union Deutsche Verlagsgesellschaft, 1992).

17 And, interestingly, one might note that the following work, *The Inaugural Dissertation*,

develops even more fully this notion of the intellect as a theoretical faculty, and argues for the possibility of a non-fallacious metaphysics through the use of the concepts of the intellect. See *The Cambridge Edition of the Works of Immanuel Kant: Theoretical Philosophy, 1755-1770*, pp. 373-415.

[18] Kant, *Dreams*, p. 354.

[19] Ibid.

[20] For a fuller treatment of this issue, see my *Kant's Doctrine of Transcendental Illusion*, p. 43.

[21] Depending on the commentator, one finds the broad suggestion that either 'Swedenborg is to be taken just as seriously as the respectable metaphysicians' or 'the metaphysicans are just as fanatical as Swedenborg'.

[22] Emanuel Swedenborg, *Arcana Caelestia*, tr. John Faulkner Potts, Fourth American Edition (New York: Swedenborg Foundation, 1949), §3348.

[23] Swedenborg, *Arcana Caelestia,* §70 as presented in George Trobridge, *Swedenborg: Life and Teaching* (New York: Swedenborg Foundation, 1992).

[24] Swedenborg, *Arcana Caelestia,* §322 as presented in Michael Stanley, *Emanuel Swedenborg, Essential Readings* (Biddles Limited, 1988).

[25] Kant, *Dreams*, p. 335.

[26] In this respect, we may agree with Laywine, that Kant is concerned with the problems associated with subjecting immaterial being to the spatio-temporal conditions under which objects of the senses are given.

[27] The passage is taken from *The Cambridge Edition of the Works of Immauel Kant: Lectures on Metaphysics* (Cambridge: CUP, 1997), p. 106.

[28] See my *Kant's Doctrine of Transcendental Illusion*, pp. 32-40.

[29] I argue at length for the claim that Kant's theory of metaphysical error is linked up with this propensity to hypostatize and project subjective ideas as objects. See my *Kant's Doctrine of Transcendental Illusion*.

[30] Kant, *Dreams*, p. 331.

[31] Ibid.

[32] This use of the term is also found in Kant's *Lectures*. See Blomberg in *The Cambridge Edition of the Works of Immanuel Kant: Lectures on Logic* (Cambridge: CUP,

1992), p. 203.

[33] Kant, *Dreams*, p. 322.

[34] Kant, *Lectures on Metaphysics*, p.104.

[35] Kant, *Dreams*, p. 358.

[36] Ibid., p. 359.

[37] Ibid., p. 358.

[38] Ibid., p. 359.

Swedenborg's positive influence on the development of Kant's mature moral philosophy *

Gregory R Johnson

K ant's rigorous and sublime system of ethics, with its emphasis on universality, consistency, autonomy, and duty for duty's sake, is one of the greatest contributions ever made to moral philosophy. 'Kantianism' is so firmly ensconced in the textbooks as one of the timeless moral archetypes that, aside from a few specialist scholars, there is very little understanding of the development of Kant's moral thinking and the figures who influenced it.[1] Wolff, Crusius, Shaftesbury, Hutcheson, Hume, and especially Rousseau are the chief influences cited. Leibniz and Pope are cited as the primary influences on Kant's thoughts about theodicy, a topic closely connected to his moral philosophy. But Swedenborg is seldom taken seriously as an influence on Kant's moral philosophy, even though it is in *Dreams of a Spirit-Seer,* Kant's 1766 book on Swedenborg, that the outlines of Kant's mature moral philosophy first emerge.[2] I wish to argue that Swedenborg did in fact influence the development of Kant's moral philosophy. This influence was, furthermore, a positive one, meaning that Kant arrived at his mature position not merely by rejecting, but by incorporating, elements of Swedenborg's thought.

1. Kant's Copernican ethics

The first stage in the development of Kant's moral philosophy is what I shall dub his 'Copernican Ethics', which I detect in his writings from 1754 to 1759, primarily his *Universal Natural History and Theory of the Heavens* (1755)[3] and his second essay on the great Lisbon earthquake of 1755, 'History and Natural Description of the Most Remarkable Occurrences Associated with the Earthquake [...]' (1756).[4] Kant's ethics in this period is 'Copernican' not in the sense of Kant's Copernican Revolution, but of Copernicus' Copernican Revolution. First, it presupposes the modern, post-Copernican vision of the cosmos in which God seems remote, his providence attenuated, and nature inhospitable to the human good. Second, just as Copernicus solved the astronomical problem of the organization of the solar system by imagining how it would look from a cosmic, rather than an Earth-centred point of view. Kant seeks to solve moral problems by recommending that we look at the human condition from a cosmic, rather than an anthropocentric point of view.

Kant's Copernican ethics is an attempt to reconcile human beings to a distant God and an inhospitable universe. It is, therefore, a theodicy: an attempt to defend the justice of divine providence by answering the classical problem of evil: How do we reconcile divine omniscience, omnipotence, and omnibenevolence with the existence of evil? This perennial philosophical problem is much intensified by the modern image of an inhospitable, mechanistic cosmos in which the achievement of value is constantly threatened by the contingencies of matter and, in the long run, is extinguished under the rule of the iron law of entropy, which dictates that all order and motion will be extinguished.

In chapter seven of his *Universal Natural History*, Kant attempts to reconcile us with this grim picture by offering us a series of cosmological hypotheses. The common thrust of all these hypotheses is to induce a sense of complacency and reconciliation by inducing the reader progressively to displace himself from the perspective of a human being suffering under the reign of contingency. One can wrest some meaning from one's suffering only by finding a higher vantage point, from which one's own misfortunes can be subsumed into the larger patterns of nature. Kant's cosmological hypotheses lead us to higher and higher vantage points, wider and wider perspectives on the cosmos, greater and greater distances from the human condition, until at last cosmological reason gives way to faith and we gain a sense of what it would be to grasp the whole from the perspective of God Himself. A similar argument is offered in the closing pages of the second earthquake essay. According to Kant's Copernican ethics, we shall cease to feel the pains of the human condition by detaching ourselves from it and identifying ourselves with the larger economy of nature and the inscrutable will of God.

Kant's Copernican ethics is not only characterized by the centrality of the theodicy problem and the moral priority of the cosmic point of view over the human point of view. It is also characterized by a concern with the hierarchical arrangement of different cognitive types. This shows up in two ways. First is Kant's 'elitist' dependence upon theoretical reasoning achievable only by the few, as opposed to practical reasoning achievable by all. Second, part three of the *Universal Natural History* is devoted to the unusual topic of extraterrestrial intelligent beings, specifically those inhabiting the other planets in our solar system (an interest shared by Swedenborg).[5] This section is significant for two reasons. First, Kant arranges the different dwellers of the planets in a hierarchy based on the relative strengths of their cognitive powers. (Human beings come out in the middle, but some of us are closer to our betters and some of us closer to our inferiors than others). Second, although Kant is concerned with hierarchy and difference, he does have an expansive, cosmic conception of a community of rational beings that includes more than just humans.

2. Rousseau and the 'Ptolemaic' counter-revolution

I shall dub the second stage of the development of Kant's moral philosophy the Ptolemaic counter-revolution in morals,[6] which I detect in the writings of 1760 to 1765, particularly the *Observations on the Feeling of the Beautiful and Sublime* (1764),[7] the 'Essay on the Sicknesses of the Head' (1764),[8] and the so-called *Remarks* of 1764-5, that Kant penned in his own copy of the *Observations*.[9] I call it 'Ptolemaic' because just as Kant's Copernican ethics proposes to solve the problems of human existence by encouraging us to displace ourselves from the point of view of the human actor to that of a cosmic spectator, the Ptolemaic counter-revolution reasserts the primacy of the human point of view over the cosmic. This is accompanied by the corollary assertion of the primacy of the practical reason of the human agent over the theoretical reason of the cosmic spectator. Because practical reason can be exercised by virtually all human beings, whereas high levels of theoretical attainment are open only to the few, this stage also marks a move from an unabashed intellectual elitism to a more egalitarian and populist moral outlook.

The grounds for this egalitarian move are already present, albeit latently, in Kant's cosmology. In the *Universal Natural History*, Kant observes that, 'All that is finite, whatever has limits and a definite relation to unity, is equally far removed from the infinite'.[10] Kant's reasoning is that, in the face of an infinite universe, all finite differences—including finite human differences—are ultimately matters of indifference; or, as Kant puts it, 'in the presence of the infinite, the great and small are small alike'.[11] This reasoning is beautifully encapsulated in the story of 'Carazan's Dream', that Kant quotes in a footnote in the *Observations*:

> One evening, as I drew up my accounts and calculated my profits, sleep overpowered me. In this state I saw the Angel of Death come over me like a whirlwind [...] I was led before the throne of the third heaven. The glory that flamed before me spoke to me thus: 'Carazan, your service of God is rejected. You have closed your heart to the love of man, and have clutched your treasures with an iron grip. You have lived only for yourself, and therefore you shall also live the future in eternity alone and removed from all communion with the whole of Creation'. At this instant I was swept away by an unseen power, and driven through the shining edifice of Creation. I soon left countless worlds behind me. As I neared the outermost end of nature, I

saw the shadows of the boundless void sink down into the abyss before me. A fearful kingdom of eternal silence, loneliness, and darkness! Unutterable horror overtook me at this sight. I gradually lost sight of the last star, and finally the last glimmering ray of light was extinguished in outer darkness! The moral terrors of despair increased with every moment, just as every moment increased my distance from the last inhabited world. I reflected with unbearable anguish that if ten thousand times a thousand years more should have carried me along beyond the bounds of all the universe I would still always be looking ahead into the infinite abyss of darkness, without help or hope of any return. In this bewilderment I thrust out my hands with such force toward the objects of reality that I awoke. And now I have been taught to esteem mankind; for in that terrifying solitude I would have preferred even the least of those whom in the pride of my fortune I had turned from my door to all the treasures of Golconda.[12]

Carazan, by limiting his perspective merely to the human realm, brought human differences, both natural and social, into the foreground. Consequently he was an elitist, a miser, a misanthrope. However, once he was exiled from the human world and cast into the sublime and infinite void, all such differences lost their importance. In the presence of the infinite, great and small became small alike.

The Ptolemaic stage of Kant's ethics could also be called Rousseauian, for although its basic principles were latent in Kant's earlier works, it was Rousseau who provided the decisive stimulus to Kant's thinking.[13] Kant records this influence in a famous *Remark* from 1764 or 1765:

I am by inclination an inquirer. I feel in its entirety a thirst for knowledge and a restless desire to increase it, along with satisfaction in each forward step. There was a time when I thought that this alone could constitute the honour of mankind, and I despised the people, who know nothing.

Rousseau set me right. This blind prejudice vanished. I learned to honour human beings, and I would be more useless than the common worker if I did not believe that this view could give worth to all others to establish the rights of mankind.[14]

Rousseau taught Kant that, contrary to the best hopes of the Enlightenment—indeed, contrary to the intellectualism of virtually the entire philosophical tradition—intellectual excellence does not automatically equal moral excellence; intellectual progress does not necessarily equal moral progress; in fact, the progress of the arts and the sciences leads, in most cases, to the increase of human unhappiness by corrupting those virtues that are more likely to be found in simple, uneducated souls.[15] The theorist's claim of moral superiority vanishes. It is important to note, however, that neither Kant nor Rousseau ever deny the ineluctable fact of intellectual inequality. They deny only that intellectual inequality is equivalent to moral inequality. Because theoretical activity is no longer regarded as necessarily or intrinsically good, it must justify itself by serving a moral purpose. The sole justification of theoretical activity becomes the service it renders to the moral and practical interests of mankind.

Kant's Rousseauian turn is characterized by a broadening of his ethical interests beyond the theodicy problem to such issues as the grounds of moral obligation and the springs of moral motivation. Another important result of Kant's encounter with Rousseau—one that is especially important in setting the stage for his encounter with Swedenborg—is his formulation of the idea of 'laws of freedom' (*Gesetzen der Freyheit*). From a strictly Newtonian materialist point of view, the laws of nature govern a wholly deterministic system of physical monads, and freedom is a violation of physical law; the idea of 'laws of freedom' is, therefore, an oxymoron. Rousseau, however, identifies human goodness with both nature and freedom, implying simultaneously that human nature is not deterministic and that human freedom is law-governed. A true-bred materialist would simply have rejected such notions outright. Kant, however, did not. Instead, Kant declared Rousseau to be the Newton of the moral world:

> Newton was the first to see order and regularity bound with great simplicity; whereas before him disorder and badly joined multiplicity was encountered, since then the comets run in geometrical courses.
>
> Rousseau was the first to discover under the multiplicity of available human forms [*Gestalten*] mankind's deeply hidden nature and the concealed law through which providence through its observation is justified. Before, the objection of Alphonso and Mani was valid. After Newton and Rousseau, God is justified and henceforth Pope's teaching is true.[16]

Kant's declaration that Rousseau is the Newton of the human world does, however, create a problem: How does the human world, with its laws of freedom, fit into the physical world, with its laws of necessity?

Kant's *Remarks* also record a serious engagement with Rousseau's identification of nature and goodness, i.e., his attempt to ground moral obligation in human nature. Kant also adopted Rousseau's understanding of human nature as free, unified, and self-determining. As Kant puts it: 'The question is whether, in order to move the affects of myself or others I should take my point of support from outside the world or within it. I answer that I find it in the state of nature, that is, in freedom'.[17] In order to reconcile the freedom, unity, and autonomy of the state of nature with the constraint, alienation, and heteronomy of the civil condition, Kant also adopted Rousseau's distinction between human beings as products of nature and human beings as products of history:

> by *man* here I do not only mean man as he is distorted by the mutable form [*Gestalt*] which is impressed upon him by the contingencies of his condition, and who, as such, has nearly always been misunderstood even

by philosophers. I rather mean the unchanging *nature* of man, and his distinctive position within the creation [...] This method of moral enquiry is an admirable discovery of our times, which, when viewed in the full extent of its program, was entirely unknown to the ancients.[18]

Rousseau claimed that the move from the state of nature to the civil condition was merely a matter of contingency, not the result of natural teleology or providence. Neither the push of our nature nor the pull of our destiny requires that man become civilized. Our hearts are just not in it. This asocial conception of man's nature gives Rousseau the vast critical distance and leverage needed to undertake a total critique of civilization. Kant, however, claims that human beings are driven into society by a natural sociability.[19] But he still retains a sufficient critical distance from the modern civil condition to offer a radical, Rousseauian critique.[20]

Like Rousseau, however, the aim of Kant's critical project is not to return us to the state of nature. This is impossible. History cannot be undone. We must try to uncover our natural state in order to put ourselves in a position outside of society. From this position, we can take stock of both the losses suffered and the gains made in our passage from nature to civilization: 'If one evaluates the happiness of the savage, it is not in order to return to the forests, but in order to determine what one has lost while in other respects one has made gains'.[21] From this position, we can also take up the task, not of destroying, but of reforming the restraints of civilization, bringing them in harmony with our natural sentiments. The purpose of *Emile*, claims Kant, is to show the way 'to remain a man of nature in society'.[22] This is Kant's purpose as well: 'My purpose will be to establish which perfection is appropriate to him [man] in the state of primitive innocence and which perfection is appropriate to him in the state of wise innocence'.[23]

To combine natural freedom and civilized constraints, Rousseau recommends that we discover those constraints that we can freely impose upon ourselves. The set of all such laws constitutes an ideal republic. Insofar as the human will naturally and necessarily wills the good, it naturally and necessarily wills this republic. Rousseau calls this will the General Will. It is what all of us, deep down, truly will. Individual human beings can bring our empirical wills into harmony with the General Will (our true wills), only by paring away the countervailing forces of irrational desires and passions. Kant too adopted this account of the moral will, and he never abandoned it. In the *Groundwork of the Metaphysics of Morals*, Rousseau's General Will appears as Kant's Holy Will: the will that necessarily wills the good. Individual human beings can bring our wills in line with the holy will by surmounting our sensuous and selfish impulses and subordinating them to the good.

Another important feature of Kant's writings of this time is his serious exploration of the relationship of morality and feeling, a task prompted by Rousseau's claim that knowledge of the natural goodness of man is accessible through the sentiments of self-esteem and pity, and Kant's populist concern to connect moral knowledge to levels of cognitive attainment available to all human beings. It is at this point in his career that Kant began his engagement with the British moral sense theorists, particularly Shaftesbury, Hutcheson and Hume.

Kant's doctrine of 'moral feeling' (*moralische Gefühl*) is, however, problematic. Feelings are clearly rooted in our physical natures. Our physical natures, however, are clearly subject to the amoral laws of nature, not the moral laws of freedom. 'Moral feeling', seems, therefore, to be as oxymoronic as 'laws of freedom'. Furthermore, feeling, insofar as it can be said to be moral at all, is traditionally associated with eudemonistic ethics. Kant, however, does not think that the pursuit of happiness is the true aim of morality. Indeed, duty often requires that we be willing to sacrifice our happiness for the sake of goodness. It is this ability to sacrifice happiness for goodness, to contravene the incentives of the entire economy of nature to heed the higher call of duty, that constitutes for Kant the true ground of human moral self-esteem. Finally, the relationship of moral feeling to the General Will is quite problematic, for it seems that we align our individual wills with the General Will only insofar as we rise above our feelings. The General Will is the same as our autonomy. Feelings, moral or otherwise, are a principle of heteronomy. How the latter are compatible with the former is unclear.

A final feature of Kant's Rousseauian turn to the human perspective is his constriction of the morally relevant community: from the *Universal Natural History*'s community of *rational beings as such* to the specifically *human* community. Virtue becomes identified with 'universal affection toward the *human* species' and 'a high feeling of the dignity of *human* nature'.[24]

3. Swedenborg and the turn toward the supersensible

Kant's early writings display an unresolved tension between two principles that he regarded as equally true. On the one hand, he was completely convinced that the world, including the human body, is a complex machine, a completely determinate system of material bodies that can be understood solely in terms of mathematical physics and requires no recourse to such explanatory principles as teleology, special providence, or spiritual influxes, including the free will. On the other hand, Kant was equally convinced of the freedom, dignity, and moral responsibility of human beings, a conviction that he received at his mother's knee and that was powerfully reinforced in his thirties by his encounter with the writings of Rousseau.

But how does the human world, with its laws of freedom, fit into the physical world, with its laws of necessity? Moral freedom and complete physical determinism cannot exist in the same world. The laws of nature and the laws of freedom cannot be reconciled within a single system. Something has to give. Susan Shell nicely sums up the problem of Kant's Rousseauian ethics:

> The 'Remarks' […] leave us with two principles of world 'unity', two forces of 'attraction' whose relation remains unresolved: a 'natural instinct of active benevolence' rooted in sexual desire (and inequality), and a non-instinctual benevolence associated with the free community of equals […] The first is 'indeterminate' and destabilising, but also dynamic; the second

is determinately bound up with the timeless concept of a perfected moral/
political whole.[25]

My suggestion is that Kant resolved these problems through a creative appropria-
tion of Swedenborg.

In *Dreams of a Spirit-Seer*, part I, chapter two, Kant offers an account of the spirit
world that he claims is based solely on his own speculations—although, he adds, it
just happens to be confirmed by Swedenborg's visions. It is clear, however, that the
two correspond so closely because Kant's account of the spirit world is nothing more
than a careful philosophical reconstruction of Swedenborg's.[26] Kant argues for the
existence of the spirit world based on the following phenomena: (1) the existence
of non-material, non-locatable animating principles (souls), (2) the existence of
a *sensus communis*, which leads us to submit our judgments for intersubjective
adjudication, and (3) the existence of distinctly moral motivations, which lead us to
thrust aside our private, selfish, and sensuous motivations and take up a universal
standpoint. Kant argues that these phenomena can best be explained by positing
the existence of a spirit world. Kant claims that the spirit world is inhabited by essentially the same kinds of beings as Swedenborg does:

> This immaterial world would [...] include, firstly, all created intelligences, some
> of them being united with matter so as to form a person, others not; the immate-
> rial world would, in addition, include the sensible subjects in all animal species;
> finally, it would include all the other principles of life wherever they may exist in
> nature [...] All these immaterial natures, whether they exercise an influence on
> the corporeal world or not, and all rational beings, of which the animal nature
> is an accidental state of their being, whether they exist here on earth or on other
> heavenly bodies, and whether they are now animating the raw stuff of matter, or
> will do so in the future, or have done so in the past—all these beings, I say, would,
> according to this account, stand in a community consonant with their nature.[27]

Kant, like Swedenborg, claims that the spirit world consists of a systematic unity or whole of spiritual beings: 'these immaterial beings, if they are directly united, may perhaps together constitute a great whole, which could be called the immaterial world (*mundus intelligibilis*)'.[28] Since spirits account for the phenomena of life and moral obligation, which cannot be reconciled with causal determinism, Kant, like Swedenborg, concludes that they must have causal laws of their own: 'The particular causal laws in terms of which they operate are called *pneumatic*, and, in so far as corporeal beings are the mediating causes of their effects in the material world, they are called *organic*'.[29] Like Swedenborg, Kant also claims the spirit world would exist outside of space and time: 'This community would not be based on the conditions which limit the relationship of bodies. It would be a community in which distance in space and separation in time, which constitute the great chasm in the visible world which cancels all community, would vanish. The human soul, already in this present life, would therefore have to be regarded as being simultaneously linked to two worlds'.[30] Finally, Kant claims that some people in this life can gain the knowledge available to their spiritual selves, a knowledge unlimited by the conditions of space and time, by means of decoding the meanings of influxes from the spirit world that clothe themselves in spatio-temporal garb. Kant's account is essentially identical to Swedenborg's.

This Swedenborgian vision of the spirit world suggested to Kant his solution to the problems of Rousseau's ethics. From the premise that moral freedom and physical determinism cannot exist in the same world, Kant concluded that if he was to preserve both freedom and determinism, he would have to split the world in two, and this he did, dividing the whole into material and spiritual, sensible and intelligible, or phenomenal and noumenal worlds. The phenomenal 'world' is the world insofar as it is given to the senses, a realm of beings perceived as in space and time and interpreted by the categories of the understanding. It is a wholly deterministic system of material bodies governed in accordance with physical laws. The noumenal 'world' is that aspect of the world that is not given to any form of intuition, sensible or intellectual, but that is only intelligible or thinkable. Whereas phenomena are always sensuously given in space and time, noumenal or intelligible beings are given independent of space and time. The noumenal realm comprises a number of things. First, all beings have a noumenal aspect just insofar as their existence transcends our consciousness of them, i.e., just insofar as their being is not exhausted by their being present to us. Second, the noumenal realm, like the phenomenal realm, is a system, a community of spiritual monads governed by pneumatic laws.

Human beings are citizens of both worlds. Insofar as we are phenomenal beings, we are members of the community of physical monads wholly determined by Newtonian laws. If, however, human beings were *merely* natural beings, we would not possess freedom, dignity, and moral responsibility. But the experience of freedom, dignity, and moral responsibility is undeniable. We find ourselves stirred by a feeling of respect for the moral law, the commandments of which might contravene the entire economy of nature; we can thrust aside the incentives of pleasure and pain, glory and shame, even the desire for self-preservation itself to heed the call of the moral law. Insofar as we can do this, we experience a dimension of ourselves that transcends the entire natural order. This noumenal dimension is our moral personality; it is the locus of freedom, dignity, and moral responsibility; it establishes our citizenship in the kingdom of rational beings governed by spiritual laws. In his mature works, Kant refers to this spiritual realm as the 'moral world', the '*corpus mysticum*' (the mystical body), the '*regnum gratiae*' (the Kingdom of Grace), the '*mundus intelligibilis*' (the intelligible world), and the 'Kingdom of Ends' (*Reich der Zwecke*).[31] It is the realm that Swedenborg claims to have seen and heard.

Kant's Swedenborgian ethics continues his Ptolemaic counter-revolution. The chief difference is that Kant retracts his 'humanist' identification of the moral community with mankind alone and reasserts his earlier, expansive account of the moral community as including all rational beings as such, expanding it even further to include not just extraterrestrials, but the spiritual aspects of embodied beings, disembodied spirits, and—taking Swedenborg as our guide—perhaps angels and demons as well.

The continuities, though, are striking. First of all, Kant's Swedenborgian ethics preserves his Rousseauian emphasis on the priority of practical reason over theoretical reason, and of the moral agent's point of view over that of the scientific spectator and technological operator. Kant, however, strips the agent's point of view down to its moral essence. He does not return to a full-blown classical teleological interpretation of nature. Kant does hold that the teleological interpretation of nature and history is absolutely essential, but he also holds that it is underdetermined by empirically accessible phenomena and can be grounded only in a form of reflective judgment that ventures out beyond what can be sensuously verified. Kant thus leaves in place the mechanistic interpretation and technological mastery of nature. (The primacy of the spirit world is not the primacy of the life world.) In short, Kant's discovery of the spirit world reverses the moral meaning of the first Copernican Revolution, while leaving its scientific meaning intact. Kant reasserts that man's true home, the spiritual world, is still the centre of the universe (morally speaking), even though our material home is but a mote whirling in the void.

Second, Kant's Swedenborgian ethics preserves his Rousseauian concern with the questions of moral justification and moral motivation. However, in opposition to Rousseau and the moral sense theorists, Kant abandons any attempt to account for moral justification and motivation by reference to feelings, for all feelings belong to our *material* nature, which is wholly determined by physical laws and thus falls outside of our moral personality. Kant does, however, preserve Rousseau's General Will and the reciprocal laws of love and respect that it legislates. But he transforms them into pneumatic laws of the spiritual world. Furthermore, Kant preserves a notion of moral feeling in the form of the feeling of respect (*Achtung*) for the moral law and for rational natures, but Kant claims that the feeling of respect is *not* a feeling in the physiological, and therefore materially determined, sense. Finally, it must be noted that Kant's Swedenborgian ethics lays the groundwork not only for Kant's mature moral philosophy, but for the *Critique of Pure Reason* as well. Kant's own Copernican Revolution—which itself is Ptolemaic insofar as it asserts the epistemological primacy of the human point of view—is made necessary by his Ptolemaic revolution in morals. In order to establish the primacy of the moral agent's point of view, i.e., the primacy of practical reason, Kant must rein in the imperialistic ambition of theoretical reason to be the sole source and criterion of truth; Kant must limit (theoretical) reason to make room for (moral) faith. Hence it is no accident that Kant first refers to the project of a critique of pure reason in *Dreams*, as well as in texts and reflections composed at the same time, in 1764-5.[32]

Conclusion: the starry heavens and the moral law

To conclude this account of Swedenborg's role in the development of Kant's mature moral philosophy, I wish to examine Kant's own conclusion to the *Critique of Practical Reason*, where—his victories secured—he looks back upon his struggles.

> Two things fill the mind with ever new and increasing admiration and awe, the oftener and more steadily we reflect upon them: the starry heavens above me and the moral law within me [...] The former begins at the place I occupy in the external world of sense, and it broadens the connection in which I stand into an unbounded magnitude of worlds beyond worlds and systems of systems and into the limitless times of their periodic motion, their beginning and their continuance [... The] view of a countless multitude of worlds annihilates, as it were, my importance as an animal creature, which must give back to the planet (a mere speck in the universe) the matter from which it came, the matter which is for a little time provided with vital force, we know not how.[33]

This is the question. The cosmos revealed by modern science annihilates our freedom, dignity, and self-esteem. How, then, do we retain our humanity?

The answer is our citizenship in another world, a community of spiritual beings, free, rational and dignified, existing under laws of spiritual harmony and perfection; this spiritual community transcends the material world in both fact and value; it therefore serves as the archetype for the progressive transformation of nature and society in its image. In Kant's words:

> The latter [the moral law] begins at my invisible self, my personality, and exhibits me in a world [i.e., the spiritual world] which has true infinity but which is comprehensible only to the understanding [i.e., it is intelligible or noumenal]——a world in which I recognise myself existing in a universal and necessary (and not only, as in the first case, contingent) connection, and thereby also in connection with all those visible worlds [insofar as these other visible worlds are homes to rational beings...] The latter [citizenship in the spiritual world...] infinitely raises my worth as that of an intelligence by my personality, in which the moral law reveals a life independent of all animality and even of the whole world of sense——at least so far as it may be inferred from the purposive destination assigned to my existence by this law, a destination which is not restricted to the conditions and limits of this life, but reaches into the infinite.[34]

The answer, in short, is Swedenborg.

NOTES

* This is a heavily revised version of a lecture delivered to the Swedenborg Seminar of the American Academy of Religion at their annual convention in Philadelphia, on

18 November 1995. I wish to thank Professor Jane K Williams-Hogan of the Academy of the New Church College in Bryn Athyn, Pennsylvania for inviting me.

[1] On the development of Kant's moral philosophy, see Paul Menzer, 'Entwicklungsgang der kantischen Ethik in den Jahren 1760-1785', in *Kant-Studien,* vol. 3 (1899), pp. 41-104; Josef Schmucker, *Die Ursprünge der Ethik Kants in seinen vorkritischen Schriften und Reflexionen* (Meisenheim: Anton Hain, 1961); Dieter Henrich, 'Hutcheson und Kant', in *Kant-Studien,* vol. 49 (1957), pp. 49-69; 'Über Kants früheste Ethik', in *Kant-Studien,* vol. 54 (1963), pp. 404-31; *Aesthetic Judgment and the Moral Image of the World: Studies in Kant* (Stanford: Stanford University Press, 1992); Paul Arthur Schilpp, *Kant's Pre-Critical Ethics* (Evanston: Northwestern University Press, 1960); Keith Ward, *The Development of Kant's View of Ethics* (New York: Humanities Press, 1972); Richard L Velkley, *Freedom and the End of Reason: On the Moral Foundation of Kant's Critical Philosophy* (Chicago: University of Chicago Press, 1989); Susan Meld Shell, *The Embodiment of Reason: Kant on Spirit, Generation, and Community* (Chicago: University of Chicago Press, 1996); and J B Schneewind, *The Invention of Autonomy: A History of Modern Moral Philosophy* (Cambridge: Cambridge University Press, 1998).

[2] Two significant exceptions are Keith Ward in *The Development of Kant's View of Ethics* and 'Kant's Teleological Ethics', in *Immanuel Kant: Critical Assessments*, ed. Ruth F Chadwick, 4 vols. (New York: Routledge: 1992), vol. III, pp. 244-6; and J N Findlay in *Kant and the Transcendental Object: A Hermeneutic Study* (Oxford: Clarendon, 1981), pp. 76-7. According to Findlay, '[Swedenborg's] spiritual world [is] perhaps the original of Kant's "kingdom of ends" ' (p. 76) and 'We are obviously here [in *Dreams*] anticipating the kingdom of ends of which so much is made in the *Metaphysic of Morals* [sic], and it is pleasing to know that this conception, though rational, is also mystical and Swedenborgian' (p. 77). The majority view, however, is represented by Schneewind, who sums up *Dreams of a Spirit-Seer* by saying, 'Well, it was not meant seriously' (*The Invention of Autonomy*, p. 505). The greatest obstacle to taking seriously the possibility that Swedenborg influenced Kant is the snide and flippant tone of *Dreams*. I offer an explanation of the literary qualities of *Dreams* and argue at length that Kant was decisively influenced by

Swedenborg in my doctoral dissertation, *A Commentary on Kant's Dreams of a Spirit-Seer* (Washington, DC: The Catholic University of America, 2001).

[3] Kant, *Universal Natural History and Theory of the Heavens*, tr. W Hastie (Ann Arbor: University of Michigan Press, 1969) (a partial translation that leaves out the book's entire third part) and *Universal Natural History and Theory of the Heavens*, tr. Stanley L Jaki (Edinburgh: Scottish Academic Press, 1981) (complete).

[4] Kant, 'History and Physiography of the Most Remarkable Cases of the Earthquake which Towards the End of 1755 Shook a Great Part of the Earth', in Kant, *Essays and Treatises*, 2 vols., tr. John Richardson (London: William Richardson, 1798-9), vol. 2, pp. 95-142.

[5] See Emanuel Swedenborg, *The Earths in Our Solar System which are Called Planets and the Earths in the Starry Heaven and their Inhabitants; also the Spirits and Angels There; from Things Heard and Seen*, tr. J Whitehead (New York: Swedenborg Foundation, 1913). This book contains excerpts from the articles appended to the chapters of the *Arcana Coelestia* which deal with the book of Exodus. We know that Kant read this material, for he refers to it in one of his lecture courses: *Fragment einer späteren Rationaltheologie nach Baumbach*, in *Gesammelte Schriften*, ed. Preussischen Akademie, 29 vols. (Berlin: Reiner, 1902-), vol. 28.2, p. 1325. Kant's *Gesammelte Schriften* henceforth cited as AK.

[6] I wish to thank John Gerard Moore for this phrase.

[7] Kant, *Observations on the Feeling of the Beautiful and the Sublime*, in Kant, *Essays and Treatises*, vol. 2, pp. 1-78 and *Observations on the Feeling of the Beautiful and Sublime*, tr. John T Goldthwait (Berkeley: University of California Press, 1960).

[8] Kant, 'Versuch über die Krankheiten des Kopfes', AK, vol. 2, pp. 257-71.

[9] Kant, *Bemerkungen zu den Beobachtungen über das Gefühl des Schönen und Erhabenen*, AK, vol. 20, pp. 1-192; henceforth cited as *Remarks*.

[10] Kant, *Universal Natural History*, tr. Hastie, p. 139.

[11] Ibid., p. 136.

[12] *Observations*, tr. Goldthwait, pp. 48-9 n.

[13] There are a number of excellent studies on the influence of Rousseau on Kant, particularly as reflected in the *Remarks* of 1764-5. See Schmucker, *Die Ursprünge*

der Ethik Kants in seinen vorkritischen Schriften und Reflexionen; Ernst Cas-
sirer, 'Kant and Rousseau', in his *Rousseau, Kant, Goethe*, tr. James Gutmann,
Paul Oskar Kristeller, and John Herman Randall, Jr (Princeton: Princeton University
Press, 1945); Dieter Henrich, 'Über Kants Entwicklungsgeschichte', in *Philosophische
Rundschau,* 13 (1965), pp. 252-63; Richard L Velkley, *Freedom and the End of
Reason*; and Susan Shell, 'Kant's Political Cosmology: Freedom and Desire in the
"Remarks" in Concerning Observations on the Feeling of the Beautiful and the
Sublime', in *Essays on Kant's Political Philosophy*, ed. Howard Lloyd Williams
(Chicago: University of Chicago Press, 1992); see also ch. 4 of her *The Embodiment
of Reason*.

14 Kant, *Remarks*, AK, vol. 20, p. 44.

15 See especially Jean-Jacques Rousseau, *Discourse on the Sciences and Arts* (First
Discourse) (1751), trs. Judith R Bush and Roger D Masters, in *The Collected Writings
of Rousseau*, vol. 2, ed. Roger D Masters and Christopher Kelly (Hanover and London:
Dartmouth College/University Press of New England, 1992).

16 Kant, *Remarks*, AK, vol. 20, pp. 58-9. On the project of Newtonian moral philosophy,
cf. the conclusion to Kant's *Critique of Practical Reason*, tr. Lewis White Beck
(Indianapolis: Bobbs-Merrill, 1956), pp. 167-8.

17 Kant, *Remarks*, AK, vol. 20, p. 56.

18 Kant, *M. Immanuel Kant's Announcement of the Programme of his Lectures for the
Winter Semester of 1765-1766*, tr. David Walford, in *Immanuel Kant, Theoretical
Philosophy, 1755-1770*, ed. and tr. David Walford with Ralf Meerbote (Cambridge:
Cambridge University Press, 1992), AK, vol. 2, pp. 311-12; Walford, p. 298; henceforth
cited as *Announcement*.

19 On this contrast, see Shell, 'Kant's Political Cosmology', p. 89.

20 See, for example, the opening pages of the 'Versuch über die Krankheiten des Kopfes',
AK, vol. 2, pp. 257-8.

21 Kant, *Remarks*, AK, vol. 20, p. 31.

22 Ibid.

23 Kant, *Announcement*, AK, vol. 2, p. 312; Walford, p. 298.

24 Kant, *Observations*, tr. Goldthwait, pp. 58, 66, emphasis added.

25 Shell, 'Kant's Political Cosmology', p. 105.

26 Kant circumspectly admits to this point in *Dreams of a Spirit-Seer Elucidated by Dreams of Metaphysics*, tr. David Walford, in *Theoretical Philosophy*, pp. 344-5 (henceforth *Dreams*); AK, vol. 2, pp. 257-9. On this point, see also Robert H Kirven, 'Swedenborg and Kant Revisited: The Long Shadow of Kant's Attack and a New Response', in *Swedenborg and his Influence*, eds. Erland J Brock et al. (Bryn Athyn: Academy of the New Church, 1988), esp. p. 114. See also C D Broad, 'Kant and Psychical Research', in his *Religion, Philosophy and Psychical Research*, 2nd edn. (New York: Humanities Press, 1969), p. 143.

27 Kant, *Dreams*, p. 319; AK, vol. 2, p. 332.

28 Kant, *Dreams*, pp. 316-17; AK, vol. 2, pp. 329; Kant's parentheses.

29 Kant, *Dreams*, pp. 316-17; AK, vol. 2, pp. 329.

30 Kant, *Dreams*, p. 319; AK, vol. 2, p. 332.

31 Kant refers to the moral world/*corpus mysticum/regnum gratiae* in the *Critique of Pure Reason*, A808/B836. He refers to the Kingdom of Ends/*mundus intelligibilis* in the *Foundations of the Metaphysics of Morals*, tr. Lewis White Beck (New York: Macmillan, 1990), pp. 49-57 (AK, vol. 4, pp. 433-8).

32 Kant, *Dreams*, p. 355; AK, vol. 2, p. 369; *Remarks*, AK vol. 20, p. 181; *Announcement*, AK, vol. 2, pp. 310-11.

33 Kant, *Critique of Practical Reason*, AK, vol. 5, p. 162; Beck, p. 166.

34 Ibid.

C S Peirce and Swedenborg

Eugene Taylor

> No man can know the theology of the nineteenth century who
> has not read Swedenborg——Henry Ward Beecher

Much has been written about Charles Sanders Peirce, William James, and the origins of American pragmatism. [1] In this literature it is generally agreed that the primary intellectual sources for Peirce's pragmatism lay philosophically in Kant, Bain, Mill and Berkeley, and personally in encounters with Nicholas St John Green and Chauncey Wright. Peirce himself states as much near the end of his career. Around the same time, however, he also left us with a re-evaluation of the pragmatic maxim, which, after thirty years, he assures us, had not weakened with the test of time. In fact, he had been ever more confirmed in his original view thanks to Royce, the two Schillers, Henry James, Sr and 'Swedenborg himself'. A few writers have explored this Swedenborgian connection, but by and large, it appears as a minor part, if not entirely absent, in accounts by most American philosophers of Peirce's career. [2]

In the mid-nineteenth century, however, no one could call himself educated who had not read Swedenborg's works or come into contact with the various Swedenborgian ideas that permeated the transcendentalist atmosphere of the day. Emerson, we know, had taken his Swedenborg mainly from Sampson Reed between 1826 and 1844, [3] while thereafter he relied mainly on the interpretations of Henry James, Sr and the biography and translations of James John Garth Wilkinson, English physician and translator of Swedenborg's scientific and medical writings.[4] Of Emerson's influence, remember in this regard what Peirce himself had written:

> I was born and reared in the neighborhood of Concord——I mean Cambridge—— at a time when Emerson, Hedge, and their friends were disseminating ideas […] The atmosphere of Cambridge held many an antiseptic against Concord transcendentalism; and I am not conscious of having contracted any of that virus. Nevertheless, it is probable that some cultured bacilli, some benignant form of the disease was planted in my soul, unawares, and that now, after long incubation, it comes to the surface modified by mathematical conceptions and by training in physical investigations. [5]

Peirce, like Emerson, had read Swedenborg, but one got it also by a kind of osmosis. Swedenborgian ideas permeated the philosophical air and were just as much translated through the chemistry of personalities as through the medium of Swedenborg's books, a process probably helped along in no small measure by the once close relationship between science, philosophy, and theology. One way to expose this influence is through the medium of chronological biography——a history taking in a psychiatric sense, that, even in its most rudimentary form, may help to reveal an important relation between the vicissitudes and triumphs of Peirce's emotional life and the evolution of his intellectual ideas. Central in this account is the mutual relationship that developed between Peirce, William James, and Henry James, Sr.

1862-70: Peirce comes under Henry James, Sr's spell

William James and C S Peirce first met in 1861, when James came to Harvard through his father's transcendentalist connections. Both were students in the Lawrence Scientific School under Agassiz when the controversy over Darwin's theory of evolution was furiously raging and the lines of battle had been clearly drawn between certain faculty members who had a vested interest in the outcome of the debate. Agassiz, the creationist, and Benjamin Peirce, the mathematician, had designs for transforming Harvard into a national scientific university along the lines of their soon-to-be-born brainchild, the National Academy of Sciences. Asa Gray, the botanist, confidant in Darwin's inner circle and therefore the foremost exponent of Darwin's ideas in America, was successfully attempting to introduce the theory of natural selection at Harvard, backed in this effort by the American Academy of Arts and Sciences. [6] William James was to side with Asa Gray on the matter, even though Henry James, Sr was deeply involved in the local literary and social scene with Emerson, Agassiz, Benjamin Peirce, and others. While C S Peirce may have himself accepted Darwin's theory from a scientific standpoint, he continued to be closely harboured under the protective wing of Benjamin Peirce, Agassiz's compatriot, and must at the time have been perceived as such.

At the very first instant of their meeting, James had written home to his parents describing Peirce as a fascinating but difficult personality, a smart fellow with a great deal of character, 'pretty independent and violent though', he had said. [7] In any event, they must have come into contact frequently. While James was studying chemistry, Peirce received his MA, and in 1863, while James was studying physiology, Peirce received the first Bachelor of Science, *summa cum laude*, to be awarded at Harvard. October of that year, Peirce married Melusina Harriet Fay, feminist writer, social organizer, and daughter of the Reverend Charles Fay, a Bostonian who became the first Episcopal Bishop of Vermont, and whose sister, Maria Fay, gave her Cambridge house as the first building to be called Radcliffe College.

Also that same year, Henry James, Sr published *Substance and Shadow* (1863), in which he set forth his interpretation of Swedenborg on the problem of morality and on the place of institutional religion as opposed to the place of the individuals in the process of Creation. [8]

Substance and Shadow was significant for several reasons. First and foremost, James subjected Kant to a severe critical analysis. Kant, and others such as Hamilton and Mill, denied cause a spiritual implication, because they resolved spiritual being itself into physical constitution. Kant, in particular, made the dissecting room the school of philosophy. 'He found life so dazzling a thing to contemplate', James said, 'that he betook himself to the unspeakable comfort of his optics'. He confused life with death. His fatal philosophic delinquency was in exteriorating object to subject. He confounded the testimony of sense with that of consciousness. He reduced philosophy to little more than a pious hiccup to a requiem over deceased hopes. He raised science, which in reality is only a handmaid to philosophy, to the throne, and then he pretended to be the Copernicus of philosophy, and his German and Scottish disciples confirmed him in this attempt. Indeed, James said, Kant had failed precisely where Swedenborg had succeeded.

Kant, you may remember, had at one point in his career tried to contact Swedenborg, and had digested much of Swedenborg's philosophy a good four years before his own inaugural dissertation was published, as evidenced by Kant's *Dreams of a Spirit-Seer*. [9] Peirce had learned his Kant at the feet of Benjamin Peirce, studied him daily for years, and then proposed a revision of Kant's categories. Thus Henry James, Sr's ideas must have been of great interest.

Another reason *Substance and Shadow* was important was because in it James enunciated Swedenborg's doctrine of the origin of evil, which he saw as part of God's plan for man's transformation. In this explanation James also set forth the basic cycle of creation, redemption and regeneration, which involves the emergence into consciousness of the repressed feminine, in both its diabolical and transcendent aspects, the *vir* which marries the *homo*, a union which leads to the fulfilment of the purpose of creation; namely, the experience of divinity in human relationships. [10]

We do not know whether William's talk of his father was the impetus, although there can be little doubt that such acts as Henry James, Sr's gift to Harvard of some forty original editions of Swedenborg must have attracted Peirce's attention. [11] But in 1863, the same year that Henry James, Sr published *Substance and Shadow*, Peirce referred to Swedenborg for the first time in an essay entitled, 'Analysis of the Ego'. What most interested Peirce there was Swedenborg's phrase referring to man as a 'bud upon the Almighty', which Peirce cited in the context of writing about the idea of a created soul. [12]

In 1864, Henry James, Sr moved his wife and two boys, Wilky and Robertson, from Newport, Rhode Island, to Boston, partly at Emerson's behest and partly to be near William and Henry, who were both attending classes in Cambridge. Sometime during this period, perhaps because of the same Boston and Cambridge literary connections, Melusina's aunt, Maria Fay gave Peirce a copy of Henry James, Sr's *Substance and Shadow* and the Harvard College Library charging records also show that Peirce was reading Henry James, Sr's *Tracts for the New Times*. [13] Around this time it was arranged that William would accompany Louis Agassiz on the Thayer Expedition to Brazil, and it was presumably during this year that William was gone that Peirce had the long conversations with Henry James, Sr that he later mentions in his papers. [14] At the same time the 1865 list of volumes in Peirce's library shows a copy of Swedenborg's *Divine Love and Wisdom*, [15] a book that summarizes Swedenborg's religious philosophy in the context of his three concepts of love, wisdom, and use, often one of the first books read by people being introduced to the Church of the New Jerusalem, the Christian religious denomination that follows Swedenborg's teachings.

When Peirce gave his Lowell Lectures the following year in 1866 on 'The Logic of Science and Induction', he made reference to Swedenborg's alleged conversations with Saint Paul,[16] while that same year the Harvard College Library charging records show Peirce reading Henry James, Sr's copy of Swedenborg's *Prodromus Philosophiae Ratiocinantis de Infinito* (1734), edited by James John Garth Wilkinson. [17] This work was Swedenborg's rational argument for the Infinite, composed during his scientific and philosophical period and before his religious enlightenment.

William James returned from the Amazon in 1866, having barely recovered from a form of typhus. Still at a loose end about his career, he immediately enrolled in the Medical School at Harvard. Henry James, Sr, meanwhile, moved his family from Boston to Quincy Street in Cambridge, on the present site of the Harvard Faculty Club, and hence was then but a stone's throw from the Lowells, just around the corner from the Holmeses, just down the street from the Peirces, and not far from the Nortons. Melusina and Charles Peirce had moved to a little house on Arrow Street in 1864, which meant that William James's house was now a three-minute walk away. Indeed the ladies of these distinguished families must have visited regularly, either at tea or through their exclusive sewing circles. The Fay sisters, friends of the Jameses, were always in and out of the Arrow Street house, much to Peirce's annoyance. Alice James with her brother Henry wrote to William, then travelling, and described a social visit to the Peirces, except, she said, that Mr Peirce was nowhere in sight,[18] and when Melusina and Charles travelled abroad, they always received newsy letters from the Fays about the activities of the James family.[19] By the end of the decade, a sense of fraternal kinship seems to have developed between the Jameses and the emotionally difficult Peirce.

Such an interpretation finds further support in the events of 1870. As an experiment designed to launch the graduate programme in philosophy at Harvard, President Eliot invited a number of speakers, Emerson and C S Peirce among them, to deliver different series of lectures.[20] Peirce lectured on the British Empiricists, and William James went to hear him speak. Within a decade, James was himself lecturing on the British philosophers, whom he eventually resurrected and renovated with his own formulation of radical empiricism. Mill and Bain, among these philosophers, had been members of Carlyle's literary circle, which, through Emerson, Henry James, Sr had been a part of in the 1840s. Also in 1870, Peirce published a review of Henry James, Sr's *Secret of Swedenborg* (1869).[21] Essentially a reiteration of his previous themes on the creation-redemption-regeneration cycle of *Substance and Shadow*, James now attempted to explicate Swedenborg's doctrine of the Divine Natural Humanity, taking another swipe at Kant on the way and, in addition, now dismissing Hegel as well. This was the book that caused William Dean Howells to say that if Swedenborg had a secret, then Henry James, Sr had certainly kept it. Peirce, in his review, was more sympathetic. He said: 'Though this book presents some very interesting and impressive religious views and the tone of it is eminently healthy, it is altogether out of harmony with the spirit of this age'. Indeed, the creationists had been soundly routed, theology was not faring well in the dialogue between science and religion, and the drift of philosophy was already toward scientific materialism. Peirce's final characterization, however, was that 'this book can be understood by the right mind with the right preparation, and that, to many a man who cannot fully understand it, it will afford, as it has to us, much spiritual nutriment'. Curiously, these are nearly the characterizations that William James had made to his sister about conversing with Peirce or hearing him lecture some years earlier.

1871-1884: The Metaphysical Club and beyond

Meanwhile, Peirce left for Sicily in 1870 with his wife to take measurements of the total eclipse. When he returned in 1871, his philosophic visits with William James and others resumed in earnest. Meetings began on a regular basis between parlours of the James and Peirce houses, and the group at various times later came to include (Professor Max Fisch tells us) in addition to James and Peirce, Chauncey Wright, Francis Ellingwood Abbott, Nicholas St John Green, Joseph Warner, Oliver Wendell Holmes, Jr, Francis Greenwood Peabody, and John Fiske. [22] They argued philosophy and seriously 'stuck to the question', as Henry James, the novelist, later described it. Peirce came to the group through Kant; Green was a student of Bentham's utilitarianism, while Wright was trying to fuse Mill with Darwin. Based particularly on the ideas of Bain, who defined belief as 'that upon which a man is prepared to act', Peirce said that he developed the idea called pragmatism at these meetings. So as to have some souvenir before the group broke up in its original form, Peirce committed some of his ideas to paper, which he published in 1878 in *Popular Science Monthly* as 'How to Make Our Ideas Clear', which marks the official beginning of the pragmatist movement.

By 1875, Peirce had become even more involved under his father in extensive research for the US Geologic Survey and went to Europe to attend an international scientific convention and to continue his pendulum investigations upon which the gravity and curvature of the earth were measured. He was again accompanied by his wife, Melusina, but she returned from France by herself, and their separation extended into a divorce some years later. Alone in Paris for nearly a year, Peirce took up with William's brother, Henry, the novelist, who wrote home telling of his adventures with this eccentric philosopher-scientist. He described Peirce as 'a very good fellow when he is not in an ill humor; then he is intolerable', saying also, 'He is leading here a life of insupportable loneliness and sterility but of much material luxury, as he seems to have plenty of money. He sees, literally, not a soul but myself and his secretary. [23]

In the years immediately following, Peirce would occasionally write to William with a closing, 'Please remember me with great respect and love to your father', [24] and later while 'swaggering at the Brevoort Hotel in New York' wrote, 'you don't say how your father and all the rest are'. [25] James was constantly wishing him back in Cambridge, but Peirce at one time wrote that it was unknown even to him if he should ever live there again or not: 'I like the place, but there is something about it [...] which I find very antagonistic to me', although he also said in the same letter that he missed the intellectual talks he could be having. [26]

As long as his father was alive and head of the US Coastal Survey, Peirce's material fortunes seemed secure, except that because of his arcane scientific interests and his eccentric personality, he seemed never able to find a real job for himself. Meanwhile, he continued to work on a major treatise on logic, which William James eagerly anticipated, although the project was never completed. As a result of James's influence, Peirce was able to secure a part-time position as Lecturer on Logic at the newly founded Johns Hopkins University, beginning in 1879. Josiah Royce had recently graduated, but among Peirce's students were a few destined to become luminaries in the history of psychology and philosophy—Christine Ladd-Franklin, Joseph Jastrow, and John Dewey, to name a few.

Peirce was also briefly concerned with Swedenborg while at Hopkins, when he began a major project to assess scientific men of genius from the eighteenth and nineteenth centuries. Characteristics of scientific personalities and samples of their work were collected and correlated with impressionistic statements from raters as to degree of greatness. Peirce then submitted the impressions to logical forms which could be mathematically quantifed. Averaging impressions, he was then able to rank in order the men of genius. Swedenborg counted among the top three hundred chosen, and it was Swedenborg whom Peirce used in his explanatory paradigm to show how the method of quantification worked. [27]

1884-1906: Peirce's increasing dependence on James

By 1883, a new era had opened for Peirce. His father had died in 1880, and in 1882 both Emerson and Henry James, Sr had passed away. In 1883, Peirce finalized his divorce with Melusina and six days later he married Juliette Froissy, a Frenchwoman whom he had known since 1878 or earlier. Newly married with a university position and a raise in salary, he took an extended lease on his home. Then suddenly in 1884, he was summarily dismissed from the University without explanation. Recent disclosures in the popular press suggest that his dismissal came as a result of news being leaked to the trustees that he had been living with Juliette while still married to Melusina, a situation unacceptable to the Baptist standards of the University. Apparently, the information was passed on to the president by an enemy of Peirce's father, who had not been able to secure Benjamin Peirce's position as head of the US Geologic Survey. [28]

Somewhat embittered, and always at loose ends financially, Peirce sold his library to the University and focused his efforts on his work for the Geologic Survey. Finally in 1887, at age forty-eight, he inherited a small amount of money and retired to the rural setting of Milford, Pennsylvania, where he and his wife lived for the rest of their lives, mostly in an economically uncertain state, as Peirce was forced to resign from the Survey in 1891, and from then on he attempted to derive his income from book reviews, journal papers, and dictionary articles.

James, meanwhile, had begun a meteoric rise to international prominence in the 1880s as his psychological work was published simultaneously in America, England, and France. A philosopher at heart, but bearing down directly on the potential of empirical science, James played a major role in moving psychology as a discipline into the domain of physiology by way of scientific laboratory investigation. In 1890, after a twelve-year delay, during which time he published his first book, a collection of Henry James, Sr's papers, William James brought out his monumental two-volume *Principles of Psychology*. The work has continued to have a far-reaching impact on psychology to this day. In 1891 Peirce reviewed *Principles* in *The Nation*. [29] Despite Peirce's assessment that it 'was probably the most important contribution that has been made to the subject for many years', he criticized James for indulging in 'idiosyncrasies of diction and tricks of language such as usually spring up in households of great talent'. Peirce went on to accuse James of being 'materialistic to the core' in a methodological sense, but not a religious one, due largely to the fact that James was 'brought up under the guidance of an eloquent apostle of a form of Swedenborgianism, which is materialism driven deep and clinched on the inside'. [30]

Peirce again took up Henry James, Sr's Swedenborgianism in a series of essays published in *The Monist* in the early 1890s. Thought to represent his more speculative cosmology, they are respectively, 'The Architecture of Theories', 'The Doctrine of Necessity Examined', 'The Law of Mind', 'Man's Glassy Essence' and 'Evolutionary Love'. James the Elder appears in this last essay, after Peirce established his understanding of how we construct theories. He then attacked determinism in science in favour of his own pragmatic method. He examined the method's implications for personality, and then stated his case for the purpose of evolution as Divine Love, a Swedenborgian idea. For the basis of his statement he drew on Henry James, Sr's solution to the problem of evil. Peirce says:

> It is no doubt very tolerable finite or creaturely love to love one's own in another, to love another in his conformity to one's self; but nothing can be

in more flagrant contrast with the Creative Love, all whose tenderness *ex vi terminus* must be reserved only for what intrinsically is most bitterly hostile and negative to itself'. This is from *Substance and Shadow: An Essay on the Physics of Creation*. It is a pity he [Henry James, Sr] had not filled his pages with things like this, as he was able easily to do, instead of scolding at his reader and at people generally, until the physics of creation was well-nigh forgot. I must deduct, however from what I just wrote: obviously no genres could make his every sentence as sublime as one which discloses for the problem of evil its everlasting solution. [31]

Peirce here had previously explained that God visits no punishment on those who love darkness, for they punish themselves by their natural affinity for the defective. The Love that God is, is not a love of which hatred is the contrary, otherwise Satan would be a coordinate power. Rather, it is a love that embraces hatred as an imperfect stage of itself——a love that even needs hatred and hatefulness as its object. For self-love is no love; so if God's self is love, that which he loves must be a defect of love; just as a luminary can light up that which otherwise would be dark.

Other sources also give us an indication of Henry James, Sr and the Swedenborgian influence on Peirce between 1893 and 1897. Because he was in particularly desperate financial circumstances, Peirce had tried to enlarge the scope of his avenues for published articles in the early 1890s. As part of this scheme, in the late summer of 1893, he had written to E L Burlingame, editor of *Scribner's Magazine*, proposing an article on Swedenborg, but the offer was declined. [32] Peirce obviously would not have based such a piece on secondary sources alone, so that it is reasonable to assume that he would have employed some combination of Henry James, Sr's interpretation with works by Swedenborg in the original. At this time, to underscore the emotional support William James was giving Peirce, we need only mention James's response to Peirce's financial proposal in 1893 to write a twelve-volume work on *The Principles of Philosophy*. James wrote, 'Count on me as a subscriber to your books', adding:

There is no more original thinker than yourself in our generation. You have personally suggested more important things to me than perhaps anyone whom I have known, and I have never given you sufficient public credit for all you have taught me. I am sure that this systematic work will increase my debt. [33]

Several years later, Peirce wrote to James from Milford in a similar laudatory vein about Henry James, Sr. Peirce said:

I am alone in the house here and have spent some of the quiet hours over *Substance and Shadow* and in recalling your father. My experiences in the last four years have been calculated to bring Swedenborg home to me very often. [34]

Such mutual regard was to continue, but in the typical Peircean fashion. The year 1898 marked the official birth of William James's version of pragmatism, honouring Peirce publicly as the founder, followed by Peirce's adamant disavowal of that movement. [35] Nevertheless, James continued to find guest lectures for Peirce, lend him books, correspond with him, and finally James arranged an anonymous subscription fund for Peirce's upkeep. [36] To show his appreciation, Peirce took the additional middle name 'Santiago', or 'St James'.

Meanwhile, Peirce was again referring to Henry James, Sr's work during this period. In an 1899 review, Peirce had criticized Crozier's *My Inner Life* for lacking 'the earnestness required to rival Emerson, Carlyle, Ruskin, or Henry James the Elder, each of whom was in the clutch of a great idea and struck with its superhuman force'.[37] And in one place of his collected works, concerning God's purpose, Peirce says:

What do you imagine the present functions of this Supreme Being toward the Universe to be? Creation, as just said; and much may also be learned from the book *Substance and Shadow* by Henry James, the father [...] In particular, the obvious solution to the problem of evil is there pointed out.

Columbus's egg is not simpler. In general, God is perpetually creating us, that is, developing our real manhood, our spiritual reality. Like a good teacher, He is engaged in detaching us from a false dependence on Him. [38]

Also in 1899, Peirce wrote a criticism of Renouvier for *The Nation*, saying of the French philosopher's metaphysics:

I rather hope that some corresponding form of Hegelism is the truth, or, better still, that, as the elder James taught, the Reasonable One sets off over against himself an irrational phantom upon which his warmth and light may be brought to pass. [39]

Two years later, in the same periodical, Peirce wrote a review of Alfred Caldecott's *Philosophy of Religion in England and America*, upbraiding the author for, among other failures, omitting even a mention of Henry James, Sr's *Substance and Shadow*'.[40] Peirce, we see, was not only sympathetic to the elder James's philosophy, but considered it significant enough to be included in a comparative analysis of the religious influences of the age.

It is interesting in this regard that in his review of Renouvier, Peirce aligns himself with Henry James, Sr as an alternative to the Frenchman whose writings on the will had played such an important part in William's recovery from a near-suicidal depression almost thirty years before. James had written Peirce in 1897, admitting that while he thought Renouvier's form atrocious, he was nevertheless thankful to him for a number of vital points of view. James there admitted also that the whole of his essay, *The Will to Believe*, was cribbed from Renouvier. Peirce, on the other hand, continued to invoke Henry James, Sr on philosophical problems of common interest.

A letter dated 23 January 1903, for instance, shows that James had sent Peirce a copy of the syllabus for his Philosophy 3 course, described as 'The Philosophy of Nature', with special reference to 'man's place in Nature, the fundamental conceptions of science, the relation of mind and body, evolution, etc.', using as texts Pearson's *Grammar of Science* and Ward's *Naturalism and Agnosticism*.[41] Peirce wrote that he thought the idea of the course extremely valuable for his own work, giving also a criticism of James's position. He said finally, 'I can't admit at all your metaphysical tychism, which seems to me untenable. The true solution to the problem of evil is precisely that of substance and shadow. There may be something over us not infinite, but *that* it is a misnomer to call *divine*'. While God may have been 'the Reasonable One' for Peirce, it is quite clear that he meant to criticize William James by using Henry James, Sr as the proper corrective.

1906: The Swedenborgian context of Pragmaticism

Finally, a note should be made about Peirce's 1906 statement, 'Consequences of Pragmaticism', appended by Professors Hartshorne and Weiss to the *Collected Papers* edition of Peirce's 1878 'How to Make Our Ideas Clear'.[42] Krolikowski has given us an admirable exegesis of this passage, showing that in its entirety it is deeply embedded in Henry James, Sr's Swedenborgian cosmology, which Peirce himself reinterpreted.[43] Peirce repeated the pragmatic maxim intact after thirty years. To it, he added:

> No doubt, Pragmaticism makes thought ultimately apply to action exclusively—to conceived action. But between admitting that and either saying that it makes thought, in the sense of the purport of symbols, to consist in acts, or saying that the true ultimate purpose in thinking is action, there is much the same difference as there is between saying that the artist-painter's living art is applied to dabbing paint upon canvas, and saying that art-life consists in dabbing paint, or that its ultimate aim is dabbing paint'.[44]

Peirce here appears to be addressing the revisionists, especially William James, who, in Peirce's eyes, was the one most responsible for defining pragmatism in the public eye as the supremacy of the act over the thought that inspired it. Thought was supreme in Peirce's system, while for James it was exactly the reverse. Ever since his 1898 Berkeley address, James had maintained that 'the ultimate test for us of what a truth means is the conduct it dictates or inspires'. Taking consequences into account was, for Peirce, a method for correcting faulty logic and not a programme for behaviour. So Peirce continues in his 1906 fragment: 'Pragmaticism makes thinking to consist in the living inferential metaboly of symbols whose purport lies in conditional resolutions to act'.

Enunciated in 1878 as a method of logic, Peirce's reiteration of the maxim in 1906 is now cast into a teleological metaphysics of evolution. He then says, 'As for the ultimate purpose of thought, which must be the purpose of everything, [it] is beyond human comprehension'. He then states how far his ideas on the matter have gone, giving the extraordinary passage where he acknowledges his most recent intellectual debts:

> but according to the stage of approach which my thought has made to it—
> with aid from many persons, among whom I mention Royce (in his *World
> and the Individual*), Schiller (in his *Riddles of the Sphinx*), as well, by the
> way, the famous poet [Friedrich Schiller] (in his *Aesthetische Briefe*), Henry
> James the Elder (in his *Substance and Shadow* and in his conversations),
> together with Swedenborg himself—it is by the indefinite replication of
> self-control upon self-control that the *vir* is begotten, and by action, through
> thought, he grows in aesthetic ideal, not for the behoof of his own poor noodle
> merely, but as a share which God permits him to have in the work of Creation. [45]

Peirce, in other words, attempts at the end to articulate some global picture of how the different elements of his system—the different fields in which he has worked in service of Reason—might fit together.

Some commentary

Although intellectually a genius, who had been exposed at an early age to private instruction and advanced learning, Peirce himself at one point acknowledged that the emotional side of his education—one that should have stressed self-control over excessive indulgence—was entirely lacking, and it was this lack, I suggest, expressed as a kind of emotional and spiritual longing, that eventually drew Peirce to Henry James, Sr. William, however, was the original impetus and the key element in the equation. Surely there must have been some intimation, even from the very beginning to Peirce himself, that James was a staunch and true friend. Eventually, James proved to be a lifelong philosophical compatriot, probably one of the only close friends Peirce was to have. James derived much stimulation from Peirce, whose rigorous logic and loyalty to the scientific method no doubt had the effect of continually reining James in, saving him from too unbridled thinking, while at the same time Peirce must have whetted James's appetite for philosophy long before James was conscious of it himself as a possible vocation. Peirce, on the other hand, seems to have developed a personal sense of kinship with James that was extended and reinforced by Henry James, Sr who in turn provided intellectual stimulation for Peirce. It would not be stretching the point too far to say that Peirce's connection to William and his father, and even Henry, the novelist, verged on an extended family relationship that strengthened Peirce emotionally, because it may have fed him spiritually, where in his personal life he needed it the most.

This gives us a clue to how Peirce refers to Henry James, Sr's Swedenborgian ideas at different points in his career. We might take Peirce seriously when, in reviewing *The Secret of Swedenborg*, he admits deriving much spiritual nutriment from the work. Of his various references to Henry James, Sr's everlasting solution to the problem of evil, I cannot agree with Trammell when he suggests that in 'Evolutionary Love', Peirce said that James, Sr had solved the problem 'once and for all' as a way to mock him. [46] Too many other passages by Peirce suggest that he was making instead a theological statement about his own beliefs. Similarly,

Krolikowski's analysis of the Peircean *vir*, while it considers the linguistic usage of the term in the writings of both James and Peirce in order to come to some objective conclusion about what Peirce could have meant, omits one other interpretation of Peirce's passage on the *vir* in 1906—that it might also have been autobiographical. For whatever intellectual justification he may have given elsewhere, and in addition to whatever pragmatic sufficiency he may have seen in the theory, Peirce may also have found in James a certain amount of self-justification. James's was probably the only theological system that gave Peirce in his darkest hours any hope, for in it he could logically account for his behaviour and the course of his life, while it still provided the possibility that his contribution—his life work—would somewhere make a difference. Why else would Peirce in his most desperate hours, bankrupt, frequently depressed, and, from the evidence, sometimes near-suicidal, continually hark back to those halcyon Cambridge days, except to derive spiritual solace from Henry James, Sr's Swedenborgian ideas?

Värilä comes close to such an interpretation when he says that Peirce, in effect, may have taken Swedenborg's ideas out of a purely Christian context and secularized them as a theistically oriented metaphysics. [47] Apel further holds that Peirce was not successful in 1906 in the step he took beyond his statement of 1878, in that the 1906 clarification did not achieve the completion of a rational system. In this, Apel notes, Peirce had the same problem as Kant in accounting for emotions and moods when he tried to show how reason becomes practical. This is as much a psychological diagnosis of Peirce's personal life as it is a comment on his philosophical achievement. [48]

Three unanswered questions

The question of whether or not personal biography has any relevance in helping to explain Peirce's intellectual ideas is a problematic one for at least two reasons. First, because a definitive biography of Peirce has yet to be written. [49] Secondly, emotional factors in a person's life are elusive and represent for the most part private experience that may parallel, interact with, and even undergird conscious intellectual life. But such factors lie beyond the scope of scientists and philosophers. They are the meat, however, of the craft plied by the biographer, the historian, and the psychologist. I would not advocate a psychoanalytic interpretation of Peirce's life, but only take my cue from William James, who believed that there can be no philosophy without autobiography. Simply put, can the evolution of Peirce's thought be made more understandable by a knowledge of what constituted his personal beliefs and values? If the answer is even a tentative yes, then Peirce's spiritual adoption into the James family becomes an important part of that story.

Another question then presents itself, namely, is there a deeper intellectual connection between Peirce's reading of Swedenborg, his belief that Henry James, Sr had once and for all solved the problem of evil, and Peirce's use of Swedenborg and Henry James, Sr to clarify the purpose of pragmatism? Even a cursory glance into Swedenborg's works that we know Peirce had in his hands is enough to see that the major Swedenborgian concepts of love, wisdom, and use are cast into the context of the importance and power of rational thought and its consequences. For Swedenborgian scholars, this represents a research project for future work. For American philosophers interested in the historical roots of pragmatism, it may mean that in addition to deriving pragmatism from the standard English and German sources, pragmatism, and consequently Swedenborgian thought, can also be seen in the more historically accurate context of its own time. Will this augur well for Swedenborg's philosophy in light of present day academic judgments against it? I would hope so, although I may be too optimistic.

From a closer consideration, then, of the influence of Henry James, Sr and Swedenborgian ideas on Peirce, is any new light shed on the origins and meaning of William James's brand of pragmatism? In the first place, we are forced to take a harder look at the Swedenborgian and transcendentalist milieu directly impinging on William James's intellectual development'. [50] When this is done, there is a small but significant shift in emphasis that corrects an impression given by Ralph Barton

Perry that the major roots of James's philosophy are of English and European origin. Rather, William James was a direct inheritor of this uniquely American legacy and it stood at the front and not in the background of his personal outlook, his philosophical ideas, and his intellectual influence in so many areas of modern culture. To understand a person's philosophy, James once said, you have to capture the centre of his vision. With regard to our understanding of William James, this is a task that still remains. How Peirce understood Swedenborg may be a further contribution to that story.

NOTES

Acknowledgements are gratefully extended to Thomas Cadwallader and especially Dick Davison for giving the original impetus for this paper; to Sylvia Mitarachi for invaluable detail of Zina Fay Peirce's relation to the Jameses; to George Dole and Marian Kirven, librarian at the Swedenborg School of Religion; to Houghton Library, Harvard, for permission to quote from the James-Peirce letters; and to Max Fisch for both information and encouragement. The research for this paper was supported by a grant from the Wesley N Gray Fund.

[1]   For instance, Ralph Barton Perry, *The Thought and Character of William James* (Boston: Little, Brown, 1935); Philip Wiener, *Evolution and the Founders of Pragmatism* (Cambridge: Harvard University Press, 1949); Max H Fisch, 'Alexander Bain and the Genealogy of Pragmatism', in *Journal of the History of Ideas*, vol. 15 (1954), pp. 413-44; Murray G Murphey, *The Development of Peirce's Philosophy* (Cambridge: Harvard University Press, 1961); Edward C Moore, *American Pragmatism: Peirce, James, and Dewey* (New York: Columbia University Press, 1961); Edward H Madden, *Chauncey Wright and the Foundations of Pragmatism* (Seattle: University of Washington Press, 1963); *The Writings of William James,* ed. John J McDermott, (New York: Modern Library, 1968); Murray G Murphey, 'Kant's Children: The Cambridge Pragmatists', in *Transactions of the Charles S. Peirce Society*, vol.

IV, no. 1, 1968, pp. 3-33; H S Thayer, *Meaning and Action: A Critical History of Pragmatism* (Indianapolis: Bobbs-Merrill, 1968); Charles Morris, *The Pragmatic Movement in American Philosophy* (New York: George Braziller, 1970); H S Thayer, 'Introduction', in William James, *Pragmatism* (Cambridge: Harvard University Press, 1975).

[2] W P Krolikowski, 'The Peircean *Vir*', in E C Moore and R S Robin (eds.), *Studies in the Philosophy of Charles Sanders Peirce: Second Series* (Amherst: University of Massachusetts Press, 1964), pp. 257-70; F H Young, *The Philosophy of Henry James, Sr* (New York: Bookman Associates, 1951); Gerd Wartenberg, *Logischer Sozialismus: Die Transformation der Kantschen Transcendentalphilosophie durch Charles S. Peirce* (Frankfurt: Suhrkamp Verlag, 1971); Richard L Trammell, 'Charles Sanders Peirce and Henry James the Elder', in *Transactions of the Charles S. Peirce Society*, vol. IX, no. 4, 1973, pp. 202-20; Karl-Otto Apel, *Der Denkweg yon Charles Sanders Peirce: Eine Einfuhrung in den amerikanischen Pragmatismus* (Frankfurt: Suhrkamp Verlag, 1975); Armi Värilä, *The Swedenborgian Background of William James's Philosophy* (Helsinki: Suomalainen Tieddeaktemia, 1977).

[3] Perry Miller maintains that Swedenborgian ideas permeated the transcendentalist movement, and that the influence of Sampson Reed on disseminating Swedenborg in America was equal to the influence of Cousin in France and Coleridge in England in disseminating the ideas of Kant. See Perry Miller, *The Transcendentalists: An Anthology* (Cambridge: Harvard University Press, 1950), p. 49.

[4] See, for instance, Raymond H Deck, 'The "Vastation" of Henry James, Sr: New Light in James's Swedenborgian Theology', in *Bulletin of Research in the Humanities*, vol. 83, no. 2 (1980), pp. 216-47; or Robert W Gladish, *Swedenborg, Fourier, and the America of the 1840s* (Bryn Athyn: Swedenborg Scientific Association, 1983), for more on the relation between James, Sr and Wilkinson, and consequently, Emerson.

[5] C S Peirce, *Collected Papers of Charles Sanders Peirce,* ed. C Hartshorne, P Weiss and A W Burks (Cambridge: Harvard University Press, 1958), vol. 6, p. 102 (hereafter cited as CSP, *Works*); also F I Carpenter, 'Charles Sanders Peirce: Pragmatic Transcendentalist', in *New England Quarterly*, March 1941, pp. 35-48.

[6] A H DuPree, *Asa Gray, 1810-1888* (Cambridge: Harvard University Press, 1959).

7   William James to his family, 16 September 1861, in *William James, Letters*, ed. Henry James, Jr (Boston: Atlantic Monthly Press, 1920), vol. I., p. 35 (hereafter cited as *Letters*).

8   Henry James, Sr, *Substance and Shadow: or, Morality and Religion in Their Relation to Life: An Essay Upon the Physics of Creation* (Boston: Ticknor & Fields, 1863).

9   Immanuel Kant, *Traume eines Geistersehers* (Konigsberg, 1766); and for the argument of Kant's borrowing from Swedenborg, see Svante Arrhenius's introduction to and A H Stroh's article in Swedenborg, *Opera Quaedam de Rebus Naturalibus*, 3 vols. (Stockholm: Royal Swedish Academy of Sciences, 1907-11), vol. II, p. 372. Kant's investigation of Swedenborg began in 1763. See also William Ross Woofenden, *Swedenborg and 20th Century Thought, Australian University Lectures (1979-1980)* (Sydney: Swedenborg Lending Library, 1981), pp. 65-80, 'Some Thought Affinities between Immanuel Kant and Emanuel Swedenborg'.

10   The similarity of *interpretatum* between James, Sr and Peirce on the sense of community has been pointed out by both Trammell and Apel. (see n. 2 above).

11   Harvard College Library Accession Lists. UAIII 50 15.70.6, pp. 137-8. Pusey Library, Harvard University Archives, by permission.

12   C S Peirce, *The Writings of Charles Sanders Peirce: A Chronological Edition*, ed. Max H Fisch, vol. I, 1857-1866 (Bloomington: University Press, 1982). Reference in manuscript, courtesy of Dr Fisch. n.p.

13   CSP, *Works*, vol. 6, p. 507. For Peirce's readings of James's *Tracts*, see Harvard College Library Charging Lists, 25 May and 14 December 1863. Pusey Library, Harvard University Archives, by permission.

14   CSP, *Works*, vol. 5, p. 402.

15   Reference courtesy of Dr Max Fisch.

16   Reference courtesy of Dr Max Fisch. (Cf. Swedenborg, *The Spiritual Diary*, §§3728, 4322 and *The Spiritual Diary (Minor)*, §4631; and R L Tafel (tr., comp and ed.), *Documents Concerning Swedenborg,* no. 232.)

17   The Harvard College Library Charging Lists show that Peirce checked out the Latin edition of Swedenborg's *Philosophical Conceptions of the Infinite* (Alcove # 23

1/2.6). The book was traced to Houghton Rare Manuscript Library QSc7.Sw331.734 p (copy B) and contains a bookplate which reads 'Gift of William James, Esq. of Boston, 21, June, 1864'. On the flyleaf is the inscription 'James John Garth Wilkinson, Store St., Bedford Sq. To Henry James Esq. with most affectionate regards'.

[18] Alice James to William James, 6 August 1867, with supporting material, quoted in Jean Strouse, *Alice James, A Biography* (New York: Houghton Mifflin, 1980), pp. 114-15.

[19] Sylvia Mitarachi, *Melusina Fay Biography Project*, unpublished MS.

[20] Francis G Peabody, 'The Germ of the Graduate School', in *Harvard Graduates Magazine*, 1916.

[21] C S Peirce, 'Review of Henry James's Secret of Swedenborg', in *North American Review*, 110, April 1870, p. 463.

[22] Max H Fisch, 'Was There a Metaphysical Club in Cambridge?', in F C Moore & R S Robin (eds.), *Studies in the Philosophy of C S Peirce: 2nd Series* (Amherst: University of Massachusetts Press, 1964), pp. 3-32.

[23] Ralph Barton Perry, *The Thought and Character of William James* (Boston: Atlantic/Little, Brown, 1935), vol. I, p. 536.

[24] C S Peirce to William James, Paris, 16 December 1875. James Papers, Houghton Library, Harvard University.

[25] Ibid., New York, 1 May 1877.

[26] Ibid., Paris, 21 November 1875.

[27] Peirce Papers, Houghton Library, Harvard University.

[28] D C Denison, 'The Greatest American Philosopher', in *The Boston Globe Magazine*, 10 March 1985, p. 8.

[29] C S Peirce, Review of James's *Principles of Psychology*, taken from *Charles Sanders Peirce's Contributions to The Nation*, ed. K L Ketner and J E Cook (Lubbock: Texas Tech Press, 1975), pt. 1, 1869-1893, pp. 104-5.

[30] Peirce gives a definition of materialism as that which is governed by blind mechanistic law in 'The Law of Mind', in *The Monist*, 1892, which I interpret as meaning that Henry James, Sr's philosophy is a justification for materialism in the egotistical phase of the creation-redemption-regeneration cycle.

[31] CSP, *Works*, vol. 6, p. 287.

32 E L Burlingame to C S Peirce, Peirce Papers, Houghton Library, Harvard University (L. 395). See also Krolikowski, p. 270, n. 9.

33 William James to C S Peirce, Cambridge, 15 March 1892. James Papers, Houghton Library, Harvard University. Peirce later published James's comments about the proposed series, but omitted this particularly praiseworthy passage, to James's regret. James appears to have been expressing a long awaited intent of honouring Peirce, which he finally succeeded in making public when he dedicated his *The Will to Believe* (1897).

34 C S Peirce to William James, Milford, 13 December 1897, James Papers, Houghton Library, Harvard University.

35 W James, 'Philosophical Conceptions and Practical Results', in *The University Chronicle* (Berkeley: University of California Press, 1898); and for Peirce's view see *Works*, vol. 5, p. 414.

36 Alexander Graham Bell, for instance, was one of the anonymous subscribers, see William James to A G Bell, 21 February and 20 March 1907, Bell Papers, Archives, Library of Congress, Washington, DC.

37 *Charles Sanders Peirce's Contributions to The Nation*, vol. 2, p. 192.

38 CSP, *Works*, vol. 6, p. 507.

39 C S Peirce, review of 'Renouvier & Prat's *La Nouvelle Monadologie*', in *The Nation*, 3 August 1899, pp. 97-8.

40 C S Peirce, 'Review of Caldecott's *Philosophy of Religion in England and America*', in *The Nation*, 73, 15 August 1901, pp. 139-40.

41 C S Peirce to William James, Milford, 23 January 1903, in Perry's *Thought and Character of William James*, vol. II, p. 425.

42 CSP, *Works*, vol. 5, p. 402, n. 3.

43 Krolikowski, 'The Peircean *Vir*', pp. 257-70.

44 CSP, *Works*, vol. 5, p. 402, n. 3.

45 Ibid.

46 Trammell, 'Charles Sanders Peirce and Henry James the Elder', pp. 202-20.

47 Värilä, *The Swedenborgian Background of William James's Philosophy*.

48 Apel, *Der Denkweg yon Charles Sanders Peirce: Eine Einfuhrung in den amerikanischen Pragmatismus*.

[49] The only chronology is J I Brent, III, 'A Study of the Life of Charles Sanders Peirce', Doctoral dissertation, UCLA, 1960.

[50] For a good beginning, see C Hartley Grattan, *The Three Jameses; A Family of Minds. Henry James, Sr, William James, Henry James* (New York: Longmans Green, 1932); Quentin Anderson, *The American Henry James* (New Brunswick: Rutgers University Press, 1957); and Howard Feinstein, *Becoming William James* (Ithaca: Cornell University Press, 1984).

Schopenhauer as reader of Swedenborg

Gregory R Johnson

A rthur Schopenhauer (1788-1860) is widely known as the first Western philosopher of note to delve seriously into the esoteric philosophies of the East, Hinduism and Buddhism in particular. [1] Although the outlines of Schopenhauer's philosophy were in place before his discovery of Eastern thought, this encounter affected the subsequent development of his philosophy in many ways. [2] Less widely known is Schopenhauer's equally broad reading in the Western esoteric tradition, including the writings of Emanuel Swedenborg. Schopenhauer's library included works by Meister Eckhart, Ramon Llull, Angelus Silesius, Nicholas of Cusa, Marsilio Ficino, Giovanni Pico della Mirandola, Henricus Cornelius Agrippa, Paracelsus, Giordano Bruno, Tomasso Campanella, Jacob Boehme, Jane Lead, John Pordage, Johannes Tauler, Johann Heinrich Jung-Stilling, Franz von Baader, and Karl von Eckartshausen, as well as Swedenborg. [3] It also included a large collection of books on animal magnetism, clairvoyance, and spirit apparitions, including the multi-volume *Archiv für den Thierischen Magnetismus* (*Archive of Animal Magnetism*). [4] Many of these works are extensively annotated in Schopenhauer's hand. The list of the books on paranormal phenomena alone occupies thirty-two pages in the catalogue of Schopenhauer's library and its marginalia published by Arthur Hübscher. [5]

In this essay, I shall focus on Schopenhauer's encounter with Swedenborg. I shall argue two points. First, Schopenhauer took Swedenborg's writings and the claim that he was a clairvoyant seriously, meaning that he looked to Swedenborg as a potential source of important truths. Second, although Schopenhauer and Swedenborg share the same basic metaphysical outlook according to which such phenomena as clairvoyance are possible, Schopenhauer's metaphysical commitment to the idea that the individual soul perishes at death is deeply incompatible with Swedenborg's visionary experiences. Thus, although Schopenhauer adamantly defends the possibility of clairvoyance, the incompatibility of Swedenborg's visions with his own outlook leads Schopenhauer in the end to reject the truth of Swedenborg's visions and to try to explain them away.

I. Schopenhauer's familiarity with Swedenborg's writings

Upon his death, Schopenhauer's library contained two volumes of Swedenborg. First is the *Prodromus Philosophiae ratiocinantis de Infinito, et causa finali creationis, deque mechanismo operationis animae et corporis (Forerunner of a Reasoned Philosophy Concerning the Infinite and the Final Cause of Creation, also The Mechanism of the Operation of the Soul and the Body).* [6] Published in 1734, this work pre-dates Swedenborg's first visions of the spiritual world. Schopenhauer's copy is now lost, so there is no way to determine whether he annotated it or what he had to say. The other Swedenborg volume is a 1782 French translation comprising *Heaven and Hell* and *Worlds in Space: Les merveilles du ciel et de l'enfer et des terres planétaires et astrals. D'après le témoignage de ses yeux et de ses oreilles (The Marvels of Heaven and Hell and the Planets in our Solar System and in the Stars. According to the Testimony of the Eyes and Ears).* [7] This volume contains an interesting note in Schopenhauer's hand that we shall examine below.

There is reason to believe that Schopenhauer also read Swedenborg's 1769 opusculum, *De Commercio Animae et Corporis (The Interaction of Soul and Body),* [8] for Schopenhauer mentions Swedenborg's encounter with Aristotle and Christian Wolff in the spiritual world, which is described in § 19 of that work. [9] There is, furthermore, evidence that Schopenhauer read Swedenborg's major 1771 work

Vera Christiana Religio (*The True Christian Religion*), [10] for he paraphrases and comments upon a passage in an unpublished manuscript that we will examine in the next section. [11]

Another source of Schopenhauer's knowledge of Swedenborg is Kant's 1766 book *Träume eines Geistersehers* (*Dreams of a Spirit-Seer*). [12] Although it is rife with snide and dismissive comments about Swedenborg, this volume, along with Kant's 1763 letter to Charlotte von Knobloch, is history's primary source of information on three of Swedenborg's most famous clairvoyant feats, which are known as the affairs of the Queen's Secret, the Stockholm Fire, and the Lost Receipt. [13] Schopenhauer's copy of *Dreams* shows evidence of careful study, particularly of part II, chapter 2, 'Ecstatic Journey of an Enthusiast Through the Spirit World', in which Kant presents his digest of Swedenborg's accounts of the spiritual world in the *Arcana Coelestia*. In the margins of Kant's exposition, Schopenhauer provides citations to the appropriate passages of the French edition of *Heaven and Hell*. [14] Schopenhauer also had access to Kant's Letter to Charlotte von Knobloch, which was first published as an appendix to Ludwig Ernst Borowski's biography of Kant, *Darstellung des Lebens und Charakters Immanuel Kants*. [15] In November 1814, Schopenhauer checked out a copy from the Dresden Public Library for a month, then later acquired his own copy. [16]

II. Swedenborg and Schopenhauer's philosophical style

Schopenhauer was primarily interested in Swedenborg as a clairvoyant and spirit-seer. Before turning to this topic, however, I wish to examine Schopenhauer's earliest recorded remark on Swedenborg, from a manuscript dated 1817:

> In the *Vera christiana religio* §400 Swedenborg says that, 'The egoistical man with his bodily eyes certainly sees the rest as men, but with his spiritual eyes he sees as men only himself and his relations, whilst the rest he sees only as masks'. According to their innermost meaning, these words are the same

as Kant's precept that, 'We should never consider others merely as means but as ends in themselves'. But how differently expressed is the idea; how vivid, sharp and to the point, graphic and immediately adequate are the words of Swedenborg (whose manner and way of thinking I do not usually find enjoyable), and how indirect, abstract and expressed through a derived connotation are the words of Kant![17]

First, it should be noted that the first set of words in quotation marks are not Swedenborg's words, but Schopenhauer's paraphrase of the gist of the first paragraph of *The True Christian Religion* §400. Second, Schopenhauer's remark that he 'usually' does not enjoy Swedenborg's 'manner and way of thinking' implies a wider acquaintance with Swedenborg's works. Furthermore, although Swedenborg's writings do contain some striking images, they are mostly rather dry, so Schopenhauer really cannot be faulted for finding Swedenborg's style to be most of the time uncongenial. (As Henry James, Sr was wont to observe, however, Swedenborg's lack of stylistic savour actually supports his veracity.[18] He is not trying too hard to persuade, which in itself is persuasive.) Third, Schopenhauer is stylistically the greatest German writer of philosophy, and one of the greatest philosophical stylists of all time. Thus for Schopenhauer to praise Swedenborg's style, albeit in a limited and qualified manner, is still high praise indeed.

The sincerest flattery, however, is the recurrence of this Swedenborgian trope more than twenty years later in §22 of Schopenhauer's 1839 treatise *On the Basis of Morality*:

Thus there is the man to whom all others are invariably non-ego, and who in fact ultimately regards only his own person as truly real, looking upon others virtually only as phantoms, attributing to them only a relative existence insofar as they may be a means or an obstacle to his ends. Thus there remains an immeasurable difference, a deep gulf, between his person and all that is non-ego. He exists exclusively in his own person, and sees all reality and the whole world perish with his own self in death. [19]

A more distant echo appears in §165 of Schopenhauer's essay, 'Additional Remarks on the Doctrine of the Affirmation of the Will-to-Live', first published in 1851 in volume two of *Parerga and Paraliomena*:

A noble character will not readily complain about his own fate; on the contrary, what Hamlet says in praise of Horatio will apply to him:

> for thou hast been
> As one, in suffering all, that suffers nothing.

This can be understood from the fact that such a man, recognising his own true nature in others and thus sharing their fate, almost invariably sees around him an even harder lot than his own and so cannot bring himself to complain of the latter. An ignoble egoist, on the other hand, who limits all reality to himself and regards others as mere masks and phantoms, will take no part in their fate, but will devote the whole of his sympathy and interest to his own; the results of this will then be great sensitiveness and frequent complaints.[20]

These stylistic echoes of Swedenborg are by no means the only ones in Schopenhauer's writings. [21] They are a far cry from signs of philosophical influence, but they do indicate that Schopenhauer read Swedenborg's works with care and sensitivity.

III. Schopenhauer's theory of spirit-seeing

The main reason Schopenhauer read Swedenborg was a deep and abiding fascination with paranormal phenomena, evinced by his library, his manuscript remains and his published writings. Schopenhauer published two accounts of paranormal phenomena. First is his chapter on 'Animal Magnetism and Magic' in his 1836 book *On the Will in Nature*. [22] Second is his extensive 1851 'Essay on Spirit-Seeing and Related Phenomena'. [23] This essay, which occupies ninety-eight pages in the Suhrkamp edition of Schopenhauer's *Collected Works* and eighty-three pages in Payne's English translation, is more than fifty per cent longer than Kant's entire book *Dreams of a Spirit-Seer* and is based on vastly more research. It also stands out as Schopenhauer's worst-written work. Rambling, prolix, disorganized and often dull, it is in need of sections and subsections for easier reading and comprehension. The subject matter demands a formal treatise, not a breezy and sometimes annoyingly digressive essay.

In the 'Essay' Schopenhauer attempts to offer a single theory that explains a number of different paranormal phenomena: (1) *animal magnetism*, now known as hypnosis, in which the hypnotist places the patient in a trance-like state which allows the hypnotist to exert his will over the patient and the patient to access levels of consciousness that are unavailable to normal waking consciousness, (2) *somnambulism*, which is not confined merely to sleepwalking, but includes any activity engaged in while unconscious or in a trance, including under hypnosis, (3) *clairvoyance*, which means sensing things that cannot be physically sensed because of great distances of time or space or a difference of metaphysical status, e.g., dead people, (4) *magic*, which means action at a distance analogous to sensing at a distance, (5) *prophecy* of the future, (6) *apparitions* of the living and the dead, and (7) *mediumship*, meaning communication with the spirits of the dead.

Schopenhauer's neo-Kantian metaphysics offers the foundation for his explanation of these phenomena. First, Schopenhauer holds to the Kantian distinction between phenomena and the thing-in-itself. These are different because the finite, determinate nature of our cognitive faculties implies that we can experience things not as they are in themselves, but only insofar as they can be given to us. Second, again following Kant, Schopenhauer argues that we experience things as spatio-

74

temporal objects subject to causal laws because it is the nature of our mind to do so. Space, time and causality constitute the structure of the phenomenal realm, not necessarily of reality in itself. While Kant was himself mostly agnostic on the nature of ultimate reality and would claim only that we cannot know if the thing-in-itself is also spatio-temporal and subject to causal laws, Schopenhauer positively affirms that the thing-in-itself lies outside of space and time and is not subject to causal laws. Third, again taking his lead from Kant but pushing beyond him, Schopenhauer affirms that the thing-in-itself is will. Furthermore, Schopenhauer argues that since the will lies outside of space and time, which are the principles of individuation, the will is undifferentiated. Insofar as each phenomenal individual has his roots in the thing-in-itself, we are all, in ourselves, one. Fourth, human consciousness has a number of levels. The highest level of consciousness is wakeful, worldly, self-conscious awareness, which is also the most individuated level of consciousness. As we descend through the gradations of consciousness, we become less self-conscious and less individuated. When we descend below the threshold of self-consciousness to the unconscious or subconscious mind, we leave individuation further behind and approach the undifferentiated will, which lies outside of space, time and the causal order.

An additional element of Schopenhauer's account is his notion of the 'dream-organ'. [24] In dreams, we experience things that are not given to our external senses. Our experiences are, therefore, generated from within, by means of the dream-organ. The dream-organ explains not only dreams, but also spirit apparitions. Spirits do not appear by stimulating our senses, but by stimulating the dream-organ while we are awake. Because we are awake when the dream-organ is stimulated, we automatically transpose the dream image into the outer realm. Yet other people cannot see these apparitions because these apparitions do not—and indeed cannot—stimulate their external senses, but only the dream-organs of those who are susceptible to apparitions. Schopenhauer's notion of the dream-organ is also derived from Kant, from *Dreams of a Spirit-Seer*. [25]

Magic, clairvoyant cognition of 'the hidden, the absent, the remote and even that which still slumbers in the womb of the future', and other paranormal phenomena seem to suspend space, time and the causal order. [26] This is not, however, incomprehensible given Schopenhauer's metaphysics, for space, time and causality are merely how the world appears to our ordinary consciousness. They are part of the world as representation. But if we leave ordinary consciousness behind, we will enter a new world where space, time, and causality are annulled. We will enter the world of the will. Schopenhauer's theory is that the paranormal phenomena listed above involve trance-like states, whether self-induced, spontaneous, or induced by another. In these trance states, we descend down the scale of consciousness and approach the realm of the undifferentiated will, where the distinctions between near and far, and between past, present and future have no meaning. In Schopenhauer's words:

Animal magnetism, sympathetic cures, magic, second sight, dreaming the real, spirit seeing and visions of all kinds are kindred phenomena, branches of one stem. They afford certain and irrefutable proof of a nexus of entities that rests on an order of things entirely different from nature. For her foundation nature has the laws of space, time and causality, whereas that other order is more deep-seated, original and immediate. Therefore the first and most universal (because purely formal) laws of nature are not applicable to it. Accordingly, time and space no longer separate individuals and their separation and isolation, which are due to those very forms, no longer place insuperable barriers in the way of the communication of thoughts and the direct influence of the will. Thus changes are brought about in a way quite different from that of physical causality with the continuous chain of its links; in other words, they are produced merely by virtue of an act of will that is brought to light in a special manner and thereby intensified to a higher potential beyond the individual. Accordingly, the peculiar characteristic of all the animal phenomena here considered is *visio in distans et actio in distans* [seeing at a distance and acting at a distance], both as regards time and space. [27]

Animal magnetism is explained by the fact that the common root of all is the will. The hypnotist, by inducing a trance-like state in his patient, puts the individual will out of commission and opens the patient up to the influxes of the universal will, through the medium of which the hypnotist exercises his will over the patient. *Somnambulism* is ultimately explained by the scale of consciousness and the relative superficiality of the self-conscious mind when compared to the vastness of the subconscious or unconscious. We know more than we know we know. We can do more than we know we can do. *Clairvoyance* is possible if we can sense things through the medium of the will, where distances of space and time do not exist. Since the normal senses are not used in clairvoyant cognition, such experiences enter consciousness through the dream-organ. *Magic* is possible if we can act on things through the medium of the will, where not only space and time, but also the laws of causality do not exist. *Prophecy* is possible if we can access the realm of the will, which is 'that mechanism which is hidden in the background and from which everything originates [...] so that which is seen externally, that is, through our optical lens of time, as merely something that will come in the future, is already at this moment present in that mechanism'. [28] Prophetic visions enter consciousness through the dream-organ. *Apparitions* of the living and the dead are caused by the will of the persons who appear. Their wills cause images of themselves to be communicated through the medium of the will and to appear in the dream-organs of parties who are susceptible to such apparitions. Finally, according to Schopenhauer's theory, *mediumship*, meaning actual communication with the spirits of the dead, is not possible.

Schopenhauer stresses again and again that apparitions of the dead are caused by dead persons while they are still alive, and their effects linger long after they are dead, like the light of burnt-out stars. He claims that an image of a person is affixed to particular places and things by their intense emotions, and these images can enter the consciousness of sensitive people through their dream-organs. Schopenhauer's examples of apparitions are the stuff of Romantic literature and opera: murder victims dressed as they were when they were killed, misers guarding their treasure hoards, dead lovers haunting their living beloveds, etc. In Schopenhauer's words:

> From what has been said, it is obvious that the immediate reality of an actually existing object is not to be imputed to a ghost that appears in this way, although indirectly a reality does underlie it. Thus what we see there is certainly not the deceased man himself, but a mere *eidolon*, a picture of him who once existed which originates in the dream-organ of a man attuned to it and is brought about by some remnant relic, some trace that was left behind [...] Accordingly, a spirit apparition of the kind we are here considering certainly does stand in objective relation to the *former* state of the person who appears, but certainly not to his *present* state, for it does not take any active part therein, and so from this the continued individual existence of the person cannot be inferred. The explanation given is also supported by the fact that the deceased persons appearing in this way are as a rule seen in the clothes they usually wore, and also that a murdered man appears with his murderer, a horse and his rider, and so on.[29]

Schopenhauer also suggests that the 'whole conception of the realm of shades [the spiritual world] probably arose from spirit apparitions'.[30] Schopenhauer resists the inference that apparitions of the dead are caused by the surviving spirits of the dead because his metaphysics commits him to denying that the individual soul survives the death of the body. The phenomenal realm, including the material body, is the realm of individuation. When the individual body perishes, the individual soul perishes as well. The only immortal element of a human being is the will, which is not individual, but common and undifferentiated.

But if the soul does not survive the death of the body, then how does Schopenhauer explain—or explain away—mediumship, in which living people carry on conversations with spirits of the dead? Swedenborg suggests that mediumship is a combination of apparitions of the dead with the imagination of the medium. The medium simply invests the dumb apparitions with imaginary personalities and then carries on conversations with them:

> In all probability, most of the ghosts seen by the clairvoyante of Prevorst are also to be reckoned among visions of this kind [mere images of the dead]. But the conversations she carried on with them are to be regarded as the work of her own imagination that furnished the text for this dumb show from its own resources and thus supplied its explanation. Thus by nature man attempts in some way to explain everything that he sees, or at any rate to introduce some connection and sequence and in fact to turn it over in his mind. Therefore children often carry on a dialogue even with inanimate things. Accordingly, without knowing it, the clairvoyante herself was the prompter of those forms that appeared to her. Here her power of imagination was in the same kind of unconscious activity with which we guide and connect the events in the ordinary insignificant dream, indeed with which we sometimes seize the opportunity for this from objective accidental circumstances, such as a pressure felt in bed, or a sound reaching us from without, an odour and so on, in accordance with which we then dream long stories.[31]

The clairvoyante of Prevorst was Frau Frederica Hauffe, née Wanner (1801-29), whose exhibitions of clairvoyance and mediumship were related by Justinus Kerner in his celebrated book *Die Seherin von Prevorst* (*The Clairvoyante of Prevorst*).[32] Schopenhauer's library contained an extensively annotated copy of the 1838 third edition of this work, as well as vols. 8-11 of Kerner's *Blätter aus Prevorst* (*Pages from Prevorst*), also annotated, and two other volumes of Kerner's on somnambulism and animal magnetism.[33]

Schopenhauer claims that the fact that a medium's spirit-conversations are often identifiably coloured by the medium's own world view is evidence in favour of his hypothesis. For instance, he writes of the clairvoyante of Prevorst:

> this explanation finds strong confirmation in the unutterable absurdity of the text of those dialogues and dramas that are alone in keeping with the intellectual outlook of an ignorant girl from the hills and with the popular metaphysics that has been drilled into her. To attribute to them an objective reality is possible only on the assumption of a world order that is so boundlessly absurd and revoltingly stupid that we should have to blush at belonging thereto. [34]

Here Schopenhauer lays his cards on the table, for the 'popular metaphysics' that he finds so 'absurd and revoltingly stupid' that he treats it as a *reductio ad absurdum* of the clairvoyante's revelations is merely the idea that the individual soul survives the death of the body and lives on in a spiritual world. He rejects this metaphysics because it conflicts with his own. He rejects mediumship, because if he took it seriously, it would constitute an empirical refutation of his metaphysical denial of the survival of the individual soul after death.

There are three serious problems with Schopenhauer's argument that mediumship is imaginary because reports of spirits are always coloured by the medium's point of view. First, it proves too much. The same argument can be used to prove that everything is imaginary, because our perception of everything is coloured by our particular points of view. Second, as Schopenhauer himself points out a few pages later in the same essay, the argument is a non sequitur: 'We often imagine we have abolished the reality of a spirit apparition when we show that it was subjectively conditioned. But what weight can this argument have with the man who knows from Kant's doctrine how large a share the subjective conditions have in the appearance of the corporeal world?' [35] For a Kantian idealist, it simply does not follow that because consciousness is subjectively conditioned, it is not consciousness of something real. Indeed, it is precisely by means of these subjective conditions that we are capable of knowing things at all. Third, not everything in a medium's reports can be reduced to his prior knowledge and point of view. Spirits sometimes report facts otherwise unknown to the medium, facts that can be tested. If these facts can be verified, and if the medium could not have learned of them by conventional means, then we have elegant proof of the veracity of at least some cases of mediumship. Robert Almeder examines a number of such cases in his *Death and Personal Survival: The Evidence for Life After Death*.[36] Schopenhauer himself lists a number of empirically testable reports by the clairvoyante of Prevorst:

> if the very prejudiced and gullible Justin Kerner had not secretly had a faint notion of the [imaginary] origin here stated of those spirit conversations, he would not have omitted always and everywhere with such irresponsible levity seriously and zealously to look for the material objects that are made known by the spirits, for example writing materials in church vaults, gold chains in castle vaults, children buried in stables, instead of allowing himself to be deterred from this by the most trifling obstacles. For this would have thrown some light on the facts.[37]

If any of these reports turned out to be true and there were no ordinary way the clairvoyante could have obtained the information, this would prove her veracity. Schopenhauer claims that Kerner did not investigate these claims precisely for fear of refuting the clairvoyante. But we could just as well accuse Schopenhauer of failing to investigate them for fear of proving her right. Such an investigation would not have been difficult for Schopenhauer. He was a man of leisure and independent means. Prevorst was not so far away and the clairvoyante was a younger contemporary who had lived entirely within Schopenhauer's own lifetime.

81

IV. Schopenhauer on Swedenborg

It is important to note that Swedenborg is nowhere mentioned in Schopenhauer's published accounts of paranormal phenomena. His name does, however, appear in Schopenhauer's preliminary notes for his 'Animal Magnetism and Magic' chapter, §106 of his notebook entitled *Adversaria*, which was begun in March of 1828. The ideas expressed in these notes also find their way into the 1851 'Essay on Spirit-Seeing':

> In general it might well be that all dreaming is a function not of the brain, but of the inner nerve-centre, a consciousness of which, however, nothing usually enters the brain as long as this is not yet absorbed in total rest and which then still acts like a spectator; it is therefore *possible* to recall dreams. This possibility, however, would cease if the brain were totally quiescent and the vital force were concentrated entirely in the ganglionic sensorium, especially if this seized control of the nerves that produce external movement. For this reason those in a deep sleep and especially magnetic as well as natural sleep-talkers and sleep-walkers have, when they are awake, no recollection of the representations or mental pictures of their sleep. Now if we assume this and regard dreams simply as the sensorial activity of the solar plexus which had as its condition the more or less complete exclusion and inactivity of the brain, then the abnormal case could also be conceived where once during wakefulness, and hence while the brain is active, the solar plexus entered a state of sensorial activity whose product, being mixed up with that of cerebral activity, would then suddenly stand out as a phantom or ghost. This, however, often vanishes when, to observe it more closely, a man focuses his attention on it and hence intensifies the cerebral activity, where at day-break it disappears like a will-o'-the-wisp. Aristotle has already observed that things like this happen [...] It is highly probable that this is what happens with all spirit-seeing and spirit-hearing. Now whether such a phenomenon

referred to anything objective, that is to say to something different from our own individuality, would depend on whether the sensorial activity of the solar plexus (so abnormally strong that it rises above cerebral activity) had no other cause than a purely physiological one, as for example with Nicolai; or an external cause such as may be the lively thoughts and desires of others, especially of the dying. Whether one who has died can have such an effect is extremely doubtful. The most striking instances of this would be Swedenborg and the clairvoyante of Prevorst [...] [38]

Schopenhauer also pairs Swedenborg and the clairvoyante of Prevorst in a note on the back end-page of his copy of the French translation of *Heaven and Hell* and *Worlds in Space*:

It appears to have been a spontaneous somnambulism and *clairvoyance*, the memory of which remained in the brain, which however, as with nearly all somnambulists, in whom earlier, and indeed very strong, brain representations were fixed, from which springs the thoroughgoing and decided Christianity of all [his] visions; from which [springs] the polyhistorical thought-tendency of the inhabitants of Mercury, for Mercury was the God of oratory, and so forth; from which [springs] encounters with Christian von Wolff, Aristotle and many others, who appear according to *Swedenborg's* capacities, and so forth. For though *Swedenborg* was a man of excellent faculties and much knowledge, the visions, since they stood under the influence of the brain, systematically and coherently failed. I would like to say: with such visions the ganglion network supplies *the dumb show*, and the brain speaks the text in addition. So also with the Seeress of Prevorst: She is probably a Seeress, but no Heareress. The same applies to Swedenborg. The spirit world of each of these two therefore corresponds exactly the sphere of their knowledge. [39]

This note requires a bit of unpacking and explanation. First, Schopenhauer thinks that Swedenborg and the clairvoyante had essentially the same sort of visions, namely 'spontaneous somnambulism and clairvoyance'. Spontaneous somnambulism is to be contrasted with induced somnambulism, whether self-induced or induced by another. Somnambulism does not refer to sleepwalking, but to any activity undertaken in a state of trance. In the case of Swedenborg and the clairvoyante, the activity is clairvoyance itself. (Swedenborg also wrote a good deal during his trance states). Second, both Swedenborg and the clairvoyante reported seeing and communicating with the spirits of the dead. Schopenhauer rejects this possibility for reasons given above. Third, Schopenhauer explains away Swedenborg's mediumship the same way he explains away that of the clairvoyante of Prevorst. He even uses the same language. Swedenborg merely saw apparitions of the dead. His imagination endowed the 'dumb show' of these apparitions with personalities, and then he imagined interacting with them. This explains why his accounts of the spiritual world are so obviously conditioned by his own interests and world view. In spite of his 'excellent faculties and much knowledge', Swedenborg was, in short, calamitously deluded and never caught on to his delusion throughout the decades of his spiritual awakening and the production of dozens of weighty volumes.

Although Schopenhauer links Swedenborg and the clairvoyante of Prevorst, it is significant that she is mentioned in his published work, but Swedenborg is not. This requires an explanation. Schopenhauer thought that Swedenborg and the clairvoyante had essentially the same sort of visions. He also rejected the veracity of their visions for the same reason. Finally, he tried to explain away their visions in essentially the same way. Since Schopenhauer did not think that the clairvoyante's visions were any more veracious that those of Swedenborg, I would suggest that the only reason he does not mention Swedenborg's visions in print is that he thought the clairvoyante's visions were far better documented. Swedenborg, of course, gives extensive first-person accounts of his visions but for the purposes of the scientific study of the paranormal the accounts of other parties are preferred, and Kerner provides voluminous documentation of just this sort.

* * *

Schopenhauer's encounter with Swedenborg has to be described as a missed opportunity. Schopenhauer looked eagerly to natural science and natural history—including the scientific study of paranormal phenomena—because he wished to evaluate his metaphysical system in the light of experience. Naturally, his strongest desire was to see his theorizing confirmed, but intellectual honesty also required him to confront evidence to the contrary as well. We need not raise the question of the ultimate veracity of Swedenborg and the clairvoyante of Prevorst in order to question Schopenhauer's handling of their testimonies. Schopenhauer was willing to believe quite a lot of testimony about paranormal phenomena that probably would not be accepted by today's rigorous scientific investigators of the paranormal, much less by axe-grinding materialist debunkers. The testimonies of Swedenborg and the clairvoyante are certainly no less credible than other testimonies accepted by Schopenhauer. Schopenhauer got off to a good start by reading Swedenborg with great care. Yet, in the end, he baulked, because if Swedenborg is right, the individual soul survives the death of the body, a possibility that Schopenhauer rejected on metaphysical grounds as 'revoltingly absurd' and 'infamously stupid'. [40] In the final analysis, Schopenhauer was un-willing to question one of his metaphysical tenets. He was, therefore, placed in a very odd position. Although he thought that animal magnetism, somnambulism, clairvoyance, magic, prophecy and apparitions of the dead were real, when it came to mediumship, he joined the ranks of debunkers.

I see Schopenhauer's rejection of Swedenborg as richly ironic. The model of Schopenhauer's 'Essay on Spirit-Seeing' is Kant's *Dreams of a Spirit-Seer*. Not only does Schopenhauer refer explicitly to *Dreams*, he also mentions it in the most subtle ways, for instance by alluding to its epigraphs. [41] I have argued extensively that Kant was deeply influenced by his encounter with Swedenborg in the early 1760s. [42] In

85

particular, I have argued that two of the very Kantian tenets that Schopenhauer uses to explain the possibility of clairvoyance—the distinction between phenomena and things-in-themselves and the ideal nature of space and time—were so well suited to that end because they were adopted by Kant from Swedenborg as Kant himself tried to come to grips with clairvoyance.[43] Thus two of the foundational principles of Schopenhauer's theory of the paranormal derive ultimately from Swedenborg, yet in the end Schopenhauer does not see fit even to mention Swedenborg in his published accounts. Another irony is that Schopenhauer's rejection of Swedenborg is ultimately based on a dual rejection of Kant. First, Schopenhauer's inference that the thing-in-itself is a single, undifferentiated will is illegitimate on Kantian grounds. From the Kantian claim that space and time (the principles of individuation) and the principle of causality are the structure of the phenomenal world, we cannot infer that the thing-in-itself is non-spatial, non-temporal, non-individuated and non-causal as Schopenhauer does. Things as they are in themselves could be exactly as they appear to us. We simply do not know. Second, Kant defended the metaphysical possibility that the individual soul survives the death of the body, and he also offered moral arguments for believing that this is so. Schopenhauer's inference that personal survival is impossible is precisely the kind of *a priori* argument about the way things-in-themselves must be that Kant's critical philosophy shows to be groundless. Perhaps if Schopenhauer had been a better Kantian he would have appreciated Swedenborg more.

NOTES

[1] For a list of Schopenhauer's collection of orientalia and his marginalia, see Arthur Schopenhauer, *Der handschriftliche Nachlaß*, vol. 5, *Randschriften zu Büchern*, ed. Arthur Hübscher (Frankfurt am Main: Waldemar Kramer, 1968), pp. 319-52. Henceforth cited as Hübscher 5.

[2] On Schopenhauer's reading and assimilation of Eastern philosophy, see Moira Nicholls, 'The Influences of Eastern Thought on Schopenhauer's Doctrine of the Thing-in-Itself', in *The Cambridge Companion to Schopenhauer*, ed. Christopher Janaway (Cambridge: Cambridge University Press, 1999).

[3] See the sections on 'Philosophie' and 'Theologie und Religionswissenschaft' in Hübscher 5.

[4] Hübscher 5, pp. 287-91.

[5] Ibid., pp. 287-318.

[6] Emanuel Swedenborg, *Prodromus Philosophiae ratiocinantis de Infinito, et causa finali creationis, deque mechanismo operationis animae et corporis* (Dresden and Leipzig: F Hekelii, 1734). In English: *Forerunner of a Reasoned Philosophy Concerning the Infinite and the Final Cause of Creaton also The Mechanism of the Operation of the Soul and the Body*, tr. J J Garth Wilkinson (London: Swedenborg Society, 1992). Hübscher 5, p. 315.

[7] Swedenborg, *Les merveilles du ciel et de l'enfer et des terres planétaires et astrals, par E S, D'après le témoignage de ses yeux et de ses oreilles*, 2 vols., tr. A J P Bin (G J Decker, 1782). The two volumes were bound together as one. Hübscher 5, p. 315.

[8] Swedenborg, *De Commercio Animae et Corporis, quod creditus fieri vel per Influxum Physicum, vel per Influxum Spiritualem, vel per Harmonium Praestabilitam* (London,1769). In English: *The Intercourse between the Soul and the Body, which is believed to be either by Physical Influx, or by Spiritual Influx, or by Pre-established Harmony*, tr. J Whitehead (New York: Swedenborg Foundation, 1913).

[9] Hübscher 5, p. 316.

[10] Swedenborg, *Vera Christiana Religio, continens universam Theologiam Novae Ecclesiae, a Domino apud Danielem cap. vii.13, 14, et in Apocalypsi cap. xxi. 1, 2, praedictae* (Amstelodami, 1771). In English: *The True Christian Religion, containing the universal theology of the New Church, foretold by the Lord in Daniel 7:13, 14, and in the Revelation 21:1, 2*, tr. W Dick (London: Swedenborg Society, 1950).

[11] Schopenhauer, *Der handschriftliche Nachlaß*, vol. 1, *Frühe Manuskripte (1804-1818)*, ed. Arthur Hübscher (Frankfurt am Main: Waldemar Kramer, 1966), §674,

p. 471. Henceforth cited as Hübscher 1. In English: *Manuscript Remains in Four Volumes*, ed. Arthur Hübscher, tr. E F J Payne, vol. 1, *Early Manuscripts (1804-1818)* (New York: Berg, 1988), §674, p. 521. Henceforth cited as Payne 1.

[12] Immanuel Kant, *Träume eines Geistersehers, erläutert durch Träume der Metaphysik* (1766), ed. Rudolf Malter (with supplemental appendices) (Stuttgart: Reclam, 1976). In English: *Kant on Swedenborg: Dreams of a Spirit-Seer and Other Writings*, ed. and tr. Gregory R Johnson (West Chester: Swedenborg Foundation, 2002).

[13] Kant, Brief an Charlotte von Knobloch, 10 August 1763, in Malter's edition of *Träume eines Geistersehers*, pp. 99-106. In English: To Charlotte von Knobloch, 10 August 1763, in *Immanuel Kant, Correspondence*, tr. and ed. Arnulf Zweig (Cambridge: Cambridge University Press, 1999), pp. 70-6.

[14] Hübscher 5, pp. 97-8.

[15] Ludwig Ernst Borowski, *Darstellung des Lebens und Charakters Immanuel Kants von Ludwig Ernst Borowski, von Kant selbst genau revidiert und berichtigt* (Königsberg, 1804).

[16] Hübscher 5, p. 19.

[17] Hübscher 1, §674, p. 471. In English: Payne 1, §674, p. 521.

[18] 'Insipid with veracity' was Henry James, Sr's customary expression.

[19] Schopenhauer, *Über die Grundlage der Moral,* in *Sämtliche Werke*, 5 vols., ed. Wolfgang Freiherr von Löhneysen, vol. 3, *Kleinere Schriften* (Frankfurt am Main: Suhrkamp, 1986), §22, p. 811. In English: *On the Basis of Morality*, tr. E F J Payne (Indianapolis: Hackett, 1995), §22, p. 213.

[20] Schopenhauer, 'Nachträge zur Lehre von der Bejahung und Verneinung des Willes zum Leben', in *Sämtliche Werke*, 5 vols., ed. Wolfgang Freiherr von Löhneysen, vol. 5, *Parerga und Paralipomena*, vol. 2. (Frankfurt am Main: Suhrkamp, 1986), §165, p. 372. In English: 'Additional Remarks on the Doctrine of the Affirmation and Denial of the Will-to-Live', in *Parerga and Paralipomena*, 2 vols., tr. E F J Payne (Oxford: Clarendon Press, 1974), vol. 2, §165, p. 315.

[21] Schopenhauer, for example, sometimes uses the term 'Geisterwelt' (spirit-world) in a manner that calls Swedenborg to mind. See, for example, the end of §58 of *Die Welt als*

Wille und Vorstellung, in *Sämtliche Werke*, 5 vols., ed. Wolfgang Freiherr von Löhneysen, vol. 1 (Frankfurt am Main: Suhrkamp, 1986), p. 443. In English: *The World as Will and Representation*, vol. 1, tr. by E F J Payne (New York: Dover, 1969), p. 323.

[22] Schopenhauer, *Über den Willen in der Natur: Eine Erörterung der Bestätigungen, welche die Philosophie des Verfassers seit ihrem Auftreten durch die Empirischen Wissenschaften Erhalten hat*, in *Kleinere Schriften*. In English: *On the Will in Nature: A Discussion of the Corroborations from the Empirical Sciences that the Author's Philosophy has Received Since its First Appearance*, tr. E F J Payne (New York: Berg, 1992).

[23] Schopenhauer, 'Versuch über Geistersehn und was damit zusammenhängt', in *Sämtliche Werke*, 5 vols., ed. Wolfgang Freiherr von Löhneysen, vol. 4, *Parerga und Paralipomena*, vol. 1 (Frankfurt am Main: Suhrkamp, 1986), pp. 275-372. In English: 'Essay on Spirit-Seeing and Related Phenomena', in *Parerga and Paralipomena*, 2 vols., tr. E F J Payne (Oxford: Clarendon Press, 1974), vol. 1, pp. 227-309.

[24] Schopenhauer, 'Essay on Spirit-Seeing', pp. 238-9.

[25] See *Dreams*, part I, ch. 3, 'Anti-Kabbalah—A Fragment of Common Philosophy to Cancel Community with the Spirit-World'. Although this chapter is cast as a reductionistic attempt to 'explain away' apparitions, Kant's account of the mechanism of apparitions is also consistent with them being genuine influxes from a spiritual world. See Gregory R Johnson, 'A Commentary on Kant's Dreams of a Spirit-Seer', Ph.D. dissertation (Washington, DC: The Catholic University of America, 2001), ch. 8.

[26] Schopenhauer, 'Essay on Spirit-Seeing', p. 263.

[27] Ibid., pp. 265-6.

[28] Ibid., p. 264.

[29] Ibid., pp. 285-6.

[30] Ibid., p. 284.

[31] Ibid., p. 286.

[32] Justinus Kerner, *Die Seherin von Prevorst. Eröffnungen über das innere Leben des Menschen und über das Hereinragen einer Geisterwelt in die unsere* (Stuttgart und Tübingen: J G Cotta, 1829).

[33] Hübscher 5, pp. 302-4.

34 Schopenhauer, 'Essay on Spirit-Seeing', p. 287.

35 Ibid., pp. 298-9.

36 Robert Almeder, *Death and Personal Survival: The Evidence for Life After Death* (Lanham: Rowman and Littlefield, 1992), ch. 5, 'Communications from the Dead'. See also ch. 2, 'Appartions of the Dead'.

37 Schopenhauer, 'Essay on Spirit-Seeing', p. 287.

38 *Arthur Schopenhauer. Der handschriftliche Nachlaß*, vol. 3, *Berliner Manuskripte (1818-1830)*, ed. Arthur Hübscher (Frankfurt am Main: Waldemar Kramer, 1970), pp. 528-9. In English: *Arthur Schopenhauer, Manuscript Remains in Four Volumes*, ed. Arthur Hübscher, tr. E F J Payne, vol. 3, *Berlin Manuscripts (1818-1839)* (New York: Berg, 1989), pp. 575-6.

39 Hübscher 5, p. 316. Translation mine.

40 Schopenhauer, 'Essay on Spirit-Seeing', p. 308.

41 Schopenhauer's epigraph for the essay is from Goethe, but Goethe himself is alluding to a quote from Virgil, *Aeneid*, Book VI. ii. 268-9, which Kant quotes near the beginning of *Dreams*, part I, ch. 2. In the closing paragraphs of the 'Essay' Schopenhauer quotes two words, 'aegri somnia' ('dreams of the sick') from Horace's *Ars Poetica* 7. Kant uses the sentence in which these words occur as the epigraph to the whole of *Dreams*.

42 See especially my Ph.D. dissertation 'A Commentary on Kant's Dreams of a Spirit-Seer' as well as my following articles: 'Kant on Swedenborg in the Lectures on Metaphysics: The 1760s-1770s', in *Studia Swedenborgiana*, vol. 10, no. 1, October 1996, pp. 1-38; 'Kant on Swedenborg in the Lectures on Metaphysics: The 1780s-1790s', in *Studia Swedenborgiana*, vol. 10, no. 2, May 1997, pp. 11-39; 'Kant's Early Metaphysics and the Origins of the Critical Philosophy', in *Studia Swedenborgiana*, vol. 11, no. 2, May 1999, pp. 29-54; 'The Kinship of Kant and Swedenborg', in *The New Philosophy*, vol. 99, nos. 3 & 4, July-December 1996, pp. 407-23; 'Did Kant Dissemble His Interest in Swedenborg?: The Esotericism Hypothesis', in *The New Philosophy*, vol. 102, no. 2, July-December 1999, pp. 529-60; and 'Swedenborg's Positive Influence on the Development of Kant's Mature Moral Philosophy' contained herein, pp. 25-44.

43 See my 'A Commentary', Preface and chs. 5 and 7.

'Swedenborg's Meaning is the truth': Coleridge, Tulk and Swedenborg

H J Jackson

oleridge was born in 1772, the year of Swedenborg's death. He must have been aware in a general way of the nature of Swedenborg's work and the rapid spread of his influence in England, but it was not until 1817, when he met Charles Augustus Tulk, that he undertook a careful study of the writings of Swedenborg and became for a short time involved in the business of the Swedenborg Society. At one point he gleefully reported to Tulk the rumour that he had experienced a religious conversion: 'They say, Coleridge! that you are a Swedenborgian!'.[1] But they both knew that it was not true. Coleridge turned 45 in 1817, Tulk 31. Though Swedenborg himself is proof that conversion may occur late in life, Coleridge was not converted by reading his work. He cannot even be properly said to have been *influenced* by Swedenborg, though he was certainly interested by him and consistently described him as a man of 'philosophic Genius'.[2] Since Coleridge came to a knowledge of Swedenborg through Tulk and since many of his statements about Swedenborg and the New Church were directly or indirectly addressed to Tulk, I want to begin by briefly retelling the story of the relationship between them before considering the nature and evolution of Coleridge's own involvement with the Swedenborgian movement.

At the time when they met (on holiday at the seaside), both men were about as prosperous and contented as they would ever be. Tulk, with a large fortune, had been happily married for ten years and had a growing family to care for. As a founder member of the Swedenborg Society, then known as the 'Society for Printing and Publishing the Writings of the Hon. Emanuel Swedenborg, instituted in London in the Year 1810', he continued a family tradition (his father, John Augustus, had been involved in the original Theosophical Society of 1783 and took an active part in the new one) and was kept busy in a good cause. He helped to organize the publication and distribution of Swedenborg's works, contributed articles to the New Church *Intellectual Repository*, chaired sessions of the Society and of the Hawkstone Meeting, and did some translating himself. As to Coleridge, he was enjoying the sheltered harbour of a surgeon's family after twenty turbulent and troubled years. Under the Gillmans' care in Highgate he had reduced his dependency on opium to a controlled dose and, thus stabilized, seemed to be picking up the pieces of his literary career. In 1816-17 he had published 'Christabel' and 'Kubla Khan', brought out an autobiography and a volume of collected poems, and contributed two 'Lay Sermons' to the current political debates. He had in the works an introduction to an encyclopedia (the 'Treatise on Method'), a three-volume revised version of his periodical *The Friend*, and an annotated selection from the works of the seventeenth-century Archbishop of Glasgow, Robert Leighton. Shortly after meeting Tulk, he began to work regularly with a young surgeon and Germanist, Joseph Henry Green, with the aim of articulating a coherent system of philosophy to displace both Newtonian materialism and post-Kantian idealism.[3]

In the period of their *close* friendship, which lasted about ten years, Tulk's and Coleridge's circumstances naturally changed. Coleridge delivered public lectures and privately gave lessons in philosophy, but was often ill. Tulk had the satisfaction of serving for six years as a Member of Parliament, but he suffered the loss of his wife Susannah in 1824 and never remarried. (Coleridge did not handle the death well: though he later said that he had written as soon as he heard the news, he did not post his letter and Tulk had to write to him some months later to find out what had happened.) [4] Realizing that they had a good deal in common, they put considerable effort into reinforcing the ties between them. In 1818 they both campaigned for better conditions for children working in the cotton factories. Tulk attended some of Coleridge's lectures, and probably mentioned them to other friends—Coleridge sent him copies of the prospectus. He assisted and advised Coleridge in difficult negotiations with the publisher John Murray. Coleridge and Gillman in turn advised him in his attempt to buy a house near them in Highgate after the death of his wife. [5]

In all these practical matters Coleridge and Tulk did what they could to support one another. But the basis of their intimacy was an intellectual affinity that had been apparent from the very beginning. Coleridge knew no half measures in friendship: he registered his excitement over meeting a kindred spirit by sending Tulk two whopping letters outlining his system of dynamic philosophy. [6] Tulk responded by lending and giving Coleridge books. The first we hear of are titles that might have been expected to appeal to Coleridge's poetic and philosophic tastes while also having connections with Swedenborg: Blake's *Songs of Innocence and of Experience*, some work of Schelling's, an Indian poem, notes on Spinoza. [7] By October 1819, Tulk had Coleridge reading Swedenborg's own works, both theological and scientific. They must have eagerly talked over Swedenborg's philosophy and theology when they had the opportunity, continuing the discussion in letters when they were apart. In January 1820, Coleridge wrote,

> If I mistake not, one formula would comprise your philosophical faith & mine—namely, that the sensible World is but the evolution of the Truth, Love, and Life, or their opposites, in Man—and that in Nature Man beholds only (to use an Algebraic but close analogy) the integration of Products, the Differentials of which are in, and constitute, his own mind and soul—and consequently that all true science is contained in the Lore of Symbols & Correspondences. [8]

Tulk sometimes rode up to Highgate, Coleridge sometimes went to stay with the Tulks for a few days. Coleridge's excitement about what he was reading spilled over in the form of literary projects.

Knowing Tulk's responsibilities, Coleridge proposed several publishing ventures for the Society, in some of which he was prepared to be personally involved. Since he considered Swedenborg to be 'illustrious tho' grossly misconceived', he made memoranda in the pages of his Latin copy of *Heaven and Hell* about ways in which the followers of Swedenborg might prevent misunderstanding in the future:

> But again I repeat my conviction, that *Swedenborg's* Meaning is the truth—— and the duty of his followers is, to secure this meaning to the Readers of his Works by collecting from his numerous Volumes those passages, in which this meaning is conveyed in terms so plain as not to be misconceived: an Introduction of 50 pages would suffice for this purpose.[9]

At the annual meeting of the Society in 1817, Tulk had been able to remind members of the Society that they had achieved a major part of the purpose for which they had joined together, namely the translation and publication of all the 'divinely illuminated writings' of Swedenborg, and that they were now embarked on second editions and new translations.[10] Coleridge's letters to Tulk suggest another direction that the Society might choose to pursue. The works were out, to be sure, but they were misunderstood; by judicious presentation, adapting the works for a nineteenth-century British readership, the Society could see to it that they were correctly understood——or, as we might put it, could attempt to control interpretation. Further suggestions in the 1820s included an octavo companion volume to *The True Christian Religion*, a blank-verse version of *Conjugial Love*, an '*introductory* Essay to the Science of Correspondences', and 'a history of the mind of Swedenborg'. The last of these Tulk is said actually to have proposed to the Society in 1825, recommending a commission of £200. The offer was rejected, allegedly because of doubts about Coleridge's doctrinal fitness for the task.[11] From the point of view of the Church, if not of Tulk, those doubts were well founded.

The survival of many of Coleridge's notebooks and annotated books, as well as a substantial portion of his side of the correspondence with Tulk, means that it is possible to trace the history of his views about Swedenborg in detail, only bearing in mind that his comments must often have been coloured by his desire to please his friend. When Coleridge said that Swedenborg had been 'grossly misconceived', he could have been describing his own situation, for he had himself misconceived Swedenborg. Before meeting Tulk, he was aware that Swedenborg had described visions of heaven and hell; he knew about the controversies surrounding the establishment of the New Jerusalem Church; and he had read some of the major critics of Swedenborgianism, certainly Kant and probably Wesley and Priestley.[12] He shared the common prejudices of his day and age and church against Swedenborg, as we can see by a couple of throwaway remarks made at some distance before and after his period of sympathetic engagement in the early 1820s. In a lecture of 1808 he referred to 'Mahometanism which is only an anomalous corruption of Christianity, like Swedenborgianism', and in a notebook entry of 1833 about the meaning of the Old Testament prophecies he asks, 'May we dare hope for a *sane* Swedenborg?'[13] It seems that his unguarded opinion, to the end of his life, was that Swedenborg was in some sense mad, and that the Church founded in his name was misguided. In 1826, describing Tulk for the benefit of another friend who was about to meet him, he expressed his pleasure in the fact that Tulk was a non-sectarian Swedenborgian who chose, like other leaders of the movement from the early years and like Swedenborg himself, to remain a member of the established Church.[14] But Coleridge vacillated between trying to conform to contemporary society, and to reform it. Attacked for obscurity and Germanic mysticism himself, he was cautious about having his name publicly connected with the Swedenborgians and avoided any positive endorsement in his published works.[15]

On the other hand, in a strange sequence of notebook entries dating from very early in Coleridge's career, a series that includes recipes, addresses, extracts from books, noteworthy jokes, and ideas for new poems and publishing projects, we encounter 'Mem. To reduce to a regular form the Swedenborgian's Reveries'.[16] (Not Swedenborg's, but the Swedenborgian's.) It is impossible to say exactly what Coleridge can have had in mind; the immediate context of the notebooks offers no help. But the idea, however sketchy, would be consistent with Coleridge's lifelong interest in dreams and dreamlike states, his conviction that they were meaningful, and his efforts to 'reduce' them to an intelligible order. If at one level of thought he was disposed to downplay the effect of Swedenborg's visions, at another he was aware of their power. Some of the latest references to Swedenborg in his letters and notebooks are allusions to those parts of *Heaven and Hell* (probably §§576-88) that describe the plurality of hells and of demons. Coleridge ruefully imagines gastric devils in his own insides, bringing him terrible dreams——'a woeful passage for me that in the Honorable Baron's Visa et Audita: for it has haunted me ever since I first read it, and *in my Sleep* I believe or at least take it for granted'.[17] The imagery of *Heaven and Hell* evidently had a lasting effect even if its doctrine did not; and this is ironic given Coleridge's conscious reservations about the imagery and his intuitive receptivity to the doctrine.

Another image that Coleridge found particularly resonant, that is associated with a warm tribute to Swedenborg and that may therefore have been prompted by *Conjugial Love* although it also has solid Platonic credentials, is the image of the androgyne, which occurs in a passage in the *Notebooks* that Virginia Woolf later made famous. Coleridge is observing that great minds often go together with unassertive manners:

> The truth is, a great mind must be *androgyne*. Great minds (Swedenborg's for instance) never wrong but in consequence of being in the right——tho' imperfectly. Such was the case with his adherence to the mechanic philosophy, even to the last——as in his notion of the human Will being placed in the *punct*[*um*] *indifferentiae* between the Heavens & the Hells——[18]

Thus Swedenborg may have contributed obliquely, through Coleridge, to the formation of a controversial concept of modern feminism.

In order to disentangle the various strands of Coleridge's ambivalent response, it is necessary to consider his comments on Swedenborg in relation to his philosophy at large. In the 1820s he was trying to work out a comprehensive philosophical system to combat what he saw as the prevailing complacent materialism of his time. He aimed to incorporate whatever was valid from other systems, going by the Leibnizian axiom that most parties in philosophy have some apprehension of the truth, and that a 'true philosophy' would 'collect the fragments of truth scattered through systems apparently the most incongruous'.[19] Another mantra for him, however, was that a partial truth could do as much damage as outright falsehood. In the *Lay Sermons* of 1816 he had declared that 'If we are a christian nation, we must learn to act nationally, as well as individually, as Christians. We must remove half-truths, the most dangerous of errors...by the whole Truth'.[20] So as he read Swedenborg, he struggled to separate wheat from chaff, in order to adopt or adapt what was valuable in a more nearly perfect philosophical whole.

Reading Swedenborg for effectively the first time, Coleridge was struck by the affinities between Swedenborg's ideas and values and those of other eminent but marginalized thinkers in an idealist and mystical tradition that extended from Plato to Schelling. Where we might be inclined to see common sources and influences, Coleridge believed he was seeing recurrent glimpses, scattered fragments as he would say, of an ultimate truth, confirmed by their reappearance in writers and visionaries remote from one another in time or place—indeed, the more remote the better. Singularity was no recommendation. Coleridge likened Swedenborg to a distinguished and, on the face of it, discordant host: to Plotinus, Porphyry, Augustine, Aquinas, Duns Scotus, Luther, Pico della Mirandola, Giordano Bruno, Boehme, George Fox, Spinoza, and recent German philosophers of nature— Schelling, Schubert, and Eschenmayer. What do they have in common? Well, not much—or rather, no one thing, but a family resemblance. Some of them were system-makers, some interpreters, some millenarians, some visionaries. Some of them advocated a new way of reading the Bible; some declared the humanity of God and the divinity of humanity; some taught the immateriality of the natural world and the reality of the spiritual world. Most of them were misfits either in their own time or in the world that Coleridge knew, and he revered them as heroic representatives of an alternative world view even though he thought their formulations were incomplete or otherwise flawed. In *Biographia Literaria*, published just before he met Tulk, he had eloquently attacked the prejudice against 'enthusiasts' like Fox and Boehme, and gratefully acknowledged their role in his own intellectual development: 'they contrived', he said, 'to keep alive the *heart* in the *head*'.[21] Coleridge kept a little list of 'revolutionary minds' that he wanted to write about in a 'Vindication of great men unjustly branded', and Swedenborg's name was soon added to it.[22]

Coleridge found much to admire in Swedenborg as a fellow warrior in the battle against philosophical materialism. On key topics he seemed to be on the right side, his insights strengthened, to Coleridge's mind, by their appearing to coincide with and thus to confirm the formulations of figures such as Plotinus, Augustine, Luther, and Boehme (which in turn acted to confirm his). He admired the coherence and comprehensiveness of the system itself, which explained the external, natural world as a product of the internal world of spirit. He acknowledged that Swedenborg's science was ahead of its time and that 'Much of what is most valuable in the physiosophic works of Schelling, Schubert, and Eschenmayer is to be found anticipated in this supposed *Dementato*'.[23] He thought that along with Luther and the Moravians, Swedenborg had got the crucial doctrine of the Logos right: the Logos was to be sought and found in 'the divine Humanity'.[24] He noted affinities between Swedenborg's three worlds and the threefold vision of Augustine and the Neoplatonists:

Augustine teaches the same doctrine as Swedenborg: there can be but three essentially different Genera of Being—Divine, Human, and Bestial. And Reason says the same/ The absolute rational, the finite Rational, and the

Irrational—or 1. the Absolute. 2. the rational Finite. 3. the irrational Finite. God, Man, and nature exhaust our conception.[25]

He applauded the Doctrine of Correspondences and the project of interpreting the Bible in a consistently spiritual sense. In a notebook entry of 1827 concerned chiefly with the prophetic books of the Old Testament and their relationship to Christian doctrine, he rather wistfully raised the possibility of an unbroken but unwritten tradition of interpretation in 'an interior and spiritual sense [...] still discoverable by a spiritual Light', which he said he would seize on if he could only 'be sure, it was more than an Opinion./The invidious epithets of Swedenborgian and Cabalistic, would not frighten me'.[26]

But Swedenborg also in many ways made Coleridge very uneasy and no positive comment comes without reservations. There were serious divergences between them on certain theological issues: Swedenborg, for instance, firmly rejected the doctrine of the Trinity of persons. Coleridge was still more at odds with Swedenborg's New Church followers, whom he accused of being materialists at heart: 'the Letter hideth the spirit from them. As they read, so they believe—both with the eyes of the body [...] For such men it is either literal or metaphorical. There is no third. For to the *Symbolical* they have not arrived'.[27] But the most important differences between him and Swedenborg were not isolated but systemic, and the root of Coleridge's objections was the way that the Swedenborgian system depended on Swedenborg's visions of angels. It was not that he took Swedenborg for a charlatan or fantasist or madman, as many of his contemporaries did. He never doubted that Swedenborg had had the experiences he described. But since his visions could not be corroborated by any second witness or any further evidence, there was the distinct risk that they might be altogether subjective and idiosyncratic. Comparing the visions of Swedenborg with the vision that converted St Paul, Coleridge pointed out that in Paul's case, there had been objective evidence in the form of a miracle in addition to his subjective experience: 'N.B. Not every revelation requires a sensible Miracle as the credential—but every Revelation of a *new* series of Credenda [does]'.[28] Worse, by representing the spirit world in distinctly physical terms, Swedenborg's account seemed to contradict itself: what could be seen and heard, if not held and touched, was not immaterial enough for Coleridge. Such appeals to the senses, he thought, were liable to lead to idolatry and pantheism.[29]

Coleridge tried by various means to salvage Swedenborg's 'meaning', which was 'truth', from the humanly flawed form in which it was embodied. His interpretative strategies can be seen most clearly in marginalia to three Swedenborgian books, the Latin copy of *Heaven and Hell* (*De Coelo...et de inferno, ex auditis et visis*); *The True Christian Religion*; and Samuel Noble's 1826 defence of the New Church, *An Appeal in behalf of the Views of the Eternal World and State,* [etc.]. (Though these books were his own property, Coleridge's library circulated freely and he knew other people would see the marginalia. He made a diplomatic effort to soften the criticism in one set of notes by observing, for the sake of 'any other eyes, but my own' that might see them, that his disagreement could well be no more than a misunderstanding arising from the lack of definitions of key terms.) [30] In his notes, Coleridge paid Swedenborg the tribute of subjecting his work to the kinds of tests that biblical scholarship was then applying to the 'inspired' writings of the Old and New Testaments. Were they internally consistent? Were they susceptible of a symbolical as well as a literal reading? Were they in harmony with the rest of the canon? How were essential doctrines to be purged of the accidental details of historical and cultural context?

On the vexed question of the visions themselves, Coleridge tried out a number of approaches. He found a ready physiological explanation for Swedenborg's experiences in new theories of mesmerism (also known as animal magnetism or zoomagnetism) which would not have been available in Swedenborg's day. Using mesmeric terminology, Coleridge repeatedly describes Swedenborg as a 'clairvoyant' or 'somnambulist'.[31] The same or a similarly rare organic condition might account, he thought, for the *forms taken* by the quite different visions of other mystics. Believers were not obliged to accept the form along with the substance of the belief. The angelic figures could therefore be dispensed with as idiosyncratic elements in the system—they were, as Coleridge puts it, not objectively subjective but individually subjective.[32] Instead of 'regarding the System as the Relation of actual Travels', therefore, the respectful reader 'would receive it as the Account of a Series of allegorical in part & in part symbolical Visions, some of which the gifted Seer had misinterpreted'.[33] It may be some mitigation of Coleridge's presumptuousness (maintaining that Swedenborg did not know what he was saying while he, Coleridge, did) to remember that he would have said the same of the prophets of the Old Testament and the Evangelists of the New, and would expect to have it said of himself by more advanced thinkers in the course of time.

Even if the physiological explanation were not correct, and Swedenborg's visions were genuine supernatural visitations, still acceptance of the truth of the whole system of belief must depend, Coleridge pointed out, on its compatibility with 'the Light of the Eternal and of the Written Word—i.e. with the Scriptures and with the sciential and the practical Reason'.[34] It had to be systematic (logically consistent) and scripturally sound. Coleridge complained that the system was not internally coherent and not immaterial enough, but when he tried to dematerialize it and to make it coherent, he tended to produce unappealing paraphrases, starting off with a formula such as 'Now if I understand Sw. aright, he means'.[35] For the concrete particulars of Swedenborg's vivid encounters with God and the angels, for example, Coleridge substituted abstract propositions:

> The Transgression consists not in the sort of Image, nor whether one Image or three, but in presenting any image at all, either to the bodily or mental Eye [...] All therefore [that] Swedenborg meant or could mean, is this—Suppose for a moment what is not however the possible subject of a rational Supposition, that the Deity could *appear totally*, or indeed *appear* at all as God—then it would be deducible [...] that the Deity would appear in the Human Form.[36]

Coleridge plainly struggled to translate the details of Swedenborg's system of belief into terms compatible with one that he found more inclusive and more universally applicable. He wanted Swedenborg's work to be less naturalistic and more rigorous, to bring it into line with what he regarded as the best thought from Plato to Kant. He thought it would benefit from a regular appeal to first principles, and from a stricter definition of terms.[37] But then the system would no longer be Swedenborg's, as becomes strikingly evident when Coleridge claims that Swedenborg could not have meant what he said about the doctrine of justification by faith, and has to override Swedenborg's explicit rejection in order to reconcile his thinking with that of Luther and 'the Founders & Fathers of the Church of Christ in England'.[38] In a well-meant, for the period broad-minded, but ultimately patronizing way, Coleridge tried to make Swedenborg over as a systematic philosopher, one of the special set of '*Christian* Philosophers' to which he declared he and Tulk belonged.[39]

Coleridge had a history of keen engagement with one new friend after another, most of these relationships going up in smoke sooner or later, vanishing altogether or leaving only a charred shell to go on with. Southey and Wordsworth are the classic cases. But a few faithful figures, perhaps less competitive or more easy-going in the first place, survived the flames. Lamb, Green and Gillman belonged to this group, and so did Tulk. He was certainly hurt by Coleridge's neglect of him after his wife's death, but they patched things up and continued to see one another. I venture to suggest that something of the same kind happened in Coleridge's relationships with books and ideas, and that the experience of enthusiasm followed by difficulties and disenchantment is not uncommon among us. Coleridge and Tulk knew what they could count on from one another; Coleridge in the end kept Swedenborg at a respectful distance. Still, a new opportunity could bring out a considered tribute, as in Coleridge's last note to Noble's *Appeal*, in 1827:

> I can venture to assert, that as a *moralist*, Swedenborg is above all praise; and that as a Naturalist, Psychologist, and Theologian he has strong and

varied claims on the gratitude and admiration of the professional and philosophical Faculties.[40]

NOTES

1   S T Coleridge, *Letters*, ed. Earl Leslie Griggs (Oxford: Clarendon Press, 1956-71), vol. V, p. 136.

2   e.g., S T Coleridge, *Marginalia*, ed. H J Jackson and George Whalley (Princeton: Princeton University Press, 1980-2001), vol. V, pp. 427, 444.

3   The manuscript that they produced between them, the *Opus Maximum*, has just been published (2002) as the final volume of the standard edition of Coleridge's *Collected Works*. Green's version of their system was published shortly after his death as *Spiritual Philosophy*, a title tellingly close to that of Tulk's magnum opus, *Spiritual Christianity*.

4   Coleridge, *Letters*, vol. V, p. 420.

5   Ibid., vol. IV, pp. 841-4, 883-4, 914-15; vol. V, pp. 281-4, 291-3; vol. VI, pp. 605-20. Both sets of negotiations were ultimately unsuccessful.

6   Ibid., vol. IV, pp. 767-76, 804-9.

7   Ibid., vol. IV, pp. 835-8, 883-4.

8   Ibid., vol. V, p. 19.

9   Ibid., vol. V, p. 17; *Marginalia*, vol. V, p. 410.

10   Society for Printing and Publishing the Writings of The Hon. Emanuel Swedenborg, *Report of the Eighth Annual Meeting* (London, 1817), p. 7.

11   Coleridge, *Letters*, vol. V, pp. 174-5, 284, 327, 89 n. The published minutes of the 1825 annual meeting, however, contain no reference to this offer.

12   There exist three copies of Kant's *Vermischte Schriften* annotated by Coleridge, all with notes on Kant's attack on Swedenborg, *Träume eines Geistersehers*: Coleridge, *Marginalia*, vol. III, pp. 317, 333, 350-3. (His last word on Kant's opinion, in a note of about 1824, is a very strange psychological interpretation which accounts for Kant's vehemence by supposing that he had been at first impressed by Swedenborg

and inclined to believe in him, but subsequently disappointed in his works—an idea for which there is no external validation or corroboration of any kind, and which appears to be a projection of Coleridge's own experience.) As a young man Coleridge had been a great admirer of Priestley and followed his theological debates closely. If he did not actually read his 1791 *Letter to the New Jerusalem Church*, he must have known it by report: his sense of the issues raised by Swedenborg and the way to approach them matches Priestley's point by point. Wesley dismissed Swedenborg as a madman, as Coleridge could have known from his *Journal* or from various biographies that appeared after Wesley's death in 1791.

[13] Coleridge, *Lectures 1808-1819 on Literature*, ed. R A Foakes (Princeton: Princeton University Press, 1987), vol. I, p. 53; and *Notebooks*, ed. Kathleen Coburn and Anthony John Harding (Princeton: Princeton University Press, 1957-2002), vol. V, no. 6764.

[14] Coleridge, *Letters*, vol. VI, pp. 583-4.

[15] Ibid., vol. V, p. 284. He was plainly nettled by a review of December 1820 that associated him with Boehme and Swedenborg, i.e., in the opinion of the reviewer, with incomprehensible mystics: *Letters*, vol. V, p. 125. In the 1818 revised edition of *The Friend* he had offered a hedged or backhanded compliment—about as close as he ever came to public endorsement. There he says that in any system of belief that becomes widely diffused there is bound to be a measure of truth. Even of such apparently far-fetched ideas as the doctrine 'of a latent mystical sense in the words of Scripture and the works of nature, according to Emanuel Swedenborg', which might well be 'a distorted and dangerous, as well as partial, representation of the truth, on which it is founded [...] I dare, and do, affirm that it always does shadow out some important truth': *The Friend*, ed. Barbara Rooke (Princeton: Princeton University Press, 1969), vol. I, p. 430.

[16] Coleridge, *Notebooks*, vol. I, no. 165 (dated 1796).

[17] Ibid., vol. V, no. 5640 (1827). See also *Notebooks*, vol. IV, p. 5460; *Letters*, vol. V, pp. 216, 388, 489, and vol. VI, p. 607.

[18] Coleridge, *Notebooks*, vol. IV, no. 4705. Virginia Woolf refers to the passage in *A Room of One's Own* (London: Grafton, 1977; repr 1987), pp. 93-4.

[19] Coleridge, *Biographia Literaria*, ed. James Engell and W Jackson Bate (Princeton: Princeton University Press, 1983), vol. I, pp. 247, 244.

[20] Coleridge, *Lay Sermons*, ed. R J White (Princeton: Princeton University Press, 1972), p. 288.

[21] Coleridge, *Biographia Literaria*, vol. I, p. 152. An important related passage appears in *Shorter Works and Fragments*, ed. H J Jackson and J R de J Jackson (Princeton: Princeton University Press, 1995), vol. II, pp. 829-30.

[22] Coleridge, *Marginalia*, vol. III, pp. 990-1; also *Shorter Works and Fragments*, vol. I, p. 770.

[23] Coleridge, *Marginalia*, vol. V, p. 427.

[24] Coleridge, *Notebooks*, vol. IV, p. 4671.

[25] Coleridge, *Marginalia*, vol. III, p. 985.

[26] Coleridge, *Notebooks*, vol. V, no. 5667.

[27] Coleridge, *Letters*, vol. V, p. 91.

[28] Coleridge, *Marginalia*, vol. V, p. 987.

[29] Ibid., vol. V, p. 406.

[30] Ibid., vol. V, p. 409.

[31] e.g., in *Marginalia*, vol. III, p. 353; vol. V, p. 467; *Notebooks*, vol. IV, no. 4908 fol. 68.

[32] Coleridge, *Marginalia*, vol. V, p. 465.

[33] Ibid., vol. V, p. 413.

[34] Ibid., vol. III, p. 991.

[35] Ibid., vol. V, p. 410.

[36] Ibid., vol. V, p. 406.

[37] Ibid., vol. V, pp. 405, 409, 418.

[38] Ibid., vol. V, pp. 466-7.

[39] Coleridge, *Letters*, vol. IV, p. 809.

[40] Coleridge, *Marginalia*, vol. III, p. 992.

Swedenborgian simile in Emersonian edification

Anders Hallengren

C onsider a scene from an assembly in uproar. In vivid figurative language, the eloquent speaker accuses leading politicians, officials, business persons and other upper-class people of high ranking, of corruption and baseness. Tables are turned. The moment is a period of internal struggle and war. The future of the nation is at stake. Civilization itself seems to be endangered, and progress is topsy-turvy. Wherever you are, and in whatever direction your thoughts may go, it is easy to recognize the incident as well as the setting. In this particular historical case—Emerson addressing America in Civil War times and during the era of Reconstruction—we will pay special attention to the revolutionary language used by the dismayed orator, who in plain speaking asseverates a home truth.

The upright and the upside down

In his lecture on American Civilization, 'Civilization at a Pinch', delivered in Boston in 1861 just after the outbreak of the war, and read again in Washington in January the following year, Emerson opens with a central Swedenborg doctrine: 'Use, labor of each for all, is the health and virtue of all beings'. In this spirit Emerson attacks the 'conspiracy of slavery' [...] called 'an institution. I call it destitution, this stealing of men and setting them to work, stealing their labor, and the thief sitting idle himself'.[1]

In his address on 'Progress of Culture', read before the Phi Beta Kappa Society at Cambridge in 1867, Emerson emphasizes that 'great thoughts come from the heart' and that 'piety is an essential condition of science', mentioning Swedenborg as an example, and a model of both.

Likewise in politics. Challenging the immorality of American public servants, he states:

> We have suffered our young men of ambition to play the game of politics and take the immoral side without loss of caste,——to come and go without rebuke. But that kind of loose association does not leave a man his own master. He cannot go from the good to the evil at pleasure, and then back again to the good. There is a text in Swedenborg which tells in figure the plain truth. He saw in vision the angels and the devils; but these two companies stood not face to face and hand in hand, but foot to foot,——these perpendicular up, and those perpendicular down.[2]

This scene illustrates the exact opposite between right and wrong, good and evil.

Swedenborg repeatedly points out that hell is built on earth, and in the next life is the abode of people who feel at home there. In his reports from the intermediary spiritual world, he observes that purposefully choosing evil is like jumping headlong, throwing oneself vertically (*perpendiculariter*) down.[3]

How is this to be understood? A *memorabile* in Swedenborg's book on the Apocalypse, *The Apocalypse Revealed* is particularly instructive,[4] since it is also repeated in his concluding theological testament, *The True Christian Religion*.[5] There he tells us how faithful people can be like dragons compared to others who believe that love is primary, belief secondary. In a spirited discussion, a representative of the latter clarifies Swedenborg's view. The relation between truth and love is as that between light and its source. If you think you can have light (insight, illumination, truth), which is secondary, before you have the source (neighbourly love, *charitas*, warmth), which is primary, you will look like someone turned upside down, with feet up and head down, or like an acrobat who walks on his hands. That is an inverted attitude. Without good works, you cannot get access to the truths of faith.

In the book on *Heaven and its Wonders, and Hell*, another book carefully read by Emerson with pen in his hand, Swedenborg explains how evil souls freely and naturally chose the reversed state since they are bent for the lower.[6] When they throw themselves down into hell from the spiritual world, they appear to fall 'backward headfirst. The reason it looks like this is that such people are in an inverted order'.[7]

The art of the genuine

In 'Being and Seeming' (1838), Emerson tells us about an experienced counsellor (Samuel Hoar) who he has heard saying, that he

> feared never for the effect upon a jury of a lawyer who does not believe in his heart that his client ought to have a verdict [...] This is that law (is it not?) whereby a work of art, of whatever kind, sets us in the same state of mind as the artist was when he made it. That which we do not believe we cannot adequately say, though we may repeat the words never so often. It was this conviction which Swedenborg expressed when he described a group of persons in the spiritual world endeavoring in vain to articulate a proposition which they did not believe, but they could not, though they twisted and folded their lips even to indignation. But say what you believe and feel, and the voluble air will become music and all surrounding things will dance attendance and coin themselves into words for sense. Every word shall be sovereign, noble, and new, and full of matchless felicities. [...] Truth always overpowers the poor nature of a deceiver [...] Trust *being* and let us seem no longer.[8]

In 'Spiritual Laws', in the first series of *Essays* (1841), Swedenborg's narrative reappears in support of Emerson's belief, that when one 'speaks the truth in the spirit of truth', the eye 'is as clear as the heavens'. The world is 'full of judgement-days', and a man passes for what he is worth. Emerson had arrived at a bright view of man and his world. He is of the opinion that truth is always advantageous, because the world is just. Furthermore, he is certain that everyone can do something better than anyone else. This is the highest benefit of self-trust: to find and fulfil one's object in life. But, as much 'virtue as there is, so much appears; as much goodness as there is, so much reverence it commands'. Man's actual success in his efforts is according to what he is worth: according to the amount of truth and goodness he has in him.

Emerson thus was struck by Swedenborg's memorable relation on the inability of angels to lie, to utter what they do not believe, contained both in *The Apocalypse Revealed*, and in *The True Christian Religion*. [9] He later bought and read the latter work in the translation published in Boston 1847. [10] More important, he secured the former work for his library, in the translation dated Boston 1836, announced in the *New Jerusalem Magazine* in October 1835, and it seems to have occupied him in early 1836. [11] His intense interest can be judged from the fact that a student who was later to become his best-informed critic among New Churchmen, the famous Benjamin Fiske Barrett, was originally introduced by Emerson to Swedenborg: Emerson advised Barrett to check out *The Apocalypse Revealed* from the Harvard College library! [12]

The relation found in that book on angels who 'distorted and folded their lips in many ways but could not articulate any other words than such as were consonant with the ideas of their thought', exceedingly attracted Emerson. [13] He quoted it several times. The way he interpreted and used this memorable relation is important: it apparently supported his concepts of the nature of Truth, of Eloquence, of Self-reliance, and of Beauty. It also explains his own imagery. Emerson thought the days of the pilgrims, the days of the founding fathers, were a season of eternal spring, like the Golden Age: 'Massachusetts, in its heroic day, had no government—was an anarchy. Every man stood on his feet'. [14]

Virtue and artistry

In Emerson's outlook there is a strong link between ethics and aesthetics. They are different sides of the same thing. Rightness or accuracy, and the accordance with natural and spiritual laws, is the essence of both.

In his influential 'American Scholar Address' (1837), Emerson called attention to Swedenborg's *literary* value. In this pioneering Cambridge oration, where he put forth a philosophy of life for the New World, he said:

> There is one man of genius who has done much for this philosophy of life, whose literary value has never been rightly estimated;—I mean Emanuel Swedenborg. The most imaginative of men, yet writing with the precision of a mathematician, he endeavoured to engraft a purely philosophical Ethics on the popular Christianity of his time. Such an attempt of course must have difficulty which no genius could surmount. But he saw and showed the connection between nature and the affections of the soul. He pierced the emblematic or spiritual character of the visible, tangible world. Especially did his shade-loving muse hover over and interpret the lower parts of nature; he showed the mysterious bond that allies moral evil to the foul material forms, and has given in epical parables a theory of insanity, of beasts, of unclean and fearful things. [15]

What is the secret of this power of imagination and the emblematic, then? In 'Poetry and Imagination', Emerson explains that the very design of imagination is 'to domesticate us' in 'a celestial nature'. [16] Therefore Emerson praises the symbol as the way of understanding, and time and again stresses its power of clarifying. 'This power is in the image because this power is in Nature. It so affects, because it so is. All that is wondrous in Swedenborg is not his invention, but his extraordinary perception;—that he was necessitated to see', and there are several quotes from Swedenborg in that important aesthetic essay.

Analogously, in his essay on 'Immortality' (1875), Emerson extols Swedenborg's moral perception, his *second sight*, and the realism of his narratives:

> The most remarkable step in the religious history of recent ages is that made by the genius of Swedenborg, who described the moral faculties and affections of man, with the hard realism of an astronomer describing the suns and planets of our system, and explained his opinion of the history and destiny of souls in a narrative form, as of one who had gone in trance into the society of other worlds. Swedenborg described an intelligible heaven, by continuing the like employments in the like circumstances as those we know; men in societies, houses, towns, trades, entertainments; continuations of our earthly experience. We shall pass to the future existence as we enter into an agreeable dream. All nature will accompany us there. [17]

In this spirit Swedenborg appears as both a bard and a lawgiver: Emerson, like Coleridge, and Baudelaire, recognized Swedenborg as a great poet. In Emerson's early lecture on 'The Poet', Swedenborg's writings were referred to as 'prose poems'. [18] Still, the 'moral insight of Swedenborg, the correction of popular errors, the announcement of ethical laws, take him out of comparison with any other modern writer and entitle him to a place, vacant for some ages, among the lawgivers of mankind'. [19] What is the connection, then? Emerson at once spells out: 'We have come into a world which is a living poem'. [20] Thus realism and imagination may combine and conflow.

Himself turning to the poetic idiom, Emerson lyrically approaches Swedenborg's significance in the poem 'Solution', published in *May-Day and Other Poems* (1867):

> Far in the North, where polar night
> Holds in check the frolic light,

In trance upborne past mortal goal
The Swede EMANUEL leads the soul.
Through snows above, mines underground,
The inks of Erebus he found;
Rehearsed to men the damned wails
On which the seraph music sails.
In spirit-worlds he trod alone,
But walked the earth unmarked, unknown.
The near bystander caught no sound,—
Yet they who listened far aloof
Heard rendings of the skyey roof,
And felt, beneath, the quaking ground;
And his air-sown, unheeded words,
In the next age, are flaming swords.

This is another way of expressing the currency and topicality of the mystic's strange wisdom, which Emerson pointed out in his programmatic 'Editor's Address', printed in *Massachusetts Quarterly Review* in December 1847:

> There are literary and philosophical reputations to settle. The name of Swedenborg has in this very time acquired new honors, and the current year has witnessed the appearance, in their first English translation, of his manuscripts. Here is an unsettled account in the book of Fame; a nebula to dim eyes, but which great telescopes may yet resolve into a system.[21]

Here, much remains to be done. Today, the editor of the present volume assumably agrees to this point, and, from a scholarly point of view, there are still ample reasons for doing so. [22]

NOTES

1 R W Emerson, *Miscellanies* (Boston and New York: Houghton, Mifflin, 1904), p. 297. To Emerson, 'use' has always a spiritual and moral meaning. Swedenborg's Doctrine of Uses was probably a doctrine that Emerson accepted in full, as I have shown elsewhere: *The Code of Concord* (Stockholm: Almqvist & Wiksell, 1994), ch. 'Uses, Utility, and Utilitarianism'; *Gallery of Mirrors* (West Chester: Swedenborg Foundation, 1998), ch. 'An American Philosophy of Use'.

2 Emerson, *Letters and Social Aims* (Boston and New York: Houghton, Mifflin, 1875); *The Complete Works of Ralph Waldo Emerson* (Boston and New York: Houghton, Mifflin, 1904), vol. VIII, p. 233 (henceforth cited as *W*).

3 Emanuel Swedenborg, *The Spiritual Diary* (London: Swedenborg Society, 2002), §2831.

4 Swedenborg, *The Apocalypse Revealed* (London: J S Hodson, 1832), §655.

5 Swedenborg, *The True Christian Religion* (Boston, 1843), §388.

6 Swedenborg, *Heaven and its Wonders, and also Concerning Hell* (London, 1823), §§510 f., 548.

7 Ibid., §510.

8 Emerson, *Early Lectures*, vol. II, pp. 300 f. (henceforth cited as *EL*); *Journals and Miscellaneous Notebooks*, vol. V, p. 396 (henceforth cited as *JMN*).

9 Emerson, *JMN*, vol. IV, p. 343. He often returned to this passage. See *The Apocalypse Revealed*, §294 and *The True Christian Religion*, §111.

10 An indication of earlier cognizance of this work: *JMN*, vol. V, p. 7.

11 Emerson, *MN*, vol. V, pp. 115 f., 168, 397. The pencil marks in Emerson's copy in the Houghton Library, compared with the earliest excerpts, show that at least the first volume was read before *Nature* (1836) was published.

12 B F Barrett, *Autobiography* (Philadelphia: Swedenborg Publishing Association, 1890), pp. 54-5.

13 Emanuel Swedenborg, *The Apocalypse Revealed*, vol. I., §294, pp. 254-5; p. 255 marked in Emerson's copy.

14 Emerson, 'Speech on the Affair in Kansas', in *W*, vol. XI, pp. 261 f.

15 Emerson, *W*, vol. I, pp. 112-13.

[16] Emerson, *Letters and Social Aims* (1875).

[17] Emerson, *W*, vol. VIII, p. 327.

[18] Emerson, *EL*, vol. III, p. 361.

[19] Emerson, *Representative Men* (London, 1850).

[20] Emerson, *W*, vol. IV, pp. 115 f.

[21] Emerson, *Miscellanies*, p. 391.

[22] Books by Emanuel Swedenborg in Emerson's extant library, now stored in Houghton Library, Harvard, and in the Concord Antiquarian Museum: *The Animal Kingdom*, vols. I-II (London: Newbery, 1843-4); *Angelic Wisdom Concerning the Divine Love and the Divine Wisdom* (Boston: Freeman and Bolles, 1847); *The Apocalypse Revealed*, vols. I-III (London, 1832; Boston 1836); *The Delights of Wisdom Concerning Conjugial Love* (Boston: Carter & Clapp, 1843); *The Economy of the Animal Kingdom* (London: Newbery, 1845-6); *Heavenly Arcana*, vols. I-XII (Boston, 1837-47); *On the Intercourse between the Soul and the Body* (Boston: A Howard, 1828); *Opuscula*, ed. J J G Wilkinson, (London: Newbery, 1846); *The Principia,* vols I-II (London and Boston, 1845-6); *A Treatise Concerning Heaven and its Wonders, and also Concerning Hell* (London: T Goyder, 1823); *The True Christian Religion* (Boston, 1843).

Swedenborg, existentialism and the active life

Gary Lachman

In writing my book, *Discovering Swedenborg*,[1] one aspect of Swedenborg's work that I was happy to reacquaint myself with, but which for sheer constraints of space I could only touch on, is what we might call Swedenborg's 'philosophy of life', his moral and ethical teachings, even what we might call his 'existentialism'. Now existentialism is not a word we usually associate with Swedenborg. We generally associate it with the writers and thinkers Jean Paul Sartre and Albert Camus, with Paris in the 1950s and the Left Bank, with Gauloises, berets, and café noir, and with a bleak, even nihilistic view of the world. But existentialism has a broader application, and in general it relates to questions about the meaning of life, and, more immediately, how we are to live now that we find ourselves here, in this strange place, without a Rough Guide. Existentialists live, generally, in Camus' phrase, 'without appeal'[2]—without appeal, that is, to a world other than this one, and without appeal to any god, or spiritual or supernatural agency. And this, clearly, is rather the opposite from Swedenborg.

Yet Swedenborg himself was very concerned about this world. Not only for the reason that it is our choices in this world that determine our life in the next—an idea that is not uncommon in other teachings, as in Eastern ideas about karma and reincarnation—but also because he recognized that our life in this world was important in itself, and that there is meaning, significance and value to be experienced and achieved here and now. It is this 'here and now' that I am interested in exploring.

Now, one of the ways in which Swedenborg's teachings share similarities with existentialism is in his ideas about the relation between knowledge and action. The existentialists have no use for 'abstract knowledge', and this is true also of thinkers who came before them and who are not usually associated with them. Knowledge that does not give us some help in dealing with the question of how to live—the choices we should make, the decisions we should take, finding ourselves 'here and now'—was useless to them. Søren Kierkegaard expressed this in his remarks about the philosophy of Hegel. Hegel's vast, metaphysical system, which includes all history and existence, and deals with abstract ideas about consciousness and the unfolding of spirit through human history, could offer no help to the unique, problematic being, Kierkegaard, who finds himself suddenly in this strange alien world, without a guide or set of instructions. Kierkegaard says that trying to orient your life using Hegel's philosophy, is like trying to find your way around Copenhagen using a map of the world, or a map so large that Copenhagen itself is only about the size of a postage stamp on it. [3] The vast, cosmic picture is there, but it is useless if I want to know how to get from the train station to my hotel. Now Swedenborg, it strikes me, is very existential when he says of his angels that they can only have knowledge about that which they can act on. As Johann Wolfgang von Goethe, who I would include among the 'other' existentialists, and who was a reader of Swedenborg, would say sometime after Swedenborg, and which seems to apply to the latter's angels: 'I hate everything that merely instructs me without augmenting or directly invigorating my activity'. [4] And I may point out that some years ago I wrote an article entitled 'Too Much Information?' dealing with the benefits and drawbacks of living in our supposed 'information age', drawing on Goethe's concern. If we set aside that Kierkegaard and the later existentialists, like Sartre and Camus, had a somewhat darker vision of life than Swedenborg's, we can see that their ideas about the relation between knowledge and action are rather similar.

everything can
use.

This, I think, is related to Swedenborg's doctrine of 'uses'. Everyone, everything, has his, her or its 'use'.[5] Even angels. This is a remarkably pragmatic view of things, a kind of spiritual utilitarianism. For us, though, I think the term 'use' can carry some unwelcome connotations. The idea of 'using' someone, for whatever noble or spiritual aim, is dubious. That is why I think 'purpose' might be a better choice. Finding one's purpose, one's vocation, one's calling is, in a way, finding one's use, but it strikes me that 'purpose', 'vocation' or 'calling' have connotations of a kind of activity on one's part, that 'use' seems to lack. Even so, the idea of 'finding' your purpose is still somewhat passive, as if it is lying around somewhere and you might by chance just come across it. The German philosopher Friedrich Nietzsche, who is not usually spoken of in connection with Swedenborg—but who was a reader of Goethe—makes a remark that is relevant here, I think. In his early book *Human, All Too Human*, Nietzsche writes, apropos of the Socratic dictum to 'know thyself' that 'Active, successful natures act, not according to the dictum "know thyself", but as if there hovered before them the commandment: *will* a self and thou shalt *become* a self. Fate seems to have left the choice still up to them; whereas the inactive and contemplative cogitate on what they *have* already chosen, on *one* occasion, when they entered into life'.[6]

Nietzsche, putting aside all the huge differences between his radically 'earthly' philosophy and Swedenborg's heavenly one, shares with Swedenborg an appreciation of what we may call 'the active life'. And again, this is something he shares with existentialist thought. Nietzsche is stressing the creative element in our lives, the idea that being a 'self' is an activity. A 'self' is something we *do*, something we make, not something we simply find and know. I cannot know my self without being that self, and that 'being' is not a static state, but an activity. One of Sartre's most important ideas is that of 'bad faith'.[7] This is when, in order to avoid the risks and dangers of freedom—of choosing how to live here and now—one instead accepts some role handed out to you, either by society, your friends, your parents, wife, husband, or even, as Nietzsche remarks on, some past idea of your self. Freedom, for Sartre, is something most people want to avoid——it is, in fact, a kind of 'hole' in life that we often hurry to 'fill' with some ready-made role or belief, much as many people cannot bear silence and feel the need to start talking whenever there is an awkward 'gap' in a conversation. And it might be of interest to note a very influential book of some years ago, *Escape From Freedom*, by the psychologist Erich Fromm, which is a variation on Sartre's theme. [8] The pressure to adhere to a role or self that one has previously adopted can be very great, and often it is our own laziness to do otherwise that keeps us fixed in place. In a novel by the writer L H Myers, who was on the margins of the Bloomsbury Set and was the son of Frederic Myers, one of the founders of the Society for Psychical Research, there is a passage which spells this out with great clarity. In *The Orissers*, published in 1922, Myers writes:

> In the conduct of everyday life each one of us likes to refer to some fairly well-defined conception of his own character in order to decide without trouble what to do, what to say, even what to think. We require some rule of thumb in our current self-manifestations; for a perpetual effort of choice would be an intolerable burden. Do we not habitually repose with a sense of satisfaction upon what we take to be our fixed characteristics——upon the supposedly fatal element within us?

But, recognizing the problem with this, Myers continues:

> But this sacrifice of variability has its disadvantages. The character develops at the expense of the perceptions and the imagination. The young man is apt to feel at times that he is investing himself in habiliments which cramp him. He would fain throw them off; but almost irresistible is the force of precedent; that is the force of interior and exterior expectation.

And Myers ends with what, I think, is a very important insight. 'Besides', he says, 'it is only in moments of unusual excitation that the ego gathers the energy to rebel. For the most part it prefers to take its ease in an inert illustration of the public personality, which has, indeed, become a second nature'. [9]

Myers, it seems clear, is talking about the same thing as Nietzsche and Sartre, and for me this puts him in the camp of the 'other' existentialists. For Sartre, as for Myers, freedom is recognizing our responsibility to make choices, to do *this* rather than *that*, and also acknowledging the irrevocableness of our choices and actions. Hence Myers is speaking of 'the perpetual effort of choice' being 'an intolerable burden'. Once made, we cannot 'take back' an action, and this is why much existential literature, like Sartre and Camus' novels, have an air of a thriller. I can say 'I'm sorry' about some misdeed, but this does not undo it. It has happened and nothing I can do can change that. So things are on the edge here, there is something at stake. Swedenborg feels likewise. The choices we make are prompted by our true affections, and it is these which will determine our experiences in the next world. But again we must remember that for Swedenborg, heaven and hell are states, not places, and through our choices we inhabit them already. They, like ourselves, are 'here, now'.

Now Swedenborg, unlike Sartre and Camus, had a compass that helped when deciding how to act. Although Sartre spoke and wrote a great deal about freedom, in reading his work, one soon finds that he really had no idea what to do with it. Sartre's writings and lectures electrified his readers and students, especially in the Paris after the liberation. He instilled the idea of freedom in the hearts and minds of his listeners, and that excitement shows us the best in Sartre. But after convincing his students that they were free—'condemned to be free', [10] in fact, as he put it—when they then asked him what they should do with their freedom, he had no answer. 'Do whatever you like', [11] he said on one occasion, which, to me at least, is something of a let-down. I would say that Sartre failed to recognize the distinction Nietzsche makes in *Thus Spake Zarathustra*, when he has Zarathustra say 'Free from what? Zarathustra does not care about that. But your eye should clearly tell me: free *for* what?' He also adds a remark that can very easily be misunderstood: 'There are many who threw off their final worth when they threw off their bondage', [12] meaning that freedom in the sense of mere 'license' is as often as not a curse as much as it is a blessing.

An idea of the anticlimax of the existential notion of freedom can be found in Simone de Beauvoir's novel *The Mandarins*, which depicts the Parisian scene after the liberation, and in which people like Sartre, Camus and others are characters. When the Nazis occupied Paris and Sartre and others like him were threatened by the Gestapo, freedom seemed an unquestionable and palpable good; yet once they were liberated, the existentialists on the Left Bank do little but drift in and out of affairs, drink and smoke a great deal, and find themselves confronting the 'absurd' and their own lack of purpose, which many of them try to deal with by moving toward communism and ideas of political engagement. And mention of the Gestapo reminds us of Myers' remark that 'it is only in moments of unusual excitation that the ego gathers the energy to rebel'. Paradoxically, Sartre remarked that he never felt so 'free' as when he was in danger of being arrested by the Gestapo. That danger somehow triggered the 'unusual excitation' and Sartre was probably more 'himself' then, than later, when the danger had vanished. This is the 'paradox of freedom' that Colin Wilson has explored in several of his books, most famously *The Outsider*. [14]

In a way, the Nazis provided Sartre with a kind of 'compass', but once they were gone, he was left adrift. There really is no moral compass in Sartre's philosophy, and that is not surprising, given its radically materialistic and atheistic character; in a famous phrase, man, Sartre tells us, is a useless passion, and it is meaningless that we live and meaningless that we die. [15] Even Camus wasn't as bleak as this, and he had a vague sense of the numinous, of something 'more', although he stopped short of any kind of belief. And this is why Sartre's later philosophy, his attempt to wed existentialism to Marxism, is something of a grand failure. His hatred of capitalism, of America, of the bourgeoisie, gave him some sense of direction. But even so, it was a dead end, as a reading of his *Critique of Dialectical Reason* [16] will, I think, show.

Swedenborg, however, avoided this. Asked for some guidance on what we should do, Swedenborg advised that we should 'Do the good that you know'. Again, here is the link between action and knowledge, between doing and knowing. Also the idea of uses, of purpose. Many people of an existential bent suffer from what we may call 'Hamlet's disease'. Knowledge for them is not an aid to action. Quite the opposite. Their knowledge inhibits their action, and makes them incapable of it. We find something similar in T S Eliot's poem 'Love Song of J Alfred Prufrock'. Here Eliot's indecisive anti-hero, who is 'no great prophet', knows that 'in a minute there is time for decisions and revisions which a minute will reverse'. His anxiety about his actions is so great that he wonders if he dares 'to eat a peach?' 'Do I dare disturb the universe?' the paralysed Prufrock asks, and more than likely he is still asking it today. [17]

Again, Nietzsche in the nineteenth century wondered if the flood of knowledge about the past would inhibit creativity in the present, and he wrote an essay about the 'use and abuse of history for life'. [18] Nietzsche's impatience with Hamlet-like dithering led him to make some extreme statements about war and other vital activities—like 'It's a good war that hallows any cause' [19]—which unfortunately were appropriated and misused by, among others, the Nazis—ironically, as Nietzsche was a fervent anti-militarist. But, taking this into account, I think we can see where he and Swedenborg shared a similar appreciation of what we might call 'the use and abuse of knowledge for life'.

This significance of 'knowledge for life' reaches, as I have said, up to heaven as well. One of the surprises I had while writing my book was that I was already familiar with much of what Swedenborg had to say about heaven through the work of one of my favourite writers, the playwright Bernard Shaw, especially his 'philosophical comedy' *Man and Superman*. There, in the 'Don Juan in Hell' section, Shaw depicts a very Swedenborgian heaven. Not only does Shaw make clear that, as Swedenborg says, heaven and hell are of our own making and that we are led to either one or the other by the choices we make, he also points out that heaven, as opposed to hell, is a very 'active' place. Hell, for Shaw, is not a place of torment and pain, but a place in which 'one has nothing to do but amuse oneself'. The souls there engage in gossip and chit-chat, take on beautiful appearances, compliment each other, and gratify their sensual appetites eternally. It is 'the home of the unreal and of the seekers of happiness'. Heaven, on the other hand, is the home of 'the masters of reality'. Here one works to help life's 'incessant aspiration to higher organisation, wider, deeper, intenser self-consciousness, and clearer self-understanding'. [20] Likewise, for Swedenborg, although his hell is a less cosy place, heaven too is a place of work. The cherubic choirs and harp-strumming angels of tradition have no place there. 'Such a life', Swedenborg tells us, 'would not be active, but idle. There is no happiness in life apart from activity'. [21] And in fact, in one of Shaw's later plays a character says something like 'I don't want to be happy. I want to be active'. [22] This is the Shavian ethic in a nutshell, which a reading of 'Don Juan in Hell' will make clear. One of Shaw's commentators, the American historian Jacques Barzun (who, at nearly 100 years of age, is a very good advertisement for the active life), wrote of the 'message' of 'Don Juan in Hell':

> Life is not a preliminary to anything except possibly a more abundant life for our descendants. Heaven and Hell are here on earth, a permanently open choice. The blest are those who prefer effort to illusion and truth to enjoyment, who would live or die for an idea rather than live for their senses in the fear of death. The damned take the path of least resistance, avoid thought and surround themselves with nice things. [23]

Aside from life not being a 'preliminary to anything', this, to me, strikes the Swedenborgian note.

Now it may be superfluous to point out that the active life that Shaw, Swedenborg, Barzun, Nietzsche and others extol is not the kind of active life we hear about today. It is not about joining a gym and working out, although, to be sure, keeping fit is not a bad thing——as I said, Barzun is nearly 100 and Shaw himself lived to be 94. It is not about rushing about, trying to fill your day with as many 'activities' as possible; that is more of a 'busy' life than an active one. And although it does not preclude this, it is not about being an 'activist' for some cause or other. Indeed, in time rich with competing causes——global warming, climate change, animal rights, ecology and so on——Swedenborg's compass of 'doing the good that you know' is a great help, because it returns us to what is at hand. Many of us may want to 'save the planet', but unfortunately, having our eyes set on such a colossal goal can often obscure what is immediately in front of us, and I personally know quite a few people who want to fight 'globalization', but who are somewhat lacking in more immediate areas of civility and consideration. It is easier to talk about saving the planet than it is to deal with the often boring necessities of living on it. As the old Buddhist saying goes, 'Talk won't cook the rice'.

Swedenborg's active life is one in which the rice gets cooked. It is a life attuned to the importance of making choices, of thinking and deciding for oneself, of using our knowledge and our will to cut a path through life, rather than depending on others to do this for us, or filling life up with so many trivialities that there is no room in it for anything else.

Although I do not know of a direct influence——Richard Lines has written a short article about this [24]——but finding a Swedenborgian note in Shaw led me to look at some other writers and thinkers who I would call existential in the broader sense, to see if I could find any other similar themes. And I found quite a lot. So what I will do in closing is share a few thoughts from some of the writers and thinkers who had a somewhat Swedenborgian feeling about the active life.

William Blake, of course, is an immediate choice, although like Nietzsche he is sometimes easy to take out of context and misapply. 'He who desires but acts not breeds pestilence' and 'Sooner murder an infant in its cradle than nurse unacted desires'[25] can seem a bit extreme, but Blake was in many ways, like Nietzsche, a frustrated man, and this is understandable. Less challenging is his insight that 'The busy bee has no time for sorrow',[26] which is like Shaw's remark that the best way to avoid misery is to stay so busy you have no time to realize you are miserable. And perhaps best known is 'Exuberance is beauty' and 'Energy is Eternal Delight'.[27]

Ralph Waldo Emerson is another reader of Swedenborg who had a lot to say about action. 'Do not be too timid and squeamish about your actions. All life is an experiment. The more experiments you make the better.'[28] (I should point out that Emerson was a favourite of Nietzsche.) 'Make the most of yourself, for that is all there is of you' is a favourite of mine, as is 'Our chief want in life is somebody who shall make us do what we can',[29] as well as 'Always do what you are afraid to do',[30] which strikes me as expressing Nietzsche's advice to 'live dangerously'.[31] 'The world belongs to the energetic',[32] agrees with Blake. And Emerson tells us to use our powers and others will be given to us.[33] Do not hide your star under a bushel, in other words. 'An ounce of action is worth a ton of theory.'

Goethe, as you would expect, has some contributions. 'What you can do or dream', he tells us, 'begin it. Boldness has genius, power and magic in it'.[34] 'Thinking is easy, acting is difficult, and to put one's thoughts into action is the most difficult thing in the world.'[35] As for 'uses': 'Man is not born to solve the problem of the universe, but to find out what he has to do, and to restrain himself within the limits of his powers of his comprehension'.[36] 'Character, in great and little things, means carrying through what you feel able to do.' 'It is not enough to have knowledge, one must also apply it. It is not enough to have wishes, one must also accomplish.'[37] 'Life is not anything but an opportunity for something.' Here are two that relate to 'doing the good that we know'. 'How can we learn self-knowledge? Never by taking thought but rather by action. Try to do your duty and you'll soon discover what you are like. But what is your duty? The demands of the day.'[38] And 'Anyone who wants to be active and busy need only consider what ought to be done at any given moment and in this way he can proceed without diffusing his energies'. [39]

And to return to Shaw, his sign of what he calls the evolutionary urge is 'an appetite for fruitful activity and a high quality of life'. [40] 'A perpetual holiday is a good working definition of hell.' [41] And again from 'Don Juan in Hell': 'A lifetime of happiness! No man could bear it; it would be hell on earth'. [42]

And to close let me quote from someone who could not possibly have read Swedenborg, the ancient Chinese sage Confucius, who tells us that 'The superior man is modest in his speech, but exceeds in his actions'. [43]

NOTES

[1] Gary Lachman, *Into the Interior: Discovering Swedenborg* (London: Swedenborg Society, 2006; repr. 2009).

[2] Albert Camus, *The Myth of Sisyphus*, tr. Justin O' Brien (Harmondsworth: Penguin, 1975), p. 53.

[3] Colin Wilson, *The Angry Years: The Fall and Rise of the Angry Young Men* (London: Robson Books, 2007), p. 161.

[4] Quoted in Friedrich Nietzsche, 'On the Uses and Disadvantages of History for Life', in *Untimely Meditations*, ed. Daniel Breazeale, tr. R J Hollingdale (Cambridge: Cambridge University Press, 1997), p. 59.

[5] Swedenborg's doctrine of uses is nicely summarized in *Arcana Caelestia*, tr. John Elliott (London: Swedenborg Society, 1983), vol. 1, §997, p. 408: 'As regards use, the situation is this: People who are governed by charity, that is, who dwell in love towards the neighbour—from which love the living delight contained in pleasure derives—have no regard for the enjoyment of pleasures except on account of the use that is served; for charity does not exist if there are no works of charity. It is in the exercise of it, that is, in use, that charity consists. Someone who loves the neighbour as himself never experiences the delight of charity except in the exercise of it, or in

use. Consequently the life of charity is a life of uses. Such life pervades the whole of heaven, for the Lord's kingdom, being a kingdom of mutual love, is a kingdom of uses. Every pleasure therefore that springs from charity finds its delight in use, and the more pre-eminent the use the greater the delight. For this reason it is the very being and nature of a use which determines the happiness that angels have from the Lord'.

6   Nietzsche, *Human, All Too Human: A Book for Free Spirits*, tr. R J Hollingdale (Cambridge: Cambridge University Press, 1996), p. 294.

7   See Jean Paul Sartre, *Being and Nothingness*, tr. Hazel E Barnes (London: Methuen, 1969), ch. 2 'Bad Faith'.

8   Erich Fromm, *Escape from Freedom* (New York: Avon Books, 1965).

9   L H Myers, *The Orissers* (London and New York: G P Putnam's Sons, 1922), pt. 3, ch. 9, pp. 330, 331.

10 Sartre, *Being and Nothingness*, pp. 129, 439, 509, 632.

11 Sartre, *Existentialism Is a Humanism*, ed. John Kulka, tr. Carol Macomber (New Haven and London: Yale University Press, 2007), p. 44.

12 Nietzsche, *Thus Spoke Zarathustra*, tr. R J Hollingdale (Harmondsworth: Penguin, 1969), p. 89.

13 Simone de Beauvoir, *The Mandarins,* tr. Leonard M Friedman (London: Collins, 1957).

14 Colin Wilson, *The Outsider* (London: Gollancz, 1956).

15 Sartre, *Being and Nothingness*, p. 615.

16 Sartre, *Critique of Dialectical Reason*, 2 vols., ed. Jonathan Rée, tr. Alan Sheridan-Smith (vol. 1), ed. Arlette Elkaim-Sartre, tr. Quintin Hoare (vol. 2) (London: Verso, 2004-6).

17 T S Eliot, 'The Love Song of J Alfred Prufrock', in *Prufrock and Other Observations* (London: The Egoist LTD., 1917), pp. 8, 6, 9, 6.

18 Nietzsche, 'On the Uses and Disadvantages of History for Life', in *Untimely Meditations*.

19 Nietzsche, *Thus Spoke Zarathustra*, p. 74.

20 George Bernard Shaw, *Man and Superman* (London: Constable and Company Limited, 1947), act III, pp. 93, 99, 123.

21 Swedenborg, *Heaven and Hell*, tr. George F Dole (New York: Swedenborg Foundation, 1984), §403, pp. 312-13.

22 Shaw, *Buoyant Billions: A Comedy of No Manners* (privately printed, 1948), act III 'The Discussion', p. 40.

23 Jacques Barzun, 'Bernard Shaw', in *A Jacques Barzun Reader: Selections from His Works*, ed. Michael Murray (New York: HarperCollins, 2002), p. 233.

24 Richard Lines, 'George Bernard Shaw and Swedenborg: A Footnote', in *Things Heard and Seen*, no. 16, Spring 2005, p. 9.

25 William Blake, *The Marriage of Heaven and Hell*, plates 7 and 10, in *Complete Writings*, ed. Geoffrey Keynes (Oxford: OUP, 1969), pp. 151, 152.

26 Ibid., plate 7 (p. 151 in *Complete Writings*).

27 Ibid., plates 10 and 4 (pp. 152, 149 in *Complete Writings*).

28 Ralph Waldo Emerson, *The Heart of Emerson's Journals*, ed. Bliss Perry (Boston and New York: Houghton Mifflin Co., 1926), p. 189. Entry for 11 November 1842.

29 Emerson, *The Conduct of Life* (Boston: Ticknor and Fields, 1863), p. 239.

30 Emerson, 'Heroism', in *Essays: First Series* (Boston: James Munroe and Company, 1850), p. 237.

31 Nietzsche, *Thus Spoke Zarathustra*, p. 29.

32 Emerson, 'Resources', in *Letters and Social Aims* (Boston: James R Osgood and Company, 1876), p. 136.

33 Cf. Emerson, *The Complete Sermons of Ralph Waldo Emerson*, vol. 2, ed. Teresa Toulouse and Andrew Delbanco (Columbia: University of Missouri Press, 1989), sermon LXXV, p. 188.

34 Johann Wolfgang von Goethe, *Faustus, A Dramatic Mystery*, tr. John Anster (London: Longman, Rees, Orme, Brown, Green & Longman, 1835), 'Prelude at the Theatre', p. 15.

35 Cf. Goethe, *Wilhelm Meister's Apprenticeship and Travels*, 2 vols., tr. Thomas Carlyle (Boston: Ticknor, Reed, and Fields, 1851), vol. II, book VIII, ch. V, p. 153: 'There are few who at once have Thought, and the capacity of Action. Thought expands, but lames: Action animates, but narrows'.

36 Johann Peter Eckermann, *Conversations with Goethe in the Last Years of his Life*, tr. S M Fuller (Boston and Cambridge: James Munroe and Company, 1852), p. 153.

37 Cf. Goethe, *Campaign in France in the Year 1792*, tr. Robert Farle (London:

Chapman and Hall, 1849), p. 257: 'he is accompanied every where with what gives him the highest enjoyment, and with a valuable means of instruction without trouble; and he has the benefit continually of a very precious possession. But to attain to such a possession, it is not enough that you wish for it; to accomplish it, you must also, above all things, be favoured by circumstances'.

[38] Goethe, *Goethe's Opinions on the World, Mankind, Literature, Science and Art*, tr. Otto Wenckstern (London: John W Parker and Son, 1853), p. 111.

[39] Goethe, *Maxims and Reflections*, ed. Peter Hutchinson, tr. Elisabeth Stopp (Harmondsworth: Penguin, 1999), no. 908, p. 119.

[40] Shaw, *The Complete Prefaces*, ed. Dan H Laurence and Daniel J Leary (London: Allen Lane, 1995), vol. 2, p. 131.

[41] Shaw, *Misalliance. A Treatise on Parents and Children* (London: Constable and Company Ltd, 1919), p. xxxix.

[42] Shaw, *Man and Superman*, act I, p. 13.

[43] Confucius, *Confucian Analects, The Great Learning & The Doctrine of the Mean*, tr. James Legge (Mineola: Dover Publications, 1972), p. 286.

II. LITERATURE

Blake and Swedenborg*

Czeslaw Milosz

lake's thought is rooted in the Fall. His interpretation of the Bible, if as allegorical as Swedenborg's, acquires a new dimension: if the Swedish visionary was a practitioner of the imagination, Blake was both theorist and practitioner, in the sense that the Imagination (capitalized) was for him the animating and redemptive power of the Human Form Divine, an emanation of the Holy Spirit. In Blake religion and poetry merge, art becomes prophecy, just as religion, before it became debased, was once prophecy—the writings of the prophets of the Old Testament and the Gospels stood for him as perfect models of inspired speech. Blake's poet is a vatic figure, a seer. But because Blake resorts to language neither as a vehicle of pure subjectivity nor as a tool of discourse, he is not a patron of what would come to be known as Symbolism or of linguistic experiments in the postmodernist phase, just as little as he would have approved of efforts to rehabilitate a 'rational' syntax on behalf of some ideology. Proper use of the poet-seer's language is made when Imagination allows him, the poet, to surmount the fallen state in which our species resides. That is why Blake's own poetry defies translation into the language of philosophy, itself a product of the Fall. Through the consistency of its correspondences (not to be confused with symbols, randomly and capriciously bestrewn), his poetry, like the books of Scripture, both demands and escapes such a transposition.

For Blake, as much as for Swedenborg, man's Fall results not from the violation of any interdiction but—if I may be allowed to simplify—from the victory of the *proprium*, of the ego. We shall sidestep the complex issue of Blake's successive Churches, or civilizations, as we shall the Blakean enigma: the placing of an equal sign between the Human Form Divine and the cosmos, in consequence of which any disruption of order in man is tantamount to a cosmic disruption. In reading Blake we are never quite certain whether the Fall occurred before or after Creation, to which Blake would have replied that both are synonymous. The mythical figures introduced by him in the *Prophetic Books* symbolize those human faculties that were designed to work in concert but are divided, which is the cause of their travail. Although Blake's writings do not lack a past dimension, they compose above all an eschatological vision in which the eighteenth century is cast as the 'abomination of desolation'. Blake, one of the most open of poets to the pleasures of the senses, a poet given to the same childlike eroticism as the Sienese painters, is also a poet of fury. Embattled with the age, he attacks and indicts where others might bemoan: a Christianity become an instrument of control in the hands of the powerful, a system of rules and punishments; the tyranny of kings who wage bloody wars; the human misery wreaked by the Industrial Revolution, then under way in England; the plight of slaves and Indians, of women and children; the puritanical hypocrisy of sexual prohibitions; prostitution. Above all, his fury was directed at that which sustained, facilitated, and sanctioned such an order, which became in a way its code, the language of the Fall: at the science and philosophy founded by Francis Bacon.

The number 4 was crucial in Swedenborg (four ages of mankind, four seasons of the year, four points of the compass, four stages of life). So, too, in Blake four mythical figures join in man to make a family; from their cleavage came calamity. The spatial relationship between these figures—as in Swedenborg's 'other space'—is of particular note: (1) *Tharmas*, or the body. Its orientation: West. Its element: water (the ocean of Time and Space). Its location: the loins. Its sense:

touch. Its art: painting. (2) *Urthona*, or the individual creative Imagination (Christ is the all-encompassing Imagination). Its orientation: North. Its element: earth. Its metal: iron. Its trade: blacksmith. Its location: the, subconscious. Its sense: hearing. Its art: poetry. (3) *Luvah*, or the emotions (love and hatred). Its orientation: East. Its element: fire. Its metal: silver. Its trade: weaver. Its location: the heart. Its art: music. And finally (4) *Urizen*, or Reason (the Lawgiver). Its orientation: South. Its element: air. Its metal: gold. Its trade: ploughman, master builder. Its location: the head. Its sense: vision. Its art: architecture. Tharmas, Urthona, and Luvah may personify the Holy Trinity in man (the human body as an image of the Father, love as an image of the Son, the imagination as an image of the Spirit), in which case Urizen, as some commentators have suggested, would be the fallen aspect of the Godhead, or Satan.

I would be the loser if the reader were to indulge these mythic personifications as literary-historical *curiosa*. In contesting the age in which he lived, Blake could not adopt its language without disarming himself. Behind the naïve lyricism of his early poems lies a scathing irony, making the young Blake a precursor of a much later generation of European poets. Not content with irony, he later invented a whole menagerie of fantastic creatures to serve as agents. A similar strategy was later used by the poet Lesmian [1] with the difference that his creatures are confined to a single poem. *Nota bene*, Blake's heroes, like those of Leśmian bear names derived from native etymologies (rarely from Greek), and in general Blake is a poet strongly rooted in the native poetic tradition, which may explain his near inaccessibility beyond the pale of English, as witnessed by his reception in France, bordering on the non-existent.

In its age-old, metaphysical origin, the evil combatted by Blake, that self-appointed heir to the biblical prophets, was entirely consistent with the age. Throughout Christianity the *mysterium iniquitatis* had pertained only to human fate, guilt, suffering, while man himself, as king of nature, had been released from nature, placed above it. When science introduced the concept of nature's laws, a new dimension was revealed: man's kinship in pain with all things living. Swedenborg's reticence on this point was a cause for Blake's disaffection with the master: Swedenborg was too 'angelic'. Yet, in his general resolution of the problem, Blake was his successor, making his allegiance to the Gnostic and Manichaean tradition all the more plausible. Christ is God. Was it God who created a universe that 'dwells in evil'? No, this state arose from a cataclysm in the Primordial Man, from a violation of the harmony once prevailing among the four elements of his psyche, one of which, Urizen, became architect of the universe, Blake's version of Satan. Urizen is present in the Book of Genesis, where he bears the name of Elohim. It was he who brought negation and drew distinctions where none were meant to be and where none would remain after the restoration of the Human Form Divine: the distinction between man and woman (the Primordial Man was both man and woman); good and evil (the temptation of the Tree of Knowledge); Heaven and Hell; body and soul (caused by death); the confusion of tongues (the Tower of Babel).

Blake's cosmology is not a retelling of Creation meant to compete with the Book of Genesis or with any scientific hypotheses. Rather, it is a poetic—read prophetic, religious—myth; its intent is to present the creation of the world, not 'factually' but as evoked by the Imagination when it abides in truth, that is, when it acknowledges God as energy and love rather than as a land surveyor, a mathematician, and a guardian of the law

Urizen, or Reason, fell through pride and broke away from Tharmas, Luvah, and Urthona, leaving him incorporeal, passionless and, most significantly, barred from the source of all workings of the Imagination: the subconscious. Urizen is thus endowed with those attributes traditionally ascribed to Satan: solitude and distance; power of the intellect and a fanatic ability to wield abstraction; despair and envy of any creature capable of reconciling the four elements—of man, in other words. He is none other than the evil spirit served by Mickiewicz's 'learned', by those who drained the 'cup of their conceit' at God's funeral. [2]

In the course of his other-worldly travels, Swedenborg was told that the Last Judgment had come to pass in 1757, a date by no means arbitrarily chosen. That earthly mortals were unaware was incidental. Blake interpreted the Last Judgment as a manifestation of the lie, which first had to achieve a state of perfection before it could be exposed. To himself, born in the year of the Judgment, he assigned a providential mission, that of a knight who, armed with pen, graving tool, and brush, would deal the dragon a mortal wound. The perfection of the lie had been achieved in his time: Urizen was venerated as the true God, both by the Christian churches and by the philosophers who, dispensing with Jesus, clung to the idea of the Creator as a Clockmaker.

A heretical Christian, Blake was non-religious (his membership in a Swedenborgian congregation in London was of short duration). A non-worshipper, in his poems he cast the Anglican churches as places dedicated to a satanic cult. (Let us note that in its sermons the clergy of Blake's time revelled in terrorizing the faithful with the punishments of hell.) Religion was reduced to a set of prohibitions, above all sexual, where its role as guardian of the established order was most nakedly manifested. The God of that religion was Urizen, a sovereign who ruled by repression and demanded self-repression of his subjects; who was continually frustrating that energy which seeks ways of realizing itself. Cold and aloof, from his throne he surveyed the city along the 'chartered Thames'. [3] If ever a phantom-city had its own history, a city of street lamps in the fog, of sobs in the dark, of slinking, wraith-like prostitutes, of drunkards, of people reeling from hunger——then the London of Blake's poetry has pride of place, ahead of Dickens's (and Norwid's)[4] London, ahead of Balzac's and Baudelaire's Paris, of Gogol's and Dostoevsky's St Petersburg. Only those subjects living in falsehood could revere the protective deity, whose antithesis was Blake's God-man, Christ. In place of the prohibitions of law, Jesus had brought freedom; instead of the punishments of hell, forgiveness; instead of repression, the ecstatic release of energy. And what was this thing they called hell? For Jesus said: 'I am the resurrection, and the life: he that believeth in me, though he were dead, yet shall he live'.[5] For Jesus said: 'All manner of sin and blasphemy shall be forgiven unto men: but the blasphemy against the Holy Ghost shall not be forgiven unto men. And whosoever speaketh a word against the Son of man, it shall be forgiven him: but whosoever speaketh against the Holy Ghost, it shall not be forgiven him, neither in this world, neither in the world to come'.[6] Only one sin, then, is truly unforgivable: the sin against the Holy Ghost. But if Swedenborg conceived of hell as a state freely willed, Blake held that not man but his sinful states were cast into eternal fire, and he accused his master of having indirectly espoused a belief in predestination. To blaspheme against the Man-Son was a serious sin, yet Blake believed that even Voltaire, guilty though he was of such a sin, was saved through his labours in the service of Imagination, something his enemies never understood. In Blake's eschatological vision, even Urizen would be saved when the Human-Divine Family was restored, that is, on the day of the great Restitution (*apokata stasis*)——just as in St Gregory of Nyssa's vision Satan is spared eternal torment.

Sexual freedom was a revolutionary catchword arising from a philosophy advocating a return to the 'natural man', and the passion with which Blake defended it is somewhat surprising for a poet of the Fall. It is indicative of his whole search for a union of opposites, not for the sake of their resolution (in which case how could there be a Heaven of 'Intellectual Hunts'?)[7] but of their transfer to a higher plane; his was not 'naturalness' per se, but a 'naturalness' transfigured——recalling Swedenborg's 'angelic sexuality'.

The guiding exemplars of science and philosophy were the three villains: Bacon, Locke, and Newton. Yet all were of a piece with the theologians of a bogus Christianity: all genuflected before Urizen, the god of this world. Blake, in other words, drew a definite analogy between the vision of a mechanistic universe and religion conceived of as a moral code. Both proclaimed the universal at the expense of the particular, be it a particular moment in time, singular and irreducible, the shape and colour of a particular plant, or the life of a particular man. Urizen, in effect, is the god of reduction who reduces everything to quantitative terms.

Hence Blake's attack on the very foundations of the 'scientific world view'. How that attack was pressed is not within my power to document. The task is made the more arduous because it would take us, as I said, outside the purely literary realm. A literary critic engaged with any of the Romantic poets hardly runs the risk of antagonizing the scientific community. The fact is that today Blake still manages to provoke and antagonize; I know of an instance in the United States where a Blakean was denied a professorship because of opposition mounted by the physics faculty, who were protective not of their theorems so much as of the language of their formulation. Here I only allude to the Blakean attack, referring the interested reader to the major studies: Northrop Frye's *Fearful Symmetry*, Ronald L Grimes's *The Divine Imagination: William Blake's Major Prophetic Visions*, and Donald Ault's *Visionary Physics: Blake's Response to Newton*.[8] The material contained in these works, like the Blakean oeuvre itself, would provide enough food for thought to last the next couple of decades. It is enough for me to signal a war mounted by a poet who was endowed, according to the experts, with an intuitive grasp of the most complicated problems of physics. The difficulty, even for his English commentators, is that a 'translation' of his symbols into discursive language is unavoidable, even though such a 'translation' must significantly diminish the richness of his symbols.

It is now time to introduce the figure of Los (a probable anagram of Sol, or Sun). Man, exiled from his homeland, strives to regain that homeland—or Eden, eternal Paradise, the eternal Golden Age—while the poet-prophet foretells and hastens that return. Of the four eternal elements of human nature, whose dissension was precipitated by the Fall, only one, Urthona (Imagination), can serve as guide for the return voyage. She is represented in time and space by Los (time) and his wedded spouse Enitharmon (space). The Manichaean doctrine held that the creation of the world was an 'act of grace', that without it the pre-cosmic Fall could not be redeemed. So it is with Blake. Los, time, has a redemptive function; it is not absolute but man-related, humanizing time, just as Enitharmon is not absolute, Newtonian space. I am inclined to see Los as rhythm, born of the heart's pulsation; as a cosmic poet who saves, by embodying in rhythm, the most infinitesimal moment and object from irrevocable loss, who forges them into incorruptible shapes. Says Los

> [...] for not one Moment
> Of Time is lost, nor one Event of Space unpermanent,
> But all remain: every fabric of Six Thousand Years
> Remains permanent, tho' on Earth where Satan
> Fell and was cut off, all things vanish & are seen no more,
> They vanish not from me & mine, we guard them first and last.
> The generations of men run on in the tide of Time,
> But leave their destin'd lineaments permanent for ever and ever.
>
> —*Milton*, Book I, plate 22 [9]

And in the following passage:

> But others of the Sons of Los build Moments & Minutes & Hours
> And Days & Months & Ages & Periods, wondrous buildings;
> And every Moment has a Couch of gold for soft repose,
> (A moment equals a pulsation of the artery),
> And between every two Moments stands a Daughter of Beulah
> To feed the Sleepers on their Couches with maternal care.
> And every Minute has an azure Tent with silken Veils:
> And every Hour has a bright golden Gate carved with skill:
> And every Day and Night has Walls of Grass & Gates of adamant
> Shining like precious Stones & ornamented with appropriate signs:
> And every Month a silver paved Terrace builded high:
> And every Year invulnerable Barriers with high Towers:
> And every Age is Moated deep with Bridges of silver & gold:

And every Seven Ages is Incircled with a Flaming Fire.
Now Seven Ages is amounting to Two Hundred Years.
Each has its Guard, each Moment, Minute, Hour, Day, Month & Year.
All are the work of Fairy hands of the Four Elements:
Every Time less than a pulsation of the artery
Is equal in its period & value to Six Thousand Years,
For in this Period the Poet's Work is Done, and all the Great
Events of Time start forth and are conceiv'd in such a Period,
Within a Moment, a Pulsation of the artery.

—*Milton*, Book I, plate 28 [10]

To quote Blake is to explain little; every few lines require commentary. I would only append a footnote: in Blake's cosmology, Beulah stands for the nocturnal realm, poetic inspiration, the subconscious, and the erotic. Beulah's daughters are the Muses of inspired poetry, as opposed to the classical Muses, which are the daughters of Mnemosyne, or memory.

Los is active as time shaped by man. Man can be a computer—to adopt our modern vocabulary—and atomize the world only at the expense of his own humanity. Fallen man, the worshipper of Urizen, conceives of the eternal as time without end. Eternity, measurable in clock seconds, trails endlessly into oblivion and reaches indefinitely into the future; it forms a chain of causes and effects reaching back to the First Cause, the false god of the Deists. It defies the imagination: an eternity of mathematical relations and laws, a spatial dimension purged of time. Infinity will then be perceived as pure duration, as time without space. The scientific mind beholden to such notions will always deduce the same product: the indefinite.

To repeat the Swedenborgian maxim: 'You see as you are'. Blake placed man at the centre, and just as the artist bodies forth his work from the essential thing in him, so God, in fashioning man, gives proof of His essence: His divine humanity. God (Jesus) beholds Nature through human eyes, but not through the eyes of fallen man. Blake's Jesus was not the bearer of lofty moral precepts but the whole man; by emulating Him, we exchange our flawed physical perception of the world for a whole one. A scientist of the Baconian, Lockian, or Newtonian school suffers the illusion that knowledge is something impersonal, disembodied—that, in other words, only one faculty, the rational, suffices. The image of the world adduced by this science is a false one. To be free of its coercive power is to refute that false eternity (an endless succession of moments lapsing into nothingness) and false infinity (of illusory space, indefinite duration), and to know true eternity and infinity as the eternal Now. This is the message of the Blakean maxim.

> The desire of Man being Infinite, the possession is Infinite & himself Infinite.
> *Application*; He who sees the Infinite in all things, sees God. He who sees the Ratio only, sees himself only.
> Therefore God becomes as we are, that we may be as he is. [11]

There is no such thing as a neutral science: its vision of the world can be benign or destructive. Both the scientists and their allies, the theologians, meet with the same opprobrium:

> He never can be a Friend to the Human Race who is the Preacher of Natural Morality or Natural Religion; he is a flatterer who means to betray, to perpetuate Tyrant Pride & the Laws of that Babylon which he foresees shall shortly be destroyed, with the Spiritual and not the Natural Sword [...]
> You, O Deists, profess yourselves the Enemies of Christianity, and you are so: you are also the Enemies of the Human Race & of Universal Nature. Man is born a Spectre or Satan & is altogether an Evil, & requires a New Selfhood continually, & must continually be changed into his direct Contrary. But your Greek Philosophy (which is a remnant of Druidism) teaches that Man is Righteous in his Vegetated Spectre: an Opinion of fatal & accursed

consequence to Man, as the Ancients saw plainly by Revelation, to the intire abrogation of Experimental Theory; and many believed what they saw and Prophecied of Jesus.

Man must & will have Some Religion: if he has not the religion of Jesus, he will have the religion of Satan & will erect the Synagogue of Satan, calling the Prince of this World, God, and destroying all who do not worship Satan under the Name of God. Will any one say, 'Where are those who worship Satan under the Name of God?' Where are they? Listen! Every religion that Preaches Vengeance for Sin is the Religion of the Enemy & Avenger and not of the Forgiver of Sin, and their God is Satan, Named by the Divine Name. Your religion, O Deists! Deism, is the Worship of the God of this World by the means of what you call Natural Religion and Natural Philosophy, and of Natural Morality or Self-Righteousness, the Selfish Virtues of the Natural Heart. This was the religion of the Pharisees who murder'd Jesus. Deism is the same & ends in the same. [. . .]

Voltaire! Rousseau! You cannot escape my charge that you are Pharisees & Hypocrites, for you are constantly talking of the Virtues of the Human Heart and particularly of your own, that you may accuse others, & especially the Religious, whose errors you, by this display of pretended Virtue, chiefly design to expose. Rousseau thought Men Good by Nature: he found them Evil & found no friend. Friendship cannot exist without Forgiveness of Sins continually. The Book written by Rousseau call'd his Confessions, is an apology & cloke for his sin & not a confession.

—*Jerusalem*, plate 52 [12]

The modern scientist, particularly one given to the extremism of the geneticist Jacques Monod, would shrug at such an obvious blurring of two distinct categories, of 'objective truth' and ethics. Yet he could hardly deny an exact correlation between eighteenth-century science and Deism. And, to be consistent, he would keep to his own domain and not encroach (as he does) on that territory designated by Blake as 'natural philosophy' and 'natural morality'. Blake's pairing of these categories is not exactly clear from my paraphrase, hence some further elaboration.

Blake was not an advocate of Mystery as something inaccessible to reason, as something circumscribing the narrow circle of our knowledge. The word 'Mystery' has a negative connotation in his vocabulary: it is a terrorizing of the mind through the religion and philosophy of Urizen. The world around us is real, not illusory; neither can it be divided into that which has been discovered and that which awaits discovery by the human mind, but only into the true, or that which is contained by the Imagination, and the false, the 'vegetative mirror' that is a parody of the former. The first is for man a living heaven, the second a hell, the Land of Ulro. I quote Northrop Frye:

There are two poles in human thought, the conception of life as eternal existence in one divine Man, and the conception of life as an unending series of cycles in nature. Most of us spend our mental lives vacillating somewhere between these two, without being fully conscious of either, certainly without any great impulse to accept either. But the rise of Deism has increased our awareness of the extent to which we are attracted by the latter. Between the beginning of life in our world and our selves, a long interval of time may have elapsed, and a great development have taken place; but the beginning of our world cannot have been, from a natural point of view, anything more than an accident in the revolving stars in the sky. As soon as our idea of a beginning of time or creation disappears into the 'starry wheels,' we have attained the complete fallen vision of the world [...] the wheel of death. [...] Such an idea, Blake insists, is a mental cancer: man is not capable of accepting it purely as an objective fact; its moral and emotional implications must accompany it into the mind, and breed there into cynical indifference, a short-range vision, selfish pursuit of expediency, and all the other diseases of the Selfhood, ending in horror and despair. But we cannot shut our eyes and deny its reality; we must see its reality as a reflected image of the eternal mental life of God and Man, the wheel of life, the auto-motive energy of the risen body. [13]

Frye comes close to paraphrasing Blake in conventional terms, in terms of recognizable concepts, though he succeeds only partially. Crucial in the passage above is the mind's inability to accede to 'objective facts' as being truly 'objective'. The tree of knowledge of good and evil, or the tree of contradictions, is the tree of scientific cognition, based on the principle of consistency. Whoever tastes of that tree is immediately beset by a series of paired negations, casting the mind into the role of an arbiter, which in the moral realm is synonymous with the triumph of arrogance (Swedenborg's *proprium*, Blake's Selfhood). In the Wheel of Death, in Ulro, man reduces other men to vacant shadows, to creatures of chance quickly consigned to oblivion; unable to believe in their reality, he becomes a captive of ego, of the 'Spectre':

The Negation in the Spectre, the Reasoning Power in Man:
This is a false Body, in Incrustation over my Immortal
Spirit, a Selfhood which must be put off & annihilated alway.
To cleanse the Face of my Spirit by Self-examination,
To bathe in the Waters of Life, to wash off the Not Human,
I come in Self-annihilation & the grandeur of Inspiration,
To cast off Rational Demonstration by Faith in the Saviour,
To cast off the rotten rags of Memory by Inspiration,
To cast off Bacon, Locke & Newton from Albion's covering,
To take off his filthy garments & clothe him with Imagination
—*Milton*, Book II, plate 40 [14]

If man in the Age of Reason lived with the vision of 'Starry Wheels', how much more susceptible to such a vision are we who have seen our Earth photographed from the Moon in the shape of a sphere? Such a vision, Blake insisted, was wrong: Earth is flat, circumscribed by the horizon and the celestial dome. This, his heresy, was not propounded by him as a 'scientific fact'. If I understand him correctly, he treated both images as constructively antithetical, in the sense of issuing from the power of the intellect, whereas man's spiritual needs are better satisfied by the 'naïve' imagination. Blake wanted man to inhabit an Earth-garden (*dichterisch*, as Hölderlin said), the same as that embodied in Mickiewicz's *Pan Tadeusz*, written several years after Blake's death:

The Sky is an immortal Tent built by the Sons of Los:
And every space that a Man views around his dwelling-place
Standing on his own roof or in his garden on a mount
Of twenty-five cubits in height, such space is his Universe:
And on its verge the Sun rises & sets, the Clouds bow
To meet the flat Earth & the Sea in such an order'd Space:
The Starry heavens reach no further, but here bend and set
On all sides, & the two Poles turn on their valves of gold;
And if he moves his dwelling-place, his heavens also move
Where'er he goes, & all his neighborhood bewail his loss.
Such are the Spaces called Earth & such its dimension.
As to that false appearance which appears to the reasoner
As of a Globe rolling thro' Voidness, it is a delusion of Ulro.
The Microscope knows not of this nor the Telescope: they alter
The ratio of the Spectator's Organs, but leave Objects untouch'd.
For every Space larger than a red Globule of Man's blood
Is visionary, and is created by the Hammer of Los:
And every Space smaller than a Globule of Man's blood opens
Into Eternity of which this vegetable Earth is but a shadow.

—*Milton*, Book I, plate 29 [15]

Swedenborg's Last Judgment took place outside what Blake called the vegetative world. Blake's major poems, on the other hand, are an anticipation of the Harvest of Wrath, of the consummation of time—the 'end of that age' when the 'dream of Albion' (mankind) is over and the four conflicting elements of human nature are restored to harmony. Blake's eschatological expectations are no less fervid than those of the Polish Messianists, [16] though their Age of the Spirit seems more a historical 'third stage' than does his Jerusalem, the title he gave to the last of his *Prophetic Books*. His symbolic holy city, Jesus' betrothed, lies beyond history. The whole power of his cranky and extravagant style (for a long time he was considered a schizophrenic) derives from such a vision, even though, we should hasten to add, the future was for him not only 'tomorrow' but a dimension of the present, now and for ever. Poetry and religion, as I have stated, are synonymous, provided they be authentic, i.e., eschatological. The only language recognized by Blake was the language of prophecy, the language of 'the final things'. As examples he cited the Gospel symbolism of fruition: the harvest, grape gathering, the nuptial ceremony. Bread from the harvest is changed into the body of Christ and wine into His blood, an event foretold by the miraculous changing of water into wine at the wedding feast at Cana.

Even a theologically trained Christian must puzzle over the Gospel references to the future Kingdom of God. For how are the words 'My Kingdom is not of this world' [17] to be reconciled with the repeated and emphatic promise that it will come to pass here on earth, at the end of this aeon? The Gospels have been invoked both by millenarianists of every persuasion and by pessimistically inclined Christians, for whom the earth will always be a valley of tears. Here again, rather than attempt to paraphrase Blake, I would rely on a quotation from Northrop Frye. Paraphrasing is laborious work; if this task has already been performed for us, there is no reason why we should not make use of it.

In the resurrection of the body the physical universe would take the form in which it would be perceived by the risen body, and the risen body would perceive it in the form of Paradise.

The complete conquest of nature implied by the words 'resurrection' and 'apocalypse' is a mystery bound up with the end of time, but not with death. When the Selfhood is asked what it wants to do; it can only answer, with the Sibyl in Petronius, that it wants to die, and it thinks of death as a resolution. To the imagination physical death isolates the part that lives in the spiritual world; but as that world is the real here and the real now, we do not have to wait to die to live in it. 'Whenever any Individual Rejects Error & Embraces Truth, a Last Judgment passes upon that Individual'. Similarly, the apocalypse could occur at any time in history if men wanted it badly enough to stop playing their silly game of hide-and-seek with nature. Visionaries, artists, prophets and martyrs all live as though an apocalypse were around the corner, and without this sense of a potentially imminent crisis imagination loses most of its driving power. The expectation of a Last Judgment does not mean that the Christians of that time were victims of a mass delusion, or that they were hypnotizing themselves in order to nerve themselves for martyrdom, but that they saw the physical universe as precariously balanced on the mental cowardice of man. And when Blake and Milton elaborate theories of history suggesting that time is reaching its final crisis during their own lives, they are only doing what Jesus did before them. [18]

This may indeed be the glad tidings which Blake brings us: for the Imagination it is unreasonable and unjustified to assent to this world, while to anticipate its end is both justified and reasonable. And because the final reaping was continually being accomplished in the here and now, the seventy-year-old Blake, in no way disillusioned by its deferment in time, could die with a hymn to Jesus on his lips.

NOTES

* This essay is from Czeslaw Milosz's *The Land of Ulro*, ch. 29, translated by Louis Iribarne and is reprinted here by kind permission of Farrar, Strauss and Giroux.

1 Bolesław Leśmian or Lesman (*c.* 1878-1937). Polish poet and artist whose verse is populated with fantastic creatures derived from, chiefly, Polish folklore.

2 Adam Bernard Mickiewicz (1798-1853), Polish Romantic poet. The 'learned' refers to Mickiewicz's poem 'The Romantic' which Milosz critiques earlier in the book this essay is extracted from, *The Land of Ulro*. The 'cup of their conceit' is a line from an 1830 Mickiewicz poem; cf. *Land of Ulro*, p. 134.

3 Blake, 'London', l. 2, p. 26, in *The Complete Poetry and Prose of William Blake*, ed. David V Erdman (Berkeley: University of California Press, 2008).

4 Cyprian Kamil Norwid (1821-83), Polish poet and artist who lived much of his life outside of Poland, including a spell in London in 1854.

5 John 11:25, 26.

6 Matthew 12:31, 32.

7 Cf. Blake, *Jerusalem*, chapter 2, plate 38, l. 31 (p. 185 in *The Complete Poetry and Prose of William Blake*).

8 Northrop Frye, *Fearful Symmetry: A Study of William Blake* (Princeton: Princeton University, 1947); Ronald L Grimes, *The Divine Imagination: William Blake's Major Prophetic Visions* (Metuchen: Scarecrow, 1972); Donald Ault, *Visionary Physics: Blake's Response to Newton* (Chicago and London: University of Chicago Press, 1974).

9 Blake, *Milton*, book I, plate 22, ll. 18-25 (p. 117 in *The Complete Poetry and Prose of William Blake*, ed. David V Erdman).

10 Ibid., book I, plate 28, l. 44-plate 29, l. 3 (pp. 126-7 in *The Complete Poetry and Prose of William Blake*).

11 Blake, 'There is no Natural Religion' [b], no. VII (p. 3 in *The Complete Poetry and Prose of William Blake*).

12 Blake, *Jerusalem*, plate 52 'To the Deists' (pp. 200-1 in *The Complete Poetry and Prose of William Blake*).

13 Northrop Frye, *Fearful Symmetry*, pp. 383-4.

[14] Blake, *Milton*, book II, plates 40-1 (p. 142 in *The Complete Poetry and Prose of William Blake*).

[15] Blake, *Milton*, book I, plate 29 (p. 127 in *The Complete Poetry and Prose of William Blake*).

[16] The Polish messianists were poets such as Mickiewicz, Juliusz Słowacki (1809-49) and Zygmunt Krasiński (1812-59) whose works were characterized by the belief that Poland's suffering was a precursor to mankind's salvation.

[17] John 18:36.

[18] Frye, *Fearful Symmetry*, p. 195.

Balzac and Swedenborg *

Saori Osuga

Introduction

Honoré de Balzac (1799-1850) was one of the earliest French writers
to recognize the importance of Swedenborg's doctrines, writing
Séraphîta, a mystical work expressing in poetic form the spiritual
elation induced by his readings of Swedenborg. Balzac was also only one of a few
men of letters to declare himself a follower of Swedenborg's religious thought.
And not only did he declare this via his fictional double, Louis Lambert, who was
given to say: 'I have come back to Swedenborg after vast studies of all religions',[1]
but he also wrote in a letter to Madame Hanska, his future wife: 'You know what
my religions are, I am not orthodox and I do not believe in the Roman Church
[...] Swedenborgianism, which is but a repetition of ancient ideas in a Christian
sense, is my religion, lifted by the incomprehensibility of God'.[2]

Certainly, after the publication of *Séraphîta* in 1835, Balzac would never again
write such a work, and this for reasons that we might suppose to include his weari-
ness and disappointment from several bitter discussions on religion with Madame
Hanska, in particular her incomprehension (as well as that of Parisians in general)
of *Séraphîta*, and also his inability to write another work which, in his own words,
required, 'exaltations that can only come at the expense of life'.[3] He later admitted:
'one can write *Goriot* any day; one writes *Séraphîta* but once in a lifetime'.[4] Nevertheless, he kept Swedenborg in mind until his last years, mentioning him in *Le Cousin*

151

Pons (1846-7): 'Swedenborg, the great Swedish prophet, said that Earth is a man'.[5] And in *L'Envers de l'histoire contemporaine* (1842-8), where he recalls 'Swedenborg's doctrine on angels' in the life of the saintly woman Madame de la Chanterie.[6]

In any case, the 1830s were an exceptional period for Balzac, who, propelled by a mystical fervour, would successively produce *Les Proscrits* (*The Exiles*) (1831), *Louis Lambert* (1832-5) and *Séraphîta* (1833-5), the more or less 'Swedenborgian' trilogy which would be brought together as one under the title *Le Livre Mystique* (1835). In this essay we will first attempt to understand which aspects of Swedenborg were appreciated by Balzac and why, and then to identify the works of Swedenborg that were read by Balzac, giving examples of the direct influence of the Swedish thinker on the French writer.

Swedenborg from Balzac's perspective

Reading Pastor Becker's discourse in *Séraphîta* alongside *Louis Lambert* and certain letters from Balzac to Madame Hanska, we might begin to understand how Balzac envisaged Swedenborg. In the first instance we find him emphasizing Swedenborg as a virtuous and scientific man. He trusted Swedenborg as 'a man of vast learning, esteemed and cherished for his virtues, always irreproachable and constantly useful',[7] and also as a scientist of the highest rank, who published 'the encyclopaedic works'[8] until the age of sixty. He admired in the Swede a lucid and mathematical spirit who never ceased to express himself clearly, and in which there are 'thousands of propositions, all numbered, none of which is contradicted'.[9] His impressions upon reading Swedenborg's theological works are evoked by Pastor Becker who expresses his emotion thus: 'I have often experienced unheard-of delights, deep emotions, inward joys, which alone can give the plenitude of truth, the evidence of celestial light. All things here below seem small indeed when the soul glances through the raging pages of these treatises'.[10] This account would have been impossible if Balzac himself had not been seized by the power of Swedenborgian words, which flowed with the spirit of both science and celestial light.

After this we find Balzac emphasizing Swedenborg the visionary, who, having opened his eyes inwardly, claimed communication with angels and the gift of conveying the marvels of heavenly truth to mankind. Through the accounts of what he had seen and heard in the world of spirits, Swedenborg answered some of the religious questions that Balzac had pondered since his youth, i.e., the existence of angels, heaven and hell, and the resurrection of the soul. In reading Swedenborg, the novelist was thus convinced that angels had all been people on earth, that they live in a heavenly society as we live on earth, and that mankind would live on after death and commence its spiritual life. Balzac was enraptured by the enduring presence of the Swede's lucid and methodical ethos in this field, as expressed not only in *Louis Lambert*: 'Thus Swedenborg's doctrine is the product of a lucid spirit who recorded the innumerable phenomena by which the angels manifest their presence among men', [11] but also in *Séraphîta*: 'Throughout the exactitude, the method, the presence of spirit, exploding and flowing down from a single fact, the existence of Angels'. [12]

Swedenborg's visionary gifts prompted Balzac to call him 'the prophet' or 'the Swedish prophet' on several occasions in *Louis Lambert* and *Séraphîta*, and according to Balzac the 'prophets'—sometimes called visionaries or messengers—are those whose internal vision records the Word of God as supreme reasoning, who come 'to push the nations to God' and, 'burning with love and faith', proclaim 'the sacred way in simple words that lead to the kingdom of heaven'. [13] From this perspective, Swedenborg is indeed a prophet: inspired by heaven, with his eyes opened internally. Unwavering in his faith and his love for the Lord and his neighbour, he gathered and studied the Word of God—the exegetic aspect of Swedenborg was also important to Balzac—and wrote in a clear and simple Latin to guide humanity towards the kingdom of heaven.

However, not happy just to call Swedenborg 'the prophet', Balzac also gave him the famous nickname 'the Buddha of the North'. [14] If he saw Buddha as the first great reformer of the primitive religions of Tibet, [15] then he saw Swedenborg as the new reformer of Christianity. But above all else he emphasized and appreciated the character of Swedenborgianism, which 'is but a repetition of ancient ideas in a Christian sense'[16] and which 'epitomizes all the religions, or rather the one religion of Humanity'.[17] This aspect is all the more important for Balzac, who was convinced that 'man has never had but one religion' and that all the prophets from a variety of religions have all held the same principles and the same ends.[18] Recognizing in his religion a sublime and mathematical system based on the principle of one single God, and in his personage a figure full of love towards God and man, the novelist discovered in the Swedish prophet the synthesis of all religions, to the point of likening him to the awakened sage of India who was geographically and chronologically the furthest away from him.

The theological works of Swedenborg read by Balzac

Despite Balzac's passionate interest in Swedenborg, his understanding of Swedenborgian thought has often been cast into doubt. This doubt arises from the claim that Balzac's knowledge of Swedenborg stems solely from his reading of *Abrégé des ouvrages d'Em. Swedenborg* (The Abridged Works of Emmanuel Swedenborg) by Daillant de La Touche (1744-1827),[19] which is refered to, exclusively, in *Séraphîta*. It is certain that Balzac 'plagiarized' this résumé, as was proven incontestably by Pauline Bernheim in her thesis entitled *Balzac und Swedenborg*.[20] Nonetheless, according to Balzac's bookbinding bill dated 12 January 1833, he also owned eight other volumes of the works of Swedenborg which he would have read or at the very least perused.[21] In his 'Lettre à M. Ch. Nodier', published in the *Revue de Paris* in October 1832, Balzac himself confided that he respects the works of the mystical authors like Swedenborg, Madame Guyon and Jacob Bœhme, and assured Nodier that he possesses them 'completely', bound and lined up on a particular shelf in his library.[22] The translations for these works were by Jean-Pierre Moët (1721-1806), the royal librarian to Versailles, who translated all of Swedenborg's theological works into French. And amongst these translations, the following twelve emerged after Moët's death, between 1819 and 1824, thanks to the care of an English Swedenborgian, John Augustus Tulk (1756-1845):[23]

1. *Du Ciel et de ses merveilles, et de l'Enfer*, Brussels, J. Maubach, 1819. (*Heaven and Hell*)
2. *La Vraie Religion chrétienne*, J. Maubach, 1819, 2 vols. (*The True Christian Religion*)
3. *Du Cheval blanc dont il est parlé dans l'Apocalypse*, J. Maubach, 1820. (*The White Horse*)
4. *De la Nouvelle Jérusalem et de sa doctrine céleste*, Paris, Treuttel and Würtz, 1821. (*The New Jerusalem and its Heavenly Doctrine*)
5. *Doctrine de la vie pour la Nouvelle Jérusalem*, Treuttel and Würtz, 1821. (*Doctrine of Life*)
6. *La Sagesse angélique sur le divin amour et sur la divine sagesse*, Treuttel and Würtz, 1822. (*Divine Love and Wisdom*)
7. *L'Apocalypse révélée*, Treuttel and Würtz, 1823, 2 vols. (*Apocalypse Revealed*)
8. *La Sagesse angélique sur la divine Providence*, Treuttel and Würtz, 1823. (*Divine Providence*)
9. *Les Délices de la sagesse sur l'amour conjugal*, Treuttel and Würtz, 1824. (*Conjugial Love*)
10. *Des Terres dans notre monde solaire, et des terres dans le ciel astral*, Treuttel and Würtz, 1824. (*The Worlds in Space*)
11. *Du Dernier Jugement et de la Babylone détruite*, Treuttel and Würtz, 1824. (*The Last Judgment*)
12. *Continuation du Dernier Jugement*, Treuttel and Würtz, 1824. (*The Continuation of the Last Judgment*)

Moët's translations are now almost forgotten, and have since been replaced by the more orthodox and precise translations of Jean-François-Étienne Le Boys des

Guays (1794-1864), who published all of Swedenborg's works in French from 1840 to 1859. However, when Balzac was writing his *Livre Mystique* trilogy, Moët's translations were the only ones available in France. Le Boys des Guays himself, having learnt that Moët had left the manuscripts of his translations, acquired them and used them as the basis for his own translations. In fact, it is said that one of Le Boys des Guays' collaborators felt 'the drawback of overly literal translations', and preferred Moët's more liberal efforts, which were a pleasure to read in French. [24]

In any case, it was Moët's translations which Balzac owned and read. Reading through his three mystical works, *Les Proscrits*, *Louis Lambert* and *Séraphîta*, we can see that he consulted at least five works by Swedenborg, namely: *Du Ciel et de ses merveilles, et de l'Enfer*; *La Sagesse angélique sur le divin amour et sur la divine sagesse*; *L'Apocalypse révélée*; *De la Nouvelle Jérusalem et de sa doctrine céleste*; and *La Vraie Religion chrétienne*. *Du Ciel et de l'Enfer*, in particular, has a striking presence in *Louis Lambert* and is commonly recognized as the first work read by Balzac. In *Séraphîta* there is a sentence which is correctly attributed to Swedenborg's *La Sagesse angélique sur le divin amour et sur la divine sagesse*, and elsewhere he demonstrates a keen interest in the spiritual interpretation introduced in the exegetic work, *L'Apocalypse révélée*, to which he accords just as much importance as St John's original text. Finally, Balzac can also be seen referring to the doctrine of Swedenborgian Christianity in *La Vraie Religion chrétienne* and *De la Nouvelle Jérusalem et de sa doctrine céleste*.

Let us now examine the ideas that Balzac drew from each work.

1) *Du Ciel et de ses merveilles, et de l'Enfer*.

In *Les Proscrits* (*The Exiles*), written in 1831 and presented as 'the peristyle of the edifice' [25] of *Le Livre Mystique*, the character of Doctor Sigier explains his theories of spheres, angels and God (who is the first principle and the source of the universe), whilst Dante also recounts the panoramic vision of the spheres, from paradise to hell.[26] Such ideas give some sense of Swedenborg, even if still only inspired by the memory of reading *Du Ciel et de l'Enfer* mixed with that of *The Divine Comedy*. However, in *Louis Lambert* the influence of *Du Ciel et de l'Enfer* is more central. For example: Louis, as a child, is described as reading a translation of this work upon meeting Madame de Staël; as a schoolboy he is said to often talk about 'heaven and hell' to his classmate, whom he tells about Swedenborg and with whom he tries to share 'his beliefs concerning angels';[27] later, he is given to explain everything 'by his system of the angels'.[28] He learns from Swedenborg that there exists in us 'two distinct creatures', one 'an internal being', the other 'an external being', and that when what we call death arrives, the internal being, in which 'the exquisite angelic nature' resides, begins its true life.[29] These ideas of angels and internal beings are so precious to the child that he cries out 'I needed to believe in a double nature and in Swedenborg's angels!'[30] And from these ideas of angels Balzac broaches ideas of 'spheres' (as he had done in his earlier work, *Les Proscrits*), recalling convincing explanations in Swedenborg that he deemed superior to those of Dante:

Apparently mingled here on earth, the creatures are there distributed according to the perfection of their *inner being*, in distinct spheres whose manners and language have nothing in common. In the invisible world, as in the real world, if some inhabitant of the lower spheres comes, all unworthy, into a higher sphere, not only can he never understand the customs and speeches there, but also his presence paralyzes the voices and the hearts. Dante, in his *Divine Comedy*, had perhaps some slight intuition of those spheres which begin in the world of torments, and rise, by an armillary movement, to the heavens.[31]

Balzac here draws upon *Du Ciel et de l'Enfer*, §35, where Swedenborg explains: there are three distinct heavens where an angel of one heaven cannot enter another heaven, and if an angel of a lower heaven ascends to a higher heaven, he 'is seized with a distress amounting to anguish', and if, on the contrary, an angel of a higher heaven descends to a lower heaven, he 'is deprived of his wisdom, hesitates in his speech and gives up in despair'. [32] Balzac was interested in the instinctive affinities and repulsions that exist between souls [33] as expressed through Lambert's: 'That man is not of my heaven'. [34] Balzac was also convinced by the theory on the difference between the spheres and of the suffering that one must endure in surroundings beneath oneself. The only difference between Swedenborg's theory and Balzac's understanding of it is the fact that Swedenborg talks of angels of the three heavens, whereas Balzac applies this theory to creatures here on earth.

If Balzac had only read *Du Ciel et de l'Enfer* when writing *Les Proscrits* and *Louis Lambert*, he most certainly began reading other works when writing *Séraphîta*. In addition to *Du Ciel et de l'Enfer* we also see him introducing *La Sagesse angélique sur le divin amour et sur la divine sagesse*, *Les Délices de la sagesse sur l'amour conjugal*, *L'Apocalypse révélée*, and *La Vraie Religion chrétienne* as 'the treatises on which the spirit of God casts its most vivid gleams', [35] and we can confirm that he consulted directly four of Swedenborg's works translated by Moët: *La Sagesse angélique sur le divin amour et sur la divine sagesse*; *L'Apocalypse révélée*; *De la Nouvelle Jérusalem et de sa doctrine céleste*; and *La Vraie Religion chrétienne*. We shall now compare the text of *Séraphîta* with Moët's translations; to this effect, we will now quote the French texts accompanied by their English translation.

2) *La Sagesse angélique sur le divin amour et sur la divine sagesse.*
At the start of his explanation of Swedenborgian angels, Pastor Becker cites a passage directly from this work, which reads: 'Les Anges ne sont donc pas Anges par eux-mêmes (*Sag. ang.* 57); ils se transforment par une conjonction intime avec Dieu'. ('The Angels are therefore not Angels as such (*Divine Love and Wisdom*, §57), they are transformed through their close conjunction with God.') [36] As Balzac indicates within the passage, this quote is lifted directly from Moët's translation at §57, which reads: 'C'est de là que les anges ne sont pas anges par eux-mêmes, mais qu'ils sont anges par cette conjonction avec Dieu-homme'. ('It

is from this that angels are not angels from themselves, but they are angels by virtue of this conjunction with the God-Man.') [37] Affected by the idea presented by Daillant—according to which 'God has not created angels specially, none exist who have not been men upon the earth. The earth is thus the nursery-ground of heaven' [38]—Balzac has inserted this sentence from Swedenborg in order to confirm the perfectibility of man which leads to him becoming an angel in proportion to his union with God.

3) *L'Apocalypse révélée.*

To show that everything in the Holy Scripture has an inner meaning, and that the 'angelic spirits' (the 'angels' according to Swedenborg) can fathom the truth of Saint John's Apocalypse, Balzac quotes the first verse from chapter XXI of the Apocalypse: 'Je vis un nouveau ciel et une nouvelle terre, car le premier ciel et la première terre étaient passés'. ('I saw a new heaven and a new earth, for the first heaven and the first earth were passed away.') [39] For this passage from St John, Balzac consulted neither *Abrégé*, nor the translation of the Bible by Lemaître de Sacy, [40] which he might have used, but rather *L'Apocalypse révélée,* translated by Moët, which read: 'Alors je vis un nouveau ciel et une nouvelle terre, parce que le premier ciel et la première terre étaient passés'. ('And I saw a new heaven and a new land, for the former heaven and the former land were passed away.') [41]

Apart from Balzac replacing 'parce que' with 'car', his sentence conforms completely with Moët's translation, including the word order in the phrases 'un nouveau ciel' and 'une nouvelle terre'. In de Sacy's translation, on the other hand, the word order differs slightly, with the adjectives coming after the nouns: 'un ciel nouveau' and 'une terre nouvelle'. Balzac also follows Moët in adopting the verb 'passer', whereas de Sacy's translation has 'disparaître'. Balzac also emphasizes Swedenborg's explanation of the horse of the Apocalypse: 'Le cheval de l'Apocalypse est, dit Swedenborg, l'image visible de l'intelligence humaine montée par la mort, car elle porte en elle son principe de destruction'. ('"The horse of the Apocalypse", says Swedenborg, "is the visible image of human intellect ridden by death, for it bears within itself its principle of destruction"'.) [42]

Having first read Daillant's summary, [43] he would have been prompted to return to the source: in verse 8 of chapter VI, Swedenborg interprets the inner meaning of the pale horse at §§320-1. (See also 'Summary of verses from Chapter VI'):

Et je vis aussitôt paraître un cheval pâle, signifie *l'intelligence de la Parole, détruite quant au bien et quant au vrai*. [...] *Celui qui était assis sur ce cheval avait pour nom la mort, et l'enfer suivait avec lui*, signifie *l'extinction de la vie spirituelle, et conséquemment la damnation*.
('And I saw and behold a pale horse' signifies the understanding of the Word destroyed as to both good and truth. [...] 'And the one sitting upon it, his name was death, and hell was following with him' signifies the extinction of spiritual life and the resulting damnation.) [44]

We see here that Balzac combines the general interpretation of the horse, a symbol of understanding, with its pale colour, a symbol of death and destruction. If Swedenborg means here that spiritual life, founded upon the knowledge of good and truth drawn from the Word, 'is extinguished when there is a denial of God, of the holiness of the Word, and of eternal life', [45] then Balzac reads into it a warning against science and human reasoning. [46] Struck by this image, Balzac later used this figure in David's apocalyptic vision: 'Enfin, la Mort est descendue de son cheval pâle et a dit: "Je t'obéirai!"' ('At last Death got off his pale horse, crying, "I will obey thee!"') [47]

4) *De la Nouvelle Jérusalem et de sa doctrine céleste.*
Although Balzac did not count this work amongst the 'treatises on which the spirit of God casts its most vivid gleams', [48] he refers to it once in Pastor Becker's dialogue explaining Correspondences in Holy Scripture:

LA PAROLE de Dieu fut entièrement écrite par pures Correspondances, elle couvre un sens interne ou spirituel qui, sans la science des Correspondances, ne peut être compris. Il existe, dit Swedenborg (*Doctrine céleste*, 26 [*sic*]), des ARCANES innombrables dans le sens interne des Correspondances.
(The WORD of God was wholly written by pure Correspondences, and covers an internal or spiritual sense, which, without the science of Correspondences, cannot be understood. 'There exist', says Swedenborg (*Celestial Doctrine*, 26 [*sic*]), 'innumerable Arcana within the internal sense of the Correspondences'.) [49]

Balzac accidentally wrote the reference '*Celestial Doctrine*, 26' instead of writing '260'. At §§261 and 260 of Moët's translation we read:

La Parole, quant au sens de la lettre, a été écrite par pures correspondances [...] Néanmoins cette science [des correspondances] est au-dessus de toutes les autres sciences, parce que sans elle la Parole est incompréhensible [...] (n° 261).
(As to the sense of the letter, the Word was composed by means of pure correspondences [...] This science, nevertheless, is more excellent than all other sciences, because apart from it the Word cannot be understood [...].)

Il y a des Arcanes innombrables dans le sens interne ou spirituel (n° 260).
(*In the internal or spiritual sense of the Word there are innumerable arcana.*) [50]

To explain that the spiritual understanding of the angelic spirits surpasses all of the human sciences, Balzac referred to this work, which condenses Swedenborg's essential doctrine, and in which the inner meaning and the Correspondences of the Word can be found.

5) *La Vraie Religion chrétienne.*
Finally, we turn to Balzac's particularly striking appreciation for Swedenborg's *La*

Vraie Religion chrétienne, where he expresses his admiration by echoing some of Daillant's words, [51] which in English translation are: 'His *True Religion* [*Vraie Religion*], which sums up his whole doctrine and is vigorous with light, was conceived and written at the age of eighty-three'. [52] Looking at this work—which Balzac saw as Swedenborg's masterpiece and therefore turned to more than any other—we can see how he introduced certain doctrinal elements and a few episodes from the *Memorabilias* from it into *Séraphîta*. To demonstrate the power of the internal being to be transported without physical constraints, he cites §157 from chapter III of *Vraie Religion chrétienne*, 'De l'Esprit saint et de la Divine Opération' ('The Holy Spirit and the Way God Works'):

> il [l'ange] a le don de se séparer de son corps, et voit les cieux comme les prophètes les ont vus, et comme Swedenborg les voyait lui-même. 'Dans cet état, dit-il (*Vraie Religion*, 136 [*sic*]), l'esprit de l'homme est transporté d'un lieu à un autre, le corps restant où il est, état dans lequel j'ai demeuré pendant vingt-six années.' Nous devons entendre ainsi toutes les paroles bibliques où il est dit: *L'esprit m'emporta*.
> (the Angel has the gift of separating himself from his body, and he sees heavens as the prophets and as Swedenborg himself saw them. 'In this state', writes Swedenborg (*True Religion*, §136), 'the spirit of a man is transported from one place to another, his body remaining where it is—a state I lived for twenty-six years'. We should understand thus all biblical words which say: *The spirit led me*.) [53]

While drawing upon the first sentence in *Abrégé*, Balzac also consults *La Vraie Religion chrétienne*, as is indicated in quotation marks in the passage, with the source given as '*Vraie Religion*, 136'. Yet, why does Balzac cite '136' instead of '157', [54] as it should be? We note two errors here: firstly, Balzac or his typographer seems to have written '136' instead of '156'; secondly, in Moët's translation the number '157' is skipped, with that section being included under §156. So, originally, Balzac had consulted §157 which reads:

> Dans cet état, l'esprit de l'homme, comme son âme, quant à la vue, peut être transporté d'un lieu dans un autre, le corps restant où il est. Cet état est celui dans lequel j'ai été pendant 26 années.
> (In that state a person's spirit, as the visual capacity of his mind, can be transported from place to place while his body remains in one place. This is the state in which I have been for the last twenty-six years [...].)

And the expression '*L'esprit m'emporta*' ('a spirit lifted me up') is also taken from §157: 'Voici ce que dit Ézéchiel: *L'esprit m'emporta* [...]'. ('Ezekiel says: "A spirit lifted me up [...]"') [55] Balzac also takes a keen interest in chapter IV of *Vraie Religion chrétienne* devoted to Holy Scripture: he cites the explanations of Exodus and Ezekiel (§§218, 219) as well as two *Memorabilias* on the subject of scripture (§§278, 279). First, through the voice of the doubter Mr Becker, he emphasizes that certain descriptions in Swedenborg's works have been a matter of scandal, giving as an example the explanation of the mysterious powers of precious stones:

> ses jardins [...] où les pierreries mystiques, la sardoine, l'escarboucle, la chrysolite, la chrysoprase, la cyanée, la chalcédoine, le béryl, L'URIM et le THUMIM sont doués de mouvement, expriment des vérités célestes, et qu'on peut interroger, car elles répondent par des variations de lumière (*VRAIE RELIGION*, 219).
> (his gardens where [...] the mystical stones, the sard, carbuncle, chrysolite, chrysoprase, jacinth, chalcedony, beryl, the Urim and Thummim, are endowed with motion, express celestial truths, and reply by variations of light to questions put to them (*True Religion*, 219).) [56]

Balzac references §219, but in the first edition of *Séraphîta*, published in the

Revue de Paris, he put '*Vraie Religion*, 218'. Balzac in fact summarizes both of these sections, §§218 and 219, which explain the meaning of the precious stones on Aaron's ephod and the King of Tyre's clothing. He follows Moët's translation, and retains the names of stones which are less well known and more mystical, leaving out the better known ones, such as diamond, ruby, sapphire and emerald. He also presents the divine power of Urim and Thummim as applying to all the precious stones. Moët's translation features 'l'escarboucle', 'la chrysoprase', 'la cyanée' and 'la chrysolithe' for Aaron's ephod, and 'le béryl', 'la sardoine' and 'la chrysoprase' for 'les pierres précieuses qui étaient dans le jardin d'Eden' ('the precious stones in the Garden of Eden'); [57] and as for Urim and Thummim, this explanation is given: the Urim and Thummim represented divine truth, and 'les réponses étaient données par les variations de lumière et en même temps par une tacite perception, ou par une vive voix qui se faisait entendre'. ('[R]eplies were given by changes in the quality of light, accompanied by an unspoken perception, or by direct speech [...].') [58]

Balzac then inserts two *Memorabilias*, one on the subject of angelic scripture (§278), the other on ancient Word (§279).

Dans un autre Mémorable, il reçoit du ciel un petit papier sur lequel il vit, dit-il, les lettres dont se servaient les peuples primitifs, et qui étaient composées de lignes courbes, avec de petits anneaux qui se portaient en haut.
(In another of these *Memorabilia*, he receives from heaven a bit of paper, on which he saw, he says, the letters of the primitive peoples, which were composed of curved lines, with small rings put over.) [59]

This *Memorabilia* seems to have made a great impression on Balzac as earlier, noting the source, he mentions Swedenborg's heavenly worlds, 'where the Word is written in *cornicule* (*True Religion*, 278)' [60] at the same time expressing doubt in saying 'I have failed to conceive the *cornicular* writing of the Angels'. [61] Balzac must have been struck by Swedenborg's very clear descriptions, insisting upon the term 'cornicule' which features in Moët's translation, §278:

> Voici le SECOND MÉMORABLE. Un jour, il me fut envoyé du ciel un petit papier couvert de lettres hébraïques, mais semblables à celles dont se servaient les primitifs, chez qui ces lettres [...] étaient [composées] de lignes courbes, avec de petit cercles ou de petits anneaux qui se portaient en haut. [...] Ils [Les anges] me disaient encore qu'ils avaient chez eux la divine Parole écrite en caractères inflexes avec des cornicules et des accents significatifs. [...] *Il ne passera pas un iotha et un accent de la loi* [...] Matth. V, 18.).
> (The second experience. Once a paper was sent down to me from heaven written in Hebrew letters, but in the script used in ancient times; the letters [...] were curved, with flourishes pointing upwards [...] They also said that they had among themselves the Word written in curved letters with flourishes and serifs which conveyed a meaning. [...] 'Not a jot nor a stroke shall pass away from the Law [...]'. Matt. 5:18.) [62]

Moët translates Swedenborg's Latin word '*corniculum*' in three different ways in this passage, trying to make it clearer, first by writing it as 'de petit cercles ou de petits anneaux' (small circles or small rings), then as 'des cornicules' (cornicules) and finally as 'un accent'. It is the second rendering that attracts Balzac's attention, all the more so for it being incomprehensible in the French to those unaware that Swedenborg's use of this word is drawn from Sebastian Schmidt's Latin version of the Gospel of Matthew. [63] Balzac had great trust in Swedenborg the exegete and the historian. Here is another *Memorabilia* (§279) which shows it:

> [Swedenborg] put reconnaître dans la Tartarie les vestiges du plus ancien livre de la Parole, nommé LES GUERRES DE JEHOVAH, et LES ÉNONCÉS dont il est parlé par Moïse dans les NOMBRES (XXI, 14, 15, 27-30), par Josué,

par Jérémie et par Samuel. LES GUERRES DE JEHOVAH seraient la partie historique, et LES ÉNONCÉS la partie prophétique de ce livre antérieur à la Genèse. Swedenborg a même affirmé que le JASCHAR ou LE LIVRE DU JUSTE, mentionné par Josué, existait dans la Tartarie Orientale, avec le culte des Correspondances.

([…] he was able to recognize the vestiges of the oldest books of the Word, namely *The Wars of Jehovah* and *The Enunciations*, spoken of by Moses in Numbers (XXI, 14, 15, 27-30), by Joshua, Jeremiah, and Samuel. *The Wars of Jehovah* may be the historical part and *The Enunciations* the prophetical part of this book anterior to Genesis. Swedenborg even affirmed that the Jaschar or the Book of the Righteous, mentioned by Joshua, was in existence in Eastern Tartary, together with the worship of Correspondences.) [64]

While basing this on Daillant's *Abrégé*, [65] a fascinated Balzac goes back to Moët's translation, and completes his exposition with this explanation: 'les parties historiques s'appelaient les GUERRES DE JÉHOVAH, et les parties prophétiques les ÉNONCÉS'. ('[I]ts historical parts are called The Wars of Jehovah, the prophetical parts The Utterances.') [66]

Finally, Balzac leaves a trail that suggests he was able to glance through the chapters on 'Charité' ('Charity') (§394) and 'Régénération' ('Regeneration') (§586). Speaking about the perfection of the internal man, he conflates two ideas from *La Vraie Religion chrétienne* that are originally given separately: 'Les Esprits Angéliques passent par trois natures d'amour, car l'homme ne peut être régénéré que successivement (*Vraie Religion*)'. ('The Spiritual Angels pass through three natures of love, because man can be only regenerated successively (*True Religion*).') [67] In Moët's translation we read: 'IL Y A TROIS AMOURS UNIVERSELS: L'AMOUR DU CIEL, L'AMOUR DU MONDE, L'AMOUR DE SOI-MÊME'. ('There are three universal loves, the love of heaven, the love of the world, and self-love.') [68] and 'L'homme ne peut être régénéré que successivement.' ('[A] person can only be regenerated by stages.') [69] Both of these passages are found in *Abrégé*, however, Balzac himself cites the source as *'Vraie Religion'*. Even if he drew these sentences from *Abrégé*, he did at least know they emerged originally from *La Vraie Religion chrétienne*.

*

Concerning Swedenborg's other works, we will comment briefly on the three works which are mentioned at least once in *Séraphîta*, namely: *Les Délices de la sagesse sur l'amour conjugal* (*Conjugial Love*), *Des Terres dans notre monde solaire, et des terres dans le ciel astral* (*The Worlds in Space*) and *Arcanes célestes* (*Arcana Caelestia*). Balzac mentions *Les Délices de la sagesse sur l'amour conjugal* once, counting it amongst the seven divine treatises, but, strangely, he does not quote a single passage from it, and neither does he show any particular interest in this work, even though the subjects dealt with in the book, such as marriage in heaven, the state of couples after death, and truly conjugial love, must have attracted his attention. As for *Des Terres dans notre monde solaire, et des terres dans le ciel astral*, he does not consider it to be amongst the divine treatises, but he does express his astonishment at the wonderful visions evoked in this work. Certainly, everything he quotes in *Séraphîta* is taken from *Abrégé*, where Daillant summarizes the concrete descriptions of the inhabitants of different planets, but, in imagining the scene where Swedenborg is lifted up by an angel for his first voyage, he attributes to it a sublimity which exceeds the epics by Klopstock, Milton, Tasso and Dante.[70] Regarding *Arcanes célestes*, he knew that it was an enormous work 'in sixteen volumes containing thirty thousand propositions' [71]—which produced a frank admiration by the novelist for the Swedish author's productivity [72]—and he also knew that the title *Arcanes célestes* represents one of the key concepts in the greater body of Swedenborgian thought. Although the French translation of this work had not yet been published at the time of writing *Séraphîta*—1841 was the year of Le Boys des Guays began the publication of his translation—he would have been able to find the title, *Arcanes célestes* in 16 volumes in the catalogue inserted at the beginning of Moët's translations. Here there was a list of published titles and titles yet to be published. He would also have learnt of it from the voluminous extracts found in *Du Ciel et de l'Enfer* and in *De la Nouvelle Jérusalem et de sa doctrine céleste*.

Conclusion

We have attempted here to shed light on Balzac's reading of Swedenborg, looking in particular at those passages where he tried to assimilate Swedenborgian thought. If *Du Ciel et de l'Enfer* formed the starting point and basis of Swedenborgian themes, where Balzac drew directly on the doctrine of angels, spheres and the internal man, then other works, sometimes doctrinal, sometimes exegetic, enabled him to gain a deeper understanding of what he had already taken from *Du Ciel et de l'Enfer*, and provided him with new subjects to develop. In *De la Nouvelle Jérusalem et de sa doctrine céleste* and *La Vraie Religion chrétienne*, Balzac consulted in particular the chapters on Holy Scripture, whilst in *L'Apocalypse révélée* he drew upon certain specific examples. Striving to reveal the inner meaning of the Bible, Balzac could, in this role at least, have been called Swedenborg's apostle. Furthermore, in consulting *La Vraie Religion chrétienne* above all else in writing *Séraphîta*, he singled out the unparalleled value of this doctrinal work, something truly rare in France of the first half of the nineteenth century.

With a knowledge of the works of Swedenborg, one can criticize several misunderstandings in the Balzacian interpretation; however, it should be understood, as K-E Sjödén points out, that at this time the Swedenborgian church did not yet exist in France.[73] His enthusiasm for Swedenborg, the person and his works, and his efforts to procure the works and to devour the Swedish prophet's ideas, bear witness to an exceptional event in the spiritual life of the French writer. We should also take into account the apology he writes in *Séraphîta*, at the beginning of the account of the Swedenborgian doctrine: 'but this summary, made from memory, would be necessarily incorrect',[74] as well as his aim which he specifies in the 'Preface to *Le*

Livre Mystique' saying that 'the author has attempted to make it [Swedenborg's incomprehensible doctrine] attractive like a modern novel [...] he hopes that the people of the world, tempted by the form, will understand the future shown to us by Swedenborg's hand pointing towards the heavens'.[75] Through this desire, he not only contributed to passing on Swedenborg's name but also a Swedenborgian atmosphere to his readers—amongst whom were writers such as Théophile Gautier, Charles Baudelaire, August Strindberg, Paul Valéry and Gaston Bachelard—and he also shared with his readers that aspiration towards the celestial world of Swedenborg that Gaston Bachelard called 'the Swedenborgian dynamism' of ascension.[76]

NOTES

* This essay has been translated from the French. References to citations from Balzac are to French editions and, when accompanied in these notes with the original French, the corresponding English translations in the main text of the essay are the work of the translator of this essay. Other Balzac citations in English have been modified by the author from standard English translations to more closely accord with Balzac's French; cross-references to these English translations are given here in the endnotes.

[1] Honoré de Balzac, *Louis Lambert*, in *La Comédie Humaine*, vol. XI, coll. 'Bibliothèque de la Pléiade' (Paris: Gallimard, 1980), pp. 655-6; cf. *Louis Lambert*, in *Séraphita*, tr. Clara Bell (Sawtry, Cambs.: Dedalus, 1995), p. 237; and *Louis Lambert*, in *La Comédie Humaine of Honoré de Balzac*, vol. XXXVIII, tr. Katharine Prescott Wormeley (Boston: Roberts Brothers, 1896), p. 97.

[2] 'Vous savez quelles sont mes religions, je ne suis point orthodoxe et ne crois pas à l'Église romaine [...] Le swedenborgisme qui n'est qu'une répétition dans le sens chrétien d'anciennes idées, est ma religion, avec l'augmentation que j'y fais de l'incompréhensibilité de Dieu': Balzac, *Lettres à Mme Hanska* (Letters to Madame Hanska), vol. I (1832-44), ed. Roger Pierrot, Robert Laffont (Paris: Laffont, 'Bouquins', 1990), 31 May 1837, p. 386.

[3] 'de ces exaltations qui n'arrivent qu'aux dépens de la vie': ibid., 1 July 1834, p. 170.

4 'On peut faire *Goriot* tous les jours; on ne fait *Séraphîta* qu'une fois dans sa vie': ibid., 11 March 1835, p. 235.

5 'Swedenborg, le grand prophète suédois, disait que la terre était un homme': Balzac, *Le Cousin Pons*, in *La Comédie humaine*, vol. VII, 'Bibliothèque de la Pléiade' (Paris: Gallimard, 1977), p. 587. This expression: 'Earth is a man' must be: 'heaven is a man'. Swedenborg actually said that 'heaven represents man' (*Heaven and Hell*, §§ 59, 65, 90, 94). Baudelaire used this sentence correctly: 'D'ailleurs Swedenborg, qui possédait une âme bien plus grande [que celle de Fourier], nous avait déjà enseigné que *le ciel est un très grand homme*' ('Moreover, Swedenborg, who was posessed of a far greater soul [than that of Fourier], had already taught us that *heaven is a great man*'): Charles Baudelaire, 'Notice sur Victor Hugo', in *Œuvres complètes*, 'Bibliothèque de la Pléiade' (Paris: Gallimard, 1961), vol. II, p. 133.

6 'la doctrine de Swedenborg sur les anges': Balzac, *L'Envers de l'histoire contemporaine,* in *La Comédie humaine*, vol. VIII, 'Bibliothèque de la Pléiade' (Paris: Gallimard, 1977), p. 318; cf. *The Seamy Side of History* (Stroud, Glos.: Nonsuch Publishing Limited, 2005), p. 104.

7 Balzac, *Séraphîta*, in *La Comédie humaine*, vol. XI, 'Bibliothèque de la Pléiade' (Paris: Gallimard, 1980), p. 765; cf. *Séraphita*, tr. Clara Bell (Sawtry, Cambs.: Dedalus, 1995), p. 44; and *Seraphita*, in *La Comédie Humaine of Honoré de Balzac*, vol. XXXIX, tr. Katharine Prescott Wormeley (Boston: Roberts Brothers, 1896), p. 56.

8 Balzac, *Séraphîta*, pp. 766, 775 (Pléiade); cf. p. 45 (Bell); p. 58 (Wormeley).

9 Ibid., p. 775 (Pléiade); cf. pp. 55-6 (Bell); p. 71 (Wormeley).

10 Ibid., p. 775 (Pléiade); cf. p. 55 (Bell); p. 70 (Wormeley).

11 Balzac, *Louis Lambert*, p. 617 (Pléiade); cf. p. 191 (Bell); p. 42 (Wormeley).

12 Balzac, *Séraphîta*, p. 775 (Pléiade); cf. p. 56 (Bell); p. 71 (Wormeley).

13 Ibid., p. 826 (Pléiade); cf. p. 117 (Bell); pp. 148-9 (Wormeley).

14 Balzac, *Louis Lambert*, p. 656 (Pléiade); cf. p. 238 (Bell); p. 98 (Wormeley).

15 Ibid., p. 656 (Pléiade); cf. p. 237 (Bell); p. 97 (Wormeley).

16 'n'est qu'une répétition dans le sens chrétien d'anciennes idées': Balzac, *Lettres à Mme Hanska*, 31 May 1837, p. 386.

17 Balzac, *Louis Lambert*, p. 656 (Pléiade); cf. p. 237 (Bell); p. 97 (Wormeley).

[18] Ibid., p. 656 (Pléiade); cf. p. 237 (Bell); p. 97 (Wormeley).

[19] François-Jean Daillant de La Touche, *Abrégé des ouvrages d'Em. Swedenborg* (The Abridged Works of Em. Swedenborg containing the doctrine of the New Jerusalem, preceded by a discourse examining the life of the author, the nature of his writings, and their relationship to the present time) (Strasbourg: J G Treuttel, 1788).

[20] Pauline Bernheim, *Balzac und Swedenborg: Einfluss der Mystik Swedenborgs und Saint-Martins auf die Romandichtung Balzacs* (Balzac and Swedenborg: Influence of the mystics Swedenborg and Saint Martin on Balzac's novels) (Berlin: Emil Ebering, 1914).

[21] This bill was discovered by Madeleine Ambrière-Fargeaud, and reads '8 Swedenborg': Madeleine Ambrière-Fargeaud, 'Madame Balzac, son mysticisme et ses enfants' (Madame Balzac, her mysticism and her children), in *L'Année Balzacienne*, 1965, p. 30; and Madeleine Ambrière-Fargeaud, *Balzac et 'la Recherche de l'Absolu'* (Balzac and 'the Search for the Absolute') (Paris: PUF, 1999), p. 202.

[22] *Revue de Paris*, 21 October 1832, p. 169; Balzac, *Oeuvres diverses*, vol. II, 'Bibliothèque de la Pléiade' (Paris: Gallimard, 1996), p. 1204.

[23] Karl-Erik Sjödén, *Swedenborg en France* (Stockholm: Almqvist & Wiksell International, 1985), p. 66.

[24] 'l'inconvénient des traductions trop littérales': ibid., pp. 68-70.

[25] 'le péristyle de l'édifice': Balzac, 'Preface to *Le Livre Mystique*', in *La Comédie humaine*, vol. XI, 'Bibliothèque de la Pléiade' (Paris: Gallimard, 1980), p. 506.

[26] Balzac, *Les Proscrits*, in *La Comédie humaine*, vol. XI, 'Bibliothèque de la Pléiade' (Paris: Gallimard, 1980), pp. 539-55; cf. *The Exiles*, in *Séraphita*, tr. Clara Bell (Sawtry, Cambs.: Dedalus, 1995), pp. 297 ff.; and *The Exiles*, in *La Comédie Humaine of Honoré de Balzac*, vol. XXXIX, tr. Katharine Prescott Wormeley (Boston: Roberts Brothers, 1896), pp. 251 ff.

[27] Balzac, *Louis Lambert*, p. 616 (Pléiade); cf. p. 190 (Bell); p. 40 (Wormeley).

[28] Ibid., p. 618 (Pléiade); cf. p. 192 (Bell); p. 43 (Wormeley).

[29] Ibid., p. 617 (Pléiade); cf. p. 190 (Bell); p. 41 (Wormeley).

[30] Ibid., p. 622 (Pléiade); cf. p. 197 (Bell); p. 49 (Wormeley).

[31] Ibid., p. 617 (Pléiade); cf. p. 191 (Bell); pp. 41-2 (Wormeley).

[32] Swedenborg, *Heaven and Hell*, tr. Doris H Harley (London: Swedenborg Society, 1989), §35, p. 24.

[33] Balzac, *Les Proscrits*, p. 540 (Pléiade); cf. p. 299 (Bell).

[34] Balzac, *Louis Lambert*, p. 677 (Pléiade); cf. p. 253 (Bell); p. 116 (Wormeley).

[35] Balzac, *Séraphîta*, p. 773 (Pléiade); cf. p. 53 (Bell); p. 67 (Wormeley).

[36] Ibid., p. 777 (Pléiade); cf. p. 57 (Bell); p. 73 (Wormeley).

[37] Swedenborg, *La Sagesse angélique sur le divin amour et sur la divine sagesse*, tr. Jean-Pierre Moët (Paris: Treuttel et Würtz, 1822), §57; Swedenborg, *Divine Love and Wisdom*, tr. Clifford Harley and Doris H Harley (London: Swedenborg Society, 1987), §57, p. 21.

[38] Balzac, *Séraphîta*, pp. 776-7 (Pléiade); cf. p. 57 (Bell); p. 73 (Wormeley); Daillant de La Touche, *Abrégé*, p. 353.

[39] Balzac, *Séraphîta*, p. 780 (Pléiade); cf. p. 62 (Bell); pp. 78-9 (Wormeley).

[40] *La sainte Bible, contenant l'Ancien et le Nouveau Testament*, tr. Louis-Isaac Lemaître de Sacy (Paris: J Smith, 1821): '[...] je vis un ciel nouveau et une terre nouvelle. Car le premier ciel et la première terre avaient disparu [...]' ('I saw a new heaven and a new earth for the first heaven and the first earth were passed away' AV).

[41] Swedenborg, *L'Apocalypse révélée*, tr. Jean-Pierre Moët (Paris: Treuttel et Würtz, 1823), §§876-7, pp. 392-4; Swedenborg, *The Apocalypse Revealed*, tr. Frank F Coulson (London: Swedenborg Society, 1970), vol. 2, §§876-7, pp. 888-9.

[42] Balzac, *Séraphîta*, p. 780 (Pléiade); cf. p. 62 (Bell); p. 79 (Wormeley). Cf. Swedenborg, *L'Apocalypse révélée*, vol. I, pp. 259, 261, 262 and §§298, 320, 321.

[43] Daillant de La Touche, *Abrégé*, p. 138, note 4.

[44] Swedenborg, *L'Apocalypse révélée*, tr. Moët, §§320-1; Swedenborg, *The Apocalypse Revealed*, tr. Frank F Coulson, vol. 1, §§320-1, pp. 278-9.

[45] Swedenborg, *The Apocalypse Revealed*, tr. Frank F Coulson, vol. 1, §321, p. 279.

[46] In chapter IV, Séraphîta develops a long discussion on the human sciences opposed to belief. See Balzac, *Séraphîta*, pp. 826-7 ff. (Pléiade).

[47] Balzac, *Séraphîta*, p. 800 (Pléiade); cf. p. 86 (Bell); p. 109 (Wormeley).

[48] See note 35 above.

[49] Balzac, *Séraphîta*, pp. 778-9 (Pléiade); cf. p. 60 (Bell); p. 76 (Wormeley).

[50] Swedenborg, *De la Nouvelle Jérusalem et de sa doctrine céleste*, tr. Jean-Pierre Moët (Paris: Treuttel et Würtz, 1821), §§261 and 260; Swedenborg, *The New Jerusalem and its Heavenly Doctrine*, tr. Rudolph L Tafel (London: Swedenborg Society, 1993), §§261 and 260, pp. 150-1 and 148.

[51] Daillant de La Touche, *Abrégé*, pp. XLV-XLVI.

[52] Balzac, *Séraphîta*, p. 775 (Pléiade); cf. p. 56 (Bell); p. 71 (Wormeley).

[53] Ibid., p. 781 (Pléiade); cf. p. 63 (Bell); p. 80 (Wormeley).

[54] Kohei Sawasaki refers to this number in the notes of the Japanese translation of *Séraphîta* (Tokyo: Kokusho kanko-kai, 1976; repr. 2004), p. 101.

[55] Swedenborg, *La Vraie Religion chrétienne*, tr. Jean-Pierre Moët (Bruxelles: J Maubach, 1819), vol. 1, §157, p. 246; Swedenborg, *The True Christian Religion*, tr. John Chadwick (London: Swedenborg Society, 1988), vol. I, §157, p. 206.

[56] Balzac, *Séraphîta*, p. 774 (Pléiade); cf. p. 54 (Bell); p. 69 (Wormeley).

[57] Swedenborg, *Vraie Religion chrétienne*, tr. Moët, vol. 1, §§218-19, pp. 331-2.

[58] Ibid., §218, p. 332; Swedenborg, *The True Christian Religion*, tr. John Chadwick, vol. I, §218, p. 277.

[59] Balzac, *Séraphîta*, p. 776 (Pléiade); cf. p. 56 (Bell); p. 72 (Wormeley). Cf. Bernheim, p. 72 and Sawasaki, p. 91.

[60] Balzac, *Séraphîta*, p. 774 (Pléiade); cf. pp. 54-5 (Bell); p. 70 (Wormeley).

[61] Ibid., *Séraphîta*, p. 775 (Pléiade); cf. p. 56 (Bell); p. 71 (Wormeley).

[62] Swedenborg, *La Vraie Religion chrétienne*, tr. Moët, vol. 1, §278, pp. 378-9; Swedenborg, *The True Christian Religion*, tr. Chadwick, vol. I, §278, pp. 318-19.

[63] *Biblia sacra, sive testamentum vetus et novum ex linguis originalibus in liguam latinam translatum, a Sebastiano Schmidt, Strasbourg* (1696); facsimile reproduction with Swedenborg's annotations in the margin (Bryn Athyn: The Academy of the New Church, 2005), in 2 volumes.

[64] Balzac, *Séraphîta*, p. 766 (Pléiade); cf. p. 44 (Bell); p. 57 (Wormeley).

[65] Daillant de La Touche, *Abrégé*, p. 135.

[66] Swedenborg, *La Vraie Religion chrétienne*, tr. Moët, vol. 1, §279, p. 379; Swedenborg, *The True Christian Religion*, tr. Chadwick, vol. I, §279, p. 319.

[67] Balzac, *Séraphîta*, p. 777 (Pléiade); cf. p. 58 (Bell); p. 73 (Wormeley).

[68] Swedenborg, *La Vraie Religion chrétienne*, tr. Moët, vol. 2, §394, p. 7; Swedenborg, *The True Christian Religion*, tr. Chadwick, vol. II, §394, p. 454.

[69] Swedenborg, *La Vraie Religion chrétienne*, tr. Moët, vol. 2, §586, p. 218; Swedenborg, *The True Christian Religion*, tr. Chadwick, vol. II, §586, p. 630.

[70] Balzac, *Séraphîta*, p. 769 (Pléiade); cf. p. 48 (Bell); p. 62 (Wormeley).

[71] Ibid., p. 779 (Pléiade); cf. pp. 60-1 (Bell); p. 77 (Wormeley). Correctly speaking, 10837 numbered sections.

[72] K-E Sjödén remarks upon this aspect in *Swedenborg en France*, p. 170.

[73] It was in 1837 that the translator, Le Boys des Guays, officially opened the religion of the New Jerusalem in Saint Amand (Cher) in central France, and the following year he founded the monthly review, *La Nouvelle Jérusalem*, which continued until 1847. In Paris, it was not until 1883 that the temple of the Society of the New Church was built with a library annexed alongside, behind the Panthéon. This Society published the monthly organ *L'Église de l'Avenir* (The Church of the Future) between 1892 and 1898. Cf. K-E Sjödén, *Swedenborg en France*, pp. 96-103, 140-3, 170.

[74] Balzac, *Séraphîta*, p. 776 (Pléiade); cf. p. 57 (Bell); p. 73 (Wormeley).

[75] 'l'auteur a tâché de la [l'incompréhensible doctrine de Swedenborg] rendre attrayante comme un roman moderne. [...] il espère que les gens du monde, affriolés par la forme, comprendront l'avenir que montre la main de Swedenborg levée vers le ciel': Balzac, 'Preface to *Le Livre Mystique*', p. 507.

[76] 'le dynamisme swedenborgien': Bachelard, *Le droit de rêver* (Paris: PUF, 'Quadrige', 2007), ch. 'Balzac: *Séraphîta*', p. 129 (text reproduced from the preface to *Séraphîta*, in *L'Œuvre de Balzac*, vol. XII (Le Club français du livre, 1955)).

Spiritualized science and the celestial artist: Nathaniel Hawthorne and Swedenborgian aesthetics

Devin P Zuber

In 1852, Ralph Waldo Emerson famously declared in his journal that 'this age is Swedenborg's', reflecting the widespread influence of the Scandinavian mystic (1688-1772) on mid-century America.[1] Swedenborg's impact on Romanticism had been profound—influencing figures as diverse as William Blake and Friedrich Schelling—but the works of the theologian found a particularly warm reception within later New England transcendentalism. F O Matthiessen acknowledged the importance of Swedenborg when he joked that his seminal *American Renaissance* could have become other books entitled *The Age of Swedenborg* and *The Age of Fourier*;[2] Perry Miller similarly argues that the Swedish seer is 'as fundamental as Coleridge and Carlyle' for the period's intellectual digest.[3] Swedenborg became one of Emerson's favourite authors—his mystical profundity was 'to be read in long thousands of years by some stream in Paradise'[4]—and largely due to Emerson's amplification, Margaret Fuller, Bronson Alcott and others in the Transcendental circle also came to read and discuss the Swedish seer.

Nathaniel Hawthorne, by comparison, initially seems to have had little interest in Emerson's representative mystic. References to Swedenborg are practically non-existent in his notebooks and letters, and only one character in the corpus—the semi-autobiographical Miles Coverdale—alludes to familiarity with Swedenborg's work. Swedenborg does not appear in the lending lists from the Athenaeum that record Hawthorne's (and his sister's) prolific reading. This apparent textual silence, however, has led to a general lacuna that omits a lively Swedenborgian background that pervaded Hawthorne's life, both private and public.

In addition to his immersion in transcendental circles, Hawthorne worked, lived and conversed with numerous Swedenborgians at Brook Farm, including Warren Burton who Hawthorne thought was 'one of the best of the brotherhood'.[5] Hawthorne would have come across various excerpts from Swedenborg's writings in Brook Farm's periodical, *The Harbinger*, as well as *The Dial*, which both attempted to align Swedenborg's vision of social regeneration with that of the French socialist Charles Fourier. Discussion and general knowledge of Swedenborg's symbolic theory of correspondences was widespread enough that Christopher Pearse Cranch (Hawthorne's wife's distant cousin) published a tribute to the concept in *The Dial* in 1841. Directly paraphrasing Swedenborg's *Heaven and Hell* (1758), Cranch's poem declared that 'every object that speaks to the senses was meant for the spirit/ Nature is but a scroll; God's handwriting thereon'.[6]

Hawthorne's fiction contains numerous moments where nature is read as a scroll for a spiritual world, from the rose bushes and the crimson meteor in *The Scarlet Letter* to the hieroglyphic 'pages of heaven and earth' that Kenyon ecstatically proclaims atop Donatello's tower in Hawthorne's last (complete) novel, *The Marble Faun*. The reflection of moonbeams in *The House of the Seven Gables* prompts the author to meditate that such things 'are always a kind of window or doorway into the spiritual world'[7] and in the privacy of his notebook years earlier, Hawthorne wrote that 'the trees reflected in the river—they are unconscious of a spiritual world so near them—so are we'.[8] While these references ostensibly stem from Romantic symbolic traditions and Hawthorne's own peculiar readings in seventeenth- and eighteenth-century Puritan typology, their expansive fluidity and particular moral valence further suggest the ways that several nineteenth-century American artists had incorporated Swedenborg's ideas into their aesthetic visions.

Hawthorne notably became close to two Swedenborgian artists during his

European sojourn, and was acquainted with several others. Both the painter Cephas Giovanni Thompson and the sculptor Hiram Powers had respectively integrated Swedenborg's concepts into theories of representation and creativity. Hawthorne's notebooks and letters record some of the numerous conversations he carried with each through the studios and salons of Florence and Rome. For Powers, Swedenborg's writings on the human form led to a notion that his marble sculpture should portray, and affect in the viewer, a regenerative process that reveals 'an idealized soul'; for Thompson (who had painted Hawthorne's portrait in 1850), Swedenborg's exegesis mediated the symbolic way that the artist read and painted passages of scripture. Hawthorne's contacts with Thompson and Powers are critical points in a constellation of ideas that lie behind the writing of *The Marble Faun,* a novel that is obsessed with artistic representation and theological symbolism.

This is not to reductively argue that there is a clear line of influence one can trace from Swedenborg's theology into Hawthorne's fiction. To colour in these backgrounds and emphasize such friendships is rather to demonstrate how integral Swedenborg was to a 'structure of feeling', to employ a Raymond Williams term, that permeated Hawthorne's time.[9] Hawthorne is notoriously elusive when it comes to pinpointing a particular world view or religious ideology; his journals do not digest his reading and reveal intellectual debts in the same way that Thoreau's, Alcott's, or Emerson's so often do. While Sophia trotted off to her Unitarian church on Sundays, Hawthorne prided himself on staying at home.[10] In the early 1840s, he complains that his 'respect for clerical people' decreased daily, and wrote that 'we certainly do need a new revelation—a new system—for there seems to be no life in the old one'.[11] Similarly disenchanted, Herman Melville perceived what many of Hawthorne's contemporaries did not—that behind his apparent 'Indian-summer sunlight', Hawthorne had a tricky, unknown metaphysical side, 'a mystical blackness' that was 'ten times black'.[12] Melville credited this to Hawthorne's Calvinist heritage with its 'Innate Depravity'; more recent scholarship by Agnes Donohue has expertly drawn out Hawthorne's tangled relationship to the religious ideas of his ancestors. Philip Gura's

The Wisdom of Words complements Donohue's work by demonstrating the critical importance of Unitarian theological debates in the earlier half of the nineteenth century, drawing an impressive connection between seemingly unrelated religious treatises by Horace Bushnell and James Marsh to the later ambiguous literary symbolism of Hawthorne and Melville.[13] However, to exclusively cast Hawthorne as a displaced Puritan, unhappily surrounded by Transcendental optimism, or to read his work as an extended dialogue with Unitarian and Trinitarian debates concerning language and symbol, runs the risk of forgetting Hawthorne's careful self-distancing from his past, and that his work is equally a complex response to contemporary currents. While virtually unheard of today, Swedenborg was inextricably part of a cultural matrix that Hawthorne was reacting to and writing out of. Even with some of the particular popular pressures which Hawthorne responds to so keenly (like mesmerism) Swedenborg's ideas were explicitly part of periodical conversations and debates.

This essay will proceed by first more fully demonstrating in what specific ways Swedenborg coloured Hawthorne's cultural background, and then secondly, to explore the possibilities of this casting a shadow across his fiction. The essay will conclude with a brief analysis of Hawthorne's close alliance with Swedenborgian artists in Boston and Italy, and how their aesthetic visions may have correspondingly affected his own shifting views on art and the role of the artist at the end of his career.

Swedenborgian texts and contexts

Hawthorne was a voracious reader. While it cannot be ascertained if a Swedenborgian work ever came directly into his hands, his known literary digest broaches topics close to the Swedish seer, and Hawthorne most certainly came across articles concerning Swedenborg in *The Dial* and *The Harbinger*.[14] The latter periodical directly allied itself with Swedenborg by choosing a quote from his *Principia* (1733) as its official frontispiece motto: 'All things, at the present day, stand provided and prepared, and await the light'.[15] Brook Farm's *Harbinger* exceeded *The Dial* in its output of material related to the Scandinavian mystic—around forty articles on the Swede during its four-year publication run.[16] Hawthorne occasionally makes general reference to reading *The Dial* (and his doppelgänger Miles Coverdale toys with writing essays for it in *The Blithedale Romance*); perhaps due to the eclectic styles of featured writers like Bronson Alcott—or even because of its dusty translations of Swedenborg—the magazine also served Hawthorne as a potent soporific for his afternoon naps.[17]

The Harbinger began as the official organ for Brook Farm, and its choice of the *Principia* quote, as well as its later editorship by the Swedenborgian Henry James, Sr, surely reflects the numbers from the 'New Church'—as the sectarian devotees of Swedenborg called themselves—who were in residence at Brook Farm when it was first founded.[18] Brook Farm was but one of several experimental communities that originally met with favourable reception from the New Church. The various clarions for societal reform meshed well with the Swedenborgian world view of an imminent new age, 'a new heaven and a new earth' that had been announced by Swedenborg. During Hawthorne's brief tenure at Brook Farm and in the immediate years thereafter, however, the relationship between social reformers and the more conservative New Church began to sour, and contentious public debates came to play out across the pages of small periodicals like *The Harbinger* and *The Dial*.

Albert Brisbane's *The Social Destiny of Man* (1840) probably did more than anything else to disseminate the ideas of Charles Fourier to American audiences, albeit in piecemeal and bowdlerized form. Several critics have further postulated that Brisbane is an important model for Hollingsworth in *The Blithedale Romance*.[19] Brisbane almost certainly targeted the New Church as the ideal audience for his book; he knew that Robert Owen's earlier endeavours had instigated a Swedenborgian commune in Ohio in 1824, even as the colossal failure of Owen's secular New Harmony in Indiana had made most Americans quite suspicious of utopian endeavours, especially those that seemed to lack a religious backbone (and moreover a Continental origin). Brisbane had studied briefly under Fourier in France before the eccentric philosopher died, and knew well that his radical views on marriage would upset American sensibilities. Brisbane had also met with Swedenborgians in Europe (including James John Garth Wilkinson, who would later doctor the Hawthorne family during their England stay) before putting *The Social Destiny of Man* together.[20] The book's careful excision of Fourier's more racy suggestions while emphasizing certain ideas that chimed in with Swedenborg's correspondence theory and his view of the cosmos as a *Maximus Homo*, a 'Grand Man', subsequently sparked great interest among Swedenborgians in the early 1840s.[21] Out at Brook Farm, George Ripley wrote that in the goings-on of the community:

> We study [Swedenborg] continually for the light he sheds on many problems of human destiny, and more especially for the remarkable correspondence, as of inner with outer, which his revelations present with the discourses of Fourier concerning Social organization, or the outward forms of life. The one is the great poet and high-priest, the other the great economist, as it were, of the Harmonic Order, which all things are preparing.[22]

Perhaps aware of Ripley's reading knowledge, in 1846 Hawthorne sent his good friend William Pike and Increase Hill, a young Swedenborgian, to converse with the Brook Farmer about religious matters.[23] Charles A Dana, the Boston novelist and newspaper editor, also shared Ripley's enthusiasm for Swedenborg during his Brook Farm stay; he effuses how 'the spirit which breathes from [Swedenborg's] works is pure and heavenly, his was a grand genius, nobly disciplined'.[24]

Hawthorne respected Ripley but certainly not his penchant for Fourier. Reading Fourier was unpleasant for Hawthorne—although he compelled himself to do so for *The Blithedale Romance*—and he seems to have found Fourier's declaration that in future ages all the oceans would turn to delicious 'limonade à cèdre' particularly absurd.[25] The anti-utopian failure of the Blithedale community in Hawthorne's novel clearly indicates how he regarded the effects of Fourier's and

Brisbane's idealist projections; his reaction to the intertwined Swedenborgian theology requires more studious unravelling.

The New Church response to Fourier, while initially quite enthusiastic, quickly waned, and Hawthorne's reported 'disgust' at Fourier was matched by many doctrinaire Swedenborgians. Two attempted Fourierist communes that were composed exclusively of Swedenborgians became catastrophic failures,[26] a fact that was broadly publicized by New Church periodicals, and as the courser elements of Fourier became more widely known, including the infamous passion-gratifying orgies that led some to derisively sneer the Frenchman's ideas were nothing but 'copulation and cookery', the Swedenborgian periodicals desperately tried to distance their own theology from the salacious scandal. This did not stop attempts like those of Charles Julius Hempel, as his later book, *The True Organization of the New Church, as indicated in the Writings of Emanuel Swedenborg and Demonstrated by Charles Fourier* (1847), makes clear. 'Let me tell you', Hempel sneered to the Swedenborgians,

> that you have not comprehended the whole scope of the Doctrines of your master, that man's regeneration is impossible without a true organization of Society and Church [...] unless the writings of Swedenborg are illustrated by the sublime teachings of Fourier, the 'Heavenly Arcana' will remain a mystical doctrine, and the glorious truths contained in those unknown and derided volumes will never have any important bearing upon the social progress of Humanity.[27]

The heterodox Fourierists at Brook Farm and elsewhere fully embraced Hempel's announcements, giving the book rave reviews even as the New Church complained 'this whole book is constantly exhaling its sickening and blasphemous effluvia to poison and paralyse the reader's perceptions'.[28] Like Hempel and others on the margins of different fringe movements for 'reform', the transcendentalists at Brook Farm continued to syncretically adapt Swedenborg's ideas when it suited them. Swedenborg's post-millennial vision seemed particularly useful for Brook Farm to further differentiate itself from contemporaneous Apocalypse-oriented utopian projects like the nearby Millerite and Shaker communities. Swedenborg had belatedly announced that the Apocalypse had already begun in 1757, and was not to be the expected fire, wrath, and brimstone, but an eventual global reordering of interior mental space.[29] Surely a partial reaction to growing secularism of the Enlightenment, Swedenborg's second coming of Christ was to be an apocalypse of individual minds, a recognition of divine and universal humanity—a notion which especially resonated with William Blake (who was further haunted by the coincidence of his 1757 birth). This anti-literalistic exegesis of Revelation and reading of Christ's return as ultimately an intellectual and social regeneration was used by Hawthorne's sister-in-law, Elizabeth Peabody, in an essay she wrote for *The Dial* during Hawthorne's stay there:

> There are men and women, who have claimed to say to one another, Why not have our daily life organized on Christ's own idea? [...] For each man to think and live on this method is perhaps the second coming of Christ itself.[30]

Hawthorne's infamously eccentric sister-in-law is one of several figures within Hawthorne's private circle who gravitated towards the Swedish mystic, and Elizabeth may have formed one of the earliest possible conduits for Hawthorne to hear about Swedenborg. Both Elizabeth and her younger sister Sophia (who became Hawthorne's wife) had been raised in an unorthodox religious household where Swedenborg was part of family theological debates and conversations.[31] In 1835, Elizabeth translated *Le Vrai Messie* (*The True Messiah*), an obscure text by Guillaume Œgger, a French Swedenborgian. Thanks to Peabody, *Le Vrai Messie* made its rounds through Concord and played a vital role for Emerson as he crafted the essays which became 'Nature'.[32] Œgger exemplified Swedenborg's correspondential approach, emphasizing that 'no fiber in the animal, no blade of grass in the vegetable kingdom, no form of crystallization in inanimate matter, is without its clear and well-determined correspondence in the moral and metaphysical world'.[33] The sole issue of Elizabeth's short-lived (but important) *Aesthetic Papers* continued her interest in Swedenborgian ideas: she gave prominent space to Sampson Reed's 'Oration on Genius' (yet another Swedenborgian text that was an 'oracle' who 'showered fire' for Emerson), and an essay by James John Garth Wilkinson on correspondences. Perhaps due to her sister's strong influence, Sophia Peabody (before she became Mrs Nathaniel Hawthorne) also seems to have been familiar with at least Sampson Reed, as one of Bronson Alcott's letters to her casually references his *Observations on the Growth of the Mind* (which subsequently became important for Alcott and Elizabeth Peabody's educational reforms).[34]

Hawthorne's antipathy for Elizabeth Peabody's eclectic enthusiasms, however, is legendary. Be it ardent abolitionism or the benefits of mesmerism, Hawthorne met his sister-in-law's passion for reform with reserve and occasional flashes of anger. This came to a heated peak when Elizabeth's interest in animal magnetism seems to have played a role in the mesmerizing of Sophia shortly before she married Hawthorne, and later on, when Elizabeth attempted to make use of Hawthorne's daughter Una as a seance medium. As Swedenborg's writings on spiritual worlds and his claim to speak with angels and devils deeply affected the tenor of nineteenth-century spiritualism, Hawthorne's strong feelings on the subject are worth scrutinizing. Moreover, even as Hawthorne declaimed many aspects of the spiritualist craze, as Taylor Stoehr has marvellously demonstrated, neither could he let it go, obsessively using the tropes of mesmerism and the seance as metonyms for his own act of creative writing. 'Unwilling', Stoehr claims,

> or unable to make up his mind whether the mesmeric phenomena are genuine or fraudulent, Hawthorne leaves the question unanswered [...] this ambivalence was probably one of the reasons why he introduced mesmerism so prominently into his works. It suited his sense of what romance ought to

be—a fantasy spun out of possibilities that were not quite actualities, though, given the right atmosphere, they might be presented as such.[35]

As with the advent of Fourierism in America, the intertwined geneses of mesmerism, animal magnetism and spiritualism were ubiquitously twinned with Swedenborgianism, turning to Swedenborg's theological corpus for authority. A mutual discourse of legitimation quickly established itself in periodicals like *The Dial* and *The Harbinger*. On the one hand, Swedenborg's teachings on the interface of spiritual worlds with human epistemology were hailed as anticipating the findings of Franz Mesmer (1734-1815), who first popularized a model of the human mind that contained layers of unseen, unknowable consciousness—thus helping to instigate a profound shift in the European understanding of the self that culminated with Freud and Jung one hundred and fifty years later. On the other hand, the bastard children of Mesmer's ideas, spiritualism and the hypnotic seance—Mesmer himself consistently denied a supernatural rationale for his theory of invisible, magnetic fluids—were originally hailed by the New Church as veritable proofs of Swedenborg's teachings on spirits' engagement with the material world. The link between spiritualistic spin-offs of Mesmer and the Swedenborgians reached an apogee in Europe in the late 1790s, especially within the pseudo-Masonic lodges that flourished across France before the Revolution.[36] In America, like other transplanted facets of Romanticism, this development came later in slightly different forms. For one, the Masonic societies in Europe tended to be radical, elitist and aristocratic (and thus another reason why Swedenborg vanishes from French intellectual conversations during the Revolution, only reviving later with Balzac and Hugo),[37] whereas the hybrid forms of animal magnetism in America that drew on Mesmer and Swedenborg quickly acquired a widespread public appeal that fired working- and middle-class imaginations: Robert Fuller even argues we should read their advent in nineteenth-century America as constituting a religious revival as profound and deep as the Great

Awakenings of the previous century,[38] a claim reiterated more recently in Catherine Albanese's work on heterodox American religious movements.[39]

For Hawthorne, the debates over the uses, dangers, or sheer quackery of spiritualism peaked during the 1840s and continued into the early 1850s. Sounding much like some of the early Swedenborgian enthusiasts, he has Clifford announce during his ecstatic train ride in *The House of the Seven Gables*, 'Mesmerism, now! Will that effect nothing, think you, towards purging away the grossness out of human life? [...] These rapping spirits [...] what are these but the messengers of the spiritual world, knocking at the door of substance?' The old man on the train curtly dismisses Clifford's proclamations (which are a reference to the Rochester rappings), as 'All humbug!'.[40] Yet Hawthorne himself continued to straddle these two poles of reception: disgusted by mesmeric and animal magnetism's pretensions to a spiritual world, yet unable to wholly dismiss its imaginative claims as sheer humbug like the old sceptical gentleman on the train. Hawthorne's famous reply to Sophia about her mesmeric headache cures in 1841 makes Hawthorne's deep emotional investment in the matter clear; it also anticipates the sexual tensions which underpin Westervelt's exploitation of Priscilla as a mesmeric medium in *The Blithedale Romance*. Hawthorne becomes deeply disturbed by any other than 'thy husband' intruding into Sophia's 'holy of holies' while under a mesmeric trance. He exhorts her:

> I am unwilling that a power should be exercised on thee, of which we know neither the origin nor the consequence, and the phenomena of which seem rather calculated to bewilder us, than to teach us any truths about the present or future state of being. [...] Now, ownest wife, I have no faith whatever that people are raised to the seventh heaven, or to any heaven at all, or that they gain any insight into the mysteries of life beyond death, by means of this strange science.[41]

The letter closes with an insightful comment on Elizabeth Peabody—who was continuing to write her Swedenborgian-sounding essays for *The Dial*—that for Sophia, 'thy sister Elizabeth would like nothing so much as to proclaim thy spiritual experiences, by sound of trumpet'.[42]

Hawthorne's immersion in Brook Farm utopian idealism, fuelled by its after-dinner table talk of Brisbane, Fourier, and Swedenborg, combined with this upsetting intrusion from afar with the mesmeric seance, certainly begins to explain the pairing of these two themes in *The Blithedale Romance*. Stoehr postulates it is precisely this combination that marks *The Blithedale Romance* as a perfect 'hybrid' novel, caught at a nexus between utopian fiction of the likes of William Dean Howells' *The Undiscovered Country* and the Gothic trope of the wicked hypnotist.[43]

Perhaps it was Elizabeth Peabody's infamous tenacity that prevented her from detecting Hawthorne's animosity towards spiritualism. Twelve years later, she felt no compunction about writing to her sister to see if she could use her niece Una as a spiritualist medium. Hawthorne did not reply himself, but his wrath can be gleamed through Sophia's decisive answer:

> My dear Lizzie [...] Thank you for your most interesting letter, received last week through Mary Mann. Mr. Hawthorne says he never [with *never* underlined six times] will consent to Una's being made a medium of communication & that he will defy all Hell rather, so that he will have to disprove the testimony of the spirits, if it comes to that. He says he cannot let you come here with Rappers in train—for he thinks it would injure Una physically and spiritually to be subjected to such influence.[44]

Again, Hawthorne cannot dismiss mesmeric spiritualism as foolish humbuggery —a darker danger lurks beneath, an ambivalent fear which came to colour the Mephistophelian shades of Professor Westervelt in *The Blithedale Romance*, or the satanic allusions that shadow the hypnotizing Maule family in *The House of the Seven Gables*, even as mesmerizing in both of these novels is simultaneously invested with aspects of Hawthorne's creative process.

During the 1840s, as Hawthorne began to gather recollections of Brook Farm and consider the need to write an account of his time there, Swedenborg's name was more than ever connected to the popular tide of spiritualism. Most prominently, Andrew Jackson Davis, a barely literate farmer's son from Poughkeepsie, New York, began a highly lucrative career as a self-proclaimed mystic who would continue Swedenborg's prophetic correspondence with the spiritual world. After being magnetized by a local tailor in 1843, Davis underwent an astonishing metamorphosis. Despite his lack of education, in his mesmerized state and subsequent communion with 'the seven rings of heaven', Davis discoursed fluently in Greek and Latin, read newspapers through his forehead, and told the time while blindfolded by passing his hand above a stopwatch.[45] During a later session of mesmerization, Davis claimed that he had levitated to a holy mountain in the Alleghenies where the two spirits of Galen and Swedenborg proceeded to hand him a glowing scroll: a heavenly commission, *à la* Swedenborg in his own writings, for Davis to prophesy for the enlightenment of the human race.[46] Though Davis's postures seem blatant parlour sleight of hand today, he met with almost instantaneous fame and fortune, becoming the most renowned spiritualist figure before the later Fox sisters in Rochester. He spent almost two years in New York City giving seance-like lectures, where his cryptic pronouncements while under trance were painstakingly written down by a team of assistants. The rambling results were collectively published as *The Principles of Nature, Her Divine Revelations, and a Voice to Mankind* (1847), a smash bestseller despite its daunting Swedenborg-sounding jargon, selling out some 34 different editions over the next thirty years.[47]

In attendance at Davis's 'lectures' beginning in 1845 were, at various times, Edgar Allan Poe and Albert Brisbane, as well as Transcendentalists like George Ripley and Parke Godwin. Ripley returned to Brook Farm to write a favourable review of Davis in *The Harbinger*——yet another indicator of how pervasive and overlapping the fields of 'reform' could be. More significantly, a noted professor of Orientalism and Hebrew from New York University, George Bush, decided to publish a long essay fully endorsing Davis. Entitled *Mesmer and Swedenborg, or the Relation of the Developments of Mesmerism to the Doctrines and Disclosures of Swedenborg* (1847), the work proceeds on exactly the same lines as Charles Julius Hempel's had with Fourierism: Mesmer presents an external, modern empirical 'proof' to indubitably verify Swedenborg's internal mystical teachings. Bush's book aroused much ire from other doctrinaire Swedenborgians, however; although Swedenborg had made marvellous claims to intercourse with people in heaven and hell, he emphatically warned against others from seeking to speak with spirits themselves. Matter-of-factly, in *Heaven and Hell*, Swedenborg relates that 'In our day, talking with spirits is rarely allowed, as it is so dangerous, for in that situation the spirits know they are with a person, which they would not know otherwise; and there are evil spirits, who by nature regard people with deadly hatred, and their only desire is to destroy people, soul and body'.[48] Drawing on such passages, once again as with Fourierism, arguments raged through the pages of the Transcendental and New Church periodicals over the legitimacy of Andrew Jackson Davis. It would have been hard for Hawthorne, located where he was near transcendental and Swedenborgian epicentres like Concord and Salem, to avoid hearing at least some of the furious crossfire. As Davis's credibility was increasingly questioned in more respectable intellectual circles—and as Davis continued to make ever more controversial pronouncements over the non-Divinity of Christ— Professor Bush quickly recanted his earlier support. Subsequent periodical essays by Bush tried to back paddle but the damage had already been done—through Davis, and continuing with his famous acolyte Thomas Lake Harris, who had publicly announced 'I AM SWEEDENBORG [sic]', Swedenborg's name became permanently grafted into the history of popular American spiritualism.[49] Perhaps Hawthorne's particular choice to make Westervelt a professor was inflected with the Bush and Davis debates; Hawthorne was perennially interested in a type of Faustian doctor-scientist (as well as the Quack), and Westervelt's dual occupation as sham professor and demonic mesmerist ambiguously waffles before Miles Coverdale's eyes—'At the same time, as if to vindicate his claim to the professorial dignity, so often assumed on questionable grounds, he put on a pair of spectacles, which so altered the character of his face I hardly knew him again'.[50]

Not surprisingly, the American notebooks and letters record little interest in figures like Davis. When Hawthorne was in London, however, the Poughkeepsie seer came up in a notable conversation with James John Garth Wilkinson. Hawthorne had been recommended to the Swedenborgian homeopath (probably by Emerson or Henry James, Sr) to seek a cure for Sophia's recurrent bronchial problems. Wilkinson, much like the elder Henry James, had steadfastly refused to become part of the organized New Church but affirmatively embraced Swedenborgian doctrines. He was close friends with leading London literary figures, including Carlyle, Dickens and Tennyson (Wilkinson even used his literary connections to secure an introduction to Coventry Patmore for Hawthorne). Henry James, Sr famously named a son after him—Wilkinson, known as 'Wilky', who went on to serve in the 54th Massachusetts black regiment during the Civil War. In London, while Hawthorne was surely displeased with Wilkinson's ultimate (but beneficial) advice about Sophia—which was to send her far away to Portugal—they nonetheless engaged in a conversation about the spiritualist fervour that Hawthorne finds again anathema to his core. After listening to Wilkinson effuse over Andrew Jackson Davis and his own witnessing of spiritualistic events, Hawthorne writes:

> Do I believe in these wonders? Of course; for how is it possible to doubt either the solemn word or the sober observation of a learned and sensible man like Dr. Wilkinson. But again, do I really believe it? Of course not; for I cannot consent to let Heaven and Earth this world and the next, be beaten together like the white and yolk of an egg, merely out of respect to Dr. Wilkinson's integrity. I would not believe my own sight or touch of the spiritual hands;

and it would take deeper and higher strains [of poetry] than those of Mr. Harris to convince me.[51]

Wilkinson was not the only intelligent acquaintance whose enthusiasm for mediums perplexed Hawthorne; his close friend William Pike also had a strong interest in 'the other world', and Hawthorne records relishing Pike's supernatural stories during their time together at the custom house, even as Pike's later embrace of the Rochester rappings caused Hawthorne to express mild alarm. 'I do long to see you', wrote Hawthorne to his good friend, 'and talk about a thousand things relating to this world and the next. I am very glad of your testimony in favor of spiritual intercourse […but] you must allow me to withhold my full and entire belief, until I have heard some of your details of your own spiritual intercourse'.[52] Pike was a restless seeker of religion, bouncing from Methodism into the Episcopal church, and ultimately coming to rest in the Swedenborgian fold of the New Church.[53] What Hawthorne thought about Pike's final committal here is unknown; Hawthorne does seem to have played a role in procuring obscure Swedish dictionaries (then a rarity) for Pike's attempts to learn the language (which coincides, unsurprisingly, with Pike's interest in the Scandinavian seer). Holgrave of *The House of the Seven Gables* might be inflected with bits and pieces of Pike's shifting character; Holgrave shares Pike's mystical and spiritualist leanings that are mixed in with changing popular currents, in addition to having the knack for telling a good story. 'The mystic language of his books was necessarily mixed up with the babble of the multitude', Hawthorne writes in the novel, and Holgrave has 'a crude, wild, and misty philosophy'.[54] Moreover, Hawthorne paints Holgrave as an idealist doomed to obscurity in the same pessimistic way he regarded his friend. 'At almost every step in life', Hawthorne writes, 'we meet with young men of just about Holgrave's age, for whom we anticipate wonderful things, but of whom, even after much and careful inquiry, we never happen to hear another word'.[55] Shortly after the novel was published, he candidly told Pike as he had written on Holgrave——'You will never, I fear [...] make the impression on the world, in years gone by, I used to hope you would. It will not be your fault, however, but the fault of circumstances. Your flower was not destined to bloom in this world. I hope to see its glory in the next'.[56] More curiously, Pike's acceptance of Swedenborg as a divine revelator was mirrored several decades later by Hawthorne's own son Julian, who located in Swedenborg's works both his religious world views and an aesthetic theory that guided his mediocre, stiffened fiction.[57]

Refracting Swedenborg in Hawthorne's fiction

In all the above examples, it would seem Hawthorne's relations to these Swedenborgian contexts were ambivalent at best: in the case of mesmerism, he became outright hostile. I have focused on Fourierism and American spiritualist movements as the primary loci where Hawthorne would have encountered presentations of Swedenborg's ideas, in addition to the obvious family and social contexts. However, other branches of the nineteenth-century 'pseudosciences' were as thoroughly inflected with Swedenborgian doctrine. Samuel Hahnemann's homeopathy, which (crudely put) tended to attribute chronic physical diseases to spiritual problems, meshed well with Swedenborg's concept of correspondence and influx, and a flurry of pamphlets on Swedenborg and homeopathy continued through the 1850s. Reflecting on the popularity of homeopathy in the nineteenth-century New Church, Elinore Peebles writes that the Swedenborgians 'found little difficulty in accepting a medical philosophy based on the immaterial and activating force of the spirit'.[58]

Sophia Hawthorne was an avid homeopath (and her father and brother practised it as a trade), but Hawthorne remains again characteristically ambivalent. Stoehr points out that Chillingsworth in *The Scarlet Letter* is, albeit anachronistically for the seventeenth century, a classic homeopath—his poisonous 'cures' for the Revd Dimmesdale proceed on explicitly homeopathic principles, as do his methods of collecting herbs and distillations.[59] In 'Rappaccini's Daughter' (1844), Rappaccini's theory that 'all medicinal virtues are comprised within those substances which we have termed vegetable poisons' is classic Hahnemmanian-sounding language, who had written that diseases can be cured by the diluted application of poisons which mimic the effects of the particular malady, thereby kick-starting the body's own healing mechanisms into gear. Stoehr concludes that at 'every point of his external relations' Hawthorne was touched by some aspect of these spirit-cum-science hybrids——and yet, 'so far as his public voice can be identified in his fiction, he withheld final judgment'.[60] Stoehr makes a special effort to analyse Hawthorne's obsessive treatment of the 'mad scientist' type which came to embody many of these different currents: Holgrave, for example, is not only a mesmerist in *The House of the Seven Gables*, but also involved in Fourierism, just as Rappaccini is aligned with an occult discourse in addition to his deadly homeopathic principles. Stoehr's connection of these figures to Hawthorne's own deep conflicted identity over being a writer of Romance is astute: 'all these figures are veiled artists, manipulating others as a novelist controls his characters', Stoehr writes, and moreover, in spite of a 'continuing condemnation of the mad scientist, Hawthorne seems more and more to project himself into just that figure'.[61]

Stoehr omits the significance of Emanuel Swedenborg for the advent of the pseudosciences and perhaps Hawthorne's own interest in a trope of the mad scientist. More than any other figure for the pre-Civil War period, the Swedish mystic embodied the attempts to meld empirical science of the Enlightenment with spiritual inquiry characteristic of the Romantics. Towards the end of 'The American Scholar' (1837) (whose importance was signalled by Oliver Wendell Holmes when he hailed it America's 'intellectual Declaration of Independence'), Ralph Waldo Emerson focuses on Swedenborg as *the* figure who brought spiritual and moral concerns into scientific pursuits of nature:

There is one man of genius, who has done much for this philosophy of life, whose literary value has never yet been rightly estimated; - I mean Emanuel Swedenborg. The most imaginative of men, yet writing with the precision of a mathematician, he attempted to engraft a purely philosophical Ethics onto the Christianity of his time [...] he saw and showed the connection between nature and the affections of his soul. He pierced the emblematic or spiritual character of the visible, audible, tangible world.[62]

Hawthorne likely did not echo Emerson's optimistic reception. If Swedenborg as scientist-mystic makes a mark in Hawthorne's fiction in the guise of the mad scientist, it is as a character type that becomes increasingly diabolical.

Hawthorne was interested early on in the doctor/scientist who touches the supernatural yet simultaneously evokes suspicions of humbuggery and fraud. In the burlesque 'The Haunted Quack' (1831), Hippocrates Jenkins trains under Doctor Ramshorne who 'was regarded, in point of occult knowledge and skill, as a second Faustus' [61] but when Jenkins continues Ramshorne's superstitious-filled practice, he comically poisons an old woman through a bungled potion. Dr Heidegger in 'Dr. Heidegger's Experiment' (1837) has more success in crafting a magical elixir of eternal life, but it too eventually fails, returning the three drinkers to old age after they have quarrelled and smashed the crystal vial containing the eternal fluid. Whether Hawthorne treats such figures satirically as quacks or imaginatively as spiritual alchemists, their scientific and medical experiments invariably fail, usually resulting in an unintended misshapen tragedy (the deaths of Georgiana in 'The Birth-Mark', or Beatrice in 'Rappaccini's Daughter' being the most exemplary). The moral here seems to run counter to the discourses of homeopathy and mesmeric medical treatments which claimed to 'spiritually' cure disease, and even sin, through their applications. As Chillingsworth facilely says to Dimmesdale in *The Scarlet Letter*, sounding like any good homeopath, 'a bodily disease [...] may, after all, be but a symptom of an ailment in the spiritual part'.[64] The germ for this lies as early as 1842, where Hawthorne sketches in his notebook the idea of 'a physician for the cure of moral diseases'.[65] In 'The Birth-Mark', Georgiana's hand-shaped disfiguration can be read as a none-too-subtle emblem of original sin; Aylmer increasingly allegorizes it as 'the symbol of his wife's liability to sin, sorrow, decay and death',[66] and his spiritualized science wreaks disastrous consequence in the attempts to remove it. Perhaps this is Hawthorne's Calvinist 'blackness' which Melville saw lurking in his friend, a sense that damning sin is always inevitable, with no panacea available in either Emerson's transcendental optimism or Swedenborgian pseudoscience. Given Hawthorne's murky and ambivalent religious beliefs, he seemed unable to remedy this moral pessimism—as Jonathan Edwards and other earlier Puritans had—with the sweet all-saving grace of a Christ.

After Hawthorne's Brook Farm experience, Hawthorne's spiritualizing scientists take on more explicitly Swedenborgian hues. Alfred Gabay argues that while Swedenborg was a Romantic constant throughout the first half of the nineteenth century, the 1840s saw a 'transatlantic revival' of particular interest in Swedenborg's scientific works.[67] This was due in no small part to the translation efforts of Wilkinson, who—financed with money from Henry James, Sr—had proceeded to bring out seminal English translations of Swedenborg's pre-visionary scientific works (which had all been written in Latin), including *The Animal Kingdom* (in 1843) and *Economy of the Animal Kingdom* (in 1844), which are both premised on a psycho-spiritual interest in using physiology and anatomy to locate the presence of the soul in the human body. During Hawthorne's compositions of both 'The Birth-Mark' and 'Rappaccini's Daughter' Wilkinson was also hard at work on his *Life of Swedenborg* (1849), an important biography that emphasized Swedenborg's scientific character, highlighting his discoveries in crystallography and mineralogy as much as the more extraordinary claims of visionary mystical experience. In the opening paragraphs of 'The Birth-Mark', the description of Aylmer is certainly inflected with Gothic tropes of the mad scientist (Mary Shelley's Victor Frankenstein being most evident), but the words equally touch upon the life and times of Swedenborg as Wilkinson had been contemporaneously describing them. Hawthorne writes:

In the latter part of the last century, there lived a man of science—an eminent proficient in every branch of natural philosophy—who, not long before our story opens, had made experience of a spiritual affinity, more attractive than any chemical one.[68]

Hawthorne's immediate inclusion of Aylmer's marriage to Georgiana in the first paragraph disturbs the parallels, as Swedenborg famously remained a bachelor throughout his long life. Still, striking propinquities poke through elsewhere. Swedenborg's work in the mining industry and his geological discoveries were aspects focused on by biographers like Wilkinson. Swedenborg was the first Swedish scientist to provide a modern notion of shifting geological strata that could account for the appearance of marine fossils on mountain peaks. [69] His mineralogical magnum opus, *The Principia*, also advanced a theory of matter based on a nebular hypothesis sixty some years before LaPlace and Kant. The later *The Animal Kingdom* marks a pivotal moment in Swedenborg's career as he took his empirical methodologies to the form of the human body, attempting to anatomically pinpoint the location of the soul so that the precise place could be unarguably shown where the spiritual made contacted with the natural. *The Animal Kingdom* shows Swedenborg to have been on the cutting edge of physiology during the Enlightenment—his spiritualized search for the soul led to several profound insights into cognitive neurophysiology. According to the neuroscientist and historian Charles Gross, Swedenborg's work anticipated subsequent nineteenth-century brain science in three significant ways. First, Swedenborg posited the instrumental role of the cerebral cortex in sensory, motor, and cognitive functions, one hundred years before this became accepted scientific fact. Secondly, he articulated something akin to a neuron doctrine, even though neurons had yet to be scientifically described, primarily through his creative use of Malphigi's earlier descriptions of cortical glands in *De Cerebri*. Finally, and perhaps most astonishingly, Swedenborg mapped out the somatotopic organization of motor functions to different regions of the cerebral cortex, outlining pathways of communication between each sense organ to parts of the cortex itself. This view was 'totally unprecedented and not to reappear until well into the nineteenth century', writes Gross, and no other suggestion of somatotopic organization of cortical functions surfaces in scientific literature until the definitive experiments of Fritsch and Hitzig in 1870.[70] Even more particularly, as Stanley Finger further points out, Swedenborg seems to have inferred that the frontal lobes of the cortex were involved in intellectual capacities of imagination, memory and thought.[71]

Both aspects of Swedenborg's achievements in biological science and natural anatomy might find themselves refracted in Hawthorne's description of Aylmer's eighteenth-century accomplishments:

> Seated calmly in this laboratory, the pale philosopher had investigated the secrets of the highest cloud-region, and of the profoundest mines; he had satisfied himself of the causes that kindled and kept alive the fires of the volcano; and had explained the mystery of fountains, and how it is that they gush forth […] Here, too, at an earlier period, he had studied the wonders of the human frame, and attempted to fathom the process by which Nature assimilates all her precious influences from earth and air, and from the spiritual world, to create and foster Man, her masterpiece.[72]

From Aylmer on, the spiritualizing scientist darkens. Rappaccini becomes more sinister than Aylmer, his 'so spiritual a love of science' poisoning the sacred familial bond between father and daughter (which is further destabilized by the story's Gothic hints of incest). By the time Professor Westervelt makes his appearance in *The Blithedale Romance*, the type has fragmented, oscillating between flattened caricatures of circus humbuggery or dangerous, Faustian necromancy—there are no claims to altruistic motives with Westervelt, or moments of redeeming regret, as there are with Aylmer and Rappaccini (and earlier, Dr Heidegger).

Was Hawthorne's reaction to Swedenborg thus wholly negative in tenor, the life of the Scandinavian mystic providing nothing more than 'a structure of feeling' for Hawthorne's mad scientists to germinate within? Hawthorne's fictionalization of Swedenborgian-steeped strands of culture certainly exhibits his canny understanding of marketplace values. Perhaps more than anything else, Hawthorne was simply writing into popular subjects that he knew would help his work sell: contemporaries like Orestes Brownson and Timothy Shay Arthur certainly milked mesmerism and the spiritualist fervour in a Gothic vein for all it was worth. An early British reviewer saw Hawthorne's spiritualizing in such economic, popularized terms:

> Mr. Hawthorne manages the supernatural so well [...] he derives profit so ingeniously from the existing tremor of the public mind, arising from what is seen and said of mesmerism, electro-biology, spirit-rappings, and Swedenborgian psychology, that we could have made no objection to one trial of his faculties for rendering nightmares compatible with daylight and open eyes [...].[73]

If it is remembered, however, that in addition to the popularization of Swedenborg's 'spiritual worlds' in various mesmeric, homeopathic and Fourierist circles, that the philosophic aspects of his ideas on correspondential symbols, nature, and human psychology were still being taken seriously by leading intellectuals of the nineteenth century, and most especially by those in the hermetic world of Concord Transcendentalism, other refractions of Swedenborgian concepts —beyond the popular spectre of a mad and mystical scientist—might be discerned within Hawthorne's work.

Hawthorne's self-imposed distance from Transcendentalist circles is exemplified in the allegorical 'The Hall of Fantasy' (1843), where Hawthorne ironizes the 'disciples of Newness' who flock around Emerson's feet and 'betray the power of his intellect by its modifying power of influence on their own'.[74] Like 'Earth's Holocaust', the story registers Hawthorne's ambivalence that the push for reform will end up effacing history, or that transcendental Idealism will lose sight of, and subsequently destroy, the sensuous nature of the earth that Hawthorne so valued. The concluding paragraphs are a materialist affirmation of 'the fragrance of flowers, and of new mown hay; the genial warmth of sunshine […] the country frolics, the homely humor […] I fear no other world can show us anything just like this'.[75] And yet, Hawthorne also moralizes we should still make 'an occasional visit' to these realms of the imagination, 'for the sake of spiritualizing the grossness of this actual life, and prefiguring ourselves to a state, in which the Idea be all in all'.[76] The transparent sketches of Hawthorne's contemporaries also waver between mocking stereotypes—the crazed Millerites, or the diffuse statements of Alcott— and genuine appreciation for the writers of his day: Hawthorne certainly performs an act of self-elevation by placing himself in the realm where Washington Irving and James F Cooper consociate and dream.

The imaginative space that the narrator and his companion traverse in 'The Hall of Fantasy' is notably framed in the text by the statues of Goethe and Swedenborg. They find themselves first surrounded by busts and effigies of great literary men; the narrator notes (as Hawthorne duly would) the decay and disappearance of many—'Oblivion comes with her broom and sweeps all from the marble floor'. But Swedenborg and Goethe remain eternally permanent, apparently side by side. They are the only two statues the characters pause to observe and comment on. 'Were ever two men of transcendent imagination more un-like?' asks Hawthorne's nameless companion, before they pass on in the hall towards the various groups of people gathered around the fountains of inspiration.

Hawthorne's pairing of Goethe and Swedenborg may reflect a short essay that appeared at the end of the January 1843 edition of *The Dial*—something Hawthorne almost certainly read, with 'The Hall of Fantasy' being composed later in the same year. The essay (probably penned by Emerson, according to Myerson), briefly compares Goethe and Swedenborg's spiritualized colour theories of light and darkness. The twinning of these seemingly unlikely figures might also explain the dual nature of Hawthorne's allegorical space in the story: on the one hand 'The Hall of Fantasy' is the realm of the Neoplatonic Ideal, or the Coleridgean Imagination, but on the other, it hints at parodies of a Swedenborgian afterlife. Swedenborg unabashedly wrote about communing with angelic spirits from other planets in his *The Worlds in Space* (1758), a shorter work excerpted from the larger *Arcana Caelestia*. As the Enlightenment aftermath unfolded further astronomical discoveries like Uranus (in 1781), and Friedrich Bessel's measurements of distances to other stars in 1830, understandings of the earth's own stature were unsettled, and further diminished by works like Lyell's *Principles of Geology*. Where was man's place in the universe if the earth was but a tiny fleck of dust within incomprehensible scopes of space and time? Swedenborg's presentation of a fully human cosmos comforted and charmed many. 'It needs to be known', he declared, 'that all spirits and angels are from the human race [...] It is a very well-known fact in the next life that there are many worlds inhabited by human beings, and there are spirits and angels who have come from them. Anyone there [...] is permitted to talk with spirits from other worlds'.[77] English translations of *The Worlds in Space* were popular in America, and as late as 1895, the artist Howard Pyle was adapting its themes for his Swedenborgian book, *The Garden Behind the Moon*.[78] In Hawthorne's 'The Hall of Fantasy', we also read of 'apartments, where the inhabitants of earth may hold converse with those of the moon. And beneath our feet are gloomy cells, which communicate with the infernal regions, and where monsters and chimeras are kept in confinement, and fed with all unwholesomeness'.[79] This comes quite close to Swedenborg's horizontal layering of geographic space in 'the infernal regions' in his *Heaven and Hell* (see §§584-6), in addition to the possibility of interplanetary communication.

If such allusions bear tangible weight in the story, they are undercut by Hawthorne's corrosive irony. It is the first person narrator who notes the statue of Goethe——the novelist of culture and sensual refinement, as he was regarded by many Americans—while it is his companion who enthusiastically speaks of Swedenborg. At the end of the tale, if one has been taking their banter seriously, Hawthorne pulls the rug out from under the reader's feet—' "It is an excellent resolve," said my companion, looking at his watch, "But come, it is the dinner hour. Will you partake of my vegetable diet?" '.[80] As a survey of Hawthorne's journals shows, he was thoroughly a meat-eating man, and here he relegates this vegetarian advocate of Swedenborg to the reform fringe along with the Millerites and Transcendentalists.

Despite these public postures that distance Hawthorne from his Concord neighbours, it is striking to note how often he writes, with absolutely no tongue-in-cheek, of finding symbols that reflect 'spiritual worlds' or signs that indicate something transcendent and immanent beyond the surface of perceived reality: 'The trees reflected in the river;—they are unconscious of a spiritual world so near them. So are we'.[81] Similarly, Pearl in *The Scarlet Letter* prances on the other side of a mirror-like stream in the forest, causing Dimmesdale to marvel that 'this brook is the boundary between two worlds'.[82] Hawthorne meditates in the famous preface to *Mosses from an Old Manse* (1846) that the glimmering shadows over his domicile 'were a kind of spiritual medium, seen through which, the edifice had not quite the aspect of belonging to the material world',[83] and the Concord River behind the house, once again, retains 'infinite spiritual capacity, and may contain the better world in its depths'.[84] If indeed 'moonbeams are always kind of a doorway into a spiritual world', as the earlier quote from *The House of the Seven Gables* tells us, just what exactly does this door open into? Hawthorne's reading of nature as supernatural signs and symbols comes out of multifarious sources, from European Romanticism to older Puritan typologies, but its final intent is murky.

Swedenborg's Neoplatonic concept of correspondence played a central role in expanding the typological framework that Hawthorne had inherited from Puritan predecessors. Philip Gura writes how Swedenborg's correspondence came to form 'the center of the transcendental metaphysic'.[85] Jonathan Edwards had looked with certitude at the natural world in the 1720s and found that 'the whole universe, heaven and earth, air and seas, and the divine constitution and history of the holy Scriptures, is full of images of divine things, as full as language is of words'.[86] A little over a century later, Hawthorne is deploying the same symbolic framework with vastly different results—instead of finding Christological and scriptural confirmations, there is ambiguity and uncertainty over what lies behind the sign. The meteor 'A' that blazons across the night sky in Salem could be Hester Prynn's Adultery, but it also signifies her role as Able and Angel. Melville similarly grappled with this theological symbolic mode and Christianized Neoplatonism when Ahab famously rages that 'All visible objects, man, are but as pasteboard masks [...] If man will strike, strike through the mask!'.[87] For both of these authors—who, we should remember, spent nights together drinking brandy, smoking and talking intensely of 'ontological matters' while they were Berkshire neighbours—the uncertainty of the symbol, its unhinging from Christian signification even as it kept the shell of its structure in place, became a goal in itself. As Gura writes, again, 'in a world where religious certainty was more and more chimerical, [Hawthorne and Melville] pioneered a rhetoric of ambiguity—later it would be called literary symbolism—that made possible discussion of man's spiritual condition in an anthropomorphic and pluralistic universe'.[88]

Swedenborg's correspondential theory ricocheted all over early transcendental literature. It appears throughout his theological corpus, articulated perhaps most clearly in *Heaven and Hell*, which was one of Swedenborg's most widely read books in the nineteenth century:

> In short, all creations that come into existence in the natural world, from smallest to greatest, are correspondences. They are correspondences because the natural world and everything belonging to it comes into existence and is kept in existence from the spiritual world, and both worlds do so from God.[89] These too [correspondences of plants] have their origin in the spiritual

world, or heaven, which is in the form of a person [. . .], and for this reason each particular item in that [vegetable] kingdom has a certain relation to elements of human life, as is well known to some people in the educated world. I have had plenty of experience to show me that everything in the vegetable kingdom is a correspondence, for often when I have been in gardens and looked closely at trees, fruits, flowers and vegetables there, I have been aware of their correspondences in heaven [. . .].[90]

Guillaume Œgger and Sampson Reed further magnified these ideas in their respective writings. Critically, the universality of Swedenborg's correspondence grew away from literalistic approaches to Judaeo-Christian texts while transforming the whole knowable universe into a potential sacred Logos. The more science one could know about the natural world, the deeper the secret spiritual insights one could gain through reading the correspondences correctly. The best angels, in Swedenborg's visionary accounts of heaven, do not learn and expand their intellect by reading books but by walking through nature, with the flowers, trees and gardens around them instructing and teaching spiritual truths.[91] Like Thoreau, Swedenborg's angels live out Emerson's declaration that even a farm could become 'a mute gospel [...] a sacred emblem from the first furrow of spring to the last stack which the snow of winter overtakes in the fields'.[92] Hawthorne's Kenyon in *The Marble Faun* similarly endorses the lay of the land as a grand sacred script. Looking down on the Tuscan landscape from Donatello's tower, Kenyon proclaims:

I cannot preach [...] with a page of heaven and earth spread before us! Only begin to read it and you will find it interpreting itself without the aid of words. It is a great mistake to try and put our best thoughts into human language. When we ascend into the higher regions of enjoyment, they are only expressible by such grand hieroglyphics as these around us.[93]

Correspondences in Swedenborg's spiritual world are further protean, shifting and changing in ways that anticipate the symbolic ambiguity of Hawthorne's language. This variation on the standard stiff Neoplatonism was immensely appealing for Emerson as he searched for an organic approach to nature that could yet maintain an idealist foundation. Emerson writes in 'The Poet' that 'before [Swedenborg] the metamorphosis continually plays. Everything on which his eyes rests, obeys the impulse of moral nature. The figs become grapes while he eats them. When some of his angels affirmed a truth, the laurel twig they held in their hand blossomed [...] He is the poet, and shall draw us with love and terror, who sees, through the flowing vest, the firm nature, and can declare it'.[94]

Hawthorne's metaphysical 'blackness', of course, differentiates his perspective from Emerson's (and Swedenborg's) positive affirmation that a 'firm nature' of intrinsic morality can still be pinned beneath the flowing vest of appearances. Nonetheless, the diffusion of Swedenborg's more organic Neoplatonic correspondence theory made an essential contribution to a general paradigm shift which opened the space for Hawthorne's expansive and ambivalent literary symbolism.

Hawthorne and the Swedenborgian artists

Swedenborg's correspondence theory affected not only symbolic discourses on language; from William Blake onwards, many nineteenth-century visual artists were attracted to the aesthetic potential in the seer's work. His claims to otherworldly visions that were yet combined with the methodologies of empirical science, as well as the scathing critiques of established Christian orthodoxy, made Swedenborg an attractive figure for the Romantics who elevated the artist into the space of the sacred and prophetic, distinctly at odds with traditional church structures. John Flaxman, Blake's more financially successful friend, became a participant of the Swedenborgian church in the late eighteenth century, and used Swedenborg's particular vision of the afterlife to work a quiet revolution in British funerary art.[95] Flaxman's well-known engravings may have been one of the first conduits where

Hawthorne encountered an aesthetic application of Swedenborgian ideas: Sophia was particularly taken with Flaxman, and the early days of the Hawthorne-Peabody courtship seemed to have involved looking over his work (and Sophia would later copy Flaxman illustrations when the couple was strapped for cash).[96]

Twelve years later, Hawthorne sat for what became his favourite portrait of himself by Cephas Giovanni Thompson. He notes immediately that Thompson is a Swedenborgian—'and I have generally found something marked in the men who adopt that faith'.[97] As Hawthorne sits with Thompson over the course of the next several days, he scrupulously records their conversations, especially their thoughts on issues involved with the representation of sacred subjects. 'I like this painter; he seems to reverence his art, and to aim at truth in it'.[98] Hawthorne's feelings of goodwill were the beginnings of an important friendship that was cemented later on by their shared time in Italy. Thompson was instrumental in securing Hawthorne's first residence in Rome, and introducing the family to 'the Roman ropes', as Julian Hawthorne put it years later.[99] During the sittings with Thompson in Boston, Hawthorne betrays his abiding interest in the visual arts as an analogue for his own creativity. He 'could recognize the feeling that was in [Thompson], as akin to what I have experienced myself, in the glow of composition'.[100] Hawthorne further effused: 'I love the odor of paint in an artist's room; his palette and his other tools have a mysterious charm for me. The pursuit has always interested my imagination more than any other; and I remember, before having my first portrait taken, there was a great bewitchery in the idea, as if it were a magic process'.[101]

Early stories like 'The Prophetic Pictures' (1837) or 'Drowne's Wooden Image' (1844) invest the visual artist's mimesis with uncanny, spiritualistic powers. Hawthorne treated the subject more extensively in *The House of the Seven Gables* where Holgrave is made a mesmeric daguerreotypist and portrait-taker. It was not until Hawthorne's full immersion in the English and American expatriate scene in Florence and Rome, however, that he addressed at great length the intersections of visual aesthetics, artistic creativity, and moral and spiritual concerns with his last complete novel, *The Marble Faun*. The composition of *The Marble Faun* is inextricably wound around his close friendships and corresponding conversations about aesthetics with several Swedenborgian artists, most notably Thompson and the sculptor Hiram Powers.

Everybody struggles to make art in *The Marble Faun*, their failures and successes mirroring Hawthorne's own embattled creative process. Kenyon works in marble, producing pieces that allude to things Hawthorne had seen in Powers' studio; Miriam makes paintings, and Hilda, like Sophia but also like Cephas Giovanni Thompson, excels at copying, recycling the essence of old masters into distilled new forms. What follows is a sketch of what a more thorough analysis of the generation of *The Marble Faun* within a Swedenborgian-infused circle of expatriates might reveal.

By the time Hawthorne wended his way to Florence, exhausted by his wintering in cold Rome, Hiram Powers had been in Italy for over twenty years. The Vermont know-it-all was instrumental in securing for the Hawthorne family their rental at the Casa del Bello, a mansion across the street from the Powers' own home and just steps away from Robert and Elizabeth Barrett Browning. The Powers apartment stood as a social nexus for the American and British artists in residence there, with institutionalized 'Thursday evening at-homes' where Powers' wife served corn bread and homemade jam to their fellow self-exiled Yankees.[102] Powers was also a loud and vocal espouser of Swedenborg's doctrines. In addition to regular Sunday Swedenborgian church services held in their house, the Powers parlour served as a locus for spiritualist seances at night. Hawthorne remained unimpressed by the craze for ghosts, writing that 'there is a mistake somewhere. So idle and empty do I feel these stories to be',[103] but he nonetheless was fascinated by Powers' garrulous discourses that ranged from harangues against Michelangelo to flying machines to attempts at fixing the failed transatlantic telegraph. Hawthorne marvels at himself——'I have hardly ever before felt an impulse to write down a man's conversation, as I do that of Mr. Powers',[104] and that he 'had no idea of filling so many pages of this journal with the sayings and characteristics of Mr. Powers; but the man and his talk are fresh, original, and full of bone and muscle and I enjoy him much'.[105]

Powers drew on many aspects of the Swedenborgian doctrines of correspondence and influx for his sculptures: most notably, he saw his unblemished, white Carrera marble nudes as 'revealed souls' which would show the highest state of perfection in a spiralling path of Swedenborgian regeneration. 'Color', Powers wrote, invoking Swedenborg-sounding language,

> adjoins a material body to form. This material body is not seen in a pure piece of marble, but the Spiritual body is seen in it. The Soul is in it but not the flesh. The painter adds the flesh but not the sentiment. To what is Spiritual he adds what is material, and to the voluptuary this would be agreeable but not to the chaste mind, who would wish to see a Venus perfectly nude and colored imperfectly, but sufficiently colored to attract the sensual.[106]

As Charles Colbert has further demonstrated, Powers' wildly popular depiction of his daughter Loulie's hands emerging out of a sunflower stemmed from his Swedenborgian world view that believed in celestial guardian spirits that watched over children.[107] Hawthorne embeds an allusion to this sculpture in *The Marble Faun*—which he saw in Powers' studio in June of 1858, remarking that it 'was very exquisite, such as I have never seen before'[108]—with Kenyon's secret sculpture of Hilda's delicate hands. Moreover, Kenyon's artwork is covertly made without Hilda's knowledge, glimpse by glimpse, in the same way that Cephas Giovanni Thompson painstakingly and secretly copied the portrait of Beatrice Cenci (a fact which Hawthorne also weaves later into *The Marble Faun*). Although Powers' success (and infamy over his titillating *Greek Slave*) has been largely forgotten today, his voluble conversational presence was responsible for instigating a widespread engagement with Swedenborg's ideas in English-speaking Florence and Rome, from Isa Blagden, the portraitist William Page to Elizabeth Barrett Browning.

In some cases, as with Page and Barrett Browning (and later on, George Inness), reading and discussing Swedenborg had a direct and marked impact on their creative output. Page derived a representational theory on the correspondences of the human figure from Swedenborg's *Arcana Caelestia* that changed his use of perspective; in Barrett Browning's *Aurora Leigh*, the heroine discusses the correspondence of plants 'to that spirit world,/Outside the limits of our space and time'; and for George Inness, as Adrienne Baxter Bell and Rachael Delue have recently shown, Swedenborg's writings on influx affected his attempts to show spiritual, non-material space in his landscape paintings.[109]

All these were currents floating across dinner tables and wafting through conversations held on moonlit rooftops and piazzas where Hawthorne was often a participant. He records talking about 'high states of being' with Powers on his roof, and listening as Powers reiterates the anthropomorphic cosmology which had appeared in Swedenborg's *The Worlds in Space*.[110] Certainly, Hawthorne was more wearied than ever by certain aspects of the Italian social scene, exhausted by his wife's incessant sightseeing and the constant flow of the literati; he also retained his sceptical detachment from the seance groups that Powers so avidly endorsed. Hawthorne was increasingly withdrawn, riven with anxiety as the ability to write something solid became increasingly difficult. A restlessness pervades the Italian journals, as shadows of the Civil War further complicate ambivalent feelings about what it would mean to ultimately go 'home' to a very different America. Still, the investments of spiritual creativity which Hawthorne lends to the trio of American artists in *The Marble Faun* refracts splintered pieces of his relationships with Powers, Thompson and other Swedenborgian artists in the Florentine/Rome circle. Moreover, the way the novel obsessively weaves its questions of art-making and morality with Miriam and Donatello's sin, its invocations of a non-Puritan kind of 'Providence' that suggests a necessary felix culpa, all the while heavily flirting with the theological attractiveness of Catholicism, has proved vexing for critics to adequately explain. Agnes Donohue finds that the novel reflects

Hawthorne's 'disturbed and distressed response to Calvinism versus Roman Catholicism'[111]—that it is Italy which ultimately unfetters the creative crucible of the damned, blackened heart that Hawthorne had gleaned from his Puritan heritage. The simplistic binary which Donohue and others have read here, that it is American Puritanism versus European Roman Catholicism, needs to be made more complex by interjecting Hawthorne's close connections with Swedenborgians who were crafting theologically infused art with the same sort of symbolic intent that Hawthorne's Romance aimed towards.

NOTES

1   Ralph Waldo Emerson, *The Journals and Miscellaneous Notebooks of Ralph Waldo Emerson*, ed. William H Gilman, et al. (Cambridge: Harvard University Press, 1960-1982), vol. 12, pp. 335-6.

2   F O Matthiessen, *American Renaissance: Art and Expression in the Age of Emerson and Whitman* (London: Oxford University Press, 1964), p. viii.

3   Perry Miller (ed.), *The Transcendentalists: An Anthology* (Cambridge: Harvard University Press, 1950), p. 49.

4   Emerson, *The Journals and Miscellaneous Notebooks of Ralph Waldo Emerson*, vol. 7, p. 255.

5   Nathaniel Hawthorne, *The Letters, 1813-1843*, ed. Thomas Woodson, et al. (Ohio: Ohio State University, 1984), vol. 15, p. 532.

6   Christopher Pearse Cranch, 'Correspondences' (1841), reprinted in *Transcendentalism: A Reader*, ed. Joel Myerson (New York: Oxford University Press, 2000), pp. 494-5.

7   Hawthorne, *The House of the Seven Gables* (New York: W W Norton, 1967), p. 281.

8   Hawthorne, *The American Notebooks*, ed. Claude Simpson (Ohio: Ohio State University Press, 1972), p. 251.

9   Popularized Swedenborgianism has played an interesting role in the formations of national and localized political identities, in the historical-material sense of

Williams' term; this essay focuses more exclusively on the aesthetic framework Swedenborg was part of (which for Williams was inescapable from the political). For an interesting discussion of the ramifications of Swedenborgianized spiritualism in relation to Abolitionism, for example, see Kenneth Silver, *The Spiritual Kingdom in America: The Influence of Emanuel Swedenborg on American Society and Culture, 1816-1860*. Ph.D. diss. Stanford (1983) (Ann Arbor: University Microfilms, 1984), pp. 176-209. Marguerite Beck Block touches on the interconnections between the Swedenborgian New Church and various political spheres in *The New Church in the New World: A Study of Swedenborgianism in America* (New York: Swedenborg Publishing Association, 1984).

[10] Hawthorne, *The American Notebooks*, p. 358.

[11] Ibid., p. 352.

[12] Herman Melville, 'Hawthorne and His Mosses' (1850), reprinted in *Moby-Dick; or, The Whale* (New York: W W Norton, 2002), p. 521.

[13] See Agnes Donohue, *Hawthorne: Calvin's Ironic Stepchild* (Ohio: Kent State University Press, 1985). Sometimes Donohue errs on reading the Puritans into a stereotypical fire-and-brimstone posture, forgetting Hawthorne's own depiction of the period as having a lively, complex spirit which his own present moment lacked (articulated most clearly in *The Scarlet Letter*). Gura's argument is more nuanced. Philip Gura, *The Wisdom of Words: Language, Theology, and Literature in the New England Renaissance* (Middletown: Wesleyan University Press, 1981), especially pp. 147-70.

[14] Between 1828 and 1850, Hawthorne (and/or his Aunt Mary) checked out from the Boston Athenaeum numerous books regarding marginal religious heterodoxies, including accounts of French ecstatic mystics and seventeenth-century Quakers. See Marion Kesselring, *Hawthorne's Reading 1828-1850* (New York: New York Public Library, 1949).

[15] Joel Myerson (ed.), *Transcendentalism: A Reader* (New York: Oxford University Press, 2000), p. 478.

[16] Alfred J Gabay, *The Covert Enlightenment: Eighteenth-Century Counterculture and Its Aftermath* (West Chester: Swedenborg Foundation, 2004), p. 179.

[17] Hawthorne, *The American Notebooks*, pp. 368, 371.

[18] See Block, *The New Church in the New World*, p. 151.

[19] Arthur Sherbo, 'Albert Brisbane and Hawthorne's Holgrave and Hollingsworth', in *The New England Quarterly*, vol. 27, no. 4, December 1954, pp. 531-4.

[20] In addition to Wilkinson, a very old Robert Owen also met with Brisbane, and surely spoke about his earlier communal experiments with Swedenborgians in Ohio. See Block, p. 150. For Wilkinson's substantial correspondence on Fourier and Brisbane, see the forthcoming *Selected Letters of James John Garth Wilkinson: England's Forgotten Philosopher* (West Chester: Swedenborg Foundation).

[21] See Robert Gladish, *Swedenborg, Fourier, and the America of the 1840's* (Bryn Athyn: Swedenborg Scientific Association, 1983), pp. 63-4.

[22] George Ripley, 'Association Not Sectarian', in *The Harbinger*, vol. 2, pp. 92-4.

[23] Hawthorne, *The Letters, 1843-1853*, ed. Thomas Woodson, et al. (Ohio: Ohio State University, 1985), vol. 1, p. 181.

[24] John Humphrey Noyes, *History of American Socialisms* (Philadelphia: J B Lippincott & Co., 1870), p. 547.

[25] See Hawthorne, *The American Notebooks*, pp. 310, 457. Characteristically, Hawthorne does not record his reaction to Fourier in his journals, but Sophia reports in a letter to her mother that her husband was 'thoroughly disgusted' with Fourier's *Traite de l'association domestique-agricole*. Letter excerpted in Julian Hawthorne, *Nathaniel Hawthorne and His Wife; A Biography* (Michigan: Scholarly Press, 1968), pp. 268-9.

[26] See Block, p. 153.

[27] Charles Julius Hempel, *The True Organization of the New Church, as indicated in the Writings of Emanuel Swedenborg and Demonstrated by Charles Fourier* (New York: William Radde, 1848), p. 36.

[28] See *The New Jerusalem Magazine*, vol. XXI, June 1848, p. 299.

[29] See Emanuel Swedenborg, *The Last Judgment* (1758), tr. John Chadwick (London: Swedenborg Society, 1992), §73, pp. 105-6: 'The future state of the world [after 1757] will be exactly the same as it has been up to now; for the mighty change which has taken place in the spiritual world does not cause any change in the external appearance of the natural world. [...] It is because people have had their spiritual freedom restored that the spiritual sense of the Word has now been disclosed, and

by this means Divine truths of a more inward kind have been revealed'. Swedenborg exegetically reads the death and destruction in the Book of Revelation as partially a prescient, allegorical demolition of erroneous Christian dogmas: that faith alone saves, or that an all-loving God would damn the un-baptized.

[30] Elizabeth Palmer Peabody, 'A Glimpse of Christ's Idea of Society', in *The Dial*, vol. II, October 1841, repr. (New York: Rusell and Russell, 1961), p. 221.

[31] Swedenborg's presence in the Peabody household is discussed by Megan Marshall in *The Peabody Sisters: Three Women Who Ignited American Romanticism* (New York: Houghton Mifflin, 2005), pp. 89-90, 96.

[32] Robert Richardson carefully traces Œgger's importance for *Nature* in *Emerson: The Mind on Fire* (Berkeley: Los Angeles Press, 1995), pp. 198-9.

[33] Guillaume Œgger, *Le Vrai Messie* (1836), repr. in Kenneth Walter Cameron, *Emerson the Essayist: An Outline of His Philosophical Development through 1836 with Special Emphasis on the Sources and Interpretation of Nature* (Raleigh: The Thistle Press, 1945), vol. 1, p. 301.

[34] A Bronson Alcott, *The Letters of A. Bronson Alcott* (Iowa: Iowa State University Press, 1969), p. 30. For analysis of Alcott's use of Swedenborg and the Swedenborgian Sampson Reed, see Kenneth Silver, *The Spiritual Kingdom in America*, pp. 100-2.

[35] Taylor Stoehr, *Hawthorne's Mad Scientists: Pseudoscience and Social Science in Nineteenth-Century Life and Letters* (New York: Archon Books, 1978), pp. 51-2.

[36] See Alfred Gabay, *The Covert Enlightenment*, pp. 43-79, as well as John S Haller, Jr, *Swedenborg, Mesmer, and the Mind/Body Connection: the Roots of Contemporary Medicine* (West Chester: Swedenborg Foundation, 2010).

[37] For a thorough exploration of Swedenborg's position within nineteenth-century Francophone literature, see Lynn Wilkinson, *The Dream of an Absolute Language: Emanuel Swedenborg and French Literary Culture* (Albany: State University of New York Press, 1996).

[38] Robert C Fuller, *Mesmerism and the American Cure of Souls* (Philadelphia: University of Pennsylvania Press, 1982), p. 73.

[39] Catherine Albanese, in her *Nature Religion in America: From the Algonquin Indians to the New Age* (Chicago: University of Chicago Press, 1990), p. 80, writes

how Swedenborg and mesmerism became 'guiding intellectual lights' for progressive movements throughout antebellum America. Swedenborg is also further investigated, albeit for different purposes, in Albanese's recent *A Republic of Mind and Spirit: A Cultural History of American Metaphysical Religion* (Cambridge: Harvard University Press, 2007).

[40] Hawthorne, *The House of the Seven Gables* (New York: W W Norton, 1967), p. 263.

[41] Hawthorne, *The Letters, 1813-1843*, vol. 15 ed. Thomas Woodson et al. (Ohio: Ohio State University, 1984), pp. 588-9.

[42] Ibid., p. 590.

[43] Taylor Stoehr, *Hawthorne's Mad Scientists*, p. 252.

[44] Ibid., pp. 175-6.

[45] Alfred J Gabay, *The Covert Enlightenment*, p. 212.

[46] Andrew Jackson Davis, *The Magic Staff: An Autobiography* (New York: J S Brown, 1857), pp. 210, 228.

[47] Alfred J Gabay, *The Covert Enlightenment*, p. 219.

[48] Swedenborg, *Heaven and Hell* (1758), tr. K C Ryder (London: Swedenborg Society, 2010), §249, p. 160.

[49] Most significantly, Arthur Conan Doyle devotes his first opening chapter to Swedenborg in his definitive *The History of Spiritualism* (New York: Doubleday, 1926).

[50] Hawthorne, *The Blithedale Romance*, p. 96.

[51] Hawthorne, *The English Notebooks*, p. 617.

[52] Hawthorne, *The Letters, 1813-1843*, vol. I, p. 466.

[53] George Henry Holden, 'Hawthorne Among His Friends', in *Harpers New Monthly Magazine*, vol. LXIII, July 1881, pp. 260-7; repr. in Kenneth Walter Cameron, *Hawthorne among his Contemporaries: a Harvest of Estimates, Insights, and Anecdotes from the Victorian Literary World* (Hartford: Transcendental Books, 1968), p. 226.

[54] Hawthorne, *The House of the Seven Gables*, p. 180.

[55] Ibid., p. 181.

[56] Hawthorne, *The Letters, 1813-1843*, vol. I, p. 466.

[57] According to Julian Hawthorne's primary biographer, Maurice Bassan, in his

Hawthorne's Son: The Life and Literary Career of Julian Hawthorne (Columbus: Ohio State University Press, 1970), p. 66, Emanuel Swedenborg 'greatly helped to shape Julian Hawthorne's "religious ideas", which were integrated with his aesthetic and political theories [...] In his writer's notebook of 1871-72, [Julian] Hawthorne discusses in detail Swedenborg's Language of Colours, the Law of Correspondences, and such occult matters as the Andramandoni, the Garden of Conjugial Love. He displays a fascination with the problem of duality and argues (with himself) for the preeminence of the Spiritual'. Philip Gura, at the end of his *The Wisdom of Words*, p. 157, argues that Nathaniel Hawthorne's daughter Rose's conversion to Roman Catholicism (becoming 'Mother Mary Alphonsa') might say something deeper about Hawthorne's own religious anxieties—what, then, are we to make of this turn of Julian's?

[58] Elinore Peebles, 'Homeopathy and the New Church', in *Emanuel Swedenborg: A Continuing Vision*, ed. Robin Larsen et al. (New York: Swedenborg Foundation, 1988), p. 472.

[59] Taylor Stoehr, *Hawthorne's Mad Scientists*, p. 104.

[60] Ibid., p. 30.

[61] Ibid., pp. 117, 131.

[62] Ralph Waldo Emerson, *Essays and Poems* (New York: Library of America, 1996), p. 69.

[63] Hawthorne, 'The Haunted Quack' (1831), in *Tales and Sketches* (New York: Library of America, 1996), p. 53.

[64] Hawthorne, *The Scarlet Letter* (New York: W W Norton, 1988), p. 94.

[65] Hawthorne, *The American Notebooks*, p. 235.

[66] Hawthorne, 'The Birth-Mark', in *Tales and Sketches*, p. 766.

[67] Alfred J Gabay, *The Covert Enlightenment*, pp. 212-13.

[68] Hawthorne, 'The Birth-Mark', in *Tales and Sketches*, p. 764.

[69] Swedenborg's findings were published as *The Height of Waters, and Strong Tides in the Primeval World* in 1719. See Cyriel Odhner Sigstedt, *The Swedenborg Epic: The Life and Works of Emanuel Swedenborg* (New York: Bookman Associates, 1952), p. 59.

[70] Charles G Gross, *Brain, Vision, Memory: Tales in the History of Neuroscience* (Cambridge: MIT Press, 1998), p. 127. Additionally, Gross catalogues, 'Swedenborg's

view of the cerebrospinal fluid was not surpassed until the work of Magendie a 100 years later. [Swedenborg] was the first to implicate the colliculi in vision, and in fact the only one until Flourens in the nineteenth century. [Swedenborg] suggested that a function of the corpus callosum was for the hemispheres to intercommunicate with each other, [and that] a function of the corpus striatum was to take over motor control from the cortex when a movement became a familiar habit or second nature' (p. 128).

[71] See Emanuel Swedenborg, *Three Transactions on the Cerebrum; a Posthumous Work* (Philadelphia: Swedenborg Scientific Association, 1938), p. 73; as well as Stanley Finger, *Origins of Neuroscience: A History of Explorations in Brain Function* (New York and Oxford: Oxford University Press, 2001), especially pp. 29-31. Other historians of science with relevant commentary on Swedenborg's neurological theories include M Ramstrom, 'Emanuel Swedenborg as an Anatomist', in *British Medical Journal*, 2 (1910), pp. 1153-5, and T H Schwedenberg, 'The Swedenborg Manuscripts', in *Archives of Neurology*, vol. 2, April 1960, pp. 407-9.

[72] Hawthorne, 'The Birth-Mark', p.769.

[73] Review of Nathaniel Hawthorne, 'American Novels', in *North British Review*, vol. XIX, May and August 1853, p. 45.

[74] Hawthorne, *Tales and Sketches*, p. 1179.

[75] Ibid., pp. 743-4.

[76] Ibid., p. 745.

[77] Swedenborg, *The Worlds in Space*, tr. John Chadwick (London: Swedenborg Society, 1997), §§1-2, pp. 1-2.

[78] For some speculations on the Pyle-Swedenborg connection, see Mary F Holahan, 'Twilight Attitudes: Howard Pyle, Swedenborg, and the Artist's Soul', in *Swedenborg and His Influence*, ed. Erland Brock et al. (Bryn Athyn: Academy of the New Church, 1988), pp. 439-47.

[79] Hawthorne, 'The Hall of Fantasy', p. 735.

[80] Ibid., p. 745.

[81] Hawthorne, *The American Notebooks*, p. 251.

[82] Hawthorne, *The Scarlet Letter*, p. 41.

[83] Hawthorne, *Tales and Sketches*, p. 1123.

[84] Ibid., p. 1127.

[85] Philip Gura, *The Wisdom of Words*, p. 91.

[86] Jonathan Edwards, *Typological Writings*, ed. Wallace E Anderson (New Haven: Yale University Press, 1993), p. 152.

[87] Herman Melville, *Moby-Dick; or, The Whale*, ed. Hershel Parker and Harrison Hayford (New York: W W Norton, 2002), p. 140.

[88] Philip Gura, *The Wisdom of Words*, p. 149.

[89] Swedenborg, *Heaven and Hell*, tr. K C Ryder, §106, pp. 69-70.

[90] Ibid., §109, p. 73.

[91] See, for example, ibid., §489.4, p. 390: '[Angels] live in gardens, where they see flower beds and lawns beautifully laid out, with rows of trees round about, with openings leading to walkways. The trees and flowers change every day. Everything they see brings a general feeling of pleasure to their minds, and constantly the variations bring them new pleasure in particular details. And because these correspond to divine attributes, and they have knowledge of correspondences, they are always being filled with fresh recognitions, and through these their spiritual power of reason is being brought closer to perfection. These are their pleasures because gardens, flower beds, lawns and trees correspond to branches of knowledge, recognitions, and understanding gained from these'.

[92] Ralph Waldo Emerson, *Essays and Poems*, p. 29.

[93] Hawthorne, *The Marble Faun, or The Romance of Monte Beni* (New York: The Modern Library, 2000), pp. 232-3.

[94] Ralph Waldo Emerson, *Essays and Poems*, p. 464.

[95] See H W Janson, 'Psyche in Stone: The Influence of Swedenborg on Funerary Art', in *Emanuel Swedenborg: A Continuing Vision*, pp. 115-26.

[96] See Brenda Wineapple, *Hawthorne: A Life* (New York: Alfred Knopf, 2003), pp. 119, 207.

[97] Hawthorne, *The American Notebooks*, pp. 498-9.

[98] Ibid., p. 497.

[99] For Hawthorne-Thompson family dynamics, see Julian Hawthorne, *Hawthorne and His Circle* (New York: Archon Books, 1968), pp. 260-6.

[100] Hawthorne, *The American Notebooks*, p. 499.

[101] Ibid., pp. 492-3.

[102] Robert Gladish, 'Tre Amici Artisti: E.B. Browning, Hiram Powers, and William Page in Florence and Rome', in *Covenant*, vol. 1, no. 4, 1998, pp. 273-91.

[103] Hawthorne, *The French and Italian Notebooks,* ed. Thomas Woodson (Ohio: Ohio State University Press, 1980), p. 399.

[104] Ibid., p. 337.

[105] Ibid., p. 314.

[106] Quoted in Richard P Wunder, *Hiram Powers: Vermont Sculptor, 1805–1873* (Newark: University of Delaware Press, 1991), vol. 1, p. 278.

[107] Charles Colbert, 'Spiritual Currents and Manifest Destiny in the Art of Hiram Powers', in *The Art Bulletin*, vol. 82, no. 3, September 2000, pp. 532-3.

[108] Hawthorne, *The French and Italian Notebooks,* p. 313.

[109] For Page's Swedenborgianism, see his standard biography, Joshua C Taylor, *William Page: The American Titian* (Chicago: University of Chicago Press, 1957); Barrett Browning's use of Swedenborg is dealt with by Linda Lewis, *Elizabeth Barrett Browning's Spiritual Progress: Face to Face with God* (Columbia: University of Missouri Press, 1998); for Inness, see Adrienne Baxter Bell, *George Inness and the Visionary Landscape* (New York: George Brazaille, 2003), and Rachael Delue's comprehensive *George Inness and the Science of Landscape* (Chicago: University of Chicago Press, 2004).

[110] Swedenborg, *The Worlds in Space,* §§378-9.

[111] Agnes Donohue, *Hawthorne: Calvin's Ironic Stepchild* (Ohio: Kent State University Press, 1985), p. 269.

The spiritual detective: how Baudelaire invented Symbolism, by way of Swedenborg, E T A Hoffmann and Edgar Allan Poe

Gary Lachman

I n *Heaven and Hell*, Swedenborg introduced the notion of correspondences. Although there was a history of similar notions depicting the
relationship between the things of this world and those of the higher,
spiritual realms—Jacob Boehme's ideas about the 'signatures of things' and the
hermetic dictum that 'as above, so below', for example—Swedenborg's account was
generally more detailed and thorough, leaving little ambiguity about his meaning.
For Swedenborg, there was a direct, one-to-one link between the elements of our
world, both natural and man-made, and the spiritual worlds 'above'. As he writes,
'The whole natural world corresponds to the spiritual world, not only the natural
world in general, but also in every particular'. The natural world for Swedenborg
meant 'everything in its whole extent that is under the sun'.[1] Just as an effect has its
roots in its cause, for Swedenborg, the entire physical world has its being and existence
in the spiritual one. And just as a cause may be inferred from its effects, so too the
spiritual origin of our world may be inferred from the proper study of its elements.
Swedenborg argued that this truth was, at an earlier time, common knowledge, but
has long been forgotten. We, people of a later age, have lost it completely, chiefly
because of our self-obsession, which draws our attention away from higher matters,
and focuses it on earthly, sensual things and the gratification of our appetites. By
Swedenborg's time, this drift away from the spiritual and toward the sensual was

moving toward its peak. With the rise of science and our increasing dependence on explanation in terms of material causation, the idea that there was some kind of spiritual blueprint for the phenomena of nature, and for human existence as well, was more and more rejected. Today we are, I believe, moving toward a kind of apogee in regard to the spiritual world, with science and popular culture (consumerism) speedily heading to the furthest extreme from any understanding of a 'higher' reality. Recent years have seen a robust movement in the philosophy of mind, as well as in neuroscience and pharmacology, to 'explain' in physical terms the most spiritual elements of human existence, our consciousness and very selves.[2] And broadly 'metaphysical' sciences, like cosmology and astrophysics—dealing with fundamental questions like the origin of the universe—have been aiming for some time now to arrive at a final 'theory of everything', that would account for reality itself, in terms of purely physical formulae. That other spiritual thinkers, like Rudolf Steiner for example, with his prophecy of an 'Ahrimanic future', voiced similar concerns, suggests that rather than being a purely subjective—or, worse still, aberrant—view of human history, Swedenborg's belief that human consciousness has moved away from an earlier direct perception of the spiritual, deserves careful study. [3]

The course of that movement needs little elaboration; even a cursory familiarity with the history of the last three centuries makes clear that there has been an increasing faith in science as the main bearer of 'truth' for our civilization.[4] Likewise, the details of Swedenborg's correspondences, fascinating as they are, are not necessary for an appreciation of this paper—and in any case, the interested reader could do no better than to go to the source itself. Two central ideas, though, are helpful to grasp before we go on. One is that for Swedenborg, as for many thinkers in the Western esoteric tradition, the natural world is a kind of language. It is something like a series of allegories or hieroglyphics. It is, then, something to be read. In a metaphor that will appear again, a forest is not only made of trees: it is also, for Swedenborg, made of signs.

Later thinkers will use the term 'symbol' rather than 'sign', and this distinction leads to the second idea it will be useful for us to grasp at this point. For Swedenborg, we can say that the direction in which the 'signs' of the natural world point is vertical, at least metaphorically. The 'signs' that Swedenborg tells us about 'point', he says, toward the higher, spiritual world.

Now, the 'direction' and 'pointing' I am speaking of are, as I say, metaphorical — and recognizing this reveals a curious fact. Because in trying to explain Swedenborg's notion of correspondences by using metaphors, I am actually employing the very notion I am trying to explain. Metaphors are terms or expressions that 'stand' for something else; in other words, they show how some things 'correspond' to other things. When I say of a beautiful woman that her face 'bloomed', I mean that the beauty of her face is like that of a rose; in other words, it corresponds to it. The same is true if I say of someone that he 'exploded' with anger. Obviously he did not literally explode; his anger was so great that its expression 'corresponded' to an explosion.

Now, metaphors make up a large part of our language and speech, so much so that it would be very difficult to convey anything without using them. And it is a curious exercise to go 'metaphor hunting', to become conscious of how many metaphors we use, but are unaware of using. Emerson called language 'petrified poetry', and Nietzsche voiced something very similar when he called everyday speech a series of worn-down metaphors, meaning that the phrases and expressions of everyday speech were at one time new and fresh metaphors but have become so commonplace that we no longer recognize them as such. So, in a way, we already know, tacitly, what correspondences are, and use them all the time. But it is a different and enlightening matter to become aware of them explicitly. Before I go on, I should make clear the distinction between a 'sign' and a 'symbol'. A sign, like a metaphor, 'stands' for something else—and an alert metaphor hunter will notice that, in using the word 'stand', I am using a metaphor to explain what a metaphor does. But there is a difference. A stop sign on the road tells us one thing:

that we need to stop at this intersection. It 'stands'——literally, in this case——for the command to stop. Likewise, an exit sign over a door: it tells us that we can leave a room or building in that direction. A symbol, however, is not so specific. A nation's flag can 'stand' for many things: your home, your nation's pride, its laws, its landscapes, and so on. And if we move on to other symbols, like the Christian cross, the Yin-Yang emblem, and other religious icons, we enter an area of much wider scope. Further still, we can speak of symbols in art, in literature, in dreams, in visions and fantasies. These are notoriously difficult to interpret, to pin down (another metaphor) to a specific meaning. So a handy distinction between a sign and a symbol is that with a sign we get greater specificity——a strong connection between the sign and what it stands for——but less meaning, and with a symbol we have the opposite: larger scope for meaning, but a corresponding vagueness about what it stands for.

As we go on I will try to show how this distinction is related to Swedenborg's 'vertical' correspondences——which strike me very much as 'signs'——and the more 'horizontal' correspondences——which strike me as 'symbols'——that the French poet Charles Baudelaire employed in his ideas about art, and which later became the basis for the aesthetic doctrine of Symbolism. The same distinction can be made, I think, between the notion of allegory, which works with a one-to-one correspondence between an image and an abstract idea, and metaphor, which strikes me as a much 'looser' arrangement between meaning and emblem.

*

We do not know exactly when Baudelaire became aware of Swedenborg's work, or which books of his he read. The first mention of Swedenborg in Baudelaire's writings is in his novella *La Fanfarlo*, which was published in 1847. In it the hero keeps a volume of Swedenborg by his bedside. In the novella, Baudelaire makes no attempt to convey Swedenborg's ideas, and the name is mentioned more or less as a means of creating atmosphere. Baudelaire himself more than likely discovered

Swedenborg through reading the novelist Balzac, who, in novels like *Séraphita* and *Louis Lambert* adopts Swedenborg's ideas and uses them to create a framework for the story. It is also possible, as Baudelaire's biographer Enid Starkie suggests, that the poet was familiar with French translations of *Heaven and Hell* and *The Doctrine of the New Jerusalem*, which were available at the time. In fact, Swedenborg's ideas, as well as those of other 'occult' thinkers like Franz Anton Mesmer, were 'in the air' in France at this time, forming part of the philosophical climate of Romanticism, so it is quite possible that Baudelaire 'picked them up' without much direct study of the original texts themselves.

What seems clear from a study of Baudelaire's life is that his interest in Swedenborg coincided with his profound discovery of the works of another poet, Edgar Allan Poe. *La Fanfarlo*, as I said, was published in 1847, and this was the year that Baudelaire first encountered Poe's work. A translation of Poe's story 'The Black Cat' by Isabelle Meunier appeared in the January 1847 issue of *La Démocratie Pacifique*. Baudelaire read this and his discovery of Poe was probably the most important event of his life. During Baudelaire's lifetime his literary reputation rested not on his work as a poet, but on his translations of Poe. Baudelaire felt a profound identification with the American poet; in Poe's work he discovered themes and ideas that he himself had entertained for some time. The 'correspondence', as it were, between Poe and Baudelaire even extended to Baudelaire finding actual sentences in Poe's work that he, Baudelaire, had written, prior to even knowing about Poe. Poe indeed became an obsession of Baudelaire's. He questioned everyone he met about the writer and, on one occasion, burst into the hotel room of an American writer who was visiting Paris, and subjected him to an impromptu quiz on Poe's career and standing in American letters. One sign of the effect Poe had on Baudelaire is that, while easily wearied when engaged in his own creative work, when working on his Poe translations, Baudelaire exhibited a diligence and industry that was unusual for him. Baudelaire went on translating Poe for nearly twenty years, wrote two long essays about his life and work as well as several shorter ones, and, as I have said, was associated in the French literary consciousness of the time with the work of the American poet and short story writer.

That association began in 1848 when Baudelaire published the first of his Poe translations, the short story 'Mesmeric Revelations'. What is curious about this story is that it purports to be a factual account of a mesmerist who puts an individual who is at the point of death into a trance, during which the mesmerized subject reports on a variety of 'occult' or metaphysical questions. Poe had a deep interest both in mesmerism[5] and in metaphysics, and the revelations conveyed in the story are a sort of trial run for Poe's longer excursion into cosmology, his 'scientific prose poem', *Eureka*. What is also curious about 'Mesmeric Revelations' is that after its publication, Poe received letters from a Swedenborgian group, thanking him for corroborating Swedenborg's insights about the after world; the group clearly believed that Poe had written a true account. Poe was a notorious trickster, given to literary hoaxing, and, as a professed rationalist, he dismissed such remarks as the praise of fools. Poe himself seems not to have read Swedenborg, or if he did, not to have thought much of him. His knowledge of mesmerism came from a book, *Facts in Mesmerism* (1840), by the Reverend Chauncy Hare Townshend, and it attracted him because of its 'scientific' approach to the phenomena of trance.

At this point, however, it is not important whether or not Poe accepted or even knew of Swedenborg's doctrines; what is crucial is to recognize that for Poe, as for Baudelaire, the poet/writer is a kind of seer, an individual privy to knowledge and insights unavailable to the average person. 'Mesmeric Revelations' conveys this idea directly; it runs, however, throughout all of Poe's work and is, paradoxically, portrayed most clearly in those works in which Poe professed his 'rationalism' most directly, his tales of detection, specifically 'The Purloined Letter'. I say that Poe's notion of the poet as a seer is conveyed most clearly in this story; but, again paradoxically, the fact that this idea is subtly 'hidden'——although it is in reality in open view——is what makes it 'clear'. This admittedly complicated situation may become more apparent as we go along.

*

But before we move onto 'The Purloined Letter', there is another writer, whose influence on Baudelaire was as profound as Poe's or Swedenborg's. Before becoming known as a poet, or even as a translator of Poe, Baudelaire had gained a reputation as an art critic. In his *Salon of 1846*, in a section exploring the effects of colour (and which contains a magnificent example of Baudelaire's poetic prose), Baudelaire introduces an idea that will be crucial to his later notion of correspondences. Remarking on a tavern whose red and green façade was, for Baudelaire's eyes, 'a source of exquisite pain', Baudelaire asks if any 'analogist has drawn up a well authenticated scale of colours and their corresponding feelings'. He then goes on to quote a passage from the German fantasist and critic E T A Hoffmann, in which Hoffmann describes how often, when on the point of sleep, but also while listening to music, he finds 'an analogy and close union between colours, sounds and scents'. 'I have the impression', Hoffmann writes, 'that all these things have been created by one and the same ray of light, and that they are destined to unite in a wonderful concert'. He then goes on to describe how the scent of brown and red marigolds produces 'a magical effect' on his being, easing him into a profound reverie, in which he hears the far-off sound of an oboe. [6] Elsewhere, Hoffmann also described his alter ego, Kapellmeister Johannes Kreisler (the pseudonym he used for some of his critical writings), as wearing a coat that was in C sharp minor, with a collar in E major. And he later wrote that 'It is no empty metaphor, no allegory, when a musician says that colour, fragrance, light appear to him as sounds, and that in their intermingling he perceives an extraordinary concert'. [7]

The phenomenon Hoffmann is describing is known as synaesthesia, when one sense is substituted for another: in some unusual psychological states, we see sounds, hear colours, feel tastes, etc. It was a phenomenon known to both Baudelaire and Poe. In his *Marginalia*, Poe remarks that 'The orange ray of the spectrum and the buzz of the gnat (which never rises above the second A), affect me with nearly similar sensations. In hearing the gnat, I perceive the colour. In perceiving the colour, I seem to hear the gnat'. [8] In a note to the poem 'Al Aaraaf', Poe remarks that 'I have often thought I could distinctly hear the sound of the darkness as it stole over the horizon'. [9] Baudelaire himself, just before quoting Hoffmann's remark, speaks of colour in musical terms, commenting on its 'harmony' and 'melody'. In our own everyday speech we adopt similar expressions, calling some colours 'loud' and others 'muted'. Perhaps less frequently, we speak of some tones as 'bright' and others as 'dark'. (Certainly we speak of 'high' and 'low' pitch, ascribing a spatial value to sounds which, if you think about it, seems a bit odd.) Hoffmann, Poe and Baudelaire were not the only artists fascinated by this curious phenomenon. Richard Wagner, another influence on Baudelaire, knew of it, and in 'Richard Wagner and *Tannhauser* in Paris', Baudelaire describes the synaesthetic effect of listening to Wagner's music. [10] The painter Wassily Kandinsky employed synaesthesia in his work, as did the composers Alexandre Scriabin and Olivier Messiaen, the playwright August Strindberg, the poet Arthur Rimbaud and the novelist Vladimir Nabokov, to name a few. [11]

Like the philosopher Arthur Schopenhauer, Hoffmann believed that music was in some way our most direct link to the higher worlds. Music, he says, is 'a universal language of nature'. It is 'the mysterious Sanskrit of nature, translated into sound'. Only through music can we perceive 'the sublime song of trees, flowers, animals, stones, water'. 'Music', Hoffmann argues when writing of Beethoven, 'reveals to man an unknown realm, a world quite separate from the outer sensual world surrounding him, a world in which he leaves behind all precise feelings in order to embrace an inexpressible longing'. [12]

So, like Swedenborg, Hoffmann also expresses the idea that the visible natural world is a kind of language, a 'Sanskrit', and that for him, music is the key to deciphering its meaning. As in the spectrum where white contains all the other colours for Hoffmann music is the primal source of all other phenomena, the 'ray of light' he speaks of in the passage quoted by Baudelaire, that contains everything else destined to be united again in a 'wonderful concert'. For Hoffmann, the phenomenon of synaesthesia is evidence of this. It is also clear that synaesthesia is another form of 'correspondence' although, unlike Swedenborg's, it is a less rigorous version. The colour orange 'corresponded' for Poe to the sound of a gnat's buzzing, but the same is not necessarily true for other people. Red and brown marigolds 'corresponded' for Hoffmann to the distant sound of an oboe. Again, although Baudelaire and others (the composer Scriabin, for example) believed that a strict 'scale of analogies' could be devised (Baudelaire believed the effect of Wagner's music on himself and others was evidence of this), it would be surprising if we all heard an oboe when faced with marigolds. This *horizontal* form of correspondence then, between the elements of the sensual world, admits a degree of subjectivity, which, to my mind, shifts the agents of correspondence from being 'signs', as in Swedenborg, to 'symbols'. [13]

*

Let us return to Poe. I have said that the notion of the poet/writer/artist as seer runs through all of Poe's work, but that it is most clearly expressed, if we know how to look for it, in the story 'The Purloined Letter'. Poe was a paradoxical character—not surprising, as most poets, writers or artists are—and while he advances the idea of the artist as seer, he was also eager to present himself as a strictly 'scientific' or 'rational' thinker. [14] The term he uses is 'ratiocination' and he even applied this approach to poetry, writing an essay on 'The Rationale of Verse'. Poe's self-professed aspirations to scientific thinking reached visionary, if flawed, heights in *Eureka*. He was, however, much more successful in embodying those aspirations in a fictional alter ego, the detective C Auguste Dupin, hero of 'The Murders in the Rue Morgue'——considered the first detective story——'The Mystery of Marie Roget', and 'The Purloined Letter'.

The type of tale Poe originated is out of fashion these days, its place being usurped by the crime novel, and although the most famous 'consulting detective' in the world is Conan Doyle's Sherlock Holmes, the average reader may be unaware that one of the models for Holmes was Poe's Dupin. Holmes differs from contemporary private eyes—or police investigators, for that matter, and this in itself is indicative of the change in sensibility—by being somewhat 'eccentric'. [15] He keeps his tobacco in a Persian slipper; when bored in between cases, he takes cocaine; he plays the violin, etc. These traits place Holmes 'outside' the normal run of things, and the same is true, to an even greater degree, of Poe's Dupin.

Funnily enough, Dupin lives in Paris—that is, for Poe's American readers, he is 'foreign', hence somewhat strange. But his oddness does not stop there. According to Poe's unnamed narrator, who appears in each story, Dupin is a somewhat isolated figure, an aristocrat fallen on hard times, a man of a higher nature who is yet destitute of material things. He lives in a 'time-eaten and grotesque mansion' in a 'retired and desolate portion of the Fauberg St. Germain'. The narrator meets Dupin in an obscure library where he discovers they are both in search of the same rare volume. They find that they share a predilection for darkness. Dupin wears coloured spectacles, even at night time (and Poe may be responsible for the practice in some circles of wearing sunglasses after dark), and during the day, Dupin draws all the shutters to his room, preferring to rely on the dim light of a few candles. He meditates in total darkness and smokes a pipe that produces a curious aroma. Dupin is only active during the night, when he leaves his apartment to seek 'that infinity of mental excitement which quiet observation can afford'. He is, naturally, contemptuous of the methods of the police force, yet his *noblese oblige* compels him to offer his services to them when needed. Where the police bungle through a case, using brute force as their preferred method, Dupin relies on his mind, which, for him, provides a greater illumination than gaslight. Although he shrouds himself in darkness, he is yet able to see things that invariably elude the authorities.

This ability to perceive things that the average individual is blind to (although Dupin himself, by normal standards, lives in darkness) is most eloquently portrayed, as I have said, in 'The Purloined Letter'. In the story, an important letter has been stolen from a person in high office; if its contents are made public, there would be profound, catastrophic consequences. Monsieur G, the Prefect of the Paris police, calls upon Dupin for help in recovering the letter. The police know who has stolen the letter, but although they have searched the thief's apartment from top to bottom several times, they have been unable to find it. Poe describes in detail the police procedure, which, in essence, is a method of analysis. Basically, the police have taken apart and peered into everything in the apartment that could possibly serve as a hiding place. Yet they have failed to uncover the document.

Now, although Poe and Dupin pride themselves on being 'scientific', the failure of the police to uncover the missing document through these methods suggests to me that Poe is making a criticism of the scientific 'method' itself. That method is analysis, the taking apart of nature in order to discover her secrets. 'We murder to dissect', as Wordsworth says. Dupin, however, employs other means. On a pretext he visits the apartment of the thief and there uses his superior mind to find the document. He first employs a kind of 'correspondence', by which he imagines himself into the mind of the thief. By adopting the facial expression of the thief, as he engages him in conversation—all the while examining the room, his eyes hidden by his dark glasses—Dupin 'feels' himself into the psyche of his opponent. The thief's facial expression corresponds to his thoughts, an insight we can also find in Swedenborg. 'The nature of correspondence', he writes, 'is visible in man in his face [...] all the mind's affections stand out visibly, in a physical form as in their imprint'. By adopting the physical form of the thief's face, Dupin is also able to have his thoughts. [16] In this fashion, Dupin is able to locate the hidden letter, which, it turns out, is not 'hidden' at all, but has been left out on a desk in open view—the last place the police would look. The secret that the police, using the scientific method of analysis, have been unable to discover, is in plain sight to the eccentric detective Dupin—who, he tells us, is 'something' of a poet. And just as the purloined letter is in plain sight, to those who know how to look for it, so too is Poe's message: that the poet/writer/artist can see things that the average person, even the scientist, cannot. Poe may present Dupin as a proponent of 'ratiocination', but he is able to discover that which is hidden in full view, because he is a poet. [17]

*

Earlier I said that Swedenborg believed that at an earlier time the correspondences between the natural and spiritual worlds were visible to everyone. [18] It is only in recent times that they have become 'hidden', or rather, that our vision has become so clouded with petty and selfish matters that we can no longer see them. The correspondences themselves remain; it is our sight that has deteriorated. Poe, Hoffmann and Baudelaire seem to be telling us that this may be true, but that there is a type of person who can, at least on occasion, still recognize the correspondences, still read the secret 'Sanskrit' of nature and see that which is 'hidden' to the rest of us. That person is the poet, the writer, the artist. He or she can 'detect' the hidden secret, find what is out of sight to the rest of us, and, what is more, help others to see it as well. This, in essence, is the central theme of Symbolism. The Symbolist artist or poet can decode the secret messages of existence. As the critic Anna Balakian writes, 'With his superior network of senses and perceptions, [the poet] is bent on deciphering, rather than conveying or communicating, the enigmas of life'. [19]

In his famous poem, 'Correspondances', Baudelaire tells us that 'Nature is a temple', a forest through which we pass 'symbolically'. Like the apartment containing the purloined letter, the hidden message of nature is there, in full view, but most of us do not see it. Those who do, the artists, Baudelaire tells us, are like children. Like the child, the artist 'enjoys to the highest degree the faculty of taking a lively interest in things, even the most trivial in appearance'. [20] Baudelaire likens this fresh, innocent appreciation of things to the sensibility of a convalescent and to support this notion, refers to Poe's story 'The Man of the Crowd'. Sitting in a coffee house in London, Poe's narrator is convalescing after months of illness. Looking out of the window he found himself 'in one of those happy moods which are so precisely the converse of *ennui*—moods of keenest appetency, when the *film from the mental vision departs* [my emphasis] [...] and the intellect, electrified, surpasses [...] its everyday condition'. He feels a 'calm but inquisitive interest in everything',[21] which, if we follow Baudelaire, is shared by children, but also by the 'reader' of life's symbols.

It is curious that the story Baudelaire chooses to emphasize the 'aesthetic' quality of convalescence is one that focuses on the city; in the rest of Poe's tale, his narrator becomes fascinated with a face seen in the crowd, which he follows throughout London for a day. In 'The Painter of Modern Life', and in other essays and poems, Baudelaire argues that not only nature, but the man-made world—'modernity'—is a kind of 'forest' of symbols, and that the poet and artist must learn to 'read' this as well. This idea of 'reading' the city had a great influence on the German-Jewish critic Walter Benjamin, who saw in the incidental, chance occurrences of urban experience, indicators of larger social and historical forces.[22] As nature corresponded to the spiritual world, so did the urban backdrop correspond to social, economic and political powers. Space does not allow more than a mention of this, but I think a possible Swedenborg—Baudelaire—Benjamin connection worth considering.

What we can gather from Baudelaire's writings on modernity, is that, like Dupin, the modern artist or poet must not take for granted what others would reject. Like children and convalescents, fascinated with everything, even what is 'the most trivial in appearance', the modern reader of nature's—or the man-made world's—Sanskrit, can discover a beauty and meaning that the rest of us may ignore. Just as there is a unity behind the correspondences of the natural and spiritual worlds, and a unity behind the plurality of senses (as evidenced by synaesthesia), Baudelaire believed there was a unity of the arts. The true aim of all poetry, all art, all music was to lead the reader or viewer or listener to this unity, which, for Baudelaire, as for Swedenborg, was a revelation of the higher worlds. Baudelaire shocked the critics of his time by arguing that this revelation could come from the most unlikely source: the shifting, inelegant, anarchic surface of urban life. But like Dupin, who was able to uncover what was hidden in full view, with his symbolism, Baudelaire was able to find the spiritual where the rest of us may find nothing.

NOTES

[1] Emanuel Swedenborg, *Heaven and Hell*, tr. J C Ager (London: Swedenborg Society, 1958), pp. 44-5.

[2] For more on the urge to 'explain' consciousness, see the introduction to my *A Secret History of Consciousness* (Great Barrington: Lindisfarne, 2003).

[3] For an account of Steiner's somewhat gloomy prognosis, see my article 'Rudolf Steiner and the Ahrimanic Future', in *Journal for Anthroposophy*, Spring 1993.

[4] Some readers may wonder how the rise of religious fundamentalism, both in the Christian West and the Islamic Middle East, can be explained in terms of an increasing dominance of materialist science. Although both movements are clearly very powerful, they are, it seems to me, reactions to the dominance I am speaking of. Their appearance strikes us as radical and extreme, precisely because both pose a challenge to the reigning rationalist materialist dogma. While that dogma needs to be challenged, it is unfortunate that its most vociferous opponents present alternatives that are equally undesirable.

[5] Poe's other classic mesmerist tales are, of course, 'The Facts in the Case of M. Valdemar' (1845) and 'A Tale of the Ragged Mountains' (1844).

[6] Quoted in Charles Baudelaire, *Selected Writings on Art and Literature*, tr. P E Charvet (London: Penguin, 1992), p. 58.

[7] E T A Hoffmann, *E T A Hoffmann's Musical Writings* (Cambridge: CUP, 1989), p. 164.

[8] Edgar Allan Poe, *Essays and Reviews* (New York: Literary Classics of the United States, 1984), p. 1322.

[9] Quoted in Patrick E Quinn, *The French Face of Edgar Poe* (Carbondale: Southern Illinois University Press, 1957), p. 150.

[10] See Baudelaire, *Selected Writings on Art and Literature*, pp. 331-2.

[11] Interest in synaesthesia was popular in Baudelaire's day. See Enid Starkie, *Baudelaire* (Harmondsworth: Penguin, 1971), pp. 271-3 for an account of 'smell concerts' and other synaesthetic events in the Paris of the 1840s.

[12] Hoffmann, pp. 94, 96.

[13] One approach to correspondences on both the sensual and spiritual planes is that employed in some forms of ceremonial magic. The notorious 'magician' Aleister Crowley devised an elegant and detailed set of correspondences, including colours, scents, astrological signs, magical symbols and much else, based on the Kabbalistic Tree of Life. See his *Liber 777*, in *The Qabalah of Aleister Crowley: Three Texts*, ed. Israel Regardie (New York: Samuel Weiser, 1973). Such correspondences were also employed in a similar fashion as a means of maintaining health and well-being by the Renaissance magus Marsilio Ficino. See his *Book of Life* (1489).

[14] In this Poe is very much like his later disciple, the weird fiction writer H P Lovecraft, who professed a strict materialist philosophy, yet wrote tales of supernatural and occult horror.

[15] Whereas the detective tale began with individuals who worked outside the law and were in many ways superior to the police (who, having failed to solve the case, turned to the amateur sleuth for help), today's dreary but obligatory 'realism' demands as 'factual' and quotidian a narrative as possible. Sherlock Holmes is a kind of superman, solving mysteries beyond the powers of the authorities; police procedural novels and television programmes plod on through every minute detail of often boring work. A further decline is evidenced in the popularity of 'real crime' programmes, which jettison the idea of story altogether, and aim a video camera at cops on the beat.

[16] In explaining his methods to his companion, Dupin also makes the very Swedenborgian remark that 'The material world […] abounds with very strict analogies to the immaterial'. Edgar Allan Poe, *Selected Writings* (Harmondsworth: Penguin, 1984), p. 344.

[17] It is curious to recall that in the story Monsieur G reminds Dupin that the thief, Minister D——, is 'a poet'. Poe may also be saying that it takes a poet to find what another poet has hidden, meaning that only one poet can understand the work of another.

[18] There is evidence to suggest that, in the first few months of life, children experience the world synaesthetically, that is, their experience of the world is not yet refracted into the different sensory modes. There is also some reason to believe that early humans had a very similar mode of experience. For more on synaesthesia and its relation to the evolution of consciousness, see my chapter 'Hypnagogia', in *A Secret History of Consciousness*.

[19] Anna Balakian, *The Symbolist Movement* (New York: New York University Press, 1977), p. 47.

[20] Baudelaire, *Selected Writings on Art and Literature*, p. 398.

[21] Edgar Allan Poe, *Selected Writings*, p. 179.

[22] See Benjamin's essay 'On Some Motifs in Baudelaire', in *Illuminations* (London: Fontana Press, 1992), pp. 152-96.

A hermeneutic key to the title *Leaves of Grass*

Anders Hallengren

I n his international bestseller *The Western Canon: The Books and School of the Ages* (first edn. 1994), Harold Bloom stresses the central position of Walt Whitman (1819-92) in American literature, and in Western poetry in general. In a chapter entitled 'Walt Whitman as center of the American Canon', the American professor overviews American contributions to art and culture. He does so in a mood of despondency:

> If one attempts to list the artistic achievements of our nation against the background of Western tradition, our accomplishments in music, painting, sculpture, architecture tend to be somewhat dwarfed. It is no question of us-ing Bach, Mozart, and Beethoven as the standard; Stravinsky, Schoenberg, and Bartók are more than enough to place our composers in a somewhat sad perspective. And whatever the splendors of modern American painting and sculpture, there has been no Matisse among us. The Walt Whitman as Center of the American Canon exception is in literature. [1]

Whitman was to influence future generations of poets, in the USA as well as in Europe. He had no direct contemporary predecessors, but for a poet-philosopher: Ralph Waldo Emerson. Harold Bloom time and again returns to the importance of

233

Emerson to Whitman.[2] Through the years, many prominent Whitman scholars have done so, too. Bringing the matter to a head, Newton Arvin observed that Emerson was as important to Whitman as Epicurus to Lucretius or Spinoza to Goethe.[3]

However momentous and monumental, prophetic, modern or timeless Whitman's work may be regarded in retrospect, things looked different in his own time. When *Leaves of Grass* was set, printed and published by the author himself in 1855, all at his own cost, that classic was as much a failure as Henry David Thoreau's *Walden* (1854), and Herman Melville's *Moby-Dick* (1851) had been. At least momentarily. There were not many people reading such odd and non-conformist literature. Their recognition came later, and was eventually to propel all three into worldwide fame.

Whitman's completely unconventional prose poems, written in a style not seen since Middle Age folk literature or Old Testament songs and verses and texts of most ancient date—and furthermore marked by a positive sensuality and undogmatic (yet far from ungodly) world-embracing piety and love—seemed as insignificant as depraved, and certainly ill-timed.

There were indeed some striking responses. One of his readers is said to have thrown his copy into the fire—the natural way of disposing of things in those days. However, there were a few favourable reactions, too, and Whitman carefully collected them as precious gems, as almost any author would have done. When he found a publisher for his book in 1856, he quoted them in print. First of all a letter from the (in)famous Emerson, who also had one of his early publications burnt and destroyed—the printed version of his similarly devout and unchurchly 'Divinity School Address' (1838); an edition that disappeared completely and for ever.

Emerson saluted Whitman's collection of poems as 'the most extraordinary piece of wit and wisdom that an American has yet contributed' [!] and greeted the young writer 'at the beginning of a great career'. Whitman quoted that letter in the second edition (1856) where he also paid tribute to Emerson, his 'Master'. Whitman's indebtedness was explicit, and the poet from Long Island seems to have been touched by the influential Concord mind already in the 1840s. In his letter,

Emerson also added that *Leaves of Grass* must have a long background some-where. Presumably he realized that he belonged to that background himself.[4]

Second, and of special interest, Whitman found that his book of poetry had been enthusiastically received by some people in his own New York neighbourhood. That review was published in *The Christian Spiritualist*, a journal founded by a group of Swedenborgians. *Leaves of Grass* was reviewed as a great work which partly embodied and realized the wisdom of Swedenborg's doctrines. That critique was accordingly quoted, and obviously appreciated by Whitman himself, in 'Leaves-Droppings'. It read:

> rare is it to find any receiver of 'the heavenly doctrines' determined to enter for
> himself into the very interiors of all that Swedenborg taught—to see, not the
> mighty reflections that Swedenborg was able to give of interior realities, but
> their originals, as they stand constellated in the heavens! [...] Ralph Waldo
> Emerson is the highest type. He sees the future of truths as our Spirit-seers
> discern the future of man. [*Leaves of Grass* is] written, as we perceive, under
> powerful influxes; a prophecy and promise of much that awaits all who are
> entering with us into the opening doors of a new Era.[5]

In this short text, a Swedenborg-Emerson-Whitman connection is perceived. The question is whether this observation can be further developed. There seem to be grounds for comparison. Emory Holloway, the well-informed editor of *The Uncollected Poetry and Prose of Walt Whitman*, remarked in a note that 'There can be little doubt that Swedenborg had a strong influence on Whitman, as likewise he had on Emerson'.[6]

In the following, I will examine the trinomial Swedenborg-Emerson-Whitman connection in some detail, and especially the more direct Swedenborg-Whitman rela-tion, to see if this can be of any importance whatsoever to the Whitman reader and to the understanding of his conception of words and objects, images and reality.

*

Both Emerson and Whitman dreamed of reproducing the expressive power of things, the omnipresent yet silent *logoi*, the poetry of nature. In their New England world a freshly built vision of Adam's primal language arose; the expressive power within things themselves and their inner essence and their meaning was reborn, revealed. It was this dream of Eden and Adamite language that Whitman framed:

> A SONG of the rolling earth, and of words according,
> Were you thinking that those were the words, those upright lines?
>   those curves, angles, dots?
> No, those are not the words, the substantial words are in the ground
>   and sea,
> They are in the air, they are in you […][7]

Whitman belonged to a generation that experienced humanity as liberated from the coils of original sin and allowed to return to the lost paradise. It now stood face to face with Nature herself, with responsibility for a world destined to elevate itself to Eden,

> To the garden the world anew ascending.

We are 'Children of Adam'.[8] 'Here's for the plain old Adam', announced Emerson; Adam should give things their names again. Every human being is latently a new Adam. The Adamite era is here and now:

> […] in the new-born millions,
> The perfect Adam lives.[9]

When Emerson delivered his six lectures on 'The Times' at the Library Society in New York in 1842, the young editor of the New York journal *The Aurora*, Walter Whitman, was on the spot as reporter. In his lecture on 'The Poet', Emerson surprisingly stated:

> After Dante, and Shakespeare, and Milton, there came no grand poet until Swedenborg, in a corner of Europe, hitherto uncelebrated, sung the wonders of man's heart in strange prose poems which he called Heaven and Hell, the Apocalypse Revealed, the Doctrine of Marriage, Celestial Secrets and so on, and which rivalled in depth and sublimity, and in their power to agitate this human heart—this lover of the wild and wonderful—any song of these tuneful predecessors. Slowly but surely the eye and ear of men are turning to feed on that wonderful intellect.[10]

Focusing on the symbolic, Emerson declared that 'All things are symbols. We say of man that he is grass'. Whitman reviewed the lecture, writing, 'The lecture was one of the richest and most beautiful compositions, both for its manner and style, we have ever heard anywhere, at any time'.[11]

Whitman mentioned Swedenborg by name in two of his works—*Democratic Vistas* (1871) and *November Boughs* (1883). In *November Boughs* Swedenborg appears together with historical notables such as Frederick the Great, Junius, Voltaire, Rousseau, Linné, Herschel, and Goethe. In the prose work *Democratic Vistas* Whitman approaches the literary pertinence of the mystic. He states that the

> culmination and fruit of literary artistic expression, and its final fields of pleasure for the human soul, are in metaphysics, including the mysteries of the spiritual world, the soul itself, and the question of the immortal continuation of our identity. In all ages, the mind of man has brought up here—and always will [...] In this sublime literature the religious tone, the consciousness of mystery, the recognition of the future, of the unknown, of

Deity over and under all, and of the divine purpose, are never absent, but indirectly give tone to all.

Even though these works are sometimes aesthetically defective, they are the highlights of world literature, since such 'poetry' towers up to literature's real heights and elevations like great mountains of the earth:

> The altitude of literature and poetry has always been religion—and always will be. The Indian Vedas, the Nackas of Zoroaster, the Talmud of the Jews, the Old Testament, the Gospel of Christ and His disciples, Plato's works, the Koran of Mohammed, the Edda of Snorro, and so on toward our own day, to Swedenborg, and to the invaluable contributions of Leibniz, Kant, and Hegel.[12]

There are other examples to show that America's most influential poet of the nineteenth century valued Swedenborg. Among some manuscripts at Duke University a newspaper clipping is preserved on 'The New Jerusalem' together with a page where Whitman, probably in 1857 or 1858, has taken down some of his thoughts regarding Swedenborg. It is a Swedenborg article written by Whitman. He especially observes how strangely unknown Swedenborg was in his time—neither Voltaire nor Rousseau noticed him. Whitman claims that Swedenborg's mission was one of major historical significance:

> He is a precursor, in some sort of great differences between past thousands of years, and future thousands. [13]

Here we are also faced with the prophetic optimism that is the keynote of Whitman's writings, an ecstatic homage to life, man, and the times; the world will be reborn before our eyes and we will retrieve the divine nature of things—these prospects are open to all of us. Like Sampson Reed and Waldo Emerson, Whitman believed in the progress of science and society, but he thought the contemporary scientist too intellectual and devoid of the awareness of divine providence and meaning.

Enthusiastically drawn to a democratic idea of equality, founded upon metaphysics, he also defended the right of the individual against the claims and limits of the state, of customs and legislation, and became a radical defender of human rights, for instance in the Civil War era. For the same reason he also combined a trust in the common man with a belief in the existence of superhuman insight and wisdom. He exalted the Self and the I in all of us, and glorified our body and the sensual world as originally divine and inviolable. He preached freedom within the limits of natural law and wanted to guide humanity en route to a new Eden where we might revive our divine nature and recapture the language of our world. In 'Song of Myself' he hails humanity. Essentially the title, as well as the message, is identical with that of *Salut au monde*!

A reader in hieroglyphics

Leaves of Grass is a reading in the hieroglyphic text of nature, of which man is a part. The grass is a *uniform hieroglyphic*, a symbolic writing, which signifies an omnipresence of seething life, among all peoples, in all humans. It means: 'Sprouting alike in broad zones and narrow zones, Growing among black folks as among white, Kanuck, Tuckahoe, Congressman, Cuff'. There is a spiritual inflow into all the living, and the grass symbolizes humanity, ultimately the vital force itself.[14]

Echoes may be described here of the old literary myth of the divine hieroglyphics, which dates back to Plutarch and Iamblichus and became current in Renaissance Neoplatonism and occultism; the history of hieroglyphic Bibles, storybooks, and picture puzzles; Champollion's deciphering of the Rosetta Stone in the 1820s; the ancient history of allegory and analogy; but no less Emerson's well-known description of Swedenborg's conception of the world as a 'a grammar of hieroglyphs'.[15] Emerson's early usage of the word 'hieroglyph' gradually became tinged with correspondential vision. The origin, no doubt, for this impulse came from his

Swedenborgian friend Sampson Reed. Reed's interest in these matters is obvious from his contributions to the Boston journal *The New Jerusalem Magazine*, where he published a paper on Egyptian hieroglyphics in 1830. The main source of this interest was Swedenborg's attempt at an outline and systematization of the connections between things and words. It was published in a treatise called *Clavis hieroglyphica* (1744; posthumously published in 1784). The first American edition of that *Hieroglyphic Key* appeared in 1813 (in *Halcyon Luminary*, Baltimore). Thus, the 'hieroglyphic' connection was profoundly Swedenborgian.

A similar source of major importance was the French Swedenborgian Guillaume Œgger, whose book on *The True Messiah* had left many traces in the basic outline of Emerson's philosophy in *Nature* (1836). Œgger's remarkable work *Le Vrai Messie, ou l'Ancien et le Nouveau Testaments examinés d'après les principes de la langue de la nature* (Paris, 1829), was an attempt to interpret the Holy Bible by means of the Book of Nature, translating things into thoughts and notions, and the other way round. This interplay of exegetics and ontology was derived from the old idea that The Author has written two books—the Word and the World—in corresponding hieroglyphs. Emerson had already read Elizabeth Palmer Peabody's manuscript translation, *The True Messiah* (published at Boston, 1842) in 1835.[16]

According to Œgger and Swedenborg, God had endowed Adam with the faculty of reading the ideographic names of the creatures from their physical forms, so that he could recognize the significant and realize the meaning from the design. This tongue, which is the nature of things, now once again can be interpreted; Œgger presents a 'hieroglyphic key', based on Swedenborg. Œgger's list is basically a short dictionary of correspondences, compiled from Swedenborg's exegetical and theosophical works, and the *Clavis hieroglyphica* is dimly seen in the background. He summarizes and exemplifies the doctrine of correspondences, laying claims to its universal applicability. Thus man himself is the divine written in cipher: 'Man is the true hieroglyphic of the Divinity', infinitely detailed even in his corporeal existence, 'since his material form itself, is but the emblem of his moral being' (the entry 'God' in 'Hieroglyphic Keys'). This approach to the human condition reverberates throughout Emerson's poetical universe. In the prologue to *Nature*: 'Every man's condition is a solution in hieroglyphic to those inquiries he would put'.

According to Œgger's 'Hieroglyphic Keys', or grouping of correspondences, the two most important faculties of man are 'Goodness' and 'Knowledge' (Swedenborg's *bonum* and *scientia*); God is 'Love' and 'Truth'; the sun in our world is 'heat' and 'light' (corresponding to the divine love and wisdom of the heavens); The wind announces wherever it advances 'the invisible action of a hidden God': it is 'spirit'.

This linguistic insight struck Emerson like lightning and was immediately turned into literary imagery. In the prophetic conclusion of *Nature*, the revolutionary impact of the spirit is described:

The sordor and filths of nature, the sun shall dry up, and the wind exhale.

Whitman preaches the new language, the regained Adamic perception. In 'A Song of the Rolling Earth' he writes:

I swear I begin to see little or nothing in audible words,
All merges toward the presentation of the unspoken meanings of the earth.
Toward him who sings the songs of the body and of the truths of the earth,
Toward him who makes the dictionaries of words that print cannot touch.

A constant theme in *Leaves of Grass* is the strange connections between the I and the World, the outward and the inward:

Locations and times——what is it in me that meets them
    All, whenever and wherever, and makes me at home?

> Forms, colors, densities, odors—what is it in me
> that corresponds to them [17]

When writing 'Good-Bye My Fancy' (1891), completed on his deathbed, Whitman was many times convinced of the concurrent text: 'In every object, mountain, tree, and star—in every birth and life[…]A mystic cipher waits infolded'.

For the same reason Emerson (as did Sampson Reed) wrote: 'my garden is my dictionary', 'life is our dictionary', and in the 'Prospects' of *Nature* declare that we are all Adam's equals. That prospect was one of 'an original relation to the universe', a state of mind when the different planes of reality and our awareness once again coincide and everything suddenly becomes 'transparent', reveals its inner nature, its truth. The Concord philosophy rings out as hymn and formula in the poem 'Correspondences', written by Christopher Pearse Cranch (1813-92) for Emerson's and Margaret Fuller's *The Dial* at the outset of the 1840s:

> Lost to man was the key of those sacred hieroglyphics,—
> Stolen away by sin,—till with Jesus restored.
> Now with infinite pains we here and there spell out a letter;
> Now and then will the sense feebly shine through the dark.
> When we perceive the light which breaks through the visible symbol,
> What exultation is ours! we the discovery have made!
> Yet is the meaning the same as when Adam lived sinless in Eden
> Only long-hidden it slept and now again is restored.[18]

The key opens the door of meaning by way of symbolic signs or signatures: the thing, the image. Therefore 'indirection' is a keyword in both Whitman and Emerson, a key through which the grammar of the universe is searched for.

*

Emerson wrote a powerful and well-informed essay on Swedenborg, the scientist and the 'mystic', two epithets which for Emerson always were prestige words. That colourful piece from the second half of the 1840s shows the remarkable intensity of both his fascination and his reaction. Its critical points were but sharpened by the fact that it was rumoured that Mr and Mrs Emerson, and she especially, were Swedenborgians.[19] Opposition is the token of impact, the idiom of the dialogue. Swedenborg made profound impressions which could not be swept away. Nor did he leave Whitman unaffected or unconcerned. In the preceding remarks I have also tried to show that Whitman, at least for some time, took an interest in Swedenborg, and that there are several—if only ambiguous—affinities between his views and Swedenborg's ideas.

Here it can be added that Dr Richard Maurice Bucke, in his analytical biography on his friend Walt Whitman (a book which Whitman partly wrote himself), adduced a document which is of some relevance to us, a private testimony. In a memorandum written for the biography, Helen E Price, who made Whitman's acquaintance in 1856, told that Whitman frequently met with one of her neighbours. That 'Mr A' (John Arnold), was 'a man of wide knowledge and the most analytical mind of anyone I ever knew. He was a Swedenborgian'. Whitman and Arnold often had long discussions and conversations. Helen Price remembered Whitman as an *exalté*. According to her, his distinctive feature was his profound spirituality: 'his *religious sentiment* [...] pervades and dominates his life'.[20]

Partly inspired by Arnold too, Whitman seems to have attended New Church meetings and studied Swedenborg's life and writings.[21] This way we may understand the earlier mentioned article and manuscript fragment on Swedenborg, where the seer is regarded as a kind of spiritual pioneer or regenerator—which appears to be a sketch for an essay Whitman wrote for the Brooklyn *Daily Times* in 1858.[22] In that comprehensive article, entitled 'Who was Swedenborg?', Whitman claimed that Swedenborg, among whose followers 'are some of the leading minds of our nation', will probably 'make the deepest and broadest mark upon the religions of future ages here, of any man that ever walked the earth'.[23]

From these pieces of writing, and from the extensive conversations with Horace Traubel during the many years of failing health in Camden, where he spent his last nineteen years, it is clear that Whitman time and again through the decades pondered upon the strange phenomenon Emanuel Swedenborg, including also the Swedish mystic's strange illumination and divine initiation — a historic event that, according to Whitman, marked the emergence of the individual consciousness in modern religious thought. Whitman observed the 'somewhat comical', 'most unromantic and vulgar' commencement of Swedenborg's very rare 'ineffable privilege': Swedenborg first came into rapport with the Lord and the spiritual world by eating a dinner at an inn in London.[24]

This certainly struck the positive and sensual Whitman's fancy. Even more than his master Emerson, he always tried to envisage the divine or transcendent qualities and meanings of the commonplace and the low. Whitman, who also paid attention to Swedenborg's perception of the correspondences between religious ecstasy and erotic desire, observed, 'I find Swedenborg confirmed in all my experience. It is a peculiar discovery'.[25]

*

But there is still another observation to be added here. If Whitman drew from Swedenborgian teachings such as the doctrine of influx and the doctrine of correspondences, as Emerson did, it is possible that Swedenborgian hermeneutics in some instances can be applied to his own wordings.[26] In that case the comprehensive English dictionaries of correspondences compiled from Swedenborg's writings by James Hindmarsh (1794) and by George Nicholson (1800) may assist us.[27] The latter work was circulated in New England in a revised edition published in Boston in 1841: *A Dictionary of Correspondences, Representatives, and Significatives, derived from the Word of the Lord*.[28] There we encounter the paradigm which is basic to all of Swedenborg's writings, according to which 'heat' is love, 'light' is truth and wisdom, 'darkness' is falsity, 'ascendancy' is an advancement towards the celestial, 'fire' is egotist love and infernal lusts; 'serpents' are sensual things, 'birds' are wandering thoughts and associations, and 'beasts' signify different affections; 'clouds' signify obscurities of the mind, whereas 'flowers' have good connotations and 'grass' signifies 'what is alive in man', which is the spiritual life force; 'leaves' are 'truths', the 'Sun' corresponds to celestial love, and 'winds' are spirits and influxes.

Then compare Emerson's use of linguistic examples and his manner of building his arguments upon such illustrations, for instance in *Nature* and in his lectures on Natural History. Emerson early used the doctrine of correspondences for his metaphors, and this usage abounds in many of his works, sometimes with salient similarities to the imagery and reasoning of Swedenborg's most well-known work: *A Treatise Concerning Heaven and its Wonders, and also Concerning Hell*. A copy of the 1823 London edition with Emerson's annotations is still to be seen in his extant library. Striking resemblances emerge between Emerson's and Swedenborg's philosophy of language, and in Emerson's usage.

In *Nature* (1836), Emerson enumerates a number of the aforementioned correspondences in the chapter called 'Language', which illustrates the Swedenborgian paradigm of reading material and spiritual meaning at the same time.

This comparison becomes still more exciting, however, if we use this key to the enigmatic, never fully explained title of *Leaves of Grass*. If we substitute 'truths' for *Leaves*, and 'what is alive in man' for *Grass*, we then get the title:

Truths of What is Alive in Man.

Such is indeed the theme and the subject of Whitman's epoch-making book; it is that of which the Singer sings his praise.

*

Those who were the first to praise Whitman, had also read Swedenborg or New Church literature with delight. Documentary evidence shows that Whitman had done so too. As in Emerson, this reading added something to the tone and meaning of figurative language and to the conception of the real in Whitman's singular poetic diction.

NOTES

[1] Harold Bloom, *The Western Canon* (New York: Riverhead Books, 1995), p. 247.

[2] Ibid., pp. 249, 254, 256-7, 259, 261, 264.

[3] Newton Arvin, *Whitman* (New York: Macmillan, 1938).

[4] See especially Henry Seidel Canby, *Walt Whitman* (Boston: Houghton Mifflin Company, 1943), pp. 120-1, and Roger Asselineau's well-informed discussion of the background of the first (1855) edition: *The Evolution of Walt Whitman* (Cambridge: Harvard University Press, 1960). Suzanne Poirier perceived the echoes of Emerson and Transcendentalism in Whitman's symbolism: ' "A Song of the Rolling Earth" as Transcendental and Poetic Theory', in *Walt Whitman Review*, vol. 22, June 1976, pp. 67-74. As pointed out by Ralph Rusk, in *The Letters of Ralph Waldo Emerson*, ed. Ralph Rusk (New York: Columbia University Press, 1939), vol. IV, p. 520, the printing of Emerson's letter, with its public use by Whitman, 'was perhaps an event of greater importance in the history of American literature than the printing of any other letter has ever been'. Emerson's letter to Whitman was written on 21 July 1855.

[5] Whitman, 'Leaves-Droppings', in *Leaves of Grass* (New York: Fowler and Wells, 1856), pp. 363 ff., quoted in Roger Asselineau, *The Evolution of Walt Whitman*, vol. I, p. 75.

[6] Emory Holloway (ed.), *The Uncollected Poetry and Prose of Walt Whitman* (London and Garden City: Curtis Brown, 1921), vol. II, p. 16 n.

[7] The introductory strophe of 'A Song of the Rolling Earth' (1856), printed in the edition of *Leaves of Grass* in which he praised and cited Emerson: *The Complete*

Poetry and Prose of Walt Whitman as Prepared by Him for the Deathbed Edition, introd. Malcolm Cowley (New York: Pellegrini and Cudahy, 1948), vol. I, p. 216.

8   Whitman, 'To the Garden of the World' (1860), first section of 'Children of Adam', in *Leaves of Grass* (p. 114 in *The Complete Poetry and Prose of Walt Whitman*, vol. I).

9   *The Complete Works of Ralph Waldo Emerson* (Boston and New York: Houghton Mifflin, 1903-4), vol. I, p. 76, vol. IX, p. 283 ('Promise'), vol. X, p. 137; Joel Porte (ed.), *Emerson in his Journals* (Cambridge: Harvard University Press, 1982), p. 99 and ch. 'Reorientation (1833-1834)', pp. 88-132; R W B Lewis, *The American Adam: Innocence, Tragedy, and Tradition in the Nineteenth Century* (Chicago: University of Chicago Press, 1955), prologue and ch. 2, 'The New Adam: Holmes and Whitman'. For another perspective on the creative mission in the New World's pristine outlying land: Henry Nash Smith, *Virgin Land* (Cambridge: Harvard University Press, 1970), ch. 'Walt Whitman and Manifest Destiny'. On the first and last Adam—the physical preceding the spiritual—1 Cor. 15:45.

10 R W Emerson, 'The Times' series of lectures, 'The Poet', in *The Early Lectures of Ralph Waldo Emerson*, ed. Stephen E Whicher and Robert E Spiller (Cambridge: Harvard University Press, 1959-72), vol. III, pp. 352, 361.

11 Gay Wilson Allen, *Waldo Emerson* (New York: Penguin Books, 1982), pp. 400-1; Joseph Jay Rubin and Charles H Brown (eds.), *Walt Whitman of the New York Aurora, Editor at Twenty-two: A Collection of Recently Discovered Writings* (Pennsylvania State College: Bald Eagle Press, 1950), p. 105. The full text of the lecture Whitman reported: *The Early Lectures of Ralph Waldo Emerson*, vol. III, pp. 347-65. Some passages from that lecture on 'The Poet' Emerson later used in the essays 'The Poet', 'Eloquence', and 'Poetry and Imagination'.

12 *The Complete Poetry and Prose of Walt Whitman*, vol. II, p. 470 resp. 263. Textual note: the spelling follows that of the *editio princeps* and most later editions.

13 Manuscript 35, #25; see Walt Whitman, *Notebooks and Unpublished Prose Manuscripts*, ed. E F Grier (New York: New York University Press, 1984), vol. VI, pp. 2034-5. The clipping is identified in Floyd Stovall, *The Foreground of "Leaves of Grass"* (Charlottesville: University Press of Virginia, 1974), p. 156, n. 17. See also Walt Whitman, *Notes and*

Fragments, ed. Richard Maurice Bucke (London, Ontario: A Talbot and Company, 1899), pp. 89-90.

[14] Whitman, 'Song of Myself', in *The Leaves of Grass* (Philadelphia: David McKay, 1891-2), p. 33; cf. John T Irwin, *American Hieroglyphics. The Symbol of the Egyptian Hieroglyphics in the American Renaissance* (Baltimore & London: Johns Hopkins University Press, 1980), pp. 19-20.

[15] John T Irwin, *American Hieroglyphics*, pp. 30 ff.; E Iversen, *The Myth of Egypt and its Hieroglyphs in European tradition* (Copenhagen: Gad, 1961); W A Clouston, *Hieroglyphic Bibles: Their Origin and History* (Glasgow: D Bryce & Son, 1894); Sampson Reed, 'Egyptian Hieroglyphics', in *New Jerusalem Magazine*, vol. IV, October 1830, p. 69. That the world to Swedenborg appeared as only 'a grammar of hieroglyphs' Emerson stated in *Representative Men* in 1850, i.e., five years before *Leaves of Grass* (*The Complete Works of Ralph Waldo Emerson*, vol. IV, p. 142).

[16] The excerpts are to be found in his Journal B, 1835, i.e., the year before his first book was published: *The Journals and Miscellaneous Notebooks of Ralph Waldo Emerson* (Cambridge: Harvard University Press, 1960-82), vol. V, pp. 65-9. On Abbé Œgger, see Karl-Erik Sjödén, *Swedenborg en France* (Stockholm: Almqvist & Wiksell International, 1985). On the Middle Age and Renaissance ideas behind this kind of hermeneutics, see Michel Foucault, *The Order of Things: An Archaeology of the Human Sciences*, ed. R D Laing (New York: Vintage, 1973), pp. 25 ff. and passim.

[17] Whitman, 'Locations and Times', in *The Leaves of Grass* (1891-2), p. 218. This theme is discussed in Christopher Collins, *The Uses of Observation: A Study of Correspondential Vision in the Writings of Emerson, Thoreau and Whitman* (The Hague and Paris: Mouton, 1971), ch. IV.

[18] Perry Miller (ed.), *The Transcendentalists: An Anthology* (Cambridge: Harvard University Press, 1950), p. 388; see also 'Correspondence' in the useful index.

[19] Ralph L Rusk, *The Life of Ralph Waldo Emerson* (New York: C Scribner's Sons, 1949), pp. 215, 220, 363: Lidian Emerson (Lydia Jackson) in fact once (during the lecture tour in England in the late 1840s) introduced herself as a Christian and Swedenborgian.

[20] Richard Maurice Bucke, *Walt Whitman* (1883) (New York and London: Johnson

Reprint Corporation, 1970), pp. 26-32. The part Whitman played in the production of the book is shown by Quentin Anderson and Stephen Railton, *Walt Whitman's Autograph Revision of the Analysis of Leaves of Grass (For Dr. R M Bucke's Walt Whitman)* (New York: New York University Press, 1974). Whitman's 'indirection': pp. 21, 76 (a characteristic term culled from Emerson: 'all goes by indirection', *The Complete Works of Ralph Waldo Emerson*, vol. VII, p. 81). Whitman's spirituality and his religiosity are obvious, even though (or still more, 'since') he considered historical churches and creeds obstacles to the divine, as did Emerson. See Whitman's sketches for a series of lectures on religion: *Walt Whitman's Workshop: A Collection of Unpublished Manuscripts*, ed. Clifton Joseph Furness (New York: Russell & Russell, 1964), pp. 39-53, 218-21. Paul Zweig's *Walt Whitman: The Making of the Poet* (New York: Basic Books, 1984) encounters the religious dimension, and even more so does David Kuebrich in *Minor Prophecy: Walt Whitman's New American Religion* (Bloomington: Indiana University Press, 1989). Kuebrich reminds us that Whitman in his time was esteemed as a religious seer as much as a poet, and views him as a prophet.

[21] See Justin Kaplan's very informative biography *Walt Whitman: A Life* (New York: Simon & Schuster, 1980), pp. 231-2.

[22] Whitman, 'Who was Swedenborg?', in *Daily Times*, 15 June 1858, repr. in Holloway (ed.), *The Uncollected Poetry and Prose of Walt Whitman*, vol. II, pp. 16-18. See also Kaplan, *Walt Whitman: A Life*, pp. 192-3. Similarities between Whitman and Swedenborg were pointed out by Frederik Schyberg, *Walt Whitman* (Copenhagen: Gyldendalske Boghandel, 1933), pp. 12, 72, 88, 278-9.

[23] Whitman, 'Who was Swedenborg?', in Holloway (ed.), *The Uncollected Poetry and Prose of Walt Whitman*, vol. II, pp. 16-18.

[24] Kaplan, *Walt Whitman: A Life*, p. 192; Whitman, 'Who was Swedenborg?', in Holloway (ed.), *The Uncollected Poetry and Prose of Walt Whitman*, vol. II, p. 16. Whitman's account of Swedenborg's initial vision, in the *Daily Times* article of 1858, shows that he was familiar with the historical version taken down in the bank executive Carl Robsahm's memoirs (1782). Swedenborg never told the whole story of the occurrences in London in 1745 except verbally to his friend Robsahm. Robsahm's

anecdotes were introduced in the USA by a fellow student of Emerson at Harvard, Nathaniel Hobart, in his documentary, *Life of Emanuel Swedenborg* (Boston: Allen and Goddard, 1831). Robsahm's account was published *in extenso* in the enlarged edition of Hobart's book issued in 1845, and in the edition printed and distributed in New York in 1850. Hobart's *Life* was the most important Swedenborg biography to Emerson when he wrote his influential lecture and essay 'Swedenborg; or, the Mystic' (written and revised 1848-9 and published in *Representative Men*, 1850). I have discussed the pertinence of Robsahm and Hobart to the reception of Swedenborg in the preface to my annotated critical edition of Robsahm's memoirs: Carl Robsahm, *Anteckningar om Swedenborg* (Stockholm: Föreningen Swedenborgs Minne, 1989). The internal evidence here shown indicates that Whitman was familiar with Hobart's documentary *Life of Swedenborg*; at least Hobart was evidently the source—directly or indirectly—of Whitman's account.

[25] Horace Traubel, *With Walt Whitman in Camden*, vol. V: 8 April-14 September 1889, ed. Gertrude Traubel (Carbondale: University of Southern Illinois Press, 1964), p. 376.

[26] Both Emerson and Whitman frequently seem to cite the teachings on spiritual influx, but their understanding of such 'inflow' is rather vague and can be derived from various sources. Swedenborg's seminal 'Doctrine of influx' was first introduced on the American scene by the publication of 'A Treatise on the Nature of Influx', a translation of *De Commercio Animæ et Corporis* published in the *Halcyon Luminary* (New York), vol. II (1813), pp. 344-7, 407-9, 437-40, 492-500, 541-5.

[27] Both dictionaries are based upon Gabriel Beyer's gigantic pioneering work *Index Initialis in Opera Swedenborgii theologica* (Amsterdam, 1779). Compare also William L Worcester, *The Language of Parable: A Key to the Bible* (1892) (New York: Swedenborg Foundation, 1984), and Alice Spiers Sechrist, *A Dictionary of Bible Imagery: A Guide for Bible Readers* (New York: Swedenborg Foundation, 1981).

[28] A second edition was published in 1847; the fourth edition in 1863; the 9th edition in 1887. Reprinted in a new edition (the fourteenth) by Swedenborg Foundation (New York, 1988).

Swedenborg and Dostoevsky: an interview *

Czeslaw Milosz

Q uestion: *You say it should be possible to write a study titled 'Swedenborg and Dostoevsky'. But there is an enormous literature about Dostoevsky in many languages and, admit it, the very fact that no one has yet come up with such an idea does not inspire confidence in your thesis.*

Answer: An entire lengthy section would have to be devoted to an explanation of why this is so. It would be a section about the 'blind spots' in people's sensibility in the first half of the twentieth century. Ultimately, the entire canon of Dostoevsky studies can be delimited roughly by the dates 1900 and 1950. I say 'canon' because that is when the basic works about this author which delineated the main methods of interpreting him were written. The first phase coincides with the period of Russian Symbolism, and it would be the main subject for discussion in the article.

Q: *Why the period of Russian Symbolism in particular?*

A: Not only Russian. Symbolism, regardless of its variations in different countries, had to be sensitive to its own genealogy. We have been taught that the great patron of Symbolism was Baudelaire. One of his works is even cited as a sort of programme. (When I was a student in Paris I had to memorize it.) This is the sonnet 'Correspondances'. But both the title and the contents of this sonnet are taken from Swedenborg. Both Balzac's generation and the generation that succeeded it—Baudelaire's—borrowed extensively from Swedenborg, though they rarely admitted this. Later on, however, the period of the 'scientific world view' developed in Europe and Swedenborg became decidedly taboo, someone who could be studied only by maniacs, his followers, members of the Swedenborgian Church of the New Jerusalem, which has been active chiefly in America. Let us not forget that Symbolism, as a literary and artistic movement, is very much entwined with the sobriety of the 'scientific world view'; after all, these poets and painters and critics were raised on positivist beliefs. In rebelling against them they often went quite far in their weird directions. Nonetheless, no one knew by then what to make of such an extreme case as Swedenborg. It is fairly symptomatic, then, that the Russian critics who wrote about Dostoevsky prior to 1914 had no interest in knowing about the great Swedish master of the imagination.

Q: *Does this mean that things changed at some point and that today there is a different perception of Swedenborg?*

A: I shall give a couple of examples of bafflement dating from the first half of the century. In 1922, Karl Jaspers published his book on schizophrenia, in which he analysed Strindberg, Van Gogh, Swedenborg, and Hölderlin as typical schizophrenics. [1] In 1936, Paul Valéry wrote an introduction to Martin Lamm's book on Swedenborg, which had been translated into French from the Swedish. [2] Lamm's book is painstaking, positivistically sober to the point of dullness in its abstention from coming to any conclusions; after reading it, however, it is difficult to agree with Jaspers's thesis that Swedenborg suffered from a mental illness. And yet the amiable Swedenborg, who was universally well liked in Stockholm social circles, wrote about his travels through heaven and hell and insisted that he could easily transport himself into the spirit world while walking, for example, in his garden. Thus, Valéry is at a loss and, rejecting suspicions of both charlatanism and madness, tries to explain Swedenborg's particular 'states' as the borderline between sleep and waking. Despite Valéry's cleverness, this is weak and unconvincing; what is more, Valéry unmasks himself, and not only himself but all his contemporaries, by confessing to a double standard. Because this is what it comes down to more or less: only the world of 'scientific laws' is real, but above it there rises an ethereal structure of epiphenomena, creations of the human mind that deserve to be treated with perfect tolerance because they are arbitrary, beyond truth and falsehood, subject only to the law of their own form.

Symbolism, impeded as it was by nineteenth-century science, had no confidence in itself; the language of images, the language of strata that are deeper than consciousness, became the centre of attention for psychologists and anthropologists somewhat later; if we are talking about a broader compass, it came much later. In this case only such cultural facts as the transfer of the polemic between the followers of Freud and the followers of Jung to Anglo-Saxon soil could favour a new reception of Swedenborg. Let us note that Swedenborg wrote almost exclusively in Latin, and although there were individuals in the Romantic generation who knew Latin quite well, he was read on the European continent in a small number of French adaptations. Later on, when knowledge of Latin declined, he became an even more inaccessible writer. But this was not the case in the Anglo-Saxon countries, where translations of his works, beginning with the earliest editions in the eighteenth century, never disappeared from the book market. In America in particular he had his admirers; one of them was the philosopher and theologian Henry James, Sr, the father of William, the philosopher and creator of pragmatism, and Henry, the novelist. Swedenborg made his first appearance in the orbit of literary studies only recently, and even then indirectly, thanks to the growing significance of Blake, who was dependent on him in many ways. But the veritable explosion of 'Blakeology' is in the second half of our century.

I do not think, however, that at present the tools that would allow us to comprehend the figure of Swedenborg have been developed anywhere. What is essential here is the seventeenth- and eighteenth-century scientific revolution and the resulting secularization of thought. Swedenborg was a general scientist, as was common at that time, for he was a geologist, a member of the Royal Mining Commission, a

253

physicist, and a physiologist, whose ideas, in the opinion of historians of science, were brilliant. Until he experienced a severe internal crisis when he suddenly realized where science was leading: to the weakening of the Christian religion and——in its further consequences——to the overthrow of all values. From this crisis a new Swedenborg emerged——a visionary and a theologian. Let us not concern ourselves here with the question of where to draw the line between 'normality' and 'abnormality'. If true schizophrenia begins where communication with other people breaks off, then any suspicion that Swedenborg or Blake was a schizophrenic is unfounded. The difficulty we encounter lies in the fact that the role of literary convention in the formation of the Swedenborgian visions, or whatever we call them, is undoubtedly highly significant but not easily defined. The eighteenth century loved to create apparently 'true' stories about travels and adventures, so it is not surprising that it also gave us, through Swedenborg's pen, descriptions of other-worldly journeys. It is just that the symbolism here achieves a truly great tension and the frustrated, subjective symbols of the poets around the year 1900 appear pallid in comparison. While Swedenborg's language (like the language of those who travelled through the extra-mundane world before him——Dante and Milton) makes use of symbols with fixed, immutable meanings, his entire system, described in this language, contains strong features of eighteenth-century rationalism——it is this fusion that so confounds and disturbs his readers.

Q: *In what sense would Dostoevsky fit into such a study?*

A: In a dual sense. First of all, one would have to consider the probable influence of Swedenborg on the author of *Crime and Punishment*. Second, Dostoevsky's Christology becomes somewhat less enigmatic when it is compared with Swedenborg's Christology.

Q: *Obviously, one would need to know if Dostoevsky was familiar with Swedenborg's writings.*

A: In Leonid Grossman's book *Seminarii po Dostoevskomu*——I am citing an authority here——we find a list of the books that the novelist had in his private library. [3] A N Aksakov's books are listed there, among others. [4] He was one of the less well-known Aksakovs, the one who was interested in spiritualism. Dostoevsky wrote about the Petersburg spiritualistic seances in his *Diary of a Writer for 1876*.[5] But we are interested in Aksakov as the translator of Swedenborg into Russian. *De Coelo et ejus mirabilis, et de inferno* was published in Leipzig in 1863 in his Russian version; an adaptation or translation (it's hard to check which since the book cannot be found) of five chapters of Swedenborg's interpretation of the Gospel according to St John was also published in Leipzig in 1864; and again in Leipzig, but much later, in 1870, Aksakov's work on Swedenborg appeared.[6] Dostoevsky had all three books in his library and was obviously interested in the subject, since he collected them. Grossman, in the commentary that accompanies his list, notes: 'Particularly worth noting is Dostoevsky's interest in Swedenborg [...] These books may have had an influence on Zosima's mystical speculations about prayer, hell, and our ties with other worlds'.[7] To the best of my knowledge, no one has followed up on Professor Grossman's suggestion.

Q: *The study of influence is a thankless field. It is usually difficult even to determine what intermediaries served to convey a particular idea or thought to a given writer.*

A: Certainly. Dostoevsky had two French editions of the works of Balzac in his library, for example. And he had read some Balzac earlier, in his youth. Although Balzac had a very poor, second-hand knowledge of Swedenborg, he admired him greatly, and we can consider Balzac's 'Swedenborgian' novels, such as *Séraphîta* or *Louis Lambert* as 'intermediaries'. Let us, however, limit the scope of our inquiry to just one of Dostoevsky's works, *Crime and Punishment*. He began writing this novel in Wiesbaden in 1865, and it is well known that during his stays abroad he was starved for Russian books. So it was probably then that he purchased or was given Swedenborg's work in Aksakov's translation, which had just been published in neighbouring Leipzig. The fabric of symbols in *Crime and Punishment* is so rich that it is difficult not to think about Swedenborgian correspondences, or, in Aksakov's translation, *sootvetstviia*. According to Swedenborg, these are 'objective' symbols that inhere in the very structure of the universe—and of language. But let us leave it to others to track them down and narrow our field even further by limiting ourselves to the figure of Svidrigailov. He is one of the most puzzling characters in Dostoevsky, beginning with his name, because how, all of a sudden, does the Lithuanian Prince Svidrigaila become transformed into a Russian *barin*? The noble Dostoevsky family, which derived its surname from the Dostoevo estate near Pinsk, which had been bestowed upon it in 1505, has left its traces in the criminal chronicles of the Grand Duchy from the sixteenth century. We know from a book written by his daughter Liubov (or Aimée, as she signed her name in emigration)—a book that is misleading and full of outright stupidities but nonetheless contains some priceless childhood memories—that Dostoevsky used to emphasize his descent from that family. [8] The surname Svidrigailov, derived from the prince who ruled the eastern (therefore, the ethnically Slavic, not Lithuanian) part of the Grand Duchy, might suggest the author's special identification with that character (although obviously Dostoevsky is all his characters). Also, let us not be too positive that the main character is Raskolnikov, because it could just as well be his gloomy alter ego, Svidrigailov. Despite Dostoevsky's fascination with crime without any pangs of conscience, which dates from the period of his imprisonment in Omsk, Raskolnikov appears to be treated with a greater distance than his diabolical acquaintance, who is never exorcized throughout the entire novel. One might even risk the assertion that there are two crimes in this novel and two punishments, and that, furthermore, the second crime, Svidrigailov's, is the 'correspondence', the equivalent of a feeling of guilt in and of itself.

For what is the source of Svidrigailov's problem? He does have human lives on his conscience, but he is only apparently a superman beyond good and evil. In fact, he hates his nature, which, in his opinion, is capable only of evil, and he believes that a man such as he deserves eternal damnation. That is, he commits the sin that theologians define as first among the sins against the Holy Spirit; 'despairing of God's mercy'. Svidrigailov moves through the pages of the novel like a phantom, as if he were already beyond life. He prepares his 'journey to America', which, on his lips and on Dostoevsky's, signifies a journey to hell—let us remember, for example, how Kirillov's and Shatov's stay in America is presented in *The Possessed*. Of course, Svidrigailov has in mind not a journey but the execution of a sentence against himself and he finally commits suicide. He is thoroughly reminiscent of the damned as described by Swedenborg, and even the similarity of the first syllables of their two names, *Swed* and *Svid*, suggests this, perhaps through involuntary association.

Swedenborg's hell is constructed from 'correspondences'; that is, everything that surrounds the damned is a *projection* of their spiritual states, and this is so because every visible and tangible object has its own secondary and even more real existence in the human imagination, where it serves as a sign of value, that is, of either good or evil. The jaws of hell that Swedenborg describes frequently have the appearance of grim streets in the poorest districts of great cities, of London in particular, where he lived for a long time. They are, then, pictures of life in time, but already preserved beyond time. At the same time, God does not condemn people to hell. The damned find images of heavenly joy repulsive and it is precisely from the book translated by Aksakov that one can learn that they flee the society of bright spirits, seeking the company of those who are like them. In *The Brothers Karamazov*, in Zosima's teaching about hell, Dostoevsky also speaks about a completely free choice of 'place', although this word is inexact, since 'place' is only the projection of an inner state.

For our purposes what is important is the multiplicity of hells in Swedenborg. There are as many of them as there are individual human beings. Let me take down from the shelf the very book that Dostoevsky read and quote from it, in English translation:

Every evil includes infinite varieties, the same as every good. That such is the fact will not be comprehended, by those who only have a simple idea respecting every evil, as respecting contempt, respecting enmity, respecting hatred, respecting revenge, respecting deceit, and respecting others of the like nature: but be it known to them, that every one of those evils contains so many specific differences, and every one of these, again, so many other specific or particular differences, that a volume would not suffice to enumerate them all. The hells are so distinctly arranged in order, according to the differences of every evil that nothing more orderly and distinct can be conceived. It may hence be evident, that the hells are innumerable. [9]

Svidrigailov, when we meet him on the pages of the novel, is already seeking places in this life that can serve as correspondences for his bored despair, his *acedia*. Despite the fact that he is wealthy, he chooses miserable furnished rooms, third-class stinking restaurants, and cheap filthy hotels. If I have said that Swedenborgian 'correspondences' have an objective character, then I should introduce a correction here, for certain phenomena are ambivalent and their function as symbols changes depending on their connection with other phenomena. This is true of rain and dampness in *Crime and Punishment*: for Svidrigailov they are not life-giving but grim, and are associated with his internal stagnation and collapse. A comparison with a similar function of rain and dampness in Dostoevsky's depressing story 'Bobok', about the conversations of the dead in a cemetery, comes to mind here. [10]

Svidrigailov imagines in a singular manner just what awaits people after death, and especially what ought to await him. The following dialogue between him and Raskolnikov is one of the strangest conversations in world literature:

'I don't believe in a future life', said Raskolnikov.

Svidrigailov sat lost in thought.

'And what if there are only spiders there, or something of that sort?' he said suddenly.

'He is a madman', thought Raskolnikov.

'We always imagine eternity as something beyond our conception, something vast, vast! But why must it be vast? Instead of all that, what if it's one little room, like a bath-house in the country, black and grimy and spiders in every corner, and that's all eternity is? I sometimes fancy it like that'.

'Can it be you can imagine nothing juster and more comforting than that?' Raskolnikov cried, with a feeling of anguish.

'Juster? And how can we tell, perhaps that is just, and do you know it's what I would certainly have made it', answered Svidrigailov, with a vague smile.

This horrible answer sent a cold chill through Raskolnikov. [11]

Q: *I admit that for the first time, because of this insertion of Swedenborg, this conversation is no longer an incomprehensible leap of Dostoevsky's fantasy, a macabre witticism, as it were.*

A: Even if this is my discovery, and I think it is, I attach greater weight to my observations about Dostoevsky's Christology than to the question of 'influences'. I'll come to that in a moment. For now, let us pursue our earlier line of reasoning. In my opinion, what testifies to a deeper, more profound, more subterranean identification of the author with Svidrigailov rather than Raskolnikov are Svidrigailov's dreams prior to his suicide. The obsessive motif of an offence against little ones, of the rape of a child, surfaces in them. Dostoevsky was not 'our Marquis de Sade', as Turgenev called him. [12] The rumours that linked this motif to Dostoevsky's biography should not concern us; it is sufficient to state that a wrong committed against a child, usually a young girl, is perceived by his heroes as a moral horror; I need only recall 'Stavrogin's Confession' from *The Possessed*.

Svidrigailov first sees in his dream a coffin covered with flowers, and in the coffin is a very young girl, practically a child. We are free to assume that this underage Ophelia drowned herself because of him. But the first dream is only a preparation for the second, which is much more horrifying. In a hotel where he is living (this is what he dreams), he finds a little girl, a five-year-old, abandoned, crying. What follows is Svidrigailov's dream about his own goodness, because he soothes her crying, lifts her up in his arms, carries her to his room, lays her on the bed, and covers her with a blanket. And then his dream about his own goodness suffers a decisive blow. Svidrigailov suddenly feels that she is looking at him from under her half-closed eyelids, and her gaze is the gaze of a courtesan. Mediated by this dream, two of his thoughts, which might be expressed as follows, break through to the surface: 'Whatever you touch is corrupted'; 'Innocence and goodness are an illusion, for even if we are inclined to ascribe them to Nature, Nature knows only those impulses that accord with her law of reproducing oneself and of death'. Similarly, the hero of 'The Dream of a Ridiculous Man', when he visits the earthly heaven, contaminates innocent prelapsarian humanity by his very presence. The link between the thoughts of Svidrigailov that I have introduced here is not terribly clear, but it does exist: Nature, that is to say, two times two equals four in *Notes from the Underground*, or the indifferent machine in *The Idiot* (the digression about Holbein's painting *Christ in the Tomb*), only deserves our protest in the name of our human values which it does not recognize. Svidrigailov says to himself more or less: 'There is nothing inside me but aggressive drives and they are in harmony with the world order, which is too evil to be God's order, and I know that no attempt at breaking out of my skin can be successful'. Svidrigailov commits suicide out of revulsion——at himself, and at everything. He is one of those who 'cannot behold the living God without hatred, and cry out that the God of life should be annihilated, that God should destroy Himself and His own creation', as Zosima says in *The Brothers Karamazov*. [13] To be sure, the reader will probably perceive a certain noble-mindedness in this moral revulsion and that is why Svidrigailov, despite the fact that he is in the power of Ahriman, is not generally numbered among the irrevocably black characters.

The rape of the child in the chapter about Svidrigailov's last night achieves the significance of a 'correspondence'——i.e., it symbolizes his sense of guilt, not necessarily because of these or other deeds, but simply because he is what he is. What Svidrigailov actually did, and whether the young lady in the coffin is his victim, we do not know, and that is not the point, just as in 'Stavrogin's Confession' one cannot be completely certain that he did not invent his rape of Matryosha. I do not want to attribute this device—the symbolism of dreams and nightmares, for example in Ivan Karamazov's conversation with the Devil—exclusively to Dostoevsky's reading of Swedenborg, because no one could prove these or any other borrowings. Let us move on to the second thread.

Q: *Would it not be appropriate to concentrate on Zosima's teachings, in accordance with Grossman's supposition?*

A: No, not in the least. It would not be a search for similarities aside from a single fundamental similarity: the intellectual situation. Swedenborg, who was born in 1688 (he died in 1772), was reacting to the great Industrial Revolution that began in western Europe in the seventeenth century. Like Pascal before him, who wanted to write a great apologia for Christianity; the notes known as *Les Pensées* are the fruits of that endeavour. Simplifying things to a certain extent, let us say that Swedenborg at the time of his crisis was seeking the strategy that the Christian should adopt toward the pressure of images derived from science. In western Europe the revolution was not so violent, because it took place gradually over the course of a couple of centuries, while the Russian intelligentsia of the nineteenth century faced those same ferments suddenly, receiving them in a conglomerated form. Dostoevsky truly wanted to be a defender of Christianity, although the enemy had already planted itself inside his internal fortress. There is a reason why Dostoevsky has been compared so frequently with Pascal. But a comparison with Swedenborg would turn out to be, I believe, no less, and perhaps even more, fruitful.

In its attack on Christianity, rationalism progressed from timid forays to an open battle: it started from so-called rational religion, sincerely propagated by people who considered themselves good Christians. When the clergy in England warned against the 'monster of Socinianism', their anxiety was well founded; even

John Locke, for example, though he denied it publicly, had many publications from Raków in his own library and read them attentively, as is demonstrated by the marginal notations in his own hand. [14] In fact, the first link in the process of secularization in Europe was the rebirth of the Arian heresy in the sixteenth century, from which a straight line leads to all the theses that proclaim, whether openly or not, that Jesus was a noble dreamer, a reformer, an ethical ideal, but not God.

Swedenborg grasped the very essence of this process, since his theological system, in conflict with the Lutheranism in which he was raised, and also with all other denominations, is the exact opposite of the Arian tendencies toward sundering the unity of the three hypostases of the Holy Trinity. Swedenborg accused all the churches of falsehood in that they appear to profess one God in the Trinity but in fact they instill in the faithful a belief in three gods, which, because this is an assault on reason, must lead to its opposite, and thus to a completely atheistic rational religion: *Deus sive Natura*. The significance that Swedenborg attached to the Gospel of St John and the Apocalypse indicates he adhered to the hermetic tradition that stretched all the way back to the Gnostics. 'In the beginning was the Word', that is, Christ, and Swedenborg proclaims the great secret: our Father in Heaven is Man. It sounds as if we were reading the old Gnostic texts. In these old texts the human quality of God is opposed to the non-human quality of the Archonts, who rule the world, or to Jehovah; man does not belong to the god of nature precisely because he has a higher ally, above the god of nature, in God-Man. There is no such dualism in Swedenborg, but it may very well be contained in his system *implicite*. In general, when someone places the highest value on the Gospel of St John and the Apocalypse among all the books of the New Testament, this should give us pause, and it is curious that these were also Dostoevsky's beloved books.

Q: *It would appear from this that one promising area of research would be Dostoevsky as a novelist of a Manichaean revival.*

A: That is too broad and specialized a topic. Following Bakhtin, we acknowledge that we are dealing with a new novelistic genre, that is, the polyphonic novel; we cannot place the statements of individual characters into the author's mouth, since the contents of those statements are negated by other, opposing voices. True, Vasily Rozanov, for example, made quite a convincing argument when he tried to prove that the Grand Inquisitor expresses the most personal, the most despairing conclusions arrived at by the author of *The Brothers Karamazov* after many years of meditation. But the Grand Inquisitor believes that the world is in the power of the Tempter, 'the great spirit of nonexistence'; he decides to serve him because the divinity incarnated in Jesus is, when measured by the order of both nature and human society, absolutely feeble, incapable of changing anything in the laws of life. However, let us consider the views of the Grand Inquisitor as only one pole, for Dostoevsky wished to create a counterweight, an opposite pole, in *The Brothers Karamazov*; the elder Zosima and Alyosha serve this purpose. Swedenborg comes in handy here because he observed that the only way to slow the progress of an atheism that identifies God with nature is to emphasize the idea of the God-Man. Dostoevsky did the same, only in his mind, which was always inclined toward extremism, this took the form of a radical 'either—or': if Jesus died and did not rise from the dead; that is, if he was only a man, then Earth is a 'diabolical vaudeville' and one should become a Grand Inquisitor in the name of pity for people—in order to transform the miserable 'rebellious slaves' into happy slaves.

Q: *A number of Orthodox writers have called Dostoevsky the greatest theologian that Eastern Christianity has given rise to.*

A: This opinion cannot be sustained. Anna Akhmatova used to call both Tolstoy and Dostoevsky 'heresiarchs', and I suspect she was not mistaken. As is well known, in Dostoevsky every negation is expressed with extraordinary power, whereas he had no idea how to produce an image of a truly good man, even less so of a God-Man. The entire development of his thought could be framed in a single question: How did he understand Christ in his youth and how did he understand Christ when he wrote his last novel? When Dostoevsky was a member of the Petrashevsky circle and read George Sand and Fourier, his ideas were the same as the ideas of the utopian socialists, for whom Jesus was an ethical ideal, the precursor of their imminent, easily realizable perfect society. Therefore, the metaphysical dimension was completely ignored. His experiences at hard labour caused Dostoevsky to understand how very much depends on whether one recognizes this dimension or not. His letter to Fonvizina, written in Omsk in 1854, is frequently cited in the literature about him, but very few people, apparently, notice the crucial, perilous decision expressed in it. Let us reach for the text again:

> I'll tell you of myself that I have been a child of the age, a child of disbelief and doubt up until now and will be even (I know this) to the grave. What horrible torments this thirst to believe has cost me and continues to cost me, a thirst that is all the stronger in my soul the more negative arguments there are in me. And yet God sometimes sends me moments at which I'm absolutely at peace; at those moments I love and find that I am loved by others, and at such moments I composed for myself a credo in which everything is clear and holy for me. That credo is very simple, here it is: to believe that there is nothing more beautiful, more profound, more attractive, more wise, more courageous and more perfect than Christ, and what's more, I tell myself with jealous love, there cannot be. Moreover, if someone proved to me that Christ were outside the truth, and it *really* were [Dostoevsky's italics] that the truth lay outside Christ, I would prefer to remain with Christ rather than with the truth. [15]

Let us consider what this means. Faith and reason have often been contrasted, but the opposition of faith and truth is quite unusual. Meister Eckhart, who is not known, after all, as an admirer of reason, said: 'If God were able to distance himself from the truth, I would hold to the truth and let God go'. Just at the same time in the mid-nineteenth century when Dostoevsky was in Siberia, in Denmark Kierkegaard was conducting his great attack on reason, but for him truth was on the side of faith. [16] Dostoevsky's choice is tantamount to granting all the trumps to his opponent, that is, to the progressive spirit of the nineteenth century, leaving for himself the figure of Christ as no more than a dream which it is difficult to live without. But one of the attributes of a dream is that it tends to get out of control, it easily loses its clear contours. In my opinion this letter is the confession of a potential heresiarch.

Q: *When do the consequences of such a choice appear?*

A: Not immediately. Briefly, I would describe the changes in the figure of Christ in Dostoevsky's works as follows: at first, Christ is the moral leader-ideal of utopian socialism; then he disappears for a long time, making himself known only indirectly, for example in *Crime and Punishment* when Sonia and Raskolnikov read the chapter from the Gospels about the raising of Lazarus from the dead or in the epilogue to the novel, when the peasants, his fellow prisoners at hard labour, hate Raskolnikov, who is an intellectual and therefore, in their opinion, an atheist; finally, Christ reappears as the hero of the Slavophile utopia and tsarist autocracy.

Dostoevsky's obsession with portraying children is eloquent in this regard. The society of children is a society of immature beings who are, however, capable of goodness if a mature and noble person should appear and succeed in organizing them. The first attempt at evangelical portraiture of their Christ-like leader is Prince Myshkin in *The Idiot*. During his stay in Switzerland he is surrounded by a group of children; through his meekness he eradicates their bad habits and changes their attitude toward the half-crazed Marie. But Dostoevsky did not succeed with Myshkin. Because Myshkin is utterly lacking in egotism, he is inhuman, and in the end he sows devastation all around him. Judging by his example, one would have to doubt the possibility of uniting the two natures—the divine and the human—and be inclined toward accepting the opinion of the Docetists, who proclaimed that Christ only seemed to have earthly features. So Dostoevsky renewed his efforts in *The Brothers Karamazov*.

There are two adult organizers of a society of children in that novel. One of them is the Grand Inquisitor or, if you prefer, the author of the poem 'The Legend of the Grand Inquisitor'—Ivan Karamazov. Let us note, how many times the Grand Inquisitor uses the word children in relation to the people whom he rules. The other is Alyosha and the fraternity of twelve schoolboys, quite obviously a foreshadowing of the Church as a theocratic community. The only problem is that however powerful and brilliant in every detail is the Legend of the Grand Inquisitor, the chapters about the boys (along with the chapter in which the excessively caricatured Poles appear) are artistically weak, melodramatic, and offensive to the reader because of their falseness. That *The Brothers Karamazov* remains a masterpiece despite these chapters testifies to Dostoevsky's greatness. It is actually a novel about power. The power of the corporeal father (Fyodor Karamazov) is opposed to the power of the spiritual father (the elder Zosima) and this antinomy holds. Even though the sceptical Lev Shestov used the word lubok (a cheap woodcut sold at fairs) to refer to both characters—Zosima and Alyosha—the biography of Zosima is convincing precisely as a genre patterned after the lives of the saints. The moral of this juxtaposition is the following: It is forbidden to rebel against secular power (the father) even when it is evil, but people (the sons) will rebel if there is no spiritual power alongside the secular. The second opposition concerns the future: a leader who is in a pact with the Devil and a leader who acts through love alone. The disproportion between the immense vision of the Legend of the Grand Inquisitor and the troop of boy scouts performing good deeds under Alyosha's leadership is jarring. Artistic failure bears witness to something: therefore, this is a focal point for those Dostoevsky scholars who suspect Dostoevsky the Orthodox publicist of hypocrisy toward himself.

Q: *Does Christ represent a specific principle of social organization in Swedenborg?*

A: Not at all. But the accusations that the Grand Inquisitor hurls at Christ are actually the accusations of a utopian socialist who had dreamed that his teacher would want to march in the vanguard and bears a grudge because he does not wish to do so. So he has a new dream: perhaps Christ will serve as a model for a society which someone will first convince about the virtues of fraternity—and so the model for the Kingdom of God on earth becomes a boy scout troop

Q: *It ought to be said in defense of Dostoevsky that there is no other exam-ple in world literature of a novelist having such boundless ambitions. He inherited the novel as a not very refined genre, and even today his admira-tion for such authors as Victor Hugo and George Sand amuses us. But he transformed this genre into an instrument for expressing the clashes among the most important ideas about man's fate and made such strides in this di-rection that quite possibly his failures can be justified, because the novel has only a limited weight-bearing capacity. A theologian or a poet has the benefit of greater powers than a novelist has.*

A: Dostoevsky the novelist defends himself quite adequately. He should also not be completely ignored in our deliberations as the publicist-author of *Diary of a Writer*, but that particular activity of his indicates how very much he requited illusions.

Q: *If I understand you correctly, the similarity between Swedenborg and Dostoevsky would have led to an exceptionally sharp consciousness of the con-sequences for religion inherent in the development of the exact sciences. This is the link between them; that is, in a certain sense, Dostoevsky was struggling with atheism in its eighteenth-century form.*

A: The atheism of old man Karamazov is: Voltairean. And the comic liberal Stepan Verkhovensky from *The Possessed*, is, if one were to measure him by the Western criteria of that time, a little like a character cut of Rousseau's romances. As a result of tempestuous historical events, above all of the Industrial Revolution, the sharpness of the religious problematic was dulled in Western Europe and the voices of a few individuals became a crying in the wilderness. In nineteenth-century *belles lettres* no one said as brutally as Dostoevsky what, it now seems to us, had to be said, especially about indifferent Nature as Law, about 'two times two equals four'. A search for other Similarities with Swedenborg would probably not be justified, because Dostoevsky's political daydreaming appears to have served him as an alibi in the confrontation with metaphysical difficulties.

NOTES

* This essay is from Czeslaw Milosz's *Beginning with My Streets: Baltic Reflections*, translated by Madeline G Levine and is reprinted here by kind permission of Farrar, Strauss and Giroux.

[1] Karl Jaspers, *Strindberg und Van Gogh: Versuch einer pathographischen Analyse unter vergleichender Heranziehung von Swedenborg und Hölderlin* (Bremen: Johs. Storm verlag, 1949).

[2] Martin Lamm, *Swedenborg*, tr. E Söderlindh, w. a preface by Paul Valéry (Paris: Stock, 1936).

[3] Leonid Grossman, Семинарий по Достоевскому [Seminarii po Dostoevskomu] (Москва [Moscow]: Петроград, 1922; repr. Letchworth: Prideaux Press, 1972), pp. 20-50.

[4] Aleksandr Nikolaevich Aksakov (1832-1903), Russian spiritualist, author, and Imperial Councillor to the Tsar. Russian censorship meant he primarily published in German and French. His works include *Animismus und Spiritismus* (Leipzig: Oswalde Mutze, 1894) and *A Case of Partial Dematerialization of the Body of a Medium*, tr. Tracy Gould (Boston: Banner of Light, 1898).

[5] Fyodor Dostoevsky, *The Diary of a Writer*, tr. Boris Brasol (London: Cassell & Co., 1949), vol. 1, entries for January 1876, ch. III, pt. 2, pp. 190-6; and April 1876, ch. II, pt. 3, pp. 301-8.

[6] The books listed in Grossman, p. 42 as nos. 175, 176, 177, are: A N Aksakov, Евангеліе по Сведенборгу (The Gospel according to Swedenborg), (Leipzig, 1864); Emanuel Swedenborg, О Небесахъ, о Мірѣ Духовъ, и объ Адѣ (*Heaven and Hell*), tr. with a Preface by A N Aksakov (Leipzig: Franz Wagner, 1863); A N Aksakov, Раліонајизмъ Сведенборга (The Rationalization of Swedenborg) (Leipzig: Franz Wagner, 1870).

[7] Grossmann, Семинари по Достоевскому, p. 9.

[8] Aimée Dostoyevsky, *Fyodor Dostoyevsky: A Study* (London: William Heinemann, 1921), ch. I, pp. 6-7.

[9] Emanuel Swedenborg, *Heaven and Its Wonders, The World of Spirits, and Hell: From Things Heard and Seen*, tr. Samuel Noble (New York: American Swedenborg Printing and Publishing Society, 1879), §588, p. 341.

[10] An English translation of Dostoevsky's 'Bobok' (1873) can be found in *The Gambler/ Bobok/A Nasty Story*, tr. Jessie Coulson (Harmondsworth: Penguin, 1966).

[11] Dostoevsky, *Crime and Punishment*, tr. Constance Garnett (London: J M Dent & Sons Ltd., 1955), pt. IV, ch. I, p. 261.

[12] Ivan Turgenev, letter to M E Saltykov-Shchedrin, 24 September (OS) / 6 October (NS) 1882, in *Letters*, tr. and ed. David Allan Lowe (Ann Arbor: Ardis, 1983), vol. 2, no. 326, p. 183.

[13] Dostoevsky, *The Brothers Karamazov*, tr. Constance Garnett (Chicago: William Benton/Encyclopaedia Britannica, Inc., 1952), pt. II, book VI, ch. 3, p. 170.

[14] See H J McLachlan, *Socinianism in Seventeenth-Century England* (London: Oxford University Press, 1951).

[15] Dostoevsky, letter to Natalya Fonvizina, end of January-third week of February 1854, in *Fyodor Dostoevsky: Complete Letters, Volume 1, 1839-1859,* tr. and ed. David Lowe and Ronald Meyer (Ann Arbor: Ardis, 1988), vol. 1, no. 90, pp. 194-5.

[16] See Søren Kierkegaard, *Concluding Unscientific Postscript*, tr. David F Swenson and Walter Lowrie (Princeton: Princeton University Press, 1941), p. 182. 'The truth is precisely the venture which chooses an objective uncertainty with the passion of the infinite'; but the above definition of truth is an equivalent expression for faith: 'Faith is precisely the contradiction between the infinite passion of the individual's inwardness and the objective uncertainty'.

Ideal homes: James, Rossetti and Swedenborg's House of Life

Hazel Hutchison

I   n 'The Art of Fiction' Henry James writes, 'Experience is never limited, and
        it is never complete; it is an immense sensibility, a kind of huge spider-web
        of the finest silken threads suspended in the chamber of consciousness,
and catching every air-borne particle in its tissue'. [1] The idea of consciousness
as an architectural space is a recurring motif in the history of thought from
the Old Testament to post-structuralist theory. [2] It flourishes especially vibrantly
in the poetry and fiction of the nineteenth century, both British and American.
The reasons for this are complex. Public structures on a new, bewildering scale,
such as the Crystal Palace built for the Great Exhibition of 1851, civic museums,
hospitals and railway stations sprang up in towns and cities as capitalist cathedrals
for the industrialized era. Urbanization and the rise of the middle classes meant
that more people owned or rented substantial houses, and the growing cultural
emphasis on individualism and privacy also placed a new focus on the success and
security of family life within the home, as celebrated by John Ruskin in *Sesame
and Lilies* (1862):

> This is the true nature of home—it is the place of Peace; the shelter, not
> only from all injury, but from all terror, doubt and division. In so far as it is
> not this, it is not home; so far as the anxieties of the outer life penetrate into

it, and the inconsistently minded, unknown, unloved, or hostile society of the outer world is allowed by either husband or wife to cross the threshold, it ceases to be home; it is then only a part of that outer world which you have roofed over, and lighted fire in. [3]

Ruskin's close connection between home life and gender politics is also echoed by many of his contemporaries. Coventry Patmore's now infamous poem cycle *The Angel in the House* (1854-61) is widely read as a manifesto of patriarchy, and has become the iconic text of the Victorian cult of domesticity. In creating his angelic figure, Patmore draws heavily on the writings of Swedish philosopher and mystic Emanuel Swedenborg. [4] In Swedenborg's vision of marriage husband and wife, joined in 'conjugial love', are fused into one spiritual being but retain separate duties and inclinations, the man towards the rational and public, the woman towards the affectionate and private. [5] The happy hearth ruled by this domestic angel is generally perceived to be the nineteenth-century ideal of the house, and is characterized by security, stasis and purity. This is certainly the familiar image of the Victorian home popularized by the novels of Charles Dickens. [6] Ironically, however, Swedenborg's work is also used by other writers of the period, not only to challenge the orthodox ideal of marriage, but also to present an image of the house that challenges Ruskin's cosy picture of 'a sacred place, a vestal temple, a temple of the hearth watched over by House-hold Gods'. [7]

Two works published in 1881, Henry James's *The Portrait of a Lady* and Dante Gabriel Rossetti's sonnet cycle 'The House of Life', both draw heavily on another of Swedenborg's images of domestic spirituality, the House of Life. In James's novel this metaphor underscores James's architectural imagery both in the novel and its preface, contributes to (and complicates) the debate about the moral value of art, and offers a clue to the riddle of the tale's ending. In Rossetti's sonnet cycle, the title phrase emphasizes the idea of love as a process open to change and flux, and reveals the structure usually seen to be missing from the poem.

While retaining the idea of the house as a spiritual zone in which the individual can most fully develop, James and Rossetti offer a radically different perspective on the image of the house from that projected by Ruskin, Dickens and Patmore. Turned inside out, as it were, their house is no haven where one escapes from the harsh realities of life, but a psychological space where 'terror, doubt and division' are manifested and confronted, where concrete materiality and abstract ideality are fused. Swedenborg's House of Life, as I shall explain, becomes for James and Rossetti a venue for personal and artistic progression and mutation. Rooms and chambers come to represent states of mind, the links and levels between them to stand for change, and apertures and vistas to allow observation. In this James and Rossetti anticipate the spatial representations of consciousness offered by the incipient science of psychology, established by Sigmund Freud and James's brother William James at the turn of the twentieth century, and signal modernist literature's preoccupation with perception and interior states of being. [8]

Emanuel Swedenborg is now a largely neglected figure but his scientific philosophy and visionary theology were widely read in the nineteenth century. His visions of heaven and musings on the nature of human love founded a new church, known rather unimaginatively as the New Church, and caught the imagination of writers from Blake, Coleridge and Emerson to Yeats and Strindberg. The house of the mind, sometimes tagged the House of Life, sometimes the Palace of Love, or the Temple of Wisdom, is a recurring image in Swedenborg's writing, and offers a meeting point between the spiritual and the material. Swedenborg's overarching project was an attempt to explain the spiritual world in scientific terms, and his work strives to explain the relation of the physical and the divine in treatises such as *The Interaction of the Soul and the Body* (1769). This desire to reconcile two apparently contradictory realms of experience is perhaps not surprising in a man who trained in scientific thought but also, like William Blake a generation later, believed he saw visions of heaven and conversed with angels.

The image of the house is essential to Swedenborg's depiction of life in the

World of Spirits, where the dwelling places which souls find for themselves after death correspond directly to the lives they have led on earth:

> They who are sordidly avaricious, dwell in cellars, and love the filth of swine, and such nidorous exhalations as proceed from undigested substances in the stomach. [...] They who take delight in adulteries, dwell in the other world in mean and squalid brothels, which they love, while they shun chaste houses and faint away if they happen to come near them. [...] They who love divine truths and the Word from interior affection, or from the affection of truth itself, dwell in the other life in light, in elevated places [...] Every thing in their houses is refulgent as if made of precious stones, and when they look through the windows, it is like looking through pure crystal. [9]

However these dwelling places are mirrored in this mortal life by a psychological house through which the individual moves as they grow in spiritual understanding.

> [A person] may be compared to a house in which are numerous chambers, one of which leads into another; those who are in truths only as to the understanding are not in any chamber of the house, but only in the court; but so far as truth through the understanding enters into the will, so far it enters into the chambers, and dwells in the house. [10]

This interior architecture of the self is in a perpetual state of change, redesigning itself to respond to events and new ideas. Life is a process of selection, decoration and extension, adapting the house to accommodate the developing soul. H L Odhner paraphrases Swedenborg's image in these terms of constant refurbishment:

> While here on earth, our mind is in constant flux, hesitant, restless, tasting many conflicting delights, choosing not only between good and evil, but

between all the varieties of each, between the subtle shadings and colorings of each. Throughout a life-time it gradually seeks out the furnishings and materials by which the house of life can be shaped; and as the ruling love is confirmed, this house is remodeled and adapted again and again to new states. [11]

This house is interiorized but not insular; it is also one of Swedenborg's recurring images for marriage. Always one to divide things neatly into threes, he describes the mind as a palace on three levels where different kinds of personal fusion or 'conjugial love' are possible and where sexual passion becomes a symbol of spiritual unity:

That palace represents the habitations of conjugial love, such as they are in human minds. Its highest part, into which the turtledoves betook themselves, represents the highest region of the mind, where conjugial love dwells in the love of good with its wisdom; the middle part, into which the birds of paradise betook themselves, represents the middle region, where conjugial love dwells in the love of truth with its intelligence; and the lowest part, into which the swans betook themselves, represents the lowest region of the mind, where conjugial love dwells in the love of what is just and right with its knowledge. [...] We in heaven call the highest region of the mind celestial, the middle spiritual, and the lowest natural; and we perceive them as stories in a house, one above another, and an ascent from one to the other by steps as by stairs [...]. [12]

This idea of the mind as a three-storied town house was taken up and further refined in the mid-1800s by the American philosopher and father of two famous sons, Henry James, Sr. After a personal spiritual crisis, James turned to the writings of Swedenborg for consolation and devoted much of his life to their study. He reworked the image of the House of Life in terms of art and culture, presenting art

275

as a necessary phase between material experience and higher spiritual knowledge.[13] Spiritual growth involves moving up the house from Nature's basement, through a level of rational, scientific and artistic education to a higher level of consciousness:

> Nature is in truth but the basement or culinary story of the Divine edifice; and when we make her primary, or allow her to dominate the house, we of course degrade the drawing and bedroom floors, filling them with sounds and odours fatal to every cultivated sense. [14]

For Henry James, Sr this representation of the house is also strongly tied to gender distinctions, but his conception of the female role is less passive than Patmore's. James, Sr's reading of Swedenborg leads him to equate the instinctive, animal side of humanity with Adam and the rational, spiritual tendency with Eve. He argues that only Adam was forbidden to eat of the Tree of Knowledge in the Garden of Eden. Eve therefore represents those inquisitive, creative impulses in human nature which lead to tragic experience, but which also make redemption and moral consciousness possible.

> Unquestionably what is mere 'instinct' in the creature will undergo conversion into will and intelligence; in other words, man will infallibly outgrow his animal consciousness, and attain at length to truly human proportions, when he will no longer blindly or instinctively, but freely or spontaneously, react to the creative impulsion. And this being the case, his moral or rational experience, his experience of selfhood or freedom (symbolised by Eve, or the woman), becomes incidentally inevitable, because his free, spontaneous, or spiritual reaction towards the creator is rigidly contingent upon such experience. [15]

Eve is therefore associated with qualities of perception, imagination and redemption. She also presides over the middle floor of the House of Life with its elements of art, culture and thought, which can tackle the unpleasant odours of Nature and allow progression to the transcendent level of the upper floors.

Handed down to his children as something of a family joke, 'Father's ideas' were nevertheless to have their effect both on the novelist Henry James and his brother. William's preference for spatial images of consciousness as a field or a house, or most famously as a stream, seems to owe a debt to his father's Swedenborgian tendency to fuse abstract and concrete concepts. Henry's novels, redolent as they are with images of doors, windows, passages, and buildings, also project the idea that one learns through material possessions, including objects of art, and other people, in pursuit of a more transcendent awareness.

In *The Portrait of a Lady* houses and openings in and out of them reveal the nature of the relationships within the novel. The story opens in Gardencourt, named after Pip's lodgings in *Great Expectations*, suggesting that a similar tale of inheritance and disillusionment awaits the idealistic heiress Isabel Archer, and setting the scene for an Edenic tragedy of consciousness. Isabel certainly possesses those qualities of imagination and spontaneity which James's father ascribes to the figure of Eve. However, James himself is more interested in the effect of the materialistic male on his heroine than vice versa. When Isabel turns down her uncle's neighbour Lord Warburton, he assumes that she does not care for his house Lockleigh (locks and bolts forming a recurring image in the novel). Isabel also rejects the young Mr Rosier despite his fascinating bibelots and ceramics, and the industrious Casper Goodwood despite his wealth and sensual desire. Her eventual and ill-advised marriage to the socially ambitious Gilbert Osmond is partly prompted by Isabel's curiosity about the aesthetic world in which he appears to move with such ease and dexterity. However it also blurs the distinction between Isabel as an audience for Osmond's collection and as an object within it. While in the process of arranging Isabel and Osmond's marriage, the worldly-wise Madame Merle insists to Isabel that material possessions cannot be overlooked:

When you've lived as long as I, you'll see that every human being has his shell and that you must take that shell into account [...] What shall we call our 'self'? Where does it begin? Where shall it end? It overflows into everything that belongs to us and back again. I know a large part of myself is the clothes I choose to wear. I've a great respect for things! [16]

The problem with Madame Merle, of course, it that she never gets any further. She can acquire but cannot renounce, and this materialism has serious consequences for those around her. Madame Merle's respect does not quite extend to people—certainly not to Isabel. However the awareness in this passage of the fluidity of human nature and its vulnerability to its environment suggests the work of William James or even Freud in its psychological perception. It also reminds us that Isabel ought to have paid more attention to Osmond's shell in choosing a husband. Fond of minutely copying pictures of coins and acquiring old china, Osmond proves to be narrow-minded, cold and ungenerous. Unable to open himself to Isabel's nature, he cannot move beyond the stage of viewing art as financial and cultural power to unlock its potential for spiritual change and growth. He is characterized by his Florentine villa that looked as though it might be difficult to get out of once you were inside, with 'jealous apertures' that 'seemed less to offer communication than to defy the world to look in'. [17] Indeed their marital home, the Palazzo Roccanera, literally 'palace of black rock', becomes symbolic of the emotional dungeon that Osmond eventually keeps her in, turning the lights out 'one by one'. Isabel eventually finds the 'infinite vista of a multiplied life to be a dark, narrow alley with a dead wall at one end', filled with a darkness of Osmond's making. Although he borrows the technique of presenting the psyches of Isabel and Osmond as architectural spaces, James reverses the Swedenborgian logic of correspondence between soul and habitation. It is Isabel who finds herself confined in the dark and squalid oubliette, while Osmond observes from a supercilious height.

Between those four walls she had lived ever since; they were to surround her for the rest of her life. It was the house of darkness, the house of dumbness, the house of suffocation. Osmond's beautiful mind gave it neither light nor air; Osmond's beautiful mind indeed seemed to peep down from a high small window and mock her. [18]

This reversal raises the question of whether James's adaptation of the imagery of the House of Life is perhaps ironic, or is at least testing the validity of his father's scheme. However, it is hard to ignore the way in which the development of Isabel's character and consciousness is facilitated by a series of windows and doorways through which she moves or observes. Our first glimpse of Isabel is of her reading by a locked door 'secured by bolts, which a particularly slender little girl found it impossible to slide'. [19] Later on it will be an open doorway that displays the true nature of Osmond's relationship with Madame Merle. [20] At the end of the novel Isabel refuses the offer of escape presented to her by Goodwood, running away from him back to the 'lights in the windows of the house' shining across the lawn at Gardencourt and from there presumably back to Osmond in Italy. [21]

This renunciation of physical passion seems to many readers an incomprehensible move, but James's insistence in the preface to the novel, written in 1908, that he conceived the work as a 'square and spacious house' constructed with an 'architectural competence' suggests that Isabel works her way through the House of Life. Indeed this is a phrase that James uses many times elsewhere in his writing. From her experience of the materially rich but artistically unendowed Lord Warburton, through the art trader Rosier and the refined intellectual Osmond, Isabel arrives at the ability to transcend her material surroundings. Her intense but non-sexual, almost 'conjugial', relationship with her doomed cousin Ralph draws her up from materialism and reason to something finer—not perhaps to a Swedenborgian rapture, but then James is writing after Darwin and without religious conviction—and the sense of movement through architectural frames and progressive levels remains impressive.

The most interesting house in the novel, however, is James's metaphor in the preface of the House of Fiction where each artistic consciousness stands at its own window, a window which facilitates but also limits his or her perspective:

> The house of fiction has in short not one window, but a million——a number of possible windows not to be reckoned, rather; every one of which has been pierced, or is still pierceable, in its vast front, by the need of the individual vision and by the pressure of the individual will. [...] He and his neighbours are watching the same show, but one seeing more where the other sees less, one seeing black where the other sees white, one seeing big where the other sees small, one seeing coarse where the other sees fine. And so on, and so on [...] The spreading field, the human scene, is the 'choice of subject'; the pierced aperture, either broad or balconied or slit-like and low browed, is the 'literary form'; but they are, singly or together, as nothing without the posted presence of the watcher——without, in other words, the consciousness of the artist. [22]

It is a well-known passage with deep implications for literary practice, and one that has been thoroughly explored elsewhere. But it does also bear a striking similarity to Swedenborg's system of psychological constructions, where windows equate with faculties of perception and upper levels represent moral or intellectual ascendancy. For both writers these images are also firmly linked to experience and are open to mutation, like the web in the 'chamber of consciousness'. James can thus be seen to be using the house not simply as an expression of artistic form, as is often claimed, but as an appeal to something more complex and internalized——a flexible architecture of the human mind.

While James's knowledge of Swedenborg is distilled through the New England transcendentalist tradition. Dante Gabriel Rossetti's knowledge of it filters through Patmore's writing and the British Romantic tradition——specifically through Coleridge, who planned at one stage a biography of Swedenborg, and through Blake who borrows heavily from Swedenborg's mythology and was briefly a member of the incipient New Church in London. Rossetti assisted in the editing of Alexander Gilchrist's biography of Blake and also owned one of Blake's notebooks. [23]

For purposes of symmetry I have given the publication date of Rossetti's sonnet cycle 'The House of Life' as 1881, but this date is misleading. The composition of the series of 101 sonnets (102 if the controversial 'Nuptial Sleep' is included) stretched through most of Rossetti's adult life and the sequence that is usually anthologized now was only crystallized after his death. 1881 was the publication of the extended second edition of the poems in which the full scope of the project became visible. The cycle is split into two sections. The first, entitled 'Youth and Change', deals with themes of love, passion and loss; the second entitled 'Change and Fate' explores art and disillusionment and once more loss, ending on a note of uncertain Hardyesque hope.

Critics have been disputing the structure (or lack thereof) governing 'The House of Life' since its publication. The poet's brother William Michael Rossetti claimed that it 'does not form one consecutive poem, but only so many sonnets of sufficiently diverse subject matter, grouped together'. [24] In the 1920s Evelyn Waugh would sneer, 'There is no hint of an intellectual process at work; it is all a sonourous re-echoing of dark perceptions'. And even as such fails to enlighten the reader. 'The revelation, one cannot help feeling, is rather depressing than stimulating'. [25] On the other hand, mid-twentieth-century critics seem intent on tracing some kind of pattern. William E Fredeman argues in 1965 that the cycle is a 'sonnet of sonnets'. He points out that 'the 101 sonnets are proportionately grouped so that Part I contains fifty-nine sonnets (sixty with 'Nuptial Sleep' restored), approximately four-sevenths of the total number, which is the ratio of the octave to the sestet within the Petrarchan sonnet'. [26] This idea is dismissed by later critics as 'ingenious', [27] which may or may not be a reason for discounting it. It is certainly the kind of formal game that might appeal to Rossetti's Renaissance imagination, and I will return to it later. However Fredeman fails to present any kind of argument or cohesion within the series or to show how the sonnets relate to each other. More recent scholars have tended to focus on those themes in Rossetti's work that feed into modernist and postmodernist concerns and discourses: time, mirrors, unity, language and the failure of art. [28]

There is of course another strain of criticism that reads the poem in purely biographical terms, tracing Rossetti's love for and loss of Lizzie Siddal, his passion for Jane Morris, wife of his friend and business partner William Morris, and his subsequent disillusionment with desire. Certainly many of the poems do deal with intensely personal themes. The recurring image of the stillborn child seems an obvious allusion to the daughter that Lizzie and Rossetti lost. Also many of the sonnets included in the 1881 edition of the cycle were composed as love sonnets to Jane Morris. Traditionally the sonnet, from Dante onwards, is a form that invites a measure of confession. But such confession is, by the nature of the sonnet's tight structure, always coded and stylized, and there is a danger in equating the voice of the speaker with the voice of the poet. The sensory and sensuous nature of Rossetti's poetry seems to present a particular temptation to critics in this regard, from Robert Buchanan's infamous attack on 'The Fleshly School of Poetry' onwards. [29] One cannot assume, however, that a chaotic personal life makes for chaotic poetry. It is perhaps more likely to make the drive for form and structure ever more urgent.

Rossetti does seem to have had an overarching plan in mind, and to have reorganized his material several times to fit it. The first set of sonnets were published in 1870 under the heading 'Sonnets and Songs Towards a Work to be Called *The House of Life*', suggesting that even at this point he envisaged a larger and more philosophical project. In the same year he wrote to a friend: 'in carrying out my scheme of the *House of Life* (if ever I do) I shall try to put in action a complete *dramatis personae* of the soul'. [30] Also in his celebrated riposte to Buchanan 'The Stealthy School of Criticism', Rossetti points out that 'Nuptial Sleep' is 'no more a whole poem, in reality, than is any single stanza of any poem', (*stanza* translating as the Italian for 'room') and cannot outline the poet's 'representative view of the subject of love'. In a phrase reminiscent of James's House of Fiction, he insists that his sonnets are products of 'the art of the inner standing point', and retain their integrity by presenting perceived sensation. He goes on, 'Any reader may bring any artistic charge he pleases against the above sonnet, but one charge it would be impossible to maintain against the writer of the series in which it occurs, and that is, the wish on his part to assert that the body is greater than the soul'. [31] Taken on its own 'Nuptial Sleep' certainly is strong stuff for a polite Victorian readership, describing the post-coital exhaustion of two lovers, but as Rossetti insists, it needs to be read in its context. Rather than providing the climax (as it were) of the cycle, it was only number VI (now VIa, having been replaced after the furore by 'The Kiss'). Rossetti's remark about the soul and the body also is pertinent here. Many of the sonnets following 'Nuptial Sleep' deal with themes of identity and selfhood, and explore the diffusion of self experienced in intense romantic passion, blurring the boundary between spiritual and bodily being. This is especially intense in the early poems such as 'Heart's Hope' (V):

> Thy soul I know not from thy body, nor
> Thee from myself, neither our love from God. [32]

But as the cycle progresses the confusion of spiritual and physical gives way to a *fusion* of the two. It becomes increasingly difficult to tell the difference between concrete realities and the sensual symbols which represent them:

> Sometimes thou seem'st not as thyself alone,
> But as the meaning of all things that are;
> A breathless wonder, shadowing forth afar
> Some heavenly solstice hushed and halcyon;

> —'Heart's Compass', XXVII [33]

and

Not in thy body is thy life at all,
But in this lady's lips and hands and eyes.

—'Life-in-Love', XXXVI [34]

The sonnets also carry a visionary quality that owes perhaps as large a debt to Swedenborg as to Dante. Emotions, states of mind, unfulfilled possibilities are personified with the painter's instinct for visual material. Rossetti here uses the technique at work in his poem 'The Blessed Damozel' (1850), later reworked as a painting, where the dead beloved retains all her physical warmth, personality and sexuality.[35] In 'The House of Life', heaven and hell are portrayed not as abstract concepts but as corporeal realities, almost tangible locations for longing, despair, consummation and a reuniting fusion such as that outlined in *Conjugial Love*.

But lo! what wedded souls now hand in hand
Together tread at last the immortal strand
With eyes where burning memory lights love home?
Lo! how the little outcast hour has turned
And leaped to them and in their faces yearned: —
'I am your child: O parents, ye have come!'

—'Stillborn Love', LV [36]

The most explicit reference to Swedenborg occurs in sonnet LVIII 'Her Heaven', stanza III of 'True Woman'. [37] Here the speaker asserts that 'to grow old in Heaven is to grow young, / (As the Seer saw and said). This is a direct quote, and probably the best-known line in Victorian times, from Swedenborg's *Heaven and Hell*,[38] a work satirized in Blake's *The Marriage of Heaven and Hell* (1792-93). In his essay on Swedenborg, Emerson points out that one of Swedenborg's favourite sayings was that 'Nature exists entire in leasts', holding that each minute part of a form contains the organic map of the whole. Emerson explains that, 'large, compound or visible forms exist and subsist from smaller, simpler and ultimately from invisible forms, which act similarly to the larger, but more perfectly and more universally'. [39] This thought brings us back to Fredeman's idea that the whole cycle is itself a sonnet. But it is the overall drift of the poem sequence that makes the most convincing case for adopting Swedenborg's House of Life as a structure for Rossetti's. From the joy of physical passion, Rossetti's soul moves up through attachment to physical objects, natural and artistic (musing on the uses of art as it goes); wrestles as in the three stanzas of 'The Choice' with the 'relations existing between body and mind'; [40] and arrives at a higher plane of understanding. The end of 'The House of Life' however, like the end of *The Portrait of a Lady* affords no celestial revelation or religious certainty. Rather the final poems, 'Newborn Death' and 'The One Hope' present a fairly bleak conception of the vanity of human desire and regret, searching for 'the gift of grace unknown'. [41]

Like James, then, Rossetti feels able to borrow Swedenborg's imagery without subscribing to his theological system. Rossetti's religious beliefs are hard to establish. They were unorthodox enough for his sister Christina to fear for his salvation, but do seem to have included some measure of metaphysical belief as well as allowing a certain amount of dabbling in the paranormal within his circle of friends. But it seems clear that Swedenborg's portrayal of the fusion of the physical and the spiritual, especially in terms of sexuality, appealed to Rossetti's sensual and visual imagination. The map presented by the House of Life in no way undermines those readings of the cycle which stress the autobiographical elements, the thematic patterns, the exploration of life and the discussion of art but it does offer an umbrella (or perhaps one should say a roof) under which these can be ordered and understood as a progression rather than as conflicting theories.

Swedenborg's thought has largely disappeared from the collective cultural consciousness. His emphasis on visionary experience and on biblical authority is hard to digest in an age where one is treated with medical drugs and the other with scepticism. However the impact of Swedenborg's language and imagery on Victorian literature should perhaps be reappraised. Certainly the image of the House of Life resonates through James and Rossetti's writings, upsetting the standard conception of Victorian views of the house, and expanding nineteenth-century perceptions of consciousness. Swedenborg's writing may have lost much of its religious credibility, but his work provides a system rich in the symbols of human experience. And the search for such symbols is, as James says, 'of the very essence of poetry'. [42]

NOTES

[1] Henry James, 'The Art of Fiction' (1884), in *Literary Criticism: Essays on Literature, American Writers, English Writers*, ed. Leon Edel and Mark Wilson (New York: Library of America, 1984), p. 52.

[2] In his essay 'White Mythology', Jacques Derrida discusses the house as one of the preferred metaphors of philosophical language, and wrestles with the problem of internalizing an exterior image: 'the borrowed dwelling [...] is a metaphor of metaphor; an expropriation, a being-outside-one's-own-residence, but still in a dwelling, outside its own residence but still in a residence in which one comes back to oneself, recognizes oneself, reassembles oneself, outside oneself in oneself'. Derrida, *Margins of Philosophy* (1972), tr. Alan Bass (Brighton: Harvester Press, 1982), p. 253.

[3] John Ruskin, 'Of Queens' Gardens', in *Sesame and Lilies* (1862; repr. Orpington: George Allen, 1887), p. 136.

[4] J C Reid, *The Mind and Art of Coventry Patmore* (London: Routledge and Kegan Paul, 1957), pp. 66-81. See also Edmund Gosse, *Coventry Patmore* (London: Hodder and Stoughton, 1905).

[5] Emanuel Swedenborg, *Conjugial Love,* tr. A H Searle (London: Swedenborg Society, 1891), §§174-7, pp. 163-5.

[6] For a discussion of Dickens's presentation of domesticity see Michael Slater, *Dickens and Women* (London: J M Dent, 1983), and Frances Armstrong, *Dickens and the Concept of Home* (Ann Arbor: UMI Research Press, 1990).

7   Ruskin, *Sesame and Lilies,* p. 137.

8   Sigmund Freud's image of the dream house is probably now the best known representation of the mind as a house. 'Rooms in dreams are usually women [...] There is no need to name explicitly the key that unlocks the room [...] A dream of going through a suite of rooms is a brothel or harem dream. But as Sachs has shown by some neat examples, it can also be used (by antithesis) to represent marriage. [...] Steps, ladders or staircases, or, as the case may be, walking up or down them, are representations of the sexual act.——Smooth walls over which the dreamer climbs, the facades of houses, down which he lowers himself——often in great anxiety——correspond to erect human bodies and are probably repeating in the dream recollections of a baby's climbing up his parents or nurse.' Sigmund Freud, *The Interpretation of Dreams* (1900) tr. James Strachey (London: Penguin, 1976), p. 471.

9   Swedenborg, *Heaven and Hell* (1758), tr. T Hartley (London: Swedenborg Society, 1893), §§488-9, pp. 266-7.

10 Swedenborg, *Arcana Coelestia* (1749-56), tr. J F Potts, rev. W O'Mant (London: Swedenborg Society, 1885), vol. XII, §10110, pp. 114-15.

11 H L Odhner, *Life in the Spiritual World* (Bryn Athyn: Academy Publication, 1968), p. 173.

12 Swedenborg, *Conjugial Love*, §270, p. 242.

13 See also Quentin Anderson, *The American Henry James* (London: John Calder, 1957), pp. 161-74.

14 Henry James, Sr, *Christianity: The Logic of Creation* (London: William White, 1857), p. 202.

15 James, Sr, *The Secret of Swedenborg* (Boston: Fields, Osgood and Co, 1869), p. 151.

16 Henry James, *The Portrait of a Lady* (1881; repr. London: Penguin, 1986), p. 253.

17 Ibid., p. 279.

18 Ibid., p. 478.

19 Ibid., p. 78.

20 Ibid., p. 457.

21 Ibid., p. 636.

22 Henry James, Preface to *The Portrait of a Lady* (1908), in *Literary Criticism: French*

Writers, Other European Writers and the Prefaces to the New York Edition (New York: Library of America, 1984), p. 1075.

23 See Jan Marsh, *Dante Gabriel Rossetti: Painter and Poet* (London: Weidenfeld and Nicolson, 1999), pp. 251-7.

24 William Michael Rossetti, *Dante Gabriel Rossetti as Designer and Writer* (London: Cassell, 1889), p. 181.

25 Evelyn Waugh, *Rossetti: His life and his Work* (London: Duckworth, 1928), pp. 156, 160.

26 William E Fredeman, 'Rossetti's "In Memoriam": An Elegiac Reading of *The House of Life*', in *Bulletin of the John Rylands Library*, XLVII (March 1965), p. 300.

27 Clyde de L Ryals, 'The Narrative Unity of The House of Life', in *Journal of English and German Philology*, 69 (1970), pp. 241-57.

28 See John Stasny, 'The Vanishing Lives and Language of Victorian Poets', in *Review*, vol. 11 (1989), pp. 81-91; Joseph H Gardner, 'Michaelangelo's Sweetness, Coleridge's Flycatchers, Ligeia's Eyes, and the Failure of Art in The House of Life', in *Journal of Pre-Raphaelite Studies*, 4 (1995), pp. 67-74; John Granger, 'The Critique of the Mirror in Rossetti's "The House of Life" ', in *Journal of Pre-Raphaelite Studies*, 4:2 (1984), pp. 1-16; John R Conners, 'A Moment's Monument: Time in "The House of Life" ', in the *Pre-Raphaelite Review*, 2:2 (1982), pp. 20-34; Paul Jarvie and Robert Rosenberg, 'Willowwood, Unity and "The House of Life" ', in *Pre-Raphaelite Review* 1:1 (1977), pp. 106-20.

29 Robert Buchanan, 'The Fleshly School of Poetry: Mr D G Rossetti', in *Contemporary Review*, 18 (October 1871), pp. 334-50.

30 Dante Gabriel Rossetti to T G Hake, 21 April 1870, in *The Letters of Dante Gabriel Rossetti*, ed. by O Doughty and J R Wahl, 4 vols. (Oxford: Clarendon Press, 1965-7), vol. 2, no. 992, p. 850.

31 Dante Gabriel Rossetti, 'The Stealthy School of Criticism', in *Athenaeum*, July-December 1871, pp. 792-4; repr. in David G Riede (ed.), *Critical Essays on Dante Gabriel Rossetti* (New York: G K Hall, 1992), p. 41.

32 Dante Gabriel Rossetti, 'Heart's Hope', no. V in the sonnet sequence 'The House of Life' (1881), in *Collected Writings*, ed. Jan Marsh (Chicago: New Amsterdam, 2000), p. 278.

33 Dante Gabriel Rossetti, 'Heart's Compass', no. XXVII in the sonnet sequence 'The House of Life' (1881), in *Collected Writings*, p. 289.

34 Dante Gabriel Rossetti, 'Life-in-Love', no. XXXVI in the sonnet sequence 'The House of Life' (1881), in *Collected Writings*, p. 294.

35 Dante Gabriel Rossetti, 'The Blessed Damozel', in *Collected Writings*, pp. 8-15.

36 Dante Gabriel Rossetti, 'Stillborn Love', no. LV in the sonnet sequence 'The House of Life' (1881), in *Collected Writings*, p. 303.

37 Dante Gabriel Rossetti, 'True Woman. III. Her Heaven', no. LVIII in the sonnet sequence 'The House of Life' (1881), in *Collected Writings*, pp. 303-4.

38 Swedenborg, *Heaven and Hell*, §414, p. 218.

39 Ralph Waldo Emerson, 'Swedenborg; or, the Mystic' (1850), in *Collected Works*, (Cambridge: Belknap Press, 1987), vol. IV, p. 64.

40 Dante Gabriel Rossetti, letter to Athenaeum (1872), referenced in Waugh, p. 159.

41 Dante Gabriel Rossetti, 'The One Hope', no. CI in the sonnet sequence 'The House of Life' (1881), in *Collected Writings*, p. 325.

42 Henry James, *Hawthorne* (London: Macmillan, 1967), p. 115.

'Through Death to Love': Swedenborgian imagery in the painting and poetry of Dante Gabriel Rossetti

Anna Maddison

If to grow old in Heaven is to grow young, / (As the Seer saw and said,) then blest were he / With youth for evermore, whose heaven should be / True Woman, she whom these weak notes have sung. / Here and hereafter […] [1]

The above quotation is from Dante Gabriel Rossetti's sonnet 'True Woman. III. Her Heaven', from the sonnet cycle 'The House of Life' (1881). Rossetti confirmed the identity of 'the Seer' in a letter to Jane Morris in 1880, two years before his death: 'The *seer* in the sonnet is Swedenborg, and the saying a very fine one'.[2] The influence of Emanuel Swedenborg's visionary writings upon the work of Rossetti has been acknowledged in brief, but has not received the full scholarly attention it deserves, despite the fact that a life of Swedenborg was amongst Rossetti's books and that it is likely he had read *Conjugial Love*.[3]

Swedenborg's ideas and imagery regarding love and heaven find their way into Rossetti's poetic and artistic imagery, particularly with regard to the theme of the dead beloved. Hitherto, Rossetti's obsession with that theme and the imagined afterlife has been primarily attributed to his interest in the work of the medieval poet Dante Alighieri, and Dante's worship of his deceased muse, Beatrice. Critics have often narrowed Rossetti's work to an interest in his namesake Dante, ignoring more contemporary influences which show him to be not just a medievalist, but very much a man of his own time and subject to the influences of the cultural climate of his age. Many in his circle were interested in Swedenborg's works and Rossetti gleaned knowledge of Swedenborgian ideas from a variety of sources. This essay discusses some of those sources, and traces several examples in Rossetti's body of work that show an engagement with Swedenborgian philosophies.

One of the earliest and most striking sources through which Rossetti must have accessed Swedenborgian ideas is the poet William Blake. On 30 April 1847, a British Museum attendant, William Palmer (brother of the Blake-influenced artist Samuel Palmer) [4] offered Blake's notebook to the eighteen-year-old Rossetti and, together with his brother William, he subsequently purchased it. It proved a great inspiration and Rossetti immediately 'proceeded to copy out, across a confused tangle of false starts, alternative forms, and cancellings, all the poetry in the book'. [5]

Rossetti would have recognized the fragments of poetry in Blake's notebook (now called the 'Rossetti manuscript') as embryonic versions of the *Songs of Experience* poems, because as William Michael Rossetti related, his brother 'was already a hearty admirer of William Blake's *Songs of Innocence and Experience*' prior to acquiring the notebook. [6] The manuscript was crammed full of Blake's notes and was clearly inspirational to the young Rossetti in more than one regard (most obviously it encouraged his Pre-Raphaelite rejection of Sir Joshua Reynolds and conventional Royal Academy practices). [7] Later when Rossetti aided Alexander Gilchrist in the 1860s with his biography of Blake, the notebook manuscript was to prove a useful resource. Rossetti prepared Blake's poetry for publication in the second section of the book and finished the biography after Gilchrist's death. [8]

Kathleen Raine has suggested in a discussion of Blake's interest in Swedenborg that 'the teachings of Swedenborg's Church of the New Jerusalem have permeated the spiritual sensibility of the English nation, through Blake'. [9] This is interesting in a discussion of Rossetti considering that much of the English nation would not be as familiar with Blake had not Rossetti, along with Gilchrist and others within his circle, such as A C Swinburne, championed him. Rossetti's purchase of Blake's notebook in 1847 can consequently be seen as a pivotal moment in terms of the dissemination of Blakean, and therefore to some degree, Swedenborgian ideas.

The Blake connection is a strong one, and a relevant one in a discussion of Rossetti and Swedenborg. However, Rossetti would have already been aware of Swedenborg prior to his discovery of Blake, and through a much closer source: his father. Gabriele Rossetti, an Italian political refugee and intellectual, was engaged in a lifelong work on Dante Alighieri. His study, which regarded Dante's writings as allegorical, was unconventional and rooted in the esoteric. Rossetti's brother William described their father's work in his memoir of Rossetti:

> Our father, when writing about the *Comedia* or the *Vita Nuova*, was seen surrounded by ponderous folios in italic type, "libri mistici" and the like (often about alchemy, freemasonry, Brahminism, Swedenborg, the Cabbala, etc.), and filling page after page of prose, in impeccable handwriting, full of underscorings, interlineations, and cancellings. [10]

This interesting quotation illustrates the natural acceptance and awareness of key mystical and occult works, including those of Swedenborg, which characterized the Rossetti children's familial environment and suggests that any subsequent contact with Swedenborg merely added richness to this early acquired knowledge: Rossetti's interest in Blake therefore merely furthered his acquaintance with Swedenborg.

The imagined dead beloved: 'The Blessed Damozel', Poe and Patmore's circle

Rossetti's poem 'The Blessed Damozel' contains particularly striking Swedenborgian imagery. The poem, which details the separation of lovers by death and gives voice to the beloved in heaven (the damozel) as she laments this separation, can be seen as one of Rossetti's key works associated with the theme of the dead beloved. It remained an important work throughout Rossetti's career having supposedly existed in embryo in his juvenilia and was rewritten (and republished) several times throughout his career. There were also two paintings completed from the poem in the 1870s. [11] One of the earliest known versions of the poem is thought to be the one Rossetti sent for approval to the poet Leigh Hunt in 1847 in the period concurrent with the Blake notebook discovery. [12] Hunt noted the obvious Dantesque imagery, but other influences can be traced in the poem, including that of Swedenborg.

It is unlikely that Rossetti had read much or directly from Swedenborg at this time, but it is highly likely that he would have been attracted to certain Swedenborgian ideas through the work of others, particularly regarding those concerning love and heaven, which would have chimed with his early fascination with the theme of the dead beloved. As Gary Lachman suggests in a discussion of Baudelaire's interest in Swedenborg: 'Swedenborg's ideas, as well as those of other "occult" thinkers like Franz Anton Mesmer, were "in the air" in France at this time, forming part of the philosophical climate [...] so it's quite possible that Baudelaire "picked them up" without much direct study of the original texts themselves'. [13] This is also true of London in the late 1840s and 1850s, and of Rossetti, whose circle of acquaintance included those interested in Swedenborg in addition to other occult ideas. Rossetti attended mesmerism demonstrations, for example, in 1851. [14]

During January 1850 'The Blessed Damozel' was rewritten, including additions, and prepared for publication in the Pre-Raphaelite magazine *The Germ*. [15] It was at this time that Rossetti's circle of acquaintance began to widen and included several Swedenborg enthusiasts. For example, in 1849 Rossetti met the poet Coventry Patmore. Already an admirer, Rossetti had extolled the virtues of Patmore's poem 'The Seasons' in a letter to his brother. [16] The poem was later published in issue 1 of *The Germ* and Patmore went on to contribute to three out of the four issues of the Pre-Raphaelite magazine. He was also honoured by a place on the Pre-Raphaelites' 'list of immortals', a list of exalted individuals with Jesus Christ at the head, which also included poets and artists that the Brotherhood considered inspirational. [17]

Patmore called Swedenborg 'A Blake upon a colossal scale' [18] and would acknowledge the influence of *Conjugial Love* upon his own poem *The Angel in the House* (1854-6). [19] By the time Rossetti became acquainted with him in November

1849, Patmore had begun his reading of Swedenborg, perhaps inspired to do so by Emerson, who had visited England in 1847-8 and lectured on Swedenborg.[20] Both Rossetti brothers socialized regularly with Patmore throughout 1849-50[21] and it is likely that discussions occurred concerning Swedenborg, as William Michael Rossetti stated in his Pre-Raphaelite journal that conversations sometimes took 'a religious turn'.[22] One can speculate an influence of Swedenborgian ideas may have emerged through the shared intellectual inquiry instigated by such conversations, and this may have been one of the sources through which Rossetti was introduced to *Conjugial Love* in particular.

A visit to Coventry Patmore's on Thursday 8 November 1849 heralded a piece of news which William Michael Rossetti deemed important enough to include in his Pre-Raphaelite journal: 'At Patmore's we heard of the reported death of Edgar Poe'.[23] Rossetti and Patmore shared a love of the writings of Edgar Allan Poe, who was a frequently discussed figure at Patmore's social evenings. Rossetti's partiality is clear from his many illustrations from Poe throughout 1847 and 1848,[24] and also from Poe's inclusion in the aforementioned PRB list of 'immortals'.[25] The influence of Poe upon 'The Blessed Damozel' has also been acknowledged, chiefly because of Hall Caine's claim that Poe's 'The Raven' (1845) was a thematic template with regard to the subject of the dead beloved that characterizes Rossetti's poem.[26] The Poe link takes on a deeper resonance because Poe too had a reported interest in the ideas and writings of Emanuel Swedenborg. Roger Forclaz in an essay from Volume XI of the journal *Poe Studies*, writes of 'Poe's interest in Swedenborg's theory of correspondences'.[27] In addition Poe's famous story 'The Fall of the House of Usher' (1839) contains a passage detailing the contents of the library of Roderick Usher. The books mentioned are a mix of actual and fictional occult volumes, a mystically inclined list that strangely echoes Rossetti's father's own collection and rather intriguingly includes 'the Heaven and Hell of Swedenborg'.[28]

Like Poe's 'The Raven', Philip James Bailey's poem on the theme of the Faust legend, 'Festus' (1839) is an acknowledged poetic influence upon 'The Blessed

Damozel'.[29] William Michael Rossetti tells us: 'Bailey's *Festus* was enormously relished […] read again and yet again' [30] and it is seen as influential primarily with regard to its supernatural elements. A sense of a literary circle with interest in Swedenborg here begins to emerge as Philip James Bailey, one of the 'spasmodic' poets, was friendly with the Swedenborgian Churchman Henry Sutton, who in turn was reportedly a 'life-long' friend of Coventry Patmore.[31] Rossetti's letters confirm that he was also familiar with Sutton's poetry. [32] Rossetti's relationship with Patmore in the early years of the Pre-Raphaelite Brotherhood was therefore an important connection: one which indicates a shared cultural climate that included knowledge of Swedenborg.

Bailey's poem 'Festus' is seen as influential upon Rossetti's 'The Blessed Damozel' particularly in its similarity as regards the shared theme of the dead beloved. The theme is explored in Bailey's poem through Festus' desire to reunite with one of his loves, Angela. In one scene Angela's physical beauty is described as Festus sees her in spirit-angel form, and like Rossetti's Damozel her beauty is unmarred by death: 'Angela! dost thou hear me? Speak to me. / And thou art there—looking alive and dead. / Thy beauty is then incorruptible'. [33]

Clearly what Rossetti found of interest in both Poe and Bailey, is what he found appealing about Dante: the idea of love surviving beyond death. An intertextual web emerges here, alongside the sense of a shared cultural climate. The theme of the dead beloved characterizes 'The Blessed Damozel', 'The Raven' and 'Festus' and all three can be said to contain a shade of Swedenborgian theology. In 'Festus' and 'The Blessed Damozel' it is the sustenance of the human substantial form after death that is particularly Swedenborgian. Swedenborg suggested people in heaven seem to themselves as they are on earth; their physical attributes appear to be retained:

> It needs to be known that after death a person ceases to be a natural man and becomes a spiritual man, but he looks to himself exactly the same, and is so much the same that he is unaware that he is no longer in the natural world.

He has the same kind of body, face, speech and senses, because in affection and thought, or in will and intellect, he remains the same. [34]

The Damozel of Rossetti's poem has a physical beauty seemingly uncorrupted by death and seems to her self as she always was. Aspects of her physical self are likened to beauties in the natural world. Her 'eyes', 'hand', 'neck' and 'back' are all referred to giving a sense of bodily substance, as is her hair, 'yellow like ripe corn' and clothing 'Her robe, ungirt from clasp to hem'. [35] When the influence of Swedenborg is acknowledged it becomes clear why Rossetti emphasizes the physical beauty of the celestial Damozel; something which some critics have sometimes suggested is incongruous in the spirit world.

The longing of the Damozel to be reunited both physically and spiritually with her beloved who is still in the natural world is Swedenborgian in essence: she is an angel waiting to experience the delights of truly conjugial love, and therefore to become truly whole: 'conjugial love makes an angel perfect, since it unites him with his partner'. [36] Swedenborg states that: 'For in heaven a couple are not called two, but one angel [...] they are no longer two, but one flesh'. [37] It is this to which Rossetti's Damozel aspires: 'We two will live at once, one life; / And peace shall be with us'. [38]

The reunion that Rossetti's Damozel anticipates, 'I wish that he were come to me' is sexual as well as spiritual. She imagines herself reunited with her beloved in the most holy of places:

We two will stand beside that shrine,
Occult, withheld, untrod,
Whose lamps tremble continually
With prayer sent up to God [39]

The Damozel's sexuality is something that has troubled critics who have predominantly seen Rossetti's poem as homage to Dante and the early Italian school.

The failure to perceive the Swedenborgian elements in the work has meant that the idea of sexual love in heaven that the poem suggests has been seen as blasphemous. For example David Riede's accusation that the Damozel's earthly love 'has little to do with any Christian heaven' and John Dixon Hunt's criticism that the Damozel and her lover's reunion 'smacks too severely of earth to be imaginable in heaven' are undermined in the light of a Swedenborgian interpretation. [40] In *Conjugial Love* Swedenborg categorically states that: 'it follows that people retain mutual and reciprocal sexual love after death'. [41] He explains why: 'Since then this tendency to union is stamped upon every detail of the male and female, it follows that it cannot be wiped out and die together with the body'. [42] A Swedenborgian heaven is a Christian heaven: 'a person lives on as a person after death […] this is even true in Christendom'. [43] This is a love that is spiritual, but which does not negate the physical: 'those who possess truly conjugial love […] have chaste sexual love, which regarded in essence is an inner spiritual friendship; this gains its sweetness from their abundant, but chaste, potency'. [44] It is therefore a love that is not inappropriate in a description of a Christian heaven.

The Damozel's feelings are not blasphemous but holy because they are chaste. This is because the love bond between the Damozel and her beloved is primarily spiritual: even when this anticipated love is described in its 'bodily' fashion, the scene remains sacred as it is the dwelling place of the Holy Spirit:

> We two will lie i' the shadow of
> That living mystic tree
> Within whose secret growth the Dove
> Sometimes is felt to be [45]

In an explanation of truly conjugial love Swedenborg describes the joys felt by those that engage in it: 'every kind of blessedness […] and gratification that the Lord the Creator could ever confer on a person are concentrated on this love of his'. [46] This sentiment appears in Rossetti's poem, as the Damozel anticipates the future reunion with her beloved:

> There will I ask of Christ the Lord
> Thus much for him and me:——
> To have more blessing than on earth
> In nowise; but to be
> As then we were,——being as then
> At peace. Yea, verily. [47]

Subsequent versions of the poem are more explicit concerning the regaining of love and resumption of chaste physical union. For example the 1870 version of the same stanza is more definite in its suggestion that the Damozel and her beloved will re-experience forever what they experienced briefly upon the earth; conjugial love:

> There will I ask of Christ the Lord
> Thus much for him and me:——
> Only to live as once on earth
> With Love,——only to be,
> As then awhile, for ever now
> Together, I and he. [48]

The painting from 1871-8 [49] is similarly explicit regarding physical union. The image of an embracing couple in heaven is repeated again and again behind the head of the Damozel; literally expressing her longing in visual terms. It also serves to lend a sort of medieval style narrative to the painting with different times of the story being represented on one surface. It is an image critically acknowledged as reminiscent of Botticelli's *Mystic Nativity* (1501), but which is characteristically Rossetti in its intimacy and Swedenborgian in its representation of the imagery of sexual love in heaven. [50] A closer look ascertains a more personal evocation of enduring love as the woman seen embracing is an image of Jane Morris, then Rossetti's beloved.

The real dead beloved: the Brownings, Dr Wilkinson and *Beata Beatrix*

In 1855 Rossetti met Robert Browning, who much to the delight of its author, quoted part of the 'The Blessed Damozel' from memory. Rossetti excitedly related the event in a letter to Ford Madox Brown: 'On Sunday I called on the Brownings [...] B. quoted to me some of that 'ere blessed "Damozel"'. [51] Both the Brownings were readers of Swedenborg and 'ideas emanating directly or indirectly from Swedenborg's religious writings had a profound impact on the work of the two poets'. [52] Therefore from this source also Rossetti may have acquired a Swedenborgian edge to his work, as he was by his own admission influenced by the work of both poets. Rossetti's letter to Elizabeth Barrett Browning from October 1855, regarding 'The Blessed Damozel', refers to this:

> Last night I copied out that old production of mine, & now enclose it [...] It was written long ago, but has been very little altered since [...] Bearing in mind my favourite readings when I wrote it, I feel some slight misgiving lest there should be any property of his or yours in it. [53]

It is quite possible that this 'property' had a Swedenborgian edge, and this would account to some degree for the Swedenborgian elements within the 1850 *Germ* version of Rossetti's 'Blessed Damozel'.

During the 1850s Rossetti and Browning were close and Rossetti visited the poet and his wife whenever their infrequent sojourns in England allowed. In a letter from November 1855 Rossetti communicated his fondness for them: 'I saw them a good many times, and indeed may boast of some intimacy with the glorious Robert by this time'. [54] It is therefore possible that it was the Brownings who introduced him to Swedenborg's *Conjugial Love*.

Robert Browning had been friendly with the Swedenborgian homeopathic physician (and brother of one time Swedenborg Society Secretary, William Wilkinson) Dr James John Garth Wilkinson since the late 1830s. [55] Wilkinson, who wrote a biography of Swedenborg, was also acquainted with Rossetti's friends the Howitts. Anna Mary Howitt was a fellow painter who like Rossetti trained at Sass's Academy, and was engaged for a time to Rossetti's friend Edward Bateman. [56] Anna's parents William and Mary Howitt were friendly with Dr Wilkinson and his wife, and Mary in her autobiography recalls having them over for Christmas. [57] William Howitt wrote about Swedenborg in his great masterwork on the supernatural: *The History of the Supernatural in all Ages and Nations* (1863).

Rossetti first became familiar with Dr Wilkinson in 1854, when, at the suggestion of the Howitts, Lizzie Siddal (who at the time was Rossetti's model, pupil and girlfriend) consulted him due to a lapse in good health. In March 1854 Rossetti wrote a letter to Ford Madox Brown in which he referred to this:

> The Howitts insisted on Lizzy's seeing a Dr. Wilkinson, a friend of theirs and I believe an eminent man. He finds that the poor dear has contracted a curvature of the spine. [58]

Rossetti's acquaintance with Dr Wilkinson lasted many years and the Swedenborg Society Library archive contains a copy of a letter from Rossetti to Dr Wilkinson eleven years after Wilkinson first treated Lizzie.

The letter, hitherto unpublished, implies a solid acquaintance. Dated 25 January 1865, from Cheyne Walk, it suggests that Rossetti had been reading some of Wilkinson's poems, it ends: 'and I should like to hear something from yourself about them, when I take advantage of your invitation, as I hope to do soon'. [59] The accompanying explanatory letter in the archive file is from Wilkinson's daughter who transcribes the letter and describes briefly the connection between Rossetti and her father: 'My dear father Dr. James John Garth Wilkinson attended the wife of D G Rossetti in her last illness. She died of consumption'. It is interesting to speculate whether Dr Wilkinson was one of the four doctors called out to see Lizzie on the eve of her death.

The contents of the letter imply more than just a professional relationship between the two men, who had a shared interest in William Blake: Wilkinson at one stage edited William Blake's poems. [60] He also wrote a life of Emanuel Swedenborg in 1849, which interestingly contained a quotation from Dante on the title page, in recognition of the similarity in themes and imagery between the medieval poet and the eighteenth-century visionary—something no doubt also noted by Rossetti.

In a letter from July 1860 Rossetti referred to a book of 'bogie-poems' by Dr Wilkinson. 'Bogie' was a Rossettian word for anything of a supernatural colouring and it is clear that he was fond of these poems, which were published under the title *Improvisations from the Spirit* in 1857:

> By the bye, I remember sending you a little book of bogie-poems in emblematic green cover, and hearing from you that you had one already. If you still have mine would you oblige me by sending it back as I sometimes think of it when I want to be surprised. [61]

The above quotation is from a letter written to the poet William Allingham, who was close to Rossetti throughout the 1850s and was a 'keen reader of Swedenborg'.[62] There are references throughout Allingham's diary to Swedenborg which provide strong evidence as to the degree of interest in Swedenborg's writings that existed in Rossetti's circle in the 1850s and 1860s. Allingham discusses Swedenborg with various figures including Tennyson, Carlyle and Alfred Russell Wallace across the years of his diary and this becomes pertinent when we realize that one of 'his chief companions' was Rossetti. [63]

Allingham was also friendly with Robert Browning. There is an anecdote from Allingham's diaries concerning a visit to Browning's when the poet read to him some of Dr James John Garth Wilkinson's published writings. [64] A sense of a widening circle of Swedenborgian acquaintance again emerges here, as Allingham's friend—the previously mentioned poet Henry Sutton—was most probably initially inspired to join the Swedenborgian church by reading Dr Wilkinson's translations, and his biography of Swedenborg. [65]

In 1862 Lizzie Siddal, then Rossetti's wife, died. Strangely this year also saw the death of Mrs Patmore, and found Robert Browning in mourning (Elizabeth had died in 1861), which signalled a new phase for all three poets. In 1863 Rossetti began work on a painting that would immortalize his late wife. The painting entitled *Beata Beatrix* would be replicated several times, but never with the same intensity of the original which was finally finished in 1871. [66] Throughout the years of the painting Rossetti's mind was occupied with matters of life and death, and what had been the imagined dead beloved in 'The Blessed Damozel', became the real one, in an eerie example of life imitating art.

Although a subject from Dante depicting Lizzie Siddal as Beatrice, there are Swedenborgian elements within *Beata Beatrix* which have been acknowledged. For example Philip Hoare has described the figure in the painting as a Swedenborgian angel:

Muse and poet, saint and sinner, Siddal seemed haunted by her sensual mortality, as if to embody the Swedenborgian belief that sexual congress was an echo of the union of two souls in Heaven needed to form a single angel. [67]

Hoare's word 'haunted' is pertinent as *Beata Beatrix* was painted across the years 1863-71: a period concurrent with Rossetti's immersion in spiritualism and seance attendance (something he again had in common with Wilkinson, Elizabeth Barrett Browning and all three Howitts) at which he tried to contact his dead wife. Rossetti's brother William kept a seance diary across the parallel years 1865-8.[68] It is as if Rossetti's painting is *his* version of a seance diary: visually capturing the influence of his other-worldly imagery drawn from a variety of sources, including Swedenborg and fusing the personal with the fictional and symbolic: a mystical masterpiece.

In the painting, Beatrice's shut eyes lead us to contemplation of sight and seeing. F G Stephens writes in his article on *Beata Beatrix* that she sees through these eyes like a blind prophet——a true 'Seer': 'the heavenly visions of the New Life are revealed to the eyes of her spirit'. [69] She prefigures her future angelic state in a distinctly clairvoyant episode that is reflective of the fashion for spiritualism in the period. Rossetti's own words support this, he described the picture thus:

> It must of course be remembered, in looking at the picture, that it is not intended at all to *represent* death, but to render it under the semblance of a trance […] She, through her shut lids, is conscious of a new world [70]

The view of the city behind Beatrice's head is bathed in an intense golden twilight. Formally it appears to the viewer as a column rising up from, or down through her head. This visually represents the idea that 'through her shut lids' she becomes conscious of a new world. Literally it is as if her mind is connected to heaven: it is illuminated with the spiritual light that Swedenborg suggests emanates from the sphere around God; the sun in the spiritual world: 'The internal sight of a man, which is the sight of his mind, receives influx from the spiritual sun'. [71] This could describe what is occurring to the character of Beatrice in the painting, as she sits like a receptacle of God's love and wisdom. It represents metaphorically the moment of artistic inspiration.

In Section II of *Conjugial Love* 'Marriages in Heaven', Swedenborg relates a visionary episode in which he meets a married couple in heaven who perfectly exemplify conjugial love:

> Then suddenly there was to be seen a chariot coming down from the

highest or third heaven, containing what seemed to be one angel. But as it approached, it seemed to have two angels in it. [72]

The two angels are husband and wife and speak to Swedenborg thus: 'We have led a blessed life in heaven from the earliest time, which you call the Golden Age. We have been perpetually in the bloom of youth, in which you see us today'. [73] This has eerie echoes with the themes and imagery in *Beata Beatrix* in which the fact is ever present that it is a parallel image of both Rossetti's Lizzie and Dante's Beatrice 'perpetually in the bloom of youth'. The married couple are described as having a 'fiery radiance' as they approach Swedenborg, which they explain, is 'from the heaven we come down from'. [74] An evocation of such fiery radiance is displayed in the first version of *Beata Beatrix* in the hazy golden light that seems to surround Lizzie/Beatrice in a kind of unconventional halo. Rossetti's brushwork has a fitting misty sfumato style lending the work a mystical atmosphere. Certainly the painting creates a sense of awe in the viewer: she seems to glow, as if we are looking at a mystical or sacred image.

Swedenborg says in this passage that the fiery light 'derives from the love of wisdom'. [75] In another of his treatises entitled *The Interaction of the Soul and Body*, Swedenborg expounds further regarding what fire symbolizes. He says: 'fire corresponds to love, and thence signifies it'. [76] Consequently it becomes significant that the figure of Love in the top left of the painting carries a flame and is surrounded by a fiery glow similar to that which surrounds Beatrice; in an image that is both from Dante and Swedenborg. [77] The red garment that love wears and the red dove reinforce the image and work together formally to echo the auburn-red of the model's hair, and to offset the earthy green tones in the painting.

The most striking example of a Swedenborgian edge to the work can be seen in the name of the work meaning 'Blessed Beatrice'. Depicting the figure in a saintly state of beatitude, and reinforcing this through the title, suggests divine revelation. However, as Robert Upstone has noted, the ecstatic pose of Beatrice is also sexual in tone:

Her facial expression, raised head, straining throat and parted lips are overtly sensual, and Rossetti evidently intends to suggest a connection between the sexual and the divine, between orgasm and revelation. [78]

This fusion of spiritual and sexual imagery is Swedenborgian and illustrates the idea that truly conjugial love in spiritual people leads to a state of unparalleled joy:

The case of spiritual people is quite different. For them the first state is an introduction to perpetual bliss, and this progressively grows, as the spiritual rational level of the mind, and as a result the natural sensual level of the body, in each person join with that of the other and unite. [79]

The Beatrice figure therefore becomes a supreme embodiment of conjugial pleasure, or bliss: an illustration of a Swedenborgian angel.

'The House of Life' and two paintings

The Swedenborgian imagery in Rossetti's work appears predominantly in subjects concerning love, particularly the reunion with the beloved after death. Much of his work contains the image of two becoming one, and the joining on earth as anticipatory of the ultimate joining in heaven to form one angel. It is here that one returns to the opening of this essay and the quotation from the sonnet cycle on love, change and fate 'The House of Life'. Rather pertinently, as Hazel Hutchison has also noted, the term 'The House of Life' can be seen as Swedenborgian: 'The house of the mind, sometimes tagged the House of Life, sometimes the Palace of Love, or the Temple of Wisdom, is a recurring image in Swedenborg's writing, and offers a meeting point between the spiritual and the material'. [80]

As Swedenborg wrote: 'A person may be compared to a house in which are numerous chambers, one of which leads into another'. [81] This analogy sits well with Rossetti's sonnet sequence in which each stanza ('room') leads thematically into another: the whole work being a house for the soul's experience or as Rossetti suggested 'a complete dramatis personae of the soul'. [82]

It is in the first part of that work, entitled 'Youth and Change' that the poet fully expresses this idea of joining. For example the lovers described are often joined both physically and spiritually as if one being. Phrases like 'two blent souls' and 'I am thine, thou'rt one with me!' pepper the sonnets.[83] Such moments express the spiritual ecstasy that parallels the physical, for example in 'Heart's Hope' (sonnet V):

> Lady, I fain would tell how evermore
> Thy soul I know not from thy body, nor
> Thee from myself, neither our love from God [84]

The love is blessed because it is from God: 'truly conjugial love is from the Lord'.[85] The couple are joined as one—indistinguishable from one another, or love, or from the source of that love; God. Much of the imagery concentrates upon a mirroring between the two lovers, emphasizing their two halves, which once joined, will complete each other: 'Two separate divided silences, / Which, brought together, would find loving voice'. [86] The sestet of the sonnet 'Mid-Rapture' expresses this:

> What word can answer to thy word,—what gaze
> To thine, which now absorbs within its sphere
> My worshipping face, till I am mirrored there
> Light-circled in a heaven of deep-drawn rays?
> What clasp, what kiss mine inmost heart can prove,
> O lovely and beloved, O my love? [87]

The imagery of mirroring and the kiss in 'The House of Life' are complemented by several pictorial images by Rossetti. It is as if this central motif becomes a kind of stylistic template across his body of work. For example, two lovers are depicted as

307

two halves of one person joined through physical and spiritual union symbolized through the kiss, and echoing each other's physical bodies in anticipation of the joining in heaven to form one angel. For example in *King Rene's Honeymoon* (1864) the two lovers form symmetry, with the figures of the two combining as to make one whole image: one eye each is shown and in the meeting of mouths, the nose and mouth seem as one.

Another design from 1864 is striking in this respect. In *Roman de la Rose* (1864) the embracing couple mimic each other closely like two halves, perfectly echoing lines from 'The House of Life': 'Two bosoms which, heart-shrined with mutual flame, / Would, meeting in one clasp, be made the same'. [88] The androgynous angel behind the couple, whose outstretched wing seems to enclose them, prefigures visually what the couple will form in heaven: one supreme angel. In addition the setting is in a rose garden, which amongst many other traditional associations, such as love, femininity and chastity, also references Swedenborg, who in *Conjugial Love* recounts a meeting in heaven with the wives of conjugial love: the setting is a rose garden which symbolizes by correspondence the charms of conjugial love. [89]

In this essay I have illustrated through discussion of aspects of both art and writing, the presence of Swedenborgian imagery in the work of Dante Gabriel Rossetti. [90] The influence of Swedenborg within Rossetti's oeuvre, whether accessed directly, or through the work of others, is a significant and hitherto critically under-acknowledged aspect in Rossetti scholarship. In doing so I have also shown the extent to which Swedenborgian ideas were present in the social, artistic and literary circles around Rossetti; indicating that the presence of such imagery in his work is an indication not just of his interest, but also how far that interest was present in the cultural milieu of the period.

NOTES

[1]   Dante Gabriel Rossetti, 'True Woman. III. Her Heaven', no. LVIII in the sonnet sequence

'The House of Life', in *Ballads and Sonnets* (Boston: Roberts Brothers, 1881), p. 220, ll. 1-5. The quotation in the title of my essay is from sonnet no. XLI, 'Through Death to Love', p. 203.

2   *Dante Gabriel Rossetti and Jane Morris: Their Correspondence*, ed. John Bryson (Oxford: Oxford University Press, 1976), p. 168.

3   Several scholars have acknowledged in brief the influence of Swedenborg upon Rossetti: Lisa Tickner, *Dante Gabriel Rossetti* (London: Tate Gallery Publishing, 2003), p. 54, and Philip Hoare, *England's Lost Eden: Adventures in a Victorian Utopia* (London: Fourth Estate, 2005), pp. 206-7; both would seem to have got their information from Robert Upstone's entry on Rossetti's *Beata Beatrix*, in *The Age of Rossetti, Burne-Jones & Watts: Symbolism in Britain 1860-1910*, ed. Andrew Wilton and Robert Upstone (London: Tate Gallery Publishing, 1997), pp. 155-7. A life of Swedenborg is listed amongst Rossetti's books in the sale catalogue of his house contents after death. See *16, Cheyne Walk, Chelsea; The Valuable Contents of the Residence of Dante Gabriel Rossetti, To Be Sold by Auction, On Wednesday, Thursday, & Friday, July 5, 6 & 7* (Wharton, Martin & co. Auctioneers Catalogue, 1882), item 614, p. 29.

4   *The Correspondence of Dante Gabriel Rossetti (2): The Formative Years 1835–1862, Charlotte Street to Cheyne Walk, Volume II, 1855–1862*, ed. William E Fredeman (Cambridge: D S Brewer, 2002), p. 583. See also *The Correspondence of Dante Gabriel Rossetti (1): The Formative Years 1835–1862, Charlotte Street to Cheyne Walk, Volume I, 1835-1854*, ed. William E Fredeman (Cambridge: D S Brewer, 2002), 51.11, n.2, p. 174.

5   William Michael Rossetti, *Dante Gabriel Rossetti: His Family-Letters with a Memoir* (London: Ellis, 1895), vol. 1, p. 109.

6   Ibid.

7   See *The Notebook of William Blake: A Photographic and Typographic Facsimile*, ed. David V Erdman (Oxford: Clarendon Press, 1973), transcripts N20, N32.

8   William Michael Rossetti summarizes the extent of Rossetti's involvement with Gilchrist's Blake biography: 'The volume was moreover the origin of all his after-concern in Blake literature; as Alexander Gilchrist, when preparing the *Life of Blake* published in 1863, got to hear of the MS. book, which my brother then entrusted to him, and, after Gilchrist's premature death, Rossetti did a good deal towards completing certain parts of the biography, and in especial edited all the poems introduced into the second Section. He again did something

for the re-edition dated 1880. At the sale of my brother's library and effects the Blake MS. sold for £110. 5 *s.*, so that the venture of ten shillings turned out a pretty good investment'. (*Dante Gabriel Rossetti: His Family-Letters with a Memoir*, vol. 1, pp. 109-10.)

9   Kathleen Raine, 'The Human Face of God', in *Blake and Swedenborg: Opposition is True Friendship, an Anthology*, ed. Harvey F Bellin and Darrell Ruhl (New York: Swedenborg Foundation, 1985), p. 89.

10   William Michael Rossetti, *Dante Gabriel Rossetti: His Family-Letters with a Memoir*, vol. 1, p. 64.

11   The Rossetti Archive contains detailed information on the poem's textual and printing history: 'The text of the poem underwent a continuous process of alteration up to the final (1881) text published in DGR's lifetime. DGR originally intended to have it printed (in 1846 or 1847) in the family magazine *Hodgepodge*, as he recollected in a letter to his mother in May 1873. That event did not come about, however, for the private periodical—initiated in 1843—was not revived in those years. So the poem was first published in *The Germ* no. 2 (Feb. 1850); again in *The Oxford and Cambridge Magazine* (1856) […] The poem also appears in the 1869 proofs and trial books for the 1870 edition of *Poems*, in different positions; first collected in a published edition in the *Poems* of 1870 and thereafter […] Two interesting minor (variant) texts were published (in the United States) between 1856 and 1870: *The Crayon* (May 1858), 124-25 and *The New Path* (Dec. 1863), 103-4. Both derive from the 1856 printing'. See, 'The Blessed Damozel: Scholarly Commentary', in *The Complete Writings and Pictures of Dante Gabriel Rossetti: A HyperMedia Research Archive*, ed. Jerome J McGann, <http://www.rossetti-archive.org/docs/1-1847.s244.raw.html> (20/2/2008). There are two painted versions of *The Blessed Damozel*. The first, commissioned by William Graham in 1871 (completed 1878), is now in the Fogg Art Museum (Harvard University Art Museums). The second (*c.*1875-81), a replica bought by Frederick Leyland, is in The Lady Lever Art Gallery. They differ significantly, with one major change: the Fogg painting has embracing lovers in the background, which were exchanged for three child angels in the Lady Lever version.

12   See Rossetti's letter to Hunt (47.5) and Hunt's reply (47.5A) and also Rossetti's letter to Aunt Charlotte Polidori (48.6 and 48.6, n.2) in *The Correspondence of Dante Gabriel Rossetti (1)*, pp. 49-52, 63, 64.

[13] Gary Lachman, 'The Spiritual Detective: How Baudelaire invented Symbolism, by way of Swedenborg, E T A Hoffmann and Edgar Allan Poe', herein, pp. 221.

[14] Rossetti was caught up in the craze for mesmerism that existed in the period and went to a demonstration in 1851. He wrote to William Michael Rossetti on 9 May 1851 regarding this: 'I believe Millais, Hunt, & self, are going tomorrow night to have another shy at seeing the Electro-biology. Do you like to come?' (*The Correspondence of Dante Gabriel Rossetti (1)*, 51.10, p. 173). In his memoir of Rossetti, William Michael suggests that it was probably one of the lectures given by Dr Marshall Hall and discusses Rossetti's interest: 'I can remember something of the "Electro-biology" to which the following note refers. It was a public display, conducted either by Dr. Marshall Hall, or by an over-plausible and fresh-complexioned Irish-American whom my brother characterized as "the Pink Owl". The Electro-biology was in the nature of clairvoyance, or what we now call hypnotism. For anything of this kind, including table-turning and spirit-rapping, my brother had a rather marked propensity and willing credence. He did not however believe in the "Pink Owl"'. (William Michael Rossetti, *Dante Gabriel Rossetti: His Family-Letters with a Memoir* (New York: AMS Press, 1970), vol. 2, p. 90.) William Michael had experimented with mesmerism on a private scale amongst friends. He refers to several incidences in the *Pre-Raphaelite Brotherhood Journal*, for example in the entry for Friday, 1 February 1850 he writes: 'I had a letter from Mrs. Patmore, inviting me for Thursday next, when I shall have a chance of being mesmerized by a friend of theirs who will be present'. (*The P.R.B. Journal: William Michael Rossetti's Diary of the Pre-Raphaelite Brotherhood 1849-1853*, ed. William E Fredeman (Oxford: Oxford University Press, 1975), p. 50.)

[15] Under the Journal entry for Friday, 25 January 1850 William writes: 'Gabriel finished up his "Blessed Damosel", to which he added 2 stanzas'. (*The P.R.B. Journal*, p. 47.)

[16] In September 1849, in a letter to his brother, Rossetti showed his admiration for Patmore's poem 'The Seasons', which was later published in issue 1 of *The Germ*. Clearly impressed he enthusiastically transcribed the poem for the benefit of William, with the epithet, 'Stunning, is it not?' (*The Correspondence of Dante Gabriel Rossetti (1)*, 49.13, p. 98.)

[17] *The P.R.B. Journal*, p. 107.

[18] Coventry Patmore, *Courage in Politics and Other Essays 1885-1896* (Oxford: Oxford University Press, 1921), p. 103.

[19] As Richard Lines has acknowledged, Swedenborg's *Conjugial Love* (1768) was an acknowledged influence upon *The Angel in the House* (1854-6): 'Patmore's best known poem, *The Angel in the House*, (hugely popular in its day as an exposition of ideal marriage) was deeply influenced by his reading of *Conjugial Love* (an indebtedness which the poet acknowledged in a footnote to the first published part of the work)'. (Richard Lines, 'Henry Sutton: Poet, Journalist, and New Church Man', in *Annual Journal of the New Church Historical Society for 2003* (Chester, 2003), pp. 40-1.) For a full discussion of Swedenborg's influence upon Patmore see Richard Lines, 'Eros and the Unknown Victorian: Coventry Patmore and Swedenborg', in *Between Method and Madness: Essay on Swedenborg and Literature*, ed. Stephen McNeilly (London: Swedenborg Society, 2005), pp. 65-79.

[20] Richard Lines, 'Eros and the Unknown Victorian', p. 66.

[21] Throughout 1849 and 50, there are references in William's journal to visits and gatherings with Patmore, e.g.: 'we went together to Coventry Patmore's' (Friday, 2 November 1849), 'Patmore was at Woolner's last night' (Thursday, 13 December 1849). See *The P.R.B. Journal*, pp. 22, 31.

[22] Ibid., p. 28.

[23] Ibid., p. 24.

[24] Julian Treuherz, Elizabeth Prettejohn and Edwin Becker, *Dante Gabriel Rossetti Exhibition Catalogue* (Zwolle: Waanders Publishers, in association with Van Gogh Museum, Amsterdam & The Walker, Liverpool, 2003), cat. nos. 2-6, pp. 142-3.

[25] See n. 17.

[26] See William Michael Rossetti, *Dante Gabriel Rossetti: His Family-Letters with a Memoir*, vol. 1, p. 107: 'In 1881 Rossetti gave Mr. Caine an account of its origin, as deriving from his perusal and admiration of Edgar Poe's *Raven*. "I saw" (this is Mr. Caine's version of Rossetti's statement) "that Poe had done the utmost it was possible to do with the grief of the lover on earth, and I determined to reverse the conditions, and give utterance to the yearning of the loved one in heaven" '.

[27] Roger Forclaz, 'Poe in Europe. Recent German Criticism', in *Poe Studies*, vol. XI, no. 2, December 1978, pp. 49-55.

[28] Edgar Allan Poe, *The Fall of the House of Usher and Other Writings* (London: Penguin Books, 1987), p. 149.

[29] For a detailed discussion of the influence of Bailey's 'Festus' upon 'The Blessed Damozel', see Alan D McKillop, 'Festus and The Blessed Damozel', in *Modern Language Notes*, vol. 34, pt. 2 (1919), pp. 93-7.

[30] *The Poetical Works of Dante Gabriel Rossetti*, ed. William Michael Rossetti (London: Ellis and Elvey, 1900), p. xxvi.

[31] Richard Lines, 'Henry Sutton: Poet, Journalist, and New Church Man', p. 40.

[32] See *The Correspondence of Dante Gabriel Rossetti (1)*, 54.57, p. 372 and 54.57 n.9, p. 374.

[33] Philip James Bailey, *Festus: a Poem*, 5th edn. (London: William Pickering, 1852), p. 32.

[34] Emanuel Swedenborg, *Conjugial Love*, tr. John Chadwick (London: Swedenborg Society, 1996), §31, p. 36. All subsequent page references to *Conjugial Love* refer to this edition.

[35] Dante Gabriel Rossetti, *Collected Writings*, ed. Jan Marsh (London: J M Dent, 1999), p. 8, see ll. 3-12. All subsequent line and page references refer to the 1850 version of 'The Blessed Damozel' from Marsh's edition, pp. 8-11, unless otherwise stated.

[36] Swedenborg, *Conjugial Love*, §52, p. 56.

[37] Ibid., §50, p. 55.

[38] Rossetti, 'The Blessed Damozel', ll. 137-8.

[39] Ibid., ll. 73-6 ('I wish that he were come to me' is line 61, p. 9).

[40] David G Riede, *Dante Gabriel Rossetti and the Limits of Victorian Vision* (London: Cornell University Press, 1983), p. 84; John Dixon Hunt, *The Pre-Raphaelite Imagination 1848-1900* (London: Routledge & Kegan Paul, 1968), p. 79.

[41] Swedenborg, *Conjugial Love*, §37, p. 40.

[42] Ibid., §46, p. 51.

[43] Ibid., §28, p. 33.

[44] Ibid., §55.7, p. 60.

[45] Rossetti, 'The Blessed Damozel', ll. 79-82.

[46] Swedenborg, *Conjugial Love*, §68.2, p. 71.

[47] Rossetti, 'The Blessed Damozel', ll. 127-32.

[48] 'The Blessed Damozel' (1870), ll. 127-32, in *Dante Gabriel Rossetti, Collected Writings*, ed. Jan Marsh, p. 15.

[49] This is the version of *The Blessed Damozel* (c.1871-8) now in the Fogg Art Museum

(Harvard University Art Museums). See also n. 11.

[50] The embracing couples in heaven of Rossetti's painting are likely to have been influenced visually by similar figures in William Blake's *Last Judgment* images, as they share a common stylized symmetry. Blake's depiction of romantic love in the afterlife owes much to his interest in Swedenborg. For a throrough discussion on these ideas see 'Heaven as a Union of Lovers', in Colleen McDannell and Bernhard Lang, *Heaven: A History* (London: Yale Nota Bene, 2001), pp. 223-57.

[51] *The Correspondence of Dante Gabriel Rossetti (2)*, 55.48, p. 66. Interestingly, both Brownings were also included in the PRB 'List of Immortals' (see n. 17).

[52] Richard Lines, 'Swedenborgian Ideas in the Poetry of Elizabeth Barrett Browning and Robert Browning', in *In Search of the Absolute: Essays on Swedenborg and Literature*, ed. Stephen McNeilly (London: Swedenborg Society, 2004), p. 23.

[53] *The Correspondence of Dante Gabriel Rossetti (2)*, 55.51, p. 69.

[54] Ibid., 55.58, p. 78.

[55] Richard Lines, 'Swedenborgian Ideas in the Poetry of Elizabeth Barrett Browning and Robert Browning', pp. 25-6.

[56] See entry on Anna Mary Howitt in Jan Marsh and Pamela Gerrish Nunn, *Pre-Raphaelite Women Artists* (London: Thames and Hudson, 1998), pp. 104-5.

[57] Mary Howitt, *An Autobiography*, ed. Margaret Howitt (London: Isbister and Company Limited, undated), p. 200.

[58] *The Correspondence of Dante Gabriel Rossetti (1)*, 54.29, p. 334.

[59] Dante Gabriel Rossetti, Copy of unpublished letter to Dr Wilkinson dated 25 January 1865 (Swedenborg Society Library Archives, K/141).

[60] *The Correspondence of Dante Gabriel Rossetti (2)*, 60.24 n. 8, p. 307.

[61] Ibid., 60.24, p. 306.

[62] Richard Lines, 'Henry Sutton: Poet, Journalist, and New Church Man', p. 41.

[63] *William Allingham's Diary 1847-1889*, ed. Geoffrey Grigson (London: Centaur Press, 2000), p. 68.

[64] Ibid., p. 373.

[65] See n. 60.

[66] The first reference to the subject of *Beata Beatrix* is in a letter from Rossetti to Ellen

Heaton dated 19 May 1863: 'I thought of a Dantesque subject which I have long meant to do […] This would be Beatrice seated by a sundial, the shadow of which should be falling on the hour of nine'. *The Correspondence of Dante Gabriel Rossetti (3): The Chelsea Years, 1863-1872, Prelude to Crisis, Volume I: 1863-1867*, ed. William E Fredeman (Cambridge: D S Brewer, 2003), 63.54, p. 51. William Michael Rossetti makes reference to this first version of *Beata Beatrix* as being 'about finished' in a diary entry of 27 January 1871 in *The Diary of W. M. Rossetti 1870-1873*, ed. Odette Bornand (Oxford: OUP, 1977), p. 41. This is why I have listed the production dates of the work as 1863-71. For a discussion of the painting and for information concerning the different versions, see 'Beata Beatrix: Scholarly Commentary', in *The Complete Writings and Pictures of Dante Gabriel Rossetti: A HyperMedia Research Archive,* ed. Jerome McGann at <http://www.rossettiarchive.org/docs/s168.raw.html>.

[67] Philip Hoare, *England's Lost Eden*, p. 206.

[68] William Michael Rossetti documented a selection of the seances, both public and private, that he and Rossetti attended from 1865 to 1868. There are several incidences of supposed contact with Lizzie recorded in the diary. For example on 12 November 1865 during a private seance at Rossetti's residence at 16 Cheyne Walk, Chelsea, and two further instances in which her name was spelled out and communication made: one on 4 January 1866 at a Mr Knightley's, Belvedere (William only present) and another on 25 February 1866 in the studio at Cheyne Walk at which Rossetti asks her spirit 'Are you now happy?'. William Michael Rossetti, *Séance Diary* (1865-8), UBC microfilm *Diaries of William Michael Rossetti*, Reel 3, series A.1.3 (Bodleian Library, Oxford).

[69] F G Stephens, 'Beata Beatrix by Dante Gabriel Rossetti', in *Portfolio: An Artistic Periodical*, vol. 22 (1891), p. 45.

[70] *The Correspondence of Dante Gabriel Rossetti (5), The Chelsea Years 1868–1872, Prelude to Crisis, Volume III: 1871–1872*, ed. William E Fredeman (Cambridge: D S Brewer, 2005), 71.43, p. 42.

[71] Emanuel Swedenborg, *The Interaction of the Soul and Body* (London: Swedenborg Society, 1996), §4.3, p. 7.

[72] Swedenborg, *Conjugial Love*, §42.2, p. 43.

[73] Ibid., §42.2, p. 44.

[74] Ibid., §42.2, p. 43.

[75] Ibid., §42.4, p. 44.

[76] Swedenborg, *The Interaction of the Soul and Body*, §6, p. 10.

[77] For the section of Dante's *Vita Nuova* in which Love holds a flaming heart, see Dante Alighieri, *The New Life*, tr. D G Rossetti (1861), ed. M Palmer (New York: The New York Review of Books, 2002), p. 6: 'And he who held her held also in his hand a thing that was burning in flames; and he said to me, *Vide cor tuum* ['Behold thy heart']'.

[78] *The Age of Rossetti, Burne-Jones & Watts: Symbolism in Britain 1860-1910*, p. 156.

[79] Swedenborg, *Conjugial Love*, §59.2, p. 66.

[80] Hazel Hutchison, 'Ideal homes: James, Rossetti, and Swedenborg's House of Life', printed herein, pp. 271-90.

[81] Swedenborg, *Arcana Coelestia* (1749-56), tr. J F Potts, rev. W O'Mant (London: Swedenborg Society, 1885), vol. XII, §10110, p. 114.

[82] See letter to Thomas Gordon Hake, 21 April 1870, in *The Correspondence of Dante Gabriel Rossetti (4), The Chelsea Years 1863–1872, Prelude to Crisis, Volume II: 1868–1870*, ed. William E Fredeman (Cambridge: D S Brewer, 2004), 70.110, p. 450.

[83] 'two blent souls' (Sonnet XIII, 'Youth's Antiphony', line 14, p. 175) and 'I am thine, thou'rt one with me!' (Sonnet III, 'Love's Testament', line 8, p. 165) in Dante Gabriel Rossetti, *Ballads and Sonnets* (Boston: Roberts Brothers, 1881).

[84] Ibid., p. 167, ll. 6-8.

[85] Swedenborg, *Conjugial Love*, §70, p. 72.

[86] Dante Gabriel Rossetti, *Ballads and Sonnets*, p. 202, Sonnet XL, 'Severed Selves', ll. 1-2.

[87] Ibid., p. 188, Sonnet XXV, 'Mid-Rapture', ll. 9-14.

[88] Ibid., p. 202, Sonnet XL, 'Severed Selves', ll. 6-7.

[89] Swedenborg, *Conjugial Love*, §§293-4, pp. 279-85.

[90] In this essay I have selected several of the major examples from Rossetti's oeuvre that indicate an influence of Swedenborgian ideas. There are also other works that can be seen as containing aspects of Swedenborgian theology and imagery, which I have not included here.

III. MYSTICISM

Swedenborg the mystic*

Czeslaw Milosz

T o speak of Swedenborg is to violate a Polish taboo that prohibits writers from taking a serious interest in religion. The penalty is already preordained in the form of the parroted cliché: 'He succumbed to mysticism'. Naturally you were always free to declare yourself a Catholic writer, but only at the risk of being classified as 'lowbrow', on a level with outdoor or juvenile literature— with a literature, moreover, politically allied with the Right. As I scan the terrain of twentieth-century Polish literature, I fail to find a single poet or prose writer who escaped the label, with the possible exception, and then only marginally, of Jerzy Liebert. [1] There was Marian Zdziechowski, [2] more a professor than a writer; the little-known Ludwik Koninski, [3] something of a private thinker; and Bolesław Micinski, [4] who might have made a contribution if he had not died at an early age. This is not to say that quasi-religious persuasions did not enjoy popularity, especially among the modernists of Young Poland [5] and their descendants. But anyone extensively read in Christian theology and philosophy ran the risk of being reproved for intellectual and verbal laxity. One exception was the poet, Bolesław Lesmian, [6] who, as a 'disinherited mind' [7] outside the Judaeo-Christian orbit, only confirms my thesis.

But for my readings of the French Catholic philosophers, I might have remained insensitive to this side of Polish literature. And but for my interest in the work of Oscar Milosz, I would be largely uninformed about Swedenborg. Nor, I hasten to add, are the French, despite what Balzac and Baudelaire may have borrowed from Swedenborg, the best informed, either. Oscar Milosz read Swedenborg in English; so, too, my years spent in America, where Swedenborg readers and admirers outnumber those in other countries, have given me easier access to the Royal Counsellor's work and to the secondary literature on him.

Let me explain in advance why Swedenborg merits scrutiny. It is a fact that the greatest poets and prose writers have borrowed liberally from him. The list is long: first Blake, as his direct spiritual descendant, then Goethe, a fervent reader of Swedenborg (as was Kant!), followed by Edgar Allan Poe, Baudelaire, Balzac, Mickiewicz,[8] Słowacki,[9] Emerson (who placed him between Plato and Napoleon in his temple of the great), and Dostoevsky, in whose work we find resonances of Swedenborg in the character of Svidrigailov and in the sermons of Father Zosima. Such obvious fascination must have its reasons. Nor are the reasons unrelated to the peculiarities of the age in which Swedenborg exerted an influence through his work. That work has attracted through the mysterious power of an imagination capable of summoning it to life. As I hope the following will show, it occupies a special place, one which I would classify as 'borderline disinherited'.

Swedenborg was widely read throughout the late eighteenth and early nineteenth centuries. A Russian version of *Heaven and Hell* appeared in the 1860s.[10] Today Swedenborg's coffin in the Uppsala cathedral probably says little to tourists, other than as a tangible sign of tribute paid one of Sweden's great sons. If his work is read by scholars and men of letters, then it is from a sense of professional duty—in conjunction with their research on Blake, for example. Circumstances (i.e., Oscar Milosz) have made me an exception, though I sense a Swedenborg revival currently in the making, not necessarily for reasons of which he himself would have approved: the Swedenborg phenomenon, in effect, belongs to those enigmas which, if ever solved, would shed light on the laws of the human imagination in general.

*

Emanuel Swedenborg (1688-1772) was a prominent scientist whose works on geology, astronomy, and physiology purportedly contain a wealth of brilliant discoveries. This immediately poses an obstacle, as it would take a historian of science to properly assess his achievement. No less an obstacle is posed by the later work dating from his illumination, at which time he began work on a new interpretation of Christianity, a multi-volumed work running into thousands of pages, and all composed in a pedantic Latin. To read it whole (so far I have explored only a fraction of it) is to wander through a hall of mirrors arousing a range of conflicting emotions: mockery abruptly turns to awe, rejection to assent and vice versa, curiosity to strenuous boredom, and acceptance to categorical rejection. One thing is certain: any suspicion of quackery is refuted by the man's exemplary life, by the conscientious way in which he discharged his civic and professional duties (as a member of the Royal Mining Commission), by his meticulous work habits, by his veracity and amiability. Emerson, unstinting in his praise of Swedenborg, alludes to mental illness as the price paid for transgressing one's allotted role, as if to remind us that there is no genius without a flaw. The twentieth century, as I said, has been neglectful of Swedenborg. Karl Jaspers devoted a chapter to him in his work on schizophrenia, along with chapters on Hölderlin, Van Gogh, and Strindberg; yet he is cautious in his diagnosis because Swedenborg's pathological symptoms became manifest only during the years of his crisis, 1743-5, after which he led a tranquil life, free of any strife or discord—unlike Hölderlin, for example.

Certain commonplaces about Swedenborg, to which he himself gave impetus, are unavoidable, and I shall begin with these. By his own testimony, he received from God the power to transport himself to the extramundane world, and daily inhabited both realms for the duration of some thirty years. As a record of his other-worldly journey, as a vision of a tripartite world in the beyond, his work stands, after *The Divine Comedy*, as the second such enterprise in Western civilization. Although Swedenborg, the son of a Swedish clergyman (to whom he owed the name Emanuel, meaning 'God is with us'), was equally critical of both Lutheran and Catholic theology, he was sufficiently Protestant to omit purgatory. His three realms are heaven, hell, and midway between the two the 'spirit world', the place to which all go after death, and where gradually, themselves unaware, their will's true 'intention' (their love) is revealed, whereby a person either ascends to heaven or descends to hell. Stylistically, Swedenborg's realism evokes comparison with the early English novel, e.g., Defoe's *Robinson Crusoe*, which, considering the work's subject matter, now and then has its comic effects; to quote Emerson, Swedenborg's other-worldly inhabitants often remind us more of elves and gnomes. The strictly reportorial passages, what the author called *Memorabilia*, lend validity to the question posed by Oscar Milosz, a careful Swedenborg reader, in the margin of his copy of *The True Christian Religion* (the English translation of *Vera Christiana Religio*), preserved in his private library: 'The work is composed of two parts: the one revealed in the *spiritual world*, the other constructed in the form of a theological-philosophical system in the *natural world*. Which came first? Did the memorabilia come before or after the system? Was the work born of a vision or an idea? Because these 'memorabilia' have the look of inventions designed as an *allegorical proof*.

A question that goes straight to the heart of the matter, but one which defies a definitive answer. As a writer, Swedenborg was susceptible to eighteenth-century conventions, among others to the authenticating device of the pseudo-memoir or pseudo-diary, the 'manuscript found in the tree trunk', etc. In other words, the role of convention in Swedenborg's artistic rendering of theological material cannot be neglected, particularly as the meticulous documenting of theological disputes in the other world serves an expressly utilitarian aim: the losers in these debates correspond to the author's earthly adversaries. On the other hand, the imaging of ideas antedates the actual process of writing. The crisis of 1743-5, profuse in visions and conversations with the dead, occurred in the absence of any system, which had yet to be elaborated; later the visions kept pace with the painstakingly composed volumes that followed in succession. That crisis might well be attributed to the fierce pressures exerted on a scientific mind suddenly caught in its own trap. Only after his previous intellectual framework had been demolished by dreams and visions did Swedenborg free himself from that trap.

Like the girl in Mickiewicz's 'The Romantic',[11] he suddenly had a vision of the extrasensory world; but the savants with their 'eyes and lenses' had more trouble with Swedenborg, who was after all one of the family, than with a village maid. If the girl of the poem could become so crazed by the loss of her Johnny as to converse with the dead, Swedenborg's visions were born of horror at a loss so immense as to affect all men. The illiterate and even the semi-illiterate, only dimly conscious of the incipient intellectual crisis, were unresponsive to Swedenborg's forebodings. But as a member of Europe's scientific elite, Swedenborg was well aware that nature, perceived as a system of mathematical relations, had begun to usurp God in the minds of the educated. The universe was construed as an infinity of absolute, void, Newtonian space (even the Cartesian vision of a space filled with 'vortices' had been rejected), whose rotating planets and planetary systems overwhelmed the mind by their infinite profusion: thus was man's dethronement, a process begun with the death of the geocentric theory, made complete. Yet the Christian religion had posited an Earth-centred, Man-centred universe. Religious faith was now professed not with the heart but with the lips only; whereas Swedenborg, and here he remained loyal to the age of reason, held that a man could not assent to anything which was contrary to reason. Christianity, in his opinion, was entering its final phase. And it was given to him, Swedenborg, at this critical moment for the human race, to see and bear witness to the truth. He had been anointed, no more and no less, as a Messiah announcing a new era.

Swedenborg's private diary dating from the years of his crisis, the only work he ever wrote in Swedish (and hence inaccessible to me), purportedly testifies to the strongly erotic character of his dreams and visions. The author, it is argued, being a pious and abstemious man, yet possessed of a powerful sensuality, became perturbed through habitual self-denial, as many ascetics have been known to do. Granted, Swedenborg's images are tinged with eroticism; granted that at the centre of his doctrine is an 'angelic sexuality'. But such fashionable explanations fail to do the work justice, for his theological works specifically address those things with which he was genuinely, dramatically engaged and which he wrote against.

'Against': that is the key. After the revelation of his mission, Swedenborg began issuing one volume after another, publishing them under his own imprint. Among men of science, especially in the smaller countries like Sweden, Latin was still in common use; Swedenborg's contemporary, the naturalist Linnaeus, wrote in Latin. But a reading public of enlightened, philosophically minded ladies and salon wits, either ignorant of Latin or deficient in it, now had to be addressed in the new international language of French. Swedenborg strove neither for immediate effects nor for public acclamation. Destined to close one era and open another, he was content to record his message in print, in the belief that his books would eventually triumph over the ideas of the age.

His ambition was nothing less than a major defence of Christianity, and it was addressed to atheists and deists as much as to the theologians. A hundred years before him, the mathematician Blaise Pascal, accurately intuiting the course which the European mind would take, set himself a similar task. A brief life cut short his apologia. The notes that have survived are known today as *Les pensées*. Pascal's reflections were centred on man as understood by humanists reared on the ancient philosophers. If, as the humanists argued, man was such a rational creature, such an integral part of the cosmic scheme, then mankind could dispense with revelation and biblical religion was rendered superfluous. By contrast, Pascal showed that man, that 'thinking reed', because of the strange pairing of opposites inherent in him, was distinct from every other living creature and alien to the galactic wastes; that he alone was endowed with consciousness and yet, because of nature, the animal part resident in him, lacking in self-governance and self-sufficiency. There is in Pascal a kind of Manichaean distrust of nature and the things of 'this world' which has made him a hero in the eyes of the pessimists, of those who later, in an era proclaiming the intrinsic good of the 'noble savage', responded with a mordant irony. Pascal's defence of Christianity is thus waged in anthropocentric terms, asserting the 'anti-naturalness' of that unique phenomenon called consciousness.

Swedenborg proceeds in like fashion. But a common strategy should not impel us to search for a shared style or sensibility. Tainted though he was by Jansenism, Pascal remained at heart a Catholic, whereas Swedenborg was manifestly rooted in a traditional Protestantism. Swedenborg, moreover, to a far greater extent than is implied by the term 'mystic', was a true son of the Enlightenment (A N Aksakov, Swedenborg's nineteenth-century Russian translator, wrote a book entitled *Swedenborg's Rationalism*;[12] similarly, in his book on Swedenborg,[13] Henry James, Sr., father of William James, the author of *The Varieties of Religious Experience*, and of the novelist Henry James, underscores the rationalist bias of his doctrine). A love of symmetry, poise, and balanced constructions is one of the marvels of Swedenborgian syntax, from which it might be said that he embodies the 'spirit of geometry' much more than the mathematician Pascal.[14]

Swedenborg focused on man's exclusive property: the written word, both as it refers to the word revealed, Holy Writ, and to language generally. He applied himself to the decoding of words found in Scripture, distinguishing between three biblical layers: the literal, the spiritual, and the celestial. His search for meanings was for him a means of enriching human language, in the broadest sense, because it was a manifestation of man's foremost power: the imagination.

The universe was created exclusively for man, for human use. Not only Earth but myriads of planets are populated by humans. But the visible world is merely a reflection of the spiritual world, everything perceived on Earth by the five senses is a 'correspondence', an equivalent of a given state in the spiritual realm. I deliberately avoid such commonplaces as 'allegory' or 'symbol', whose field of reference is not always commensurate with that which Swedenborg assigned to the word *correspondentia*. That some flowers, beasts, trees, landscapes, human faces are beautiful and others ugly derives from the fact that they are spiritual values; shapes, colours, and smells, by supplying the stuff of human speech, fulfil a function analogous to human speech. Here Swedenborg is heir to the medieval, Platonic-inspired axiom 'as above, so below', which held that the whole of creation was one of the two languages in which God spoke to man—the other was Holy Writ. This would explain why Swedenborg felt so drawn to the artistic sensibility. In effect, his system constitutes a kind of 'meta-aesthetics', to borrow a term applied to that system by Oscar Milosz.

But that is not all. Swedenborg appeared at a time when the entire spatial order had been challenged, first by the debunking of the geocentric theory, later by theories expanding the interplanetary void to infinity. The Christian vision had traditionally relied on a heaven and hell endowed with space. As far back as the fourth century, St Gregory of Nyssa traced the vision of hell of his contemporaries to pagan sources and deplored the belief in a Hades-type of hell as unworthy of a Christian. Yet for centuries the Hades image persisted, and Dante's *Inferno* shows to what extent such images were contingent on a belief in Earth's primacy and the existence of subterranean realms.

Swedenborg restored that space. But how? To treat his immaterial world as spatial, to take every verb of motion literally ('he ascended', 'he went', 'he landed', etc.) would be to make of him an ordinary lunatic. The truth is immensely more complex. Those caves; those miasmic barrens; those slums where the damned knife each other in the streets; those subterranean concentration camps where the condemned slave day in and day out for their niggardly portion; those celestial houses with their luscious gardens, summer cottages, and arbours nestling in trees: whatever the landscape portrayed, it is always of the same physical texture as that visited by the little heroine of *Alice in Wonderland*. A man's internal condition, determined by the intention of his will (his love), assumes a form corresponding to his sensuous experiences of earth; an afterlife, in the objective sense, does not exist, only the good or evil in man. 'You are what you see': if nature is composed of signs, those signs now become liberated to form an alphabet of joy or anguish. Swedenborg's space is *internal*. The reports of his other-worldly odyssey figure rather as illustrations within the totality of the Swedenborgian *oeuvre*. But our imagination is continually locating things through juxtaposition, relative to something else, as evidenced in painting and poetry, or even in music where the sequence of sounds in time bears a decidedly architectural, sculptural quality. In this sense, internal space is not an illusion; on the contrary, it is more real than the material one governed by time and space. If Swedenborg did not glorify art, he nonetheless effected a shift from object to *subject*, whereby the role of the artist became exalted, something readily seized upon by Blake. Blake's faith in the eternal life of the Imagination implied, after all, that the workings of the imagination (those infusions of Holy Spirit) were a prefiguring, a promise of the imagination freed of the corporeal and of nature, by analogy with the creative process itself which was, in a very real sense, a 'release from the body'. Blake regarded Swedenborg's heaven and hell exactly as he did Dante's—as real *because* imagined.

If inner space is a purely subjective creation, it follows that the number of heavens and hells is legion. But since the moral order (defined as the will propelled either toward the Creator or to its *proprium*) is constant, all such spatial realms are relative to a centripetal Spiritual Sun (whose 'correspondence' is the sun of our planetary system). How Swedenborg can deduce from these subjective states a map of the beyond is not altogether clear: if 'you are what you see', on what does he base his topography? Would not each realm be possessed of its own? Not necessarily. True, the damned see everything in distorted perspective, but he who dwells in truth, as Swedenborg did, charts with his infallible compass the land of visions where space is space only by analogy. That land, as implied by the words 'sublime' and 'base', is vertically structured. The closer the proximity to God, manifested as the Spiritual Sun, the higher the celestial realm occupied. Midway lies the 'spirit world', which is so analogous to the terrestrial one that newcomers are hardly aware they have died. And hell below. Swedenborg then reveals a remarkable secret—namely, that heaven, the sum of myriads of personal heaven projections, is Man-shaped. The universe was created that heaven might be tenanted with spirits from countless planets and planetary civilizations (except for the saved and the damned, Swedenborg did not recognize angels or devils).

Here a serious misconception must be revised. Without enumerating what Towianski [15] and the Polish Romantics borrowed from Swedenborg, such pronouncements as 'all is fashioned by and for the Spirit, nothing serves a fleshly purpose'—this culled from Słowacki—read like a Swedenborgian maxim. [16] Yet, despite certain surface similarities, Słowacki's is a vastly different sensibility. Odd as Swedenborg's vision may appear, his sentences are perfectly structured, and one has only to grasp the thread of his argument to arrive at a coherent whole. If our Polish taboo ('He succumbed to mysticism') was initially invoked by the Positivist intelligentsia in reaction to Słowacki's philosophical writings and to other works of a similar vein, it can be faulted only with a lack of discrimination. Słowacki's philosophical prose has a distinctly hallucinatory quality to it and, despite occasional moments of grandeur, is frankly unreadable. The Romantics (with the exception of Blake)—and not only Polish—misinterpreted Swedenborg's 'spirituality', which is why Balzac's *Séraphîta*, a work which purports to be an exposition of the Swedenborgian doctrine in fictive form, could become a perversion of it. But Słowacki went even further in his pursuit of the 'spiritual'. His retelling of the sin of Adam and Eve (conveyed in a letter to J N Rembowski), perhaps unique in the history of the treatment, is illustrative: as interpreted by Słowacki, Adam and Eve were so much of the spirit as to dispense with eating; by persuading Eve to eat the apple, the tempter bound them to the life of matter.

Far from being ethereal, Swedenborg, that loyal subject of his Royal Majesty engaged with the mundane affairs of his fellow citizens, construed brotherly love in an active sense, as utility (*usus*); that is, he exalted man's earthly duties toward society—its enrichment by tradesmen and merchants, its technological advancement by science, its defence by soldiers in times of peril. His heaven, populated by communities bound by shared earthly dispositions, was a realm of unceasing 'action' where love of the good was manifested solely as *usus*. Since 'proximity' in analogous space is defined in terms of shared tastes, spirits congregate on the basis of their wills' deepest 'intention'. Swedenborg's more realistic passages derive from the axiom 'as above, so below', which remains incomplete so long as it is not inverted—'as below, so above'.

In school I was taught that in his mystical phase Słowacki combined the Lamarckian theory of evolution with the primacy of the soul—'bowed by the body's travail' [17] —that he 'spiritualized' it, in effect, just as somewhat later he would season it with a belief in metempsychosis. His *Genesis from the Spirit*, which I read in those days, must certainly have had its effect on my intellectual growth, premised, like that of my contemporaries, on the tacitly assumed postulates of the natural sciences. Słowacki was like a foretaste of Teilhard de Chardin—read much later—whose muddle-headedness I cannot abide. Today I am of the opinion that Słowacki has nothing to offer the religiously minded person, that he has inflicted great harm by ensuring in Poland a disaffection with religious thought in general, for which even the language would seem poorly suited: under Słowacki's pen and those of other messianists, the language turns flaccid, mushy.

The tension between Swedenborg's pedestrian style, stripped of poetic fancy, and the substance of his message conceals a richness difficult to name, before which we stand as before Escher's geometric drawings exploiting the paradoxes of three-dimensional space. Despite his cloying repetitiveness and manifold tautologies, Swedenborg makes profitable reading, even if one is in no way moved to become a Swedenborgian. I share Oscar Milosz's antipathy for Polish messianism, pre-eminently that of Słowacki, which he characterized by such epithets as *fadasse* (sickly) and *désossé* (boneless). I can well understand, too, why he respected Swedenborg, in which he would not lack for company—even if born much earlier.

*

For the theologian Swedenborg, the prophecy contained in the Apocalypse had come to pass in his own time. Of the Christian Church all that was left was 'the abomination of desolation'. The decline of religion—the mouthing of words in which the heart no longer believed—was, in his opinion, facilitated by two doctrines. The first, the doctrine of the Trinity, adopted by the Council of Nicaea in 325 as a weapon against the heresy of Arius, constituted an enigma resolved only by the mind's imposition of three gods instead of one. Christianity, in effect, became polytheistic, the consequences of which would not become apparent until centuries later. Although a rationalist, Swedenborg refused to concede the Arian argument that Christ was a man only. On the contrary, there was no other God but the God-man, Creator of heaven and earth, who was born of a virgin, died, and was resurrected. Christ, in other words, was not *consubstantialis* (the term proposed at the Council by Emperor Constantine) with the Father but was himself Father; hence that 'Divine Human' signifying the Creator of the universe. This was the great secret revealed to Swedenborg: our heavenly Father is a man, heaven has a human shape. The second fatal doctrine was the act of redemption by which Christ obtained God's forgiveness for the sins of mankind. From Mary, Christ received a human, that is, sinful nature, and His life was a succession of temptations overcome, thanks to which human nature became divinized. Here Swedenborg was challenging the Catholics, for whom Christ's human nature was without sin, and the Lutherans, who professed that man was saved by faith alone, that salvation was made possible through Christ's bloody atonement. The fallacy of both doctrines, it would appear, lay in the way in which they interfered with a decidedly anthropocentric vision of Godmanhood (the God-man and human nature divinized).

Human will is free. But man is unmitigatedly evil and by himself can only effect evil. Whatever good he does is a result of divine 'influx' (Swedenborg avoids the term 'grace'), which he is free to accept or reject. Swedenborg's cosmology and ethics are built around two correspondences: fire equals love, light equals truth. Christ-God is a trinity in the sense that fire and light, which are correlative, are expressed in action. Man is saved when he concedes that by himself he is incapable of love and truth; doomed when he ascribes that ability to his own *proprium*. Of particular note is Swedenborg's pessimistic critique of human nature in combination with his defence of free will. Being quintessentially a man of the eighteenth century, he rejects the will-impairing effects of original sin. In his allegorical reading of the Book of Genesis, Adam and Eve are symbolic not of our first parents (primordial man lived in a state of bestiality) but of the first Church (or civilization). There have been four such Churches, as foretold in the biblical prophecy of Daniel and as symbolized in the Greek legend of the four ages: golden, silver, bronze, and iron. Each Church had its revelation: God revealed in human form, God as the 'angel of Jehovah', as voice, and as fire. The fall of the first civilization, when man ascribed to himself the power to do good, broke the bond between God and man, thus ending the Golden Age, which rupture signalled the first of hell's victories and wreaked the flood. The next civilization—or Church—also had its revelation, to which the Bible makes allusion (in the 'Books of Yasher'). The third was that of Israel. The human race grew in wickedness and the powers of hell became so powerful as to threaten heaven. Swedenborg's afterlife, as I said, is 'action', movement in analogous space. No one is condemned by God to hell, each dwells in the company and setting of his choice, according to his will's intention. The damned, when surrounded by the saved, suffer revulsion and anguish. (A similar hell is painted by Father Zosima in *The Brothers Karamazov*, and the following words, attributed to Zosima, bespeak familiarity with Swedenborg: 'On earth, indeed, we are as it were astray, and if it were not for the precious image of Christ before us, we should be undone and altogether lost, as was the human race before the flood. Much on earth is hidden from us, but to make up for that we have been given a precious mystic sense of our living bond with the other world, with the higher heavenly world, and the roots of our thoughts and feelings are not here but in other worlds'.)[18] Swedenborg believed the 'higher'

331

world to be so threatened that, if not for Christ-God's descent to earth, mankind would have suffered annihilation. Of all the planetary civilizations, only Earth was deemed worthy of the Incarnation, making it a privileged planet. To the fourth, the Christian Church, was announced the Second Advent and those events prophesied by St John. Swedenborg posited the year 1757 as the year of the Last Judgment, assigning a strictly allegorical meaning to the Apocalypse. The Judgment took place in the other world; neither Earth nor mankind would come to an end, because the higher world could exist without mankind as little as mankind could exist without the higher world. The Second Advent had also come to pass, not literally but as the truth incarnated in Swedenborg's writings, which became the foundation of a Fifth Church, the New Jerusalem. Swedenborg thus transposed the biblical story of Creation and 'the final things' to a purely spiritual plane. His theology admits neither to the resurrection of bodies, with the exception of Christ, nor to the other extreme, that of metempsychosis. Only through misinterpretation, therefore, could he have been invoked by the Polish Romantics.

Swedenborg's theology, as just outlined, betrays its heretical affinities. The historian of religion will easily recognize certain centuries-old motifs. The Creator's manlike divinity evokes the Gnostic and Manichaean image of a Primal Man in heaven, conceived by the King of Light, and the Adam Kadmon of the Jewish Kabbalists. The four ages are resonant of the ubiquitous myth of Paradise, fusing a cyclical view of history with a strongly chiliastic bias.

Here I question the value of such a summary and wonder whether it is not merely a waste of time. Swedenborg's theological system, however important to its author, fails to explain why Oscar Milosz called him a second Faust, a Faust without a personal tragedy. By summarizing it, perhaps I am intent on doing justice to its most implausible ideas, which, given the large number of prominent figures who confided in their own messianic destiny, need not astonish. Swedenborg's importance lies not in his theology so much as in his effort to decode the Bible, to build a 'verbal space', as Osip Mandelstam once said of Dante. [19] Though non-poetic in style, Swedenborg's work, no less than *The Divine Comedy*, is a vast honeycomb built by the bees of the imagination and obeying a certain imperative. A man must abide somewhere, a physical roof over his head is not enough; his mind needs its bearings, its points of reference, vertically as well as horizontally. Do we not speak of *edifying* readings?

Moreover, if the Last Judgment meant that in the 'spirit world' there was to be a strict distinction—hitherto increasingly effaced—between salvation and damnation, then we should have no quarrel with the year 1757. It coincides with the rise of the Industrial Revolution, along with its concomitant, that of spiritual disinheritance. In his rescue operation, Swedenborg drew on certain religious attitudes from an earlier phase of civilization, one not without analogy to our own: the Hellenized part of the Roman Empire in the first centuries after Christ. In his study of Gnosticism,[20] Hans Jonas attributes the success of gnosis—the attainment of salvation through secret knowledge—to, among other factors, the disintegration of the *polis* and the atomization of the masses under imperial rule; to the decline of a religion and philosophy which perceived the world as an order, a *kosmos*; to an inchoate vision, in other words, of man's alienation from the universe. A God responsible for such an evil world was either not good or not omnipotent; the Gnostics chose the good God, who was now transformed into the Other God, the Unknown God, while the Jehovah of the Old Testament received the title of a lower demiurge. Earlier figures had sought a covenant between man and the Other God, a pre-cosmic covenant against the world ruled by the Archon of Darkness. The concept of a Primal Man, found in the second-century Gnostic, Valentinus of Alexandria, and later taken up by the religion of Mani in the third century, was essentially aimed at humanizing the very premise of existence. I quote:

> To the Gnostics the existence of a pre-cosmic god 'Man' expressed one of the major secrets of their Knowledge, and some sects even went so far as to call the highest godhead himself 'Man': 'This [according to one branch of

333

the Valentinians] is the great and hidden secret, that the name of the power that is above all things, the forebeginning of everything, is Man.' [21]

In Gnostic and Manichaean speculation, Christ is sometimes cast as the suffering and pre-cosmic Man. Swedenborg's Christ is God the Father-Man incarnate, a vision that nonetheless betrays nothing of Docetism, the doctrine which held that Christ only appeared to be born, to lead a corporeal life, to die and be resurrected.

The eighteenth-century cosmos: myriads of planets spinning around in an infinite and absolute space. Easily said; but let us try to imagine, to locate our home in that infinity. Swedenborg understood that the only refuge lay in assigning a central place to the Divine Human. And what distinguished the human if not the mind and imagination—the *inner* life of a subject, in other words—whence that other world, the subjective, which was not only parallel to the objective world but was its reason and purpose. Here we have a vague foreglimpse of Hegel and the makings of an anti-Hegelian vaccine. It was, after all, the rational premise of existence, which in Hegel would obtain to the self-conscious element in man, that laid the foundation for an atheistic Prometheanism. Dostoevsky ('Vsyo v budushchem stoletii'—'All depends on the next century') [22] would be right in reducing the dilemma of the age, both his own and the succeeding one, to a choice between the God-man and the Man-god. [23] Those in the 'exact' sciences might reply, along with Jacques Monod, that religion, whether religion proper or such pseudo-religions as Hegelianism and Marxism, is a relic of the 'animistic tradition', and that 'objective truth' can assent to one as little as to the other of the two warring sides. Alas, on closer scrutiny, 'scientific truth' is not what it once was, either.

A Swedenborgian concept that had great appeal for the Romantics was the *arcanum* of marriage, which referred as well to the marriage of spirits since, in Swedenborg's heaven, angels were of both sexes. The literature of Romanticism has accustomed us to interpreting his 'bonding of souls' in an asexual way, even though Swedenborg advocated rather a purified sexuality. For Swedenborg, earthly marriage was a 'correspondence' central to Christianity, corresponding to the celestial marriage between love (*Amor*) and wisdom (*Sapientia*). Hence, too, the importance attached by him to a monogamous union, which, when it yields a harmony of the spiritual-carnal, is heaven on earth. This is the theme of Swedenborg's *Delitiae Sapientiae de Amore Conjugiali* (*The Delights of Wisdom Concerning Conjugial Love*), which expounds a fundamental interpretation of the Adam and Eve relationship, in particular of those aspects illuminating the spiritual differences between man and woman. I shall return to this later, because Swedenborg's *arcanum* of marriage provides a key to some of Oscar Milosz's work.

NOTES

* This article is from chapters 26 and 27 of Czeslaw Milosz's book *The Land of Ulro* (New York: Farrer, Strauss & Giroux Inc, 1985), tr. Louis Iribarne. The version here first appeared in *Temenos*, 4, 1983.

[1] Jerzy Liebert (1904-31) was a poet who studied literature at Warsaw University.

[2] Marian Zdziechowski (1861-1938) was a philosopher, philologist, historian and professor at the Jagiellonian and Vilnius Universities.

[3] Karol Ludwik Koninski (1891-1943). Literary critic, short story writer, and journalist. He edited the anthology of folk literature *Pisarze ludowi* (Peasant Writers) (1938), whilst his stories include *Straszny czwartek w domu pastora* (A Horrible Thursday in the Pastor's House) (1939).

[4] Bolesław Micinski (1911-43) was a philosopher, essayist and poet.

[5] Young Poland (also known as Moderna) was a modernist and neo-Romantic period in Polish art, literature and music roughly spanning 1890-1918.

[6] Bolesław Lesmian or Lesman (*c*. 1878-1937). Poet and artist. His verse includes *Łaka* (The Meadow) (1920) and *Napój cienisty* [Shadowy Drink] (1936).

[7] See Erich Heller's *The Disinherited Mind: Essays in Modern German Literature and Thought* (Cambridge: Bowes & Bowes, 1952).

[8] Adam Bernard Mickiewicz (1798-1853). Romantic poet whose works *Dziady* (1823-

32) and *Pan Tadeusz* (1834) bear traces of Swedenborg's influence.

[9] Juliusz Słowacki (1809-49). Romantic poet and author of *Godzina Mysli* (*The Hour of Thought*) (1833) and *Genezis z Ducha* (*Genesis from the Spirit*) (1844).

[10] Translated with a Preface by A N Aksakov (Leipzig: Wagner, 1863).

[11] Mickiewicz, 'Romantycznose' (1822), tr. W H Auden in *About the House* (New York: Random House, 1965), pp. 66-8.

[12] Alexandr Nikolaevich Aksakov, *The Rationalism of Swedenborg: A Critical Analysis of His Teachings on the Holy Writ* (Leipzig, 1870).

[13] Henry James, Sr., *The Secret of Swedenborg: Being an Elucidation of his Doctrine of the Divine Natural Humanity* (Boston: Fields, Osgood, & Co., 1869),

[14] Cf. Pascal, *Pensées*, no. 21.

[15] Andrzéj Towianski (1799-1878), Polish philosopher and mystic.

[16] Cf. Słowacki, *Genesis from the Spirit*, tr. with a commentary by K Chodkiewicz (London: Col. K Chodkiewicz, 1966), no. 12, p. 28.

[17] Słowacki, 'Odpowiedz na Psalmy pryszlosci' ('Reply to the Psalms of the Future') (written 1845, publ. anon. 1848).

[18] Fyodor Dostoevsky, *The Brothers Karamazov*, tr. Constance Garnett (Chicago: William Benton/Encyclopaedia Britannica, Inc., 1952), book VI, ch. 3, p. 168.

[19] Osip Emilyevich Mandelstam (1891-1938), Russian poet and essayist. For 'verbal space' see Mandelstam's 'Conversations about Dante', in *The Collected Critical Prose and Letters*, tr. and ed. Jane Gray Harris (London: Collins Harvill, 1991), p. 406.

[20] Hans Jonas, *The Gnostic Religion: The Message of the Alien God and the Beginning of Christianity* (Boston: Beacon Press, 1958).

[21] Jonas, *The Gnostic Religion*, p. 217. The square brackets are supplied by Jonas.

[22] Dostoevsky, *The Unpublished Dostoevsky: Diaries and Notebook*, tr. A Bayes and C Froffer, vol. II, notebook ix (1875-6), p. 133.

[23] Cf. Dostoevsky, *Devils*, tr. Michael R Katz (Oxford and New York: Oxford University Press, 1992), part 2, ch. 1, p. 251.

Jacob Boehme, Emanuel Swedenborg and their readers

Ariel Hessayon

Behmen and Swedenborg saw that things were representative.
—Ralph Waldo Emerson, *Representative Men* (1850)

I n his lecture series on six European 'great men' who served as the strongest lenses 'through which we read our own minds', the American author and Transcendentalist Ralph Waldo Emerson (1803-82) chose Swedenborg to represent the mystic—that class of persons concerned with 'the world of morals'. Emerson attached great importance to the 'moral sentiment' believing it, rather than institutional Christianity which he rejected, to be the basis of true religious thought. According to Emerson, Swedenborg's 'moral insight', 'correction of popular errors' and 'announcement of ethical laws' placed him among the 'lawgivers of mankind'. Boehme by contrast, he regarded as a poet, sage and mystic who, 'tremulous with emotion', listened 'awestruck with the gentlest humanity to the Teacher' whose lessons he conveyed. In his estimation, however, Swedenborg and Boehme both failed 'by attaching themselves to the Christian symbol, instead of to the moral sentiment, which carries innumerable christianities, humanities, divinities in its bosom'. But whereas Boehme was 'healthily and beautifully wise'—'notwithstanding the mystical narrowness and incommunicableness', Swedenborg was 'disagreeably wise' and for all his 'accumulated gifts' paralysed and repelled because he lacked poetic expression. [1] Though Emerson sometimes lumped them with Plato, Plotinus, George Fox, Madame Guyon and others, his occasional coupling of Swedenborg with Boehme is instructive. Both were raised in northern Europe as Lutherans, the sons of devout men. Both claimed to have experienced life-transforming visions which formed the basis of their extensive theological writings. Both were denounced by local clergymen but still attracted followers. Indeed, their deaths served only to increase the auras surrounding their life and teachings. Thus a legend took shape of Boehme as a simple, pious, barely literate artisan who had been given the gift of 'Universall knowledge' and shown the 'Centre of all Beings', while Swedenborg was held to have been a clairvoyant whose corpse—rather like that of the fabled Christian Rosencreutz—was discovered to be remarkably well preserved when first exhumed. [2]

This essay should be considered as part of a larger question: how were Continental millenarian, mystic and hermetic texts received and adapted in contexts for which they had not been intended? Its purpose is twofold—specifically to assess the extent of Boehme's and Swedenborg's influence by comparing the responses of English-speaking readers to their works. More generally, by focusing on continuities between early modern religious ideas and the Romantic imagination, it explores some of the routes through which certain beliefs traversed the Enlightenment. It will suggest that while the evidence for Swedenborg's detailed knowledge of Boehme and his interpreters is largely inconclusive, these writings nonetheless form an important context for appreciating the initial reception of Swedenborg's teachings. Mapping this readership also enables us to go beyond the boundaries of traditional Swedenborgian studies which have tended to emphasize denominational developments at the expense of wider contexts.

I. Swedenborg as a possible reader of Boehme and Boehme's interpreters

On 25 September 1766 Swedenborg wrote from Stockholm to Dr Gabriel Beyer (d. 1779), principal lecturer in theology at Gothenburg. Responding to Beyer's question concerning his opinion of Boehme's writings, Swedenborg declared 'I can pass no judgment, since I have never read them'. Following another query on the subject, probably from Beyer's brother-in-law, Swedenborg replied from Stockholm on 6 February 1767:

> My opinion concerning Boehme and L[aw?]. I have never read them, and I was forbidden to read dogmatic and systematic books in theology before heaven was opened to me, and this for the reason that otherwise unfounded opinions and notions might easily have insinuated themselves, which afterwards could have been removed only with difficulty. [3]

Swedenborg died at London on 29 March 1772. Eight years later it appears that while in London Augustus Nordenskjöld (1754-92), a prominent Scandinavian follower and alchemist, heard an anecdote which in 1782 was published by Antoine-Joseph Pernety (1716-96), a former Benedictine monk and French translator of Swedenborg:

> A certain man, a great admirer of Böhme, asked him in London, what he thought of that author. 'He was a good man', answered Swedenborg, 'it is a pity that some errors crept into his writings, especially with regard to the Trinity'. [4]

Although a nineteenth-century editor rejected Pernety's account because it contradicted what Swedenborg had stated to Beyer, the issue has not been satisfactorily resolved. Boehme himself claimed he had not received instruction from men or knowledge from reading books, but had written 'out of my own Book which was opened in me, being the Noble similitude of God'. Yet he also acknowledged having read the writings of 'very high Masters, hoping to find therein the ground and true depth'. [5] Similarly, Swedenborg's sources remain only partially researched because few students of philosophy have taken his ideas seriously since Immanuel Kant dismissed him as a fanatic in *Dreams of a Spirit-Seer* (1766). [6] Moreover, Swedenborg's voluminous output ranging from treatises on mathematics, longitude, anatomy, physiology, chemistry, cosmology, geology, metallurgy, mineralogy, philosophy and theology to journals recording his dreams and spiritual experiences, coupled with his inaccessible style—even in translation—has tended to discourage all but the committed specialist reader. Hence many older biographies, notably those by members of the church he never intended to found, are essentially a form of Protestant hagiography. His compatriots, however, have long recognized him as an extremely significant Swedish author and accordingly produced valuable critical studies like Inge Jonsson's *Visionary Scientist* (1971) and Lars Bergquist's *Swedenborg's Secret* (2005).

It is noteworthy that during the eighteenth century a number of Boehme's treatises were anonymously translated into Swedish, probably from Johann Wilhelm Ueberfeld's German edition *Theosophia Revelata* (1730). Apparently unpublished, these survive in manuscript.[7] Furthermore, *The Way to the Sabbath of Rest* by Thomas Bromley (1630-91), one of Boehme's foremost English interpreters, was anonymously translated into Swedish, probably from a German version issued at Amsterdam in 1685, as *Wägen till Hwilo-Sabbaten Igenom Siälens Fortgång uti Nya Födelsen* (1740). The censor Gustaf Benzelstjerna (1687-1746) had noted in his journal that when checking an auction catalogue on 13 May 1738 he had crossed out some writings—including two English works by Bromley.[8] Significantly, Benzelstjerna corresponded with another censor, Erik Benzelius the younger (1675-1743), Bishop of Linköping and Swedenborg's brother-in-law and patron.[9] Despite the censor's attention, Bromley's work spread among Pietist circles, particularly a small group gathered around the brothers Johan and Erik Eriksson in Stockholm. Benzelstjerna, however, appears to have been responsible for preventing the publication of 'Den sig nu brytande och fördelande himmelska skyn' (n.d.), an anonymous Swedish translation of *The Heavenly Cloud now Breaking*, probably from a German version issued at Amsterdam in 1694. This work was by another of Boehme's notable English interpreters, Jane Lead (1623-1704).[10]

According to his *Journal of Dreams* and from his own later account, Swedenborg's visions of the spiritual world began about autumn 1743, after arriving in Amsterdam on a journey from Stockholm. [11] Swedenborg may—or may not—have been familiar with the Swedish translations of Bromley, Lead and perhaps also Boehme that had begun circulating, but it is important to emphasize that while visiting Copenhagen in July 1736 he had remarked in his *Journal of Travel*:

> The town is infected with pietism or Quakerism. They are mad enough to believe that it is well pleasing to God to do away with oneself and others, of which many instances are on record. [12]

Yet a passage in *The Spiritual Diary* of 1747 concerning the deceased Benzelius and Benzelstjerna is equally revealing. Scratching his itchy anus during the night Swedenborg apprehended their irrational spirits, censuring them for proudly supposing they were wiser than others. [13]

Ten years after Swedenborg's demise his reputation was attacked in John Wesley's periodical *The Arminian Magazine*. He was charged with insanity and, in a reworking of a well-known if unsubstantiated statement about Isaac Newton, ploughing with '*Jacob Behmen*'s heifer, and that both in philosophy and divinity'. [14] The latter claim was echoed in 1789 by Christian Wilhelm Schneider, editor of a Weimar publication, who maintained that in his youth Swedenborg had read not only Boehme but also Jane Lead and John Pordage (1607-81), another leading English Behmenist. [15] The question was also discussed in the Swedenborgian periodical *The Intellectual Repository for the New Church* by Robert Hindmarsh (1759-1835), preacher, printer, bookseller and former pupil at Wesley's school. Remembering in September 1814 that 'many years ago' he had been asked his opinion, Hindmarsh recalled his unfavourable reaction and Boehme's ignorance concerning the notion of 'divine influx'. Boehme's style he pronounced 'singularly uncouth and obscure', whereas Swedenborg's was remarkable for its 'clearness, simplicity, and orderly arrangement'. Condemning Boehme's fallacies, he concluded that Swedenborg's doctrines were much superior, 'as the brightness of the sun is to the reflected light of the moon'. [16] By the time Alfred Roffe responded in the pages of the same periodical Hindmarsh had been dead several years. Observing that followers of both men were strongly partisan, Roffe carefully pointed out many striking '*agreements*' as well as '*differences*' between the two—particularly their understanding of the Trinity, free will, angelic and Adamic nature, and cosmology. Stressing their 'Individuality and Originality', he subsequently criticized the theosopher Christopher Walton (1809-77) for insisting that Swedenborg had been indebted to Boehme. In addition, he dismissed the charge that Swedenborg had stolen his 'mysticism' from Lead. [17]

Modern scholarship has done much to contextualize this relationship between the 'Teutonic Philosopher' and the 'Baron'. Thus Signe Toksvig and more recently Arthur Versluis have located Swedenborg's theological studies within an esoteric tradition that included Johann Georg Gichtel (1638-1710), a Dutch theosopher influenced by Boehme, Pietism and Kabbalah, whose massive *Theosophia Practica* (1722) could have been consulted by Swedenborg in the libraries of Leipzig, Dresden, Amsterdam or London. [18] Swedenborg's acquaintance with the writings of Boehme's principal eighteenth-century English interpreter William Law (1686-1761), however, remains very uncertain despite David Katz's assertion that there were obvious similarities. [19] More contentious still are Marsha Schuchard's far-fetched claims that Swedenborg was a crypto-Jacobite and Freemason who later associated with Samuel Jacob Hayyim Falk (*c*.1710-82), an alchemist and Kabbalist known as the 'Baal Shem of London'. These have usually been treated with caution—and rightly so, for her work generally rests on unsubstantiated connections made through uncritical readings of problematic evidence. [20] Even so, she has shown how Benzelius' extensive network facilitated Swedenborg's entry into learned circles in Hanover, Leipzig and London. [21] Inge Jonsson and his predecessor Martin Lamm have also established that Swedenborg referred to classical authors such as Aristotle, Cicero, Diogenes, Euclid, Homer, Ovid, Plato, Plutarch and Seneca. Moreover, Swedenborg disagreed with the Neoplatonist Plotinus about the freedom of the will and the origin of evil, but was deeply interested in Augustine whom he regarded as a Father of the Church of enlightened judgment. Among his near and immediate contemporaries Swedenborg was familiar with texts by the Italian anatomists Giorgio Baglivi, Giovanni Borelli and G B Cortesius as well as George Berkeley, Thomas Burnet, René Descartes, Hugo Grotius, Thomas Hobbes, John Locke, Nicolas Malebranche, Marcello Malpighi, Michel de Montaigne, Isaac Newton, Blaise Pascal, Christopher Polhem and Baruch Spinoza. In addition, he knew both Gottfried Wilhelm Leibniz's philosophical and scientific work and that of the mathematician Christian Wolff, which he excerpted copiously. [22] Indeed, an auction catalogue of Swedenborg's library and other evidence such as annotated books indicates that he possessed titles in English, French, German, Greek, Hebrew, Latin and Swedish with an emphasis on anatomy, chemistry, geometry, metallurgy, mineralogy and scriptural exegesis. [23]

In the same way, our understanding of the background of Swedenborg's early followers together with the fluid milieu they inhabited has been greatly enhanced. Swedenborg's influence on French society and literary culture has been discussed by Karl-Erik Sjödén and Lynn Wilkinson, while English Swedenborgians are the subject of a pioneering doctoral dissertation by Peter Lineham and an important article by Clarke Garrett which locates them within the 'mystical' Enlightenment. [24] Further studies, notably by E P Thompson and R W Rix, have tended to concentrate on Swedenborg's most famous early reader—William Blake. There is also Alfred Gabay's *The Covert Enlightenment* (2005), which synthesizes the secondary literature. [25] Accordingly, it is now known that some English Swedenborgians had been Methodists, others were Freemasons, and that several had interests in hermeticism, the Rosicrucians, alchemy, Kabbalah and Animal Magnetism. A few, like Swedenborg himself, were also mostly vegetarians. In addition, as its name indicated, the New Jerusalem Church (Revelation 21:1-2) established on 31

343

July 1787 linked separatist Swedenborgians with late eighteenth-century English millenarianism. That Behmenism comprised an aspect of this lively world should therefore come as no surprise.

II. The reception of Swedenborg's writings among English readers of Boehme and other 'Mystic authors'

In 1749 the first volume of Swedenborg's *Arcana Cœlestia* was printed by the Moravian John Lewis (d. 1755) and sold from his shop in Paternoster Row, Cheapside, as well as in the Strand and on Ludgate Hill. Seven more were to follow together with an additional treatise published by Lewis' son, Swedenborg's *De cœlo et ejus Mirabilibus* (1758). In his advertisement of the *Arcana* Lewis affirmed that the author—as yet unknown—was undoubtedly a 'very learned and great man' who did not seek financial gain. This prompted an enquiry from the 'ingenious and pious' Stephen Penny (d. 1780) of Dartmouth, who having read it with an 'extraordinary degree of pleasure', wondered if the 'illumined' writer was William Law. [26] As a young man Penny had been afflicted with smallpox, experienced financial hardship and mental distress. While in Rotterdam, however, he became acquainted with that 'man of wonders', Jacob Boehme. In a long letter to his sister written in August 1742 Penny recounted his spiritual growth, recalling that after browsing through an English extract and a number of epistles he progressed to a Dutch version of Boehme's first work *Aurora*, or 'Morning Light'. Despite its obscurity he became captivated with this 'enchanting' book, learning how to live in a manner that prepared him for the 'enjoyment of eternal happiness'. [27] Afterwards Penny corresponded with Law, informing him of some 'simple and illiterate sort' of people he knew in Dartmouth familiar with Boehme. Law in turn revealed his intention to undertake a new English translation of Boehme from the original German, together with the apparatus—notes and introductions—'to prepare and direct the reader in the true use of these writings'. [28] Although Law did not live to see the publication of the first volume of *The Works of Jacob Behmen* (1764), it was probably among 'the works of that wonderful man . . . the Teutonic Theosopher' contained in 'twelve different size volumes' in German and English bequeathed by Penny to a Bristol merchant. [29]

Law himself owned seven volumes of Swedenborg's *Arcana* and by April 1758 wanted one to complete the set—even though he would 'never go through them'. [30] He had also met, corresponded and eventually disputed with John Wesley, who subsequently published his critical *A Letter to the Reverend Mr. Law: Occasioned by some of his late writings* (1756). Wesley began by asserting that in 'Matters of Religion' he regarded 'no Writings but the inspired'. Boehme and a 'whole army of Mystic authors' were nothing compared with St Paul. Censuring Law for continually blending philosophy with religion, he concluded by imploring him:

> To spue out of your Mouth and out of your Heart that *vain Philosophy*, and *speak* neither higher nor lower Things, neither more nor less than the *Oracles of GOD*: To renounce, despise, abhor all the high-flown Bombast, all the unintelligible Jargon of the Mystics, and come back to the plain Religion of the Bible. [31]

Entries in Wesley's *Journal* and references in his other letters, notably one sent to the editor of the *London Chronicle* in September 1760, indicate the same attitude towards what he considered to be Boehme's unscriptural, irrational, contradictory, 'affectedly mysterious', 'most sublime nonsense'. [32] Furthermore, Wesley thought that studying Boehme confused his own followers. Indeed, during a conversation with Wesley in April 1761 the poet John Byrom (1692-1763) mentioned that six men had been expelled from the Methodists for 'reading Jacob Behmen and Mr. Law'. [33] Similarly, a former bearded vegetarian turned Methodist named Ralph Mather (1750?-1803) reported in November 1775 that a farmer and several poor people living at Leigh, Lancashire loved 'J. Behme and Wm. Law'. [34] Wesley feared that Mather had been 'almost driven out of his senses by Mystic Divinity' and after 'falling into mysticism and Quakerism' Mather admitted that he had been 'driven allmost to stark madness . . . For an hour one evening language is out of the question to describe the Glory that surrounds me'. [35] A reader of Jane Lead, he ultimately became an ordained Swedenborgian minister. [36]

Wesley appears to have become acquainted with Swedenborg's writings in February 1772, noting in his *Journal* that he thought him 'one of the most ingenious, lively, entertaining madmen that ever set pen to paper'. Further entries indicate that Wesley believed Swedenborg to be a pious, raving lunatic. [37] He said much the same in a contribution to *The Arminian Magazine* for May 1782, pronouncing his opinions absurd, 'blasphemous nonsense', 'the whims of a distempered imagination':

> Who illuminated, either *Jacob Behmen*, or *Emanuel Swedenborg* [. . .] Certainly it was, the spirit of darkness [. . .] And with what face can any who profess to believe the Bible, give any countenance to these dreamers [. . .] let the dreams of Baron *Swedenborg*, SINK INTO THE PIT FROM WHENCE THEY CAME. [38]

In December 1772 the Moravian minister Francis Okely (1719-94) wrote to Wesley regarding the 'riddle' of Swedenborg, agreeing that 'he speaks many great and important truths; and as certainly seems [. . .] to contradict Scripture in other places'. [39] An acquaintance of Byrom and Law, Okely began reading Swedenborg's *De cœlo et ejus Mirabilibus* in 1767. Finding its contents both 'new and surprising' he secured two interviews with the 'Latin author' in September 1771 after his co-religionists Mary Lewis (1703-91), widow of the printer John Lewis, and her printer son-in-law Henry Trapp (1739-90) persuaded Swedenborg of Okely's good character. During their first conversation, which moved from English to Latin and finally German, Swedenborg showed an aversion to the Quakers and expressed an equally low opinion of the Moravians, whose services at their chapel in Fetter Lane he had attended in 1744. He also censured Count Nikolaus Ludwig von Zinzendorf

(1700-60), benefactor of a Moravian community at Herrnhut, Saxony with whom Swedenborg claimed to have had 'several interviews' in the spiritual world. Although Okely thought Swedenborg had been insane when he began having visions of the spiritual world, he nonetheless bought another of his Latin treatises which he read carefully before sending him about January 1772 'a full written sheet' of what he was 'obliged to disapprove'. [40] In September 1781 Okely transcribed a review of Swedenborg's writings together with an account of him on the fly leaves of a volume containing three minor works by Swedenborg so that 'every impartial reader should see everything as well against as for the Baron's singular pretension'. [41]

As Ralph Mather observed, Okely professed 'great love to the mystics'. [42] Significantly, his translation from the German of a short book by Johanna Eleonora von Merlau (1644-1724), future wife of the Pietist Johann Wilhelm Petersen, was sold by Mary Lewis—as were several of Okely's own writings and his versification of select passages from the works of William Law. Moreover, Okely translated the *Evangelical Conversion* of the German Dominican and mystic Johannes Tauler (*c.* 1300-61), the *Divine Visions* of the Lutheran John Engelbrecht (1599-1642), and *A Faithful Narrative of God's Gracious Dealings with Hiel* with Hendrik Jansen van Barrefelt (d.1594?), a prominent member of the Family of Love who used the name Hiël (the 'Life of God'). In addition, Okely translated *Memoirs of the Life, Death, Burial and Wonderful Writings, of Jacob Behmen* (1780). He introduced these by affirming his belief that 'the Holy Scriptures, Jacob Behmen, Mr. Law, and every other *truly spiritual Writer*' possessed 'a sound and good Sense'—even on those occasions when it had not been granted him to penetrate it. Yet he also warned against putting Boehme's writings in the hands of people '*not properly disposed*' to them, for some readers had turned out 'real conceited *Enthusiasts*' while others had become perplexed to the point of '*Distraction*'. [43]

Another minister known for his 'attachment' to the 'Mystic Writers' was Thomas Hartley (*c.* 1709-84), rector of Winwick, Northamptonshire. [44] Twelve years before his death Hartley recalled that it was reading the works of William Law, 'the

Apostle of England', which 'first set him going'. [45] An acquaintance of Law and
Selina Hastings, Countess of Huntingdon, to whom he dedicated his *Sermons
on Various Subjects* (1754), Hartley praised Law's 'excellent Treatises' for their
usefulness, being well suited 'to promote Piety'. He particularly admired Law's
The Way to Divine Knowledge [...] *As preparitory to a new Edition of the
works of Jacob Behmen* (1752), declaring that 'the sacred Truths of our Religion
have their sure Foundations in the Depths of a Divine Theosophy'. [46] Indeed, it
is noteworthy that Hartley's *A Discourse on Mistakes concerning Religion,
Enthusiasm, Experiences* was reprinted with Thomas Bromley's *The Way to the
Sabbath of Rest* (1759). [47] Moreover, in *Paradise restored* [...] *To which is added,
a short defence of the mystical writers* (1764), Hartley admonished Wesley for
the 'obloquy' he poured on those 'excellent men', insisting that they taught the
way to 'Christian perfection' on 'surer principles' than Wesley had done. As for
that 'wonderful man *J. Behmen*', Wesley had never understood either him or his
'incomparable book' *Mysterium Magnum*. [48] In the same vein, Hartley chided
William Warburton, Bishop of Gloucester, for rashly censuring Boehme's writings
as nonsensical, maintaining that while some found them unintelligible, others
discerned profound meaning—at least in a 'great part' of them:

> But however this wonderful man came by his knowledge (for he was an
> original and no copy) it certainly was above the ordinary course of nature
> that God opened in his soul such an amazing treasure of wisdom, as taught
> him so many and great mysteries, brought him acquainted with the birth of
> all things, unlocked to him the secrets of universal nature, and enlightened
> his mind with such a deep knowledge of the Scriptures. [49]

Nonetheless, Wesley was dissatisfied with Hartley's vindication of the mystic writers,
bemoaning his 'vehement attachment' to them. [50] Afterwards Hartley conversed
and then corresponded with Swedenborg, requesting biographical information

to protect Swedenborg's reputation from possible slander as well as offering him a home in England should he need to leave Sweden because of religious persecution. [51] Hartley's interest in Swedenborg's teachings was shared by his acquaintance William Cookworthy (1705-80), with whom he had corresponded. An eminent Quaker minister, distinguished chemist, druggist and porcelain manufacturer of Plymouth, Cookworthy had probably read Swedenborg's *Arcana Coelestia* at the behest of his friend Stephen Penny. [52] Described as a sensible, learned man with an 'amazing Memory', Cookworthy conducted experiments on Devon cider and advocated using divining rods to discover metal, limestone and water hidden in the earth. [53] He was, moreover, a hearer of Methodist preachers and the millenarian May Drummond, whom he regarded as a 'strange phenomenon' of 'surprising Genius'. [54] Cookworthy may have rendered Béat Louis de Muralt's *The Divine Instinct, Recommended to Men* (1751) from French into English and also appears to have completed one of the earliest English translations of Swedenborg's works, *The Doctrine of Life* (1772). [55] His version of *A Treatise concerning Heaven and Hell* (1778) was revised and finished by Hartley, but published at Cookworthy's expense. [56] Hartley himself translated Swedenborg's *A Theosophic Lucubration on the Nature of Influx* (1770) and supplied a preface to Swedenborg's *True Christian Religion* (1781), which was rendered from Latin into English by John Clowes (1743-1831). [57]

A kinsman of Edward Byrom, the poet's son, Clowes accepted his cousin's offer of the rectory of the newly built St John's, Manchester in 1769. [58] Like John Byrom, Clowes read William Law's works with 'great diligence and much affection', finding that they 'tended to produce a pure, holy, and peaceable frame of mind'. [59] Though he came to disagree with Law's preference for a contemplative life and his ideas concerning the Trinity, the Scriptures and the human soul, it was through Law that Clowes became acquainted with several of the mystics. [60] According to his autobiography Clowes found much 'to love & to admire' in the writings of among others, Guyon, Engelbrecht, Hiël, Tauler, Boehme, Bromley and Lead. [61] Regarded as 'a pious solid young man', Clowes was introduced to Swedenborg's writings in 1773 by Edward Byrom's executor Richard Houghton (1732-80) of Liverpool. A friend of Wesley and correspondent of Hartley, Houghton recommended the work that Clowes would translate—*Vera Christiana Religio*. [62] In 1778 Clowes formed a Swedenborgian reading group at Whitefield near Manchester where, despite the doubts of older readers, word began circulating of 'a man who had been in heaven and hell, who had seen angels and devils, and talked of departed spirits'. [63] Four years later he began visiting a similar coterie at the cotton-spinning village of Bolton, Lancashire. This 'small society':

> who read the theosophic Behmen and the pious Law, caught the triumphant news; and though some with temerity and fear examined the invaluable treasure, yet others with avidity embraced the gift of heaven. [64]

In 1782 the Manchester Printing Society was established and soon began issuing Clowes' translation of Swedenborg's *Arcana* in monthly instalments and then half-volumes. [65] These activities were reported to Beilby Porteus, Bishop of Chester, who summoned Clowes only to dismiss him, as the latter recalled, with a warning to be 'prudent and circumspect in his conduct'. [66] Clowes chose to remain in the Church of England and even went to London in 1787 to dissuade separatist Swedenborgians from founding the New Jerusalem Church. [67] Although unsuccessful his influence in Manchester remained undiminished, for an ecclesiastical visitation article of 1804 referred to some townspeople:

> who are of a sober turn & who mind their Own Business & yet disregard public Worship, who talk of *Internal Worship* of the Kingdom of God within them &c such as mystics, Swedenborgians, readers and admirers of Jacob Behmen, Madame Bourignon, Madame Guion & others of that Class & of Rev Mr. Law. [68]

III. The reception of Swedenborg's writings continued— the Theosophical Society, Illuminati and New Jerusalem Church; Kabbalah, Freemasonry and Animal Magnetism

In 1764 the first volume of *The Works of Jacob Behmen* was printed for a publisher in Paternoster Row. Three more were to follow, as well as extracts from several of Boehme's treatises issued in 1769 by 'a gentleman retired from business'. Next appeared *A Compendious view of the grounds of the Teutonick Philosophy* (1770), printed by Mary Lewis of 1 Paternoster Row. Significantly, she also printed two early English translations of Swedenborg's works, *A Brief Exposition of the Doctrine of the New Church* (1769) and *A Theosophic Lucubration on the Nature of Influx* (1770)—which prompted a reviewer to class the author with Boehme, Law and 'other mystic writers'. [69] During the 1770s a further work appeared in English by Swedenborg, *A Treatise concerning Heaven and Hell* (1778). Printed in London by the Quaker James Phillips, it was also available in Bristol from the bookseller Thomas Mills (*c.* 1735-1820). [70] Formerly a clerk at one of the Countess of Huntingdon's chapels where he preached 'in the Methodist way', Mills had issued *The Life of Nicholas Lewis, Count of Zinzendorf* (1773), Boehme's *The Way to Christ Discovered* (1775) and *The Worship of God, in Spirit and in Truth* (1775) by Madame Guyon—an author admired by Wesley. In 1778 Mills became a Quaker, but continued selling English titles by Swedenborg until he was disowned in 1789. Maternal grandfather of the historian and essayist Thomas Babington Macaulay, Mills' grandchildren remembered him as 'an old man of imposing appearance, with long white hair, talking incessantly of Jacob Boehmen'. Moreover, Mills was acquainted with Francis Okely and sold his translations of writings by Engelbrecht and Hiël as well as his edition of *Memoirs of the Life, Death, Burial and Wonderful Writings, of Jacob Behmen* (1780). [71] These were published by James Lackington (1746-1815), a former Methodist.

After Wesley's death Lackington noted in his memoirs that many Methodist preachers and hearers had already gone over to the Swedenborgians, which he regarded as 'a proof of the fondness of mankind for novelty, and the marvellous, even in religious matters'. [72] In 1778 Lackington had entered into a short-lived partnership with John Denis (c. 1735-85), an oilman in Canon Street who provided the capital for the new firm's successful bookselling enterprise. Following the partnership's dissolution Denis, with his son and namesake, sold volumes in English and French by Swedenborg from their premises near Fleet Street. According to Lackington, the elder Denis' private library of old and valuable 'mystical and alchymical' books was the best of its kind 'collected by one person'. Denis was said to have 'prized these kinds of books' above everything and his son, who continued selling works by Swedenborg yet died a young man, shared this interest in the 'Occult Sciences'. [73] Denis' Catalogue of Ancient and Modern Books (1787) indicates the wide range of his father's collection, which listed nearly 8,000 titles including works by Swedenborg, Guyon, Boehme, Bromley, Pordage, Lead and Law. [74] One noteworthy item offered for sale was 'Two Epistles of Theaura John'. This was a volume bound in sheep leather containing four tracts by TheaurauJohn Tany (1608-59), self-proclaimed High Priest and Recorder to the thirteen Tribes of the Jews, and Boehme's most impenetrable interpreter. Each tract has been annotated by either the elder or younger Denis, whose monogram is inscribed at the beginning and end of the volume: 'J.D. cost 15 shillings 1768', 'J.D. 1789'. Furthermore, Tany's *THEAURAUJOHN His Aurora* (1651)—the title alluded to Boehme's most famous book—was commended for its 'intrinsic value' and praised as 'A great Treasure tho' in an earthen vessell'. [75]

While this volume was in the elder or younger Denis' possession it was consulted more than once over a period of several years by Henry Peckitt (1734?-1808), who made extensive extracts in a notebook from each of the four tracts. A former physician and apothecary, Peckitt lived in retirement at 50 Old Compton Street, Soho. Described as 'a very worthy character' and 'profound scholar', he was said to be an antiquarian, astronomer and lover of natural history with knowledge of Hebrew and Arabic. In the earlier part of his life Peckitt had studied the 'mystic writers', notably Boehme and Guyon, but this was superseded by his interest in Swedenborg. [76] He took an active part in the early affairs of the separatist Swedenborgian New Jerusalem Church and was President of its first general conference held at London in April 1789. Peckitt's 'most valuable' library consisted of thousands of volumes including a rare collection of mystical books. His house, however, was consumed by fire in June 1785 and an estimated full wagon load of books lost to the flames. [77] Among the surviving manuscripts were the second volume of Swedenborg's *Apocalypsis Explicata*, which was subsequently published at Peckitt's expense, and extracts from Swedenborg's *Diary*. This contains Peckitt's note, 'A certain Philosopher (1620) calls the Rainbow a certain reflex contra glance of the Sun'—a quotation from John Sparrow's translation of Boehme's *Mysterium Magnum*. [78] Also extant are a transcript of an account of Jane Lead's last hours and the excerpts from Tany's writings, which has Peckitt's concluding remark:

> I H:P: cannot rely upon this Mans declarations, as I do upon the honerable Emanuel Swedenborg's writings. [79]

Among Peckitt's Swedenborgian acquaintances was Benedict Chastanier (*c.* 1739-*c.* 1818), a Huguenot surgeon and pharmacist. Educated at the Catholic Collège de St Barbe in Paris and, after running away to escape their 'savage persecution', at the Hôtel Dieu, Paris, Chastanier came to England in October 1763 aged about twenty-four. [80] He failed to settle in London, however, experiencing a 'remarkable' vision the night before he was to relocate in the vicinity of Northampton. In January 1768 Chastanier began studying the '*Mystic Writers*' and learned German to enable him to read Georg von Welling's *Opus Mago-Cabbalisticum* (1735). He may have been influenced by Francis Okely who ministered to a small Moravian congregation at Northampton. [81] Yet since the early nineteenth century, historians of Freemasonry have maintained that during Swedenborg's lifetime Chastanier and other 'friends of the New Jerusalem' in France founded a quasi-masonic society of 'Illuminés theosophes' with seven grades:

1. Apprenti theosoph (apprentice)
2. Compagnon theosoph (journeyman)
3. Maitre theosoph (master)
4. Theosophe illumine (enlightened theosophist)
5. Frère bleu (blue brother)
6. Frère rouge (red brother)
7. Sublime Ecossais ou le Jerusalem celeste (sublime Scotch). [82]

Although it has been claimed that Chastanier was master of the lodge 'Socrate de la Parfaite Union' at Paris and that in 1767 he introduced his system of illuminated theosophists into England, there is apparently no record of his membership of a London lodge. [83] Indeed, the chronology of this supposed fusion of Freemasonry and Swedenborgian doctrines is problematic, for only in mid-1768 did Chastanier start reading part of *Arcana Cœlestia* in translation. Nor did he accompany his alchemist friends when they visited Swedenborg in London. In March 1776, however, he enquired about Boehme's *Signatura rerum* at a Holborn bookseller's and was instead handed a copy of Hartley's translation of Swedenborg's treatise *On the Nature of Influx*. [84] Having accepted its doctrines as the fulfilment of another vision, Chastanier gathered that same year a group to assist in the translation and publication of Swedenborg's manuscripts. He himself transcribed 'Worship and Love of God' (1778) and 'Continuation of the Last Judgment' (1781). [85] Afterwards he edited and issued several French translations of Swedenborg's works: *De la Nouvelle Jérusalem et de sa Doctrine Céleste* (1782); *Du Commerce établi entre l'Ame et le Corps* (1785); *Traité de la Vie* (1787); *Doctrine de la Nouvelle Jérusalem, touchant le Seigneur* (1787); *Du Dernier Jugement* (1787); *Continuation du Dernier Jugement* (1787). [86] The last four appeared in Chastanier's *Journal Novi-Jérusalémite*.

Significantly, *Journal Novi-Jérusalémite* was addressed to all lovers of the truth, particularly Freemasons, who 'are free and open-hearted' and whom Chastanier had the 'honour' of calling his 'brethren'. He also mentioned circulars which the Grand Orient in Paris had dispersed, presumably to lodges affiliated with it. [87] While Chastanier's plan to establish a quasi-masonic '*Société Universelle*' consisting of the elite among alchemists, Kabbalists, Freemasons and students of the occult sciences was undated, there is an intriguing reference to 'la société Universelle' in a letter written 14 June 1784 to Lieutenant-General Charles Rainsford (1728-1809). [88] A correspondent of Chastanier as well as a Freemason and fellow reader of Swedenborg, Rainsford was said to have attended an international masonic congress under the auspices of the Order of Philalèthes convened at Paris intermittently between August 1784 and May 1785. [89] It is noteworthy that he shared Chastanier's interest in Georg von Welling's *Opus Mago-Cabbalisticum* and Boehme, transcribing passages from *The Way to Christ Discovered* (1775). [90] Indeed, Rainsford made extensive extracts from a number of works by or attributed to alchemical, mystic and Rosicrucian authors such as Bernard of Treviso, Arthur Dee, Robert Fludd, Johann Grasshof, Heinrich Khunrath, Ramon Llull, John Pordage, Michael Sendivogius, George Starkey, Basil Valentine, Thomas Vaughan, Johann Otto von Hellbig, Johann Friedrich von Meinstorff and Johannes Weidenfeld. [91]

Equally important was Chastanier's connection with a peculiar masonic group known as the Illuminati. Founded at Berlin in 1779 by Antoine-Joseph Pernety under the protection of Prince Henry, brother of Frederick II of Prussia, it attracted people with interests in alchemy, astrology and Kabbalah. These included an English-speaking merchant of French extraction named William Bousie, who had apparently attended the masonic congress at Paris with Rainsford, and the wealthy Polish nobleman Thaddeus Grabianka (1740-1807), who adopted the title 'King of the New Israel'. In 1782 Pernety supposedly received a divine command to re-establish his circle in a new location forty days' journey from Berlin. He identified this as Avignon, a papal enclave where Scottish Jacobite exiles gathered around Charles Stuart had founded a lodge. His circuitous route went by way of Boehme's grave at Görlitz in Upper Lusatia. [92] Chastanier probably learned of the

355

Illuminati through Carl Fredrik Nordenskjöld, a Scandinavian Swedenborgian, Freemason and correspondent of Pernety who visited London in 1783. [93] Chastanier certainly knew the '*Mago-Cabbalist*' Pernety's '*falsificated Translation*' of Swedenborg's *Les merveilles du ciel et de l'enfer* (1782) which, at the suggestion of the brothers Carl and Augustus Nordenskjöld, contained anecdotes supplied by Christopher Springer (1704-88), Swedish consul at London. [94] Writing to Rainsford on 22 July 1785, Chastanier warned him that the Illuminati's interpretations were 'as far from the principles of Swedenborg as the Orient is from the Occident'. [95] Even so, when Grabianka arrived in London on 7 December 1785 he immediately met with Chastanier at a hotel in the Adelphi. [96] Having worshipped with several groups of believers in an imminent spiritual millennium Grabianka departed for The Hague on 7 November 1786. Eventually he reached Avignon from where on 12 February 1787 his Society addressed the Swedenborgians at London in millenarian language as the 'Children of the New Kingdom'. This was received on 5 March 1787 and a copy subsequently printed by Robert Hindmarsh as *A Letter from a Society in France to the Society for promoting the Heavenly Doctrines of the New Jerusalem Church in London*. [97] The separatist Swedenborgians later broke with the Avignon group over doctrinal issues, accusing them of promoting a 'Jesuitical scheme' which required recognizing the Virgin Mary as the fourth divine person in the Godhead and worshiping the angels Raphael, Gabriel, Michael and others. [98] Yet Chastanier maintained his links with continental Freemasons, directing his attention to a Society in Moscow and to the Exegetic and Philanthropic Society of Stockholm, among whose members was Swedenborg's nephew Karl Göran Silfverhjelm. [99] Furthermore, in a work dedicated to the Archbishop of Paris entitled *Tableau analytique et raisonné de la Doctrine Céleste de l'Église de la Nouvelle Jerusalem* (1786), Chastanier noted that Boehme, Lead, Law, Guyon and other good mystics had perceived the distant dawn of this beautiful day, but only the enlightened Swedenborg had demonstrated its true nature and the next state of existence. [100]

While visiting London Grabianka had met with the Swedenborgian Theosophical Society at the home of Jacob Duché (1738-98), chaplain and secretary to the Asylum for Female Orphans in St George's Fields, Lambeth. [101] A member of one of Philadelphia's wealthiest families, Duché had served as rector of two Philadelphia churches and as chaplain to the Continental Congress in 1776. Loyal to the Church of England yet also sympathetic to the colonists' grievances, he injudiciously wrote to George Washington urging him to persuade Congress, by force if necessary, to rescind its Declaration of Independence. After Washington turned the letter over to Congress Duché went into exile in England with his family. [102] Renowned for his elegant sermons and literary accomplishments, Duché had a long-standing interest in Boehme and his interpreters. Hence a fellow clergyman described him in 1764 as 'enthusiastic and mystical, a follower of Behmen and William Law'. Similarly, Duché's successor in Philadelphia recollected:

A few years after his ministerial settlement he took to the mysticism of Jacob Behmen and William Law. From this he became detached for a time [. . .] He relapsed, however, to the theory of the mystics, and continued in it until the troubles which drove him from his native country. [103]

Duché himself recounted his spiritual odyssey in a long letter written in 1767 to the London publisher John Payne (d. 1787), recalling that he was 'sometimes a deist and sometimes a Christian' before providence acquainted him with William Law's writings:

My mind which had hitherto been unsettled, dark, doubting, and yet anxious to find the Truth, became serene calm and sweetly composed. I seemed as if I had got into another world, with a new set of objects and a new set of Ideas, notions and sensibilities. [104]

By 1785 Duché had become a Swedenborgian, declaring that the 'New Church from above, the Jerusalem of Revelation is come down upon Earth [...] Look henceforth for an Internal Millennium'. [105] His son the artist Thomas Spence Duché (1763-90) likewise accepted this doctrine and may even have introduced his father to it. [106] Fascinated by Grabianka's account of the Illuminati, Thomas departed for the continent in 1788. [107] During his six-month visit he passed through a number of places where there were 'religious Societies' which were 'all to be united to the Society in London, and a constant intercourse by letters to be kept up between them'. The Moscow and Avignon Societies were even said to have been united to the London Society for 'some time past'. [108] Moreover, Thomas was said to have returned with 'a mind highly improved & advanced by close Communion with the Lord and Conversation with some characters of High Rank in this World'. So much so that he found 'great Openings of this Kingdom everywhere unconfined to any religious Sects & Denominations'. [109] Among his illustrious acquaintances was Rainsford, with whom he corresponded concerning alchemical authors:

> I [...] have found a great clearness in them, and consistency with the mystical Writers—and am disposed to believe Jacob Behmen when he says that a Man must be purified into a divine Magus, before he can have such a command over nature as to effect the Philosophical Change. [110]

It also appears that Thomas Duché visited Avignon for he (or his father) was mentioned there by John Wright, a carpenter from Leeds. [111]

Attracted by the Swedenborgian preaching of Ralph Mather and Joseph Salmon in Yorkshire, Wright had attended a New Jerusalem Church service at their chapel in Maidenhead Court, Great East Cheap. While in London he became acquainted with William Bryan, a Shrewsbury-born bookseller turned copperplate printer and former Quaker. Bryan had probably met Grabianka during a Theosophical Society meeting at Jacob Duché's home for he wrote a letter to the Avignon Society which was translated by William Bousie. After seeking divine guidance they replied on 16 April 1788, Chastanier translating their response at Bryan's request. [112] In January 1789 Bryan and Wright departed London for Avignon, lodging with Bousie en route at Paris. By April they had reached their destination. Tiemann von Berend, a Saxon said to be a Major in the Russian army whom Bryan had seen in England two years before, acted as interpreter until Bousie's arrival. The pair were employed making extracts from the Society's journals and learned of their remarkable prophecies about 'the Lord's second coming, and the restoration of his people, the whole house of Israel'. [113] In June Wright received a vision *concerning the knowledge of the spirits and the spiritual world*, while Bryan claimed that a heavenly communication had shown the Society that Swedenborg's interpretation of his own revelations was no longer correct and that God himself would form a new church. [114] Each member of the Society was also 'distinguished by a particular number' (Bryan was probably 1,4,7 and Wright 1,2,3). [115] The two Englishmen returned to their families in September but in late November two Swedish nobles arrived at Avignon—Baron Gustaf Adolph Reuterholm and Karl Göran Silfverhjelm. Both were members of a masonic order known as the Templars. [116]

Wright and Bryan later became followers of Richard Brothers (1757-1824), a former naval officer who proclaimed himself Prince and Prophet of the Hebrews and Nephew of the Almighty. Suggestively, extracts from a 1656 edition of a compilation of Boehme's writings entitled *Mercurius Teutonicus, or, A Christian information concerning the last times* were reprinted in 1795 together with other *Prophetical passages, concerning the present times* as a sign that Richard Brothers was 'the Elijah of the present day, the bright star to guide the Hebrews'. [117] Furthermore, Brothers' likeness above the legend 'Prince of the Hebrews [. . .] the Man whom GOD has appointed' was engraved in April 1795 by the Swedenborgian William Sharp (1749-1824). [118] Politically sympathetic with the revolutionary forces in America and France, a member of the Society for Constitutional Information and an associate of Thomas Paine, Sharp had been examined on treasonable charges by the Privy Council in 1794. Afterwards he became a follower of the prophetess Joanna Southcott (1750-1814), whose likeness he also drew and engraved. It is noteworthy that Sharp had apparently taught Bryan copperplate printing and supported Bryan's family during his absence at Avignon. [119] Moreover, Sharp's earlier work included an engraving used as the frontispiece to Jacob Duché's *Discourses on Various Subjects* (1779), and an engraving done from Thomas Duché's portrait of the first Protestant Bishop of the United States, Samuel Seabury. [120]

According to Hindmarsh's posthumously published *Rise and Progress of the New Jerusalem Church*, Sharp was one of a number of respectable gentleman who from about 1784 found their way to Swedenborgian meetings. His name appears on a composite and dateless list together with the 'celebrated' sculptor John Flaxman (1755-1826) and François Hippolyte Barthélémon (1741-1808). [121] An accomplished violinist, Barthélémon collaborated with his friend Thomas Duché in composing the music for a hymn sung at the Asylum for Female Orphans. Barthélémon was also a member of a French lodge known as L'Immortalité de l'Ordre which had been constituted on 16 June 1776 at 'The Crown and Anchor' in the Strand. Memoranda and extracts from their byelaws are preserved in Rainsford's papers. [122] One of Barthélémon's executors was Manoah Sibly (1757-1840), an ordained minister of the New Jerusalem Church. Raised as a Particular Baptist, Manoah was an autodidact who was said to have learned Hebrew, Greek, Latin and Syriac, as well as shorthand. In the 1780s he was a bookseller in Goswell Street specializing in Swedenborg's publications and the 'occult sciences', particularly astrology, alchemy and magic. [123] His elder brother Ebenezer Sibly (1751-99), who had been initiated into Freemasonry at Portsmouth, shared these interests. [124] In 1789 Ebenezer founded what became known as the Lodge of Joppa, which met at 'The Globe' in Hatton Garden, the same area where a New Jerusalem Temple was erected in 1796. [125] A prolific author—his published works come to approximately 2,500 quarto pages, Ebenezer compiled several popular books including *A New and Complete Illustration of the Occult Sciences* (1790), dedicated to the 'Ancient and Honourable Fraternity of Free and

Accepted Masons'. This defence of astrology contained Swedenborg's horoscope in which Ebenezer praised his 'attempts to pry into the depths of Eternal Nature, and to solve the visions of the Deity' while defending him from the charge of insanity. [126] Ebenezer also transcribed a number of works concerning alchemy, astrology, magic, Kabbalah and the Rosicrucians. Some of these texts, notably letters erroneously attributed to Michael Sendivogius copied in 1791, and extracts from Georg von Welling made in 1793, were probably obtained from Rainsford. [127] In addition, Ebenezer had four pen drawings taken from a manuscript by Dionysius Andreas Freher (1649-1728), a German draughtsman who wrote extensive commentaries on Boehme's treatises. [128] Manuscript copies of Freher's works were also in the possession of the artist and collector Richard Cosway (1742-1821). An admirer of Rubens and a reader of Swedenborg, Cosway owned some of Freher's 'Serial Elucidations' of Boehme's 'Philosophy and Theology'. However, either through ignorance or in an attempt to increase the value at auction of Freher's treatise on 'Microcosmo or the Little World, Man, in his Primaeval and fallen State', someone—most likely Cosway or his wife Maria—inserted an engraved portrait of Rubens and added 'Faithfully translated from the Original Latin written by Petrus Paulus Rubenius' to the title page. [129]

Other notable attendees at Swedenborgian meetings were the mathematical instrument maker George Adams (1750-95), the musical instrument maker Benjamin Banks (1727-95), the engraver John Emes (1762-1808), the miniature painter John Sanders (1750-1825), and the Alsatian artist Philippe Jacques de Loutherbourg (1740-1812). [130] A former scene designer at Drury Lane Theatre and an elected member of the Royal Academy, [131] de Loutherbourg painted Swedenborg's portrait in oils—probably from engravings rather than life. [132] About 1787 he also painted *Tableau de la Loge des Compagnons* in watercolour. This illustration was designed for the notorious advocate of 'Egyptian' Freemasonry, Count Alessandro Cagliostro, generally accepted as an alias of the Sicilian Giuseppe Balsamo (1743?-95), whom de Loutherbourg entertained at his London residence. After accompanying Cagliostro's wife on a journey to join her husband in Switzerland

and then occupying himself by painting *Falls of the Rhine at Schaffhausen*, de Loutherbourg returned to London. [133] Before his departure de Loutherbourg, 'bewitched' with the 'phantasies of an unsettled mind', had conducted alchemical experiments in search of the philosopher's stone. Perhaps this led him to believe that he had become an 'adept in the art of healing' for in July 1789 he was reported to have 'turned an inspired physician' with three thousand patients. Suggestively, his 'panacea' of barley water was mockingly likened to 'mesmerism'—coined after the Viennese doctor Franz Anton Mesmer (1734-1815), whose notion concerning a mutual influence which existed as a universally distributed and continuous fluid between heavenly bodies, animate bodies and the Earth, he termed Animal Magnetism. [134] A pamphlet by 'a Lover of the Lamb of God' dedicated to the Archbishop of Canterbury listed a few cures performed by de Loutherbourg and his wife Lucy 'without medicine' at their home in Hammersmith Terrace, Chiswick. Its author Mary Pratt believed that the couple:

> have been made by the Almighty power of the Lord Jehovah, proper Recipients to receive divine Manuductions, which heavenly and divine Influx coming from the Radix *God*, his divine Majesty has most graciously condescended to bestow on them, (*his blessing*) to diffuse to *all* who have faith in the Lord as mediator, be they Deaf, Dumb, Lame, Halt, or Blind. [135]

Although the de Loutherbourgs had intended to dispense their services primarily to the poor, admission tickets to their 'public healing room' were touted at inflated prices causing a riot. Their patients were of all ages and resided locally, ranging from the wife of a man living with the French ambassador to a female vocalist, an apprentice to a gentleman. Significantly, among them was Rainsford's son, for whose recovery the 'handsome young' Lucy prayed. [136] Yet during a crowded debate held at Coachmakers' Hall in September 1789 it was decided that de Loutherbourg could not have performed any 'Cures by a Divine Power' without medical treatment. This outcome echoed the findings of a public enquiry held at Paris in 1784 which had determined that 'touch, imitation, and imagination' were the 'three greatest causes of the effects attributed to magnetism'. [137]

Discredited in France and then England, the practice of Animal Magnetism nonetheless flourished at London during the intervening period. One of its foremost exponents was the Irish-born surgeon and midwife John Boniot de Mainauduc (c.1750-97), a former student of Mesmer's opponent Charles Deslon, whose thriving clinic at Bloomsbury Square attracted aristocrats and the wives of Quaker industrialists. According to the watercolour painter George Cumberland (1754-1848), de Mainauduc had many pupils pretending to be able 'to cure diseases by Sympathy' including the Duke of Gloucester and Richard and Maria Cosway:

> Loutherbourg is at the head of this Sect—who I suspect have a Scheme to empty the pockets of all the credulous christians they can find. [138]

Chastanier too had been 'initiated' by de Mainauduc, possibly at Grabianka's suggestion, acting as his 'powerful' and 'constant' assistant for six months before setting up an alternative clinic specializing in the treatment of nervous diseases, gout, deafness, convulsions and the like at his home on 62 Tottenham Court Road. [139] Afterwards he reprinted the Marquis du Thomé's views on Magnetism, which had been communicated to the *Journal Encyclopédique*. Another Swedenborgian the diplomat William Gomm recommended the practice and translated a letter on the subject. [140] Likewise, Rainsford translated a treatise on somnambulism and an account of 'Magnetic Healing', describing himself as an 'Admirer and Student in animal magnetism'. [141] His correspondent Ebenezer Sibly claimed to be a Fellow of the Harmonic Philosophic Society at Paris and was a defender of Mesmer. [142] Swedenborg's nephew Silfverhjelm also wrote a brief introduction explaining the phenomena of Animal Magnetism and somnambulism (1787). [143] This association between Swedenborgians and supporters of Magnetism was emphasized in an anonymous work issued at Avignon and by a pamphleteer who maintained that 'Swedenborgian doctrines' had help spread the practice. But as the vogue for Animal Magnetism began to wane so several of its prominent Swedenborgian adherents repudiated it. Even de Loutherbourg resumed painting. [144]

In 1796 de Loutherbourg acquired a copy of Jane Lead's *The signs of the times* (1699). Altogether he owned five or more works by Lead, one of which—*A fountain of gardens* (1696)—had been in the possession of John Denis the elder. [145] Like de Loutherbourg, Mary Pratt also read Lead as well as Boehme, Guyon, the Welsh preacher William Erbery (1604-54), the Cambridge Platonist Peter Sterry (1613-72), and 'many (almost all) Hermetic books'. Pratt's 'persecuting' husband was a 'strenuous follower' of the 'visionary' Swedenborg whose 'deluded society' was 'spreading contagion' in London. Moreover, she had no fellowship with him in religion because 'the writings of the Baron militate against the pure doctrine and experience of God manifested in the flesh'. [146] He has been identified as a contributor to *The New Magazine of Knowledge concerning Heaven and Hell* (1790) and *The New Jerusalem Journal* (1792) under the pseudonym 'Ignoramus'. [147]

IV. William Blake (1757-1827)

In 1790 William Blake began *The Marriage of Heaven and Hell*, a heterodox illuminated book combining prose, poetry and pictures. Its title was a reworking of Swedenborg's *A Treatise concerning Heaven and Hell*, with the striking addition of the term 'Marriage'. Ridiculing Swedenborg's belief that a spiritual equilibrium between heaven and hell had been restored and the Last Judgment fully accomplished in 1757 (the year of Blake's birth), he noted that it was now thirty-three years since the advent of 'a new heaven' yet the 'Eternal Hell revives'. Moreover, Blake charged Swedenborg with making vain boasts, insisting that he had not written 'one new truth' but 'all the old falshoods'. Thus Swedenborg's 'conceited notions' were 'a recapitulation of all superficial opinions, and an analysis of the more sublime—but no further'. Indeed, according to Blake:

Any man of mechanical talents may, from the writings of Paracelsus or Jacob Behmen, produce ten thousand volumes of equal value with Swedenborg's, and from those of Dante or Shakespear an infinite number. [148]

There is no evidence—despite repeated claims by Marsha Schuchard to the contrary—that Blake's father was a Swedenborgian. [149] Nor can it be substantiated, as E P Thompson suggested, that his mother's first husband was kin to a Muggletonian. [150] Even so, important recent discoveries by Keri Davies and Schuchard appear to prove that Blake's mother Catherine and her first husband Thomas Armitage were briefly members of the Moravian congregation that worshipped at Fetter Lane. [151] While this raises interesting questions about early influences on Blake's religious and artistic development it remains unlikely that he is to be identified with the 'Mr. William Blake' who subscribed to Jacob Duché's *Discourses on Various Subjects* (1779). For as a young journeyman copy engraver he probably lacked the means. [152] Similarly, suggestions that Blake heard Duché preach at Lambeth and that he could have attended meetings of the Theosophical Society at Duché's home seem extremely doubtful. [153] Blake and his wife Catherine did live at 13 Hercules Buildings, Lambeth close to the Asylum for Female Orphans, but they moved there in March 1791—by which time Duché, who had resigned his post on 1 January 1789, was living at 63 Sloane Street, Chelsea. [154] Yet a 'W. Blake' and 'C. Blake' did sign the Minute Book of the New Jerusalem Church at their first general conference held at Great East Cheap on 13 April 1789. That this was William and Catherine Blake is generally accepted. [155]

Blake was never baptized and admitted into the New Jerusalem Church—unless this is recorded in the destroyed portion of the Minute Book. Furthermore, Blake's annotations in his copies of Swedenborg's *The Wisdom of angels concerning Divine Love and Divine Wisdom* (1788) and *The Wisdom of angels concerning Divine Providence* (1790) show growing disapproval of the doctrines. [156] Nonetheless, Blake returned to Swedenborg in his prophetic poem

Milton (1804-8), depicting him as 'strongest of men, the Samson shorn by the Churches', while in *A Descriptive catalogue* (1809) he observed that 'the works of this visionary are well worthy the attention of Painters and Poets'. [157] In 1810 the diarist Henry Crabb Robinson (1775-1867) noted that Blake had been invited to join the Swedenborgians but declined, 'notwithstanding his high opinion of Swedenborg'. [158] Robinson also believed that Blake was 'not so much a disciple of Jacob Böhmen and Swedenborg as a fellow visionary', elsewhere remarking that Blake regarded Boehme as 'a divinely inspired man'. [159] It may have been the sculptor John Flaxman who, before departing for Italy in 1787, told Blake of Swedenborg's writings, [160] and it was to Flaxman in September 1800 that Blake addressed some autobiographical lines:

> Paracelsus & Behmen appear'd to me, terrors appear'd in the Heavens above And in Hell beneath, & a mighty & awful change threatened the Earth. The American War began. All its dark horrors passed before my face Across the Atlantic to France. Then the French Revolution commenc'd in thick clouds. [161]

V. Directions for future research

According to *An Inquiry into the Commission and Doctrine of the new Apostle Emanuel Swedenborg* (1794), the 'Baron's followers' had 'from their infancy a predilection to the marvellous and surprising' and were but 'old turncoats' from 'enthusiasts' such as Boehme and the Shakers. [162] Although several prominent Anglicans and Methodists, some Moravians, a handful of Particular and General Baptists and a Huguenot émigré were attracted to Swedenborg's writings it was the Quakers, as Thomas Hartley recognized, who were the 'likeliest people' to adopt and spread Swedenborgian doctrines. That so few did was because Swedenborg held the sacraments of Baptism and the Lord's Supper necessary as 'a connecting link between the spiritual and material worlds', whereas Quakers denied their validity. Significantly, this issue had also been at the heart of seventeenth-century doctrinal disputes between Quakers and English Behmenists. [163] As early Quakerism had been marked by dominant personalities, dissension and schism, so too was English Swedenborgianism. Moreover, just as the Quakers had archived their history by recording testimonies, preserving and copying letters, collecting and cataloguing publications, so Swedenborg's followers established organizations for transcribing, translating and disseminating his writings. Indeed, just as the Quaker leadership had used institutional mechanisms to enforce conformity eventually recasting themselves within society and remodelling their origins, so Hindmarsh's *Rise and Progress of the New Jerusalem Church* marginalized the contribution of non-separatist Swedenborgians and foreigners, minimizing the importance of alchemy, Animal Magnetism, astrology, Freemasonry, Kabbalah, magic, mysticism, numerology, the Rosicrucians and Behmenism to a number of Swedenborg's early readers. The process of recovering these influences, of restoring them in the history of the Swedenborgians is still not complete. While The Swedenborg Society's archives have been explored by several scholars much remains to be done on a national and local level, particularly in London. A new and revised edition of Rudolph Tafel's *Documents concerning the Life and Character of Emanuel Swedenborg* (1877) would be one forward step, a biographical dictionary of Swedenborg's readers another.

NOTES

* I would like to thank Richard Lines and Lara Muth (Swedenborg Society), Jane Muskett (Chetham's Library), Martin Cherry (Library and Museum of Freemasonry), Gunnar Lantz (Grand Lodge of Sweden) and Lorraine Parsons (Moravian Church) for their help in answering research enquiries. I am also grateful to Phil Baker, Mario Caricchio, Lorenza Gianfrancesco, Richard Lines, Stephen McNeilly, John Morrill, Ian O'Neill and James Wilson for their useful comments and suggestions.

1   Ralph Waldo Emerson, *Representative Men. Seven Lectures* (1850; repr., ed. Andrew Delbanco, Cambridge, 1996), pp. 3, 4, 53, 70, 76, 80; see also, L Braham, 'Emerson and Boehme: A comparative study of mystical ideas', in *Modern Language Quarterly*, 20 (1959), pp. 31-5; A Hallengren, 'The Importance of Swedenborg to Emerson's Ethics', in Erland Brock, E B Glenn, Carroll Odhner et al. (eds.), *Swedenborg and His Influence* (Bryn Athyn, 1988), pp. 229-50; E Hurth, 'The Uses of a Mystic Prophet: Emerson and Boehme', in *Philological Quarterly*, 70 (1991), pp. 219-36; A Hallengren, 'Swedenborgian simile in Emersonian edification', in Stephen McNeilly (ed.), *In Search of the Absolute— Essays on Swedenborg and Literature* (London, 2004), pp. 15-22.

2   *A reall and unfeigned Testimonie, concerning Iacob Beme* (1649), p. 2 (printed with *The Epistles of Jacob Behmen*, tr. J[ohn] E[llistone] (1649)).

3   Emanuel Swedenborg, *Small Theological Works and Letters*, ed. John Elliott (London, 1975), pp. 217, 219, 221; cf. Lars Bergquist (ed.), *Swedenborg's Dream Diary*, tr. Anders Hallengren (West Chester, 2001), p. 217. According to the *New-Jerusalem Magazine*, 1, no. 2 (1790), p. 73, 'L' was supposed to be Johann Caspar Lavater (1741-1801), with whom Swedenborg corresponded.

4   Emanuel Swedenborg, *Les merveilles du ciel et de l'enfer*, tr. Antoine-Joseph Pernety (Berlin, 1782), p. 64, in Rudolph Tafel (ed.), *Documents concerning the Life and Character of Emanuel Swedenborg*, 2 vols. (London, 1875-7), vol. 1, pp. 62, 650; cf. S Sandel, *An Eulogium on the lately deceased Mr. Emanuel Swedenborg* (1784), p. 24.

5   Jacob Boehme, *The Epistles of Jacob Behmen*, tr. J[ohn] E[llistone] (1649), 2.10, 2.14, pp. 20, 21; Jacob Boehme, *Aurora, That is, the Day-Spring*, tr. John Sparrow (1656), 10.45, p. 184.

6   Gregory Johnson (ed.), *Kant on Swedenborg. Dreams of a Spirit-Seer and Other Writings* (West Chester, 2002).

7   British Library, London, Add. MS 40,058, Jacob Boehme, 'Christosophia eller Wägen til Christum, författad i nio små Böcker som nu äro sammandragna i åtta'; BL, Add. MS 40,059, Jacob Boehme, miscellaneous works, translated into Swedish.

8   Anders Bygden, Carl Lewenhaupt and Erik Lind (eds.), *G. Benzelstjernas Censorsjournal, 1737-1746* (Stockholm, 1884-5), p. 41; Nils Thune, *The Behmenists and the Philadelphians. A Contribution to the Study of English Mysticism in the 17th and*

18th Centuries (Uppsala, 1948), pp. 54, 150.

9   Johan Hinric Lidén (ed.), *Brefwäxling imellan ärke-biskop Eric Benzelius den Yngre och dess broder cencor librorum Gustaf Benzelstierna* (Linköping, 1791).

10 Bygden et al. (eds.), *Benzelstjernas Censorsjournal*, p. 272; Thune, *Behmenists and Philadelphians*, pp. 150-1.

11 Cf. J K Williams-Hogan, 'Swedenborg: A Biography', in Brock, Glen and Odhner et al. (eds.), *Swedenborg and His Influence*, p. 14; Inge Jonsson, *Visionary Scientist: The Effects of Science and Philosophy on Swedenborg's Cosmology*, tr. Catherine Djurklou (West Chester, 1999), pp. 124-7.

12 Tafel (ed.), *Documents*, vol. 2, pt. i, p. 79; cf. Emanuel Swedenborg, *The Spiritual Diary*, §5764.

13 Swedenborg, *The Spiritual Diary*, §4851; cf. ibid., §§4760, 5962.

14 John Wesley, *A check to the Delusive and Dangerous Opinions of Baron Swedenborg*, ed. W Williams (High Wycombe, 1797), pp. 10, 12.

15 E P Thompson, *Witness Against the Beast. William Blake and the Moral Law* (Cambridge, 1994), p. 133 n. 12.

16 R Hindmarsh, 'A comparison between Jacob Behmen and Emanuel Swedenborg, particularly on the subject of divine influx', in *Intellectual Repository for the New Church*, 2 (1815), pp. 188-90.

17 A Roffe, 'Mr. Hindmarsh and Jacob Behmen', in *Intellectual Repository and New Jerusalem Magazine*, n.s. 8 (1847), pp. 328-31, 385-90; A Roffe, 'Jacob Behmen', in *Notes and Queries*, 2nd series, 2 (1856), p. 92; A Roffe, 'Jane Lead and Swedenborg', in *Notes and Queries*, 2nd series, 2 (1856), pp. 470-1; cf. Christopher Walton, *Notes and materials for an adequate Biography of the celebrated divine and theosopher, William Law* (1854), p. 158; Anne Penny, *Studies in Jacob Böhme* (1912), pp. 75-85.

18 Signe Toksvig, *Emanuel Swedenborg: Scientist and Mystic* (New Haven, 1948), p. 83; Arthur Versluis, *The Esoteric Origins of the American Renaissance* (New York, 2000), p. 19.

19 J H Overton, *William Law, Nonjuror and Mystic* (1881), p. 422; David Katz, *God's Last Words. Reading the English Bible from the Reformation to Fundamentalism* (New Haven, 2004), pp. 172-3.

20 M K Schuchard, 'Swedenborg, Jacobitism and Freemasonry', in Brock, Glenn, Odhner et al. (eds.), *Swedenborg and His Influence*, pp. 359-79; M K Schuchard, 'Yeats and the "Unknown Superiors": Swedenborg, Falk, and Cagliostro', in Marie Roberts and Hugh Ormsby-Lennon (eds.), *Secret Texts: The Literature of Secret Societies* (New York, 1995), pp. 114-68; M K Schuchard, 'Emanuel Swedenborg: Deciphering the Codes of a Celestial and Terrestrial Intelligencer', in Eliot Wolfson (ed.), *Rending the Veil: Concealment and Secrecy in the History of Religions* (New York, 1999), pp. 177-208; M K Schuchard, 'Jacobite and Visionary: The Masonic Journey of Emanuel Swedenborg', in *Ars Quatuor Coronatorum*, 115 (2003), pp. 33-72.

21 M K Schuchard, 'Leibniz, Benzelius and Swedenborg: The Kabbalistic Roots of Swedish Illuminism', in Allison Coudert, Richard Popkin and Gordon Weiner (eds.), *Leibniz, Mysticism and Religion* (Dordrecht, 1998), pp. 84-106.

22 Jonsson, *Visionary Scientist*, pp. 11, 12, 23-4, 27, 30, 38, 40, 46, 56, 64, 75, 79, 80-1, 119, 190-1.

23 Alfred Stroh (ed.), *Catalogus Bibliothecae Emanuelis Swedenborgii* (Stockholm, 1907); Lars Bergquist, *Swedenborg's Secret, A Biography* (London, 2005), pp. 469-82.

24 Karl-Erik Sjöden, *Swedenborg en France* (Stockholm, 1985); Lynn Wilkinson, *The Dream of an Absolute Language: Emanuel Swedenborg and French Literary Culture* (Albany, 1996); Peter Lineham, 'The English Swedenborgians, 1770-1840: a study in the social dimensions of religious sectarianism', unpublished University of Sussex D.Phil, 1978; C Garrett, 'Swedenborg and the Mystical Enlightenment in Late Eighteenth-Century England', in *Journal of the History of Ideas*, 45 (1984), pp. 67-81; P J Lineham, 'The origins of the New Jerusalem Church in the 1780s', in *Bulletin of the John Rylands Library*, 70 (1988), pp. 109-22.

25 W R Ward, 'Swedenborgianism: heresy, schism or religious protest?', in *Studies in Church History*, 9 (1972), pp. 303-9; J F C Harrison, *The Second Coming. Popular Millenarianism 1780-1850* (New Jersey, 1979), pp. 21, 72-3; M K Schuchard, 'The Secret History of Blake's Swedenborg Society', in *Blake: An Illustrated Quarterly*, 26 (1992), pp. 40-51; Thompson, *Witness Against the Beast*, pp. 129-45; Brian Gibbons, *Gender in Mystical and Occult Thought: Behmenism and its Development in England* (Cambridge, 1996), pp. 198-204; R W Rix, 'Healing the Spirit: William Blake

and the Magnetic Religion', in *Romanticism On the Net*, 25 (2002), 37 pars., <http://www.erudit.org/revue/ron/2002/v/n25/006011ar.html>; R W Rix, 'William Blake and the radical Swedenborgians', in *Esoterica*, 5 (2003), pp. 96-137, <http://www.esoteric.msu.edu/VolumeV/Blake.htm>.

[26] *The New Magazine of Knowledge*, 1 (1790), pp. 395-401; John Clowes, *Remarks on the Assertions of the Author of the Memoirs of Jacobinism* (Philadelphia, 1800), pp. 6-8; 'Miscellaneous information', in *Intellectual Repository for the New Church*, n.s. 2 (1827), pp. 179-80; Tafel (ed.), *Documents*, vol. 2, pt. i, pp. 498-9; Robert Hindmarsh, *Rise and Progress of the New Jerusalem Church, in England, America, and other parts*, ed. Edward Madeley (1861), pp. 2-6.

[27] Stephen Penny, *Stephen Penny's letter, to his sister Martha Penny* (1780), pp. 27-39.

[28] Dr Williams's Library, London, MS I.1.43, printed in Walton, *Notes and materials*, pp. 45-6 n., 597-8; Lineham, 'English Swedenborgians', pp. 36-8; Harrison, *Second Coming*, p. 22.

[29] National Archives, London, Prob 11/1077, will of Stephen Penny (probate 19 April 1781), fol. 130v.

[30] Walton, *Notes and materials*, p. 592; Tafel (ed.), *Documents*, vol. 2, pt. i, p. 498 n; Lineham, 'English Swedenborgians', pp. 34-5.

[31] John Wesley, *A Letter to the Reverend Mr. Law* (1756), pp. 5, 102.

[32] John Wesley, *The Works of John Wesley*, 3rd edn., 14 vols. (1831), vol. 1, pp. 375-6, vol. 2, p. 46, vol. 3, pp. 18-20, 160, 502-3, vol. 10, pp. 179, 184; John Telford (ed.), *The Letters of the Rev. John Wesley*, 8 vols. (1931), vol. 2, pp. 118-19, vol. 3, pp. 107, 321, vol. 4, pp. 105-7, vol. 5, p. 342, vol. 6, p. 328.

[33] Richard Parkinson (ed.), *The Private Journal and Literary Remains of John Byrom*, 2 vols. forming vols. 32, 34, 40, 44 of the publications of the Chetham Society (Manchester, 1854-7), vol. 2, pt. I, p. 629.

[34] DWL, MS I.1.43, printed in Walton, *Notes and materials*, pp. 595-6; Desirée Hirst, *Hidden Riches. Traditional Symbolism from the Renaissance to Blake* (1964), p. 241; Lineham, 'English Swedenborgians', pp. 116, 119.

[35] W R Ward and Richard Heitzenrater (eds.), *The Works of John Wesley. Journal and Diaries* (Nashville, 1993), vol. 22, pp. 386, 387-8, 397, 399; Telford (ed.), *Letters of John*

Wesley, vol. 6, pp. 67-8; Lineham, 'English Swedenborgians', pp. 65, 129-31; Garrett, 'Swedenborg and Mystical Enlightenment', pp. 77-81.

[36] DWL, MS I.1.43, printed in Harrison, *Second Coming*, p. 23; Hindmarsh, *Rise and Progress of the New Jerusalem Church*, pp. 64-5, 138; C H Odhner, 'Ralph Mather', in *New Church Life*, 16 (1896), pp. 154-5, 168-70.

[37] Ward and Heitzenrater (eds.), *Works of John Wesley. Journal and Diaries*, vol. 22, pp. 216-17, 301-2; Wesley, *Works*, vol. 4, pp. 149-50; Tafel (ed.), *Documents*, vol. 2, pt. ii, pp. 1213-14; cf. Hindmarsh, *Rise and Progress of the New Jerusalem Church*, pp. 62-3.

[38] Wesley, *A check to the Delusive and Dangerous Opinions of Baron Swedenborg*, pp. 10-38; S J Rogal, 'Swedenborg and the Wesleyans: Opposition or Outgrowth?', in Brock, Glenn, Odhner et al. (eds.), *Swedenborg and His Influence*, pp. 295-307.

[39] *The Arminian Magazine*, 8 (1785), p. 552, repr. in Tafel (ed.), *Documents*, vol. 2, pt. ii, p. 696; Lineham, 'English Swedenborgians', p. 41.

[40] W B Hayden, 'A Document concerning Swedenborg', in *The Monthly Observer and New Church Record*, 6 (1862), pp. 95-101; Bergquist (ed.), *Swedenborg's Dream Diary*, pp. 30-8, 53, 299-302; Bergquist, *Swedenborg's Secret*, pp. 169-70, 205-6.

[41] Tafel (ed.), *Documents*, vol. 2, pt. ii, p. 1244; Lineham, 'English Swedenborgians', p. 42.

[42] Walton, *Notes and materials*, p. 596.

[43] *Memoirs of the Life, Death, Burial, and Wonderful Writings, of Jacob Behmen*, tr. Francis Okely (Northampton, 1780), pp. vi-ix.

[44] James Hervey, *A collection of letters, by the late Reverend James Hervey*, 2nd edn., 2 vols. (1784), vol. 1, p. 240.

[45] T Compton, 'Thomas Hartley', in *New Church Magazine*, 10 (1891), p. 134.

[46] Thomas Hartley, *Sermons on Various Subjects: with a prefatory discourse on mistakes concerning religion* (1754), pp. xxxiii-xl.

[47] Cf. Emanuel Swedenborg, *A Treatise concerning Heaven and Hell*, tr. William Cookworthy and Thomas Hartley (1778), p. ii.

[48] Thomas Hartley, *Paradise restored...To which is added, a short defence of the mystical writers* (1764), pp. 394-5.

[49] Hartley, *Paradise restored*, pp. 443-7; cf. William Warburton, *The Doctrine of Grace*, 2 vols. (1763), repr. in William Warburton, *The Works of the Right Reverend William*

Warburton, Lord Bishop of Gloucester, 7 vols. (1788), vol. 4, pp. 625-6.

50 Wesley, *Works*, vol. 3, p. 160; Telford (ed.), *Letters of John Wesley*, vol. 4, p. 234; A Douglas Selleck, *Cookworthy 1705-80 and his circle* (Plymouth, 1978), pp. 106-7.

51 Swedenborg, *Small Theological Works and Letters*, pp. 309-31; R L Tafel, 'New documents concerning Swedenborg', in *New Church Magazine*, 4 (1885), pp. 374-5, 387-9; C Odhner, 'Thomas Hartley', in *New Church Life*, 15 (1895), pp. 136-7; Lineham, 'English Swedenborgians', pp. 42-3.

52 *Gentleman's Magazine*, 50 (1780), p. 495; Swedenborg Society, London, MS A/143, partly printed in J Clowes, 'Memoir of Mr. W. Cookworthy', in *Intellectual Repository for the New Church*, n.s. 1 (1825), pp. 439-47; Anon., 'Swedenborg and the late William Cookworthy', in *Intellectual Repository and New Jerusalem Magazine*, 3 (1856), p. 412; Tafel (ed.), *Documents*, vol. 2, pt. ii, pp. 1166, 1170-3; Lineham, 'English Swedenborgians', pp. 48-50.

53 K Morgan (ed.), *An American Quaker in the British Isles* (1992), pp. 109-10; Francis Geach, *A reply to Dr. Saunders's pamphlet, relative to the dispute concerning Devonish cider* (1768), pp. 8, 9-18; William Pryce, *Mineralogia Cornubiensis* (1778), pp. 116-17, 120.

54 Swedenborg Society, MS K/120, William Cookworthy to Richard Kingston (Plymouth, 24 December 1744; Plymouth, 1 August [no year]).

55 Hindmarsh, *Rise and Progress of the New Jerusalem Church*, p. 6; cf. Lineham, 'English Swedenborgians', p. 49.

56 Compton, 'Thomas Hartley', p. 132; Theodore Compton, *William Cookworthy* (1895), pp. 56-7; Selleck, *Cookworthy 1705-80 and his circle*, p. 109; Lineham, 'English Swedenborgians', pp. 45-6.

57 Tafel (ed.), *Documents*, vol. 2, pt. i, pp. 500-1; A E Beilby, *Rev. Thomas Hartley, A. M. Rector of Winwick, in Northamptonshire* (1931), p. 47; Lineham, 'English Swedenborgians', pp. 43-4.

58 Theodore Compton, *The Life and Correspondence of the Reverend John Clowes, M.A.* (3rd edn., 1898), pp. 11-16; Lineham, 'English Swedenborgians', pp. 75-6, 78-9.

59 Elizabeth Fletcher, *Autobiography of Mrs Fletcher of Edinburgh* (1875), pp. 40-4; Compton, *Life and Correspondence of John Clowes*, p. 120.

[60] Compton, *Life and Correspondence of John Clowes*, pp. 17-19; Lineham, 'English Swedenborgians', pp. 81-2.

[61] Chetham's Library, Manchester, Mun A 3.51-2, John Clowes, 'Autobiography', fol. 49, printed in John Clowes, *A Memoir of the late Rev. John Clowes, A.M.* (2nd edn., 1849), pp. 14-15; cf. Swedenborg Society, MS A/4, John Clowes, 'Memoirs', copy in the hand of G Harrison, p. 29; Lineham, 'English Swedenborgians', p. 82.

[62] DWL, MS I.1.43, printed in Walton, *Notes and materials*, pp. 595-6; Hirst, *Hidden Riches*, p. 242; Harrison, *Second Coming*, p. 22; Clowes, *Memoir*, p. 27; Compton, *Life and Correspondence of John Clowes*, pp. 19-25; Lineham, 'English Swedenborgians', pp. 83-4.

[63] *Aurora*, 1 (1799-1800), pp. 317-18; Lineham, 'English Swedenborgians', p. 121; Garrett, 'Swedenborg and Mystical Enlightenment', p. 79.

[64] *Aurora*, 1 (1799-1800), p. 134; James Dakeyne, *History of the Bolton New Church Society from 1781 to 1888* (Bolton, 1888), p. 2; *Life and Correspondence of John Clowes*, pp. 37-9; Carl Odhner, *Annals of the New Church vol. I. 1688-1850* (Bryn Athyn, 1904), p. 116; Lineham, 'English Swedenborgians', pp. 119, 121; Garrett, 'Swedenborg and Mystical Enlightenment', pp. 73-4, 79.

[65] Hindmarsh, *Rise and Progress of the New Jerusalem Church*, pp. 7, 67; Odhner, *Annals of the New Church*, pp. 117, 120.

[66] Compton, *Life and Correspondence of John Clowes*, pp. 38-45; C Higham, 'The Rev. John Clowes and his Diocesan', in *New Church Magazine*, 33 (1914), pp. 364-9; 'An Anonymous Letter', in *New Church Magazine*, 97 (1978), pp. 14-17; Alfred Gabay, *The Covert Enlightenment. Eighteenth-Century Counterculture and Its Aftermath* (West Chester, 2005), pp. 63-4.

[67] Hindmarsh, *Rise and Progress of the New Jerusalem Church*, pp. 54-5; Compton, *Life and Correspondence of John Clowes*, p. 48; Odhner, *Annals of the New Church*, pp. 131, 133; Lineham, 'English Swedenborgians', p. 230.

[68] Cheshire and Chester Archives, Chester, EDV 7/3, quoted in Lineham, 'English Swedenborgians', p. 80.

[69] Hindmarsh, *Rise and Progress of the New Jerusalem Church*, p. 6; *Monthly Review*, 42 (1770), p. 448.

[70] Hindmarsh, *Rise and Progress of the New Jerusalem Church*, p. 9.

[71] George Trevelyan, *The Life and Letters of Lord Macaulay* (1909), p. 15; A Hessayon, 'Jacob Boehme and the early Quakers', in *Journal of the Friends Historical Society*, 60 (2005), p. 215.

[72] James Lackington, *Memoirs of the forty-five first years* (9th edn., 1794), p. 180.

[73] Lackington, *Memoirs*, pp. 207, 209; NA, Prob 11/1125, will of John Denis the elder (probate 19 January 1785), fols. 106v-07v; John Nichols, *Literary Anecdotes of the Eighteenth Century*, 9 vols. (1812-15), vol. 3, p. 641.

[74] *Denis's Catalogue of Ancient and Modern Books* (1787), pp. 18, 38, 109, 131, 133-4.

[75] Ibid., p. 31, no. 808; Folger Shakespeare Library, Washington, shelfmark T 151; Ariel Hessayon, *'Gold Tried in the Fire'. The Prophet TheaurauJohn Tany and the English Revolution* (Aldershot, 2007).

[76] *Gentleman's Magazine*, 78 (1808), pp. 172, 848; NA, Prob 11/1474, will of Henry Peckitt (probate 5 February 1808), fols. 240r-45v; Anon., 'Epistolary correspondence of the earlier members of the Church', in *The Monthly Observer*, 1 (1857), pp. 419-20; Hindmarsh, *Rise and Progress of the New Jerusalem Church*, p. 15; Tafel (ed.), *Documents*, vol. 2, pt. ii, pp. 1191-2.

[77] Swedenborg Society, MS D/41, Henry Peckitt's memorandum of the fire (1785); Hindmarsh, *Rise and Progress of the New Jerusalem Church*, pp. 18-19, 31-3; Tafel (ed.), *Documents*, vol. 2, pt. i, pp. 542-6, pt. ii, pp. 712-13.

[78] Swedenborg Society, MS A/45, 1, Henry Peckitt, extracts from the 'Diarum' of Emanuel Swedenborg; cf. Jacob Boehme, *Mysterium Magnum*, tr. John Ellistone and John Sparrow (1656 edn.), 33.32, p. 208, 'Of this the Rain-bow is a type and figure, for it is a reflex [Antitype] or contra-glance of the Sun'.

[79] Swedenborg Society, MS A/25, Henry Peckitt MSS (n.d.).

[80] *New-Jerusalem Magazine*, 1 (1790), p. 112; Benedict Chastanier, *A Word of Advice to a Benighted World* (1795), pp. 15, 18-19; Anon., 'Epistolary correspondence of the earlier members of the Church', in *The Monthly Observer*, 1 (1857), p. 419; J Hyde, 'Benedict Chastanier and the Illuminati of Avignon', in *New-Church Review*, 14 (1907), p. 185; Lineham, 'English Swedenborgians', pp. 141-2.

[81] Chastanier, *Word of Advice*, pp. 16-18.

82 R L Tafel, 'Swedenborg and Freemasonry', in *New Jerusalem Messenger*, October 1869, p. 267; Samuel Beswick, *Swedenborg Rite and the Great Masonic Leaders of the Eighteenth Century* (New York, 1870), pp. 127-32; Tafel (ed.), *Documents*, vol. 2, pt. ii, p. 1176; Hyde, 'Benedict Chastanier', pp. 191-2; Lineham, 'English Swedenborgians', pp. 143-4.

83 Claude Antoine Thory, *Acta Latomorum, ou Chronologie de l'Histoire de la Franche-Maçonnerie française*, 2 parts (Paris, 1815), pt. 1, pp. 89, 308, 318, 501; information from Diane Clements, Director of the Library and Museum of Freemasonry.

84 Chastanier, *Word of Advice*, pp. 21-4; Hyde, 'Benedict Chastanier', pp. 186-8; Lineham, 'English Swedenborgians', pp. 142-3.

85 Anon., 'The Heavenly Life—Spiritual Aphorisms', in *Intellectual Repository and New Jerusalem Magazine*, n.s. 9 (1848), p. 409; R McCully, 'Benedict Chastanier: an early New Church worthy', in *New Church Magazine*, 9 (1890), pp. 527-8; Hyde, 'Benedict Chastanier', pp. 188-9.

86 Chastanier, *Word of Advice*, pp. 24-5; Tafel (ed.), *Documents*, vol. 2, pt. ii, pp. 1177-8; Hyde, 'Benedict Chastanier', pp. 189-90.

87 Benedict Chastanier, *Annonce d'un journal Novi-Jérusalémite* (1787), pp. i, vii; Tafel (ed.), *Documents*, vol. 2, pt. ii, p. 1176; Lineham, 'English Swedenborgians', p. 197.

88 [Benedict Chastanier], *Plan Général d'une Société Universelle* (no date); BL, Add. MS 23,669, fol. 92r-v; G P G Hills, 'Notes on the Rainsford Papers in the British Museum', in *Ars Quatuor Coronatorum*, 26 (1913), p. 107; Lineham, 'English Swedenborgians', pp. 144, 196; cf. M K Schuchard, *Why Mrs Blake Cried. William Blake and the Sexual Basis of Spiritual Vision* (2006), pp. 186-7.

89 G P G Hills, 'Notes on some Masonic personalities at the end of the Eighteenth Century', in *Ars Quatuor Coronatorum*, 25 (1912), p. 156; Hills, 'Notes on the Rainsford Papers', p. 95; Lineham, 'English Swedenborgians', pp. 198-9; Garrett, 'Swedenborg and Mystical Enlightenment', p. 75.

90 Library of the Duke of Northumberland, Alnwick Castle, MS 624; Wellcome Institute for the History of Medicine, London, MS 4037, no foliation.

91 Wellcome Institute, MSS 4032-4039; Alnwick Castle, MS 600.

92 Clarke Garret, *Respectable Folly. Millenarians and the French Revolution in France*

and England (Baltimore, 1975), pp. 99-104; M L Danilewicz, ' "The King of the New Israel": Thaddeus Grabianka (1740-1807)', in *Oxford Slavonic Papers*, n.s. 1 (1968), pp. 48-56; Lineham, 'English Swedenborgians', pp. 201-2.

93 Swedenborg Society, MS K/144, Antoine-Joseph Pernety to Carl Frederik Nordenskjöld (Berlin, 30 October 1781) [German copy]; BL, Add. MS 23,669, fols. 1r-2r, Antoine-Joseph Pernety to Carl Frederik Nordenskjöld (Berlin, 30 October 1781) [incomplete English translation]; Auguste Viatte (ed.), *Les sources occultes du romantisme: Illuminisme-théosophie, 1770-1820*, 2 vols. (Paris, 1928), vol. 2, pp. 279-83; Swedenborg Society, MS K/140, Antoine-Joseph Pernety to Carl Frederik Nordenskjöld (Berlin, 15 February 1782); Tafel (ed.), *Documents*, vol. 2, pt. ii, p. 1177; Danilewicz, 'King of the New Israel', pp. 55-6; Garret, *Respectable Folly*, p. 104; Lineham, 'English Swedenborgians', pp. 202-3; J Williams-Hogan, 'The Place of Emanuel Swedenborg in Modern Western Esotericism', in Antoine Faivre and Wouter Hanegraaff (eds.), *Western Esotericism and the Science of Religion* (Leuven, 1998), p. 235.

94 Benedict Chastanier, *Tableau analytique et raisonné de la Doctrine Céleste de l'Église de la Nouvelle Jerusalem* (1786), p. 32 n.; Chastanier, *Word of Advice*, p. 25; S Sandel, *An Eulogium on the lately deceased Mr. Emanuel Swedenborg* (1784), pp. 31-6; Tafel (ed.), *Documents*, vol. 1, pp. 637-8; Hyde, 'Benedict Chastanier', pp. 189-90; Garret, *Respectable Folly*, pp. 109-10; Williams-Hogan, 'Place of Emanuel Swedenborg in Modern Western Esotericism', p. 236.

95 BL, Add. MS 23,669, fol. 99r-v, translated from the French in Garrett, 'Swedenborg and Mystical Enlightenment', p. 75; Hills, 'Notes on the Rainsford Papers', p. 111.

96 Chastanier, *Word of Advice*, pp. 25-7; Hyde, 'Benedict Chastanier', p. 192; Lineham, 'English Swedenborgians', p. 204.

97 BL, Add. MS 23,675, fols. 24r-v, 26r-v; Chastanier, *Word of Advice*, pp. 34-5; Hindmarsh, *Rise and Progress of the New Jerusalem Church*, pp. 41-7; Hills, 'Notes on the Rainsford Papers', p. 111; Danilewicz, 'King of the New Israel', pp. 58-63; Garrett, 'Swedenborg and Mystical Enlightenment', p. 76; Lineham, 'English Swedenborgians', pp. 204-6.

98 Chastanier, *Word of Advice*, p. 36; Hindmarsh, *Rise and Progress of the New Jerusalem Church*, p. 44; Hyde, 'Benedict Chastanier', pp. 194-5; Lineham, 'English Swedenborgians', p. 203.

99 'Annals of the New Church', in *New-Jerusalem Magazine*, 1 (1790), p. 175; BL, Add. MS 23,670, fol. 275r; Tafel (ed.), *Documents*, vol. 2, pt. ii, pp. 1177, 1179; Garret, *Respectable Folly*, p. 113; Lineham, 'English Swedenborgians', p. 196; Williams-Hogan, 'Place of Emanuel Swedenborg in Modern Western Esotericism', p. 238.

100 Chastanier, *Tableau analytique*, p. 40 n.; cf. [Benedict Chastanier?], *Emmanuel Swedenborg's New-Year's Gift to his Readers* (1791), p. 27.

101 *Gentleman's Magazine*, 52 (1782), p. 360; Hindmarsh, *Rise and Progress of the New Jerusalem Church*, pp. 40-2; cf. Francis Dobbs, *A Concise View from History and Prophecy* (Dublin, 1800), pp. 258-60.

102 Anon., 'The Rev. Jacob Duché', in *The Monthly Observer*, 1 (1857), pp. 79-82; W B Hayden, 'Rev. Jacob Duché', in *The New Jerusalem Magazine*, 38 (1865-6), pp. 496-503, 561-9, 615-22; C Higham, 'The Rev. Jacob Duché, M.A.', in *New Church Review*, 22 (1915), pp. 210-25, 404-20; C Garrett, 'The Spiritual Odyssey of Jacob Duché', in *Proceedings of the American Philosophical Society*, 119 (1975), pp. 143-55; Lineham, 'English Swedenborgians', pp. 164-9.

103 E D Neill, 'Rev. Jacob Duché, the First Chaplain of Congress', in *Pennsylvania Magazine of History and Biography*, 2 (1878), pp. 62-3; Bird Wilson, *Memoirs of the life of the Right Rev. William White, D.D.* (Philadelphia, 1839), pp. 28-9.

104 DWL, MS I.1.43, partly printed in Walton, *Notes and materials*, pp. 423-4, and quoted in Garrett, 'Spiritual Odyssey of Jacob Duché', p. 145; Lineham, 'English Swedenborgians', p. 32.

105 Library of the Historical Society of Pennsylvania, Jacob Duché to Mary Hopkinson (5 May 1785), quoted in Garrett, 'Swedenborg and Mystical Enlightenment', p. 73; Lineham, 'English Swedenborgians', p. 166.

106 A F Gegenheimer, 'Artist in exile: the story of Thomas Spence Duché', in *Pennsylvania Magazine of History and Biography*, 79 (1955), pp. 3-26.

107 Chastanier, *Word of Advice*, p. 27.

108 Gegenheimer, 'Artist in exile', pp. 20-1; Garrett, 'Spiritual Odyssey of Jacob Duché', p. 153; Lineham, 'English Swedenborgians', p. 206; Garrett, 'Swedenborg and Mystical Enlightenment', p. 76.

109 Maryland Historical Library, Baltimore, Redwood Collection, Jacob Duché to William

White (30 August 1788), quoted in Hayden, 'Rev. Jacob Duché', p. 618; Garrett, 'Spiritual Odyssey of Jacob Duché', p. 153; Garrett, 'Swedenborg and Mystical Enlightenment', p. 76.

[110] BL, Add. MS 23,669, fols. 129r-130v, 101r-3r; Hills, 'Notes on the Rainsford Papers', p. 109.

[111] John Wright, *A Revealed Knowledge of some things that will speedily be fulfilled in the World* (1794), p. 61; Hyde, 'Benedict Chastanier', pp. 195, 200; Lineham, 'English Swedenborgians', p. 207.

[112] Wright, *Revealed Knowledge*, pp. 3-5, 59-60; William Bryan, *A Testimony of the Spirit of Truth* (1795), p. 20; Chastanier, *Word of Advice*, pp. 27, 37-8; Garret, *Respectable Folly*, p. 160.

[113] Wright, *Revealed Knowledge*, pp. 5-22; Bryan, *Testimony of the Spirit of Truth*, pp. 20-8; Hindmarsh, *Rise and Progress of the New Jerusalem Church*, pp. 47-8; Danilewicz, 'King of the New Israel', p. 64; Garret, *Respectable Folly*, pp. 110-12; Lineham, 'English Swedenborgians', pp. 206-7.

[114] Wright, *Revealed Knowledge*, p. 44; NA, PC 1/18/19.

[115] Wright, *Revealed Knowledge*, p. 59.

[116] Garret, *Respectable Folly*, pp. 103-4, 113; Williams-Hogan, 'Place of Emanuel Swedenborg in Modern Western Esotericism', p. 238.

[117] *Prophetical passages, concerning the present times* (1795).

[118] Timothy C F Stunt, 'Brothers, Richard (1757-1824)', in *Oxford Dictionary of National Biography* (Oxford, 2004).

[119] *Gentleman's Magazine*, 94 pt. ii (1824), pp. 469-72; *European Magazine*, 86 (1824), pp. 191-6; Anon., 'Epistolary correspondence of the earlier members of the Church', p. 423; Hindmarsh, *Rise and Progress of the New Jerusalem Church*, pp. 123-4; Garret, *Respectable Folly*, pp. 161-2, 176; Richard Sharp, 'Sharp, William (1749-1824)', in *Oxford Dictionary of National Biography* (Oxford, 2004); Schuchard, *Why Mrs Blake Cried*, pp. 255-6.

[120] A Graves, 'Portrait of Samuel Seabury', in *Notes and Queries*, 6th series, 5 (1882), p. 318; Higham, 'Rev. Jacob Duché', pp. 405, 414.

[121] Hindmarsh, *Rise and Progress of the New Jerusalem Church*, p. 23 n.; Lineham, 'English Swedenborgians', p. 156.

[122] Higham, 'Rev. Jacob Duché', pp. 413-14; information from Diane Clements; BL, Add. MS 23,675, fols. 1, 3, 25; Hills, 'Notes on the Rainsford Papers', pp. 94, 126.

[123] NA, Prob 11/1483, will of François Hippolyte Barthélémon (probate 5 August 1808), fols. 305v-6r; 'Obituary', in *Intellectual Repository and New Jerusalem Magazine*, n.s. 2 (1841), pp. 40, 140-4, 238; Thomas Robinson, *Remembrancer and Recorder of Facts and Documents Illustrative of the Genius of the New Jerusalem Dispensation* (Manchester, 1864), pp. 105-8; Tafel (ed.), *Documents*, vol. 2, pt. ii, pp. 1219-21; Lineham, 'English Swedenborgians', pp. 173, 177, 178-9.

[124] A G Debus, 'A Further Note on Palingenesis: The Account of Ebenezer Sibly in the Illustration of Astrology (1792)', in *Isis*, 64 (1973), pp. 226-30; A G Debus, 'Scientific Truth and Occult Tradition: The Medical World of Ebenezer Sibly (1751-1799)', in *Medical History*, 26 (1982), pp. 259-78; Patrick Curry, 'Sibly, Ebenezer (1751-c.1799)', in *Oxford Dictionary of National Biography* (Oxford, 2004); Susan Mitchell Sommers, 'Dr. Ebenezer Sibly (1751-99), Masonic Polymath', in A Prescott (ed.), *Marking Well. Essays on the Occasion of the 150th anniversary of the Grand Lodge of Mark Master Masons of England and Wales and its districts and lodges overseas* (Hersham, 2006).

[125] Lineham, 'English Swedenborgians', p. 261.

[126] Ebenezer Sibly, *A New and Complete Illustration of the Occult Sciences* (1790), pp. 821-8; Lineham, 'English Swedenborgians', pp. 177-8.

[127] Wellcome Institute, MSS 3203, 4594; Grand Lodge Library, London, MS 1380 SIB; John Rylands University Library, Manchester, MS 40; Alnwick Castle, MS 624; Glasgow University Library, Glasgow, MSS Ferguson 25, 99, 305, 310; BL, Add. MS 23,670, fol. 353r.

[128] Glasgow UL, MS Ferguson 25, fol. 2v.

[129] Walton, *Notes and materials*, pp. 684, 685; Glasgow UL, MS Ferguson 125.

[130] Hindmarsh, *Rise and Progress of the New Jerusalem Church*, p. 23 n.

[131] Christopher Baugh, 'Loutherbourg, Philippe Jacques de (1740-1812)', in *Oxford Dictionary of National Biography* (Oxford, 2004); J Gage, 'Loutherbourg: mystagogue of the sublime', in *History Today*, 13 (1963), pp. 332-9; J H Kunin, 'The Date of Loutherbourg's "Falls of the Rhine at Schaffhausen"', in *The Burlington Magazine*, 114 (1972), pp. 554-5.

[132] Swedenborg Society, M/4, portrait of Emanuel Swedenborg; cf. Schuchard, *Why Mrs Blake Cried*, pp. 169-70.

[133] R Joppien, 'A Visitor to a Ruined Churchyard——A Newly Discovered Painting by P J de Loutherbourg', in *The Burlington Magazine*, 118 (1976), pp. 296, 299; [Monsignor Barberi], *The Life of Joseph Balsamo, commonly called the Count Cagliostro* (1791), pp. 77 n., 144.

[134] Anthony Pasquin (pseud. John Williams), *Memoirs of the Royal Academicians* (1796), pp. 80-1; W S Lewis et al. (eds.), *The Correspondence of Horace Walpole*, 48 vols. (New Haven, 1937-83), vol. 34, pp. 50-1; Schuchard, *Why Mrs Blake Cried*, p. 199.

[135] Mary Pratt, *A list of a few cures performed by Mr. and Mrs. de Loutherbourg* (1789), sig. A2.

[136] Pratt, *List of a few cures*, pp. 3-9; BL, Add. MS 23,668, fols. 25v-26r; Hills, 'Notes on the Rainsford Papers', p. 112.

[137] 'London debates: 1789', in *London debating societies 1776-99*, London Record Society (1994), pp. 246-73; cf. *The Times*, 16, 17, 24 September 1789; *Gentleman's Magazine*, 54 pt. ii (1784), pp. 944-6.

[138] P Fara, 'An Attractive Theory——Animal Magnetism in Eighteenth-Century England', in *History of Science*, 33 (1995), pp. 138-42; G E Bentley, 'Mainaduc, Magic, and Madness: George Cumberland and the Blake connection', in *Notes & Queries*, 236 (1991), pp. 294-6.

[139] Chastanier, *Word of Advice*, p. 30; William Spence, *Essays in Divinity and Physic* (1792), p. 58; Daniel Lysons (ed.), *Collectanea: or, A collection of advertisements and paragraphs from the newspapers*, 2 vols. (n.d.) [BL, C.191.c.16], vol. 1, pt. ii, fols. 156v, 157r; Lineham, 'English Swedenborgians', p. 185; Schuchard, *Why Mrs Blake Cried*, pp. 213-14, 220.

[140] Chastanier, *Tableau analytique*, pp. 245-53; Beswick, *Swedenborg Rite*, pp. 198-9; Anon., 'Epistolary correspondence of the earlier members of the Church', p. 420.

[141] Alnwick Castle, MS 616, 1, 2; BL, Add. MS 23,675, fols. 34-6; Hills, 'Notes on the Rainsford Papers', pp. 110, 116; Lineham, 'English Swedenborgians', pp. 182-3; Schuchard, *Why Mrs Blake Cried*, p. 262.

[142] Debus, 'Scientific Truth and Occult Tradition', pp. 261, 274-7; Sommers, 'Dr. Ebenezer Sibly', p. 112; Fara, 'Attractive Theory', pp. 155, 177 n. 198.

[143] Odhner, *Annals of the New Church*, p. 139.

[144] Anon., *Observations sur le Franc-Maçonnerie: le Martinisme, les visions de Swedenborg, le magnétisme* (Avignon, 1786); *The New Magazine of Knowledge*, 1 (1790), pp. 123-7, 279-80, 401-6; Anon., *Wonders and mysteries of animal magnetism displayed* (1791), pp. 7, 9-10, 17; Fara, 'Attractive Theory', pp. 151, 173 n. 172.

[145] Jane Lead, *The Enochian walks with God* (1694) [BL, 4105.de.2(10)]; Jane Lead, *A message to the Philadelphian Society* (1696) [BL, 4378.a.32]; Jane Lead, *A fountain of gardens* (1696) [BL, 4412.i.25]; Jane Lead, *The signs of the times* (1699) [BL, 3185.i.22(1)]; Jane Lead, *A living funeral testimony* (1702) [BL, 4409.de.32]. He also owned a copy of Richard Coppin, *A blow at the serpent* (1763?) [BL, 4139. bbb.52(1)].

[146] DWL, MS I.1.43, printed in Walton, *Notes and materials*, pp. 587-91; Hirst, *Hidden Riches*, pp. 259-60, 276-81; Thompson, *Witness Against the Beast*, pp. 43-4, 138-9.

[147] *The New Magazine of Knowledge*, 2 (1791), p. 311; *The New Jerusalem Journal* (1792), pp. 36-9, 91-2, 196; Thompson, *Witness Against the Beast*, p. 139.

[148] Geoffrey Keynes (ed.), *William Blake. Complete Writings* (Oxford, 1976), pp. 149, 157-8; cf. M Schorer, 'Swedenborg and Blake', in *Modern Philology*, 36 (1938), p. 160; M D Paley, ' "A New Heaven is Begun": Blake and Swedenborgianism', in Harvey Bellin and Darrell Ruhl (eds.), *Blake and Swedenborg: Opposition is True Friendship* (West Chester, 1985), p. 26; Thompson, *Witness Against the Beast*, pp. 45, 141, 172; Schuchard, *Why Mrs Blake Cried*, pp. 241-3.

[149] D Erdman, 'Blake's early Swedenborgianism: A Twentieth-Century Legend', in *Comparative Literature*, 5 (1953), pp. 247-57; Hirst, *Hidden Riches*, p. 212; Lineham, 'English Swedenborgians', p. 194; Paley, 'New Heaven is Begun', in Bellin and Ruhl (eds.), *Blake and Swedenborg*, p. 15; cf. Schorer, 'Swedenborg and Blake', pp. 157-8; Schuchard, *Why Mrs Blake Cried*, pp. 7, 8, 145.

[150] Thompson, *Witness Against the Beast*, pp. 107, 120-1.

[151] K Davies, 'William Blake's Mother: A New Identification', in *Blake: An Illustrated Quarterly*, 33 (1999), pp. 36-50; Schuchard, *Why Mrs Blake Cried*, pp. 8, 13-15, 31, 55-7, 126-7, 342-4.

[152] Cf. Higham, 'Rev. Jacob Duché', p. 405; Garrett, 'Swedenborg and Mystical Enlightenment',

p. 72; Paley, 'New Heaven is Begun', in Bellin and Ruhl (eds.), *Blake and Swedenborg*, p. 16.

[153] Garrett, 'Swedenborg and Mystical Enlightenment', p. 73; Thompson, *Witness Against the Beast*, pp. 42, 132; cf. Harrison, *Second Coming*, p. 72.

[154] Higham, 'Rev. Jacob Duché', p. 416; D Erdman, 'Lambeth and Bethlehem in Blake's Jerusalem', in *Modern Philology*, 48 (1951), pp. 184, 186-9; Hirst, *Hidden Riches*, p. 213; Garrett, 'Spiritual Odyssey of Jacob Duché', p. 154; Lineham, 'English Swedenborgians', p. 238.

[155] Emanuel Swedenborg, *The Wisdom of angels* (1788) [BL, C.45.e.1]; C Higham, 'Blake and the "Swedenborgians"', in *Notes and Queries*, 11th series, 11 (1915), pp. 276-7; Erdman, 'Blake's early Swedenborgianism', p. 253; G E Bentley, 'Blake and Swedenborg', in *Notes and Queries*, 199 (1954), pp. 264-5; Hirst, *Hidden Riches*, pp. 213-14; Lineham, 'English Swedenborgians', p. 234; Paley, 'New Heaven is Begun', in Bellin and Ruhl (eds.), *Blake and Swedenborg*, p. 16; Thompson, *Witness Against the Beast*, pp. 125, 129-30, 133.

[156] Schorer, 'Swedenborg and Blake', p. 159; Erdman, 'Blake's early Swedenborgianism', pp. 248, 253-4; Hirst, *Hidden Riches*, pp. 214-15; Lineham, 'English Swedenborgians', pp. 234, 281; Paley, 'New Heaven is Begun', in Bellin and Ruhl (eds.), *Blake and Swedenborg*, pp. 17-21; Thompson, *Witness Against the Beast*, pp. 130-1.

[157] Schorer, 'Swedenborg and Blake', pp. 159-60; Erdman, 'Blake's early Swedenborgianism', p. 253; Hirst, *Hidden Riches*, pp. 217-18, 225; K Raine, 'The Human Face of God', in Bellin and Ruhl (eds.), *Blake and Swedenborg*, p. 101.

[158] Erdman, 'Blake's early Swedenborgianism', p. 252; D J Sloss and J P R Wallis (eds.), *The Prophetic Writings of William Blake*, 2 vols. (Oxford, 1926), vol. 1, p. 9.

[159] Henry Crabb Robinson, *Diary, reminiscences, and correspondence*, 3 vols., ed. Thomas Sadler (1869), vol. 2, pp. 305, 323; cf. Alexander Gilchrist, *Life of William Blake, 'Pictor Ignotus'*, 2 vols. (1863), vol. 1, pp. 15-16; Lineham, 'English Swedenborgians', p. 195.

[160] Erdman, 'Blake's early Swedenborgianism', pp. 255-7; Lineham, 'English Swedenborgians', p. 194.

[161] Keynes (ed.), *Blake. Complete Writings*, p. 799; Thompson, *Witness Against the Beast*, p. 130; Schuchard, *Why Mrs Blake Cried*, pp. 161, 167.

[162] Anon., *An Inquiry into the Commission and Doctrine of the new Apostle Emanuel Swedenborg* (1794), p. 14.

[163] T Compton, 'Thomas Hartley', in *New Church Magazine*, 10 (1891), p. 134; A Hessayon, 'Jacob Boehme and the early Quakers', in *Journal of the Friends Historical Society*, 60 (2005), pp. 208, 210.

'The Swedishman at Brother Brockmer's': Moravians and Swedenborgians in eighteenth-century London

Keri Davies

A t first glance, it might seem unlikely that there should be any connection between Moravians and Swedenborgians. English Moravians looked back to the origins of their church amongst the followers of Jan Hus, martyred in Prague in 1415, and were proud that in 1748 the English Parliament had recognized them as 'an ancient protestant episcopal church'. [1] Zinzendorf, in a speech to Synod in 1752, stressed the 'Oriental Extraction of the Brethren's Church', presumably alluding to the Church's origins in the Czech lands evangelized by SS Cyril and Methodius in the ninth century. [2] Swedenborg, on the other hand, believed that he had witnessed the Last Judgment in the spiritual world, along with the inauguration of a 'New Church'. He prophesied that the year 1757 would be the 'beginning of a new world', and the dawning of a new era—not so much an apocalyptic ending of human history, as the opening of a new chapter of a divinely inspired theory of history. In this paper, I shall tell something of the man Emanuel Swedenborg, how he came into contact with the Moravians, how his writings were received by them, and the subsequent evolution of Swedenborgianism and its separate New Jerusalem Church.

The Swedish philosopher, scientist and visionary, Emanuel Swedenborg, was born in Stockholm, 29 January 1688, and died in Clerkenwell, London, 29 March 1772. He was the son of Jesper Swedberg, a Lutheran bishop, and Sara Behm, who came from a family of mine owners. (In 1719, the children of Bishop Jesper Swedberg were ennobled and their name changed to Swedenborg.) Swedenborg grew up in the higher ranks of Swedish society, and was educated at Uppsala University. His intellectual ability was evident from the start, and he extended his education, under the influence of Christopher Polhem (1661-1751), 'the Archimedes of the North', and Erik Benzelius (1675-1743), who had married Swedenborg's elder sister, travelling widely in Europe. In 1724 he was offered chairs of astronomy and mathematics at Uppsala University, but declined, saying that he had mainly dealt with geometry, chemistry and metallurgy during his career. He also noted that he did not have the gift of eloquent speech because of a speech impediment, a stammer. He chose instead a post of the Swedish Board of Mines where he felt he could be of greater service to his nation. [3]

As assessor-extraordinary on the Swedish Board of Mines, Swedenborg played an important part in Sweden's economic and technological growth, introducing Newcomen's steam engine and devising a method of determining longitude. But this was also the time when the theologians Friedrich Breckling (1629-1711) and J C Dippel (1673-1774) introduced radical Pietism into a religious society dominated by a rigid Lutheranism. Out of this, combined with extensive reading of Leibniz, Malebranche and Wolff, whose attempts to bridge the gap between the physical and spiritual worlds influenced him, emerged a turmoil of thought that resulted in his *Opera philosophica et mineralia* of 1734. [4] This and his later works brought Swedenborg uneasy respect, but in 1743-4 a growing spiritual crisis culminated in a vision of union with Christ, at Easter, 6-7 April 1744, that transformed his life. Nevertheless, he continued to participate in political affairs, was consulted daily by the prime minister, Anders Johan von Höpken (1712-89), and contributed memorials to the Swedish parliament.

In June 1747, Swedenborg resigned his post as assessor of the Board of Mines. He explained that he was obliged to complete a work he had begun, and requested to receive half his salary as a pension. He took up again the study of Hebrew and began to work on the interpretation of the Bible with the goal of interpreting the spiritual meaning of every verse. From sometime between 1746 and 1747, and for ten years following, he devoted all his energy to this task. The foundation of Swedenborg's theology was laid down in *Arcana Cœlestia*, or 'Heavenly Secrets', the Latin text of which he had printed anonymously in London in eight volumes between 1749 and 1756.[5] In 1765, at Gothenburg en route for Amsterdam, he met Gabriel Beyer, who was so moved by his teaching as to launch a cult of Swedenborg's doctrines.

In the decades after Swedenborg's death, in 1772, his ideas excited considerable interest, especially in England. His conception of a divine influx that illumines the spiritual man as the sun illumines the natural man interested eighteenth-century artists and poets as diverse as Blake, Goethe, and Coleridge. We know for instance that William Blake read some of Swedenborg's religious works in the 1780s, and that he and his wife attended the first conference of the Swedenborgian New Jerusalem Church in London in April 1789. But in *The Marriage of Heaven and Hell* (1790), Blake is savage in his satire on Swedenborg, and it has been the almost unanimous view amongst Blake scholars that Blake abandoned his Swedenborgian beliefs shortly after the conference and at once became very critical of his former religious inspiration. It is also commonly stated that Blake to some degree returned to Swedenborgian ideas later in his life, perhaps twenty years on from his attendance at the New Church conference. In December 1825, the lawyer Henry Crabb Robinson recorded a conversation with the sixty-eight-year-old William Blake: 'Incidentally Swedenborg was spoken of. He was a divine teacher'; however, 'Parts of his scheme are dangerous. His sexual religion is dangerous'.[6] (The reference here is presumably to Swedenborg's doctrine of Conjugial Love, his great work on sex and marriage. Blake's early association with the New Jerusalem Church coincided with a fierce internal dispute over the status of concubinage.)[7]

Swedenborg propounded 'a highly idiosyncratic and occult form of Christianity which attached itself to certain branches of Masonry'.[8] In 2001, Marsha Keith Schuchard, a historian of Freemasonry, visited the Moravian Church Library and Archive at Muswell Hill, in London, intending to search for possible records of Swedenborg's participation in the Fetter Lane (City of London) Moravian congregation. Swedenborg was resident in London in 1744-5, and had a number of close friends from within the Moravian Church. [9] However, what Dr Schuchard found, in the Church Book of the Congregation of the Lamb (the Fetter Lane church), were instead the records of the membership of Catherine Wright Armitage, mother of the poet William Blake, and of Thomas Armitage, her first husband. My own later research uncovered fuller documentation relating to Catherine and Thomas, and possibly other connections of the Blake family. [10] Only in 2007, did I locate a document, dated 4/15 May 1745, apparently referring to Swedenborg's involvement with the Moravian Community. The entry in the Fetter Lane archives simply notes:

> The Swedishman at Br Brokmer's, that was lately besides himself is now better again, and goes out. [11]

Swedenborg's attendance at Fetter Lane is confirmed in later accounts but this is the only known reference in contemporary Moravian records. The presence of the Blake family in the same congregation is significant. If Swedenborg's Moravian encounters were, as I suggest, crucial for the development of his ideas, what the Swedenborgians stress is that individual Moravians read Swedenborg's writings and were themselves influenced by him. It seems likely that there was just such a crossover from Moravianism to Swedenborgianism within the Blake family. [12]

Swedenborg had come into contact with the Moravians in 1744 while in London to publish the third part of his *Regnum animale* or *The Animal Kingdom*. [13] A small group of Moravian missionaries had arrived in London a few years previously, in 1738. [14] For them, England was intended as merely a staging post for their missions in the British colonies, but while in London they made contact with a religious fellowship group, the Fetter Lane Society (including John and Charles Wesley), meeting at the bookshop of James Hutton (1715-95), and out of this there developed a permanent

Moravian Congregation in London. By 1742, the Fetter Lane Society's meeting room had become too small. James Hutton therefore leased a Meeting House, also off Fetter Lane. The Brethren's Chapel, Fetter Lane (as it became known) was to be the Moravians' London centre for the next two hundred years. [15]

Swedenborg had actually become interested in Moravianism some years earlier, through his friend Arvid Gradin, whose book on the Moravians he owned. [16] Indeed, he claimed a 'precognitive' vision of the Fetter Lane chapel while still in Holland in 1743. By 1744, when he arrived in England, there were regular meetings of both English and German-speaking congregations at Fetter Lane.

On his voyage to England from Holland, Swedenborg had met a 'pious shoemaker', Johann Senft (1688-1752), known in England as John Seniff, who was Warden of the Moravian's German Congregation in London. [17] When Swedenborg asked him to recommend a place of lodging in London, Seniff named a fellow Moravian, John Paul Brockmer, a gold watchcase chaser of Salisbury Court, Fleet Street (one of a number of Moravians in this specialized luxury trade). [18] Swedenborg first stayed with Brockmer from May to July 1744, at a time when meetings of the Brethren were held in Brockmer's home. Brockmer also invited Swedenborg to services at the Fetter Lane chapel.

Decades later, John Wesley recounted some of the anecdotes about Swedenborg's behaviour while a lodger at Brockmer's:

Many years ago the Baron came over to England, and lodged at one Mr. Brockmer's: who informed me (and the same information was given me by Mr. Mathesius, a very serious Swedish clergyman, both of whom were alive when I left London, and, I suppose, are so still,) that while he was in his house he had a violent fever; in the height of which, being totally delirious, he broke from Mr. Brockmer, ran into the street stark naked, proclaimed himself the Messiah, and rolled himself in the mire. I suppose he dates from this time his admission into the Society of Angels. From this time we are undoubtedly to date that peculiar species of insanity which attended him, with scarce any intermission, to the day of his death. [19]

Wesley also printed Brockmer's more formal recollections of this period which he had communicated to the Swedish Lutheran minister in London, the Revd Aron Mathesius. Wesley introduces this account with the following words:

> The following authentic account of a very great man was given me by one of his countrymen [Mathesius]. He is now in London, as is Mr. Brockmer also, and ready to attest every part of it. In the Baron's writings are many excellent things; but there are many likewise that are whimsical to the last degree. And some of these may do hurt to serious persons whose imagination is stronger than their judgment.
>
> 1. 'Some time in the year 1743, a Moravian Brother, by name Seniff, in his return to London from Holland, where he had been visiting his children, became acquainted in a packet-boat with Baron Emanuel de Swedenborg; who desired to be recommended to a family in London, where he could live retired. Mr. Seniff brought him to Mr. Brockmer. This gentleman was very easily prevailed upon to take him under his roof.
>
> 2. 'The Baron behaved very decently in his house: he went every Sunday to the chapel of the Moravians in Fetter Lane. Though he lived very recluse, he nevertheless would often converse with Mr. Brockmer, and was pleased with hearing the Gospel in London. So he went on for several months, continually approving of what he heard. At last he came to Mr. Brockmer, and told him, that he rejoiced that the Gospel was preached to the poor; but lamented over the learned and the rich, who he said must all go to hell.
>
> 3. 'Some months after, he told Mr. Brockmer he was writing a pamphlet in the Latin language, which he would send gratis to all learned men in the universities.

4. 'After that he did not open his chamber-door for two days, neither would permit the maid to come in to make the bed and sweep the room.

5. 'One evening Mr. Brockmer was at a coffee-house, and the maid came to fetch him home, informing him, that something extraordinary had happened to Mr. Swedenborg: that she knocked several times at his door, but he had not opened it: upon this Mr. Brockmer came himself and knocked; calling him by his name, he jumped up from bed. Mr. Brockmer asked, whether he would not let the maid make the bed? He answered, No: and desired to be left alone, for he was about a great and solemn work.' [20]

These accounts of Swedenborg's madness have occasioned great controversy among his followers and their veracity is often doubted. [21] The terse note in the Fetter Lane archive ('The Swedishman at Br Brokmer's, that was lately besides himself is now better again') provides crucial confirmatory and contemporary evidence of Swedenborg's mental breakdown in 1744/5. As far as the Congregation at Fetter Lane was concerned, Emanuel Swedenborg was 'besides himself'——in a condition of extreme mental distress——though they did not recognize this condition as one that leads to visionary experience. [22] But then this period coincides with the disruptive arrival of French Prophets at the open meetings:

Monday 13ᵗʰ May 1745 [...] Yesterday there was many French Prophets at Fetter Lane & many strangers in yᵉ Afternoon [23]

The trances and ecstatic convulsions of the French Prophets, descendants of the Camisards, were not what the London Moravians saw as acceptable or authentic of spiritual influx. In their early years in England, the Moravians are sometimes referred to as 'the still brethren'. For them, stillness, under the influence of Philip Henry Molther (1714-80), consisted in waiting quietly for God's grace. It was Wesley's dissension from what he saw as a depreciation of the ordinances of the

Church that in part caused his withdrawal from the Fetter Lane community. [24] Perhaps it was the ecstasies of the Prophets as much as Wesley's enthusiasm that led Molther to lay such stress on stillness.

'Swedenborg', wrote Czeslaw Milosz, 'was a true son of the Enlightenment'. [25] Like Zinzendorf and Rousseau, he is a typical product of the eighteenth century (and not a mere reaction against it) as much as Voltaire and the *encyclopédists*. Having begun his career as a scientist and inventor before turning theosopher, Emanuel Swedenborg offered a mysticism for the eighteenth century, a way of describing visionary experiences that took an Enlightenment form. As with his scientific research, Swedenborg recorded every detail of his visionary experiences in empirical terms, claiming to report accurately things he had experienced on his spiritual journeys. 'His ideas of spiritual life', wrote Judith Penny, 'are as calm and composed as the curls of his eighteenth-century wig'. [26]

In 1745, Swedenborg had ended his long series of scientific works by the publication, in London, of *The Worship and Love of God*. [27] This book is an embodiment, in a story, of its author's scientific doctrines. In a connected narrative, it treats of the origin of the earth, the birth, infancy, and love, of Adam; and of the soul in its state of integrity, in the image of God. It 'remains to mark the point of intellectual development at which Swedenborg had at this time arrived, and in this respect it will always have a strong interest to those who delight in tracing the growth and education of his mind'. [28] Over the next twenty-five years Swedenborg wrote another fourteen works of a spiritual nature. There was tight censorship in Sweden of works of religious controversy and all Swedenborg's theosophical writings were published in either London or Amsterdam.

Moravians were likely to have been the earliest readers of Swedenborg's writing.[29] Though Swedenborg strictly maintained the anonymity of his spiritual writings until 1768, the first translation of any of his religious works, a translation into English of part II of *Arcana Cœlestia*, by John Marchant, was published in 1750 by the Moravian publisher John Lewis (d. 1755). [30] Swedenborg had presumably made Lewis's acquaintance through attendance at Fetter Lane services. Later works were published by Lewis's widow Mary (1703-91), and by Henry Trapp (1739-90), married to their daughter Martha. All were members of the Moravian Congregation at Fetter Lane.

One early reader was the Moravian minister at Northampton, Francis Okely (1719-94), who had become acquainted with Swedenborg's works as early as 1767.[31] He writes about his discovery of Swedenborg's writings and his later acquaintanceship with the man himself in a letter to his brother John Okely of Bethlehem, Pennsylvania:

My first knowledge of the Baron was in the year 1767, and I received it in [the] following manner:

At the time I taught Latin &c. to a few select young gentlemen. Being at a loss for some better books with respect to matter than are usually taught in grammar schools, I looked over most of the catalogues printed and published in London. In one of them I met with a book having this extraordinary title: *De Coelo et ejus Mirabilibus, et de Inferno, ex auditis et visis*; that is, 'Concerning Heaven and its Wonders, and concerning Hell, from hearing and seeing.' This I bought and read in part. He expresses himself thus at the beginning of the book (which I thus translate out of the original Latin):

'It was given me to be together with the angels, and to converse with them as one man does with another; and withal to see the things which are in the heavens and also those that are in the hells, and this for thirteen years past; [i.e., from the year 1743; for I suppose his manuscript to have been written in that year, though not printed till 1758] and thus now to write them down from objects themselves both seen and heard by me; hoping that thereby ignorance would be enlightened and incredulity dissipated. That such an immediate revelation actually exists at this day is, because it is the very thing that is meant by the coming of the Lord.'

This was to me both equally new and surprising. On further inquiry, after a while I found the author of this piece written in Latin was Baron Swedenborg; and the printer in London, Mr. Lewis of Pater Noster Row.

From his relict, Mrs. Lewis, I was informed of more particulars respecting this extraordinary person, and afterwards, in the year 1771, in September, I had an interview with him at his lodgings in Cold Bath Fields. [32]

Okely was in London for the Moravian Provincial Synod in 1771, being the afternoon preacher at Fetter Lane Chapel on successive Sundays, 1 and 8 September, during the Synod. [33] His letter continues:

I called on Mrs. Lewis and her son-in-law, Henry Trapp.

They had promised to let me see the Baron's book concerning Marriages in Heaven, and I accordingly went to fetch it. No sooner was [I] entered their book shop, but they told me that had I come a few minutes earlier, I should have seen the Latin Author (so they called him). He was just arrived from Holland, and would be there again on Saturday. (This was Tuesday, September 10, 1771.) I replied that, as glad as I should be to see him, yet could I not hope it, being to return to North[amp]ton to attend my official duty there, that very day. But [I] said, if God should see it needful, either on my own, or on the acc[ount] of any other, for me to see him he could in the interim bring it about notwithstanding. I dined that day at my friend Mr. Edmond's. Just in the midst of dinner time, a note from Mr. Trapp was handed me, whereby I was informed that no sooner had I turned my back but the Latin Author returned; that then they proposed an interview with me, which at first he declined; but on a further explanation of my character, he accepted it, and appointed 4 o'clock in the afternoon of the same day. I went then, and was courteous[ly] introduced by him to his lodgings, up on[e] pair of stairs, and spent at least two hours with him, at first in English and Latin, but last and for the most part in German, that being the most fluent language to him.

Okely himself professed 'great love to the mystics'. [34] His translation from the German of *The Nature and Necessity of the New Creature in Christ* (1772), a short book by Johanna Eleanora von Merlau (1644-1724), future wife of the Pietist Johann Wilhelm Petersen, was sold by Mary Lewis—as were several of Okely's own writings and his versification of select passages from the works of William Law. [35]

It was through the translations of William Law that Okely had been introduced to the writings of the German cobbler and mystic Jacob Boehme. Okely's translation of the *Memoirs of the Life, Death, Burial and Wonderful Writings, of Jacob Behmen* (1780) celebrated 'the divine *Ground* and radical Philosophy' of Christ embodied in Boehme's writings. [36] He introduced these latter by affirming his belief that 'the Holy Scriptures, Jacob Behmen, Mr. Law, and every other *truly spiritual Writer*' possessed 'a sound and good Sense'—even on those occasions when it had not been granted him to penetrate it. Yet he also warned against putting Boehme's writings in the hands of people '*not properly disposed*' to them, for some readers had turned out 'real conceited *Enthusiasts*' while others had become perplexed to the point of '*Distraction*'.

Moravian spirituality and Behmenist mysticism seem to have been particularly compatible; at least three Moravian societies were established on existing Behmenist reading groups, and Moravianism helped further spread the influences of Continental mysticism in England. [37] Okely was a prolific translator of sixteenth- and seventeenth-century mysticism, not out of antiquarian interest, but because he believed it to be useful for the readership of his spiritually-fallen fellow citizens in eighteenth-century England. [38] In 1781, he translated (with extensive commentary) *A Faithful Narrative of God's Gracious Dealings with Hiel*, by Hendrik Jansen van Barrefelt (d. 1594?), a Dutch Familist schismatic who used the name Hiël (the 'Life of God'). [39] The German translation of Hiël's complete works was published in Amsterdam between 1687 and 1690, and read in the circle gravitating round William Law. From then on Hiël was regarded by a number of Englishmen with an interest in mysticism as a precursor of Boehme. Okely's translation was read by

Moravians, Methodists and Swedenborgians and, short-lived though the English interest in him was, it sheds light on the late eighteenth-century reception of mysticism in England and on the influence of continental Pietism. [40]

In addition, and quite significantly, Okely translated *The Divine Visions of John Engelbrecht*, otherwise the Lutheran visionary Hans Engelbrecht (1599-1642), often seen as a seventeenth-century precursor of Swedenborg, or 'Der teutsche Swedenburg'. [41]

I return to Okely's letter to his brother:

To relate the whole conversation would be too difficult a task now. Let this suffice at present. He had just published the book entitled True Christian Religion, then lying before him; and pointed to several passages in it, asking my thoughts about them. He told me that he had had several interviews with C. Zinzendorff in the world of spirits, who was as erroneous and peremptory about faith without love as ever was Luther at his first arrival there. He expressed no very good opinion of the Brethren; and is equally averse to the Quakers. I told him a little of my own experience, and particularly of our Savior's manifestation of Himself to me as the wounded Lamb of God, etc., etc., in a divine dream, in the year 1751. Which he congratulated me upon; and assured me that he had appeared to him likewise; and told him he should, by writing, because his speech was faltering, be his messenger and servant; and that he was every day of his life in the spiritual world and more conversant with it than in this. His eyes were bleared with much writing; but he was very composed in his countenance and whole demeanor. But there is no denying that, in the year 1743, when he first was (as he said) introduced into the spiritual world, he was, for a while, insane. He then lived with Mr. Brockmore (a gentleman well known) in Salisbury Court. As Mr. J. Wesley has published an account of this in his Arminian Magazin for Jan., 1781: pages 46-49, I refer you to it. There is little doubt but you will meet with it among some of the now numerous Methodists on your side of the water. As I rather suspect J. W.'s narratives, they being always warped to his own inclination, I inquired since of Mr. Brockmore concerning it, and have found all the main lines of it truth. [42]

Okely also wrote of this visit in a letter (10 December 1772) to John Wesley:

Baron Swedenborg is to me a riddle. Certainly, as you say, he speaks many great and important truths; and as certainly seems to me to contradict Scripture in other places. But, as he told me, I could not understand his *Vera Christiana Religio* without a Divine illumination; and I am obliged to confess that I have not yet a sufficiency of it for that purpose. I am thankful, my present course does not seem absolutely to require it.

We conversed in the High Dutch; and notwithstanding the impediment in his speech, I understood him well. He spoke with all the coolness and deliberation you might expect from any, the most sober and rational man. Yet what he said was out of my sphere of intelligence, when he related his sight of, and daily conversations in, the world of spirits, with which he declared himself better acquainted than with this.

The letter to Wesley concludes:

I heartily wish, that the real designs which an Omnipotent and Omniscient God of Love might have, either by him (Swedenborg), or by any other of his sincere servants of whatsoever sort or kind, may be truly obtained. May His Kingdom come, and His will be done once in earth, as it is done in heaven! [43]

It is important to point out that there was no 'Swedenborgianism' before 1768, which was the first time Swedenborg's name appeared on his spiritual writings.

He broke his anonymity in 1768 with the publication of *Amore conjugiale*, after which his friends—aided by Swedenborg's personal physician, Dr Husband Messiter—published two more English translations under his name, printed as usual by Mary Lewis. [44]

The first group set up to promote Swedenborg's teaching in London was a quasi-Masonic society which went under the name of the London Universal Society. It was formed in 1776, partly on the initiative of Benedict Chastanier, a French physician and high-ranking Freemason then residing in London. Though all the members of the Universal Society were Masons, they do not, however, seem to have had any rites or Masonic degrees. [45] Chastanier had come to England in October 1763 aged about twenty-four. He failed to settle in London, however, experiencing a 'remarkable' vision the night before he was to move to Northampton. In January 1768 Chastanier began studying the 'Mystic Writers', in which he may have been influenced by Francis Okely, minister to the Moravian congregation at Northampton since 1767. [46] That same year Chastanier discovered Swedenborg's works, albeit, at first, without knowing who the author was. The main purpose of the Universal Society was missionary in the Masonic philanthropic sense, working for Universal Regeneration. Members were closely involved in the translation and printing of Swedenborg's works.

An initially more modest but ultimately more successful organization was a Swedenborgian reading group founded, in London, by Robert Hindmarsh in 1783. At about the same time, a Church of England clergyman named John Clowes began to proclaim, from the pulpit of St John's Church in Manchester, the coming of Swedenborg's spiritual New Jerusalem. In both London and Manchester, Swedenborg's disciples prepared to disseminate his doctrines through the translation, publication, and distribution of his voluminous writings. The London group organized themselves into *The Theosophical Society, instituted for the purpose of promoting the Heavenly Doctrines of the New Jerusalem by translating, printing, and publishing the Theological Writings of Emanuel*

Swedenborg. Hindmarsh was a printer who, in 1782, at the age of twenty-three, met with some of Swedenborg's writings, and, as he assures us, 'read them with the utmost avidity, and instantly perceived their contents to be of heavenly origin'. Straightway he began to search out other readers of the same mindset 'in order to form a Society for the purpose of spreading the knowledge of the great truths contained in them'. His success was small at first—'I was absolutely laughed at, and set down as a mere simpleton, and infatuated youth, and little better than a madman, led away by the reveries of an old enthusiast and impostor'. [47]

On Sunday mornings, in 1783, Hindmarsh began to hold meetings at his house in Clerkenwell Close, then after a variety of moves and an increase of numbers, chambers were rented in New Court, Middle Temple, in 1784, and meetings held on Sundays and Thursdays, at which portions of Swedenborg were read and discussed. Of the many persons who either joined the Theosophical Society or sympathized with its objects, I shall draw attention to just two—Jacob Duché, Chaplain to the Orphan Asylum, St George's Fields, and the miniature painter Richard Cosway.

Jacob Duché, Jr (1737-98) is remembered today as the Anglican chaplain to the First and Second Continental Congresses who turned against the Revolution in 1777 and was forced by the ensuing public outcry to join the 7,000 or more Americans who went into exile in England. On 8 October he had written a personal letter to George Washington, urging him to persuade Congress to rescind its Declaration of Independence. The letter, in effect, destroyed Duché's career. [48]

It is a curious coincidence that the person who had first interested Duché in the mystical tradition was the great Moravian bishop, Augustus Spangenburg, whom Duché had met when he sailed to England in 1762 to receive his ordination. [49] During the fifteen years Duché served as an ordained clergyman in Philadelphia he was a committed adherent to the mystical writings of Jacob Boehme and William Law. In exile, in the early 1780s, when he had come to the painful realization that he could not return to the United Churches of Philadelphia, nor even to the United States, he encountered the revelations of Swedenborg. He was converted, and 'in the spiritual New Jerusalem of the Swedish prophet found the religious haven he had been seeking all his life'. [50]

The fashionable Regency artist Richard Cosway RA (1742-1821), had moved initially in Moravian circles. Cosway remained a close friend of James Hutton, Moravian leader in England, and painted Hutton's portrait in 1784. [51] But he can also be linked to the Universal Society (he had lived while a student at Dr Messiter's home) and became a foundation member of the Theosophical Society. [52] Cosway's circle included the Swedenborgian General Charles Rainsford (1728-1809), Duché, the artist Philip James de Loutherbourg (1740-1812), the engraver William Sharp (1749-1824), and James Bruce (1730-94), the African explorer. Bruce employed as his amanuensis Benjamin Henry La Trobe (1764-1820), the Moravian architect and political radical, whose Moravian uncle (a physician-missionary in Egypt) helped Bruce during his journey to Ethiopia. La Trobe also seems to have been part of Cosway's circle. [53]

The Theosophical Society later met at the Orphan Asylum, where they worshipped at the Sunday services and then gathered in the evening in Duché's apartment, where Duché led discussions of Swedenborg's writings. [54] Robert Hindmarsh recalled those Sunday evenings with Duché when upwards of thirty persons, male and female, had spent the evening 'in a truly delightful manner, receiving from his lips the most impressive lessons of instruction'. Over the decade of the 1780s, the Theosophical Society and Duché's gatherings, together became a conduit for a heady blend of mystical ideas and radical Masonic politics. Universal Society members were regular guests at Duché's Sunday evening discussions, and some also attended meetings of the Theosophical Society, with whom they cooperated in publishing Swedenborg's works, even sharing the same printing press. [55]

Swedenborg spoke of a 'new church' that would be founded on the theology in his works, but he himself never tried to establish an organization. On 7 May 1787, 15 years after Swedenborg's death, Robert Hindmarsh was instrumental setting up the first New Church chapel in Great Eastcheap, London, appointing himself its minister. In forming a church, English Swedenborgians gradually acquired such characteristics of institutional status as baptism, the ordination of ministers and a catechism for children.[56] The first General Conference of the New Church, held on 14-17 April 1789, was attended by seventy-seven persons, among them William Blake and his wife Catherine, who signed as sympathizers the forty-two propositions for separation from the Established Church.

Prior to the founding of the Swedenborgian New Church, people moved freely between Fetter Lane and the Theosophical Society, particularly those persons with only informal affiliation to the Moravian Congregation. Thus James Blake, father of the poet, was, according to Keynes, an 'original member of The Theosophical Society founded by Robert Hindmarsh in 1783 for the study of Swedenborg', and my own research suggests he should also be placed among the 'constant hearers' who attended the preaching services at Fetter Lane.[57] The crucial rupture came in 1787 with the lapse of part of the Swedenborgian movement into sectarianism with the formation of the New Jerusalem Church and the enunciation of doctrines incompatible with Moravian belief.

As Robert Rix has pointed out in his recent book, assessment of the historical conditions for the reception of religious ideas 'should not presume that those who were attracted to religious, mystical or prophetic movements at the time held rigid ideological positions'.[58] Religious loyalties were often fickle and ideas received second-hand. Much history of religion is written from the point of view of systematic theology. This view 'from above' fails to register the common hybridization of ideas on the level of individual seekers with little or no formal theological education. Zinzendorf, in that 1752 speech to Synod I quoted at the beginning, had instructed the Brethren 'That our Call is, to love & honour the Christian Denominations about us, all that can be look'd upon as Christian' and 'That the Inability of most of the Congreg^n-Members to defend the Congreg^n controversially, clear up Facts, & answer Objections, has proceeded from a noble Cause, viz. that they have only had Jesus & his Grace set before them, & have not been troubled with Enlargements upon intricate & more barren Topicks & Circumstances'.[59] For such readers of Swedenborg as the Anglican clergyman John Clowes, an emphasis on inner spirituality tended to convert all external matters into mere *adiaphora*. Francis Okely thought that 'the time is not yet come, when any particular Denomination can, with Truth, claim the exclusive Privilege of being the only infallible CHURCH OF CHRIST'. [60]

By 1797, when Okely's son William (1762-1830), also a Moravian minister, published *Pyrology; or, the Connexion between Natural and Moral Philosophy*, the father's puzzled respect for Swedenborg had been replaced by the son's scorn:

> The noted Swedenborg was originally a man of superior understanding and information, became in the progress of life a ridiculous visionary, and ended a complete lunatic. [61]

I suggest that there's a specific reason for this hostility. I have concentrated in this paper on Moravian-Swedenborgian meetings on the temporal plane. But Swedenborg also maintained a *Spiritual Diary*, which recorded his meetings with Zinzendorf in heaven, and his visions of the Moravian Church on the spiritual plane, including charges of antinomianism, promiscuity, etc. Though the *Spiritual Diary* was not published until 1844, with an English translation following shortly after, the Masons in the Universal Society had studied the manuscript diary and proposed publication as early as in 1791. Maybe word of Swedenborg's secret hostility towards his friends in the Moravian Church had leaked out. [62]

The question remains. Did the Moravian Church contribute to the development of Swedenborgianism? Swedenborg's and Zinzendorf's theologies diverge in their own ways from a common inheritance of Pietism, that wing of German Lutheranism that laid stress on the depth and sincerity of personal faith and direct union with God, a spiritual thirst that could not be quenched by rationality. As Brian Gibbons has pointed out, 'the tendency of Swedenborg's hagiographers to see his work as created *ex nihilo* is clearly untenable'. [63] For example, and despite Swedenborg's denial that he had ever read Jacob Boehme, further research on the relationship between Swedenborgianism, Moravianism and Behmenism might well pay a dividend. John Wesley was quite clear about it:

> I [Wesley] took an extract thereof from the beginning to the end, that I might be able to form a more accurate judgment. And one may trace through the whole, remains of a fine genius, 'Majestic, though in ruins!' From the whole I remark, that what Mr. Law oddly imputes to Sir Isaac Newton, is truly immutable to the Baron. He 'ploughed with Jacob Behmen's heifer,' and that both in Philosophy and Divinity. But he far exceeded his master: his dreams are more extraordinary than those of Jacob himself. [64]

The tradition to which Boehme and Swedenborg belonged was founded on the premise that the divine must be mystically experienced in order to be known. This theosophical Christianity was a vibrant cultural mode in which the impact of Jacob Boehme permeated the Pietistic movements of the seventeenth and eighteenth centuries. Gibbons writes that Behmenism might be regarded as the occult philosophy reformed to meet the needs of the early modern period; Swedenborgianism was a further reform, tailoring the occult philosophy to the requirements of the modern world. [65]

However, Swedenborg's own theology is in many points diametrically opposed to that of Zinzendorf, and Swedenborgianism as a religious movement absorbed elements from a wide range of sources. Ariel Hessayon has pointed out 'the importance of alchemy, Animal Magnetism, astrology, Freemasonry, Kabbalah, magic, mysticism, numerology, the Rosicrucians and Behmenism to a number of Swedenborg's early readers. The process', he adds, 'of recovering these influences, of restoring them in the history of the Swedenborgians is still not complete'. [66] It may well be, as Schuchard has alleged, that it was through those friendships formed at Fetter Lane that such ideas entered Swedenborgian thought. [67]

403

NOTES

1   *An act for encouraging the people known by the name of Unitas Fratrum or United Brethren, to settle in his Majesty's colonies in America* (22 Geo.2, c.30): 'the said congregation are an ancient protestant episcopal church, which has been countenanced and relieved by the Kings of England, your Majesty's predecessors'.

2   Moravian Church Archive and Library: C/36/7/6, Congregation Diary, vol. VI: 1 January 1752-31 December 1752, p. 64 (12 August 1752).

3   The best modern account of Swedenborg's life and work is Lars Bergquist's, *Swedenborg's Secret: The Meaning and Significance of the Word of God, the Life of the Angels and Service to God: A Biography* (London: Swedenborg Society, 2005). Bergquist's account is comprehensive, if impeded by the need to account simultaneously for Swedenborg's mundane and spiritual progress. The records of Swedenborg's life, career, and reputation are published in R L Tafel (ed.), *Documents concerning the Life and Character of Emanuel Swedenborg, collected, translated, and annotated*, 2 vols. in 3 (London: Swedenborg Society, 1875-7), including details of Swedenborg's residence in London in 1744-5, and his friendships with members of the Moravian Community.

4   Swedenborg, *Opera philosophica et mineralia*, 3 vols. (Dresdae; Lipsiae: sumptibus F Hekelii, 1734). Contents: vol. 1, pt. 1 Principia rerum naturalium—vol. 1, pt. 2 Examen principiorum rerum naturalium—vol. 1, pt. 3 Principiorum rerum naturalium—vol. 2, pt. 1 Regnum subterraneum sive minerale: De ferro—vol. 2, pt. 2 Regnum subterraneum sive minerale: De vena et lapide ferri—vol. 2, pt. 3 Regnum subterraneum sive minerale: De variis cum ferro et ejus victriolo—vol. 3, pt. 1 Regnum subterraneum sive minerale: De cupro et orichalco—vol. 3, pt. 2 Regnum subterraneum sive minerale: De vena et lapide cupri—vol. 3, pt. 3 Regnum subterraneum sive minerale: De variis cum cupro et orichalco.

5   *Arcana cœlestia: quae in scriptura sacra, seu verbo Domini sunt, detecta: hic primum quæ in Genesi,* 8 vols. ([London: John Lewis], 1749-56). A commentary with the Latin text of Genesis and Exodus in the Vulgate version.

6   Arthur Symons' extracts from Crabb Robinson's diary and reminiscences are reprinted in Joseph A Wittreich, *Nineteenth-Century Accounts of William Blake* (Gainesville:

Scholars' Facsimiles & Reprints, 1970). For the quotes cited, see pp. 255-63.

[7] Marsha Keith Schuchard, *Why Mrs Blake Cried: William Blake and the Sexual Basis of Spiritual Vision* (London: Century, 2006).

[8] Christopher McIntosh, *The Rose Cross and the Age of Reason: Eighteenth-Century Rosicrucianism in Central Europe and its Relationship to the Enlightenment* (Leiden: Brill, 1992), p. 41.

[9] See Tafel (ed.), *Documents concerning the Life and Character of Emanuel Swedenborg* (London, 1875-7), *passim*.

[10] These discoveries were presented in the following papers: Keri Davies, 'William Blake's Mother: A New Identification', in *Blake/An Illustrated Quarterly*, vol. 33, no. 2, Fall 1999, pp. 36-50. Established for the first time the maiden name of Blake's mother, and name and place of birth of her first husband. Keri Davies and Marsha Keith Schuchard, 'Recovering the Lost Moravian History of William Blake's Family', in *Blake/ An Illustrated Quarterly*, vol. 38, no. 1, Summer 2004, pp. 36-43. First publication of the Moravian links of the Blake family. Keri Davies, 'The Lost Moravian History of William Blake's Family: Snapshots from the Archive', in *Literature Compass*, vol. 3, no. 6, November 2006, pp. 1297-1319. Presents systematically the extensive archival data relating to Catherine Wright Armitage Blake, mother of the poet.

[11] Moravian Church Library and Archive: AB38 (Minutes of Saturday Conferences, 1744-5). A later hand, probably J N Libbey's, has added the words 'i.e. Swedenborg? Yes!'.

[12] Claims that Blake's father and brother became Swedenborgians after their Moravian participation are made by Thomas Wright, *The Life of William Blake* (Olney: T Wright, 1929), vol. I, p. 2, and by Margaret Ruth Lowery, *Windows of the Morning: a Critical Study of William Blake's Poetical Sketches, 1783* (New Haven: Yale University Press; OUP, 1940), pp. 13-15. D V Erdman, in an influential paper, 'Blake's Early Swedenborgianism: A Twentieth-Century Legend', in *Comparative Literature*, vol. V (1953), pp. 247-57, attempted to demolish these claims. Erdman overstated his case and evidence is beginning to emerge that suggests that the Blake family were indeed early followers of Swedenborg—long before the adult William Blake and his wife Catherine Boucher attended the first conference of the Swedenborgian New Jerusalem Church in 1789.

13 *Emanuelis Swedenborgii, sacræ regiæ majestatis regnique Sueciæ collegii metalici assessoris regnum animale anatomice, physice et philosophice perlustratum. Pars tertia. De cute, sensu tactus, & gustus; et de formis organicis in genere, agit* (Londinii, 1745).

14 See Colin Podmore, *The Moravian Church in England, 1728-1760* (Oxford: Oxford University Press, 1998), especially pp. 133-6. Podmore provides a modern, comprehensive and scholarly account of the early years of Moravianism in England.

15 Colin Podmore, *The Fetter Lane Moravian Congregation, London 1742-1992* (London: Fetter Lane Moravian Congregation, 1992), p. 3.

16 Arvid Gradin, *A Short History of the Bohemian-Moravian Protestant Church of the United Brethren: Written by Arvid Gradin, a Member of the said Church. In a letter to the Archbishop of Upsal, Primate of Sweden. Translated from the Latin manuscript* (London: printed for James Hutton, at the Bible and Sun in Little Wild-Street, near Lincolns Inn Fields, 1743).

17 Tafel (ed.), *Documents concerning the Life and Character of Emanuel Swedenborg*, vol. I, p. 194. See also Daniel Benham, *Memoirs of James Hutton: comprising the annals of his life and connection with the United Brethren* (London: Hamilton, Adams, 1856), p. 91. Seniff's unpublished obituary appears in Moravian Church Archive and Library: C/36/7/5, Congregation Diary, vol. V: 1 January 1751-31 December 1751, p. 30 (May 1751).

18 Benham, *Memoirs of James Hutton*, p. 90. For Moravians prominent in the watchcase chasing trade, see Richard Edgcumbe, *The Art of the Gold Chaser in Eighteenth-Century London* (Oxford: Oxford University Press in association with the Victoria and Albert Museum, 2000).

19 Tafel (ed.), *Documents concerning the Life and Character of Emanuel Swedenborg*, vol. II, p. 584. Transcribed from John Wesley, 'Thoughts on the Writings of Emanuel Swedenborg', in *Arminian Magazine*, vol. VI (1783), pp. 437 ff.

20 Tafel (ed.), *Documents concerning the Life and Character of Emanuel Swedenborg*, vol. II, pp. 586-7. There is a fuller version of Brockmer's testimony to Mathesius in Bergquist's edition of the dream diary, *Swedenborgs drömbok: glädjen och det stora kvalet* (Stockholm: Norstedt, 1988); tr. Anders Hallengren as *Swedenborg's*

Dream Diary (West Chester: Swedenborg Foundation, 2001).

[21] Both William White, *Emanuel Swedenborg: His Life and Writings*, 2nd revised edn. (London: Simpkin Marshall, 1868), p. 134, and Tafel (ed.), *Documents concerning the Life and Character of Emanuel Swedenborg*, vol. II, p. 1241, claim that Brockmer retracted his account of Swedenborg's madness; we will see later that this is denied by Francis Okely.

[22] Compare Christopher Smart in *Jubilate Agno*: 'For I am under the same accusation with my Saviour——for they said, he is besides himself'.

[23] Moravian Church Archive and Library: C/36/11/5, Helpers Conference Minute Book (15 October 1744-23 May 1748).

[24] See Podmore's discussion of the stillness controversy in *The Moravian Church in England, 1728-1760*, pp. 57, 59-65, 67-9.

[25] Czesław Miłosz, 'Swedenborg the Mystic', in *The Arms of Morpheus: Essays on Swedenborg and Mysticism,* ed. Stephen McNeilly (London: Swedenborg Society, 2007), p. 6 and herein p. 325.

[26] Ann Judith Penny, *Studies in Jacob Böhme* (London: John M Watkins, 1912), p. 78. Penny is referring to the Swedenborg displayed in his formal publications of the eighteenth century. With the Swedenborg of the diaries, published later, the wig is quite blown away, revealing turbulence, paranoia, jealousy, sexual obsession, and bizarre descriptions of his enemies being placed in the anus of the Grand Man, etc.

[27] *De cultu et amore Dei*, 2 vols. (Londini: Joh. Nourse & Richard Manby, 1745).

[28] William White, *Swedenborg: His Life and Writings* (London: William White; Bath: Isaac Pitman, 1856), p. 22.

[29] Robert Rix, *William Blake and the Cultures of Radical Christianity* (Aldershot: Ashgate, 2007), pp. 51-2.

[30] *Arcana cœlestia: or, Heavenly Secrets, which are in the Sacred Scripture, or, Word of the Lord, laid open* (London, 1750). See the discussion in J G Davies, *The Theology of William Blake* (Oxford: Clarendon Press, 1948), p. 31.

[31] Rod Evans, *An Index of Ministers, Provincial Officials, etc., serving in the British Province of the Moravian Church from 1740 to 1998* (Stockport: The Author, 1998): 'OKELY, Francis (1719-1794) b. Bedford 27 Mar; d. Bedford 9 May. Educ. St.

John's Coll., Cambridge. Joined Mor. Ch. 1745. Min. Bristol 1748; Dukinfield 1755-; Wyke 1756; Bedford (n.d.); Northampton 1767-94. F of W (b. 1762) and gf of WI (b. 1804). [m. Elizabeth Collins, b. Chatham 20 Nov 1725]'.

32 Document 1465.11 from Book 9 of the Green Books in the Digital Collection of Swedenborg Library in Bryn Athyn. First published by W H Benade in *New Jerusalem Messenger* (New York), 28 December 1861; then in *Monthly Observer*, vol. 6, 1862, p. 95.

33 London. Moravian Church Library and Archive, C/36/7/17, Congregation Diary, vol. XVII: 1 April 1771-31 December 1771, pp. 50-2.

34 Ralph Mather, cited in Ariel Hessayon, 'Jacob Boehme, Emanuel Swedenborg and their readers', herein p. 347.

35 [Johanna Eleonora Petersen], *The Nature and Necessity of the New Creature in Christ: stated and described, according to heart's experience and true practice. By Joanna Eleonora de Merlau. Translated from the German, by Francis Okely.* (London: printed for the editor; and sold by M Lewis; also by J Lacy and R Smith, at Northampton, 1772).

36 *Memoirs of the Life, Death, Burial, and Wonderful Writings, of Jacob Behmen: now first done at large into English, from the best edition of his works in the original German. With an introductory preface of the translator, directing to the due and right use of this mysterious and extraordinary theosopher. By Francis Okely, Formerly of St. John's College, Cambridge* (Northampton: Printed by Tho. Dicey for the translator, and for J Lackington (no. 46) Chiswell-Street, Moorfields, London. Sold also at Bristol by T Mills, and at Leeds by J Binns, 1780). The life by A von Franckenberg, with the narrative of C Weissner.

37 Podmore, *The Moravian Church in England, 1728-1760*.

38 Rix, *William Blake and the Cultures of Radical Christianity*, pp. 2-3.

39 *A Faithful Narrative of God's Gracious Dealings with Hiel: By which, in a very searching and affecting Manner, he describes both his Worldly and Religious course; terminating at length in a Radical Conversion to God in Christ: ... Englished from the High-Dutch, ... by Francis Okely,* (Northampton: printed by Thomas Dicey, for the translator; and sold by J Lackington, [London]; J Denis and

Son, London; T Mills, at Bristol; and J Binns, at Leeds, 1781).

40 On Hiël and his English reputation, see Alistair Hamilton, 'Hiël and the Hiëlists: The Doctrine and Followers of Hendrik Jansen van Barrefelt', in *Quaerendo*, 7 (1977), pp. 243-86, and Alastair Hamilton, 'Hiël in England 1657-1810', in *Quaerendo*, 15 (1986), pp. 282-303.

41 Okely's translation: *The Divine Visions of John Engelbrecht, a Lutheran Protestant, whom God Sent from the Dead to be a Preacher of Repentance and Faith to the Christian World*, 2 vols. (Northampton: Thomas Dicey, 1780). A later German edition: *Der teutsche Swedenburg: oder: Hans Engelbrechts außerordentliche Aussichten in die Ewigkeit; nebst deßen merkwürdigen Leben und sonderbaren Schriften; als ein Pendant zu Swedenburgs sämmtlichen Werken* (Amsterdam: auf Kosten guter Freunde, 1783).

42 Document 1465.11 from Book 9 of the Green Books in the Digital Collection of Swedenborg Library in Bryn Athyn. First published by W H Benade in *New Jerusalem Messenger* (New York), 28 December 1861; then in *Monthly Observer*, vol. 6 (1862), p. 95. Printed in part by White, *Emanuel Swedenborg: His Life and Writings*, 2nd edn. (1868), p. 133, citing the Revd Francis Okely's 'Reflections on Baron Swedenborg's Works', printed in *New Jerusalem Messenger* (New York), 28 December 1861.

43 Tafel (ed.), *Documents concerning the Life and Character of Emanuel Swedenborg*, vol. II, p. 696. Okely's letter was printed by Wesley in the *Arminian Magazine*, vol. VIII (1775), p. 552.

44 *Deliticæ sapientiæ de amore conjugiali; post quas sequuntur voluptates insaniæ de amore scortatorio* (Amstelodami, 1768). *A Brief Exposition of the Doctrine of the New Church: understood in the Apocalypse by the New Jerusalem; Wherein is also demonstrated, that throughout all the Christian World the worshipping of Three Gods is received, from the Creed of St. Athanasius. By Emanuel Swedenborg, A Native of Sweden* (London: printed by M Lewis, (no. 1.) Pater-Noster-Row, 1769). Translated from the Latin by John Marchant. *A Theosophic Lucubration on the Nature of Influx: as it respects the Communication and Operations of Soul and Body. By The Honourable and Learned Emanuel Swedenborg. Now first translated from the original Latin* (London: printed and sold by M Lewis, no. 1.

Pater-Noster-Row; and W Heard, in Piccadilly, 1770). Translated by T Hartley.

[45] Marsha Keith Schuchard, 'The Secret Masonic History of Blake's Swedenborg Society', in *Blake/An Illustrated Quarterly*, vol. 26 (1992), pp. 40-51, and her 'Blake and the Grand Masters (1791-1794)', in *Blake in the Nineties*, ed. Steve Clark and David Worrall (London: Macmillan, 1999), pp. 173-93.

[46] Ariel Hessayon, 'Jacob Boehme, Emanuel Swedenborg and their readers', p. 353 herein.

[47] White, *Emanuel Swedenborg: his Life and Writings*, 2nd edn. (1868), p. 683.

[48] Clarke Garrett, 'The Spiritual Odyssey of Jacob Duché', in *Proceedings of the American Philosophical Society*, vol. 119, no. 2, 16 April 1975, p. 143.

[49] Ibid., p. 144.

[50] Ibid., p. 149.

[51] On Hutton, his connection with Moravianism in England, and his portrait by Cosway, see: C J Podmore, 'Hutton, James (1715 1795)', in *Oxford Dictionary of National Biography* (Oxford: Oxford University Press, 2004) <http://www.oxforddnb.com/view/article/14303>. Cosway's wonderful portrait of the English Moravian leader James Hutton remained in his studio and was offered after his death to the Moravian Church by his widow Maria. The painting is now at Church House, Muswell Hill.

[52] See Al Gabay, 'The Stockholm Exegetic and Philanthropic Society and Spiritism', in *The New Philosophy*, July-December 2007 <http://thenewphilosophyonline.org> for Cosway's residence with Dr Messiter. There is a list of members of the Theosophical Society given by White in his *Emanuel Swedenborg: his Life and Writings*, vol. II, pp. 598-9: Meetings were held on Sundays and Thursdays, at which portions of Swedenborg were read and discussed. Amongst those who either joined the Society or sympathized with its object, we find the names of: John Flaxman, Sculptor, Wardour Street; William Sharp, Engraver, Bartholomew Lane, City; and P J Loutherbourg, Painter, Stratford Place, Piccadilly. Loutherbourg lived in The Mall, Hammersmith, and Cosway in Stratford Place, Oxford Street, after 1798. Stratford Place certainly isn't in Piccadilly, though when the Theosophical Society was active (1783 onwards) Cosway would have been resident at Schomburg House, Pall Mall, very near Piccadilly. I interpret White's confusion here as meaning that both

Loutherbourg and Cosway attended meetings of the Theosophical Society. White also lists a 'Benjamin Hutton, Merchant, Friday Street'. Could he possibly have been James Hutton's younger brother?

53 According to Schuchard, in *Why Mrs Blake Cried*.

54 Garrett, 'The Spiritual Odyssey of Jacob Duché', pp. 143-55.

55 Gabay, 'The Stockholm Exegetic and Philanthropic Society and Spiritism'.

56 Marilyn Butler, *Romantics, Rebels and Reactionaries: English Literature and its Background 1760-1830* (Oxford: Oxford University Press, 1981), p. 46.

57 Personal communication from M K Schuchard. I have been unable to locate the original reference.

58 Rix, *William Blake and the Cultures of Radical Christianity*, p. 2.

59 Moravian Church Archive and Library: C/36/7/6, Congregation Diary, vol. VI: 1 January 1752-31 December 1752, p. 64 (12 August 1752).

60 Cited by B J Gibbons, *Gender in Mystical and Occult Thought: Behmenism and its Development in England* (Cambridge: Cambridge University Press, 1996), p. 7.

61 William Okely, *Pyrology; or, the Connexion between Natural and Moral Philosophy: with a short Disquisition on the Origin of Christianity* (London: printed for J Johnson, 1797), p. 342.

62 *Proposals for printing by subscription, Emanuel Swedenborg's spiritual diary: or, a collection of his experiences and aphorisms, from the year 1746, to 1764 ... faithfully translated from his manuscripts ... By a society of gentlemen* ([London: Hindmarsh], 1791). *Eman. Swedenborgii Diarii spiritualis, partis primae volumen primum [-quintum]: e chirographo ejus in Bibliotheca Regiae Universitatis Upsaliensis asservato* (Tubingae: curam administrat 'Verlagsexpedition'; and Londini: William Newbery, 1844-60). *The Spiritual Diary of E. Swedenborg; or, a brief record, during twenty years, of his supernatural experience. Lately published from the Latin manuscripts of the author by Dr J F I Tafel ... Translated from the original by J H Smithson* (London: Newbery, 1846).

63 Gibbons, *Gender in Mystical and Occult Thought*, p. 200.

64 Tafel (ed.), *Documents concerning the Life and Character of Emanuel Swedenborg*, vol. II, p. 586.

[65] Gibbons, *Gender in Mystical and Occult Thought*, p. 200.
[66] Hessayon, 'Jacob Boehme, Emanuel Swedenborg and their readers', p. 367 herein.
[67] Schuchard, *Why Mrs Blake Cried*.

Handel, Hogarth and Swedenborg: manners and morals in eighteenth-century London [1]

Richard Lines

Introduction

George Frideric Handel and Emanuel Swedenborg both arrived in London for the first time in the latter half of 1710. [2] Handel was twenty-five years old and Swedenborg twenty-two. Both were northern Europeans professing the Lutheran faith. Swedenborg's father, Jesper Swedberg, was a clergyman who became a bishop and who was, by 1710, one of the most important men in Sweden. Handel's maternal grandfather, Georg Taust, who died in 1685, was also a pastor. [3] Both Handel and Swedenborg were to achieve fame in very different spheres and were to become two of the greatest men of the eighteenth century. The third protagonist of this essay, the artist William Hogarth, a Londoner, was only thirteen in 1710. He was to begin his artistic career three years later as an engraver's apprentice, as William Blake, 'Swedenborg's unruly disciple', [4] was to do later in the century. Handel and Hogarth between them seem to epitomize early Georgian London, particularly during the reign of George II (1727-60). Both men are associated as patrons of the Foundling Hospital in Bloomsbury, established by Royal Charter in 1739 as a result of the determined efforts of Thomas Coram, a retired sea captain. The hospital was an early example of benevolence and charity in a harsh and, despite almost universal religious practice, rather ungodly age.

Little is known of Handel's religious beliefs (his last known participation in Holy Communion was in 1703) [5] and he was no theologian, but his anthems and other church music and his oratorios, above all *Messiah*, have affected deeply the Christian sensibility of the British nation. It is difficult for anyone with even a slight knowledge of *Messiah* not to hear Handel's music in one's head when reading passages from Isaiah such as 'For unto us a child is born' (9:6). The achievements of Swedenborg, a scientist who became a theologian and a visionary, are much less well known, but it has been argued that his religious notions have, through Blake and other poets, also 'permeated the spiritual sensibility of the English nation'. [6] Both Handel and Swedenborg extolled the religious freedom that existed in England. It was said of Handel that, while he was a professed Lutheran 'he was not such a bigot as to decline a general conformity with that of the country which he had chosen for his residence' and that he regarded it as 'one of the great felicities of his life that he was settled in a country where no man suffers any molestation or inconvenience on account of his religious principles'.[7] In his description of the British in the spiritual world, Swedenborg wrote that the 'better' of the British occupied 'the very centre' of the Christians; they had 'inward intellectual light' which they received from 'the freedom they have to think, and so to speak and write'.[8]

1710: Queen Anne's London

Handel and Swedenborg may have both been young north European Protestants making their first visits to London in the autumn of 1710, but in most respects their positions were quite different. Although Handel always considered himself a Saxon, Halle where he was born in 1685, was by that time within the territory of the Electorate of Brandenburg (which became the Kingdom of Prussia in 1701). In 1710 Handel was already a well-established composer. He had spent four fruitful years in Italy where *il caro Sassone* ('the dear Saxon') had composed cantatas and a number of operas, including his early masterpiece *Agrippina* which was composed and first performed in Venice in late 1709/early 1710.[9] In Venice Handel had met Prince Ernst of Hanover, younger brother of the Elector Georg, and through him and the Baron Kielmansegge, the Elector's Deputy Master of the Horse, he was able to obtain the post of Kapellmeister to the court of Hanover to which he was appointed in June 1710. The Dowager Electress Sophia, the Elector's mother, eighty years old, was the heir presumptive to the British throne pursuant to the Act of Settlement 1701. Sophia, who had married Ernst Duke of Brunswick and later Elector of Hanover, was the twelfth child and youngest daughter of Elizabeth of Bohemia, daughter of James I and husband of Frederick V, Elector Palatine and briefly King of Bohemia. [10] It was the acceptance of the crown of Bohemia by Frederick that had precipitated the Thirty Years War in 1618, a war that later saw the rise of Sweden as a major military power under its king Gustavus Adolphus who was killed at the Battle of Lützen (1632). It was his connection with the Hanoverian court that would bring Handel to London again after the Elector Georg became King George I of Great Britain in 1714. (The Dowager Electress predeceased Queen Anne by only a few months, dying in 1714 at the age of eighty-four.) But the reason for Handel's visit in 1710 was to stage an opera with the Italian opera company at the new Queen's Theatre in Haymarket (built by John Vanbrugh the architect of Blenheim Palace). His opera Rinaldo, based on incidents from Torquato Tasso's *Gerusalemme liberata* (*Jerusalem Delivered*), [11] was first performed there on 24 February 1711. [12]

Swedenborg, with a letter of introduction to the Swedish ambassador Count Carl Gyllenborg in his pocket, came to London as a student of science. 'I read Newton daily, and I wish also to meet and to hear him', he wrote to his brother-in-law and mentor Erik Benzelius shortly after his arrival. [13] It is not recorded that he met Newton, but he did travel to Greenwich to meet the Astronomer Royal John Flamsteed at the Royal Observatory. At Greenwich he might have seen the work in work in progress of Hogarth's future father-in-law James Thornhill on the magnificent Painted Hall at Greenwich Hospital. He may well have seen Thornhill's grisaille panels inside the dome of the newly completed St Paul's Cathedral. [14] Whether or not the Swedish student saw Handel's *Rinaldo* or any other opera in London is not known, but he was well-educated musically and, like Handel, was briefly a church organist. [15] When Swedenborg visited Venice in 1738 he recorded that he attended operas, although he does not say what he saw. [16]

In his letter to Benzelius Swedenborg mentions Dr Henry Sacheverell and says that 'his name is on everyone's lips, everywhere people are talking about him, and his book is being read in every coffee house'. [17] Here Swedenborg takes us to the heart of the turbulent English politics of the day, although he does not expand on his comment. Henry Sacheverell (1674-1724) was an Anglican clergyman of High Church Tory views and a Fellow of Magdalen College Oxford. On 5 November 1709, the anniversary both of the Gunpowder Plot in 1605 and of the landing at Torbay of William of Orange in 1688, Sacheverell preached a sermon in St Paul's Cathedral in the presence of the Lord Mayor of London which attacked Whigs and Dissenters in violent terms. It was seen by the Whig ministry and their supporters as an attack on the Glorious Revolution, the Act of Settlement and the prospective Hanoverian succession and Sacheverell's impeachment by Parliament was ordered. The trial, which was held in Westminster Hall, unleashed fierce partisan passions in the capital. Although the House of Lords decided narrowly that Sacheverell was guilty, the mildest of punishments, a three-year ban on preaching, was imposed. His sermon was ordered to be burnt by the public hangman, but this ceremony did not prevent its wide circulation. [18]

By unleashing an unwise prosecution of Sacheverell the Whigs brought about their own downfall. The War of the Spanish Succession had been in progress since 1702 and now the country was exhausted and war-weary. Marlborough had won a string of victories beginning with Blenheim in 1704, but his victory at Malplaquet in September 1709 on the modern French/Belgian border had been won, it was felt, at too great a cost in British casualties. In August 1710 Queen Anne, encouraged by her confidante Abigail Masham, took advantage of the turmoil caused by the Sacheverell agitation to dismiss her Whig ministers and bring in the Tories under Robert Harley, later Earl of Oxford, and Henry St John, later Viscount Bolingbroke. A General Election was called for October that year which resulted in a large Tory majority in the House of Commons. Sacheverell was rewarded with the living of St Andrew's Holborn, one of the richest in the country. [19] St Andrew's was a medieval church rebuilt by Christopher Wren after the Great Fire of London. Thomas Coram, founder of the Foundling Hospital, was to be buried there and the church now houses Handel's organ which was originally in the Hospital. St Andrew's Holborn is very near to Fetter Lane where Swedenborg was to worship in the Moravian chapel in the 1740s.

Bolingbroke opened negotiations with France, which was even more exhausted by the long war, and in doing so abandoned his Dutch and Austrian allies. Marlborough was dismissed as commander-in-chief in December 1711 and replaced with the ineffective Duke of Ormonde, a Tory supporter. Bolingbroke's greatest achievement was the Treaty of Utrecht (1713) which put an end to the long series of wars and, as G M Trevelyan put it, 'The fortunate Eighteenth Century was well launched upon its reasonable and civilized course'. [20] There followed a long period of peace between Britain and France, a period which allowed the music of Handel to flourish and in which Swedenborg was to enjoy the freedom to publish his works in London and Amsterdam. Handel celebrated the Peace of Utrecht with a *Te Deum* and a *Jubilate* performed in St Paul's Cathedral at a Thanksgiving Service on 7 July 1713, but he was to come into his glory when the Elector of Hanover succeeded to the British throne on the death of Queen Anne in August 1714. Bolingbroke overplayed his hand, flirted with the 'Old Pretender' ('James III') in Paris in an attempt to achieve a Jacobite restoration in the vain hope that James would renounce his Roman Catholic faith and fled there to avoid retribution from the Whigs who had returned to power with the Hanoverian succession. Although he broke with the Pretender and eventually returned to England, Bolingbroke never held power again, nor was he permitted to take his seat in the House of Lords, instead having to content himself with a career outside Parliament, and often abroad, as a political philosopher and pamphleteer. The Tory Party of Harley and Bolingbroke was reduced to an ineffective rump and a long period of Whig supremacy prevailed.

It is not known what view the young Swedenborg took of these events, although it has been suggested that he may even have met Bolingbroke who, as Secretary of State for the Northern Department, had close relations with Gyllenborg, and there is evidence that Swedenborg's cousin and close companion Andreas Hesselius did meet the Secretary of State. [21] Sweden was already in political turmoil when Swedenborg first came to England. The young warrior king Charles XII, a second 'Lion of the North', [22] had been defeated by the Russians at Poltava (1709) and had fled to Turkey, returning later to Sweden to pursue more wars. He was killed by a bullet on 30 November 1718 while besieging the fortress of Fredrikshal in Norway. In July that year Swedenborg had been involved in directing the work of transporting warships overland to assist in the siege using rollers and planks of wood, the normal sea passage through the Skagerrak being blocked by Danish warships. [23] In his later career Swedenborg was a strong supporter of 'close and friendly relations with France', [24] although this did not prevent him from choosing to publish his books in Amsterdam and London (where comparative freedom of the press prevailed) and spending considerable periods in both cities.

Swedenborg's first visit to England lasted over two years. In January 1712 he travelled to Oxford and met the astronomer Edmond Halley, famous for 'Halley's Comet' and his charts showing the latitude and longitude of the English colonies in America. [25] By early 1713 he was in Holland and visited Utrecht where the great peace conference had been in session for a year. At Utrecht he met the Swedish ambassador to The Hague, Baron Johan Palmqvist, with whom he discussed algebra. [26] The Treaty of Utrecht was finally signed on 31 March Old Style, 11 April New Style 1713. [27]

London in the 1740s

Swedenborg did not return to England until May 1744 when he was already fifty-six. He arrived at Harwich from Holland where he had been staying to arrange for the publication in Amsterdam of his work *The Animal Kingdom*, the first two volumes of which had left the press. [28] The year 1744 was the period of his *Dream Diary*, a private journal written in Swedish and not intended for publication. It was published in 1859 on the initiative of a Swedish librarian, G E Klemming, and translated into English ten years later by the eminent English Swedenborgian, James John Garth Wilkinson. The diary shocked its nineteenth-century readers by the frankness with which Swedenborg described his erotic thoughts and feelings.[29] It now appears that Swedenborg, an eminent scientist and Assessor of the Royal Board of Mines in Stockholm, was going through a spiritual crisis. It is a period of his life that is difficult to fathom and one that has given rise to controversy. Meeting on his journey a German shoemaker living in London and a member of the Moravian congregation there, [30] John Seniff, the latter invited him to his own home and shortly afterwards arranged for him to lodge with another member of the Moravian congregation, a gold watch engraver called John Paul Brockmer who lived just off Fleet Street. [31] Swedenborg certainly attended services in the Moravian chapel in Fetter Lane, although he never joined the congregation. It appears that while staying at Brockmer's house Swedenborg suffered some kind of temporary mental breakdown, an incident that gave rise to later rumours that Swedenborg was at least temporarily insane. [32] Out of this spiritual crisis came Swedenborg's 'call' to interpret the Scriptures. For the rest of his life he abandoned his study of science and devoted himself to this task. The first volume of his immense biblical exegesis, *Arcana Caelestia*, was published in London by the Moravian printer and publisher, John Lewis, in 1749.

By contrast, for both Handel and Hogarth the 1740s was the period when they were at the height of their powers and produced some of their greatest and most characteristic work. For Handel, the 1740s was the decade of most of his great English oratorios. The last of his forty-two Italian operas, *Deidamia*, was first performed in 1741. Later that year he composed *Messiah* (in three weeks, between 22 August and 14 September) and it was first performed in Dublin in April 1742. Most of the oratorios had biblical subjects and texts, *Messiah* itself, *Samson*, *Solomon* and others, but *Semele* (1744) comes from Greek mythology with a libretto originally written by William Congreve (out of Ovid) for an opera by John Eccles and adapted for Handel by Alexander Pope. It tells the story of Jupiter's love for a mortal girl, Semele, daughter of Admetus and Harmonia, the king and queen of Thebes, and her destruction when the god, at her request, appears in his real form. *Semele* contains some of Handel's most sensuous music. The arias 'Where'ere you walk', 'Endless pleasure, endless love' and 'O sleep, why dost thou leave me' are famous in their own right. [33]

Hogarth first became famous for his series of etchings *A Harlot's Progress* (1732) telling in six plates the tragic story of an innocent country girl who comes to London, is ensnared by a procuress, becomes a prostitute, is imprisoned in Bridewell and finally dies from venereal disease. [34] Hogarth's depictions of low life in London, including his later *Gin Lane* and *Beer Street* (both 1751), have given rise to the epithet 'Hogarthian', but he had a serious moral purpose, to show the futility of a life of libertinism and to improve the manners and morals of contemporary society. *A Rake's Progress* (1735) is a series of etchings and engravings that show how habitual drunkenness causes a loss of rational self-control that eventually makes a man a raving lunatic and a patient at Bedlam. [35] His prints telling the parallel lives of the Industrious and Idle Apprentices were published in 1747. The industrious apprentice, called 'Goodchild', works hard and adopts virtuous habits. He makes his fortune and becomes Lord Mayor of London. His companion, 'Thomas Idle', is lazy and dissolute. He is led into a life of depravity and crime and in the last print ends his life on the gallows at Tyburn. [36]

During the 1730s Hogarth became acquainted with Thomas Coram, a former sea captain who had conceived the idea of establishing a hospital for the care, upbringing and education of some of London's many foundling children. It was established by Royal Charter in 1739 and Hogarth became a foundation governor. Its ideals are exemplified by the fine oil painting Hogarth presented to the hospital, *Moses brought before Pharaoh's Daughter* (1746). In the biblical story in Exodus chapter 2, Pharaoh's daughter goes with her maidens to bathe in the Nile and finds the baby

Moses hidden in his ark of bulrushes. The baby's sister is nearby keeping watch and she brings the mother to Pharaoh's daughter who asks her to bring up the child in return for wages. In verse 10, illustrated in Hogarth's painting, the child's mother brings him to Pharaoh's daughter who adopts him and names him Moses, 'Because I drew him out of the water' (AV). The symbolism of the painting is obvious. In *Arcana Caelestia* Swedenborg interprets the 'spiritual' sense of the words 'And she brought him to Pharaoh's daughter' as meaning 'an affection for factual knowledge', [37] something that seems to accord well with the rational philanthropy of Coram and Hogarth. Handel became associated with the Foundling Hospital some years later, becoming a governor in 1750. The usual entry fee of £50 was waived because the Hospital had already received more than £1,000 from proceeds of performances of Handel's works, as well as the organ that he presented to the chapel. [38] A concert of Handel's music to raise funds was given in the hospital chapel on 27 May 1749 in the presence of the Prince and Princess of Wales. The programme included part of the *Royal Fireworks Music*, 'a considerable slab of music from *Solomon*', and an anthem that concluded with the 'Hallelujah' chorus from *Messiah*, probably then still unfamiliar to a London audience. [39] Swedenborg is unlikely to have been present on this occasion (indeed there is no evidence that he ever listened to Handel's music), but he commended the establishment of orphanages in his unpublished manuscript posthumously published as *On the Divine Love, On the Divine Wisdom* where he mentions this as an example of practical charity:

> Amongst general uses, too, is the expenditure of money and labour on the building and maintaining of orphanages, hospitable lodges, educational and other institutions of the kind [40]

In his series of prints *Marriage A-la-Mode* (1743-5) Hogarth depicts the decline of two families following the marriage of a wealthy City alderman's daughter to the son of a gouty aristocrat. Not for the last time, the son of a peer marries a girl from a lower social class in an attempt to restore his family's fortune. The peer's son is the aptly named 'Viscount Squanderfield'. The greed for possessions, a fine London house and expensive art, was as alive in the eighteenth century as it is in ours. [41] Once again, Hogarth is giving a moral lesson in showing the disastrous results of greed, but his artistic skill and his human sympathies prevent it becoming a sermon.

Hogarth, the only one of our three protagonists to marry, had married for love, eloping with Jane Thornhill, daughter of the artist Sir James Thornhill in 1728. Handel never married and never seems to have had any intimate connection with a woman. His first English biographer John Hawkins wrote that,

> his social affections were not strong and to this it may be imputed that he
> spent his whole life in a state of celibacy; that he had no female attachment
> of another kind may be ascribed to a better reason. [42]

Yet, as has been shown, Handel was capable of writing sensuous music describing the emotions of erotic love. In a note about the reissue on compact disc of a 1950s recording of *Solomon* by Sir Thomas Beecham, Lindsay Kemp has observed:

> [Beecham] knew what many in his time had yet to realise: that Handel was
> not a pious and imposing Victorian moralist, but an 18th-century man of
> the world who could express in music the finest shadings of human feeling,
> of love and compassion perhaps above all. [43]

But in composing the scene where Solomon judges the case of the disputed parentage of a baby Handel designates the disputants as 'women' in the score instead of 'harlots', [44] as they are called in the word book and as they are described in the Authorized Version (1 Kings 3:16).

Swedenborg was also an eighteenth-century man of the world. His *Dream Diary* shows that he was not a stranger to the pleasures of sex and, late in life, he admitted to his friend the Danish general Tuxen that he had kept a mistress in Italy. [45] In the same conversation Swedenborg asked Tuxen if he and his family were musical, whereupon Tuxen's daughter played a 'difficult and celebrated sonata' on the harpsichord and Swedenborg beat the measure with his foot while sitting on the sofa. Then, with her mother, she sang for Swedenborg, 'a few Italian duets, and some French airs'. [46]

In about 1743 he wrote, as a separate volume of his *The Animal Kingdom*, a long treatise called *The Generative Organs*, but this was not published in his lifetime and was only translated into English in the middle of the nineteenth century. [47] While *The Generative Organs* is a detailed account synthesizing the current medical knowledge, it is no dry textbook. Its language is often quite poetic. In his earlier work *The Five Senses*, explaining why the treatment of the generative organs was being left to a later date he wrote:

> these generative organs are organs of a more perfect nature, as it were: for they are the campus for the exercises of Loves, and are the native land, or Cyprus of Venus, and thus the Olympus of all delights.

Continuing in this baroque vein, he writes that we do not come into the use of the sexual organs until 'about the time of youth, or rather, of adult years':

> Moreover, they constitute a new and, as it were, more pleasant, happy and heavenly life; as is apparent in the case of insects, which, as worms, live long for their appetite and stomach, but finally put off their first life, and put on the life of Venus, when, under another form, they are furnished with wings, like butterflies, and give their labour to procreation. Therefore, we leave this part as yet, until we shall come to a knowledge of superior things, and shall have grown a little older in the knowledge of things; herein imitating Nature herself, who teaches us the way. [48]

In a remarkable passage in *Arcana Caelestia*, Swedenborg describes how in the 'Grand Man', his description of heavenly society, those who live in communities to which the generative organs correspond enjoy greater peace than all the others. [49] Swedenborg clearly thought that sexual love between a man and a woman who truly love one another and are united in what he called 'conjugial' (or true marriage) love was a holy thing. Perhaps he was influenced by the practices of the Moravians who regarded marital sexual intercourse almost as a sacrament, although there were excesses in their community which shocked him?

Handel, Hogarth and Swedenborg lived in a worldly age where kings and leading statesmen alike kept mistresses. Both of Handel's English royal patrons had mistresses. George I had two and George II, despite a spirited and intellectual wife, Caroline of Ansbach, an ally and friend of the Prime Minister Sir Robert Walpole, preferred the company of his mistress Mrs Henrietta Howard, later Countess of Suffolk, for whom he provided a beautiful Palladian villa on the banks of the Thames at Twickenham, Marble Hill House. [50]

King Fredrik I of Sweden, to whom Swedenborg dedicated his treatise on copper in 1734 'with admiration and respect', took a sixteen-year-old mistress, Hedvig Taube, when he was fifty-four and had several children by her. [51]

In his early days Bolingbroke was a notorious rake and was said to have kept a Miss Gumley 'the most expensive lady of her profession in London', [52] but he later married a wealthy French marquise and enjoyed domestic happiness. Walpole married his mistress immediately after the death of his first wife. [53] George III, who succeeded his grandfather just a year after Handel's death, was respectable and uxorious. Perhaps there was already a change in the moral climate?

Swedenborg was not to publish his inspired work on love and marriage, *Conjugial Love*, [54] until 1768 when he was eighty years old, but his earlier work shows how seriously he took the subject. Always recognizing the power of the sex drive, especially in males, and generous in the exceptions he makes for human weakness, he nevertheless points to monogamous and faithful marriage as the ideal field for the expression of sexual love. Handel, Hogarth and Swedenborg, I believe, all contributed in different ways to a reformation in manners and morals that was taking place towards the middle of the eighteenth century, yet none of them had a hint of 'Victorian' prudery about them.

NOTES

1   This essay was originally conceived as a contribution to a proposed volume of essays on 'Swedenborg and London'. I am grateful to Nora Foster for helpful comments and suggestions.

2   In 1710 Handel was still Georg Friedrich Händel (he was naturalized as a British subject pursuant to an Act of Parliament in 1727 and anglicized his name at that time.) Swedenborg was Emanuel Swedberg until the family was ennobled in 1719 and took the name Swedenborg, but for ease of reference I use the names they later adopted and by which they are now known. Handel is still called Händel in Germany and Haendel in France.

3   Donald Burrows, *Handel* (Oxford: Oxford University Press, 1994), pp. 4-5, fig. 1, where Handel's lineage is set out. Georg Taust had married Dorothea Cuno, daughter of Johann Christoph Cuno. In late 1768 Swedenborg became acquainted in Amsterdam with the German botanist (he was also acquainted with Linnaeus) and businessman, Johann Christian Cuno (1708-83), who left an important memoir of recollections of Swedenborg which has been described as 'the most detailed account of Swedenborg's personality that we have': C O Sigstedt, *The Swedenborg Epic* (London: Swedenborg Society, 1981), p. 362. Cuno's manuscript is in the Library of Brussels: Sigstedt, p. 474. It is an intriguing possibility that Swedenborg's friend may have been related to Handel.

4   This epithet was applied to Blake by Jorge Luis Borges.

5   Burrows, *Handel*, p. 382. The occasion was in Halle on 6 April 1703 when Handel was eighteen.

6   Kathleen Raine, 'The Human Face of God', in *Blake and Swedenborg: Opposition is True Friendship*, ed. Harvey F Bellin and Darrell Ruhl (West Chester: Swedenborg

Foundation, 1985), p. 89. Raine mentions only Blake, but note should be taken also of Swedenborg's influence on leading Victorian poets, such as Tennyson, the Brownings, Coventry Patmore and Dante Gabriel Rossetti: Richard Lines, 'Swedenborgian Ideas in the Poetry of Elizabeth Barrett Browning and Robert Browning', in *In Search of the Absolute—Essays on Swedenborg and Literature*, ed. Stephen Mcneilly (London: Swedenborg Society, 2004), pp. 23-43; Richard Lines, 'Eros and the Unknown Victorian: Coventry Patmore and Swedenborg', in *Between Method and Madness: Essays on Swedenborg and Literature*, ed. Stephen McNeilly (London: Swedenborg Society, 2005), pp. 65-79; Richard Lines, 'Angels and Authors: Some Influences of Swedenborg on Victorian Literature', in *Presidential Address to the Swedenborg Society* (London: Swedenborg Society, 1993); and Anna Maddison, ' "Through Death to Love": Swedenborgian Imagery in the Painting and Poetry of Dante Gabriel Rossetti', herein at pp. 291-316.

[7] John Hawkins, *A General History of the Science and Practice of Music* (London, 1776), vol. II, p. 911.

[8] Emanuel Swedenborg, *The Last Judgment*, tr. John Chadwick (London: Swedenborg Society, 1992), p. 133. The comments on the British appear in Swedenborg's tract *Continuatio de Ultimo Judicio* published in 1763.

[9] Burrows, *Handel*, p. 37.

[10] Carola Oman, *Elizabeth of Bohemia* (London: Hodder and Stoughton, 1938), p. 458 (genealogical table). Elizabeth, renowned for her beauty and charm was sometimes called (like a much later English princess) 'the Queen of Hearts'. She spent most of later life in exile in The Hague.

[11] Torquato Tasso (1544-95) was an Italian poet. *Jerusalem Delivered* (1580-1) is an epic poem dealing with the siege of Jerusalem during the First Crusade (1099).

[12] Burrows, *Handel*, pp. 61 and 65.

[13] *The Letters and Memorials of Emanuel Swedenborg*, tr. and ed. Alfred Acton, 2 vols. (Bryn Athyn: Swedenborg Scientific Association, 1948-55), vol. I, p. 13.

[14] Swedenborg refers to St Paul's, then just completed, in his letter to Benzelius.

[15] Sigstedt, *The Swedenborg Epic*, p. 16. This was at Brunsbo in central Sweden where his father Jesper Swedberg had his residence as Bishop of Skara. For Swedenborg's musical knowledge and interests, see Anders Hallengren, 'Music, Metaphysics, and

Modernity', in his *Gallery of Mirrors: Reflections of Swedenborgian Thought* (West Chester: Swedenborg Foundation, 1998), pp. 3-16.

[16] Lars Bergquist, *Swedenborg's Secret* (London: Swedenborg Society, 2005), p. 156. Bergquist comments that Swedenborg would have seen operas by Vivaldi and perhaps by Pergolesi.

[17] *The Letters and Memorials of Emanuel Swedenborg*, vol. I, p. 14.

[18] G M Trevelyan, *England Under Queen Anne*, vol. 3, *The Peace and the Protestant Succession* (London: Longmans, Green & Co, 1934), pp. 45-60.

[19] *Hidden Magdalen*, ed. David Roberts and Richard Sheppard (Oxford: Magdalen College, 2008). Note by Ralph Walker at p. 58.

[20] Trevelyan, *The Peace and the Protestant Succession*, Preface, p. viii.

[21] Marsha Keith Schuchard, 'Swedenborg, Jacobitism, and Freemasonry', in *Swedenborg and his Influence*, ed. Erland J Brock (Bryn Athyn: Academy of the New Church, 1988), p. 364. Schuchard quotes a Swedish source for the meeting.

[22] This epithet had been applied to Gustavus Adolphus for his role in the Thirty Years War.

[23] Bergquist, *Swedenborg's Secret*, p. 71.

[24] Ibid., p. 362.

[25] Sigstedt, *The Swedenborg Epic*, p. 23.

[26] *The Letters and Memorials of Emanuel Swedenborg*, vol. I, p. 51.

[27] Trevelyan, *The Peace and the Protestant Succession*, p. 226.

[28] Sigstedt, *The Swedenborg Epic*, p. 189.

[29] A modern English translation is *Swedenborg's Dream Diary*, tr. Anders Hallengren and ed. with a long introduction by Lars Bergquist (West Chester: Swedenborg Foundation, 2001).

[30] The Moravians were a sect within the Lutheran Church originating in the province of Moravia adjacent to Bohemia. Their leader at that time was the Saxon nobleman, Count Zinzendorf. For a highly readable, but very controversial, account of the eighteenth-century Moravians in London and their sexual beliefs and practices, see Marsha Keith Schuchard, *Why Mrs Blake Cried: The Sexual Basis of Spiritual Vision* (London: Century, 2006). Dr Schuchard's work is remarkable for the discovery

she made in Moravian archives showing that William Blake's mother and her first husband were members of the Fetter Lane Moravian congregation from 1749 to 1751.

31 Sigstedt, *The Swedenborg Epic*, p. 189.

32 Ibid., p.190. Bergquist gives a helpful commentary on Swedenborg's apparent breakdown in his introduction to Swedenborg's *Dream Diary* at pp. 52-9.

33 Burrows, *Handel*, p. 312.

34 Matthew Craske, *William Hogarth* (London: Tate Publishing, 2000), pp. 7-8.

35 Ibid., p. 43.

36 Ibid., p. 15.

37 Swedenborg, *Arcana Caelestia*, tr. John Elliott, 12 vols. (London: Swedenborg Society, 1983-99), vol. 9, §6750, p. 56.

38 Burrows, *Handel*, p. 299.

39 Ibid., pp. 299-300.

40 Swedenborg, *On the Divine Love, On the Divine Wisdom*, tr. E C Mongredien (London: Swedenborg Society, 1986), p. 148.

41 Craske, *William Hogarth*, p. 68.

42 John Hawkins, *A General History of the Science and Practice of Music*, vol. II, pp. 911-12. Burrows, *Handel*, p. 374 comments that by 'a better reason' Hawkins meant that the fact that Handel did not keep a mistress could be ascribed to his blameless morals.

43 Handel, *Solomon* (EMI Records Ltd compact disc, 2005).

44 Burrows, *Handel*, p. 323.

45 R L Tafel (ed.), *Documents concerning the Life and Character of Emanuel Swedenborg* (London: Swedenborg Society, 1875-7), vol. II, p. 437. Tafel reprinted the English translation of Tuxen's account by Augustus Nordenskjöld which appeared as an appendix to the *New Jerusalem Magazine* for 1790, pp. 257-65. Tafel, who can certainly be described as 'a pious and imposing Victorian', argued that the story that Swedenborg had a mistress in Italy could not be true.

46 R L Tafel (ed.), *Documents concerning the Life and Character of Emanuel Swedenborg*, vol. II, pp. 437-8.

47 The translation was by James John Garth Wilkinson who later translated the *Dream Diary*.

[48] Swedenborg, *The Five Senses*, §10, quoted in Swedenborg, *The Organs of Generation*, tr. Alfred Acton (Philadelphia: Boericke & Tafel, 1912), p. 14.

[49] Swedenborg, *Arcana Caelestia*, vol. 7, §§5050-3, pp. 55-6.

[50] Marble Hill House, now a property of English Heritage, was the home of the leading English Swedenborgian Charles Augustus Tulk from 1812 to 1817. Tulk was a good singer and a lover of Handel. His friend and biographer Mary Catherine Hume recalled him singing 'the glorious airs of Handel with an expression and a feeling surpassed by few': *A Brief Sketch of the Life, Character, and Religious Opinions of Charles Augustus Tulk*, ed. Charles Pooley (London: James Speirs, 1890), p. 20.

[51] Bergquist, *Swedenborg's Secret*, pp. 390-1.

[52] F S Oliver, *The Endless Adventure* (London: Macmillan, 1930), vol. I, p. 297.

[53] Ibid.

[54] The most recent translation is that by John Chadwick (London: Swedenborg Society, 1996).

Jung and his intellectual context: the Swedenborgian connection

Eugene Taylor

> He looked at his own Soul with a telescope. What seemed all irregular,
> he saw and shewed to be beautiful constellations, and he added to the
> consciousness hidden worlds within worlds—Coleridge, *Notebooks*

I t is perhaps inconceivable, in the latter half of the twentieth century, to suggest that Carl Gustav Jung, Swiss psychiatrist, folklorist and philologist, should be associated with any other name than Sigmund Freud, the founder of psychoanalysis. For after all, wasn't Jung Freud's most eminent disciple? Didn't Freud discover the unconscious and Jung therefore follow in his footsteps as an acolyte and heir apparent to the psychoanalytic throne? Didn't Jung learn all about dynamic theories of the unconscious from Freud, and then break away to develop his own errant interpretations of psychoanalytic theory, thus classing him with the likes of Rank, Horney and Adler as one of the neo-Freudians?

Recent historical evidence suggests that the answer to all these questions might actually be a resounding 'No!' and that Jung's thought, in fact, should be interpreted not within the context of Viennese psychoanalysis, but in light of the indigenous history of Swiss psychology and its more enduring connections to the so-called French-Swiss and Anglo-American psychotherapeutic axis that flourished in the late nineteenth and early twentieth century.

As the details of this interrelation are only now being spelled out, it is possible that Jung's early attraction to the writings of Emanuel Swedenborg, rather than being seen as just some isolated incident, provides yet another clue to the myriad ways that Jungian thought actually has closer affinities to a uniquely English and American rather than Viennese psychology of the subconscious.

To begin with, the great contention between Freud and Jung was allegedly based on their differences over the nature of *libido*, or psychic energy. In the stereotypic picture of their relationship, Freud espoused a detailed and systematic theory of childhood sexual development, which, as long as dynamic processes of the unconscious unfolded in a normal way, led to mature and well-adjusted sexual behaviour in adulthood. Should traumatic incidences or psychic conflict over sexual matters occur, however, depending on their nature and severity, developmental fixation of unconscious processes would occur, and the resulting emotional (and sexual) stunting would produce characteristic neuroses in adulthood. Jung, the stereotype suggests, had come to Freud in 1906 knowing very little about the unconscious, learned everything at the feet of the master, but then broke with Freud and his circle in 1912 over the sexual emphasis given to the development of the neurosis.

Jung, it is supposed, had begun to advocate—only after a long tenure under Freud—that the nature of psychic energy was spiritual. In his view, sexual adjustment was certainly a part of human maturation, but far more important was a predictable struggle between the ego and the self that develops over control of the personality within the psychic life of each person. The urge toward wholeness, or individuation, as Jung called it, gave consciousness a teleological function. Neurosis therefore was not based on faulty adjustment to external material reality, but on an incomplete or thwarted process of personality transformation, where transcendence of the ego has not been accomplished.

We may well wonder where Jung got some of these ideas and, again, the general wisdom is that, viewing him now in our own post-positivist age, he was a unique personality with an eccentric outlook, whose theories of a spiritual psychology were underived. [1] We have ample evidence, however, that psychology and religion in Switzerland continued to enjoy a lively dialogue long after positivistic reductionism first established its stranglehold on German science. In numerous instances, an amicable fusion occurred—to one degree or another—in the theoretical systems of such notables as August Forel, a modern pioneer in brain neuropathology who had been Eugen Bleuler's predecessor as head of the Berghölzli Asylum;[2] Adolf Meyer, Forel's most distinguished student, who became a pioneer in the psychobiosocial approach in American psychiatry; Paul Dubois, the neurologist whose early text the *Psychic Treatment of Nervous Disorders* became a bible in American psychotherapeutic circles after 1905; Theodore Flournoy, Switzerland's most distinguished experimental psychologist at the turn of the century; Edouard Claparède, the child psychologist who had been a student and colleague of Flournoy (and also a relative); Oskar Pfister, minister and Freudian lay analyst;[3] and Jean Piaget,[4] the noted developmental psychologist and student of Claparède. To this list, the new scholarship suggests, must be added the psychology of Carl Jung.[5]

A number of important conceptualizations linked Jung particularly with French, English and American efforts to develop a dynamic theory of the unconscious. Primary among these was the Protestant myth of the Ascension as a driving force behind the iconography of transcendence in personality development. In numerous models of personality that flourished at the turn of the century, normality was considered imperfect, blighted and insufficient, and it was only by the transformation from a lesser, undeveloped state to a higher, more sacralized and spiritual one, that the best qualities of our humanity could become actualized in the person. It was not lost on Jung, as well as others, that such a motif within Christian cultures is based on belief in the myth of the resurrection of Jesus, accepted as either a real physical occurrence or as a numinous projective symbol suggesting the possibility of transcendence.

The question of transcendence had been a burning one for Jung. Even as a young man, he was called upon to reconcile the intense spirituality of his father, a Protestant clergyman, who had been a *seelsorge*, or pastoral counsellor, in the Swiss asylums, and the psychic abilities of his mother, a deeply intuitive woman, with the dictates of the new and emerging empirical sciences. He sensed there was some important and as yet unrevealed connection between such phenomena as the transcendent experience, mediumship and psychopathology. These states stand in enigmatic relation to waking consciousness, and he was impelled early on to understand them.

In this search, at the very beginning of his career, Jung discovered the works of Emanuel Swedenborg. He later proclaimed Swedenborg 'a learned and highly intelligent man, and a visionary of unexampled fertility'. [6] Jung first discovered the writings of the Swedish seer during his student days in the late 1890s, when he remembered himself as being most intellectually alive, full of explosive argument, and preoccupied with the problem of evil. At that time Jung considered himself a theological agnostic with 'an absolute conviction when speaking of the soul as immaterial, transcendent, outside time and space—and yet to be approached scientifically'. [7] Puzzled by the absence of any serious analysis of the psyche in traditional psychology, he studied somnambulism, hypnosis and spiritualism. Jung says in his autobiography that besides reading DuPrel, Eschenmayer, Passavant, Kerner and Gorres, he had excitedly read through seven volumes of Swedenborg, although we are not told which ones. [8] In the beginning, he found these authors weird and questionable, but they were the first objective accounts he had read of inner psychological phenomena. [9]

From here, Jung turned to modern scientific investigations of the occult, which had flourished since the 1880s through the English and American Societies for Psychical Research and through the experimental work of such men as Theodore Flournoy, a much older colleague in Geneva, F W H Myers in England, and their close friend, William James in America. Beginning in the 1880s, psychical research had proven to be an important vehicle for applying empirical methods to the investigation of the subconscious and as such, had helped spread the views of the new French dynamic psychiatry of Charcot, Janet, Bernheim and Liébeault throughout Europe and America.

Flournoy's major work, for instance, *From India to the Planet Mars*, was an analysis of subconscious processes revealed in the intensive study of the trance medium, Hélène Smith. [10] F W H Myers, one of the principal investigators of the English Society for Psychical Research, developed his conception of the subliminal consciousness from a study of automatic writing. He described this region below the threshold of consciousness as containing a spectrum of states from pathological to transcendent and he maintained that the inner strata had a mythopoetic function in elevating common thought to the level of guiding visions. [11]

One of the most important sources for Jung became the work of William James in America. Drawing first from James's *Principles of Psychology* (1890), Jung was particularly attracted to the analysis of two cases of double personality.

First was the Revd Ansel Bourne, whom James had studied with Richard Hodgson in their official capacity as investigators for the American Society for Psychical Research. Bourne had suddenly disappeared from his home one day and turned up a year later in another state, confused and in a daze. In the interim he had become a merchant with a separate identity and lifestyle, who had no knowledge of his former self as a minister. Upon reawakening to the identity of Ansel Bourne, he had no idea where he was or who he had been in the capacity of a merchant. His circumstance had attracted the attention of the ASPR and after investigating the veracity of the man's claims and the events as reported, James was able to help the man partially recover some of his lost memories through hypnosis.

The other was the case of Mary Reynolds, a young girl who would pass off into a second personality for months at a time. Reynolds was of particular interest because James indicated that the second personality to emerge was actually superior to the normal one. Eventually the second personality became permanent and Mary lived out the remainder of her life in this new identity.

James's conjectures on these cases led him to a number of important conclusions about the nature of the subconscious which later influenced Jung's writings. Many years later, Jung would hark back to James's claim:

I cannot but think that the most important step forward that has occurred in psychology since I have been a student of that science is the discovery, first made in 1886, that […] there is not only the consciousness of the ordinary field, with its usual center and margin, but an addition thereto in the shape of a set of memories, thoughts, and feelings, which are extramarginal and outside of the primary consciousness altogether, but yet must be classed as conscious facts of some sort, able to reveal their presence by unmistakable signs. [12]

James was for Jung a man of psychological vision and pragmatic philosophy who would on more than one occasion become an inner guide. Jung at one point had said of James: 'It was his far-reaching mind which made me realize that the horizons of human psychology widen into the immeasurable'. [13]

Jung drew on these resources for his own early investigations, beginning with his medical dissertation in 1902, 'The psychology and pathology of so-called occult phenomena'. This was an intensive study of his cousin Hélène Preiswerk. Jung had investigated her alleged occult powers at the urging of Eugen Bleuler in order to elucidate certain problems of psychopathology and the unconscious. Numerous aspects of Jung's later psychology appear in this early investigation. Among them, Hélène depicted to Jung 'a spirit revelation of the forces of this world', in the form of a mandala, or circle, thus presaging an important vehicle Jung would use in his own self-analysis and as a technique for self-exploration which he would eventually advocate for his patients.

Once he had graduated from the University at Zurich, Jung began looking around for a suitable contemporary psychology that was scientifically based and wide enough to accommodate his interests. Myers had recently died and James had by then passed off into a period of philosophical metaphysics. Thus, Jung turned back to Europe. During the winter of 1901-2, he served a brief apprenticeship under the physician, philosopher, and foremost student of Charcot, Pierre Janet, seeking first-hand knowledge of methods derived from the French experimental psychology of the subconscious. But he came away disappointed. The prevailing French model of dissociation theory, without the vision of James and Myers, was still too limited for the range of phenomena that required explanation. [14] During this time, Flournoy, at least, remained an important compatriot.

Then in 1906, Jung made his first contacts with Freud, whose conceptions of the unconscious, as revealed in *The Interpretation of Dreams*, seemed far-reaching and sufficiently different enough from the prevailing views to attract him. It was the force of Freud's substantial personality, however, that eventually captivated Jung and drew him ever deeper into the psychoanalytic circle. In a sort of *folie à deux*, the two corresponded personally and met frequently for six years. Jung saw Freud's work as a significant scientific investigation of the unconscious and lauded Freud for introducing psychology into modern psychiatry. Freud believed Jung to be the brightest mind of his psychoanalytic group and mentioned to Jung directly on several occasions that he had tapped him as successor to the throne. But all this came to an abrupt end in 1912, when Jung published *Transformations and Symbols of the Libido*, in which Jung for the first time in his own words postulated the existence of the collective unconscious. Freud could not tolerate the reinterpretation of his theories, and they mutually agreed to cease further personal contact.

While this account is satisfactory as far as it goes, recently several scholars have put forth evidence to show that Jung already had developed his own views before he had ever met Freud, that Jung discussed many of these ideas with Freud when they first met, and that Jung in fact never told Freud anything at the end of their relationship that he had not already broached from the beginning. [15] While Freud was willing to allow broad verbal discussions, he did make it known in manifold ways to everyone, some not always indirect, that only certain topics were acceptable. What must have galled him the most was that Jung had actually gone into print under the apparent guise of psychoanalysis with ideas that were clearly not Freud's own.

Moreover, the source of the material for Jung's 1912 book had been Flournoy, who had translated the Miller fantasies from French into German and sent them to Jung. Miss Frank Miller, a young, intelligent American woman of an independent bent, had travelled widely, but had been hospitalized for nervous disorders on at least two occasions. She composed a phenomenological essay reflecting the images of her inward journey and Flournoy had published it in his *Archives de Psycholgie*, in the same issue in which articles had appeared by William James and Edouard Claparède. Jung analysed the material and saw in the archetypal images the portent of a coming psychotic breakdown. His analysis of the material occurred during an acute identity crisis of his own, just at a point when he knew that the break with Freud was imminent. His personal identification with the Miller fantasies led him to raise the issue of the repressed feminine in his own psyche and thus to formulate for the first time the possibility that this personal crisis had forced him into an encounter with his own anima. [16]

We cannot escape the conclusion that his break with Freud and the narrow interpretations of psychoanalysis caused him to return to the wider frame of reference of his original Swiss and Anglo-American context. Jung tells us as much in the preface to his Fordham University lectures, delivered just after the split with Freud, when he writes:

It has been wrongly suggested that my attitude signifies a 'split' in the psychoanalytic movement. Such schisms can only exist in matters of faith. But psychoanalysis is concerned with knowledge and its everchanging formulations. I have taken as my guiding principle William James's pragmatic rule: 'You must bring out of each word its practical cash value, and set it at work within the stream of your experience'. It appears less as a solution, then, than as a program for more work, and more particularly as an indication of the ways in which existing realities can be changed? [17]

So Jung had been guided by Flournoy back to William James. James, of course, had died in 1910; thus, I suggest that this reference should be taken in the sense of a symbolic return to Jung's original intellectual and spiritual lineage from which he first derived a dynamic psychology of the subconscious, [18] James had cast the philosophical categories of mental life into the context of physiology while at the same time arguing for the efficacy of consciousness in the evolutionary process. The teleological argument remained alive in biology for James because consciousness was a fighter for ends. Myers adapted this interpretation of evolution to the reality of psychic phenomena in the subliminal consciousness, saying that the appearance of such higher forms of functioning in particular individuals was simply a harbinger of what the species was to become as a whole. Jung applied this same teleological paradigm to the evolution and transformation of consciousness within the individual.

At the same time, James was preoccupied enough with the physiology of consciousness to have only broached the symbolic hypothesis, that specific physical symptoms of the neurosis were in some sense symbols of the original trauma, and in this he largely followed Janet rather than Myers. While both Myers and Flournoy did articulate the mythopoetic function of the subliminal, it was left to Jung to expand on it. His task was to create a more complex depth psychology in the twentieth century that was sophisticated enough to rival psychoanalysis in the post-modern period. Jung did this by not only incorporating the older ideas embracing the teleological aims of consciousness, but also by reinterpreting the function of the symbolic process. Just as the traumatic etiology of the neurosis ushered in an unprecedented era of psychotherapy, he now showed the necessity of constructing a mythic structure if personal transformation is to take place. Growth and health meant not simply adjustment to external social norms, but a new era of understanding the importance of education for transcendence.

All of this had existed in his thought in germinal form from the beginning, and had been quickened by the projective and highly unconscious nature of the relationship Jung had maintained with Freud. But Jung's direct encounter with the unconscious only began when the break with Freud had finally occurred. Once he and Freud had severed their contacts Jung resigned his teaching position at the University of Zurich in 1913 because, he said, he was in such personal turmoil and uncertain about his own self-identity. While he continued to maintain a flourishing private practice, he then embarked upon a six-year self-experiment in an attempt to understand the fantasies emerging from his unconscious. To record all that happened, he began a detailed log, the famous *Red Book*, which he filled with archetypal paintings of the inner landscape during this period.

He ended this experiment with publication of *Seven Sermons to the Dead* (1921) and immediately thereafter produced his first mandala, which he represented as a map of his own psyche. The rest is history. Beginning in 1922, with publication of *Psychological Types*, he embarked upon the career for which he has become best known, as an interpreter of dreams, fantasies, myths, alchemical symbols, and religious iconography, during which he produced the bulk of the eighteen volumes that compose his collected works.

Jung and Swedenborg

Thus, it is no accident that after his break with Freud, Jung returned periodically to delve into Swedenborg's books. He also read biographies and comments on Swedenborg's life, and he cited Swedenborg on numerous occasions in his own collected works. There are two explanations why this might be so.

First, the intellectual and spiritual lineage Jung had used to construct a psychology of the unconscious was sympathetic to Swedenborgian thought. William James's father had written some dozen works on Swedenborg, had been instrumental in introducing Swedenborg to the New England transcendentalists, and had evolved a religious philosophy based on the Swedish seer's works that formed the bulwark of the literary legacy inherited by his sons, William and Henry. Then William himself authored almost a dozen more works on psychology and philosophy implicitly answering his father's Swedenborgian metaphysics. Jung, we know, drew particularly from James's *Principles of Psychology*, from his *Varieties of Religious Experience*, and from his *Pragmatism*.

F W H Myers, as well, was no stranger to Swedenborg and referred to him in several places. He believed that Swedenborg was a precursor to the mesmerists, who themselves led eventually to a more thorough scientific investigation of the paranormal. At the same time, Swedenborg's accounts not only gave credibility to the thesis that communication from mind to mind was possible independent of the senses, but also, Swedenborg himself was proof that there could be knowledge and memory of a spirit world without actual spirit possession. In his major work, *Human Personality and Its Survival of Bodily Death* (1903), Myers devotes several pages of personal opinion to Swedenborg's writings, concluding that what he wrote concerning sight, feelings, and experiences of the other world corroborated in many important ways a mass of literature by other sensitives, while Swedenborg's dogmatic statements as to the true internal meaning of the books of the Bible appeared as arbitrary projections of his own preconceived ideas. [19]

Flournoy, as well, has left us a clue. After *From India to the Planet Mars*, Flournoy's second most important text was *Spiritism and Psychology* (1911). In it, Flournoy was considering a classification of various types of mediumship, and under the category of those who were not morbid types, but rather in most robust health, he named Swedenborg.

In contrast, we do not find much sympathy for Swedenborg from Freud and his followers. [20] There is also one small piece of evidence from Jung to Freud suggesting the extent of the psychoanalysts' distance from the material. In a reference that particularly annoyed Jung, Adler and Stekel had referred in print to the Swedish seer as 'Schwedenberg'. [21]

Second, for Jung, Swedenborg's ideas also represented a teleological and mythopoetic iconography of personal transformation. This is most cogently represented in the details of their respective biographies. Both had come from intensely religous families. Both had first turned to science and then ended in religion. Both had made the transition after an extended struggle with the unconscious that led to life-transforming experiences. Both evolved a mythic vision of the interior world that had great pragmatic usefulness in their respective careers. Jung thus used Swedenborg in a number of ways to corroborate aspects of his own psychology of the unconscious.

Visionary Experience

Jung was forever attracted to an investigation of personalities whose biography showed that the normal process of growth and transformation was accompanied by, and I will use Huxley's terms, an opening of the doors of perception. At every given moment, we live in a wider and deeper world than normal waking awareness usually reveals. Progress, in the sense of mastering the struggle for self-understanding, or completing the inner work that uniquely confronts every person, can only proceed if we have a way to regard inner experience. When Jung said that the terms of this discourse were of a visionary nature, he meant that the engulfing power of psychic experience had to be mediated by symbols appropriate to the task. The numinous quality of transformation could make itself seen through a variety of forms: one could find it through waking imagery, through the use of dreams, through the interpretation of religious visions and psychotic hallucinations (actively sought for or unbidden), or through active identification with images from mythology, both personal and collective in nature.

In this search, among numerous other examples, Jung refers in his collected works to Swedenborg's life and visions. He was particularly attracted to the description of Swedenborg's vision of Christ in April 1744, and he quotes extensively in at least two places Swedenborg's clairvoyant experiences and discusses their implications. [22] In another place, he compares Swedenborg's conversations with the dead and recently departed as similar to those found in the Tibetan *Bardo Thodol*. [23]

Synchronicity

Synchronicity was for Jung a philosophical way in which the problem of causality could be approached. Direct relationships in which a cause and effect sequence could have an explainable effect were the common stock of science, he said. But what of those occurrences, psychic in nature, which appear together in consciousness but have no apparent causal connection, and yet they have great significance for the inner life of the individual?

As a simple example Jung gave the case where he had ordered a white tuxedo for the opera a week in advance. The day of the performance he received news that a close friend had died and the funeral would be the next day. Almost simultaneously the tuxedo he had ordered a week before arrived, but the tailors had made the mistake of sending a suit of the wrong colour—in this case, black, just what he needed for the funeral. Jung was less interested in the explanation that there was some mysterious force at work in the universe, behind the scenes, directing these events, than he was in the purport of his own psychic state.

He found a similar case in Swedenborg's ability to describe in detail the progress of the Stockholm fire. [24] That Swedenborg could have had some role in starting the fire by having the thought was ludicrous to Jung. A more plausible explanation was that Swedenborg experienced a fall of the threshold of consciousness and corresponding images became activated in his brain. The archetypal connection had to do more with Swedenborg's immediate psychic state, which gave him access to 'absolute knowledge'. [25]

Alchemical Symbolism

Jung's interest in alchemy also included comparisons with Swedenborg. Jung had been first attracted to alchemical symbolism through his friend, the sinologist, Richard Wilhelm. Wilhelm had translated a Chinese Taoist text on yoga, *The Secret of the Golden Flower*, in 1931 and asked Jung to add a psychological commentary.[26] Fascinated with the implication that alchemy involved not formulas for the chemical change of lead into gold, but a complex symbolism for the transmutation of the baser elements of the personality into the more noble, Jung began a study of his own European alchemical tradition, which eventually led him to deciphering the psychological and spiritual meaning of the European texts.

Jung's collected works contain numerous references comparing Swedenborg's life and ideas to the symbolism in alchemy. In particular, Jung was attracted to Swedenborg's idea of the *maximus homo*. In one place, Jung described Swedenborg's formulation as 'a gigantic anthropomorphism of the universe'.[27] In another place, he refers to Swedenborg's *maximus homo* as a 'matrix or organizing principal of consciousness'. [28] In yet another he suggests that such symbolism expresses a single all-embracing consciousness, the 'greatest man', in support of the idea that the individual psyche is derived from the collective. [29]

Finally, in an interesting reference to a patient that he treated who was influenced by Swedenborgianism, Jung compared Swedenborg's idea of the *maximus homo* with the alchemical image of being devoured by the serpent, the *anima mundi* that the patient had reproduced in a dream. Jung then adds some comments on Swedenborg, himself:

> Swedenborg was not a real alchemist, but he was influenced by the mediaeval philosophy of nature and had at one time partially succumbed to a tragic invasion of the unconscious; I refer to the psychic attack during his stay in London, for which there is unmistakable evidence in his own diary. I will not deny that Swedenborg's peculiar mental condition had an influence on the general conscious attitude of my patient. But anyone with a sufficient knowledge of Swedenborg's chief writings will know that it is very unlikely that he could have infected my patient with alchemistic philosophy, or that she could have reproduced it by cryptomnesia. [30]

He was, in other words, suggesting that while the symbolism of Swedenborgians and that of alchemy may carry a similar meaning, there are no grounds for asserting that the patient's exposure to Swedenborg's idea of the *maximus homo* could have spontaneously caused her to reproduce a related symbol from the alchemical tradition. Also, his comments on Swedenborg's vision should be taken in the context that Jung typically saw visionary experience in a tragic mode, since the entire process was one in which the psyche wages a battle against the forces of its lesser nature, the outcome of which, that is, individuation, was never certain, especially in light of the gargantuan nature of the task.

Jung's affinity with Swedenborg is unmistakable. What is new may be the context in which the attraction can now be understood. Jung stands not in the shadow of Freud and Viennese positivism, but in the light of a more all-encompassing depth psychology of personal transformation that has a long past and an enduring presence far beyond the epistemological borders of psychoanalysis.

*

Acknowledgements are gratefully extended to Mr Sonu Shamdasani, of London, England, for invaluable materials on Jung, Flournoy and Miss Frank Miller; Dr John Haule from the C G Jung Center of Boston for materials linking Jung and Janet; and to Dr Fernando Vidal, University of New Hampshire, for background conversations on psychology and religion and the Protestant tradition in Switzerland.

NOTES

[1] While there can be little doubt that Jung's system, like Freud's, was built around a personal mythology, only Freud hypostatized his internal structure, and by elevating it to a formal system, projected it out onto the world as a scientific psychology. Jung, at least, called on his followers to formulate their own mythology of the unconscious and warned them not to borrow his. 'I can only hope and wish that no one becomes

"Jungian". […] I proclaim no cut-and-dried doctrine and I abhor "blind adherents". I leave everyone free to deal with the facts in his own way, since I also claim this freedom for myself'. Letter from Jung to a Dutch colleague, 14 January 1946, quoted in *C G Jung, Word and Image*, ed. Aniela Jaffé (Princeton: Princeton University Press, 1979), p. 58.

2   John Paul Vader, *For the Good of Mankind: August Forel and the Baha'i Faith* (Oxford: George Ronald, 1984).

3   The German language backdrop to Pfister's view is presented in J Cornell, 'When Science Entered the Soul: German Psychology and Religion, 1890-1914' unpublished Ph.D. dissertation in History, Yale University (1991).

4   Fernando Vidal, 'Jean Piaget and the Liberal Protestant Tradition', in *Psychology in Twentieth-Century Thought and Society*, ed. Mitchell G Ash and William R Woodward (New York: Cambridge University Press, 1987), pp. 271 ff.

5   Most cogently put forward by Mireille Cifali, 'Le fameux couteau de Lichtenberg', in *Le Bloc-Notes de la psychanalyse*, 4 (1984), pp. 171-88.

6   C G Jung, *Collected Works* (Princeton: Bollingen/Princeton University Press, 1957-78), vol. 18, p. 299.

7   V Brome, *Jung* (New York: Atheneum, 1978), p. 65.

8   C G Jung, *Memories, Dreams and Reflections* (New York: Pantheon, 1969), p. 99.

9   Brome, *Jung*, p. 65.

10 Mireille Cifali, 'Theodore Flournoy, la decouverte de l'inconscient', in *Le Bloc-Notes de la psychanalyse*, 3 (1983), pp. 111-31; and her 'Une glossolale et ses savants: Élise Müller alias Hélène Smith', in Sylvain Auroux et al. (eds.), *La Linguistique fantastique* (Paris: Clims-Denoël, 1985), pp. 236-44.

11 Described in Eugene Taylor, *William James on Exceptional Mental States: Reconstruction of the 1896 Lowell lectures* (New York: Charles Scribner's Sons, 1982; repr. Amherst: University of Massachusetts Press, 1984). See pp. 41-3, for instance.

12 William James, *Varieties of Religious Experience* (1902), quoted in Jung's essay 'On the Nature of the Psyche' (1946), in *Collected Works*, vol. 8, p. 167. Jung added the coda: 'The discovery of 1886 to which James refers is the positing of a "subliminal consciousness" by Frederick W. H. Myers'.

[13] Quoted in Eugene Taylor, 'William James and C G Jung', in *Annual of Archetypal Psychology and Jungian Thought*, Spring 1980, p. 166.

[14] Two exceptional articles on the not inconsiderable extent of Janet's influence are by John R Haule: 'Archetype and Integration: Exploring the Janetian Roots of Analytical Psychology', in *Journal of Analytical Psychology*, 28 (1983), pp. 253-67; and 'From Somnambulism to the Archetypes: The French Roots of Jung's Split with Freud', in *The Psychoanalytic Review*, 71:4 (1984), pp. 635-59.

[15] Andrew Paskauskas, 'The Conspiracy Against Jung in Freud's Circle', unpublished paper presented to the History Division of the American Psychological Association, Los Angeles, California, 26 August 1985.

[16] Sonu Shamdasani, 'Miss Frank Miller: Jung's Paradigm Case of Schizophrenia as Seen Through her American Confinement', unpublished paper presented to the History of Psychiatry Section, New York Hospital/Cornell Medical Center, 3 April 1991.

[17] Quoted in Eugene Taylor, 'William James and C G Jung', p. 163.

[18] Sonu Shamdasani, 'Jung, Flournoy, Myers, and the Mediums: Somnambulist Choreographies', unpublished paper presented to the Analytical Psychology Society of Western New York, 29 March 1991.

[19] F W H Myers, *Human Personality and Its Survival of Bodily Death* (1903), ed. Susy Smith (New York: University Books, 1961), pp. 22, 23, 346, 353-5. Myers also recounts the critique of Swedenborg in Kant's *Dreams of a Spirit-Seer*.

[20] For an analysis of the pejorative attitude Freud maintained toward religion, see Edwin R Wallace, IV, 'Freud and Religion: A History and Reappraisal', in *The Psychoanalytic Study of Society*, 10 (1984), pp. 113-61.

[21] C G Jung to S Freud, 29 October 1910, in *The Freud-Jung Letters: The Correspondence between Sigmund Freud and Carl Jung*, ed. William McGuire (Princeton: Princeton University Press, 1974), p. 366.

[22] See C G Jung, *Collected Works*, vol. 18, p. 295, for instance.

[23] C G Jung, *Collected Works*, vol. 11, p. 519.

[24] This refers to a clairvoyant experience of Swedenborg. Kant refers to it in his *Dreams of a Spirit-Seer*.

25   See Jung's essay, 'On Synchronicity', in *Collected Works*, vol. 8, p. 481.

26   For a review of Jung's interpretation of Asian sources, see Eugene Taylor, 'Contemporary Interest in Classical Eastern Psychology', in A Paranjpe, D Ho and R Rieber (eds.), *Asian Psychology: Contemporary Perspectives* (New York: Praeger, 1988).

27   C G Jung, *Collected Works*, vol. 15, p. 9.

28   Ibid., vol. 9, pt. 1, p. 198.

29   Ibid., vol. 10, p. 86.

30   C G Jung, 'A Study in the Process of Individuation', in his *The Integration of Personality* (New York: Farrar & Rinehart, 1939), p. 47.

SELECT BIBLIOGRAPHY

INDEX

Select bibliography

Essays

Abelkis, Kai, 'Emanuel Swedenborg's Influence on Daniel H Burnham's Planning Philosophy and the Plan of Chicago', in *Arcana*, vol. II, no. 3, pp. 53-61.

Altschule, Mark D, 'Swedenborg and Stahl: Opposite——and Wrong——Sides of the Same Coin', in *Studia Swedenborgiana*, vol. 6, no. 3, July 1988, pp. 72-82.

Avens, Robert, 'Blake, Swedenborg, and the Neoplatonic Tradition', in *Arcana*, vol. II, no. 2, pp. 29-47.

——'The Subtle Realm: Corbin, Sufism, and Swedenborg', in *Emanuel Swedenborg: A Continuing Vision*, ed. Robin Larsen et al. (New York: Swedenborg Foundation, 1988), pp. 392-401.

Báez-Rivera, Emilio R, 'Swedenborg and Borges: the Mystic of the North and the Mystic *in puribus*', in *In Search of the Absolute——Essays on Swedenborg and Literature*, ed. Stephen McNeilly (London: Swedenborg Society, 2004), pp. 71-88.

Bell, Reuben, 'Swedenborg and the Kabbalah', in *The arms of Morpheus——Essays on Swedenborg and Mysticism*, ed. Stephen McNeilly (London: Swedenborg Society, 2007), pp. 95-105.

Bergquist, Lars, 'Subjectivity and Truth: Strindberg and Swedenborg', in *In Search of the Absolute——Essays on Swedenborg and Literature*, ed. Stephen McNeilly (London: Swedenborg Society, 2004), pp. 61-9.

——'Linneaus and Swedenborg', in *Arcana*, vol. III, no. 3, pp. 23-39.

Bernstein, Andrew, 'D T Suzuki and Swedenborg', in *Arcana*, vol. I, no. 4.

Böhme, Hartmut and Böhme, Gernot, 'The Battle of Reason with the Imagination', in *What is Enlightenment? Eighteenth-Century Answers and Twentieth-Century Questions*, ed. James Schmidt (Berkeley: University of California Press, 1996), pp. 426-52.

Cameron, Kenneth Walter, 'Swedenborg in Boston. Emerson and the New Church through 1836', in K W Cameron, *Young Emerson's Transcendental Vision: An Exposition of his World View with an Analysis of the Structure, Backgrounds, and Meaning of* Nature *(1836)* (Hartford: Transcendental Books, 1971), pp. 228-52.

Cerullo, John J, 'Swedenborgianism in the Works of Joseph Sheridan Le Fanu: Desocialization and the Victorian Ghost Story', in *Swedenborg and His Influence*, eds. Erland J Brock et al. (Bryn Athyn: The Academy of the New Church, 1988), pp. 91-100.

Chadwick, John, 'Swedenborg and his Readers', in *Swedenborg and His Readers: Selected essays by John Chadwick*, ed. Stephen McNeilly (London: Swedenborg Society, 2003), pp. 1-8.

Deck, Raymond H, Jr, 'New Light on C A Tulk, Blake's Nineteenth-Century Patron', in *Studia Swedenborgiana*, vol. 3, no. 3, January 1979, pp. 5-34.

Dole, George F, 'The Ambivalent Kant', in *Studia Swedenborgiana*, vol. 10, no. 2, May 1997, pp. 1-10.

Doyle, Arthur Conan, 'The Story of Swedenborg', in *Between Method and Madness—Essays on Swedenborg and Literature*, ed. Stephen McNeilly (London: Swedenborg Society, 2005), pp. 95-108.

Duban, James, 'Pragmatism Lost: Moralism, Disinterestedness, and Swedenborgian "Use" in the Philosophy of Henry James, Sr', in *Studia Swedenborgiana*, vol. 14, no. 2, April 2005, pp. 1-16.

Dunér, David, 'Daedalus of the North: Swedenborg's Mentor Christopher Polhem', in *The New Philosophy*, vol. CXIII, nos. 3-4, July-December 2010, pp. 1077-98.

Erdman, David, 'Blake's Early Swedenborgianism: A Twentieth-Century Legend', in *Comparative Literature*, vol. 5, 1953, pp. 247-57.

Florschütz, Gottlieb, 'Swedenborg's Hidden Influence on Kant', in *The New*

Philosophy, vol. XCVI, nos. 1-2, January-June 1993, pp. 171-225; vol. XCVI, nos. 3-4, July-December 1993, pp. 277-307; vol. XCVII, nos. 1-2, January-June 1994, pp. 347-96; vol. XCVII, nos. 3-4, July-December 1994, pp. 461-98; vol. XCVIII, nos. 1-2, January-June 1995, pp. 99-108; vol. XCVIII, nos. 3-4, July-December 1995, pp. 229-58; vol. XCIX, nos. 1-2, January-June 1996, pp. 341-85.

Fox, Leonard, 'The Poems of Angelus Silesius in Light of Swedenborg's Writings', in *Arcana*, vol. I, no. 1, pp. 12-21.

Gabay, Al, 'Swedenborg, Mesmer, and the "Covert" Enlightenment', in *The New Philosophy*, vol. C, nos. 3-4, July-December 1997, pp. 619-90.

Gardiner, Perry F, III, 'Cassirer, Swedenborg, and the Problem of Meaning', in *Studia Swedenborgiana*, vol. 3, no. 1, January 1978, pp. 5-21.

Garrett, Clarke, 'Swedenborg and the Mystical Enlightenment in Late Eighteenth-Century England', in *Journal of the History of Ideas*, vol. 45, 1984, pp. 67-81.

Gladish, Robert W, 'Elizabeth Barrett Browning and Swedenborg', in *New Church Life*, vol. 85, 1965, pp. 506-13 and 559-70.

——'Tre Amici Artistici: E.B. Browning, Hiram Powers, and William Page in Florence and Rome', in *Covenant*, vol. 1, no. 4, 1998, pp. 273-91.

Gladish, Stephen, 'Thoreau and Transcendentalism', in *The New Philosophy*, vol. LXXXVI, no. 4, October-December 1983, pp. 210-13.

Gladish, Sylvia M, 'Pascal and Swedenborg', in *The New Philosophy*, vol. LXXVII, no. 1, January-March 1974, pp. 1-15.

Goerwitz, Emanuel F, 'Swedenborg in Goethe's Faust', in *The New-Church Review*, vol. IX, no. 2, April 1902, pp. 222-44.

Gyllenhaal, Martha, 'John Flaxman's Illustrations to Emanuel Swedenborg's *Arcana Coelestia*', in *Studia Swedenborgiana*, vol. 9, no. 4, April 1996, pp. 1-71.

Hall, Dorothy Judd, 'The Mystic Lens of Robert Frost: Bent Rays from Swedenborg', in *Studia Swedenborgiana*, vol. 9, no. 1, October 1994, pp. 1-26.

Hallengren, Anders, 'The Importance of Swedenborg to Emerson's Ethics', in *Swedenborg and His Influence*, eds. Erland J Brock et al. (Bryn Athyn: The Academy of the New Church, 1988), pp. 229-50.

——'Swedenborgian simile in Emersonian edification', in *In Search of the*

Absolute—Essays on Swedenborg and Literature, ed. Stephen McNeilly (London: Swedenborg Society, 2004), pp. 15-22.

Harding, Brian, 'Swedenborgian Spirit and Thoreautic Sense', in *Journal of American Studies*, 7, pp. 64-79.

Hayward, Margaret, 'Plagiarism and the Problem of Influence: Pauline Bernheim, *Balzac und Swedenborg*', in Studies in Memory of J G Cornell, *Australian Journal of French Studies*, vol. XXIX, no. 1, 1992, pp. 41-51.

Hjern, Olle, 'Carl Jonas Love Almqvist—Great Poet and Swedenborgian Heretic', in *Swedenborg and His Influence*, eds. Erland J Brock et al. (Bryn Athyn: The Academy of the New Church, 1988), pp. 79-90.

Hotson, Clarence Paul, 'Coleridge's "Hamlet" and Emerson's "Swedenborg"', in *The New-Church Magazine*, vol. LIII, no. 512, April-June 1934, pp. 99-112.

——'Emerson and the "New-Church Quarterly Review"', in *The New-Church Magazine*, vol. LIII, no. 513, July-September 1934, pp. 169-83 and no. 514, October-December 1934, pp. 239-53.

——'Emerson and the Swedenborgians', in *Studies in Philology*, vol. 27, no. 3, July 1930, pp. 517-45.

——'Emerson's Biographical Sources for "Swedenborg"', in *Studies in Philology*, vol. 26, no. 1, January 1929, pp. 23-46.

——'Emerson's Boston Lecture on Swedenborg', in *The New-Church Magazine*, vol. LI, no. 504, April-June 1932, pp. 91-101.

——'Emerson's Manchester Lecture on Swedenborg', in *The New-Church Magazine*, vol. LII, no. 507, January-March 1933, pp. 48-58.

—— 'Emerson, Swedenborg, and B F Barrett', in *The New-Church Magazine*, vol. L, no. 502, October-December 1931, pp. 244-52 and vol. LI, no. 503, January-March 1932, pp. 33-43.

——'George Bush and Emerson's Swedenborg', in *The New-Church Magazine*, vol. L, no. 499, January-March 1931, pp. 22-34 and no. 500, April-June 1931, pp. 98-108.

——'Prof. Bush's Reply to Emerson on Swedenborg', in *The New-Church Magazine*, vol. LI, no. 505, July-September 1932, pp. 175-84 and no. 506, October-December 1931, pp. 213-23.

——'A Salford Reply to Emerson's Manchester Lecture on Swedenborg', in *The New-Church Magazine*, vol. LIII, no. 511, January-March 1934, pp. 46-57.

——'Smithson's Reply to Emerson's Manchester Lecture on Swedenborg', in *The New-Church Magazine*, vol. LII, no. 509, July-September 1933, pp. 174-85 and no. 510, October-December 1933, pp. 232-43.

Johnson, Gregory R, 'Did Kant Dissemble His Interest in Swedenborg', in *The New Philosophy*, vol. CII, nos. 3-4, July-December 1999, pp. 529-60.

——'Kant on Swedenborg in the *Lectures on Metaphysics*, Part 1, 1760s-1770s', in *Studia Swedenborgiana*, vol. 10, no. 1, October 1996, pp. 1-38.

——'Kant on Swedenborg in the *Lectures on Metaphysics*, Part 2', in *Studia Swedenborgiana*, vol. 10, no. 2, May 1997, pp. 11-39.

——'Kant's Early Metaphysics and the Origins of the Critical Philosophy', in *Studia Swedenborgiana*, vol. 11, no. 2, May 1999, pp. 29-54.

——'The Kinship of Kant and Swedenborg', in *The New Philosophy*, vol. XCIX, nos. 3-4, July-December 1996, pp. 407-23.

——'William James on Swedenborg: A Newly Discovered Letter', in *Studia Swedenborgiana*, vol. 13, no. 1, June 2003, pp. 61-7.

Jones, P Mansell, 'Swedenborg, Baudelaire and their Intermediaries', in his *The Background of Modern French Poetry: Essays and Interviews* (Cambridge: CUP, 1951), pp. 1-37.

Kegler, Adelheid, 'Elements of Swedenborgian Thought in Symbolist Landscapes: with reference to Sheridan Le Fanu and George MacDonald', in *Between Method and Madness—Essays on Swedenborg and Literature*, ed. Stephen McNeilly (London: Swedenborg Society, 2005), pp. 45-63.

King, Kristin, 'The Power and Limitations of Language in Swedenborg, Shakespeare, and Frost', in *Studia Swedenborgiana*, vol. 11, no. 3, November 1999, pp. 1-63.

Kirven, Robert H, 'Swedenborg and Kant Revisited: The Long Shadow of Kant's Attack and a New Response', in *Swedenborg and His Influence*, eds. Erland J Brock et al. (Bryn Athyn: The Academy of the New Church, 1988), pp. 103-20.

Kurtz, Benjamin P, 'Coleridge on Swedenborg with Unpublished Marginalia on the Prodromus', in *University of California Publications in English*, 14

(Berkeley: University of California, 1943), pp. 199-214.

Lachman, Gary, 'Rudolf Steiner and the Hypnagogic State', in *The arms of Morpheus—Essays on Swedenborg and Mysticism*, ed. Stephen McNeilly (London: Swedenborg Society, 2007), pp. 57-70.

——'Space: the Final Frontier. O V de Lubicz Milosz and Swedenborg', in *Between Method and Madness—Essays on Swedenborg and Literature*, ed. Stephen McNeilly (London: Swedenborg Society, 2005), pp. 81-93.

Lawrence, James F, 'Swedenborg's Trail in the Coleridgean Landscape', in *Studia Swedenborgiana*, vol. 11, no. 2, May 1999, pp. 55-66.

Leonard, Jennifer L, 'Singing Masters of the Soul: Swedenborg's and Blake's Influence on William Butler Yeats', in *Emanuel Swedenborg: A Continuing Vision*, ed. Robin Larsen et al. (New York: Swedenborg Foundation, 1988), pp. 169-72.

Lines, Richard, 'Darwin, Wallace, Tennyson and Swedenborg: Religion and Science in the Nineteenth Century', in *The New Philosophy*, July-December 2009, pp. 893-910.

——'Eros and the Unknown Victorian: Coventry Patmore and Swedenborg', in *Between Method and Madness—Essays on Swedenborg and Literature*, ed. Stephen McNeilly (London: Swedenborg Society, 2005), pp. 65-79.

——'The Feminine Mysticism of Madame Guyon: A Modern Perspective, including Comparisons with Swedenborg', in *The arms of Morpheus—Essays on Swedenborg and Mysticism*, ed. Stephen McNeilly (London: Swedenborg Society, 2007), pp. 71-93.

——'Swedenborgian ideas in the poetry of Elizabeth Barrett Browning and Robert Browning', in *In Search of the Absolute—Essays on Swedenborg and Literature*, ed. Stephen McNeilly (London: Swedenborg Society, 2004), pp. 23-43.

Lundeberg, Axel, 'August Strindberg's "Conversion": A Psychological Study', in *The New-Church Magazine*, vol. LV, no. 521, July-September 1936, pp. 171-81, no. 522, October-December 1936, pp. 220-8 and vol. LVI, no. 523, January-March 1937, pp. 43-51.

McCluskey, Robert, 'Luther, Swedenborg, and the Modern Appearance of Freedom', in *Studia Swedenborgiana*, vol. 8, no. 1, January 1993, pp. 1-19.

Martz, Erin C, 'Dostoyevsky's Christianity: Emanuel Swedenborg's Contribution', in *The New Philosophy*, vol. XCI, no. 4, October-December 1988, pp. 669-82.

Milosz, Czeslaw, 'Dostoevsky and Swedenborg', in *Emanuel Swedenborg: A Continuing Vision*, ed. Robin Larsen et al. (New York: Swedenborg Foundation, 1988), pp. 159-68.

Nemitz, Kurt P, 'Christian Wolff', in *The New Philosophy*, vol. CII, nos. 1-2, January-June 1999, pp. 391-412.

——'The Development of Swedenborg's Knowledge of and Contact with Wolff', in *The New Philosophy*, vol. CII, nos. 3-4, July-December 1999, pp. 467-527.

——'The German Philosophers Leibniz and Wolff in Swedenborg's Philosophic Development', in *The New Philosophy*, vol. XCVII, nos. 3-4, July-December 1994, pp. 411-25.

——'Leibniz and Swedenborg', in *The New Philosophy*, vol. XCIV, nos. 1-2, January-June 1991, pp. 445-88.

Nugent, Charles R, 'The Influence of Swedenborg upon Goethe', in *The New-Church Review*, vol. VII, no. 4, October 1900, pp. 541-7.

Odhner, Hugo Lj., 'Christian Wolff and Swedenborg', in *The New Philosophy*, vol. LIV, no. 4, October 1951, pp. 237-51.

Pacheco, José Antonio Antón, 'Ibn 'Arabi and Swedenborg: Proposals for a Figurative Philosophy', in *The arms of Morpheus—Essays on Swedenborg and Mysticism*, ed. Stephen McNeilly (London: Swedenborg Society, 2007), pp. 125-36.

Prickett, Stephen, 'Swedenborg, Blake, Joachim, and the Idea of a New Era', in *Studia Swedenborgiana*, vol. 7, no. 4, June 1992, pp. 1-30.

Rix, Robert, 'William Blake and the Radical Swedenborgians', in *Esoterica*, vol. 5, 2003, pp. 96-137.

Rowlandson, William, 'Borges's reading of Dante and Swedenborg: Mysticism and the Real', in *Variaciones Borges*, no. 32, October 2011, pp. 59-85.

Schorer, Mark, 'Swedenborg and Blake', in *Modern Philology*, vol. 36, 1938, pp. 157-78.

Schuchard, G C L, 'The Last Scene in Goethe's *Faust*', in *The New Philosophy*, vol. LXXXV, nos. 1-2, January-June 1982, pp. 31-63.

Schuchard, Marsha Keith, 'Leibniz, Benzelius, and Swedenborg: The Kabbalistic Roots of Swedish Illuminism', in *Leibniz, Mysticism, and Religion*, eds. Allison P Coudert, Richard H Popkin and Gordon M Weiner (Boston: Kluwer, 1998), pp. 84-106.

——'The Secret History of Blake's Swedenborg Society', in *Blake: An Illustrated Quarterly*, vol. 26, 1992, pp. 40-51.

——'Swedenborg, Jacobitism and Freemasonry', in *Swedenborg and His Influence*, eds. Erland J Brock et al. (Bryn Athyn: The Academy of the New Church, 1988), pp. 359-79.

——'Yeats and the "Unknown Superiors": Swedenborg, Falk, and Cagliostro', in Marie Roberts and Hugh Ormsby-Lennon (eds.), *Secret Texts: The Literature of Secret Societies* (New York: AMS Press, 1995), pp. 114-68.

Silver, Ednah C, 'Maeterlinck and Swedenborg', in *The New-Church Review*, vol. XII, no. 3, July 1905, pp. 416-22.

Simpson, David, 'Return from the Unknown Country: A Swedenborgian Key to Dostoevsky's *Crime And Punishment*', in *The New Philosophy*, January-June 2009, pp. 791-833.

Sjödén, Karl-Erik, 'Balzac et Swedenborg', in *Cahiers de l'Association internationale des etudes françaises*, March 1963, no. 15, pp. 295-307.

——'Remarques sur le swedenborgisme balzacien', in *L'Année balzacienne*, 1966, pp. 33-45.

Steiner, Rudolf, 'The Interplay of Various Worlds', lecture VII on Swedenborg, Jacob Boehme and Paracelsus, 25 August 1923, in *The Evolution of Consciousness* (London: Rudolf Steiner Press, 2006), pp. 148-64.

Stockenström, Göran, '"The Great Chaos and the Infinite Order:" The Spiritual Journeys of Swedenborg and Strindberg', in *Swedenborg and His Influence*, eds. Erland J Brock et al. (Bryn Athyn: The Academy of the New Church, 1988), pp. 47-78.

——'Strindberg and Swedenborg', in *Emanuel Swedenborg: A Continuing Vision*, eds. Robin Larsen et al. (New York: Swedenborg Foundation, 1988), pp. 137-58.

Sugden, Emily Robbins, 'Swedenborg in English Literature: Coleridge', in *The New-Church Review*, vol. XVI, no. 4, October 1909, pp. 514-22.

——'Swedenborg in English Literature III: Thomas De Quincey', in *The New-Church Review*, vol. XVII, no. 1, January 1910, pp. 70-82.

Sutton, Eric A, 'Swedenborg and Browning', in *The New-Church Magazine*, vol. XLIX, no. 495, January-March 1930, pp. 1-8.

Taylor, Eugene, 'Emerson: The Swedenborgian and Transcendentalist Connection', in *Emanuel Swedenborg: A Continuing Vision*, eds. Robin Larsen et al. (New York: Swedenborg Foundation, 1988), pp. 127-36.

—— 'Jung on Swedenborg, Redivivus', in *Jung History*, vol. 2, no. 2, 2007, pp. 27-31.

—— 'Peirce and Swedenborg', in *Studia Swedenborgiana*, vol. 6, no. 1, June 1986, pp. 25-51.

—— 'Some Historic Implications of Swedenborg's Spiritual Psychology', in *Studia Swedenborgiana*, vol. 4, no. 4, January 1983, pp. 5-38.

—— 'Swedenborgian Roots of American Pragmatism: The Case of D T Suzuki', in *Studia Swedenborgiana*, vol. 9, no. 2, May 1995, pp. 1-20.

—— 'William James and Helen Keller', in *Studia Swedenborgiana*, vol. 4, no. 1, January 1981, pp. 7-26.

Tobisch, Othmar, 'Lavater and Swedenborg', in *The New-Church Review*, vol. XL, no. 4, October 1933, pp. 210-33.

Treuherz, Francis, 'The Origins of Kent's Homeopathy: The Influence of Swedenborg', in *Arcana*, vol. VI, no. 3, 2001, pp. 10-38.

Wake, Wilma E, 'Swedenborg and Andrew Jackson Davis', in *Studia Swedenborgiana*, vol. 11, no. 2, May 1999, pp. 1-7.

Walsh, Arlene M Sanchez, 'Warren F Evans, Emanuel Swedenborg, and the Creation of New Thought', in *Studia Swedenborgiana*, vol. 10, no. 3, September 1997, pp. 13-35.

Williams-Hogan, Jane, 'Light and Dark in the Art of Edgar Allan Poe (1809-1849)', in *The Dark Side: Proceedings of the Seventh Australian and International Religion, Literature and the Arts Conference, 2002*, eds. Christopher Hartney and Andrew McGarrity (Sydney: RLA Press, 2004), pp. 25-40.

—— 'The Place of Emanuel Swedenborg in Modern Western Esotericism', in Antoine Faivre and Wouter Hanegraaff (eds.), *Western Esotericism and the Science of Religion* (Leuven: Peeters, 1998), pp. 201-52.

Wilson, James, 'Swedenborg, Paracelsus, and the Dilute Traces: A Lyrical and

Critical Reflection on Mysticism, Reform, and the Nature of Influence', in *The New Philosophy*, July-December 2011, pp. 175-206.

Wright, Theodore F, 'Balzac and Swedenborg', in *The New-Church Review*, vol. 3, no. 4, October 1896, pp. 481-503.

——'Boehme and Swedenborg', in *The New-Church Review*, vol. II, no. 2, April 1895, pp. 214-32.

——'Kant and the Spirit-Seer', in *The New-Church Review*, vol. 7, no. 3, July 1900, pp. 428-32.

Yeats, William Butler, 'Swedenborg, Mediums and the Desolate Places', in *Between Method and Madness—Essays on Swedenborg and Literature*, ed. Stephen McNeilly (London: Swedenborg Society, 2005), pp. 1-30.

Zuber, Devin, 'Edwards, Swedenborg, Emerson: From Typology to Correspondence', in Richard Hall (ed.), *The Contribution of Jonathan Edwards to American Culture and Society: Essays on America's Spiritual Founding Father (The Northampton Tercentenary Celebration 1703-2003)* (Lampeter: Edwin Mellen Press, 2008), pp. 109-24.

——'A Spiritual World in Sensation: Joseph Sheridan Le Fanu and Emanuel Swedenborg's Mystical Theology', in Kimberly Harrison and Richard Fantina (eds.), *Victorian Sensations: Essays on a Scandalous Genre* (Columbus: The Ohio State University Press, 2006), pp. 74-86.

Books and Dissertations

Adams, Hazard, *Blake's Margins: An Interpretive Study of the Annotations* (Jefferson: McFarland & Co, 2009).

Albanese, Catherine L, *A Republic of Spirit. A Cultural History of American Metaphysical Religion* (New Haven: Yale University Press, 2007).

Ankarsjö, Magnus, *William Blake and Religion: A New Critical View* (Jefferson: McFarland & Co, 2009).

Arnold, Paul, *Esoterisme de Baudelaire* (Paris: Vrin, 1972), esp. ch. VII 'Baudelaire et le Swedenborgisme'.

Bellin, Harvey F and Ruhl, Darrell (eds.), *Blake and Swedenborg: Opposition is True Friendship* (New York: Swedenborg Foundation, 1985).

Benz, Ernst, *Emanuel Swedenborg: Visionary Savant in the Age of Reason*, tr. Nicholas Goodrick-Clarke (West Chester: Swedenborg Foundation, 2002).

Bernheim, Pauline, *Balzac und Swedenborg. Einfluss der Mystik Swedenborgs und Saint-Martins auf die Romandichtung Balzacs* (Berlin: Emil Ebering, 1914).

Bishop, Paul, *Synchronicity and Intellectual Intuition in Kant, Swedenborg, and Jung* (Lampeter: Edwin Mellen Press, 2000).

Blake, William, *Blake's Illuminated Books*, volume 3, *The Early Illuminated Books: All Religions Are One, There Is No Natural Religion, The Book Of Thel, The Marriage Of Heaven And Hell, Visions Of The Daughters Of Albion*, ed. David Bindman (London: Tate Gallery Publications, 1993).

Brock, Erland J et al. (eds.), *Swedenborg and His Influence* (Bryn Athyn: The Academy of the New Church, 1988).

Bush, George, *Mesmer and Swedenborg* (New York: John Allan, 1847).

Chambers, Leslie, *The Swedenborgian Influence on William Blake* (Open University Press, 1993) Ph.D. Thesis.

Corbin, Henry, *Swedenborg and Esoteric Islam*, tr. Leonard Fox (West Chester: Swedenborg Foundation, 1995).

Deck, Raymond H, Jr, 'Blake and Swedenborg', dissertation (Brandeis University, 1978).

Edmisten, Leonard Martin, 'Coleridge's Commentary on Swedenborg', dissertation (University of Missouri, Columbia, 1954).

Emerson, Ralph Waldo, *Swedenborg: Introducing the Mystic*, ed. Stephen McNeilly (London: Swedenborg Society, 2009)

Fiut, Aleksander, *The Eternal Moment: The Poetry of Czeslaw Milosz*, tr. Theodosia S Robertson (Berkeley: University of California Press, 1990).

Florschütz, Gottlieb, *Swedenborg and Kant: Emanuel Swedenborg's Mystical View of Humankind, and the Dual Nature of Humankind in Immanuel Kant*, tr. George F Dole (West Chester: Swedenborg Foundation, 1993).

Frye, Northrop, *Fearful Symmetry: A Study of William Blake* (Toronto: University of Toronto Press, 2004).

Gabay, Alfred J, *Covert Enlightenment: Eighteenth-Century Counterculture and its Aftermath* (West Chester: Swedenborg Foundation, 2005).

Gladish, Robert W, *Swedenborg, Fourier and the America of the 1840s* (Bryn Athyn: Swedenborg Scientific Association, 1983).

Gerding, J L F, *Kant en het paranormale* (Utrecht: Psychologisch Instituut, 1993).

Gyllenhaal, Martha, *Emanuel Swedenborg's Influence on the French Symbolist Movement* (Philadelphia: Temple University, 1999).

—*William Blake's A Vision of the Last Judgment. A Swedenborgian Interpretation* (Philadelphia: Temple University, 1999).

Hallengren, Anders, *Code of Concord: Emerson's Search for Universal Laws* (Stockholm: Almqvist & Wiksell, 1994).

—*Deciphering Reality: Swedenborg, Emerson, Whitman and the Search for the Language of Nature* (Minneapolis: University of Minnesota Press, 1992).

—*Gallery of Mirrors: Reflections of Swedenborgian Thought* (West Chester: Swedenborg Foundation, 1998).

—*The Grand Theme and Other Essays* (London: Swedenborg Society, 2013).

Haller, John S, Jr, *Swedenborg, Mesmer, and the Mind/Body Connection: The Roots of Complementary Medicine* (West Chester: Swedenborg Foundation, 2010).

Hanegraaff, Wouter J, *Swedenborg, Oetinger, Kant: Three Perspectives on the Secrets of Heaven* (West Chester: Swedenborg Foundation, 2007).

Horn, Friedemann, *Schelling and Swedenborg: Mysticism and German Idealism*, tr. George F Dole (West Chester: Swedenborg Foundation, 1997).

Hotson, Clarence Paul, 'Emerson and Swedenborg', dissertation (Harvard University, 1929).

Johnson, Gregory R (tr. and ed.), *Kant on Swedenborg: Dreams of a Spirit-Seer and Other Writings* (West Chester: Swedenborg Foundation, 2002).

Jonsson, Inge, *Visionary Scientist. The Effects of Science and Philosophy on Swedenborg's Cosmology* (West Chester: Swedenborg Foundation, 1999).

Keane, Donna Dee, *Spiritual Therapy: A Comparison Between Swedenborg's and Jung's Psychodynamic Models as They Function in Pastoral Counseling* (Andover Newton Theological School, 1988).

Lamm, Martin, *Emanuel Swedenborg: the Development of his Thought*, tr. Tomas Spiers and Anders Hallengren (West Chester: Swedenborg Foundation, 2000).

Larsen, Robin et al. (eds.), *Emanuel Swedenborg: A Continuing Vision* (New York: Swedenborg Foundation, 1988).

Lawrence, James F, (ed.) *Testimony to the Invisible: Essays on Swedenborg* (West Chester: Chrysalis Books, 1995).

Lee, Jun-chol, *A Search for the Origin of Evil: Swedenborg & Jung* (2000).

Lineham, Peter, 'The English Swedenborgians, 1770-1840: A Study in the Social Dimensions of Religious Sectarianism' (University of Sussex, 1978) Ph.D. thesis.

McFarland, John Sylvester, *Baudelaire and Swedenborg: The Unity of the Symbolic Tradition* (Harvard University, 1950).

McNeilly, Stephen, (ed.) *On the True Philosopher and the True Philosophy: Essays on Swedenborg* (London: Swedenborg Society, 2002).

——(ed.) *Swedenborg and His Readers: Selected essays by John Chadwick* (London: Swedenborg Society, 2003).

——(ed.) *In Search of the Absolute—Essays on Swedenborg and Literature* (London: Swedenborg Society, 2004).

——(ed.) *Between Method and Madness—Essays on Swedenborg and Literature* (London: Swedenborg Society, 2005).

—— (ed.) *The arms of Morpheus—Essays on Swedenborg and Mysticism* (London: Swedenborg Society, 2007).

Milosz, Czeslaw, *The Land of Ulro*, tr. Louis Iribarne (New York: Farrar, Straus & Giroux, 1984).

Milosz, O V de L, *The Noble Traveller: The Life and Writings of O V de L Milosz*, ed. Christopher Bamford (West Stockbridge: Lindisfarne Press, 1985).

Morris, H N, *Flaxman, Blake, Coleridge, and Other Men of Genius Influenced by Swedenborg* (London: New-Church Press, 1915).

Nathan, Leonard and Quinn, Arthur, *The Poet's Work: An Introduction to Czeslaw Milosz* (Cambridge: Harvard University Press, 1991).

Osuga, Saori, *Séraphîta et la Bible. Sources scripturaires du mysticisme balzacien* (Paris: Honoré Champion Éditeur, 2012).

Pacheco, José Antonio Antón, *The Swedish Prophet: Reflections on the Visionary Philosophy of Emanuel Swedenborg*, tr. Steven Skattebo (West Chester: Swedenborg Foundation, 2012).

—*Visionary Consciousness: Emanuel Swedenborg and the Immanence of Spiritual Reality*, tr. Robert E Shillenn (Charleston: Arcana Books, 2000).

Palmquist, Stephen, *Kant's Critical Religion* (Aldershot: Ashgate, 2000).

Raine, Kathleen, *Blake and the New Age* (London: Allen and Unwin, 1979).

—*Blake and Tradition*, 2 vols. (Washington: Princeton University Press, 1968).

—*The Human Face of God: William Blake and the Book of Job with 130 illustrations* (London: Thames and Hudson, 1982).

—*William Blake* (London: Thames and Hudson, 2000).

Ramella, Christina, *Balzac (Séraphîta et Louis Lambert), Strindberg (Inferno et Journal occulte), lecteurs de Swedenborg*, mémoire de DEA, Université Paris IV, etudes scandinaves, année 1998-9.

Reed, Sampson, *Primary Source Material for Emerson Studies*, ed. George F Dole (West Chester: Swedenborg Foundation, 1993).

Rix, Robert, *William Blake and the Cultures of Radical Christianity* (Aldershot: Ashgate, 2007).

Rose, Jonathan et al. (eds.), *Scribe of Heaven: Swedenborg's Life, Work, and Impact* (West Chester: Swedenborg Foundation, 2005).

Rowlandson, William, *Borges, Swedenborg and Mysticism* (Oxford: Peter Lang, 2012).

Schuchard, Marsha Keith, *Why Mrs Blake Cried. William Blake and the Sexual Basis of Spiritual Vision* (London: Century, 2006).

Siegel, Eli, *James & the Children: A consideration of Henry James's 'The Turn of the Screw'* (New York: Definition Press, 1968).

Sjödén, Karl-Erik, *Swedenborg en France* (Stockholm: Alqvist & Wiksell, 1985).

Suzuki, D T, *Swedenborg: Buddha of the North*, tr. Andrew Bernstein (West Chester: Swedenborg Foundation, 1996).

Sznajder, Anna, *Mysl Emmanuela Swedenborga w poezji i esejach Czesława Miłosza* (Krakow: Dissertation from Jagiellonian University's Faculty of Polish Studies, 2006).

Taylor, Eugene, *William James on Exceptional Mental States: The 1896 Lowell Lectures* (New York: Charles Scribner's Sons, 1983).

Thompson, E P, *Witness Against the Beast. William Blake and the Moral Law* (Cambridge: University of Cambridge, 1993).

Varila, Armi, *The Swedenborgian Background of William James' Philosophy* (Helsinki: Suomalainen Tieddeaktemia, 1977).

Wilkinson, Lynn R, *Balzac, Baudelaire and the Popularization of Swedenborgianism in France* (Berkeley: University of California, 1983) Ph.D. Thesis.

—*The Dream of an Absolute Language: Emanuel Swedenborg and French Literary Culture* (Albany: State University of New York Press, 1996).

Woofenden, William Ross, *Swedenborg's Philosophy of Causality* (Missouri: St. Louis University, 1970), Ph.D. Thesis.

Index

mis seis recurrentes → volver al colegio es no edad
                    → Padre no violentos,

La biblioteca del psicoanálisis estaba llena de enfermedades
de muchas civilizaciones.

Les decía que leyó más arqueología que psicología.
Necesariamente se le presentó la analista del
psicoanálisis como una excavadora

Psicoanálisis a method of treatment or neurosis

• International journal of psychoanalysis)

Si no sueña en ella, ¿está fuera de su deseo?

→ sobre la possibilidad del encuentro
    espiritual

        "Guys, I think this guy can actually break my heart"

Un libro se puede y sugiere